2011—2012 TOWNSEND **PRESS**

Sunday School
Commentary
Based on the International Lessons Series

SUNDAY SCHOOL PUBLISHING BOARD
NATIONAL BAPTIST CONVENTION, USA, INC.

DR. KELLY M. SMITH JR.,
EXECUTIVE DIRECTOR

KING JAMES
VERSION

NEW
INTERNATIONAL
VERSION

91

ninety-first edition

Dr. Julius R. Scruggs, *Convention President;* Dr. Kelly M. Smith Jr., *Executive Director,* Mrs. Kathlyn Pillow, *Associate Director;* Rev. Debra Berry, *Director of Publishing Administration.*
Writers: Dr. William Franklin Buchanan; Dr. Forrest E. Harris Sr.; Dr. Geoffrey V. Guns; *Editors:* Rev. Wellington A. Johnson Sr.; Rev. Michael Woolridge; Rev. Emmanuel Reid; *Copy Editors:* Yalemzewd Worku, Tanae C. McKnight Murdic, Lucinda Anderson; *Layout Designer:* Royetta Davis.

ISBN: 1-932972-24-2

CONTENTS

Fall Quarter, 2011—Tradition and Wisdom

Winter Quarter, 2011-2012—God Establishes a Faithful People

Spring Quarter, 2012—God's Creative Word

Summer Quarter, 2012—God Calls for Justice—Old Testament Survey

2010–2016 SCOPE AND SEQUENCE—CYCLE SPREAD
Arrangement of Quarters According to the Church School Year,
September through August

FALL 2010 GOD **The Inescapable God** Exodus; Psalms 8, 19, 46, 47, 63, 66, 90, 91, 139	*WINTER 2010–2011* HOPE **Assuring Hope** Isaiah; Matthew; Mark	*SPRING 2011* WORSHIP **We Worship God** Matthew; Mark; 1 & 2 Timothy; Philippians; Jude; Revelation	*SUMMER 2011* COMMUNITY **God Instructs the People of God** Joshua; Judges; Ruth
FALL 2011 TRADITION **Tradition and Wisdom** Proverbs; Psalms 16, 25, 111, 119; Ecclesiastes; Song of Solomon; Esther	*WINTER 2011–2012* FAITH **God Establishes a Faithful People** Genesis; Exodus; Luke; Galatians	*SPRING 2012* CREATION **God's Creative Word** John	*SUMMER 2012* JUSTICE **God Calls for Justice** Exodus; Leviticus; Deuteronomy; 1 & 2 Samuel; 1 & 2 Kings; 2 Chronicles; Psalm 146; Isaiah; Jeremiah; Ezekiel
FALL 2012 FAITH **A Living Faith** Psalm 46; 1 Corinthians 13:1-13; Hebrews; Acts	*WINTER 2012–2013* GOD: JESUS CHRIST **Jesus Is Lord** Ephesians; Philippians; Colossians	*SPRING 2013* HOPE **Beyond the Present Time** Daniel; Luke; Acts; 1 & 2 Peter; 1 & 2 Thessalonians	*SUMMER 2013* WORSHIP **God's People Worship** Isaiah; Ezra; Nehemiah
FALL 2013 CREATION **First Things** Genesis; Exodus; Psalm 104	*WINTER 2013–2014* JUSTICE **Jesus and the Just Reign of God** Luke; James	*SPRING 2014* TRADITION **Jesus' Fulfillment of Scripture** Zechariah; Malachi; Deuteronomy; Matthew	*SUMMER 2014* COMMUNITY **The People of God Set Priorities** Haggai; 1 & 2 Corinthians
FALL 2014 HOPE **Sustaining Hope** Jeremiah; Habakkuk; Job; Ezekiel; Isaiah 52	*WINTER 2014–2015* WORSHIP **Acts of Worship** Psalm 95:1-7; Daniel; Matthew; Mark; Luke; John; Ephesians; Hebrews; James	*SPRING 2015* GOD: THE HOLY SPIRIT **Work of the Spirit** Mark; John; Acts; 1 Corinthians 12–14; 1 John; 2 John; 3 John	*SUMMER 2015* JUSTICE **God's Prophets Demand Justice** Amos; Micah; Isaiah; Jeremiah; Ezekiel; Zechariah; Malachi
FALL 2015 COMMUNITY **The Community of Believers Comes Alive** Matthew; John; 1 John	*WINTER 2015–2016* TRADITION **Traditions of Israel** Leviticus; Numbers; Deuteronomy	*SPRING 2016* FAITH **The Gift of Faith** Mark; Luke	*SUMMER 2016* CREATION **Toward a New Creation** Genesis; Psalms; Zephaniah; Romans

LIST OF PRINTED TEXTS

The Printed Scriptural Texts used in the *2011-2012 Townsend Press Sunday School Commentary* are arranged here in the order in which they appear in the Bible. Opposite each reference is the page number on which Scriptures appear in this edition of the *Commentary*.

PREFACE

The *Townsend Press Sunday School Commentary*, based on the International Lessons Series, is a production of the Sunday School Publishing Board, National Baptist Convention, USA, Incorporated. These lessons were developed consistent with the curriculum guidelines of the Committee on the Uniform Series, Education Leadership Ministries Commission, National Council of the Churches of Christ in the United States of America. Selected Christian scholars and theologians—who themselves embrace the precepts, doctrines, and positions on biblical interpretation that we have come to believe—are contributors to this publication. By participating in Scripture selection and the development of the matrices for the Guidelines for Lesson Development with the Committee on the Uniform Series, this presentation reflects the historic faith that we share within a rich heritage of worship and witness.

The format of the *Townsend Press Sunday School Commentary* lessons consists of the following: the Unit Title, the general subject with age-level topics, Printed Text from the *King James Version* and the *New International Version* of the Bible, Objectives of the Lesson, Unifying Lesson Principles, Points to Be Emphasized, Topical Outline of the Lesson—with the Biblical Background of the Lesson, Exposition and Application of the Scripture, and Concluding Reflection (designed to focus on the salient points of the lesson), Word Power, and the Home Daily Bible Readings. Each lesson concludes with a prayer.

The *Townsend Press Sunday School Commentary* is designed as an instructional aid for persons involved in the ministry of Christian education. While the autonomy of the individual soul before God is affirmed, we believe that biblical truths find their highest expression within the community of believers whose corporate experiences serve as monitors to preserve the integrity of the Christian faith. As such, the Word of God must not only be understood, but it must also be embodied in the concrete realities of daily life. This serves to allow the Word of God to intersect in a meaningful way with those realities of life.

The presentation of the lessons anticipates the fact that some concepts and Scripture references do not lend themselves to meaningful comprehension by children. Hence, when this occurs, alternative passages of Scripture are used, along with appropriate content emphases, that are designed to assist children in their spiritual growth. There will, however, remain a consistent connection between the children, youth, and adult lessons through the Unifying Principle developed for each session.

We stand firm in our commitment to Christian growth, to the end that lives will be transformed through personal and group interaction with the Word of God. The challenge issued by the apostle Paul continues to find relevance for our faith journey: "Do your best to present yourself to God as one approved by him, a worker who has no need to be ashamed, rightly explaining the word of truth" (2 Timothy 2:15, NRSV). May we all commit ourselves to the affirmation expressed by the psalmist, "Your word is a lamp to my feet and a light for my path" (Psalm 119:105, NIV).

ACKNOWLEDGMENTS

The *Townsend Press Sunday School Commentary* is recognized as the centerpiece of a family of church-school literature designed especially to assist teachers in their presentation of the lessons as well as to broaden the knowledge base of students from the biblical perspective. Our mission has been and will always be to provide religious educational experiences and spiritual resources for our constituency throughout this nation, as well as many foreign countries. To achieve this end, the collaborative efforts of many people provide the needed expertise in the various areas of the production process. Although under the employ of the Sunday School Publishing Board, personnel too numerous to list approach their respective tasks with the dedication and devotion of those who serve God by serving His people. This *Commentary* is presented with gratitude to God for all those who desire a more comprehensive treatment of the selected Scriptures than is provided in the church-school quarterlies, and it is intended to be a complementary resource to the quarterlies.

We acknowledge the Executive Director of the Sunday School Publishing Board in the person of Dr. Kelly M. Smith Jr., who has given a charge to the publishing family to focus on QTC—Quality, Timeliness, and Customer Care—in our interaction with our constituency. Special appreciation is appropriately accorded to Dr. Smith for his continued insightful and inspiring leadership and motivation. Through Dr. Smith's tenure at the Sunday School Publishing Board, the SSPB continues to prosper. It continues as the publisher and printer for the National Baptist Convention, USA, Inc. and its constituent components. There is a greater emphasis on addressing issues germane to the local, national, and international communities, utilizing the latest technologies to promote and distribute our materials—and doing all this based on Christian principles for the advancement of the kingdom of Jesus Christ.

The Sunday School Publishing Board consists of employees with expertise in their assigned areas whose self-understanding is that of "workers together with God" and partners with those who labor in the vineyard of teaching the Word of God in order to make disciples and nurture others toward a mature faith.

Our gratitude is expressed to Dr. William F. Buchanan, expositor for the Fall Quarter, to Dr. Forrest E. Harris, expositor for the Winter and Spring Quarters, and Dr. Geoffrey V. Guns, expositor for the Summer Quarter, for their devotion to the development of the respective lessons. These three writers bring diversity and a broad spectrum of ministerial and educational experience to bear on the exposition and application of the Scripture.

Appreciation is also expressed to Dr. Kelly M. Smith Jr., Executive Director, Mrs. Kathy Pillow, Associate Director, and Rev. Debra Berry, Director of Publishing Administration, for their ongoing leadership. It is a credit to their leadership that the employees have embraced the mission of the Sunday School Publishing Board with a self-perspective that enhances their personal commitment to the cause of Christ as they interact with one another and intersect with the greater community of faith.

The task in which we are all involved would be meaningless and fruitless were it not for the many readers for whom this publication has been so diligently prepared. The faithfulness of our constituency has been enduring for over a century, and we consider ourselves blessed to be their servants in the ministry of the printed Word exalting the living Word, our Lord and Savior Jesus Christ. We pray that God's grace will complement our efforts so that lives will be transformed within and beyond the confines of classroom interaction as the Spirit of God manifests Himself through the intersection of teaching and learning. It is our prayer that God may grant each of us the power to live for Him and be witnesses to the saving grace of the One who died for us, even Jesus Christ, our Lord and Savior.

Wellington A. Johnson Sr.
Associate Director of Curriculum Publishing

Reverend Dr. William F. Buchanan ▼
Fall Quarter

William F. Buchanan was born in Broxton, Georgia—the third of four children born to the late Millinease and John L. Buchanan. He spent his formative years in Georgia, but later the family moved to Florida, where he graduated from high school. In 1976, he received a Bachelor of Science degree from Bethune-Cookman College. He later matriculated at the University of Florida's business school in Gainesville. In 1983, he received a Master of Divinity degree in Pastoral Counseling from the Morehouse School of Religion–Interdenominational Theological Center. Subsequently, he was a Proctor-Booth Fellow at United Theological Seminary, where he earned the Doctor of Ministry degree in 1995.

Dr. Buchanan was ordained into the ministry in 1985, and from 1985 to 1988 served as youth minister at Greenforest Baptist Church in Decatur, Georgia, and as a chaplain intern at Emory University Hospital in Atlanta. He was called to be the senior pastor of First Baptist Church in Huntington, West Virginia, in 1988. In 1994, he was called to the pastorate of the historic Fifteenth Avenue Baptist Church in Nashville, Tennessee.

Since coming to Fifteenth Avenue, Dr. Buchanan has transformed this church into a beacon of light for all persons in the community. The church continues to grow spiritually and numerically, and to serve as a model for twenty-first-century ministry.

Dr. Buchanan has received many awards and honors. He was most recently honored with being named the recipient of the Lily Foundation's Clergy General Grant, which allowed him to take a brief sabbatical to study at Harvard University's School of Divinity. He is a board member of the Nashville Housing Fund, Oasis, Saint Thomas Pastoral Care Advisory Board (chairman), Vanderbilt Divinity School Board of Visitors, and Operation Andrew Group (former board chairman). Dr. Buchanan is an adjunct professor at American Baptist College in Nashville, and a Field Education supervisor at Vanderbilt University's School of Divinity. Additionally, he is in great demand as a preacher, lecturer, and facilitator at churches throughout the nation.

In addition to his busy schedule as a pastor and teacher, Dr. Buchanan is the loving husband of Audrey Cave Buchanan. They are the parents of four children—Kwame, Shani, Dashan, and Aubrey Buchanan—and have six grandchildren.

Reverend Dr. Forrest E. Harris Sr. ▼
Winter and Spring Quarters

Forrest Harris was born August 24, 1949, in Memphis, Tennessee, to Wilbur T. and Sallie Mae Harris. Harris's siblings include a twin brother and seven other sisters and brothers.

Harris matriculated at Knoxville College in Knoxville, Tennessee, where he completed a Bachelor's degree in Psychology and Sociology in 1971.

From 1971 to 1979, he was a Federal Compliance Officer with the Energy and Research Development Administration in Oak Ridge, Tennessee. During his tenure as an employee with the federal government, Harris responded to a call to professional Christian ministry. In 1979, he completed a Th.B. (Bachelor of Theology) at American Baptist College in Nashville, Tennessee. He earned a M.Div. (Master of Divinity) and D.Min. (Doctor of Ministry) from Vanderbilt University Divinity School in 1983 and 1989, respectively. At Vanderbilt, Harris was a Benjamin E.

Mays Fellow and a recipient of the Florence Conwell prize for preaching.

Harris was ordained in 1975 at the Oak Valley Baptist Church in Oak Ridge, Tennessee. While a seminary student at Vanderbilt, he served as the pastor of this church. During this pastorate, Harris brought together several community organizations and founded the Oak Valley Development Corporation. He also served a three-year term as president of the Oak Ridge Branch of the NAACP. From 1985 to 1987, he taught at Roane State Community College, where he initiated a black studies curriculum and co-ordinated social outreach programs and special events.

Since 1988, Harris has served on the Vanderbilt Divinity School faculty. He is the Director of the Kelly Miller Smith Institute on Black Church Studies, Assistant Dean for Black Church Studies, and Assistant Professor for the Practice of Ministry. His teaching responsibilities include courses in the theology of ministry in the black church tradition. Under Harris's leadership, the endowment of the Kelly Miller Smith Institute on Black Church Studies has grown to be in excess of one million dollars.

In 1999, Harris was appointed President of American Baptist College in Nashville. During his presidency, the College's endowment has increased by 65 percent.

In addition to his presidential duties, Harris is a husband and father. He is married to Jacqueline Borom Harris, a research nurse at Vanderbilt University Medical Center. They have four children: Kara, Elliot Jr., Morgan, and Alexis.

Reverend Dr. Geoffrey V. Guns ▼
Summer Quarter

Dr. Geoffrey V. Guns is a native of Newport, Rhode Island. He is the son of a retired Baptist pastor and co-pastor. Dr. Guns received his elementary and secondary education in the Norfolk public school system. He earned his B.S. degree in Business Administration from Norfolk State University in 1972.

In 1981, he earned his Master of Divinity degree from the School of Theology, Virginia Union University, graduating *summa cum laude*. He earned his Doctor of Ministry degree from the School of Religion, Howard University in Washington, D.C., in 1985.

Dr. Guns is the senior pastor of Second Calvary Baptist Church in Norfolk, Virginia, where he has served for over twenty-five years. He is active in his denomination, the National Baptist Convention, USA, Inc. Dr. Guns served as the president of the Virginia Baptist State Convention (VBSC) from 1997 to 2001 and is currently the moderator for the Tidewater Peninsula Baptist Association.

He has written articles for the *Christian Education Informer* of the Division of Christian Education of the Sunday School Publishing Board. Dr. Guns also serves as vice chairman of the Council of Christian Education for the Division of Christian Education of the Sunday School Publishing Board of the NBC. He works with the Home Mission Board of the NBC and serves as the regional representative for the Southeast region.

Dr. Guns is the author of two books: *Church Financial Management* (1997), which is published by Providence House Publishers; and *Spiritual Leadership: A Practical Guide to Developing Spiritual Leaders in the Church* (2000), published by Orman Press, Inc.

He is married to the former Rosetta Harding of Richmond, Virginia. Mrs. Guns is a licensed social worker and works as a school social worker.

Tradition and Wisdom

GENERAL INTRODUCTION

The study this quarter is a survey of Old Testament Wisdom Literature.

There are eight lessons in **Unit I**, *Teaching and Learning*. As is characteristic of Wisdom Literature, these books make little reference to covenant or religious life. They are focused instead on human wisdom and transmit lessons learned from experience and tradition. They are the words of a teacher to a student, or a parent to a child—words of wisdom passed on from one generation to another. The first five lessons draw on the wisdom collected by the writers of the book of Proverbs. The next two lessons consider the wisdom of the book of Ecclesiastes. The final lesson comes from the book of Song of Solomon.

Unit II, *Jesus Teaches Wisdom*, has five lessons. These lessons are examinations of Jesus' Sermon on the Mount and its relationship to the traditional teaching of Mosaic Law. The first four lessons, taken from Matthew 5 and 6, give attention to what Jesus says to disciples about living, forgiving, loving, and praying. The final lesson is an invitation for the participants to hear anew Jesus' words about worry-free living.

LESSON 1   **September 4, 2011**

RIGHTEOUSNESS AND WISDOM

DEVOTIONAL READING: **Psalm 115:3-11**
PRINT PASSAGE: **Proverbs 3:1-12**

BACKGROUND SCRIPTURE: **Proverbs 3:1-35**
KEY VERSE: **Proverbs 3:5**

Proverbs 3:1-12—KJV

MY SON, forget not my law; but let thine heart keep my commandments:

2 For length of days, and long life, and peace, shall they add to thee.

3 Let not mercy and truth forsake thee: bind them about thy neck; write them upon the table of thine heart:

4 So shalt thou find favour and good understanding in the sight of God and man.

5 Trust in the LORD with all thine heart; and lean not unto thine own understanding.

6 In all thy ways acknowledge him, and he shall direct thy paths.

7 Be not wise in thine own eyes: fear the LORD, and depart from evil.

8 It shall be health to thy navel, and marrow to thy bones.

9 Honour the LORD with thy substance, and with the firstfruits of all thine increase:

10 So shall thy barns be filled with plenty, and thy presses shall burst out with new wine.

11 My son, despise not the chastening of the LORD; neither be weary of his correction:

12 For whom the LORD loveth he correcteth; even as a father the son in whom he delighteth.

Proverbs 3:1-12—NIV

MY SON, do not forget my teaching, but keep my commands in your heart,

2 for they will prolong your life many years and bring you prosperity.

3 Let love and faithfulness never leave you; bind them around your neck, write them on the tablet of your heart.

4 Then you will win favor and a good name in the sight of God and man.

5 Trust in the LORD with all your heart and lean not on your own understanding;

6 in all your ways acknowledge him, and he will make your paths straight.

7 Do not be wise in your own eyes; fear the LORD and shun evil.

8 This will bring health to your body and nourishment to your bones.

9 Honor the LORD with your wealth, with the firstfruits of all your crops;

10 then your barns will be filled to overflowing, and your vats will brim over with new wine.

11 My son, do not despise the LORD's discipline and do not resent his rebuke,

12 because the LORD disciplines those he loves, as a father the son he delights in.

BIBLE FACT

Righteousness is a recurring theme throughout the Scriptures. Through progressive revelation, the understanding of the nature of righteousness shifted from works to relationship. Generally, Old Testament righteousness meant "right works." In the New Testament, Paul taught righteousness by faith, or "right relationship." Our cumulative understanding, then, is that right relationship produces right works.

UNIFYING LESSON PRINCIPLE

People want their lives to have purpose and meaning. Is there a way of living that really works toward that end? The book of Proverbs is rooted in a tradition of instruction that encourages godly living.

TOPICAL OUTLINE OF THE LESSON

I. Introduction
A. Wisdom, Then and Now
B. Biblical Background

II. Exposition and Application of the Scripture
A. Principles for Living Purposeful and Meaningful Lives (Proverbs 3:1-2)
B. Living According to Divine Wisdom (Proverbs 3:3-4)
C. Trusting God (Proverbs 3:5-8)
D. Principles to Help Us Make the Right Choices (Proverbs 3:9-12)

III. Concluding Reflection

LESSON OBJECTIVES

Upon the completion of the lesson, the students will be able to:

1. Find a deeper purpose and meaning in their lives;
2. Reassure those who no longer believe that life has meaning or purpose; and,
3. Find meaningful and purposeful ways to live life to its fullest—in their search for spiritual guidance.

POINTS TO BE EMPHASIZED

ADULT/YOUTH
Adult Topic: **Wisdom for Living**
Youth Topic: **Living Right**
Adult/Youth Key Verse: **Proverbs 3:5**
Print Passage: **Proverbs 3:1-12**

—The parental tone of Proverbs 3, seen in the address to "my child" (Proverbs 3:1, NLT), suggests that the context for teaching God's wisdom in this passage may be the family or tribe.
—The phrase "wise in your own eyes" in Proverbs 3:7 points to those who have no respect for the wisdom of the community.
—The admonition to "fear the LORD" is the theological heart of the wisdom and teachings in the book of Proverbs.
—"Fear of the Lord" means much more than terror or being afraid. It also means respect and obedience and is equated with hatred of evil, humility, knowledge of God, loyalty, and faithfulness.
—Obedience and loyalty to God bring blessings.
—God is a reliable source of wisdom and guidance for our lives.
—God can bless you in more ways than material prosperity.
—God disciplines those whom He loves.

CHILDREN
Children Topic: **Pleasing God**
Key Verse: **Proverbs 3:5**
Print Passage: **Proverbs 3:1-12**

—Loyalty and faithfulness are character qualities of wise persons.
—Trusting God helps us make important decisions.

—Honor the Lord with all that you have.

—Wisdom involves listening to and learning from parents and teachers.

—God has given us laws to direct our paths.

—Just as an earthly parent does, the Lord must sometimes discipline us.

I. INTRODUCTION

A. Wisdom, Then and Now

The book of Proverbs is a part of a genre of Hebrew writings called *Wisdom Literature*. One of the pillars of Old Testament Jewish religion is Hebrew wisdom—and wisdom was considered a high achievement of culture. The book of Proverbs was considered as moral instructions for children and was intended to help them live life to its fullest. It was to this end that Wisdom Literature in ancient Israel had at least six important elements: knowledge, imagination, discipline, piety, order, and moral instruction.

However, the parent (sage) sharing the literature with a child made no claim of heavenly revelation; rather, many of the proverbs are lessons that life and experience teach. These proverbs were intended to be earthy, and not to require any special intellectual gifts to understand, nor great spiritual maturity to grasp. As a matter of fact, consider this definition of wisdom: "the right use of knowledge." Conversely, *foolishness* is "the wrong use of knowledge"—acting in ways the opposite to being wise! For the parent (sage), the right uses of knowledge will invariably lead to a good life. Wisdom Literature in ancient Israel was for the guidance of children.

B. Biblical Background

We are now a society that processes information rather than one that ponders it. However, the book of Proverbs is to be pondered and should serve as an admonition to a child: "Do not be wise in your own eyes" (Proverbs 3:7, NIV). Although the sage addressed the learner as a "child," the designation was not intended to be demeaning or insulting; rather, it invites the reader to live free of the anxiety that is one of the defining characteristics of adult life. The warning is that exclusive reliance on one's own understanding to get where one wants to go in life has proven impossible for the sage. Therefore, this lesson (Proverbs 3:1-10) contains both admonitions and prohibitions. "Do not let loyalty and faithfulness forsake you; bind them around your neck, write them on the tablet of your heart" (Proverbs 3:3, NRSV).

The operative words are *loyalty* and *faithfulness*. Loyalty in the wisdom tradition is demonstrated by the learner's faithful obedience to what is being taught and is expressed in the recognition of the lordship of Yahweh. Our text (Proverbs 3:1-12) can be divided into six sections (teachings or strophes): verses 1-2, 3-4, 5-6, 7-8, 9-10, and 11-12. These teachings (instructions) emerge out of the covenant community of Israel that was bound together by two virtues: "faithfulness" and "steadfast love." Israel's communal "faithfulness" and Yahweh's "steadfast love" (*hesed*) are the foundations of wisdom. Thus, "faith" in the context of the covenant community is analogous to "trust" and is deeply embedded within Israel's oral tradition. It is also verified by experience (see the book of Exodus). The Israelites' faithfulness to Yahweh was a major cornerstone of who they were as the people of God. Therefore, for the sage, wisdom has nothing to do with intellect, but with faithfulness. So, the sage admonished, "Trust in the LORD with all your heart and lean not on your own understanding" (Proverbs 3:5, NIV). By trusting in God, one renounces the vanity of one's own wisdom.

II. EXPOSITION AND APPLICATION OF THE SCRIPTURE

A. Principles for Living Purposeful and Meaningful Lives

(Proverbs 3:1-2)

MY SON, forget not my law; but let thine heart keep my commandments: For length of days, and long life, and peace, shall they add to thee.

Chapter 3 opens with the admonition to keep the parent's instruction and commandment. The child is to take them to heart. In other words, the instruction and the commandments of the father must not be taken lightly. The aim of the moral teaching of the parent or sage was to help the child avoid the pitfalls and the negative consequences of his or her generation and live a good life. A common school of thought among almost every generation is that their parents are "old-fashioned." By this they mean that their parents do not relate to their age group. But the sages are clear that wisdom is time-neutral and is relevant for every generation. Dr. Raymond C. Van Leeuwen, in his reflections on the book of Proverbs, refers to wisdom as the "cosmic standard." In other words, wisdom comes to us (on earth), but it is from beyond us (heavenly).

Verse 2 (NIV) includes the promise of a long and a good life—"for they will prolong your life many years and bring you prosperity."

The key word is *prosperity*; however, this word has been compromised by contemporary religious culture to mean wealth and success, which is not the case. Even in late biblical times, *prosperity* in the Greek language (*euodoo*) meant "to bring to a good conclusion" or "to lead on a good path." As we look at the waywardness and threats facing so many of our young people (AIDS, premature death, incarceration, illiteracy, and a general sense of aimlessness), it appears that too many are not being guided by wisdom.

One of the elements of wisdom is experience. Many of our parents lived and learned from the "school of hard knocks" and have attempted to pass their lessons on to us. There is an old adage: "There is nothing new under the sun" (Ecclesiastes 1:9, NIV), and indeed this is true. Temptation is temptation, danger is danger, and consequences are consequences in every age and can be best navigated through wisdom. So the promise in these verses is that wisdom will prolong one's life and bring it to a good conclusion. A good life for the child is to live a purposeful, meaningful, and full life that will honor God and parents. Wisdom "will prolong your life many years and bring you prosperity." There are two principles that, if kept by the child, will be a blessing to the child: *obedience* and *loyalty*. These are covenant terms that were essential in the life of Israel's covenant relationship with Yahweh. Likewise, obedience was like bedrock and foundational to the covenant community of Israel. These laws were based on obedience to God and parents. "If you do not obey the LORD your God and do not carefully follow all his commands and decrees I am giving you today, all these curses will come upon you and overtake you" (Deuteronomy 28:15, NIV). "If you fully obey the LORD your God and carefully follow all his commands I give you today, the LORD your God will set you high above all the nations on earth. All these blessings will come upon you and accompany you if you obey the LORD your God: You will be blessed in the city and blessed in the country" (Deuteronomy 28:1-3, NIV). "Obedience is better than sacrifice" (see 1 Samuel 15:22).

The second principle is loyalty. The word *loyalty* can also be understood as *fidelity*. The child must prove loyal to the teachings of the parents and the commands of the Lord. Hence, the child must trust that instructions come from the parents because they know best. Also, actions speak louder than words; obedience was a demonstration of loyalty. For the sage in ancient Israel these were inseparable principles and were part of one's character and would lead to a meaningful and purposeful life.

B. Living According to Divine Wisdom
(Proverbs 3:3-4)

Let not mercy and truth forsake thee: bind them about thy neck; write them upon the table of thine heart: So shalt thou find favour and good understanding in the sight of God and man.

"Let love (loyalty) and faithfulness never leave you; bind them around your neck, write them on the tablet of your heart. *Then* you will win favor and a good name in the sight of God and man" (NIV). The rewards of obedience and loyalty are the approval of God and humans. Now, care must be taken in the translation of the word *favor* because of its colloquial usage. The word *favor*, in its original language, meant "to rejoice" or "a feeling of festive joy." The promise in these verses is to find "favor" or "festive joy" in life, as opposed to dread. Yet, this festive joy is a conditional joy that comes with how one appropriates the wisdom handed down to the child. Verse 3 reads, "Let not loyalty and faithfulness forsake you." The binding of the instructions and commandments around one's neck and writing them on their hearts was a metaphor for a deep commitment and faithfulness to the instructions of the father. Likewise, the *heart* is a metaphor for the seat of the human personality and is the seedbed for all thoughts and actions. The sage believed that it was the heart—and not the mind—that governed human behavior. The writer of the book of Proverbs said, "It is out of the heart that flows the issues of life" (see Proverbs 4:23). Verse 3b is connected by the term *then*. There are consequences for heeding the instructions and keeping the commandments of the father. This was a practical matter; living in loyalty and faithfulness according to the father's wisdom would lead to both favor and a good reputation with God and humanity. So if one follows the instructions outlined in verse 3a, then one will reap the benefits and promises of loyalty and faithfulness: favor and a good reputation.

C. Trusting God
(Proverbs 3:5-8)

Trust in the LORD with all thine heart; and lean not unto

thine own understanding. In all thy ways acknowledge him, and he shall direct thy paths. Be not wise in thine own eyes: fear the LORD, and depart from evil. It shall be health to thy navel, and marrow to thy bones.

These verses are some of the most noted and recited proverbs by believers today. As a matter of fact, they have been a staple for many pastors in stewardship meditations. "Trust in the LORD with all thine heart; and lean not unto thine own understanding. In all thy ways acknowledge him, and he shall direct thy paths" (verses 5-6). Proverbs 1:7 reads, "The fear of the LORD is the beginning of [wisdom]." For the sage, fearing (having reverence for) the Lord is essential to trusting in the Lord, which is in contrast to self-reliance and trusting in one's own insights. The son (child) could not be expected to make the right choices at opportune times with only his own insights. The sage was aware of human limitations, thus he admonished his son to trust in the Lord with all his heart and not to rely on his own understanding. To trust God in this context means to rely upon the trustfulness and integrity of God for His promises.

Again, the essence of this language is located in the traditions of Israel and its covenant with Yahweh (see Deuteronomy 6:1-6). The entire community of Israel as a striving nation was undergirded by an abiding trust in the God of Abraham, Isaac, and Jacob. So not only was the cumulative wisdom of their ancestors communicated to each subsequent generation, but also the meta-narratives (like the Red Sea, the walls of Jericho, and so forth) were passed on. A "way out of no way" spoke of their God with whom nothing was impossible. The message was clear to the child: trust in Yahweh and lean not on one's own understanding when challenges seem insurmountable and impassable

and when one thinks one has it all figured out. Finally, another way of saying "acknowledge Him" is "in all your ways know him." According to many scholars, "ways" refers to human conduct in the world with all of its diversity. The child's knowledge or lack thereof would be revealed by his or her response to the divine standards of justice and righteousness in the world. Whatever one is doing and whatever the challenges are, one's knowledge of Yahweh will direct one's ways.

D. Principles to Help Us Make the Right Choices (Proverbs 3:9-12)

Honour the LORD with thy substance, and with the firstfruits of all thine increase: So shall thy barns be filled with plenty, and thy presses shall burst out with new wine. My son, despise not the chastening of the LORD; neither be weary of his correction: For whom the LORD loveth he correcteth; even as a father the son in whom he delighteth.

There are concrete ways of honoring Yahweh. Often, we are prone to "lip service." But, the rubber meets the road at the place where we are willing to honor God with our substance. It was true then and it is true today. We are by nature selfish creatures and hoarders of resources. Self-reliance is considered as an American virtue. But the Bible presents a paradox. We increase through giving. Yahweh has so ordained it that the gateway to sustained blessings is through honoring Him by giving of our increase to Him. Good living requires making the right choices in life.

Robert Frost, in his poem "The Road Less Traveled," wrote, "I shall be telling this with a sigh. Somewhere ages and ages hence: Two roads diverged in a wood, and I, I took the one less traveled by, and that has made all the difference." Robert Frost, the sage, believed that our actions (choices) would make all the difference. Of course, we must keep in mind that the book of Proverbs is also poetry and bears the characteristic of poetic language, which is figurative and not literal. "So your barns will be filled with plenty, And your vats will overflow with new wine" (verse 10, NKJV) is a promise of divine protection from the famine and pestilence that haunted the farmer by day and by night (see Malachi 3:10-14). God blesses in multiple ways when we honor Him.

III. CONCLUDING REFLECTION

Hebraic wisdom was passed on through the medium of wisdom saying and the African-American slave used slave songs later known as "spirituals" to pass on their wisdom. Both forms were based in the loyalty (righteousness) and faithfulness of God and the experiences of the people. Dr. Wyatt T. Walker, in his book, *Hush, Somebody's Calling My Name: Black Sacred Music and Social Change!*, says, "Music became, for the slave, the medium of all yearning for peace and freedom. That which slaves dared not breathe in public, they disguised in song, thereby keeping a vital part of their humanity and their hope alive." One such song was "Keep a Inching"—*Keep a inching like a poor inch-worm, Jesus will come by and by.* This song inspired hope that change does come, though slowly—it does come. So, it was indeed the embedded wisdom of the slave song that enabled the slaves to live life to its fullest, with their own unique perspectives of the world without the compromising of their beliefs.

PRAYER

"How little, O God, we trust in Thee. Forgive the weakness and the feebleness of our minds and our spirits. Accept, O God, the joy of our hearts for the light that breaks in us when we have heard thy whisper. Dismiss us with Thy spirit, and grant unto us Thy peace, Our Father." (Prayer by Howard Thurman in *The Growing Edge*).

WORD POWER

Heart *(kardia)*—the seat of feeling, desires, and passion. The seat of the will.
Favor *(charitoo)*—festive joy; the reward for faithfulness.
Prosperity *(euodoo)*—"to lead on a good path" or "to bring to a good conclusion."

HOME DAILY BIBLE READINGS
(August 29–September 4, 2011)

Righteousness and Wisdom

MONDAY, **August 29: "The Sun of Righteousness" (Malachi 4:1-6)**
TUESDAY, **August 30: "Remember All the Commandments" (Numbers 15:37-41)**
WEDNESDAY, **August 31: "God Is Our Help and Shield" (Psalm 115:3-11)**
THURSDAY, **September 1: "God's Abundant Blessings" (2 Corinthians 9:6-12)**
FRIDAY, **September 2: "Wisdom in Relationships" (Proverbs 3:27-35)**
SATURDAY, **September 3: "The Profit from Wisdom" (Proverbs 3:13-26)**
SUNDAY, **September 4: "Trust in the Lord" (Proverbs 3:1-12)**

LESSON 2 | September 11, 2011

FROM GENERATION TO GENERATION

DEVOTIONAL READING: **Jeremiah 31:7-11**
PRINT PASSAGE: **Proverbs 4:10-15, 20-27**

BACKGROUND SCRIPTURE: **Proverbs 4:1-27**
KEY VERSE: **Proverbs 4:13**

Proverbs 4:10-15, 20-27—KJV

10 Hear, O my son, and receive my sayings; and the years of thy life shall be many.
11 I have taught thee in the way of wisdom; I have led thee in right paths.
12 When thou goest, thy steps shall not be straitened; and when thou runnest, thou shalt not stumble.
13 Take fast hold of instruction; let her not go: keep her; for she is thy life.
14 Enter not into the path of the wicked, and go not in the way of evil men.
15 Avoid it, pass not by it, turn from it, and pass away.

…..

20 My son, attend to my words; incline thine ear unto my sayings.
21 Let them not depart from thine eyes; keep them in the midst of thine heart.
22 For they are life unto those that find them, and health to all their flesh.
23 Keep thy heart with all diligence; for out of it are the issues of life.
24 Put away from thee a froward mouth, and perverse lips put far from thee.
25 Let thine eyes look right on, and let thine eyelids look straight before thee.
26 Ponder the path of thy feet, and let all thy ways be established.
27 Turn not to the right hand nor to the left: remove thy foot from evil.

Proverbs 4:10-15, 20-27—NIV

10 Listen, my son, accept what I say, and the years of your life will be many.
11 I guide you in the way of wisdom and lead you along straight paths.
12 When you walk, your steps will not be hampered; when you run, you will not stumble.
13 Hold on to instruction, do not let it go; guard it well, for it is your life.
14 Do not set foot on the path of the wicked or walk in the way of evil men.
15 Avoid it, do not travel on it; turn from it and go on your way.

…..

20 My son, pay attention to what I say; listen closely to my words.
21 Do not let them out of your sight, keep them within your heart;
22 for they are life to those who find them and health to a man's whole body.
23 Above all else, guard your heart, for it is the wellspring of life.
24 Put away perversity from your mouth; keep corrupt talk far from your lips.
25 Let your eyes look straight ahead, fix your gaze directly before you.
26 Make level paths for your feet and take only ways that are firm.
27 Do not swerve to the right or the left; keep your foot from evil.

UNIFYING LESSON PRINCIPLE

People want to live life to its fullest. Are there ways to live that will make that happen? It is suggested in the book of Proverbs that those who make good choices and keep a righteous path will find fulfillment in life.

TOPICAL OUTLINE OF THE LESSON

I. **Introduction**
   A. Wisdom: Powerful Simplicity
   B. Biblical Background

II. **Exposition and Application of the Scripture**
   A. A Father's Plea
      (Proverbs 4:10-13)
   B. A Father's Warning
      (Proverbs 4:14-15)
   C. A Father's Insistence
      (Proverbs 4:20-23)
   D. A Father's Simple Directions
      (Proverbs 4:24-27)

III. **Concluding Reflection**

LESSON OBJECTIVES

Upon the completion of the lesson, the students will be able to:
1. Instruct those who desire and are seeking fulfillment in life;
2. Understand that a fulfilled life is largely dependent on the choices that we make in life;
3. Understand that the choices that we make can mean the difference between life and death, failure and success; and,
4. Show that the choices we make do matter.

POINTS TO BE EMPHASIZED
ADULT/YOUTH
Adult Topic: **The Wise Path**
Youth Topic: **Learn to Listen**
Adult/Youth Key Verse: **Proverbs 4:13**
Print Passage: **Proverbs 4:10-15, 20-27**

—Proverbs 4 is an extensive encouragement to follow the path of wisdom and righteousness. It uses the model of parental teaching handed down from one generation to the next to encourage readers to walk the path of righteousness and wisdom.

—Proverbs 4 relies heavily on direct commands that tell the reader or listener what to do. For example, "Keep straight the path of your feet" (see 4:26).

—Proverbs 4 sharply contrasts the ways of wisdom and righteousness with the way of wickedness, in order to encourage the reader to walk God's path of righteousness.

—Proverbs 4 asserts that following the teachings about wisdom and righteousness leads to life and healing, which is another way of talking about a fulfilling life.

CHILDREN
Children Topic: **Knowing Right from Wrong**
Key Verse: **Proverbs 4:14**
Print Passage: **Proverbs 4:10-15, 20-25**
—It is good to pursue wisdom daily.
—Children gain wisdom by listening to their parents.
—Doing right is the heart of wisdom.
—Turn your back on evil.
—Life is influenced by one's feelings and desires.
—Be careful of the company you keep, avoiding evil at all costs.

I. INTRODUCTION

A. Wisdom: Powerful Simplicity

Proverbs 4 serves as encouragement to the student to hold fast to the instructions of the father. These moral teachings will lead to the good path of life. According to ancient thought, it was the father's responsibility to instruct his children in the ways of wisdom. The concept of wisdom sounds simple, but it is essential if one wants to have a good life. There is an inherent goodness in following wisdom. So this text teaches the paths of life—the straight path and the path of the wicked. The sage (teacher) knew that the road to destruction was appealing and fraught with danger that would ultimately shorten a person's life. There was a general understanding in Old Testament days that evildoers died young, while the good lived to a ripe old age (verse 10). Therefore, for the sage, wisdom is the guardian of life—and if one follows it then this will lead to a long life.

B. Biblical Background

The central theme of Proverbs 4 is tradition. Wisdom is something that is passed on from generation to generation. In the ancient Israelite culture, information was passed along primarily orally. There were no publishing companies, books, or copier machines. Only the upper class and affluent were learned and had access to education. Most of the population was illiterate and passed information and knowledge through oral narratives. The frequency of the admonition to "listen" (verses 1, 10, and 20) illustrates that these messages were passed down by word of mouth. Specifically, verse 20 shows the sage (parent) being emphatic when he said, "Pay attention" (NIV). "Listen" in the Hebrew language is *shama,* which means "to hear intellectually with attention toward obedience"; "Hear, O Israel: The LORD our God is one" (Deuteronomy 6:4). This is not hearing for the sake of hearing—this is listening that transforms.

Wisdom, therefore, was considered the treasure of the ages passed down from one generation to the next. Each generation's success was predicated upon the sages' (parents') getting it right. Thus, the admonition was to listen—because wisdom was too valuable to be taken lightly.

Chapter 4 is an invitation to get wisdom. The child can inherit wisdom from the parent, thus being enabled to live a secure and stable life. These moral teachings were handed down from generation to generation in order to preserve the rich legacy of a covenant people, enabling the child to sustain the inheritance secured from the parent. This point is illustrated in the life and death of Barbara Hutton. According to *Time* magazine in its May 21, 1979, obituary of Barbara Hutton, the granddaughter of F. W. Woolworth, Barbara inherited several million dollars from her grandfather's estate at the age of twelve. Yet, her money did not make her happy. She was married to seven different men, including famed movie star Cary Grant. Her life was not only plagued by poor decisions and poor health, but she died as a recluse, reportedly weighing only eighty pounds. Her epitaph in newspapers across the country was, "Barbara Hutton, the poor little rich girl." Barbara's life circumstances are all too commonplace in the lives of men and women in the world whose obituaries could read "poor young, poor old incomplete life." So for the sage, wealth without wisdom is a heavy burden that can do more harm than good in one's life. Finally, we will note that chapter 4 has three segments, and each opens with an admonition to *listen* (verses 1-9, 10-19, and 20-27).

II. EXPOSITION AND APPLICATION OF THE SCRIPTURE

A. A Father's Plea
(Proverbs 4:10-13)

Hear, O my son, and receive my sayings; and the years of thy life shall be many. I have taught thee in the way of wisdom; I have led thee in right paths. When thou goest, thy steps shall not be straitened; and when thou runnest, thou shalt not stumble. Take fast hold of instruction; let her not go: keep her; for she is thy life.

These verses put the onus on the child (listener) to live a disciplined life and choose the straight path. There is much dialogue taking place around the nation concerning the role of the church in the lives of many young people who have made and are making harmful decisions. These decisions came with consequences that include death or prison. Funerals and court dates for those under the age of twenty-five are all too frequent for all of us parents, grandparents, and the church community. But it is made clear in the book of Proverbs that the first line of instruction is in the home. "Listen, my son, accept my words and you will live many years" (see verse 10). The implication is that the conduit of wisdom for the child is the parent. So the church's role is to reinforce the teachings (wisdom) of the parents and not supplant it, or even to be the original source of a child's wisdom.

Second, the child must be disciplined enough to hold onto the parents' teachings. Verse 13 reads, "Hold on to instruction, do not let it go; guard it well, for it is your life" (NIV). The word *instruction* means "discipline." The idea is to keep hold like a professional athlete who commits to the regimen of exercises. The concept is not punitive in nature; rather, it is freedom to walk through life without stumbling (verse 12). So the argument in this section is that the responsibility for the listener is to listen with all due diligence and then appropriate the lessons into a disciplined lifestyle. However, many young people have dismissed the teachings of their parents as old-fashioned, as if the teachings by their very nature will impede their freedom and individuality. Contrarily, wise instruction is not a hindrance to freedom, but a precondition of it.

B. A Father's Warning
(Proverbs 4:14-15)

Enter not into the path of the wicked, and go not in the way of evil men. Avoid it, pass not by it, turn from it, and pass away.

This section warns against the path of the wicked. "Do not set foot on the path of the wicked or walk in the way of evil men" (verse 14, NIV). Many of the wisdom sayings were probably nearly universally taught among

Hebrew households. This section mirrors the admonition of Psalm 1:1 (NKJV): "Blessed is the man who walks not in the counsel of the ungodly, Nor stands in the path of sinners, Nor sits in the seat of the scornful." Just as Proverbs 4:13 opens with an emphatic statement about instruction, so does verse 14 open with an emphatic warning for the child: "Do not set foot on the path of the wicked" (NIV). The way of the wicked can only lead to destruction.

Many young people make life decisions that land them in deep trouble, which their parents have to bail them out of. To those who are wise, their actions may seem strange. But sages knew long ago that young people were prone to do foolish things, and if left to themselves would walk in places where there "ain't no light." Light of dawn and deep darkness characterize the contrasting paths of righteousness (wisdom) and wickedness.

Last, the inference is that the child does not know what lies ahead, and if he or she follows the wisdom of the ages, he or she will be able to navigate the unknown and unforeseeable places that lie ahead of him. Only a fool walks where he cannot see and goes headlong into the unknown. This is essentially what a child does when he or she tries to live life without the benefit of the parent's instructions. In summary, a long and fruitful life is the promise of obedience.

C. A Father's Insistence
(Proverbs 4:20-23)

My son, attend to my words; incline thine ear unto my sayings. Let them not depart from thine eyes; keep them in the midst of thine heart. For they are life unto those that find them, and health to all their flesh. Keep thy heart with all diligence; for out of it are the issues of life.

This time, the admonition to the child is to "pay attention" (NIV) as if the parent had observed the child's losing focus—his mind beginning to drift and wander. So the parent, knowing how important the subject matter is, shouts, "Pay attention!" As children, we have all heard the instruction to "Pay attention!" more than a few times, and we know well what this means. This is the meaning of verse 20. "Pay attention to what I say; listen closely to my words" (NIV). The parent knows the importance of the lessons being taught. Thus, the inference is that wisdom is too precious to go unheeded! Second, the parent's words are to be kept in the heart, to inner self; that is the fountain of life. Again, the sage reiterated the importance of the heart as the well-spring from which good and evil choices are made.

Wisdom cannot be merely an intellectual activity for the child, for it is what is in the storehouse of the heart that governs the child's behavior. The mind might forget or rationalize, but the heart is the seat of moral discernment and decision making. This is the difference between knowing right from wrong, and actually doing what is right. The mind informs, but the heart convicts! Therefore, the admonition is to guard it. This image of guarding the heart is a powerful and provocative image. It is the image of someone standing as sentry over something that is important, valuable, and off-limits. It is a military security guard standing over a weapons depot, or a basketball player playing defense trying to keep the opposing player from scoring a basket. The child must guard his or her heart of wisdom with the diligence of a soldier or a basketball player. "Above all else, guard your heart"—this is serious business, so verse 23 is framed with a sense of urgency!

D. A Father's Simple Directions
(Proverbs 4:24-27)

Put away from thee a froward mouth, and perverse lips put far from thee. Let thine eyes look right on, and let thine eyelids look straight before thee. Ponder the path of thy feet, and let all thy ways be established. Turn not to the right hand nor to the left: remove thy foot from evil.

Finally, if the first thirteen verses instruct and contrast the two ways, the last four verses are instructions on practical ways to walk in the way of righteousness (wisdom). The story is told of an old crab who told a young crab to straighten up and walk straight. The young crab said to the old crab, "Show me how and I will." The last four verses are the how-to part of the instruction to the child. So notice the positive action phrases in each of these last four verses (NIV): "Put away" (verse 24); "Look straight" (verse 25); "Make level" (verse 26); and "Do not swerve" (verse 27).

The child is to put away perversity from his or her mouth and corrupt talk from his or her lips. There is a correlation between language and behavior. There is an element of rap music that glorifies vulgarity and violence. One should understand that it is not representative of all of the rap music industry; nevertheless, it has created a subculture of violence in the industry and among its consumers. Several years ago, when "gangsta' rap" was most popular, its language promoted a corresponding lifestyle of death and violence that ultimately led to the death of Biggie Smalls and Tupac Shakur. It is as much the language of any culture that gives definition to the culture as anything else. We identify people according to their language or dialect, although there are other ways of identifying people. It is as much the language of the individual that defines the character of the individual in many circles and the culture that he or she represents. Therefore, the sage instructed the child not only to guard his or her heart (see verse 23), but also to put away perversity from his or her mouth and corrupt talk from his lips. The idea is to "put away" words that are distorted, false, and injurious—and talk that does not promote healing. These cannot lead to a full life.

The second admonition is to look straight ahead and fix one's gaze directly before one. This is not tunnel vision; rather, it is a way to focus on what is before us on the road ahead. With cell phones and text messaging has come a rise in automobile accidents due to distracted drivers; hence, many states have enacted laws against texting while driving. There are certain activities that require us to pay attention and look straight ahead. This is the advice of the sage: "Keep your eyes looking straight ahead; fix your gaze directly before you" (see verse 25).

The third admonition is to take only the firm pathways of life (verse 26). The sage knows that all ground is not the same, for there is some that look solid, but is not. The implication in this warning is that looks can be deceiving, so the child must look straight ahead so he can discern and choose (make) the level paths that will lead to righteousness. The final admonition (verse 27) is that once you have chosen the right path, do not swerve to the left or to the right—but stay on the right path. It is not enough to *get* on the right path; one must *stay* on the right path. The teachings of the sage (parent) were to adhere to the path of wisdom and be careful and diligent in seeing to it that one does not stray. Living the moral life is a lifelong pursuit!

III. CONCLUDING REFLECTION

The wise path is not some arbitrary or objective choice to be made by each generation; rather, it is a strictly defined way that one must travel in order to come to a good conclusion. The sharp polarity of the two paths is fundamental to the Judeo-Christian heritage. The books of Psalms and Proverbs offer several teachings contrasting the way of the righteous and the way of the wicked. Likewise, in many of His parabolic illustrations, Jesus drew comparisons between two gates, two houses, and different soils. Howard Thurman, in his book *Deep Is the Hunger*, says, "There are certain options available to us when we are young, as the beginning of life and all the world stretches out before us, boundless and unexplored. But there is one option that remains ever available—I can select the things against which I shall stand with life and the things for which I shall stand." Wisdom makes the distinctions clear that with choices come consequences; so, "Choose for yourselves this day whom you will serve" (Joshua 24:15, NIV).

PRAYER

"*Lord, grant me the serenity to accept the things I cannot change, the courage to change the things I can, and the wisdom to know the difference*" ("Serenity Prayer," by Reinhold Niebuhr).

WORD POWER
Listen—to hear or to obey.
Guard—a lifeguard or a king's security guard.

HOME DAILY BIBLE READINGS
(September 5-11, 2011)

From Generation to Generation

MONDAY, September 5: "Guard Your Heart and Mind" (Proverbs 23:15-19)

TUESDAY, September 6: "Walk Uprightly" (Psalm 84:8-12)

WEDNESDAY, September 7: "Keep God's Commandments" (Joshua 23:1-8)

THURSDAY, September 8: "Lifelong Protection" (Psalm 91:9-16)

FRIDAY, September 9: "Walk in Your Parents' Paths" (Proverbs 1:8-15)

SATURDAY, September 10: "Prize Wisdom" (Proverbs 4:1-9)

SUNDAY, September 11: "Walk the Straight Path" (Proverbs 4:10-15, 20-27)

LESSON 3　　　September 18, 2011

TEACHING VALUES

DEVOTIONAL READING: **Proverbs 1:1-7**
PRINT PASSAGE: **Proverbs 15:21-33**

BACKGROUND SCRIPTURE: **Proverbs 10:1–15:33**
KEY VERSE: **Proverbs 15:32**

Proverbs 15:21-33—KJV

21 Folly is joy to him that is destitute of wisdom: but a man of understanding walketh uprightly.
22 Without counsel purposes are disappointed: but in the multitude of counsellors they are established.
23 A man hath joy by the answer of his mouth: and a word spoken in due season, how good is it!
24 The way of life is above to the wise, that he may depart from hell beneath.
25 The LORD will destroy the house of the proud: but he will establish the border of the widow.
26 The thoughts of the wicked are an abomination to the LORD: but the words of the pure are pleasant words.
27 He that is greedy of gain troubleth his own house; but he that hateth gifts shall live.
28 The heart of the righteous studieth to answer: but the mouth of the wicked poureth out evil things.
29 The LORD is far from the wicked: but he heareth the prayer of the righteous.
30 The light of the eyes rejoiceth the heart: and a good report maketh the bones fat.
31 The ear that heareth the reproof of life abideth among the wise.
32 He that refuseth instruction despiseth his own soul: but he that heareth reproof getteth understanding.
33 The fear of the LORD is the instruction of wisdom; and before honour is humility.

Proverbs 15:21-33—NIV

21 Folly delights a man who lacks judgment, but a man of understanding keeps a straight course.
22 Plans fail for lack of counsel, but with many advisers they succeed.
23 A man finds joy in giving an apt reply—and how good is a timely word!
24 The path of life leads upward for the wise to keep him from going down to the grave.
25 The LORD tears down the proud man's house but he keeps the widow's boundaries intact.
26 The LORD detests the thoughts of the wicked, but those of the pure are pleasing to him.
27 A greedy man brings trouble to his family, but he who hates bribes will live.
28 The heart of the righteous weighs its answers, but the mouth of the wicked gushes evil.
29 The LORD is far from the wicked but he hears the prayer of the righteous.
30 A cheerful look brings joy to the heart, and good news gives health to the bones.
31 He who listens to a life-giving rebuke will be at home among the wise.
32 He who ignores discipline despises himself, but whoever heeds correction gains understanding.
33 The fear of the LORD teaches a man wisdom, and humility comes before honor.

BIBLE FACT

Discipline in all its forms is one of the glaring marks of an authentic believer in Christ. Christians can be corrected when wrong. We can issue correction where it is needed. We can exercise constraint consistently. We can maintain routines in order to mature or lead. Discipline does not *make* us Christians; it *shows* that we are Christians.

People need good and effective advice in order to live well. Where can we find good advice? The book of Proverbs is full of advice that can guide us toward a godly life.

TOPICAL OUTLINE OF THE LESSON

I. **Introduction**
   A. Rewards and Punishment
   B. Biblical Background

II. **Exposition and Application of the Scripture**
   A. The Power of Words (Proverbs 15:21-24)
   B. The Lord Knows Our Hearts (Proverbs 15:25-26)
   C. The Righteous and the Wicked (Proverbs 15:27-29)
   D. Eyes and Ears, Heart and Soul (Proverbs 15:30-33)

III. **Concluding Reflection**

LESSON OBJECTIVES

Upon the completion of the lesson, the students will be able to:

1. Become acquainted with sayings that promote effective living;
2. Talk about their experiences of following wise teachings; and,
3. Apply godly principles to their lives.

POINTS TO BE EMPHASIZED

ADULT/YOUTH

Adult Topic: **Good Advice**
Youth Topic: **What's Wrong with Your Thinking?**
Adult/Youth Key Verse: **Proverbs 15:32**
Print Passage: **Proverbs 15:21-33**

—Proverbs 10:1–15:33 teaches values, using two-part verses that demonstrate contrasts between righteousness and wickedness.
—Proverbs makes strong connections between people's character and behaviors and the outcomes they experience.
—While the general attitude toward wealth is positive, the Proverbs urge kindness, generosity, and justice for the poor (see 11:24-25; 19:7; 21:13; 22:9; 31:8-9).
—Foolish people enjoy doing foolish things.
—God is pleased with the righteous and unhappy with the unrighteous.
—People who are wise heed and give good advice.
—God is not pleased with people who try to exploit others.
—To gain wisdom, a person must be humble and show respect to God.

CHILDREN

Children Topic: **Words for Living**
Key Verse: **Proverbs 15:13**
Print Passage: **Proverbs 15:13-22**

—A strong desire for discovering truth is a mark of wisdom.
—A mental diet is as important as a physical diet.
—Attitudes color one's personality.
—Seek the advice of people who can enlarge your vision and broaden your perspective.

I. INTRODUCTION

A. Rewards and Punishment

Proverbs 15 consists of a series of wisdom lessons. It is difficult to interpret these verses as a block of knowledge; however, if there is one unifying theme that runs the course of these wisdom sayings, it would be the moral philosophy of divine retribution. God rewards the wise (righteous) for their well-ordered behavior and language, while punishing the wicked (foolish) for their perverse language disrupting the social order. Chapter 15 contrasts the behavior and rewards of the righteous with the behavior and punishments of the wicked fool. Moreover, as purported by the sage, language, more than any other sphere of human activity, has the capacity to heal or to hurt at the deepest level. The right words can restore us to a place of harmony with God and with one another, whereas the wrong words can disrupt the balance of community and the world. Humanity's greatest innate capacity is its ability to use language creatively. Perhaps it is this gift—both creative and destructive language—that illustrates what it means to be created in the image and likeness of God. "The tongue that heals is the tree of life, but a devious tongue breaks the spirit" (see Proverbs 15:4). Language figures prominently in chapter 15.

B. Biblical Background

There are Old Testament theologians who reason that the language in this chapter is a direct reference to the language in the Garden of Eden. On the one hand, it was language that created reality, according to John 1. On the other hand, it was language (words) that ultimately led to the fall in the Garden of Eden (see Genesis 3). The world came into existence by the power of words and was declared to be "good and very good." Likewise, it was the persuasive power of perverted or demonic words that tempted Adam and Eve to be disobedient. It was also Adam's deceptive words that accused Eve of duping him into disobedience. The Garden of Eden's image characterizes wise speech as the mark of wisdom that leads to the "tree of life" (Proverbs 15:4). Conversely, the outcome of perverse speech (foolishness) is destruction.

II. EXPOSITION AND APPLICATION OF THE SCRIPTURE

A. The Power of Words
(Proverbs 15:21-24)

Folly is joy to him that is destitute of wisdom: but a man of understanding walketh uprightly. Without counsel purposes are disappointed: but in the multitude of counsellors they are established. A man hath joy by the answer of his mouth: and a word spoken in due season, how good is it! The way of life is above to the wise, that he may depart from hell beneath.

These verses connect the consequences of both appropriate and inappropriate speech. "A man who delights in foolishness lacks judgment, but a man of understanding keeps a straight course" (see verse 21). A fool is a person who thinks that rude and uncouth behavior is funny. There is no sense of etiquette or social graces when it comes to the treatment of others. What such a person does leads to destruction, but that person finds delight in it. A classic example of this idea is summed up in the phrase "ignorance is bliss." For the sage, there was a hairline difference between judgment and understanding. The word *judgment* is often understood in the Old Testament as "discernment—the capacity to know right from wrong." Verse 22 contains one of the many marks of one who demonstrates wisdom. A person of wisdom will seek the advice of the wise before making a decision. A wise person will not take it upon himself or herself to make important decisions without the wise counsel of another. Proverbs 11:14 (NIV) reads, "For lack of guidance a nation falls."

Conversely, success springs from the good counsel of many advisers. A person of wisdom knows that he or she does not have all of the sense or answers, so the wise thing to do is to seek the advice of another before engaging in an important project. These verses are not set as a contrast (as are many of the proverbs); rather, they are set as a reality for the wise.

Verse 23 again establishes that the mark of a wise person is seen in how he or she uses words to build up himself or herself and others. As a matter of fact, a person finds joy (pleasure, gladness) because he or she knows the effect of a good word. The wise person knows that what he or she says builds others up—it does not tear them down.

One of the troubling developments in American politics over the past few years is the intentional use of divisive language that has created great differences of opinion in our nation. The *Nashville Scene* newspaper carried the following story of Walt Baker, CEO of the Tennessee Hospitality Association: He sent a "joke e-mail," comparing First Lady Michelle Obama to Tarzan's chimp Cheetah. Baker then quoted comedian Larry the Cable Guy: "I don't care who you are! This is funny!" Baker sent the e-mail to prominent Nashvillians. It turned out to be no laughing matter for Baker, who was fired. He apologized but never seemed to get it, calling it "political humor" and did not understand the uproar. His e-mail joke was not appropriate or timely for any season. The sages might say that such crass political "humor" is the stuff of which folly is made, and the fool does not know the difference.

Finally, verse 24 brings the reader back to the straight path or the path of life, which is wisdom personified. On the other hand, folly leads to the grave (*sheol*). Yes, we will all die; it is the fate of creation since the Fall—all things must die—but the implication in this verse is that the foolish die young. For the sage, this is a premature death. For the wise, the path of life leads upward to a full and useful life. Although some might suggest that this upward path is eternal life, this is not the theology of the sage. Speech, behavior, and wisdom go together like hand-in-glove and when used appropriately will lead to a fulfilling life.

B. The Lord Knows Our Hearts
(Proverbs 15:25-26)

The LORD will destroy the house of the proud: but he will establish the border of the widow. The thoughts of the wicked are an abomination to the LORD: but the words of the pure are pleasant words.

"The LORD will destroy the house of the proud: but he will establish the border of the widow. The thoughts of the wicked are an abomination to the LORD: but the words of the pure are pleasant words" (verses 25-26). Verse 25 discusses two different kinds of persons: the proud and the widow. Accordingly, the Lord does not honor the proud and promises to destroy them, as opposed to blessing the widow. The widowed woman in Old Testament times was one of God's most lowly and humble creatures on the earth. Therefore, special provisions were made on Israel's Law for the widow. The sage used the widow, who had no inheritance in the community and was dependent upon the goodwill of others for survival, as an example of modesty and humility that pleases the Lord.

Conversely, the Lord says that He will destroy the proud. The Lord would tear down the proud man's house—not literally his house, but his or her life. His house could be his place of abode or his family or his friendships or his business; nevertheless, the Lord will bring it to ruin. The sage said, "Pride goes before destruction" (Proverbs 16:18, NIV).

The sage shifted the spotlight from the wise to the blessings of the Lord on the community that feared Him. Wisdom is of the Lord and the Lord acts in the blessings of the wise. Success, happiness, joy, and a good life are by-products of that wisdom. But there is also a negative reaction from the Lord toward those who do not fear Him. The Lord despises the proud and detests the thoughts of evil persons. Therefore, the Lord's reaction to the behavior of the wicked is set in juxtaposition to the Lord's reaction to the behavior of the wise (humble).

The outcomes of the wise and the wicked are obviously different. The Lord despises evil thoughts, but in contrast the Lord keeps the boundaries of the widow intact and "pure thoughts" are pleasing to the Lord.

C. The Righteous and the Wicked (Proverbs 15:27-29)

He that is greedy of gain troubleth his own house; but he that hateth gifts shall live. The heart of the righteous studieth to answer: but the mouth of the wicked poureth out evil things. The LORD is far from the wicked: but he heareth the prayer of the righteous.

One translation of the word *greed* (*batsa*) in Hebrew means "to plunder" or, in some instances, "unjust gain." Neither of these meanings suggests goodness; they both infer an unjust act. God created the earth and all of its resources for the good of all the people, and not just for an elite few. The language and the wisdom of these proverbs are theologically grounded in the Creation narrative in which the earth and everything in it belong to Yahweh and are to be used and shared for the advancement of the community for the good of all humankind. Greed upsets the ecological design of the Creator.

Greed may take away what others need, and although one might have the resources to buy more and more and more, in our excess someone else is being deprived. The sage considers greed an act of plundering that is taking by force or deception that which rightly belongs to another. Verse 29 concludes this section with another contrast between the Lord's response to righteousness and wickedness: "The LORD is far from the wicked: but he heareth the prayer of the righteous." "Far," in this context, does not mean spatial (as in time and space). An omnipresent God cannot be far from any of us (literally); rather, "far" is figurative and points to the moral distance between the righteousness of God and those who do wickedness!

"A greedy man brings trouble to his family" (verse 27, NIV). Greed is one of the seven deadly sins in Catholic theology. It has never been a good thing, even though we are living in an age where the lines are often blurred between want and greed. We are saturated 24/7 with media market forces designed to whet our appetites. Hence, we are a society of competitive excesses. Our buying habits are stimulated not by our needs as much as by our greed! It is often best asked, tongue-in cheek, "How many pairs of shoes can one wear at a time? Or how many cars can one drive at a time?" Yet, there is a perceived correlation in our society between things and success. The more things we can accumulate, the more successful we appear. But greed is a tornado; its force cannot be contained and will ultimately destroy everything in its path—even families and communities. Many families have been undone and communities destroyed by the addictive lifestyles of parents, community leaders, and others.

The theological intent of the sage is evident in verse 29b: "He heareth the prayer of the righteous." While the wicked are far from God, God hears the prayers of the righteous! God is sensitive to the concerns of the righteous and hears their prayers, but the concerns of the wicked "fall on deaf ears."

D. Eyes and Ears, Heart and Soul
(Proverbs 15:30-33)

The light of the eyes rejoiceth the heart: and a good report maketh the bones fat. The ear that heareth the reproof of life abideth among the wise. He that refuseth instruction despiseth his own soul: but he that heareth reproof getteth understanding. The fear of the LORD is the instruction of wisdom; and before honour is humility.

Notice the prominence of the heart in the teachings of the sage. The word *heart* is used four times (in verses 14, 15, 28, and 30) in chapter 15 and is the seedbed of all human behavior. The heart is like a mirror of the human personality that can only reflect what is in it! This is why what is in the heart is important to God. The sage closed in verse 33 (NIV) with one of the key themes of the book of Proverbs: "The fear of the LORD teaches a man wisdom" (see also Proverbs 1:7). Reverence (fear) of the Lord teaches wisdom. Again, for the sage, wisdom had its foundation in Israel's covenant laws. The Word of the Lord is an elixir for the people of God; when obeyed, it will lead to a good end (see Deuteronomy 10:11). This is the work of wisdom, and one's lifestyle can be summarized by the presence or the absence of wisdom. A song made popular by the late Johnny Mathis describes the wisdom of this chapter succinctly: "Fools rush in where wise men fear to tread."

III. CONCLUDING REFLECTION

It was the ability of African-American people under oppression and struggle to use words wisely to inspire hope, even in the midst of hopelessness. What they could not say in any other public forum they could say in music without the consequences meted out by cruel overseers (taskmasters). Humanity's greatest innate capability is its ability to use language creatively. So the sage in Proverbs 15 was certain that the evidence of wisdom was in the tongue.

Rev. Dr. Wyatt Walker, in his book *Somebody's Calling My Name,* writes, "It is safe to say that the Freedom Movement in the South is a 'singing Movement.' This is somewhat to be expected when one considers that music has the strange power to evoke various emotional responses in us. Somehow, the literature and idiom of music makes possible the restoration of lost hopes; it binds up the wounds of the broken-hearted." The freedom fighters in the South would sing, "I ain't going to let nobody turn me around. I'm going to keep on a walking, keeping on a marching...." The words rallied the black communities throughout the South, even though many of the fighters were not connected by the same social demographics; the words of the freedom songs became the common bond for all of the freedom fighters, regardless of race, creed, or ethnicity.

PRAYER

God of grace and God of mercy, be ever present with us as we attempt to discern Your will and Your way for our lives and the lives of our communities, our nation, and our world. Make pure our hearts and grant us wisdom to walk uprightly before you. In Jesus' name we pray. Amen.

WORD POWER

Greed *(batsa)*—to plunder or to covet, taking something that justly belongs to another.
Folly *(ivveleth)*—silliness in the sense that it violates God's law, or in speaking it refers to foolish chatter.
Righteous *(tsadaq)*—doing that which is just; this is a legal term and refers to the person who is just in all his or her relations.
Understanding *(towbunah)*—This is a wisdom word that connotes discretion. Understanding is the practical expression of wisdom.
Counselor *(yaats)*—prudence, or one who is skilled in law (God's law).

HOME DAILY BIBLE READINGS
(September 12-18, 2011)

Teaching Values

MONDAY, **September 12: "A Wise Child" (Proverbs 10:1-5)**

TUESDAY, **September 13: "Wise Words" (Proverbs 10:18-22)**

WEDNESDAY, **September 14: "Wisdom and Health" (Proverbs 10:23-28)**

THURSDAY, **September 15: "The Wicked and the Foolish" (Proverbs 12:12-16)**

FRIDAY, **September 16: "A Righteous Life" (Proverbs 14:27-34)**

SATURDAY, **September 17: "The Better Way" (Proverbs 15:15-19)**

SUNDAY, **September 18: "Instruction in Wisdom" (Proverbs 15:21-33)**

LESSON 4   September 25, 2011

WISDOM AND DISCERNMENT

Devotional Reading: **1 Kings 3:5-14**
Print Passage: **Proverbs 25:1-10**

Background Scripture: **Proverbs 25:1-28**
Key Verse: **Proverbs 25:9**

Proverbs 25:1-10—KJV

THESE ARE also proverbs of Solomon, which the men of Hezekiah king of Judah copied out.

2 It is the glory of God to conceal a thing: but the honour of kings is to search out a matter.

3 The heaven for height, and the earth for depth, and the heart of kings is unsearchable.

4 Take away the dross from the silver, and there shall come forth a vessel for the finer.

5 Take away the wicked from before the king, and his throne shall be established in righteousness.

6 Put not forth thyself in the presence of the king, and stand not in the place of great men:

7 For better it is that it be said unto thee, Come up hither; than that thou shouldest be put lower in the presence of the prince whom thine eyes have seen.

8 Go not forth hastily to strive, lest thou know not what to do in the end thereof, when thy neighbour hath put thee to shame.

9 Debate thy cause with thy neighbour himself; and discover not a secret to another:

10 Lest he that heareth it put thee to shame, and thine infamy turn not away.

Proverbs 25:1-10—NIV

THESE ARE more proverbs of Solomon, copied by the men of Hezekiah king of Judah:

2 It is the glory of God to conceal a matter; to search out a matter is the glory of kings.

3 As the heavens are high and the earth is deep, so the hearts of kings are unsearchable.

4 Remove the dross from the silver, and out comes material for the silversmith;

5 remove the wicked from the king's presence, and his throne will be established through righteousness.

6 Do not exalt yourself in the king's presence, and do not claim a place among great men;

7 it is better for him to say to you, "Come up here," than for him to humiliate you before a nobleman. What you have seen with your eyes

8 do not bring hastily to court, for what will you do in the end if your neighbor puts you to shame?

9 If you argue your case with a neighbor, do not betray another man's confidence,

10 or he who hears it may shame you and you will never lose your bad reputation.

BIBLE FACT

Integrity—the "men of Hezekiah" copied this section of the book of Proverbs, possibly to preserve them for posterity. They were careful to acknowledge that the proverbs were "of Solomon." They did not attempt to take credit for themselves, or try to attribute the work to King Hezekiah. They could have easily done these things, yet they exercised *integrity*. Doing the right thing when one can just as easily benefit oneself is a mark of integrity.

UNIFYING LESSON PRINCIPLE

People need principles by which to conduct their relationships in society. Where do we find such principles? The proverbs of Solomon suggest principles for developing good and equitable relationships.

TOPICAL OUTLINE OF THE LESSON

I. Introduction
   A. The Origin of the Proverbs
   B. Biblical Background

II. Exposition and Application of the Scripture
   A. God's Glory and Kings' Honor (Proverbs 25:1-3)
   B. Purging Wickedness from Leadership (Proverbs 25:4-5)
   C. Wisdom in Social Graces (Proverbs 25:6-7)
   D. Wisdom in Conflict Resolution (Proverbs 25:8-10)

III. Concluding Reflection

LESSON OBJECTIVES

Upon the completion of the lesson, the students will be able to:

1. Examine the wisdom of following godly advice in dealing with other people;
2. Reflect on what it means to treat others as we desire to be treated; and,
3. Take steps to live in humility before God and in harmony with others.

POINTS TO BE EMPHASIZED

ADULT/YOUTH

Adult Topic: **Neighborly Advice**
Youth Topic: **So You're Always Right**
Adult/Youth Key Verse: **Proverbs 25:9**
Print Passage: **Proverbs 25:1-10**

—The Background Scripture (Proverbs 25:1-28) teaches how to discern the appropriate behaviors for a number of specific social settings and situations.
—Proverbs 25:6-7 emphasizes the value of humility before the king. Such humility has positive application to a wide variety of relationships. In Luke 14:7-11, Jesus refers to this teaching.
—Proverbs 25:7-10 encourages thoughtful response rather than hasty reactions to situations.
—Proverbs 25:9 points to honesty, discretion, and respect as principles for settling differences.
—God can do anything He wants because of who He is; God does not have to explain what He is doing or has done.
—Let others exalt you rather than exalting yourself.
—Don't be too hasty to accuse someone, such as your neighbor; always discuss the matter in private, or you may be embarrassed.

CHILDREN

Children Topic: **Treasures in God's Word**
Key Verse: **Proverbs 25:11**
Print Passage: **Proverbs 25:1-10**

—God is greater than the mind can imagine.
—A major task is to work for good and justice.
—Humility is the mark of one who puts God first in life.
—Treat others as you wish to be treated.
—Make your life a fit dwelling place for God.

I. INTRODUCTION

A. The Origin of the Proverbs

When Prince William of England announced his engagement to Kate Middleton in November of 2010, the English media referred to her as a "commoner," to which many in the American media took exception. But in nations, such as ancient Israel, whose political structure was centered on a royal family or families, all others outside of the royal court are "commoners" and abide by the protocol of domestic behavior set by the royal court. However, this protocol had very little impact on most commoners, who in most instances lived agrarian lifestyles away from the palace—the seat of power. For many persons, the Proverbs are viewed as religious sayings, but according to many scholars, these proverbs were written to the children of the royal court to enable them to maintain their status quo. So, these royal teachings used spatial images of heights and depths to quantify the distances between the divine and kings, and kings and their subjects. The sage was sure about the order of sovereignty—God is sovereign above the king, and the king was sovereign above his subjects. Nevertheless, there is something in these teachings for the reader today. When the one who is judging is God, humility is called for by all who are subject to the authority.

B. Biblical Background

According to verse 1 of Proverbs 25, these wise sayings were authored by King Solomon in ancient times and were used in the royal court of King Hezekiah, and perhaps even edited by the court scribes. This was the ancients' way of footnoting and giving credit to the original author, King Solomon. These sayings were given to establish political and social order within the kingdom. The hierarchy was established and the people of the kingdom were to abide—Jehovah (God), the king, and then the people.

Solomon's wisdom established the hierarchy of social mobility as well as how political decisions were made in his kingdom. No one was to enter the king's presence without an invitation from the king (verse 7).

Foundational in the teachings of the book of Proverbs is that righteousness exalts a nation, but sin is a reproach (see 14:32). Perhaps it was this teaching that inspired the apostle Paul as he encouraged the Corinthian Christians to settle their disputes among themselves, rather than in a court of law. The righteous would have to settle with each other justly without the king's judgment.

II. EXPOSITION AND APPLICATION OF THE SCRIPTURE

A. God's Glory and Kings' Honor
(Proverbs 25:1-3)

THESE ARE also proverbs of Solomon, which the men of Hezekiah king of Judah copied out. It is the glory of God to conceal a thing: but the honour of kings is to search out a matter. The heaven for height, and the earth for depth, and the heart of kings is unsearchable.

Hezekiah, king of Israel, was a wise ruler who brought about major religious reforms in Israel after the death of his father, Ahaz (see 2 Kings 18:5-7a), who was wicked and brought idolatry to Israel. It was perhaps during this reform that the scribes of King Hezekiah rewrote the proverbs of Solomon. These verses distinguish the ways of kings and the ways of God. God conceals, while kings do not conceal. God's concealing represents His awesome greatness, while the king searches out the truth. The verb to *conceal* means "to hide by covering." God conceals His awesome greatness and the greatness of His wisdom. But the king's searching refers to the king's judicial function of bringing to light the hidden nature of the king's heart. Elsewhere in the Bible the word *unsearchable* is used of God and the vastness of creation (see Psalm 145:3; Isaiah 40:28). However, it referred to the king's heart. There is an adage that goes, "No one knows what is in a person's heart." This is the idea here in verse 3.

This concealing is not a matter of God's not wanting humanity to know; rather, it is a necessity borne out of the great chasm that exists between the mind of God and the mind of man! So, the sage said that God conceals the mysteries of creation that boggle the mind. An example of God's greatness and man's inability to comprehend is illustrated in *My Stroke of Insight,* by Jill Bolte Taylor, PhD—a brain scientist. She says, "As a member of the same human species, you and I share all but 0.01 percent (1/100 of 1 percent) of identical genetic sequences. So biologically, as a species, you and I are virtually identical to one another at the level of our genes (99.99 percent). Looking at the diversity in the world, only 0.01 percent accounts for a significant difference in how we look, think, and behave." If creation is this unsearchable, then how much more is the Creator? How do we understand and explain that of the billions of people on planet earth, 1/100 of 1 percent of the gene pool of humanity account for our being different and unique from each other? It is the glory of God to conceal a matter. But to search out a matter is what kings do. Thus, the sage was contrasting (and not comparing) God and kings. God conceals and kings search. The sage in verse 3 was not saying that the king's heart was not searchable as God is not searchable; rather, no one could know what was in the heart of the king as he made decisions (verse 2). We are the glory of God in creation, made a little lower than the angels, but the best are light years away from the greatness of the Creator.

B. Purging Wickedness from Leadership
(Proverbs 25:4-5)

Take away the dross from the silver, and there shall come forth a vessel for the finer. Take away the wicked from before the king, and his throne shall be established in righteousness.

During the process of refining silver, *dross* (or impurities) must be extracted from silver ore before a silversmith can make silver vessels.

Likewise, a king must remove wickedness from his court, if his court was to rule in justice and righteousness. This is a powerful image of the contamination of righteousness. One cannot reach a place of peace, justice, and morality without an intentional process separating corruption from righteousness. It was not unusual for a king to surround himself with counselors or advisors to instruct him in matters pertaining to the kingdom. The sage said that the king must drive out wickedness from his presence, because ultimately evil advice will lead to evil conclusions. As a silversmith could not make a precious vessel without the process of purifying the ore, neither could a king make a wise decision without sound advice. Unfortunately, King Rehoboam, son of Solomon, ascended to the throne of King David after the death of his father. King Rehoboam rejected the advice of elders of his court, who advised him to serve the people. He chose, rather, to take the advice of his peers, who advised him to be a tough taskmaster. Consequently, all of Israel rebelled against his throne (see 2 Kings 12). In too many instances, leaders surround themselves with "yes" people to give them the advice that they want to hear. The practical advice of the sage is to be intentional and weed out persons who are corrupt and who offer corrupt advice.

C. Wisdom in Social Graces
(Proverbs 25:6-7)

Put not forth thyself in the presence of the king, and stand not in the place of great men: For better it is that it be said unto thee, Come up hither; than that thou shouldest be put lower in the presence of the prince whom thine eyes have seen.

Years ago, a president of the National Baptist Convention commented on those who sat on the stage at the Convention: "It is better to be invited up than asked down." Beware of false assumptions and taking the king's court for granted. In spite of the distance we live today from royal courts, there is a word in this for us. We have become a people with many false assumptions about personal freedoms and others, even the church.

There is a gulf between those in high places and those who are not. Although we do not have a monarchy here in the United States of America, there is, nevertheless, a tremendous gulf between the president of the United States and the people of the state! There are certain areas of government that are off-limits to its citizens, except by invitation only. In 2009, a couple crashed an invitation-only function at the White House. They were summarily criticized, ridiculed, and investigated by both the FBI and the Secret Service for violating the protocol of the White House's social policy.

It was Jesus who picked up on this wisdom saying in Luke's gospel (see 14:1-11). Speaking a parable about the Pharisees, Jesus advised His followers, "When someone invites you to a wedding feast, do not take the place of honor....But when you are invited take the lowest place, so that when your host comes, he will say to you, 'Friend, move up to a better place'" (Luke 14:8, 10, NIV). Jesus concluded His parable with this saying: "Everyone who exalts himself will be humbled, and he who humbles himself will be exalted" (verse 11, NIV). This is practical advice about protocol and public graces. We must not assume that others think as highly of us as we think of ourselves. There is a thin line between humility and humiliation!

But there is also a spiritual element in this verse that points beyond itself to the work of

Jesus Christ. The doctrine of our salvation hinges on the reality that there was a great gulf between the righteousness of God and the unrighteousness of humanity. God bridged that great gulf via Jesus the Christ. Now all believers have access to the throne of grace, because of the work that Jesus did on Calvary (see Hebrews 4:14-16). The believer has a seat of honor in Christ Jesus!

D. Wisdom in Conflict Resolution (Proverbs 25:8-10)

Go not forth hastily to strive, lest thou know not what to do in the end thereof, when thy neighbour hath put thee to shame. Debate thy cause with thy neighbour himself; and discover not a secret to another: Lest he that heareth it put thee to shame, and thine infamy turn not away.

These sayings concern legal and domestic matters or disputes. The first seven verses in our lesson for today concern God and kings; the last three concern neighborliness. Good neighborly advice is to not meddle in the affairs of another—and if one must participate in the resolution of such matters then he or she should be honest and not violate confidentiality. The greater humiliation will come when the king (person in authority) adjudicates the matter and discovers the deception and dishonesty and shames one. In today's vernacular, this proverb is a warning against busybodies and gossipers who like meddling in the affairs of others.

We should all be forewarned not to violate the confidentiality of another by sharing secret knowledge with others. Clearly for the sage, such behavior, when discovered by an authority figure, could lead to being disgraced or taunted by the one settling the case. Years ago, before the advent of DNA testing, a young man was taken to court by a woman who claimed that he had fathered her child. The young man denied that the child was his. On the day of the trial, he encouraged his buddies to be his witnesses in court. They testified that they, too, had been intimate with the young lady. They tried to put her sexual history and character into question. The judge hearing the case discerned their deception, and since all of them claimed to have had sex with the young lady, all of them were ordered to pay child support. And so, the last laugh was on the young man and his friends. They were the laughingstock of the community! This story illustrates the folly that the sage was warning against.

III. CONCLUDING REFLECTION

Neighborly advice is common-sense advice for maintaining the proper social graces with people of authority and with one another. Humility is the condition that binds together this teaching. Honor will come to those who humble themselves in the presence of authority and in the settling of disputes in courts of law or with neighbors. There are some who will argue that there is an *integrity* crisis in America, but perhaps it is a *humility* crisis. Citizens cannot be trusted to be honest in domestic, economic, and political matters. What drives this behavior? It is driven as much by arrogant selfishness that asks "What's in it for me?" as it is by a lack of integrity. It is believed by many sociologists that it is "excessive individualism" that is leading to the demise of our society as we have known it.

Recent years have found our country

embroiled in a conversation over the use of political rhetoric that seems to be fanning the flames of hatred. Politicians are using war images and combative rhetoric to attack their opponents, and although Sarah Palin and Sean Hannity had no direct connection with the Tucson, Arizona, shooting of Representative Gabrielle Gifford, a nine-year-old girl, a federal judge, and several other bystanders, they have been accused of fanning the flames of hatred via politics in the country. Even in the face of such tragedy, both political sides are still trying to argue their particular points while calling for civility; hence, we are experiencing anything but neighborliness in the country. The late Archbishop Oscar Romero said, in his book *The Violence of Love,* "We must overturn so many idols; the idol of self first of all, so that we can be humble and only from our humility can learn to be redeemers, can learn to work together in the way the world really needs." This is the point of this lesson on neighborly advice.

PRAYER

Eternal God our Father, humble us this day so that we can serve You more perfectly, as we serve others. In Jesus' name we pray. Amen.

WORD POWER

Search *(chaqar)*—to examine, to seek out. This term is used in a court of law of a judge when a witness is examined to ascertain the truth.

Conceal *(cathar)*—to hide by covering. This term has to do with divine revelation and how God conceals truth, so that only those who want the truth can discover it.

HOME DAILY BIBLE READINGS
(September 19-25, 2011)

Wisdom and Discernment

MONDAY, September 19: "The Creator's Hiddenness" (Isaiah 45:9-17)

TUESDAY, September 20: "Asking for Wisdom" (1 Kings 3:5-14)

WEDNESDAY, September 21: "Humbly Seeking God" (2 Chronicles 7:12-18)

THURSDAY, September 22: "Words Fitly Spoken" (Proverbs 25:11-15)

FRIDAY, September 23: "Wisdom with Neighbors" (Proverbs 25:16-20)

SATURDAY, September 24: "The Wisdom of Self-control" (Proverbs 25:21-28)

SUNDAY, September 25: "Wisdom and Government" (Proverbs 25:1-10)

LESSON 5   October 2, 2011

AN ORDERED LIFE

DEVOTIONAL READING: **Deuteronomy 1:9-17**
PRINT PASSAGE: **Proverbs 29:16-27**

BACKGROUND SCRIPTURE: **Proverbs 28:1–29:27**
KEY VERSE: **Proverbs 29:25**

Proverbs 29:16-27—KJV

16 When the wicked are multiplied, transgression increaseth: but the righteous shall see their fall.
17 Correct thy son, and he shall give thee rest; yea, he shall give delight unto thy soul.
18 Where there is no vision, the people perish: but he that keepeth the law, happy is he.
19 A servant will not be corrected by words: for though he understand he will not answer.
20 Seest thou a man that is hasty in his words? there is more hope of a fool than of him.
21 He that delicately bringeth up his servant from a child shall have him become his son at the length.
22 An angry man stirreth up strife, and a furious man aboundeth in transgression.
23 A man's pride shall bring him low: but honour shall uphold the humble in spirit.
24 Whoso is partner with a thief hateth his own soul: he heareth cursing, and bewrayeth it not.
25 The fear of man bringeth a snare: but whoso putteth his trust in the LORD shall be safe.
26 Many seek the ruler's favour; but every man's judgment cometh from the LORD.
27 An unjust man is an abomination to the just: and he that is upright in the way is abomination to the wicked.

Proverbs 29:16-27—NIV

16 When the wicked thrive, so does sin, but the righteous will see their downfall.
17 Discipline your son, and he will give you peace; he will bring delight to your soul.
18 Where there is no revelation, the people cast off restraint; but blessed is he who keeps the law.
19 A servant cannot be corrected by mere words; though he understands, he will not respond.
20 Do you see a man who speaks in haste? There is more hope for a fool than for him.
21 If a man pampers his servant from youth, he will bring grief in the end.
22 An angry man stirs up dissension, and a hot-tempered one commits many sins.
23 A man's pride brings him low, but a man of lowly spirit gains honor.
24 The accomplice of a thief is his own enemy; he is put under oath and dare not testify.
25 Fear of man will prove to be a snare, but whoever trusts in the LORD is kept safe.
26 Many seek an audience with a ruler, but it is from the LORD that man gets justice.
27 The righteous detest the dishonest; the wicked detest the upright.

BIBLE FACT

The Scriptures encourage temperance in all things. We are warned against greed, just as we are warned against the unchecked surrender of our resources. Christian disciples must rein in anger, fear, haste, and countless other vices. Then we will find peace and see the hand of God working on our behalf.

TOPICAL OUTLINE OF THE LESSON

I. Introduction
   A. God's Justice in Our World
   B. Biblical Background

II. Exposition and Application of the Scripture
   A. Wicked People Create a Wicked Place (Proverbs 29:16-17)
   B. Visionaries and Examples (Proverbs 29:18-19)
   C. Haste Makes Waste (Proverbs 29:20-21)
   D. Anger and Pride (Proverbs 29:22-23)
   E. Self-hate or Trust in God (Proverbs 29:24-25)
   F. Whose Side Are You On? (Proverbs 29:26-27)

III. Concluding Reflection

LESSON OBJECTIVES

Upon the completion of the lesson, the students will be able to:

1. Discover the relationship between an orderly life and trust in God;
2. Reflect on what it means to live an ordered life; and,
3. Reevaluate their priorities in light of God's wisdom.

POINTS TO BE EMPHASIZED
ADULT/YOUTH

Adult Topic: Law and Order
Youth Topic: Discipline Me?
Adult/Youth Key Verse: Proverbs 29:25
Print Passage: Proverbs 29:16-27

—Proverbs 28:1–29:27 presents the wicked or greedy persons as those who disrupt harmony and security by ignoring God's laws. Specific examples show a variety of illustrations of the principle.
—Proverbs 29:25 teaches that those who honor God's laws in their lives find harmony and security.
—Proverbs 29:16 teaches that wickedness and unrighteousness affect the entire community. It also teaches that that righteousness will ultimately prevail.
—Wicked leaders will eventually fall.
—The prophet communicates God's will to the people.
—Proverbs 29:26 points to God and God's laws as the ultimate source of justice.
—Proverbs 29:27 expresses the tension and conflict that emerge when people confront injustice with God's righteousness and justice.
—A nation that keeps God's laws will be happy and not suffer moral decay.

CHILDREN

Children Topic: Follow the Right Path
Key Verse: Proverbs 29:26
Print Passage: Proverbs 29:16-27

—A disciplined life leads to happiness and peace of mind.
—Responsible citizens follow the law of God first.
—Actions speak louder than words.
—God provides us with safety.
—Humility leads to honor, while pride leads to disgrace.
—Think right thoughts before you speak or act.

I. INTRODUCTION

A. God's Justice in Our World

In 1997, while traveling down I-65 from Nashville, Tennessee, to South Florida to visit my father, I decided to stop in Montgomery, Alabama. My memory of the horrific days of the Civil Rights struggle was awakened when I visited Dexter Avenue Baptist Church, a small, red, brick church sitting at the foothills and in the shadow of the State Capitol of Alabama that had become a symbol of the struggle for "peace and justice for all." I recalled that moment in history when then-Governor George Wallace stood on the steps of the capitol building, declaring, "Segregation yesterday, segregation today, and segregation forever" to a rancorous, rebel flag-waving and cheering crowd.

The Rev. Dr. Martin Luther King Jr., in his "I Have a Dream" speech, characterized the hateful rhetoric of that era, when he said that the governor's lips were "presently dripping with the words of interposition and nullification." As I drove across the state of Alabama and other states, I observed that in almost every town and "hamlet" there was a street or a road or bridge that bore the name of Rev. Dr. Martin Luther King Jr. Today, a person would have to look hard and long to find a city that does not have a street named after this civil rights icon.

Conversely, the only place, even in Alabama, that I have seen a street or anything else named after the late Governor George Wallace, the face of southern racism and its resistance to "peace and justice for all," was in Montgomery, Alabama, around the State Capitol. God orders our lives according to the righteous judgment of God. Social structures might disrupt and oppress, but in the end it is the Lord who orders the ultimate steps of us all.

B. Biblical Background

Chapter 29 is a part of a section of the book of Proverbs that consists of what appears to be arbitrary wisdom sayings, with seemingly no connection to one another. But the contrary is true; there is a common theme. It is the contrast between the ways of the Lord and the ways of the wicked. These contrasts are between God and humanity, the righteous and the wicked in power, and the wise (justice) and the foolish (injustice). Proverbs 28:25 (NIV) reads, "A greedy man stirs up dissension, but he who trusts in the LORD will prosper." Leo G. Perdue, in his *Commentary on the Proverbs*, calls these varying wisdom sayings "antithetical."

These sayings are also set against the backdrop of several failed monarchies in the dynasty of David. In the northern kingdom, no dynasty succeeded in taking root, so the history of its kingship was one failure after another (read the books of 1 and 2 Kings; 1 and 2 Chronicles). The sage wanted to assure the student that there was security in trusting in the Lord. A recurring theme throughout Wisdom Literature is to "trust in the LORD with all your heart and lean not on your own understanding;…and he will make your paths straight" (Proverbs 3:5, 6, NIV). Israel reached a point in her history when she violated her covenant with God. They were disobedient and would not trust in the God of their fathers—Abraham, Isaac, and Jacob. This lack of trust ultimately led to the demise of both the southern kingdom (to Babylonian captivity) and the northern kingdom (to Assyrian captivity). Therefore, for the sage, a well-ordered life is the consequence of a healthy, trusting relationship with God. We learn that it does not matter that the wicked seem to triumph; the righteous will have the final word.

II. EXPOSITION AND APPLICATION OF THE SCRIPTURE

A. Wicked People Create a Wicked Place (Proverbs 29:16-17)

When the wicked are multiplied, transgression increaseth: but the righteous shall see their fall. Correct thy son, and he shall give thee rest; yea, he shall give delight unto thy soul.

There is a correlation between the prevalence of wicked people and sin within the community. Wicked people's doing wicked things is synonymous with sin in verse 16. When those who are without God thrive, so does sin. Sin is defined as missing the divine mark. Those who are without the Lord will cause sin to thrive. Some have questioned the relevance of the church today, but this test makes clear that sin increases as the number of people who are without God increases. It is the presence of God-fearing people that makes for a better community.

There is an implicit contrast in this verse—the outcome of the foolish will be witnessed by the righteous; they will see the downfall of the wicked. However, the downfall of the wicked is a consistent theme in the Bible, especially in the Old Testament. There will be a day of judgment for the wicked. King David declared, "My feet had almost slipped; I had nearly lost my foothold. For I envied the arrogant when I saw the prosperity of the wicked....then I understood their final destiny" (Psalm 73:2, 17b).

Too many of us, especially in our youth, have been attracted to ungodly lifestyles. We have made poor choices that have proven to be most dangerous and deadly, such as drug trafficking, strip dancing, and supporting music that denigrates women and promotes vulgarity. The ill-gotten or immoral gains from these enterprises have proven to be only for a season. In time, such actions often result in death, jail, and/or fractured relationships. But whatever they are coming to, it is a painful witness to have to visit them in jail or to say good-bye to them at the cemetery.

Verse 17 seems disconnected from verse 16, but the common denominator is that wise people should discipline their children so that they do not meet the fate of the wicked and thus bring sorrow to the parents. A wise son will do wise things and bring delight to the soul of the parent, but a wicked son will bring regret.

B. Visionaries and Examples (Proverbs 29:18-19)

Where there is no vision, the people perish: but he that keepeth the law, happy is he. A servant will not be corrected by words: for though he understand he will not answer.

This very familiar proverb reads, "Where there is no vision, the people perish" (verse 18). Another interpretation of this verse is, "Where there is no prophetic vision the people cast off restraint" (*Orthodox Jewish Bible*). Yet another translation is, "Where there is no vision, the people cast off restraint" (EVB). But for the sage, wisdom came from the Lord; hence, where there was no vision, there was no word from the Lord; and with no word, there was no wisdom. And without wisdom, the people will perish (cease). However, the *New Living Translation* (NLT) captures the idea best: "When people do not accept divine guidance, they run wild." Yet, the underlying presupposition in these verses is that the servant learns from the behavior of the master more than just from the words of the master. The Law was not just to be recited; it must be lived. Israel was admonished to "obey" all that God had commanded her. Her blessing was in her obedience.

There is an old adage in African-American southern culture to "Do as I say, and not as I do." This would be problematic for the teacher, because many of us are visual learners and learn from observing the behavior of those who have influence over us. Verse 19 reads, "A servant will not be corrected by words." Truth is best understood when it is applied! An old proverb tells the story of an old crab saying to a young crab, "Straighten up and walk straight." The young crab said, "Show me how to walk straight and I will." We learn best by example.

C. Haste Makes Waste
(Proverbs 29:20-21)

Seest thou a man that is hasty in his words? there is more hope of a fool than of him. He that delicately bringeth up his servant from a child shall have him become his son at the length.

Benjamin Franklin made famous the saying "Haste makes waste." This is the teaching of the sage. There is a connection between speaking in haste and speaking in folly. Please note that the absence of the Holy Spirit in one's life leads to folly. Patience is the opposite of haste. Therefore, the Bible admonishes us to live patient lives. A line from a poem by Alexander Pope (made famous in a song by Frank Sinatra)—"Fools rush in where wise men fear to tread"—captures the essence of verse 20. The parent must teach the child discipline and patience, which are the fruits of the wise. For the sage, haste in speech and in behavior was the height of folly (see Proverbs 17:27-28).

D. Anger and Pride
(Proverbs 29:22-23)

An angry man stirreth up strife, and a furious man aboundeth in transgression. A man's pride shall bring him low: but honour shall uphold the humble in spirit.

Nothing good comes from an imprudent man, either for himself or for the community. Notice the implied correlation between how one man's demeanor can affect the harmony of a community. An angry man stirs up dissension within the community. Yet, the hotheaded man, in his arrogance (opposite of humility), is oblivious to his impending downfall. But a humble spirit "will gain honor" in time. There will be a reversal of fortune—high becomes low, and the proud will be humbled. How much better off our families, communities, nation, and world would be if this wisdom guided our living. Anger does not just affect the one who is angry, but it impacts the community in negative ways. Most atrocities in the world begin with some sense of anger toward a particular group of people. Historians have noted that it was the anger of Hitler toward the Jewish people that kindled and led to the genocide of millions of Jews in Europe. One angry person can incite the masses to riot.

E. Self-hate or Trust in God
(Proverbs 29:24-25)

Whoso is partner with a thief hateth his own soul: he heareth cursing, and bewrayeth it not. The fear of man bringeth a snare: but whoso putteth his trust in the Lord shall be safe.

The criminal will trust his accomplice, but in the end it will be his accomplice who will turn over evidence to the state to save his own hide. The reality of this proverb is witnessed daily in criminal courts around the country. There is a crime series on cable television entitled *Gangsters*. In this series, many of the mafia chieftains were brought down by an insider who usually was apprehended by the FBI for a lesser crime. Under investigation, that insider would often strike a plea deal and turn over evidence to the state in exchange for a lesser sentence. He would "rat on" the crime family boss. John Gotti was convicted by the testimony of an underboss who made such an exchange to save himself. In one such case, an extortionist and murderer plea-bargained himself into the witness protection program at the government's expense in exchange for his testimony against his friends. Although there is a code of ethics and secrecy within these crime organizations, under the right pressure many criminal partners have "ratted" on their bosses to save their own necks. An accomplice will confess his own crimes as well as the crimes of others under the right conditions and pressure. This is why it is called "plea bargain" in the

court of law. The lesson is that no one can be trusted in partnership with wickedness, rather to do good and trust in the Lord.

Verse 25 is very practical. Often people are intimidated into committing various criminal or wicked behaviors by others who are perceived to have authority or power over them. In the days of these proverbs, "subjects of the kingdom" would look to the king or those near the seat of power to determine their behavior. If the king was a tyrant, then usually there was a trickle-down effect to the next social level. Don't fear those who sit in seats of authority; rather trust in the Lord, our Maker. Trusting in the Lord is the only assurance that any of us has that we will be kept safe. Rulers will come and go, but the Lord reigns forever.

F. Whose Side Are You On?
(Proverbs 29:26-27)

Many seek the ruler's favour; but every man's judgment cometh from the Lord. An unjust man is an abomination to the just: and he that is upright in the way is abomination to the wicked.

We live in a culture in which people are big on name dropping, networking, and hobnobbing. Unfortunately, we can become too reliant on these political/social connections and not trust in the One who makes all of these realities possible for us—the Lord. In antiquity, to have an audience with the king was an indication that one was well-connected and had influence. But the sage would say, "Trust in the Lord, who is the maker of us all." A modern adage says that "birds of a feather flock together." Likewise, "The righteous detest the dishonest; the wicked detest the upright" (verse 27, NIV). Jesus said that a person cannot serve two masters; either he will love one and hate the other, or cling to one and despise the other. Yet, we seem to be living in an age when good people are prone to compromise their values, if not condone unrighteous behaviors in the name of political alliance and friendship. But according to verse 27, a litmus test of true righteousness is how one feels about the behavior of the wicked regardless of what mode it takes or in whom it is found. The assumption is that the righteous align themselves with the divine perspective on good and evil. Righteousness and wickedness are antithetical points of view!

III. CONCLUDING REFLECTION

Two extreme currents seem to be engaged in combat for the souls of humanity. Perhaps this is why the apostle Paul said, "We wrestle not against flesh and blood, but against principalities" (Ephesians 6:12). These are factions that are invisible and mysterious to all of us. These factions draw us, even when we want to do the opposite. The late Benjamin E. Mays, president of Morehouse College, said in his book *Quotable Quotes*, "A man may and does lie, but he clings to truth as an ideal. Men are dishonest, some more than others, but man declares that 'honesty is the best policy.' The drunkard may not be able to stop drinking, but if he could choose for his son, he would choose for him a life of sobriety and temperance. The mother who has a questionable character prays that her daughter will be chaste." This lesson is on achieving a balanced life, so for the sage, this is done through listening to the wisdom of those whose lives have taught them how to walk straight and avoid the traps that can ensnare and hinder one from living a full life.

PRAYER

Eternal God, our Father, thank You for Your divine guidance. May our hearts be ever receptive to the teachings of Your wisdom. Also, enable us to impart Your wisdom to our children so that they, too, might live full and abundant lives. In Jesus' name we pray. Amen.

WORD POWER

Justice (tsedaka; Hebrew: *[tsed aw kaw]*)—rightness or virtue. Another meaning of this word is "prosperity." This understanding is a departure from the general belief that prosperity is material or other abundance. Rather, it is bringing righteousness and virtue to every area of one's life as God's grace empowers.

HOME DAILY BIBLE READINGS
(September 26–October 2, 2011)

An Ordered Life
MONDAY, September 26: "Impartiality in Judgment" (Deuteronomy 1:9-17)
TUESDAY, September 27: "The Danger of Pride" (2 Chronicles 32:20-26)
WEDNESDAY, September 28: "The Wisdom of Justice" (Proverbs 28:1-5)
THURSDAY, September 29: "Wisdom in Wealth and Poverty" (Proverbs 28:8-16)
FRIDAY, September 30: "Walking in Wisdom" (Proverbs 28:20-28)
SATURDAY, October 1: "The Wisdom of the Righteous" (Proverbs 29:2-11)
SUNDAY, October 2: "Wisdom in Practice" (Proverbs 29:16-27)

LESSON 6   October 9, 2011

THE SUPERIORITY OF WISDOM

Devotional Reading: **Psalm 33:13-22**
Print Passage: **Ecclesiastes 9:13-18**

Background Scripture: **Ecclesiastes 9:13–10:20**
Key Verse: **Ecclesiastes 9:16**

Ecclesiastes 9:13-18—KJV

13 This wisdom have I seen also under the sun, and it seemed great unto me:

14 There was a little city, and few men within it; and there came a great king against it, and besieged it, and built great bulwarks against it:

15 Now there was found in it a poor wise man, and he by his wisdom delivered the city; yet no man remembered that same poor man.

16 Then said I, Wisdom is better than strength: nevertheless the poor man's wisdom is despised, and his words are not heard.

17 The words of wise men are heard in quiet more than the cry of him that ruleth among fools.

18 Wisdom is better than weapons of war: but one sinner destroyeth much good.

Ecclesiastes 9:13-18—NIV

13 I also saw under the sun this example of wisdom that greatly impressed me:

14 There was once a small city with only a few people in it. And a powerful king came against it, surrounded it and built huge siegeworks against it.

15 Now there lived in that city a man poor but wise, and he saved the city by his wisdom. But nobody remembered that poor man.

16 So I said, "Wisdom is better than strength." But the poor man's wisdom is despised, and his words are no longer heeded.

17 The quiet words of the wise are more to be heeded than the shouts of a ruler of fools.

18 Wisdom is better than weapons of war, but one sinner destroys much good.

BIBLE FACT

In addition to what this lesson teaches, the Bible declares wisdom's superiority in several other ways:

- Wisdom is better than money (see Proverbs 16:16).
- Wisdom is better than foolishness, as much as light is better than darkness (see Ecclesiastes 2:13).
- Having wisdom is better than having power (see Ecclesiastes 9:16, 18).
- Godly wisdom is "ten times better" than fortune telling (see Daniel 1:20).
- The Spirit of wisdom empowers us to know the Lord better (see Ephesians 1:17).

UNIFYING LESSON PRINCIPLE

People are drawn in by loud voices that make an impression, even though these voices lack true wisdom. To whom should we listen? The book of Ecclesiastes teaches that we should not ignore the quiet, thoughtful words of the wise.

TOPICAL OUTLINE OF THE LESSON

I. Introduction
   A. The Truth about Wealth and Wisdom
   B. Biblical Background

II. Exposition and Application of the Scripture
   A. Poor with Wisdom (Ecclesiastes 9:13-15)
   B. Wisdom Is Better (Ecclesiastes 9:16-18)

III. Concluding Reflection

LESSON OBJECTIVES

Upon the completion of the lesson, the students will be able to:

1. Explore the story of a person, wise and poor, who delivered a city;
2. Recognize the superiority of wisdom over might;
3. Seek the great value of wisdom by asking God for wisdom and understanding; and,
4. Understand that riches and wealth are not the "be all to end all" in life.

POINTS TO BE EMPHASIZED

ADULT/YOUTH

Adult Topic: **Subversive Wisdom**
Youth Topic: **Wisdom versus Foolishness**
Adult/Youth Key Verse: **Ecclesiastes 9:16**
Print Passage: **Ecclesiastes 9:13-18**

—Gaining wisdom is a process of discernment to be used rather than a certain content to be mastered.
—The book of Ecclesiastes records *aphorisms* (personal observations) rather than *proverbs* (collective wisdom of the community).
—The book of Ecclesiastes does not offer solutions but poses penetrating questions.
—Looking at examples of wisdom helps us see how important it is to listen to a wise person.
—A poor, wise person saved the town, but he was not recognized because of his low economic status.
—The poor, wise person was able to save the town without using force.
—Words of wisdom spoken softly are better than loud words of foolishness.
—Foolish words can do a lot of damage.
—Acting in wisdom is better than using strong force.

CHILDREN

Children Topic: **An Example of Wisdom**
Key Verses: **Ecclesiastes 9:16 (18)**
Print Passage: **Ecclesiastes 9:13-18**

—Although wisdom is of great value, not everyone recognizes or accepts it.
—People honor wealth, success, and beauty above wisdom.
—People listen to the loudest voice backed by the most powerful weapon.
—Wisdom is better than strength and weapons of war.
—One person can greatly influence many.
—How one lives is a testimony of one's life in the Lord.

I. INTRODUCTION

A. The Truth about Wealth and Wisdom

Recently, a televangelist was heard preaching a sermon about material wealth from this text. He interpreted "the poor man" in verse 15 as one who had no money, was "broke," and was without means; and no one remembered him. His conclusion was that "no one remembers people who have no money. If you want to be remembered in life you must have money." His sermon was about the superiority of having wealth. Obviously, he did not recall history where "poor" people such as Martin Luther King Jr., Gandhi, and Mother Theresa not only were remembered, but left indelible marks on history. Neither did he do his homework on the word *poor*. *Poor* in the context of this Scripture does not refer to a lack of money. Rather, it is a metaphor for one deprived of influence and importance. Of course, the theme of the book of Ecclesiastes is that wisdom is better than folly and in the final analysis everything in creation is meaningless (see Ecclesiastes 1:2). For the ancient sage, there was no difference between the haves and the have-nots: "The LORD is the maker of them all" (Proverbs 22:2).

B. Biblical Background

According to its opening salutation, the book of Ecclesiastes was written by King Solomon. Professor Ellen F. Davis says that this book in its entirety is a book of incongruities. In chapter 2, the writer (also called the Teacher) lamented that there is no remembrance of the wise, yet triumphed that the use of wisdom leads to a useful life. The Teacher wrote from the experiences of both the ups and the downs of life and then imparted to the student the wisdom of many years. He concluded, "All is vanity and vexation of spirit" (Ecclesiastes 1:14). The underlying assumption of the Teacher was that the end goal of life was not wealth and materialism—because neither would bring fulfillment in life. In the final analysis, the Teacher concluded, "The end of the matter; all has been heard. Fear God, and keep his commandments, for this is the whole duty of man. For God will bring every deed into judgment, with every secret thing, whether good or evil" (Ecclesiastes 12:13-14, RSV).

The theme of chapter 9 is that life is in the Lord's hand, and that all people share a common destiny. In the kingdom of God, there is no social or political caste system. There are those who are good and bad, righteous and wicked, clean and unclean, but their distinctions were not in what they had. Rather, it is in the richness of the creature's relationship with the Creator (verses 1-2). This is what would make for a good life both now and later in the afterlife.

The second part of chapter 9 contains an assertion that wisdom is better than folly. The Teacher drew from the wealth of his experiences "under the sun" and what he had seen in life. He shared with us a parable of a man without influence who saved a city, yet by non-conventional means—and his deeds were soon forgotten. Israel in all of her rich history had many miracles through which the divine worked through ordinary persons, and rather than having an appreciation for the prophets, the people sought to persecute them. They showed no appreciation for that which we do not understand. God uses the seemingly illogical to confound those who are wise in their own eyes. The sage's understanding of wisdom is the right use of knowledge and is the synergy of both knowledge (divine and human) and experience. Conversely, folly is the misappropriation of knowledge. "A fool has said in his heart 'there is no God'" although the fool sees the evidence of God's handiwork in creation.

II. EXPOSITION AND APPLICATION OF THE SCRIPTURE

A. Poor with Wisdom
(Ecclesiastes 9:13-15)

This wisdom have I seen also under the sun, and it seemed great unto me: There was a little city, and few men within it; and there came a great king against it, and besieged it, and built great bulwarks against it: Now there was found in it a poor wise man, and he by his wisdom delivered the city; yet no man remembered that same poor man.

These verses tell the story of a poor, wise man who saved an entire city during a siege by an enemy king, and yet in the end the community forgot the poor man. Here, the Teacher gave an example of wisdom that impressed him. The story of the poor man is merely an example of the power of wisdom to effect unbelievable change. Again, if we are not careful, we will focus on the social location of the poor man and miss the point of the Teacher. People do not appreciate wisdom for what it is and what it does. Wisdom is not treasured by the masses. This eternal truth is expressed through this example of how fickle humanity can be toward the things that God values. The might of great men or women can be no match for a man or woman of wisdom. It is said in verse 14b that a powerful king, a king of great political capital and military might, laid siege on a small city, but it was wisdom, not might, that delivered the city.

Also, this teaching is consistent with the Old Testament narratives in which the Lord God of Israel used ordinary men and women to gain victory over great nations (for example: Joshua's wall of Jericho; the defeat of the imposing armies of the Syrian nation; and the destruction of the prophets of Baal). The prophet Zechariah said, "'Not by might or by power, but by My Spirit,' says the LORD" (Zechariah 4:6, NASB). This is the emphasis of these verses. If we are not careful, in a society that has come to view wealth and political clout with a sense of awe, we will forget the "poor wise man" altogether. In other words, we will not appreciate wisdom for wisdom's sake.

But indeed, God's ways are not our ways, and God's thoughts are not our thoughts. How many schools are named after J. Paul Getty, Howard Hughes, or Aristotle Onassis? These were the world's richest men at one time in history, but years after their deaths their names are not household names anymore. On the other hand, Mary McLeod Bethune, Booker T. Washington, and Nannie Burroughs are persons that history has long remembered because of their contributions to the uplifting of all of humanity. These names almost have become sacred as communities all over the world continue to recognize the principles and virtues for which they stood. Yet, by any measure of contemporary standards, these were poor persons. God used the foolishness of this world to confound the wise. He that was weak would become strong; she that will become great must be the servant—and in order to receive, one must first give. There is strangeness in the wisdom of God that confounds rational human thinking. The poor are those who have no money, yet demonstrate the spirit of the righteousness of God: they value the things of God rather than those things that are temporal.

B. Wisdom Is Better
(Ecclesiastes 9:16-18)

Then said I, Wisdom is better than strength: nevertheless the poor man's wisdom is despised, and his words are not heard. The words of wise men are heard in quiet more than the cry of him that ruleth among fools. Wisdom is better than weapons of war: but one sinner destroyeth much good.

It is obvious from verse 16 that the contrast in this text is not between the rich and poor, but it is between wisdom and strength. The History Channel often runs programs on the World Wars. When one considers the loss of lives and the trillions of dollars, and sheer destruction caused by these wars with the same problem yet persisting, we can see why "Wisdom is better than weapons of war" (verse 18). The sage was right: might and strength have proven inadequate to win and dominate the world, yet we continue to settle disputes through might instead of following God's precepts.

The war in Iraq has cost America ten billion dollars a month for several years, and the world is still no safer. Then the U.S. followed up by also fighting in Afghanistan. To what end? Years ago the United States engaged in *détente* (peaceful coexistence) during the Cold War with the Soviet Union. *Détente* came about between America and the Soviet Union because both countries had suffered economic hardship from their support of the Vietnam War. Therefore, in 1972, President Richard Nixon and the Soviet Union's Prime Minister Alexei Kosygin agreed on the Salt I Treaty that limited nuclear armament. It was economic hardship that eventually contributed to the demise of the Soviet Union. The sage was right: wisdom can do what bombs and bullets cannot do—if we would only heed its call.

Likewise, the quiet words of the wise are to be heeded over the shouts of the fool. But the reality of humanity is that we like the boisterous words of men speaking loudly and saying nothing more than we like the quiet, humble spirit of a wise person who, though speaking almost in gentle monotones, manages to say something significant. We must not be persuaded by the *loudness* of speech, but by the *soundness* of speech! Wisdom is superior to many things that the cultures of this world value. Yet, the sage knew that all of the good that a wise person could do could be quickly undermined by folly. In the vernacular of our culture, a wise saying goes, "one rotten apple can spoil the whole bunch."

III. CONCLUDING REFLECTION

In *Aesop's Fables,* there is the story of a farmer who discovered that he owned a goose that laid golden eggs. Initially, he thought that it was a joke, until he learned that the eggs were solid gold. It was not long afterward that he became a very rich man. Each morning, he would collect from the nest a golden egg that the goose had laid. After a while, he came up with the brilliant idea of killing the goose and getting all of the gold at one time. So, he killed the goose that laid the golden eggs, only to discover that there was nothing inside it. Like the farmer, what appeared to be obvious to human reasoning is often the farthest thing from it. Wisdom is the capacity to discern the difference between reality and fantasy. When we are driven by sheer greed, we can miss the obvious. Therefore, in a world fascinated by might and power, we must heed the words of Jesus that command us to "seek first the kingdom of God and all of its righteousness, and all else will be added to us."

PRAYER

Eternal Father, giver of every good and perfect gift, we pray for wisdom to know the difference between being that which You value and desiring the things that the world values. Help us to be mindful in our daily living that if we seek first Your kingdom, then our living will not be in vain. In Jesus' name we pray. Amen.

WORD POWER

Remember (Hebrew: *zakar* [zaw kahr])—to mention; to mark. This word is also connected to the words *memoir* and *memorial*. In application to our text, the citizens of the city who escaped destruction failed to remember that their freedom was secured by one of their own. They even failed to speak casually about having the good fortune of the presence of such great wisdom among them.

HOME DAILY BIBLE READINGS
(October 3-9, 2011)

The Superiority of Wisdom

MONDAY, October 3: "Hope in God's Steadfast Love" (Psalm 33:13-22)

TUESDAY, October 4: "Two Are Better than One" (Ecclesiastes 4:4-12)

WEDNESDAY, October 5: "Fear God!" (Ecclesiastes 5:1-7)

THURSDAY, October 6: "Consider the Work of God" (Ecclesiastes 7:1-14)

FRIDAY, October 7: "Wisdom and Success" (Ecclesiastes 10:5-11)

SATURDAY, October 8: "Wisdom with Words" (Ecclesiastes 10:12-20)

SUNDAY, October 9: "Wisdom Is Better than Might" (Ecclesiastes 9:13-18)

LESSON 7   October 16, 2011

WISDOM FOR AGING

DEVOTIONAL READING: **Psalm 71:1-12**
PRINT PASSAGE: **Ecclesiastes 11:9-10; 12:1-7, 13**

BACKGROUND SCRIPTURE: **Ecclesiastes 11:7–12:14**
KEY VERSE: **Ecclesiastes 12:13**

Ecclesiastes 11:9-10; 12:1-7, 13—KJV

9 Rejoice, O young man, in thy youth; and let thy heart cheer thee in the days of thy youth, and walk in the ways of thine heart, and in the sight of thine eyes: but know thou, that for all these things God will bring thee into judgment.

10 Therefore remove sorrow from thy heart, and put away evil from thy flesh: for childhood and youth are vanity.

.....

REMEMBER NOW thy Creator in the days of thy youth, while the evil days come not, nor the years draw nigh, when thou shalt say, I have no pleasure in them;

2 While the sun, or the light, or the moon, or the stars, be not darkened, nor the clouds return after the rain:

3 In the day when the keepers of the house shall tremble, and the strong men shall bow themselves, and the grinders cease because they are few, and those that look out of the windows be darkened,

4 And the doors shall be shut in the streets, when the sound of the grinding is low, and he shall rise up at the voice of the bird, and all the daughters of musick shall be brought low;

5 Also when they shall be afraid of that which is high, and fears shall be in the way, and the almond tree shall flourish, and the grasshopper shall be a burden, and desire shall fail: because man goeth to his long home, and the mourners go about the streets:

6 Or ever the silver cord be loosed, or the golden bowl be broken, or the pitcher be broken at the fountain, or the wheel broken at the cistern.

7 Then shall the dust return to the earth as it was: and the spirit shall return unto God who gave it.

.....

Ecclesiastes 11:9-10; 12:1-7, 13—NIV

9 Be happy, young man, while you are young, and let your heart give you joy in the days of your youth. Follow the ways of your heart and whatever your eyes see, but know that for all these things God will bring you to judgment.

10 So then, banish anxiety from your heart and cast off the troubles of your body, for youth and vigor are meaningless.

.....

REMEMBER YOUR Creator in the days of your youth, before the days of trouble come and the years approach when you will say, "I find no pleasure in them"—

2 before the sun and the light and the moon and the stars grow dark, and the clouds return after the rain;

3 when the keepers of the house tremble, and the strong men stoop, when the grinders cease because they are few, and those looking through the windows grow dim;

4 when the doors to the street are closed and the sound of grinding fades; when men rise up at the sound of birds, but all their songs grow faint;

5 when men are afraid of heights and of dangers in the streets; when the almond tree blossoms and the grasshopper drags himself along and desire no longer is stirred. Then man goes to his eternal home and mourners go about the streets.

6 Remember him—before the silver cord is severed, or the golden bowl is broken; before the pitcher is shattered at the spring, or the wheel broken at the well,

7 and the dust returns to the ground it came from, and the spirit returns to God who gave it.

.....

All people experience the aging process. Is there a way to appreciate the fullness of life without regard to our ages? The book of Ecclesiastes concludes that the only thing that makes life worth living is to remember and honor our creator God all the days of our lives.

13 Let us hear the conclusion of the whole matter: Fear God, and keep his commandments: for this is the whole duty of man.

13 Now all has been heard; here is the con-clusion of the matter: Fear God and keep his commandments, for this is the whole [duty] of man.

TOPICAL OUTLINE OF THE LESSON

I. Introduction
    A. The Vanity of Life
    B. Biblical Background

II. Exposition and Application of the Scripture
    A. Guidelines for Enjoying Your Youth/Enduring Old Age (Ecclesiastes 11:9-10)
    B. Party Now, Pay Later (Ecclesiastes 12:1-5)
    C. The Broken Life (Ecclesiastes 12:6-7)
    D. The Conclusion of the Matter (Ecclesiastes 12:13)

III. Concluding Reflection

LESSON OBJECTIVES

Upon the completion of the lesson, the students will be able to:

1. Discover the wonder and futility of life expressed in the book of Ecclesiastes;
2. Reflect on the meaning of life even as we move toward death; and,
3. Decide and act on a plan to honor God with mind, body, and soul.

POINTS TO BE EMPHASIZED
ADULT/YOUTH

Adult Topic: Life worth Living
Youth Topic: Enjoy Life while You Are Young
Adult/Youth Key Verse: Ecclesiastes 12:13
Print Passage: Ecclesiastes 11:9-10; 12:1-7, 13

—Death is the only certainty, and it ends all good things.
—The book of Ecclesiastes encourages people not only to enjoy life while they can but also to fear God and keep God's commandments.
—We should reflect on the meaning of life, even in youth.
—We should realize that wisdom comes from God.
—We should remember that God is the creator of all life.
—We must give an account of the life we live.
—We should listen to a wise person or teacher.

CHILDREN

Children Topic: Remember Your Creator
Key Verse: Ecclesiastes 12:1
Print Passage: Ecclesiastes 11:9-10; 12:1-7, 13

—We are not our own; we belong to God.
—Remembering God while one is young is the wise way to live.
—Make your strength available to God while you are still young.
—Some choices in life are irreversible.
—Respect for God's way is everyone's duty.
—Death may come early in life and it is final.

I. INTRODUCTION

A. The Vanity of Life

The primary purpose of the book of Ecclesiastes was to teach. There is much debate on who the author was; however, the author was a wisdom teacher who sought to impart to his young pupils practical advice that he had gathered over the years. The Teacher was aware of the potential danger of hoarding wealth or even enjoying it. He tried to teach his students how to avoid the consequences of greed and how to shun folly, because both were vanity. There was an ancient maxim: "Eat, drink, and be merry, for tomorrow you may die." The Teacher said, "So I commend the enjoyment of life, because nothing is better for a man under the sun than to eat and drink and be glad" (Ecclesiastes 8:15, NIV). The point is that the student was to enjoy life and not take it too seriously, because in the end all achievements, (in life) great and small will come to naught. Psalm 49:2 reads, "Both low and high, rich and poor alike." And Proverbs 22:2 reads, "Rich and poor have this in common: The LORD is the Maker of them all." The implication is that both will return to dust, for nothing in nature can change humanity's ultimate destiny.

B. Biblical Background

It was important for the Teacher that his students remember their Creator while they were young. The inference is that since the fear or reverence of the Lord is the beginning of wisdom, as the pupil grows older he will also grow wiser. Another understanding of this text is to enjoy life while one can because the day will come when one finds no pleasure in it. How many old persons have had to live with the consequences and regrets of foolish decisions they made when they were young? Most of them have summarily said, "If I could only live my life over, I would live it differently."

A hospital patient at a large metropolitan hospital suffered from a disease which made it necessary for him to use an oxygen tank in order to breathe. He asked the hospital's chaplain to pray that God would take his life because he did not want to live with emphysema. He bemoaned his years as a chain smoker. This sad story illustrates the gist of this lesson: what seems like the good life for a young person becomes the bane of old age, bringing with it pain and no pleasure.

The Teacher warned the pupil that life was fleeting and would be over before he or she realized it. The Teacher used several metaphors in chapter 12 to describe the process of growing old. It would not happen overnight; rather, aging is a slow process. First, the eyes grow dim and then the hearing grows faint, and the person stops finding pleasure in the things of his or her youth. Growing old is like an approaching storm: it is coming, but one cannot be sure of the exact moment of its arrival. The second warning is to shun anxiety from their hearts because it adds nothing to their lives. It is indeed interesting the things that many people get anxious or stressed about. Usually, it is something of a temporal nature and, according to Jesus, anxiety undermines their faith.

II. EXPOSITION AND APPLICATION OF THE SCRIPTURE

A. Guidelines for Enjoying Your Youth/Enduring Old Age
(Ecclesiastes 11:9-10)

Rejoice, O young man, in thy youth; and let thy heart cheer thee in the days of thy youth, and walk in the ways of thine heart, and in the sight of thine eyes: but know thou, that for all these things God will bring thee into judgment. Therefore remove sorrow from thy heart, and put away evil from thy flesh: for childhood and youth are vanity.

Although verses 7 and 8 are not part of the lesson Scripture, they will be expounded upon as background information (for further clarity on the lesson subject).

W. Sibley Towner, in his *Commentary on Ecclesiastes,* says, "The sage offers an assessment of the losses and terror of old age contrasted with opportunities that are presented to youth." Youth must be diligent in taking advantage of being young, because the day will come when their days will pass as the night season. Live and enjoy life and everything in it, because time is fleeting, and what once was will be no more. But we must be sure that today this is a qualified enjoyment and not a blank check to live without constraints.

Verse 9 contains instruction on how to live while being young. The young are advised to "Be happy…while you are young, and let your heart give you joy" (NIV). However, we are living in a culture whose parental teachings seem to be antithetical to the wisdom of this teacher. We encourage our children to live in the fast lane; hence, we have taken from them the opportunity to *be* young. We enroll our children in everything from ballet to AAU basketball, and these activities consume all of their free time. So when they are not in school they are in pursuit of their life's goals. Children are encouraged to live their lives with a sense of urgency and to grow up fast. But this teaching is antithetical to the attitude about life explained in our text. We do not have to rush life, because there is a time and season for everything under the heaven. A child ought to enjoy being a child, and a youth ought to enjoy being a youth.

Verse 10 (NIV) reads, "Banish anxiety from your heart." The meaning of *anxiety* in the Greek language (which is applicable here in this Hebrew text) is "those cares or concerns that cause one to lose sleep, and refuge is sought through drink or other solicitous behavior." *Banish* is a strong word that implies that one could be put away for good, as in exile. In simple words, children and youth ought not worry about adult things, because adulthood has enough of its own concerns and will come soon enough.

These are strange instructions for youth when we view them against the backdrop of today's culture. There are so many perils that youth have to deal with today. What was enjoyment five thousand years ago is not enjoyment today. Enjoyment is relative to the times! The road to adulthood today is fraught with danger for our children and our children's children. When I lived and taught in middle school in Atlanta years ago, the horrendous stories twelve- and thirteen-year-olds would share with me were mind-boggling. These young boys and girls, at even such young ages, boasted of weekends of robbery, shoplifting, sex, and drugs. They would say that they were "having fun." I am sure that this was not the case with all these young people; nevertheless, they shared many of the perils that all youth are exposed to today. The opportunities for mischief are much greater today than they were even fifty years ago. Yet, we are to encourage youth to be youthful and enjoy their young years, for the day is coming when the days of their youth will be over. The enjoyment of life was to be bracketed by the reality that God will bring all behavior into judgment. One day, we will all have to give an account for our behavior, whether good or bad.

B. Party Now, Pay Later
(Ecclesiastes 12:1-5)

REMEMBER NOW thy Creator in the days of thy youth, while the evil days come not, nor the years draw nigh, when thou shalt say, I have no pleasure in them; While the sun, or the light, or the moon, or the stars, be not darkened, nor the clouds return after the rain: In the day when the keepers of the house shall tremble, and the strong men shall bow themselves, and the grinders cease because they are few, and those that look out of the windows be darkened, And the doors shall be shut in the streets, when the sound of the grinding is low, and he shall rise up at the voice of the bird, and all the daughters of musick shall be brought low; Also when they shall be afraid of that which is high, and fears shall be in the way, and the almond tree shall flourish, and the grasshopper shall be a burden, and desire shall fail: because man goeth to his long home, and the mourners go about the streets.

Verse 1 (NIV) reads, "Remember your Creator in the days of your youth." This is not an easy verse to interpret because the Hebrew word for "creator" is not as explicit as it is in

English. There are several different translations of the word *creator*. For example, your health or well-being is just two to cite. Neither is the phrase "remember your creator" consistent with the verses that follow. So perhaps, the interpretation of the words *well-being* is more in line with the context of these verses. The Teacher instructed his pupils to guard their well-being while they were young, because the days would come when they would find no pleasure in being old.

According to verse 2, there would be a loss of vision and then depression would begin to set in. There would be a loss of health in all people from youth to old age. So the Teacher wanted the student to consider how he lives his life. Youthful years will not last forever, and the inference is that there will be a longing for those days.

Another reality of growing old was that youthful indiscretions would have a direct impact on life in old age. I believe that the evidence of this wisdom can be seen in many former professional athletes who, once their playing days are over, suffer from many different debilitating injuries that have made their lives difficult. A famous football player known as the "iron man" with the Pittsburgh Steelers was reckless and played although he was injured. Years after his career was over, he took his own life because he could no longer live with the pain. An autopsy revealed that his brain was similar to that of a person who had experienced a violent head-on collision. Perhaps the Teacher was saying that there is a correlation between the lifestyle of one's youth and the years of one's old age. Our bodies will fail us without any help from us accelerating the process of growing old. The Teacher was sure that we are all creeping toward our common destiny—dust.

C. The Broken Life
(Ecclesiastes 12:6-7)

Or ever the silver cord be loosed, or the golden bowl be broken, or the pitcher be broken at the fountain, or the wheel broken at the cistern. Then shall the dust return to the earth as it was: and the spirit shall return unto God who gave it.

The Teacher used an analogy of a broken cord, a shattered pitcher, and a broken wheel to teach about the fragility of life and finality of death. The images of a silver cord severed, a golden bowl broken, and a broken wheel that cannot be mended illustrate things that can no longer serve the purposes for which they were created. This is what life is like when one is old and has not lived a good life. Age cannot be undone, just as a silver cord or a golden bowl cannot be put back together again. Neither can a fruitless life be relived! Likewise, once a thing is broken or shattered, it no longer has the same use or value as it had when unbroken. The teacher emphasized that life has no greater value than it does in its youth; the pupil is encouraged to be a good steward of his youth, because spilled water cannot be reclaimed and a broken cord cannot be unbroken. This is the way it is with life; it all comes to a common end, so one should guard the years of one's life carefully because what is done cannot be undone.

D. The Conclusion of the Matter
(Ecclesiastes 12:13)

Let us hear the conclusion of the whole matter: Fear God, and keep his commandments: for this is the whole duty of man.

This verse could be the conclusion for all of Wisdom Literature. Once all is said and done, all wisdom boils down to these two instructions: "Fear God," and keep his commandments." Likewise, this verse also summarizes the Law of Israel (Mosaic Laws; see Deuteronomy 6:3-6), which had as its foundation the reverence of God and the keeping of the Lord's commandments. This sense of fear is more of what Rudolph Otto, in his book the *Idea of the Holy,* talks about is the *awe* of God. Humanity stands in *awe* of the otherness of God. The very holiness of God is so different from what we are that God's presence ought to inspire *awe* in each of us. This is the consistent theme of both the Old Testament and New Testament. God is holy and to be worshipped—not just in organized ritual, but in reverent attitudes toward God. This is the end of all instruction, the summation of all that can be said about life and wisdom. Finally, in the end God will bring all things into judgment, good or evil, and will have the final word. In the end, justice will prevail for both rich and poor, young and old, and good and evil. There will be a day of reckoning!

III. CONCLUDING REFLECTION

Often, we value our words and political power more than we ought to do, but in the end they are all meaningless. It does not matter how powerful one becomes or how profound one's words are. In the final analysis, they are all meaningless. As we listen to the political rhetoric that drives much of the social commentary today, it is laced with both false promises and slander. Some of the hardcore politicos make it seem that they have all of the answers and that all others are wrong. Some of the most hateful rhetoric one would ever want to hear is being heard over the airways. But in the grand scheme of God's creative design, it is all meaningless and will come to nothing.

It is clear from this lesson that God is a God of justice and will bring all things into judgment. So the people of goodwill must not grow weary at the appalling attacks and determinations of evil men and women. Archbishop Oscar Romero said, "The present form of the world passes away, and there remains only the joy of having used this world to establish God's rule here. All pomp, all triumphs, all selfish capitalism, all false successes of life will pass with the world's form. What does not pass away is love. In the evening of life, you will be judged on love." All else, the sage said, is "Meaningless! Meaningless! all is meaningless and vexation of the spirit."

PRAYER

Oh Lord, our Lord, how excellent is Your name in all of creation. We are humbled by the reality that all things are in Your hands and that our best will come to nothing! Now, God, we pray that our lives will be worthy of Your honor so that You will be glorified in us. Thank You, Lord, for all expressions of Your grace and mercy in our lives. In Jesus' name we pray. Amen.

WORD POWER

Vanity or meaningless *(mataios)*—deceptive, empty, or pointless.
Remember *(mnema)*—When used of humanity, it carries the idea of a memorial that constantly reminds; or to commemorate something. It is more than a mental act.
Judgment *(krino)*—a legal term that means "to seek justice or to resolve."

HOME DAILY BIBLE READINGS
(October 10-16, 2011)

Wisdom for Aging

MONDAY, October 10: "Do Not Forsake Me" (Psalm 71:1-12)

TUESDAY, October 11: "Nothing New under the Sun?" (Ecclesiastes 1:1-11)

WEDNESDAY, October 12: "Nothing to Be Gained?" (Ecclesiastes 2:1-11)

THURSDAY, October 13: "Toiling for the Wind?" (Ecclesiastes 5:10-20)

FRIDAY, October 14: "Everything Has Its Time" (Ecclesiastes 3:1-8)

SATURDAY, October 15: "Ignorance of God's Work" (Ecclesiastes 11:1-8)

SUNDAY, October 16: "Remember Your Creator" (Ecclesiastes 11:9–12:7, 13)

LESSON 8   October 23, 2011

TRADITION AND LOVE

DEVOTIONAL READING: Genesis 2:18-24
PRINT PASSAGE: Song of Solomon 4:8-16; 5:1a
KEY VERSE: Song of Solomon 4:16

BACKGROUND SCRIPTURE: Song of Solomon 4:8–5:1a

Song of Solomon 4:8-16; 5:1a—KJV

8 Come with me from Lebanon, my spouse, with me from Lebanon: look from the top of Amana, from the top of Shenir and Hermon, from the lions' dens, from the mountains of the leopards.

9 Thou hast ravished my heart, my sister, my spouse; thou hast ravished my heart with one of thine eyes, with one chain of thy neck.

10 How fair is thy love, my sister, my spouse! how much better is thy love than wine! and the smell of thine ointments than all spices!

11 Thy lips, O my spouse, drop as the honeycomb: honey and milk are under thy tongue; and the smell of thy garments is like the smell of Lebanon.

12 A garden inclosed is my sister, my spouse; a spring shut up, a fountain sealed.

13 Thy plants are an orchard of pomegranates, with pleasant fruits; camphire, with spikenard,

14 Spikenard and saffron; calamus and cinnamon, with all trees of frankincense; myrrh and aloes, with all the chief spices:

15 A fountain of gardens, a well of living waters, and streams from Lebanon.

16 Awake, O north wind; and come, thou south; blow upon my garden, that the spices thereof may flow out. Let my beloved come into his garden, and eat his pleasant fruits.

…..

I AM come into my garden, my sister, my spouse.

Song of Solomon 4:8-16; 5:1a—NIV

8 Come with me from Lebanon, my bride, come with me from Lebanon. Descend from the crest of Amana, from the top of Senir, the summit of Hermon, from the lions' dens and the mountain haunts of the leopards.

9 You have stolen my heart, my sister, my bride; you have stolen my heart with one glance of your eyes, with one jewel of your necklace.

10 How delightful is your love, my sister, my bride! How much more pleasing is your love than wine, and the fragrance of your perfume than any spice!

11 Your lips drop sweetness as the honeycomb, my bride; milk and honey are under your tongue. The fragrance of your garments is like that of Lebanon.

12 You are a garden locked up, my sister, my bride; you are a spring enclosed, a sealed fountain.

13 Your plants are an orchard of pomegranates with choice fruits, with henna and nard,

14 nard and saffron, calamus and cinnamon, with every kind of incense tree, with myrrh and aloes and all the finest spices.

15 You are a garden fountain, a well of flowing water streaming down from Lebanon.

16 Awake, north wind, and come, south wind! Blow on my garden, that its fragrance may spread abroad. Let my lover come into his garden and taste its choice fruits.

…..

I HAVE come into my garden, my sister, my bride.

UNIFYING LESSON PRINCIPLE

People find it difficult to express their feelings about love and life. How can we find words to describe our feelings? The books of Ecclesiastes and Song of Solomon use poetry and figurative language to talk about love and life.

TOPICAL OUTLINE OF THE LESSON

I. Introduction
   A. Sex: Business versus Truth
   B. Biblical Background

II. Exposition and Application of the Scripture
   A. Swept by a Glance
      (Song of Solomon 4:8-10a)
   B. Like a Garden—a Fountain
      (Song of Solomon 4:10b-15)
   C. The Consummation
      (Song of Solomon 4:16; 5:1a)

III. Concluding Reflection

LESSON OBJECTIVES

Upon the completion of the lesson, the students will be able to:

1. Enjoy the music of love found in the book of Song of Solomon;

2. Realize and accept the beauty and wonder of love shared in a committed relationship; and,

3. Act on building a relationship that honors a marriage commitment.

POINTS TO BE EMPHASIZED

ADULT/YOUTH
Adult Topic: A Kiss Is Still a Kiss
Youth Topic: Love in a Committed Relationship
Adult Key Verse: Song of Solomon 4:16
Youth Key Verse: Song of Solomon 4:10a
Print Passage: Song of Solomon 4:8-16; 5:1a

—The book of Song of Solomon is an extended love song or poem, graphic in its metaphorical references to romantic love.

—Traditional interpretations of the book of Song of Solomon have seen it as an allegory of the relationship between God and Israel, or between Jesus and the church—the bride of Christ.

—When read in the context of Israel's covenant tradition, the song can represent God and Israel's mutual longing.

—Scripture affirms marriage as the full expression of the love between a man and a woman.

—The king treasured his bride's love and thought it was the best thing that ever happened to him.

—The king cherished his bride's physical beauty.

—His bride invited him into her garden, where he could have first choice in all he wanted from her—both to his delight and to be refreshed forever.

CHILDREN
Children Topic: God Gives Good Gifts
Key Verses: Ecclesiastes 3:12, 13
Print Passage: Ecclesiastes 3:9-15

—Order, harmony, and beauty are characteristics of God's works.

—The things of the world do not bring lasting satisfaction.

—Doing good is the hallmark of happiness.

—People are to make proper use of God's good gifts.

—What God does lasts forever.

—God has placed eternity in the hearts of people.

I. INTRODUCTION

A. Sex: Business versus Truth

Sex is a flourishing industry in this nation. In its special, "Selling the Girl Next Door," television network CNN interviewed a young woman at a brothel in Las Vegas. The young woman called prostitution a vocation and said that she had been in the vocation since she was thirteen years old. She said, "Once I lost my virginity I said, 'What the heck, sex is no longer sacred.'" The owner of the brothel said that women can make between $100,000 to $600,000 a year in the business of sex. Love has indeed been made cheap by an industry that exploits and capitalizes on sex as a commodity. However, the young woman on CNN was correct: legitimate intimacy brings us into contact with the sacred. Sex is sacred!

We are not only spiritual beings, but also sexual beings. Therefore, it is impossible to understand our own humanity and our religious capacity to love God, love self, and love others without an awareness of both our spirituality and our sexuality. Ellen F. Davis is very poignant in her description of the message of sexuality in the book of Song of Solomon: "What the Bible tells us about God's love can help us come to recognize sexual love as an arena for the formation of the soul. Like the love of God, profound love of another person entails devotion of the whole self." The book of Song of Solomon is love poetry about an intimate and sexual relationship between the lover and the beloved. A kiss is a kiss? Perhaps it depends on the motive behind the kiss.

B. Biblical Background

The purpose of the book of Song of Solomon is to invite the reader to share the spirit of intimacy as an aspect of one's own life with God. The song affirms the incomparable joy of a faithful relationship with God and one's chosen mate. The adult topic of the lesson is "A Kiss Is Still a Kiss." The image of two lovers kissing is what it is—a symbol of deep intimacy that reaches to the depth of who they are as human beings. Also, it is believed by some scholars that this text was pointing toward Israel's infidelity with God, who had married Israel. Israel had been found wanting and lacking in her relationship with Yahweh.

However, the poetic prose of the book of Song of Solomon is not that different from the language in the story of the prophet Hosea and Gomer, in which Gomer was guilty of sexual infidelity. Her infidelity is a simile for Israel's infidelity to Yahweh. Therefore, the book of Song of Solomon affirms the great innate need that humanity has for intimacy with another and with God, and God's longing for intimacy with humanity. God, as a lover, is calling us, the beloved, into a faithful and intimate relationship with Him.

Also there are some images from the Garden of Eden of the lushness of a pristine environment in which love can flourish, pure and uncontaminated by sin. The images of Lebanon were relevant to the first readers of this book. Lebanon was known for its cedars and flourishing forests, teeming with animal life. Lebanon, therefore, became synonymous with fertility and was prominent in Greek mythology as a symbol of the goddess of fertility. Finally, Lebanon was a code word in Old Testament prophecy for Jerusalem as the glory of God's dwelling place (see Isaiah 60:13). The book of Song of Solomon is rich in its figurative language, but in the end it all points to Yahweh as the lover beckoning the beloved to faithfulness.

II. EXPOSITION AND APPLICATION OF THE SCRIPTURE

A. Swept by a Glance

(Song of Solomon 4:8-10a)

Come with me from Lebanon, my spouse, with me from Lebanon: look from the top of Amana, from the top of Shenir and Hermon, from the lions' dens, from the mountains of the leopards. Thou hast ravished my heart, my sister, my spouse; thou hast ravished my heart with one of thine eyes, with one chain of thy neck. How fair is thy love, my sister, my spouse!

This is a love song that continues from its opening verse: "How beautiful you are, my darling! Oh, how beautiful!" (Song of Solomon 4:1, NIV). The love song escalates throughout the chapter as the lover invited the beloved to follow him from Lebanon. He called her his bride, which suggests that the two had entered into a covenant vow with one another. Verses 6 and 7 set up and clarify verse 8. The bride was without flaw. Her beauty was compared to the fragrance and the ointments of Mount Lebanon. We cannot imagine what these words meant in the lover's day; nevertheless, they are words of endearment. It may be that the lover was striking at the power of a scent to transport our minds to a special memory in a different time and place. Myrrh and frankincense were precious and raw ointments (perfumes) and were treasured even in the days of Jesus many hundreds of years later. These were two of the gifts that the magi from the East brought to Jesus when they came to visit Him (see Matthew 2). But the beloved also was a woman with charm. Her charm arrested him; it sounds like "love at first sight." The writer also lavished praise on his beloved.

There is a love language that ought to accompany the love relationship between two people. It invariably includes "terms of endearment" in which the lover lavishes the beloved with intimate and loving words. The writer affirmed his lover and made her feel good about herself. It is not certain that she would be as beautiful to us as his words lead us to believe, but we are sure that she was beautiful to him. She was all of this to him, and that is the only thing that really matters in a love relationship. How do you feel about your mate? When was the last time you lavished praise on your mate? When was the last time that you said or did something special for your mate? What woman does not want to hear her man calling her beautiful and affirming her womanhood? What man does not want to hear his woman calling him handsome and affirming his manhood? Recently, I was in the presence of a man who spoke with great affection about his wife of over fifty years. With years taking a toll on her body and mind and his having to care for her like a child, he said with voice cracking and tears in his eyes, "She is just as beautiful today as when we met almost sixty years ago." It was with this kind of intimacy that the book of Song of Solomon speaks. Anybody can kiss, but is there any intimacy of the soul behind the kiss? The kiss merely affirms the language of endearment, the covenant vow of a love relationship.

B. Like a Garden—a Fountain
(Song of Solomon 4:10b-15)

How much better is thy love than wine! and the smell of thine ointments than all spices! Thy lips, O my spouse, drop as the honeycomb: honey and milk are under thy tongue; and the smell of thy garments is like the smell of Lebanon. A garden inclosed is my sister, my spouse; a spring shut up, a fountain sealed. Thy plants are an orchard of pomegranates, with pleasant fruits; camphire, with spikenard, Spikenard and saffron; calamus and cinnamon, with all trees of frankincense; myrrh and aloes, with all the chief spices: A fountain of gardens, a well of living waters, and streams from Lebanon.

The writer used images from nature to further enhance his description of his bride. He used wine, spices, nectar, honey and milk, cedar wood, pomegranates, myrrh, and henna to describe her. These herbs can be expected to be found in a garden. "[Her] lips drop sweetness as the honeycomb… milk and honey are under [her] tongue" (verse 11, NIV). What erotic images he painted! For the lover, merely describing her appearance could not express how lovely she was in his eyes, so he borrowed images that were unquestionably wonderful to all who read his description of his bride. It is the same kind of image found in God's description of the Promised Land, "a land flowing with milk and honey" (Exodus 3:8). Without a doubt, God wanted the people to know that the land was excellent beyond question. Since "beauty is in the eye of the beholder," the lover wanted the image of his beloved to be beyond question.

Some scholars call this a "garden poem," a reference to the Garden of Eden with all of its beauty. The "garden" was well-watered— "a well of living waters" (verse 15). Perhaps the writer was hinting at the passion that he experienced in intimacy with the beloved. It was a mysterious passion that was only of her. According to some commentaries, this verse is an allusion to the theme found in Proverbs 5:16-19 (RSV), in which the sage warned against adultery with strange women: "Should your springs be scattered abroad, streams of water in the streets? Let them be for yourself alone, and not for strangers with you. Let your fountain be blessed, and rejoice in the wife of your youth, a lovely hind, a graceful doe." He warned that sexual intimacy is not a frivolous or meaningless matter to be taken likely and sought after in non-covenant relationships (strangers). There is a mystery to intimacy to be found only in the beloved.

The word *fountain* takes the place of *garden* and is also synonymous with intimacy. Something mysterious was taking place between the lover and the beloved. He could not explain the energy that they shared; all he knew was that it was "love at first sight" (verse 1). So the best that he could do was to find images from creation to illustrate his passion and how she made him feel.

She was like a fountain of running water, a soothing sensation to both mind and touch. What a powerful metaphor a fountain of running water is! Years after these images were written, there is still a fascination with fountains and running water. It is not unusual to find fountains and running water in homes and offices, to quiet the spirit. Finally, the book of Song of Solomon is trying to describe the ecstasy that happens when two become one flesh. But clearly, we are in an age in which marriage is no longer a covenant between two people but a contract that can be broken at any inconvenience. The rate of divorce in America is 41 percent, and according to George Barna, president and founder of Barna Research Group, "It may be alarming to discover that born-again Christians are more likely than others to experience a divorce."

C. The Consummation
(Song of Solomon 4:16; 5:1a)

Awake, O north wind; and come, thou south; blow upon my garden, that the spices thereof may flow out. Let my beloved come into his garden, and eat his pleasant fruits. …I AM come into my garden, my sister, my spouse.

In these verses, we hear the voice of the beloved (her) for the first time. It brings to mind a love ballad in which the man sings the first few bars, but then the female voice is heard in response to what has been said. It is a call-and-response. She now invited the lover to enter her "locked garden." She asserted authority over her garden and granted the lover access to it. He eagerly accepted her invitation. Again, in chapter 5, the lover responded and came to her garden, and affirmed her: "I come…I gather…I eat" (verse 1).

Some scholars interpret these verses to mean that the lover and the beloved were consummating their marriage. The lover gathered all the sensuality that the beloved had to offer. Nothing was spared from his caress and indulgence. The marriage was consummated. In antiquity, marriage were consummated by sexual intercourse and not by a legal wedding certificate. This point is illustrated in the story of Jacob, Leah, and Rachel. Jacob preferred Rachel, but her father Laban duped him and gave him Leah first. Jacob's marriage to both Leah and Rachel were consummated by intercourse. However, this love song and narratives are not intended to be pornographic in nature; rather, they point the reader to a deeper spiritual reality—what it means to love absolutely and unconditionally is like the love that Yahweh has for His people! But, there is also a reasonable expectation of intimacy and fidelity between God and God's people. God is a jealous God (see Exodus 20:5); "You shall have no other gods before me" (Exodus 20:3). God was married to Israel, just as the church is the bride of Christ; and in both relationships, God expects fidelity (faithfulness).

III. CONCLUDING REFLECTION

Interpreting the book of Song of Solomon is difficult at best because of its figurative language. The writer used objects from the Garden of Eden to describe the lushness of the sensual body parts of the beloved. It is in the context of purity and innocence, when love is not contaminated by the lusts of the flesh. However, in a world such as ours, in which so much emphasis is placed on the human body, the meaning of this text can easily be misunderstood because figurative language is open for interpretation.

However, one thing that we can be certain of is that the lover in the book of Song of Solomon called the beloved to make a covenant vow with him. She accepted his invitation and they entered into intimacy together. The act of sexual intimacy is a sacred act when perpetrated in covenant union with one's soul mate. For the writer it is not a frivolous act to be indulged in with strangers.

The underlying theme of the book of Song of Solomon is the faithfulness of the lover and the beloved to each other. God is the lover calling the beloved (Israel and Christians) into a faithful relationship with Him. It is interesting that in the early years the opposition to the book of Song of Solomon as a sacred writing and its inclusion in the Bible was that there was no reference to God or a prophecy. But it appears that the entire book is a truth "type" that points beyond itself and to a great spiritual truth. The lover's love points to God's love for all of humanity. The greatest commandment is "to love the Lord your God with all your heart, with all your soul, and with all your mind, and to love your neighbor as yourself" (see Matthew 22:37-39). The book of Song of Solomon is a call to all believers to love the Lord with their total beings. However, this love must also be modeled in intimacy with and faithfulness to one's earthly mate. Jesus asked the question of us, "How can you only love God whom you have not seen, and despise your brother or sister whom you see daily?" (see 1 John 4:20). We are to love God as we love our mates. If we cannot perfect the latter, how can we master our first love, God, whom we have not seen?

PRAYER

Gracious God, we are grateful that You first loved us and called us to love You. We express our love to You and accept Your invitation to enter Your garden of love. May our lives be ones of faithfulness to You, and may we forever honor our covenant vow to You. In Jesus' name we pray. Amen.

WORD POWER

Bride (Hebrew: *kallah* [kal law])—It is translated as "spouse" in the KJV. This word easily translates to "wife" or "bride." But what is interesting—and more impactful—is its root word. It means "to complete." We are made complete by our spouses. This is not to be confused with being made whole; we are not half a person when we are single. Just as bread and ham can stand on their own, they cannot be a complete sandwich until they come together.

HOME DAILY BIBLE READINGS
(October 17-23, 2011)

Tradition and Love

MONDAY, October 17: "God Blessed Them" (Genesis 1:26-31)
TUESDAY, October 18: "One Flesh" (Genesis 2:18-24)
WEDNESDAY, October 19: "The Consequences of Unfaithfulness" (Jeremiah 3:1-5)
THURSDAY, October 20: "A Covenant of Love" (Hosea 2:16-23)
FRIDAY, October 21: "The Source of Love" (1 John 4:7-12)
SATURDAY, October 22: "The Expectations of Love" (1 Corinthians 13)
SUNDAY, October 23: "How Sweet Is Love!" (Song of Solomon 4:8–5:1a)

LESSON 9   **October 30, 2011**

LIVING AS GOD'S PEOPLE

DEVOTIONAL READING: **James 5:7-11**   BACKGROUND SCRIPTURE: **Matthew 5:1-12**
PRINT PASSAGE: **Matthew 5:1-12**   KEY VERSE: **Matthew 5:6**

Matthew 5:1-12—KJV

AND SEEING the multitudes, he went up into a mountain: and when he was set, his disciples came unto him:

2 And he opened his mouth, and taught them, saying,

3 Blessed are the poor in spirit: for theirs is the kingdom of heaven.

4 Blessed are they that mourn: for they shall be comforted.

5 Blessed are the meek: for they shall inherit the earth.

6 Blessed are they which do hunger and thirst after righteousness: for they shall be filled.

7 Blessed are the merciful: for they shall obtain mercy.

8 Blessed are the pure in heart: for they shall see God.

9 Blessed are the peacemakers: for they shall be called the children of God.

10 Blessed are they which are persecuted for righteousness' sake: for theirs is the kingdom of heaven.

11 Blessed are ye, when men shall revile you, and persecute you, and shall say all manner of evil against you falsely, for my sake.

12 Rejoice, and be exceeding glad: for great is your reward in heaven: for so persecuted they the prophets which were before you.

Matthew 5:1-12—NIV

NOW WHEN he saw the crowds, he went up on a mountainside and sat down. His disciples came to him,

2 and he began to teach them, saying:

3 "Blessed are the poor in spirit, for theirs is the kingdom of heaven.

4 Blessed are those who mourn, for they will be comforted.

5 Blessed are the meek, for they will inherit the earth.

6 Blessed are those who hunger and thirst for righteousness, for they will be filled.

7 Blessed are the merciful, for they will be shown mercy.

8 Blessed are the pure in heart, for they will see God.

9 Blessed are the peacemakers, for they will be called sons of God.

10 Blessed are those who are persecuted because of righteousness, for theirs is the kingdom of heaven.

11 Blessed are you when people insult you, persecute you and falsely say all kinds of evil against you because of me.

12 Rejoice and be glad, because great is your reward in heaven, for in the same way they persecuted the prophets who were before you."

BIBLE FACT

The "Sermon on the Mount" would more aptly be named the "Teaching on the Kingdom." Jesus mentioned the kingdom or the kingdom of heaven eight times in Matthew 5–7. Indeed, Jesus began here to lay out what it means to be a kingdom citizen, both in this life and the next.

UNIFYING LESSON PRINCIPLE

People seek happiness in their lives. Is there a way to satisfy the search? In the Beatitudes, Jesus lists nine ways that God blesses those who seek first the kingdom of God.

TOPICAL OUTLINE OF THE LESSON

I. Introduction
   A. Christian or Churchgoer?
   B. Biblical Background

II. Exposition and Application of the Scripture
   A. Jesus Begins to Teach about the Kingdom (Matthew 5:1-3)
   B. Happiness in Humility (Matthew 5:4-6)
   C. Happiness through Character (Matthew 5:7-9)
   D. Happiness in Tribulation (Matthew 5:10-12)

III. Concluding Reflection

LESSON OBJECTIVES

Upon the completion of the lesson, the students will be able to:

1. Present Jesus' teachings on blessings at the Mount;
2. Experience the blessings of God's reign already present on the earth; and,
3. Look for the blessings of the Beatitudes in everyday life.

POINTS TO BE EMPHASIZED
ADULT/YOUTH

Adult Topic: Seeking True Happiness

Youth Topic: What's with This Sermon?

Adult Key Verse: Matthew 5:6

Youth Key Verse: Matthew 5:12

Print Passage: Matthew 5:1-12

—A parallel statement of the Beatitudes is found in Luke 6:20-23.

—The key words *heaven* (verses 3, 10) and *righteousness* (verses 6, 10) highlight the divine and human dimensions of blessedness.

—Jesus expects disciples to live by kingdom blessings today rather than waiting for a future life.

—The inner life (meekness, purity) and the outer life (merciful, peacemaking) form a holistic way to live.

—Jesus affirms that those who embody the "blessed" life will face opposition, but will be rewarded ultimately.

—*Beatitude* is a Latin word meaning "happy" or "blessed."

—Following the Beatitudes will help us develop godly character.

—Living a godly life is not always going to be easy.

—Happiness and blessings are defined differently in the kingdom of heaven than they are in the world.

—The Beatitudes are part of the Sermon on the Mount.

CHILDREN

Children Topic: What a Blessing!

Key Verse: Matthew 5:12

Print Passage: Matthew 5:1-12

—Jesus went up on a mountain to teach.

—Nine times Jesus used the word *blessed*—meaning happy or satisfied—to describe the ideal person in Matthew's community.

—In verses 3-5, Jesus declares that God is with those who are poor in spirit, those who mourn, and those who are powerless and poor.

—Jesus declares in verse 6 that those who long for righteousness will receive it.

—In verses 7-12, Jesus affirms the social actions of some believers, actions that sometimes result in persecution; however, God rewards the faithful.

—Verses 7-12 uphold the qualities of those who seek mercy, sincerity, and peace, or who are persecuted for their actions.

I. INTRODUCTION

A. Christian or Churchgoer?

Living as God's people means abiding by rules and regulations that come to us from God. They are for us, but not from us. Over the next few Sundays the lessons will provide instructions on how to live as God's people. Areas of discussion include the following: Christian living requires more than mere lip service to please God. It will require the learner to move beyond worldly or carnal understandings of Christianity and hear what Jesus demands of us. To live up to the standards of the kingdom of God requires the believer to walk to the "beat of a different drummer."

Christianity for too many of today's churchgoers has become a religion of verbiage and not of living. It has been taught that a good Christian is one who has the right set of beliefs, like the Virgin Birth, the Resurrection, and the inerrancy of the Scriptures. Yet, while these beliefs are foundational, they cannot be held absent from the mandate of Jesus to love God and love our neighbors as ourselves.

The indictment that Christianity is one of talk more than action may seem harsh, but all we have to do is examine history to see that some of the most hideous acts and hideous times were periods when church attendance was at historical highs. Yet, crimes and immoral acts were being committed against other human beings by Bible-toting "Christians." Legend has it that the famous picture of the hanging of a Negro in a city in Nebraska was witnessed by a church congregation on Sunday morning. Worship was dismissed so that the congregants could witness the hanging event. Many of the killings and atrocities committed against the Negro were done by "good church folk," as in the case of the killing of the three civil rights workers in Philadelphia, Mississippi. Edgar Ray "Preacher" Killen, a Baptist minister, was convicted in 2005 of organizing the Ku Klux Klan mob that kidnapped and murdered the three workers in Philadelphia, Mississippi. To live as God's people requires more of us than just possessing right *beliefs*; we must also engage in right *practices*; we must live according to the principles of the kingdom of heaven.

B. Biblical Background

The gospel of Matthew was written to a Jewish community, announcing that the prophecy of the long-awaited Messiah was indeed fulfilled in Jesus. Matthew's gospel opens with the genealogy of Jesus and goes back to God's promise to Abraham, which was confirmed in King David. "This is the genealogy of Jesus the Messiah the son of David, the son of Abraham" (see Matthew 1:1). The first four chapters of the book of Matthew contain the narration of Jesus' birth, the flight to Egypt, the baptism of Jesus by John the Baptist, the testing of Jesus in the wilderness, and the call of His disciples. But then chapter 5 begins the teaching of Jesus on what it means to be part and parcel of the kingdom of heaven. For the Jew, the strict observance of the Law of Moses was necessary for salvation, but Jesus declared that they were guilty of observing the letter of the Law while missing the spirit of the Law.

The Sermon on the Mount in Matthew 5–7 consists of teachings and the reinterpretation of old sayings by which the Jewish community had been living. The first twelve verses of chapter 5 are known as the Beatitudes and indicate the way to blessings for Christians. Joan Chittister, in her book *Welcome to the Wisdom of the World,* says, "In the Beatitudes Jesus brings us beyond and above the motives that drive a world bent on power and greed, on profit and control. Instead, Jesus draws for us a template of godly happiness that is based on humility, compassion, justice, mercy, singleness of heart, peacemaking, and the willingness to pour ourselves out, to spend ourselves to make it all happen."

The aim of this lesson is to enable the student to move beyond the things that motivate him or her to live above the norms of a culture that glorifies power and greed.

II. EXPOSITION AND APPLICATION OF THE SCRIPTURE

A. Jesus Begins to Teach about the Kingdom (Matthew 5:1-3)

AND SEEING the multitudes, he went up into a mountain: and when he was set, his disciples came unto him: And he opened his mouth, and taught them, saying, Blessed are the poor in spirit: for theirs is the kingdom of heaven.

Jesus was very deliberate in His approach to His ministry. Here in the opening verses of Matthew 5, Jesus saw the crowd and grasped the opportunity to give some foundational teachings about authentic Christianity. He positioned Himself geographically so that His voice would resonate and carry so that the gathered crowd could hear Him. He "went up on a mountainside."

The meaning of the word *blessed* is a much-debated issue. It carries with it an unusual meaning in its original definition, but the translation of "happiness" seems to be the best of several possible meanings. *Happiness* is the state of peace that comes from living under God's rule. Christians find happiness not according to the world's standards, but according to the moral principles that Jesus outlined in these verses.

In verse 3, Jesus said, "Blessed are the poor in spirit, for theirs is the kingdom of heaven." The poor in spirit would be happy—their happiness comes from the assurance of having the presence of God, both now and in the world to come. However, the word *poor* has been used in an economic or financial sense, but this was not the thought of Jesus. He was not pointing to those who were destitute of the world's possessions. He used *poor* as a metaphor for those who were humbled and whose dependence was on God and not on material possessions. The psalmist had declared that God is near to "a broken and contrite spirit" (51:17, ASV; see 34:18). This is the gist of this verse: that God will not despise those who are of humble spirits and who understand that they are dependent on God.

After each "blessed are" comes what the blessing will be—"see God...be comforted," and so forth. Therefore, the Beatitudes are both for future and present assurance of blessedness. The poor in spirit will see God, both now and later.

B. Happiness in Humility
(Matthew 5:4-6)

Blessed are they that mourn: for they shall be comforted. Blessed are the meek: for they shall inherit the earth. Blessed are they which do hunger and thirst after righteousness: for they shall be filled.

Verse 4 reads, "Blessed are they that mourn: for they shall be comforted." There is a belief that God is biased toward those who have been dispossessed and exploited by systems and structures of injustice. Indeed, God's comforting of the dispossessed is one of the key themes that runs throughout both the Old and the New Testaments. Thus, Jesus granted assurance that there would be a day of reckoning in the kingdom of God for those who have been oppressed. Those who are citizens of the kingdom of heaven and are afflicted by the injustices of this world will be comforted. In the words of Howard Thurman, this is the Gospel message that speaks to "persons whose backs are against the wall." Mourning is not the end in and of itself; those who mourn would have something beyond this experience to look forward to.

Verse 5 reads, "Blessed are the meek: for they shall inherit the earth." The word *meek* does not mean a spiritless, weak, or cowardly person. *Meekness* in the kingdom of God is compatible with courage and great strength; it is a word used to describe a person who has a subservient and trusting attitude toward God. Also, meekness is demonstrated via a humble and gentle spirit in dealing with the hatred of others. The Bible characterizes Moses and Jesus as men of meekness (see Numbers 12:3; Matthew 11:29). There was a social system in Jesus' day whereby the aristocracy—the royalty, governmental figures, and military classes—were considered the most influential and important groups. All others were without influence and were a part of the underclass. Persons with position and power tended toward arrogance; therefore, this verse is saying that arrogant people will not inherit the earth; rather, the meek shall.

This does not mean that the meek will possess the earth and all of its wealth and power. The image of "inherit the earth" comes to us from Revelation 21, in which John saw a new heaven and new earth in which the old order would pass away and a new order would be established. In the kingdom of God, those who are meek in spirit will inherit the things that God has in store for the just, but will not be the recipients of a transfer of wealth.

Finally, verse 6 (NIV) reads, "Blessed are those who hunger and thirst for righteousness, for they will be filled." Normally, we do not think of those who are hungry or thirsty as being blessed. But Jesus used two metaphors to which the listeners could relate; to be hungry or thirsty in the desert region of Palestine was a serious matter. There was nothing blessed about being destitute of food or water in the desert region in which the multitude lived, so Jesus used two human conditions to emphasize the gravity of what He was saying. In the kingdom of God, righteousness is as essential for His followers as the need for food and drink. Just as humanity cannot live without food or drink, neither can those who desire to be a part of the kingdom of heaven live without righteousness. There must be a yearning for the righteousness of God. Likewise, these images of hunger and thirst cannot be separated from the images of Jesus the Christ in John's gospel in which Jesus is characterized as the Bread of Life and the Water of Life. "I am the bread of life. He who comes to me will never go hungry, and he who believes in me will never be thirsty" (John 6:35, NIV). They will be filled.

C. Happiness through Character (Matthew 5:7-9)

Blessed are the merciful: for they shall obtain mercy. Blessed are the pure in heart: for they shall see God. Blessed are the peacemakers: for they shall be called the children of God.

"Blessed are the merciful: for they shall obtain mercy" (verse 7). Mercy is one of the moral attributes of God. God is merciful and gives all of us the hand of forgiveness in dealing with our sins. William Shakespeare said of mercy:

"The quality of mercy is not strain'd.
It droppeth as the gentle rain from heaven,
Upon the place beneath. It is twice blessed:
It blesses him that gives and him that takes.
'Tis mightiest in the mightiest;
It becomes the throned monarch
better than his crown.

According to Shakespeare, mercy has the following qualities: impartiality, gentleness, and abundance. So as citizens of the kingdom of heaven we must be merciful, just as our heavenly Father is merciful.

Verse 8 reads, "Blessed are the pure in heart: for they shall see God." According to the Bible, the heart is the center of human personality. Jesus said it is "out of the overflow of the heart the mouth speaks" (Matthew 12:34b, NIV). Then in Matthew 15:19 (NIV), Jesus said, "Out of the heart come evil thoughts, murder, adultery, sexual immorality, theft, false testimony, slander." Only God can cleanse our hearts from these impurities. God is a righteous and just God, and only those who are pure in heart will see God. This promise is similar to the promise of Psalm 1 to those whose "delight is in the law of the LORD" (verse 2); "For the LORD watches over the way of the righteous" (verse 6, NIV). The promise was that they would see God, which is obviously an allusion to the age to come and a confirmation recognizing God's presence in the present age as well. Ultimately, those whose lives are not corrupted or contaminated by the systems of this world will have a part in God's eternal plan for a new heaven and a new earth.

Verse 9 reads, "Blessed are the peacemakers: for they shall be called the children of God." We live in a country that believes in intimidation and violence as a means to obtaining political ends. Over the past year, we have listened to the political rhetoric against President Obama. He is accused of being soft on leaders of other countries that historically have had hostile relationships with America. During the recent Egyptian revolt of 2011, the president was roundly criticized as being too passive. Likewise, he was ridiculed for saying that he would seek dialogue with the Prime Minister of Iran to iron out foreign policy differences. However, contrary to the beliefs of those who criticized President Obama, Jesus encouraged His followers to be peacemakers. A *peacemaker* is one who seeks harmony with another. The interesting thing about this virtue is that it has been demonstrated in our relationship with God toward us. We are to pass these virtues on to others, because we first experienced them in our relationship with Jesus the Christ. We are to seek peace and not war, and as peacemakers we will be called the children of God.

D. Happiness in Tribulation
(Matthew 5:10-12)

Blessed are they which are persecuted for righteousness' sake: for theirs is the kingdom of heaven. Blessed are ye, when men shall revile you, and persecute you, and shall say all manner of evil against you falsely, for my sake. Rejoice, and be exceeding glad: for great is your reward in heaven: for so persecuted they the prophets which were before you.

Verse 10 reads, "Blessed are those who are persecuted for righteousness' sake, for theirs is the kingdom of heaven." In these verses are the assurance and comfort for those whose "backs are against the wall." Here, Jesus was speaking to a multitude—mostly Jews—who knew firsthand what it meant to be persecuted. Palestine, the country in which Jesus and His people lived, was under Roman rule. During Jesus' lifetime, Caesar Augustus was emperor of Rome and had given Herod the Great and his sons political power to rule over Palestine. They were ruthless rulers who ruled with iron fists. Therefore, many in the multitude knew persecution personally, either from Caesar's political puppets or at the hands of the religious rulers of Judaism. In the book of Acts, the followers of Jesus were routinely persecuted for righteousness' sake (the stoning of Stephen in Acts 7:54-58, and the imprisonment of Peter in Acts 12 are two examples). Acts 12:1 (NIV) reads, "It was about this time that King Herod arrested some who belonged to the church, intending to persecute them." However, it must be clear that the persecution of which Jesus spoke was for righteousness' sake; not all persecution is for righteousness' sake. Persecution and suffering for righteousness will not be in vain, but it has a redemptive quality, just as Jesus' suffering on the cross was redemptive.

Finally, verses 11-12 are the continuation of the teaching in verse 10. In these two verses, Jesus gives specific examples of the ways in which His followers might be persecuted. "Blessed are you when people insult you, persecute you and falsely say all kinds of evil against you because of me. Rejoice and be glad, because great is your reward in heaven, for in the same way they persecuted the prophets who were before you" (NIV). False accusations were the means by which persons were put in prison or stoned to death. The Pharisees and Sanhedrin Council looked for people to bring false accusations against Jesus when they were trying to put Him to death. The blessing, here, is that when the believer is persecuted, he or she joins an elite company of God's agents in the world. Rejoice and be glad, because God will ultimately reward those who sacrifice themselves for the kingdom's sake, just as God rewarded the prophets before us.

III. CONCLUDING REFLECTION

The governance of the kingdom of God resides with God and not with humankind. There are many differences between the ways and standards of the world and the ways and standards of the kingdom of heaven. As believers, Jesus challenges us to live up to a standard that will not be appreciated by the world, and is contrary to its standards. These standards, if lived up to, might bring persecution and ridicule to the believer, but will be pleasing to God. So the relevant question of our age is this: What does it mean to be Christian? Jesus said, "Very truly I tell you, whoever believes in me will do the works I have been doing, and they will do even greater things than these because I am going to the father" (see John 14:12). To live as God's people means to live according to divine standards of justice, humility, gentleness, and purity of heart, and to have a yearning for the things of God. As the people of God, we are to live to glorify God on earth.

PRAYER

Lord God our Father, we are Your children, humbled by Your grace and mercy toward us. Grant us now Your peace that we may indeed be Your peacemakers in a world economically, socially, and politically fragmented and broken by conflict. Heal our land through us. In Jesus' name we pray. Amen.

WORD POWER

Merciful *(eirenopoios)*—describes one who seeks harmony with another or to bring to peace. Peace is produced in communion with God.

Blessed *(eneulogeo)*—often translated as "happy," but means "to confer a benefit." There is a benefit in living in communion with God.

Meek *(praios)*—a mildness of disposition or a person who wholly relies on God and not on one's own strength to defend against attack or injustice.

Poor *(ptochos)*—used in a qualified or relative sense of those who live under straitened circumstances.

Mourn *(pentheo)*—a grief or lament that cannot be hidden. A passionate lamenting that cannot be hidden. Also used to describe the lament of one's sin.

HOME DAILY BIBLE READINGS
(October 24-30, 2011)

Living as God's People

MONDAY, October 24: "A Lowly Spirit" (Proverbs 16:16-20)

TUESDAY, October 25: "Comfort for All Who Mourn" (Isaiah 61:1-7)

WEDNESDAY, October 26: "The Inheritance of the Meek" (Psalm 37:10-17)

THURSDAY, October 27: "The Way of Righteousness" (Isaiah 26:7-11)

FRIDAY, October 28: "Be Merciful" (Luke 6:32-36)

SATURDAY, October 29: "The Strength of My Heart" (Psalm 73:10-26)

SUNDAY, October 30: "Blessed by God" (Matthew 5:1-12)

LESSON 10   November 6, 2011

FORGIVING AS GOD'S PEOPLE

DEVOTIONAL READING: **Psalm 32:1-5**
PRINT PASSAGE: **Matthew 5:17-26**

BACKGROUND SCRIPTURE: **Matthew 5:17-26**
KEY VERSES: **Matthew 5:23-24**

Matthew 5:17-26—KJV

17 Think not that I am come to destroy the law, or the prophets: I am not come to destroy, but to fulfil.
18 For verily I say unto you, Till heaven and earth pass, one jot or one tittle shall in no wise pass from the law, till all be fulfilled.
19 Whosoever therefore shall break one of these least commandments, and shall teach men so, he shall be called the least in the kingdom of heaven: but whosoever shall do and teach them, the same shall be called great in the kingdom of heaven.
20 For I say unto you, That except your righteousness shall exceed the righteousness of the scribes and Pharisees, ye shall in no case enter into the kingdom of heaven.
21 Ye have heard that it was said by them of old time, Thou shalt not kill; and whosoever shall kill shall be in danger of the judgment:
22 But I say unto you, That whosoever is angry with his brother without a cause shall be in danger of the judgment: and whosoever shall say to his brother, Raca, shall be in danger of the council: but whosoever shall say, Thou fool, shall be in danger of hell fire.
23 Therefore if thou bring thy gift to the altar, and there rememberest that thy brother hath ought against thee;
24 Leave there thy gift before the altar, and go thy way; first be reconciled to thy brother, and then come and offer thy gift.
25 Agree with thine adversary quickly, whiles thou art in the way with him; lest at any time the adversary deliver thee to the judge, and the judge deliver thee

Matthew 5:17-26—NIV

17 "Do not think that I have come to abolish the Law or the Prophets; I have not come to abolish them but to fulfill them.
18 I tell you the truth, until heaven and earth disappear, not the smallest letter, not the least stroke of a pen, will by any means disappear from the Law until everything is accomplished.
19 Anyone who breaks one of the least of these commandments and teaches others to do the same will be called least in the kingdom of heaven, but whoever practices and teaches these commands will be called great in the kingdom of heaven.
20 For I tell you that unless your righteousness surpasses that of the Pharisees and the teachers of the law, you will certainly not enter the kingdom of heaven.
21 You have heard that it was said to the people long ago, 'Do not murder, and anyone who murders will be subject to judgment.'
22 But I tell you that anyone who is angry with his brother will be subject to judgment. Again, anyone who says to his brother, 'Raca,' is answerable to the Sanhedrin. But anyone who says, 'You fool!' will be in danger of the fire of hell.
23 Therefore, if you are offering your gift at the altar and there remember that your brother has something against you,
24 leave your gift there in front of the altar. First go and be reconciled to your brother; then come and offer your gift.
25 Settle matters quickly with your adversary who is taking you to court. Do it while you are still with him on the way, or he may hand you over to the judge,

UNIFYING LESSON PRINCIPLE

People wonder if good, harmonious relationships are possible. Can't we all just get along? Jesus teaches us that forgiveness is crucial to Christian living.

to the officer, and thou be cast into prison. 26 Verily I say unto thee, Thou shalt by no means come out thence, till thou hast paid the uttermost farthing.

and the judge may hand you over to the officer, and you may be thrown into prison. 26 I tell you the truth, you will not get out until you have paid the last penny."

TOPICAL OUTLINE OF THE LESSON

I. Introduction
   A. The Truth about Forgiveness
   B. Biblical Background

II. Exposition and Application of the Scripture
   A. Godly Righteousness (Matthew 5:17-20)
   B. Murder by Mouth (Matthew 5:21-22)
   C. Kingdom Citizens Forgive Others (Matthew 5:23-26)

III. Concluding Reflection

LESSON OBJECTIVES

Upon the completion of the lesson, the students will be able to:

1. Recount Jesus' teaching about reconciliation;
2. Experience the joy of forgiving and being forgiven; and,
3. Work toward making reconciliation a priority in their lives.

POINTS TO BE EMPHASIZED

ADULT/YOUTH

Adult Topic: Living in Harmony with Others

Youth Topic: Should I Forgive?

Adult/Youth Key Verses: Matthew 5:23-24

Print Passage: Matthew 5:17-26

—Promise and fulfillment are important biblical themes—that is, Christ fulfills the Law and Prophets.

—Jesus asserted His role as teacher in reinterpreting the application and intent of the Law.

—In response to the prior grace of God, believers worship with thankful hearts and obedient lives. True worship requires faithful, consistent ethical behavior among worshippers.

—Jesus criticized scribes and Pharisees because of their inconsistent practice of faith that impeded the faith of those for whom they had responsibility (see Matthew 23).

—Jesus assured the disciples that He did not come to abolish the Old Testament laws, but to fulfill them.

—It was important to Jesus that the people have the right attitude toward the Law.

—Keeping the Law is more than just obeying it outwardly; it also includes having a change within the heart.

—Jesus said that anger needs to be properly managed and dealt with.

—Repentance and reconciliation are top priorities with Christ.

CHILDREN

Children Topic: Can I Really Forgive?

Key Verse: Matthew 5:24

Print Passage: Matthew 5:17-26

—Jesus is the fulfillment of the Law and the Prophets.

—Jesus teaches that keeping the commandments and teaching others to do the same leads to greatness in the kingdom of heaven.

—Jesus taught that showing anger toward or insulting another person would have dire consequences.

—Jesus taught that the act of forgiveness and reconciliation precedes giving a gift at the altar.

—Jesus taught that reaching an agreement with an opponent is better than fighting the opponent in court.

I. INTRODUCTION

A. The Truth about Forgiveness

Forgiveness is a tough act of grace, yet God has given us grace and calls us to forgive one another (see Matthew 6:12-14). However, we live in a culture and society that teaches us to hold grudges. Our system is punitive, and teaches revenge and retribution against wrongdoers. We do not teach forgiveness in our culture. Instead, we have cliques that promote restraint against a forgiving spirit. We "forgive, but we don't forget. The first offense is on me, but the next one is on you." In a conversation about a conflict between two men, one man said to a counselor, "I can't forgive the person who offended me until he comes to me and asks for it." But this is not biblical. In the Bible, forgiveness is initiated by the offended and not the offender. If one has to ask for it then it is not forgiveness. Forgiveness is what God does for us. The apostle Paul wrote to the church in Rome: "But God demonstrates His own love for us in this: While we were still sinners, Christ died for us" (Romans 5:8, NIV).

As Jesus began teaching a different way of looking at religion, at the top of His list was forgiveness. As we study these lessons, it is interesting that these principles that were being taught by Jesus find their genesis in the character of God. Forgiveness is vital in the kingdom of heaven, because it is what gains us entry into heaven—God's forgiving us. Consequently, God commands and expects us to forgive others. As we struggle with the act of forgiveness, the question that we all must ponder and that is at the heart of the ministry of Jesus is, "Can there be redemption without forgiveness?" Both Jesus and the Bible say no.

B. Biblical Background

This lesson is a continuation of the Sermon on the Mount, but Jesus shifted His focus from the principles of governance for the kingdom of heaven to challenging some of the traditional teachings of Judaism. Over the centuries, the Jewish leaders had developed commentaries (Midrash) to give interpretation of the Law of Moses. These laws became codified in Jewry and the people were expected to live according to them. The Sadducees, the Pharisees, the Essenes, and other groups inside Judaism disagreed about various passages in the Law and how they should be interpreted and applied. What does it mean to remember the Sabbath in order to keep it holy? Who is one's neighbor? And what does it mean to use the Lord's name in vain? The subsequent interpretations became a rigid oral tradition that was enforced by the religious leaders. So a key phrase in the Sermon on the Mount and in this chapter (see Matthew 5:21, 27, 31, 33, 38, and 43) is, "You have heard that it was said." Over time, these interpretations—written and oral—were many and varied and the people could not keep track of all of them. Therefore, Jesus began in verse 17 challenging the status quo of the importance of these oral traditions. Over time the oral tradition began to overshadow the written laws of Moses. The religious leaders were honoring the letter of the Law, but missed the spirit of the Law.

The Sermon on the Mount is divided into units according to the issues involved in these interpretations that needed to be clarified. Why Jesus chose this time to clarify these traditions is not certain. Perhaps He was drawing on personal experience from having lived among the people for thirty years and hearing these oral traditions repeated over and over, yet difficult to follow. Jesus established a new code of ethics for the people of God to live by; yet, He wanted to be clear that He did not come to destroy these traditions, but to fulfill (*plerosia*) the Law that they sought to expand upon or clarify.

II. EXPOSITION AND APPLICATION OF THE SCRIPTURE

A. Godly Righteousness
(Matthew 5:17-20)

Think not that I am come to destroy the law, or the prophets: I am not come to destroy, but to fulfil. For verily I say unto you, Till heaven and earth pass, one jot or one tittle shall in no wise pass from the law, till all be fulfilled. Whosoever therefore shall break one of these least commandments, and shall teach men so, he shall be called the least in the kingdom of heaven: but whosoever shall do and teach them, the same shall be called great in the kingdom of heaven. For I say unto you, That except your righteousness shall exceed the righteousness of the scribes and Pharisees, ye shall in no case enter into the kingdom of heaven.

After establishing His mission as it pertained to bringing clarity to the oral tradition and interpretation of the Law, Jesus summarized this section in verse 20 (NIV) as He dealt with the true righteousness of God: "For I tell you that unless your righteousness surpasses that of the Pharisees and the teachers of the law, you will certainly not enter the kingdom of heaven." The Pharisees were the guardians of the laws for the Jews; yet, much of their living was primarily for public display. In the words of Jesus, they did things to be "seen of men"; hence, Jesus called them hypocrites (Matthew 6:5). For the Jews, righteousness was achieved by observing the Law—over six hundred laws. It was impossible to remember them all or to abide by them all. So, in the words of the apostle Paul, these religious sects tried "to establish their own the righteousness but not according to righteousness of God" (see Romans 10:3).

Righteousness (dikaiosune) is "the quality of being right that conforms to the revealed will of God." Righteousness is one of the moral attributes of God. Thus, Jesus said that one's righteousness cannot be fabricated, but is the result of one's having a right relationship with God. The righteousness of the Pharisees was predicated upon the observance of rituals and traditions that did not speak for God nor represent Him. Jesus said that the righteousness of God's people must exceed their righteousness. In our society, this is tantamount to religion without principles. It is fascinating how Christianity does not seem to demand much of us in America. A good Christian is described as one who attends church, believes the doctrines of the church, and pays tithes; yet, there are very few demands of social responsibility. But Jesus ushered in a different expectation. He called us to live beyond the trappings of the public display of religion, and to abide by another standard of ethical behavior.

B. Murder by Mouth
(Matthew 5:21-22)

Ye have heard that it was said by them of old time, Thou shalt not kill; and whosoever shall kill shall be in danger of the judgment: But I say unto you, That whosoever is angry with his brother without a cause shall be in danger of the judgment: and whosoever shall say to his brother, Raca, shall be in danger of the council: but whosoever shall say, Thou fool, shall be in danger of hell fire.

Douglas R. A. Hare, in his commentary on the book of Matthew, calls these sayings of Jesus "antitheses whose intent is to place Jesus over against other Jewish interpretations of the Torah." The first two antitheses relate to the Decalogue (Ten Commandments). "You shall not murder and you shall not bear false witness against your brother" (see verses 21-22). But Jesus says, "You have heard that it was said to the people long ago, 'Do not murder, and

anyone who murders will be subject to judgment'" (verse 21, NIV). What Jesus is saying is that use of abusive and insulting language toward another is unacceptable in the kingdom of heaven. He uses two words, *raka* and *fool*, which were considered as abusive language in Jesus' day. *Raca* is an Aramaic term and meant "contempt." To call a person a *fool* was to profane the person. We live in a society today that promotes the speaking of one's mind. Many see it as honorable to speak one's mind, even if this is hurtful and insulting to another. But Jesus deemed such a practice as inappropriate if it is injurious to one's brother or sister. He likened these inappropriate expressions of anger to murder.

Obviously, this is not a blanket indictment against anger, because the Bible says, "Be angry, but sin not" (Psalm 4:4, RSV). Jesus was stirred to anger by the moneychangers in the Temple, and took a whip and drove them out. Anger must be appropriate and non-injurious to one's brother or sister. If not, it has the same capacity to destroy the spirit of a person as murder does in the physical sense. When people use injurious language against others, the will of God for God's people is being denied. This is the tone and the tenor of Jesus' statement in these verses. So Jesus said that one who was accused of such contempt against his brother would have to answer to the Sanhedrin Council, the "Supreme Court" of ancient Israel. They were granted certain legal powers by the Roman Empire in order to maintain Roman peace among the Jews. Jesus said that when contempt was uttered against a brother, the offending party must answer to the Sanhedrin Council. But to call someone a fool was a greater offense and the offending party must give an account to God. Jesus was contrasting behavior under the Law versus that in the kingdom of heaven. It is not the act that constitutes the sin; rather, it is the conception of the sin in one's heart.

In our society, we use the phrase "character assassination" to refer to instances in which a person's reputation has been sullied by innuendos and misinformation. Well, what Jesus is saying is that murder can be both literal and figurative. The literal act of murder speaks for itself, but there are other ways in which we can destroy a person. It is indeed interesting what Jesus is trying to do. He is not saying that murder is synonymous with character assassination, but that inappropriate language toward another is also a serious matter and must not be taken lightly. Just as the Ten Commandments were given to regulate life in the community of Israel, so are the teachings of the Sermon on the Mount. Jesus gives these ethical principles to regulate life within the new community of the kingdom of heaven.

C. Kingdom Citizens Forgive Others (Matthew 5:23-26)

Therefore if thou bring thy gift to the altar, and there rememberest that thy brother hath ought against thee; Leave there thy gift before the altar, and go thy way; first be reconciled to thy brother, and then come and offer thy gift. Agree with thine adversary quickly, whiles thou art in the way with him; lest at any time the adversary deliver thee to the judge, and the judge deliver thee to the officer, and thou be cast into prison. Verily I say unto thee, Thou shalt by no means come out thence, till thou hast paid the uttermost farthing.

Finally, the theme of this lesson is for God's people to be forgiving. The key word in verse 24 is *reconciled*. It is obvious that Jesus was reflecting on some of the practices He had seen in His day of how people resolved conflict. Many attempted to resolve conflict through legal processes without an awareness of one's moral obligation to be a peacemaker. The people's behavior could be divided into the categories of *sacred* and *secular*. The people would offer gifts at the altar of God, while harboring malice and un-forgiveness in their hearts. Their religious demeanor remained unchanged. Jesus was saying that reconciliation is as important as offering gifts on the altar of God. Life for Jesus could not be lived on two distinct tracks—the religious and the secular.

One's relationship with another must be informed by his relationship with God. "If someone says, 'I love God,' and hates his brother, he is a liar; for the one who does not love his brother whom he has seen, cannot love God whom he has not seen" (1 John 4:20, NASB). Citizens of the kingdom of heaven must love God and love their neighbor as they love themselves (see Matthew 22:37-39). "All the Law and the Prophets hang on these two commandments" (Matthew 22:40). Jesus gave the multitude a lesson on forgiveness by using an illustration in verse 25 of how matters ought not to be settled. Forgiveness is an act of grace and its crimson thread runs through the Gospel message and culminates on the Cross of Calvary. "Settle matters quickly with your adversary" (verse 25, NIV). Just as there can be consequences for not reconciling with one's adversary in the court of law, God will also hold us accountable for how we treat each other.

III. CONCLUDING REFLECTION

The Quaker community in Pennsylvania demonstrated one of the most profound acts of forgiveness in modern public life. On October 2, 2006, lone gunman Charles C. Roberts IV walked into an Amish community schoolhouse in Nickel Mines of Lancaster

County, Pennsylvania. He shot ten little schoolgirls—killing five of them—and then took his own life. The Amish community's response to this tragedy was remarkable and almost other-worldly. Jack Meyer, a member of the community, explained, "I don't think there's anybody here that wants to do anything but forgive and not only reach out to those who have suffered a loss in the way but to reach out to the family of the man who committed these acts." The day of the killings, the father and grandfather of one of the little murdered girls visited the home of Roberts to comfort his widow, parents, and in-laws. Later, they set up a charitable fund for the family of the shooter. It was asked how the Amish community could be so willing to forgive someone who had violated their community in such a heinous way. A grandfather of one of the murdered girls said, "Forgiveness is a way of life within our culture, so forgiveness was our only option."

This was a profound demonstration of what Jesus is calling His followers to do. Forgiveness is not an option; rather, forgiveness is an act of grace. If one has to ask for it, then it is no longer forgiveness. Archbishop Desmond Tutu said, "In the act of forgiveness, we are declaring our faith in the future of a relationship and in the capacity of the wrongdoer to make a new beginning on a course that will be different from the one that caused us the wrong. We are saying here is a chance to make a new beginning." True Christians who aspire to citizenship in the kingdom of heaven see forgiveness as an essential part of their beings.

PRAYER

Lord God Almighty, You have forgiven us and reconciled us unto Yourself. We pray now that Your Spirit will nurture in us the spirit of forgiveness, so that we will be quick to forgive others who transgress against us. In Jesus' name we pray. Amen.

WORD POWER

Righteousness *(dikaiosune)*—**the character of being right that conforms to the revealed will of God.**
"Raca"—**an Aramaic term that means "contempt."**

HOME DAILY BIBLE READINGS
(October 31–November 6, 2011)

Forgiving as God's People

MONDAY, October 31: "A Covenant of Forgiveness" (Hebrews 10:11-18)

TUESDAY, November 1: "Rejoicing in God's Forgiveness" (Psalm 32:1-5)

WEDNESDAY, November 2: "The Prayer of Faith" (James 5:13-18)

THURSDAY, November 3: "Forgive and Be Forgiven" (Luke 6:37-42)

FRIDAY, November 4: "How Often Should I Forgive?" (Matthew 18:21-35)

SATURDAY, November 5: "Forgiveness Begets Love" (Luke 7:40-47)

SUNDAY, November 6: "First, Be Reconciled" (Matthew 5:17-26)

LESSON 11   November 13, 2011

LOVING AS GOD'S PEOPLE

DEVOTIONAL READING: **Matthew 22:34-40** BACKGROUND SCRIPTURE: **Matthew 5:43-48**
PRINT PASSAGE: **Matthew 5:43-48**   KEY VERSES: **Matthew 5:44-45**

Matthew 5:43-48—KJV

43 Ye have heard that it hath been said, Thou shalt love thy neighbour, and hate thine enemy.

44 But I say unto you, Love your enemies, bless them that curse you, do good to them that hate you, and pray for them which despitefully use you, and persecute you;

45 That ye may be the children of your Father which is in heaven: for he maketh his sun to rise on the evil and on the good, and sendeth rain on the just and on the unjust.

46 For if ye love them which love you, what reward have ye? do not even the publicans the same?

47 And if ye salute your brethren only, what do ye more than others? do not even the publicans so?

48 Be ye therefore perfect, even as your Father which is in heaven is perfect.

Matthew 5:43-48—NIV

43 "You have heard that it was said, 'Love your neighbor and hate your enemy.'

44 But I tell you: Love your enemies and pray for those who persecute you,

45 that you may be sons of your Father in heaven. He causes his sun to rise on the evil and the good, and sends rain on the righteous and the unrighteous.

46 If you love those who love you, what reward will you get? Are not even the tax collectors doing that?

47 And if you greet only your brothers, what are you doing more than others? Do not even pagans do that?

48 Be perfect, therefore, as your heavenly Father is perfect."

BIBLE FACT

In dozens (if not hundreds) of statements throughout the Gospels, Jesus contrasted the way of the world with the way of the Father. Here are a few:

- The Jews taught, "Do not commit adultery." But Jesus said that the person who lusts after another person is guilty of adultery (see Matthew 5:28).
- The world teaches retaliation; Jesus teaches non-violence (see Matthew 5:38-39).
- The world promotes people based on appearances; Jesus looks at the heart (see Matthew 7:15).
- Humanity is aware of its own limitations; Jesus taught that God has no such limits (see Mark 10:27).
- Jesus chastises the stingy and blesses the generous (see Luke 7:35-48).
- Jesus said that people are more apt to accept a self promoter than a God promoter (see John 5:43).

UNIFYING LESSON PRINCIPLE

People usually find it hard to love—even to like—those who are their enemies. Is there any help that would encourage us to change our attitudes toward those who hurt us? Jesus taught the disciples to pray for those who are unjust and evil.

TOPICAL OUTLINE OF THE LESSON

I. Introduction
   A. Different Types of Love
   B. Biblical Background

II. Exposition and Application of the Scripture
   A. Oral Tradition or Godly Truth?
      (Matthew 5:43-45)
   B. A Greater Love
      (Matthew 5:46-47)
   C. Jesus Commands "Perfection"
      (Matthew 5:48)

III. Concluding Reflection

LESSON OBJECTIVES

Upon the completion of the lesson, the students will be able to:

1. Explore Jesus' teachings concerning loving and praying for one's enemies;
2. Recognize and appreciate the relationship between loving one's enemies and being a child of God; and,
3. Participate in activities, such as prayer—which is designed to show love and concern for one's enemies.

POINTS TO BE EMPHASIZED

ADULT/YOUTH

Adult Topic: **Adopting an Attitude of Love**
Youth Topic: **Love My Enemies?**
Adult Key Verses: **Matthew 5:44-45**
Youth Key Verse: **Matthew 5:44**
Print Passage: **Matthew 5:43-48**

—Jesus defined the word *neighbor* in the story of the Good Samaritan (see Luke 10:25-37).
—Jesus asserted that values of the Christian community are different from Old Testament values.
—Gentiles honor and live by values that maintain relationships in their communities.
—The goal of believers is to emulate the love of God the Father in daily life.
—There was a "saying" attached to the Law which indicated that one should love his or her neighbor but hate his or her enemies.
—Jesus taught that we should love and pray for our neighbors and our enemies.
—Jesus demonstrated His superiority over the Law.
—God makes the sun to shine and the rain to fall on everyone.
—Jesus said that we should be perfect, as God is perfect.

CHILDREN

Children Topic: **Love Your Enemies**
Key Verse: **Matthew 5:44**
Print Passage: **Matthew 5:43-48**

—Jesus acknowledged that most people learn to love their neighbors and hate their enemies.
—Jesus intentionally turned that teaching around and challenged His hearers to love and pray for their enemies.
—Those who love their enemies give evidence that they are God's children.
—Jesus challenges His hearers to strive to be more like God.

I. INTRODUCTION

A. Different Types of Love

Is it possible to love everybody? If we claim that we love people in the way that God intends, then most of us are probably mistaken. Love is not some abstract concept that can be applied to people like paint to a wall. We must love one another concretely. The Bible uses four distinct Greek words for *love*, and when they appear in a passage, it is always in a significant context. The first word is *agape* and refers to "the kind of love that God gives." It is love without condition or variableness. This love loves in spite of the spirit or condition of the beloved (see John 3:16). Second, the word *eros* refers to "love expressed in sexual relationships between two people." Third, the word *storge* refers to "family love." This is the love that parents have for their children and vice versa. It only appears in the Scriptures translated as "without natural affection," "without love," or "heartless." Finally, *philia* is "brotherly love." It is the root word of *Philadelphia* (also known as "the City of Brotherly Love") and *philanthropy* (love for humanity). These four words address the nature of all human relationships. Thus, there is always a face and a circumstance attached to the beloved; love is never in the abstract. Therefore, we cannot love everyone in general but no one in particular. Likewise, Jesus drew inference from how His Jewish tradition had interpreted the Ten Commandments. The ninth and tenth commandments address one's relationship with one's neighbor. In practice, the people had a limited concept of *neighbor*. But Jesus calls the believer to love all who fall within our sphere of influence.

B. Biblical Background

The background for verses 43-48 is the Beatitudes. Jesus set the tone and the tenor for the rest of the Sermon on the Mount (chapters 5–7) in the first twelve verses of chapter 5. The Jews had a very narrow concept of who was one's neighbor during the time of Jesus' ministry and perhaps did not include Roman centurions who routinely persecuted them—or prosecutors who would slap the defendant with the back of his hand as an insult in courts of law. Were these persons their neighbors, and were they to be treated with neighborliness? Many of the Jews did not think so. But Jesus elevated the ethical codes of Judaism to another level of interpretation. The prevailing question in the days of Jesus was, "Who is my neighbor and whom do I love?" The Law said, "You shall love your neighbor" (Leviticus 19:18, NKJV); but where does "and hate your enemy" come from? It is not in the Law, so that law was embellished over time and became a part of the Jewish oral tradition.

Thus, Jesus gave us a different standard that redefines the boundaries of our neighborhood and who we are to love. It is easy to love people who are next door and who are kind, friendly, and cordial toward us—but what of a hostile and contrary neighbor?

Douglas Hare raises the question: "What does it mean to love a person whose hostility threatens us and whose behavior we heartily abhor?"

In this lesson, Jesus teaches that His followers must strive to be peacemakers and reconcilers in the world.

II. EXPOSITION AND APPLICATION OF THE SCRIPTURE

A. Oral Tradition or Godly Truth?
(Matthew 5:43-45)

Ye have heard that it hath been said, Thou shalt love thy neighbour, and hate thine enemy. But I say unto you, Love your enemies, bless them that curse you, do good to them that hate you, and pray for them which despitefully use you, and persecute you; That ye may be the children of your Father which is in heaven: for he maketh his sun to rise on the evil and on the good, and sendeth rain on the just and on the unjust.

Jesus opened this section by referencing the oral tradition of Judaism. The first mandate was to love one's enemy. Jesus implores us to exercise the supreme, unconditional, unqualified love. This is the Greek concept of an undeniable love that has no boundaries and cannot be inhibited by the external force of another. Of course, Jesus was alluding to the kind of love that God has demonstrated toward us. The apostle Paul said, "But God demonstrates his own love for us in this: while we were still sinners, Christ died for the ungodly" (see Romans 5:8). Love is an attribute of God, and the believer is commanded to love as God loves. Jesus also made love of God and love of neighbor the fundamental commands on which all else depends (see 22:34-40). It is said that this command is without parallel, in that Jesus extended this *agape* love even to one's enemies. There is a reward for those who love as God loves. Jesus said that those who do such things will be called sons of the Father. This is a high distinction. It denotes a very special relationship with the Father, and

it is not just that we can claim the Father, but that the Father can claim us as His children.

The believer's conduct must be appropriate to his or her status as a child of God. Rev. Dr. Martin Luther King Jr., in his sermon "Love in Action," said, "Jesus' dying word from the cross, 'Father forgive them; for they know not what they do' was Jesus matching words with action. One of the greatest tragedies of life is that men seldom bridge the gulf between practice and profession, between doing and saying." Perhaps what Jesus was asking believers to do was to counter human inclinations to only love those who love them. So He modeled unconditional love and commands His followers to follow His example.

B. A Greater Love
(Matthew 5:46-47)

For if ye love them which love you, what reward have ye? do not even the publicans the same? And if ye salute your brethren only, what do ye more than others? do not even the publicans so?

Although they are not a part of this lesson, it would behoove the student to begin his or her reading with verse 38.

One of the most despised people in the Jewish community was the tax collector. Tax collectors were usually Jewish men whose vocation it was to collect taxes from the Jewish people for Caesar. The tax collector in many instances would extract extra taxes to pad his own pockets. This person would take property when taxes could not be paid. So Jesus used one of the most hated persons in the community as an example of whom His disciples must love. To love a tax collector was the height of what it meant to love one's enemy. This is what the love ethic of Jesus means. This is important to Jesus, because when we were unlovable, God loved us and now those who have experienced His love must pass it on!

A rhetorical question is raised in verse 46 (NIV): "If you love those who love you, what reward will you get? Are not even the tax collectors doing that?" There was a hierarchy among tax collectors; the publican was usually the one in charge of the individual tax collectors who collected the taxes from the people. The burden on the people and the assessment of taxes came from the publican. But Jesus said that as despised as the publicans were, they were to be loved. Therefore, Jesus was saying that while the tax collectors could be worthwhile examples for believers to follow, the believer would be called to a higher standard of love in the world. So, just as Jesus drew a contrast between the righteousness of the Pharisees and that of the kingdom of heaven (verse 20), He also drew a contrast between the believer's love and the love ethic of the publicans (verse 46).

Divine love loves in spite of the moral conduct or character of the beloved.

C. Jesus Commands "Perfection" (Matthew 5:48)

Be ye therefore perfect, even as your Father which is in heaven is perfect.

Jesus drew a contrast in verse 20 between the righteousness of the Pharisees and the new standard of righteousness in the kingdom of heaven. And in verse 46, He contrasted the love ethic of the tax collectors to that of the kingdom of heaven. Alexander Maclaren said, "The sum of religion is to imitate the God whom we worship." We are to imitate God's expression of love, because even the best example of human love is imperfect.

Therefore, verse 48 reads, "Be perfect, therefore, as your heavenly Father is perfect" (NIV). Often the word *perfect* in this verse has been interpreted to mean "to be without flaw." But the Greek word *teleios* (translated as "perfect") here means "whole or undivided." When the word *perfect* is used in reference to God's love (in 1 John 4:18), it means "full," or "unlimited," or "not leaving any room for anything else." The believer's love ought not to have room for subjective reasoning which causes him or her to love conditionally. This is the perfection that Jesus expects from us. Howard Thurman said, in his book *For the Inward Journey*, "To love means dealing with persons in the concrete rather than in the abstract. In the presence of love, there are no types or stereotypes, no classes and no masses." This is what Jesus is calling us to! Perfect love drives out fear of not being loved in return.

III. CONCLUDING REFLECTION

Martin Luther King Jr. said, "It is pretty difficult to like some people. Like is sentimental and it is pretty difficult to like someone bombing your home; it is pretty difficult to like somebody threatening your children; it is difficult to like congressmen who spend all of their time trying to defeat civil rights. But Jesus says love them, and love is greater than like." This is where the rubber meets the road for Jesus and for us. The love of which Jesus speaks is more than mere emotion; it is an extension of the core values of Jesus.

Unfortunately, we live in a culture that views love primarily as emotion. There was a young lady who told her counselor that her marriage was over because she had "outgrown" her husband. Likewise, we have heard people say as they separate from a significant other that they have "fallen out of love" with the other. These and many others are reasons why people tend to give for breaking off tenured relationships. Yet, these are flimsy reasons and show the lowly esteem to which love has fallen in our society. Jesus calls the believer to love beyond the personal traits we look to admire in others and to love people for who they are and not for whom we would have them to be.

We must love in accordance with the standards of the kingdom of heaven, because we are to be "the light of God sitting on a hill that cannot be hidden." Jesus said to His disciples, "A new command I give you: Love one another. As I have loved you, so you must love one another. By this everyone will know that you are my disciples, if you love one another" (see John 13:34-35). This is the quality of love to which Jesus called us as He ushers in a different standard by which the believer is to live.

PRAYER

Father God, we hear Your call to us to love one another as You have loved us. We pray now that You will give us the courage and the fortitude to love concretely as You have loved us, so that indeed we will be known as Your children on the earth. In Jesus' name we pray. Amen.

WORD POWER

Perfect *(teleios)*—means "whole or undivided."
Love *(agape)*—refers to the God kind of love. It is love without condition or variableness.

HOME DAILY BIBLE READINGS
(November 7-13, 2011)

Loving as God's People

MONDAY, November 7: "The Greatest Commandment" (Matthew 22:34-40)

TUESDAY, November 8: "Loving Your God" (Deuteronomy 6:1-9)

WEDNESDAY, November 9: "Loving Your Neighbor" (Leviticus 19:13-18)

THURSDAY, November 10: "Loving the Alien" (Leviticus 19:33-37)

FRIDAY, November 11: "Loving Your Wife" (Ephesians 5:25-33)

SATURDAY, November 12: "Loving Your Husband and Children" (Titus 2:1-5)

SUNDAY, November 13: "Loving Your Enemies" (Matthew 5:43-48)

LESSON 12   November 20, 2011

PRAYING AS GOD'S PEOPLE

DEVOTIONAL READING: **Isaiah 12**
PRINT PASSAGE: **Matthew 6:5-15**

BACKGROUND SCRIPTURE: **Matthew 6:5-15**
KEY VERSE: **Matthew 6:6**

Matthew 6:5-15—KJV

5 And when thou prayest, thou shalt not be as the hypocrites are: for they love to pray standing in the synagogues and in the corners of the streets, that they may be seen of men. Verily I say unto you, They have their reward.

6 But thou, when thou prayest, enter into thy closet, and when thou hast shut thy door, pray to thy Father which is in secret; and thy Father which seeth in secret shall reward thee openly.

7 But when ye pray, use not vain repetitions, as the heathen do: for they think that they shall be heard for their much speaking.

8 Be not ye therefore like unto them: for your Father knoweth what things ye have need of, before ye ask him.

9 After this manner therefore pray ye: Our Father which art in heaven, Hallowed be thy name.

10 Thy kingdom come. Thy will be done in earth, as it is in heaven.

11 Give us this day our daily bread.

12 And forgive us our debts, as we forgive our debtors.

13 And lead us not into temptation, but deliver us from evil: For thine is the kingdom, and the power, and the glory, for ever. Amen.

14 For if ye forgive men their trespasses, your heavenly Father will also forgive you:

15 But if ye forgive not men their trespasses, neither will your Father forgive your trespasses.

Matthew 6:5-15—NIV

5 "And when you pray, do not be like the hypocrites, for they love to pray standing in the synagogues and on the street corners to be seen by men. I tell you the truth, they have received their reward in full.

6 But when you pray, go into your room, close the door and pray to your Father, who is unseen. Then your Father, who sees what is done in secret, will reward you.

7 And when you pray, do not keep on babbling like pagans, for they think they will be heard because of their many words.

8 Do not be like them, for your Father knows what you need before you ask him.

9 This, then, is how you should pray: 'Our Father in heaven, hallowed be your name,

10 your kingdom come, your will be done on earth as it is in heaven.

11 Give us today our daily bread.

12 Forgive us our debts, as we also have forgiven our debtors.

13 And lead us not into temptation, but deliver us from the evil one.'

14 For if you forgive men when they sin against you, your heavenly Father will also forgive you.

15 But if you do not forgive men their sins, your Father will not forgive your sins."

UNIFYING LESSON PRINCIPLE

People want to make a good public appearance. What is the benefit of looking good on the outside? Jesus taught that it is more important to develop our inner relationship with God through prayer.

TOPICAL OUTLINE OF THE LESSON

I. **Introduction**
   A. What Is Prayer?
   B. Biblical Background

II. **Exposition and Application of the Scripture**
   A. Jesus' Critique on Public Prayer (Matthew 6:5-8)
   B. Jesus Gives a Prayer Model (Matthew 6:9-13)
   C. It's about Forgiveness (Matthew 6:14-15)

III. **Concluding Reflection**

LESSON OBJECTIVES

Upon the completion of the lesson, the students will be able to:

1. Help others become familiar with Jesus' teachings about prayer and fasting;
2. Create time to enjoy the fruit of authentic prayer and fasting; and,
3. Create opportunities for practicing authentic prayer and fasting.

POINTS TO BE EMPHASIZED
ADULT/YOUTH

Adult Topic: **Valuing the Inner and Outer Actions**
Youth Topic: **Talking to Father**
Adult Key Verse: **Matthew 6:6**
Youth Key Verse: **Matthew 6:7**
Print Passage: **Matthew 6:5-15**

—Prayer is an expression of an intense relationship between God and His disciple.
—In this model prayer, disciples understand that all of life's concerns are of interest to God.
—This prayer serves as a model that disciples use in developing full, rounded lives before God.
—Intimacy with God is dependent on honesty, openness, and humility. Secrecy in our piety and prayer enables us to have intimate relationships with God.
—Luke 11:2-4 is a parallel rendering of this prayer.
—Jesus wants us to be sincere when we pray.
—Our prayers should reflect our dependence on God.
—Jesus wants us to watch our motives for praying and make sure that they are not for selfish reasons.
—Jesus made the act of forgiveness an integral part of our prayer lives.

CHILDREN

Children Topic: **Pray This Way**
Key Verse: **Matthew 6:6**
Print Passage: **Matthew 6:5-15**

—Jesus said that people who love to make a show of their faith in public will receive the proper reward.
—Jesus urged His followers to pray in private so that God could reward them privately.

—Jesus urged His disciples not to use many words in praying, because God knows what we need before we even ask.

—Jesus gave His disciples the Lord's Prayer as a model for how we should pray.

—Jesus emphasized for a second time the importance of our forgiving others: so that God will forgive us.

I. INTRODUCTION

A. What Is Prayer?

There have been many volumes written on the subject of prayer. One would think that we as Christians would have mastered the prayer life. But to the contrary—many still struggle with prayer. Perhaps you are one of those who struggle, especially in public settings, with prayer. It is quite amazing how often church leaders are intimidated by the thought of giving a public prayer; on the other hand, it is amazing how rote and predictable some public prayers are. Many public prayers are too showy and appear to be more to impress the audience than to reach heaven. But Jesus said that when the believer prays he or she "must not be like the hypocrites. For they love to stand and pray in the synagogues and at the street corners, that they may be seen by others" (see Matthew 6:5). Jesus does not want our prayers to become vain attempts that yield nothing from the Father. Thus, comfort and consistency in prayer begin with a clear understanding of what prayer is and is not.

There are many definitions of prayer: Khalil Gibran, in *The Prophet,* said, "What is prayer but the expansion of yourself into the living ether?...for your delight to pour forth the dawning of your heart." Thomas Merton, a Catholic mystic, said, "Prayer is seeking the presence of God." Still another definition is that of George A. Butterick, who said, "The heart of religion is in prayer—the uplifting of human hands, the speaking of human lips, the expectant waiting of human silence in direct communion with the eternal." These definitions get to the heart of what prayer is and is not. Prayer is not a technique or a skill or an understanding of one's best theology. Prayer is always an intimate conversation with God, the eternal one. This is the context of this lesson—to clarify the meaning and purpose of prayer in the kingdom of heaven.

B. Biblical Background

Jesus continued to clarify what it meant to live as a believer in the kingdom of heaven. He debunks popular misinterpretations of some of the oral laws and practices of Judaism. Often it is easy to lose sight of the fact that in the first century the people did not have access to written Bibles (just the Old Testament at that time) as we do today. Most people were illiterate and information was passed down by oral tradition. Consequently, it was difficult to identify and challenge the many faulty sayings that evolved over time that completely missed the point of the Law. In today's text, Jesus corrected the misinterpretations and the practices of prayer. We can only reason that in verse 5, Jesus was referring to the Pharisees when He said, "You must not be like the hypocrites." It was not unusual for Jesus to call many of the acts of the Pharisees hypocritical. They were the ones known for praying in the synagogues and on street corners—and doing religious things to draw attention to themselves.

Jesus followed His critique of these customs with examples of the appropriate way to pray. So, after telling the multitude how not to pray, Jesus then told them how to pray (verses 9-13).

II. EXPOSITION AND APPLICATION OF THE SCRIPTURE

A. Jesus' Critique on Public Prayer
(Matthew 6:5-8)

And when thou prayest, thou shalt not be as the hypocrites are: for they love to pray standing in the synagogues and in the corners of the streets, that they may be seen of men. Verily I say unto you, They have their reward. But thou, when thou prayest, enter into thy closet, and when thou hast shut thy door, pray to thy Father which is in secret; and thy Father which seeth in secret shall reward thee openly. But when ye pray, use not vain repetitions, as the heathen do: for they think that they shall be heard for their much speaking. Be not ye therefore like unto them: for your Father knoweth what things ye have need of, before ye ask him.

Jesus made it clear that personal prayer ought to be private between the one praying and the heavenly Father (verse 6). However, Jesus was not teaching against all forms of public prayer—because even in His day, prayers were offered in the Temple and in the synagogue during the liturgy and at the hour of prayer. During congregational services in the synagogues, the "cantor" led congregational prayers. As a matter of fact, the synagogue was called "the house of prayer." So Jesus' critique was not against the act of public prayer, only that it ought not to be showy and for personal recognition. Prayer should be a sincere expression of love and thanksgiving to God.

In verse 7, Jesus deviated from His previous custom of critiquing His own customs to now critiquing the Gentile practices of prayer. In the Middle East, the Muslim community can be heard and seen in Jerusalem, offering prayers during their hour of prayer. However, in the days of Jesus, Islam was not a religious order, so He was referring to other pagan religious practices in His day. "And in praying, do not heap up empty phrases as the Gentiles do; for they think that they will be heard for their many words" (RSV). He gave a harsh warning: "Do not be like them, for your Father knows what you need before you ask him" (verse 8, RSV). Our prayers must line up with our theology; if God knows all and sees all (He is omniscient), then clearly God knows our concerns even before we speak. God is not ignorant of who we are and what our needs are!

B. Jesus Gives a Prayer Model
(Matthew 6:9-13)

After this manner therefore pray ye: Our Father which art in heaven, Hallowed be thy name. Thy kingdom come. Thy will be done in earth, as it is in heaven. Give us this day our daily bread. And forgive us our debts, as we forgive our debtors. And lead us not into temptation, but deliver us from evil: For thine is the kingdom, and the power, and the glory, for ever. Amen.

Jesus gave the disciples the Model Prayer as a guide for how His disciples ought to pray. Of course, many biblical scholars have dissected this prayer many different ways, but they all seem to agree that the opening verse (verse 9) is adoration. The word *adoration* means "to ascribe honor and worthiness to God who is in heaven." The Jewish prayers in the first century addressed God as "Father," so true to His Jewish heritage, Jesus taught His disciples to pray as the Jews prayed, "Our Father who art in heaven." The title "Father" is consistent with the language in Matthew 5:9, in which Jesus says that as peacemakers, His disciples would be called the children of God, and the believers throughout the New Testament were called the sons or daughters of God.

"Father" was a term of endearment, so Jesus said that when we pray we are to say, "Our Father who art in heaven." The phrase "in heaven" is distinctive because pagans often built physical representations of their gods. This practice can be seen famously in the book of Daniel, in which King Nebuchadnezzar erected a golden image in the plain of Dura of Babylon. Pagan gods were local or territorial and not viewed as rulers of heaven and earth (cosmos). So in this Model Prayer, Jesus acknowledged not only the fatherhood of God, but also that He is Lord over all! When the believer prays, he or she must not only acknowledge his or her kinship with God, but also recognize the supremacy of God.

Of course, "Our Father" is not the only term of endearment that the believer can use to ascribe worth to God. *Lord* (or *Adonijah*) was a common noun in the Psalms that ascribed worthiness to God. In Psalm 8:1, "O LORD, our Lord" ascribes adoration to the only true and living God. These psalms are used today in both public and private prayers.

Second, verses 10-12 constitute petitions. In praying the Model Prayer, we petition God for four things: 1) We ask for divine intervention to help usher into the world the love ethic of Jesus—where there is conflict, injustice, malice, or sickness; "Your will be done on earth as it is in heaven." 2) We petition God for our daily sustenance; "Give us this day our daily bread." Daily bread was much more of an important commodity in the first century than it is today in a nation as prosperous as the United States. Hunger is still a significant issue for too many people in this nation, but it need not be so. Because of the waste and the excess of resources in the hands of the few, hunger is still an issue in significant pockets of our nation and the world. This petition is consistent with the teachings of Jesus at the end of this chapter in verse 33, in which Jesus instructed to "Seek ye first the kingdom of God, and his righteousness; and all these things shall be added unto you." Our petitions must be inclined with the will of God for His kingdom. This is the essence of this petition—that we trust God for our most primal needs. 3) We petition God for our forgiveness. Some call this petition the confession of sins. The believer must confess his or her sins and transgressions and ask for forgiveness. However, it is paramount that he or she understands that God's forgiveness is tied to his or her willingness to forgive others of their sins. Verse 12 (NIV) reads, "Forgive us our debts, as we also have forgiven our debtors." Forgiveness is the bedrock of our relationship with God, but we must ask for it—and when we do, we acknowledge our shortcomings and trespasses. 4) The final petition is for deliverance. Verse 13 reads, "Lead us not into temptation, but deliver us from evil." On the surface, it appears that Jesus is suggesting that God might lead us into temptation. Other biblical scholars do not believe that such an interpretation would be consistent with other biblical passages that say otherwise. James said that God does not tempt us with evil (see James 1:13-14). Frank E. Gaebelein, in his commentary on the book of Matthew, admits that this phrase is a difficult one to interpret and perhaps is best interpreted as, "Let us not be brought into temptation, by the evil devil." Yet we can all agree that temptation and trials are a part of the believer's sojourn—and if we are to be delivered from the temptations of this world, then the Lord must do it for us. God is the only one who can keep us and protect us from the wiles of the evil one.

C. It's about Forgiveness
(Matthew 6:14-15)

For if ye forgive men their trespasses, your heavenly Father will also forgive you: But if ye forgive not men their trespasses, neither will your Father forgive your trespasses.

From these verses, we learn the conditional nature of our forgiveness. The lesson from November 6, "Forgiving as God's People," addressed the subject of forgiveness. It might be beneficial as you study this lesson to review the comments on forgiveness there. "For if you forgive men when they sin against you, your heavenly Father will also forgive you. But if you do not forgive men their sins, your Father will not forgive your sins" (verses 14-15, NIV). Use of the "if" clause in verses 14 and 15 suggests that forgiveness is conditional. We as believers

determine the measure of divine forgiveness that we receive from God. Verse 15 is explicit; if we do not forgive others their sins, God will not be inclined to forgive us. Perhaps you might ask why this is so. Forgiveness is a virtue that flows to us from God; hence, God holds us accountable for forgiving others. There are many ways of understanding forgiveness, but in a nutshell it is God's grace to us, because without forgiveness, reconciliation with God would be impossible.

III. CONCLUDING REFLECTION

A great expression of forgiveness can be seen in the incident where a young man robbed and murdered a young woman in California in 1980. In 1983, he was convicted and sentenced to death at San Quentin State Prison. The young woman was the only child of single mother Gayle Blount. While visiting other death-row inmates at San Quentin, the mother discovered that the murderer of her daughter was housed there. She wrote him and eventually became his pen pal and visited him four times a year while he was on death row. He wrote and asked for her forgiveness! She shared a letter she wrote to the young man with Colman McCarthy in his article "Mother Forgives, Befriends a Murderer" published in the *National Catholic Reporter* (1992).

> "Twelve years ago, I had a beautiful daughter named Catherine. She was a young woman of unusual talents and intelligence.... she radiated with love and joy.... The violent way she left this earth was impossible for me to understand. I was saddened beyond belief. This does not mean

that I think you are innocent or that you are blameless for what happened. What I learned is this: You are a divine child of God. You carry the Christ-consciousness within you. You are surrounded by God's love even as you sit in your cell. The Christ in me sends blessings to the Christ in you."

Over time, she worked to get him off death row and then worked to get him probation. She was able to accomplish both and subsequently adopted the man that murdered her daughter. She said on "60 Minutes" as they reported her story: "I lost a daughter, but gained a son that I never had." Once he was paroled, she provided a home for him and helped him find a job.

Perhaps this act of forgiveness is most uncommon and seems other-worldly for many of us, because our culture teaches revenge and retaliation against those who transgress against us. But in the kingdom of heaven, what Gayle Blount did is exactly what God did for us and calls us to do for others.

PRAYER

Increase our faith, O Lord. May we never forget the great measure of love that You have for us. And now help us to find Your spirit of love in our hearts, so that we will be able to forgive others as You have forgiven us. In Jesus' name we pray. Amen.

WORD POWER

Adoration—to ascribe honor and worth to someone.
Transgression *(parabasis)*—"stepping over" sin in relation to overstepping the law.
Forgiveness *(aphesis)*—to release or to leave in peace. It is what God does for us through the blood of Jesus Christ.

HOME DAILY BIBLE READINGS
(November 14-20, 2011)

Praying as God's People

MONDAY, November 14: "A Prayer for Deliverance" (Genesis 32:6-12)

TUESDAY, November 15: "A Prayer for Forgiveness" (Numbers 14:13-19)

WEDNESDAY, November 16: "A Prayer for God's Blessing" (2 Samuel 7:18-29)

THURSDAY, November 17: "A Prayer for Healing" (1 Kings 17:17-23)

FRIDAY, November 18: "A Prayer of Thanksgiving" (Isaiah 12)

SATURDAY, November 19: "God's Assurance for Prayer" (Jeremiah 29:10-14)

SUNDAY, November 20: "The Practice of Prayer" (Matthew 6:5-15)

LESSON 13   November 27, 2011

FACING LIFE WITHOUT WORRY

DEVOTIONAL READING: **Psalm 37:1-8**
PRINT PASSAGE: **Matthew 6:25-34**

BACKGROUND SCRIPTURE: **Matthew 6:25-34**
KEY VERSES: **Matthew 6:33-34**

Matthew 6:25-34—KJV

25 Therefore I say unto you, Take no thought for your life, what ye shall eat, or what ye shall drink; nor yet for your body, what ye shall put on. Is not the life more than meat, and the body than raiment?
26 Behold the fowls of the air: for they sow not, neither do they reap, nor gather into barns; yet your heavenly Father feedeth them. Are ye not much better than they?
27 Which of you by taking thought can add one cubit unto his stature?
28 And why take ye thought for raiment? Consider the lilies of the field, how they grow; they toil not, neither do they spin:
29 And yet I say unto you, That even Solomon in all his glory was not arrayed like one of these.
30 Wherefore, if God so clothe the grass of the field, which to day is, and to morrow is cast into the oven, shall he not much more clothe you, O ye of little faith?
31 Therefore take no thought, saying, What shall we eat? or, What shall we drink? or, Wherewithal shall we be clothed?
32 (For after all these things do the Gentiles seek:) for your heavenly Father knoweth that ye have need of all these things.
33 But seek ye first the kingdom of God, and his righteousness; and all these things shall be added unto you.
34 Take therefore no thought for the morrow: for the morrow shall take thought for the things of itself. Sufficient unto the day is the evil thereof.

Matthew 6:25-34—NIV

25 "Therefore I tell you, do not worry about your life, what you will eat or drink; or about your body, what you will wear. Is not life more important than food, and the body more important than clothes?
26 Look at the birds of the air; they do not sow or reap or store away in barns, and yet your heavenly Father feeds them. Are you not much more valuable than they?
27 Who of you by worrying can add a single hour to his life?
28 And why do you worry about clothes? See how the lilies of the field grow. They do not labor or spin.
29 Yet I tell you that not even Solomon in all his splendor was dressed like one of these.
30 If that is how God clothes the grass of the field, which is here today and tomorrow is thrown into the fire, will he not much more clothe you, O you of little faith?
31 So do not worry, saying, 'What shall we eat?' or 'What shall we drink?' or 'What shall we wear?'
32 For the pagans run after all these things, and your heavenly Father knows that you need them.
33 But seek first his kingdom and his righteousness, and all these things will be given to you as well.
34 Therefore do not worry about tomorrow, for tomorrow will worry about itself. Each day has enough trouble of its own."

TOPICAL OUTLINE OF THE LESSON

I. **Introduction**
   A. The Trap of Worry
   B. Biblical Background

II. **Exposition and Application of the Scripture**
   A. Trusting God for the Basics (Matthew 6:25-27)
   B. Trusting God beyond Status Symbols (Matthew 6:28-30)
   C. Trusting One Trinity for the Other (Matthew 6:31-34)

III. **Concluding Reflection**

LESSON OBJECTIVES

Upon the completion of the lesson, the students will be able to:

1. Survey Jesus' teachings about God as the great provider;
2. Understand that money can do much, but it cannot relieve worry and stress; and,
3. Work out a plan to lean more and more on God to provide for our needs.

POINTS TO BE EMPHASIZED

ADULT/YOUTH

Adult Topic: Putting Worry in Its Place
Youth Topic: Why Worry?
Adult Key Verses: Matthew 6:33-34
Youth Key Verse: Matthew 6:33
Print Passage: Matthew 6:25-34

—God assists those who worry by calling attention to a broader frame of reference—that is, nature.
—Faith and trust in God's provision for human needs counteracts worry.
—God wants all humans to experience the adequacy of God's provisions for life and meaning.
—God places high value on living "one day at a time."
—Striving for life's basics can lead to worry; striving for God's kingdom relieves worry. When we put first things first, worry and anxiety diminish.
—If God supplies the needs of the birds, then God will surely supply the needs of human beings, who were made in God's image.
—God is aware of His roles as Father and provider.
—It takes faith to trust God; thus, our worrying indicates that we have little trust in God.
—When we put God first, our other needs are taken care of.

CHILDREN

Children Topic: Do Not Worry
Key Verse: Matthew 6:25
Print Passage: Matthew 6:25-34

—Jesus taught the disciples not to worry about daily necessities.
—Just as God takes care of nature, God will take care of human needs.
—God knows the things we really need and provides them.
—Instead of worrying about everyday things, we should

strive first for the kingdom of God and God's righteousness.

—Trusting God to meet our needs demonstrates our faith in and understanding of God.

—Trust God as you deal with today, rather than worrying about tomorrow.

I. INTRODUCTION

A. The Trap of Worry

There is a Travelers Insurance television commercial in which a cute, white dog cannot rest because he is worrying about his bone. This brief commercial is set against the backdrop of a song by Ray Lamontagne: "*Trouble, trouble, trouble trouble; Trouble been doggin' my soul since the day I was born. Worry, worry, worry, worry, worry, worry. Worry just will not seem to leave my mind alone. Worry, oh worry, worry, worry, worry. Sometimes I swear it feels like this worry is my only friend. Oh…ah.*" The tag line goes, "When it comes to things you care about, leave nothing to chance."

In psychological theory, one of the elements of anxiety disorder is *worry*, and it can lead to mental disorders such as depression or despondency. Jesus was not a psychologist, but He understood the psychology of human behavior. Thus, He taught that materialism should not be a priority in our lives. He told us to "seek first the kingdom of heaven." He concluded that worry is useless and does not solve problems. The people of God must trust that He will add to the believer's life what he or she needs. However, we as a people are status seekers, and our culture teaches us that we can find status in things.

B. Biblical Background

In this lesson, Jesus again dealt with one of the common concerns that had been afflicting the people for ages—concern for worldly possessions. In the earlier lessons, Jesus' concerns were theological (forgiveness, love, and prayer), but in later lessons He shifted to the physical/psychological. Perhaps Jesus was trying to teach that human life cannot be compartmentalized into the spiritual and the physical. The human personality is body, mind, and soul, and Jesus came to minister to the total person—with all of his or her needs. However, it is indeed interesting that when Jesus was talking about the spiritual, some Bible scholars call "worry" an enemy of faith, because it undermines one's trust in God. After admonishing the multitude about worry, Jesus said, "Oh ye of little faith."

But, again, we cannot understand this block of Scripture (verses 25-34) without reading and considering other Scriptures in chapter 6—especially verses 19-24, which address human motives. These verses (19-24) are actually the antecedent to our text. Verse 21 reads, "For where your treasure is, there will your heart be also." The heart is the center of human motive: "As water reflects a face, so a man's heart reflects the man" (Proverbs 27:19, NIV). This lesson is about the motives of the heart. The believer is encouraged to let his or her heart seek for the things of God and not the things that the world systems count as status and value. However, the deeper warning comes to us from Matthew 6:24b (NLT): "You cannot serve both God and money." We are not to worry about things that are of no consequence to us. Perhaps this is another way in which our righteousness can exceed the righteousness of the Pharisees.

II. EXPOSITION AND APPLICATION OF THE SCRIPTURE

A. Trusting God for the Basics
(Matthew 6:25-27)

Therefore I say unto you, Take no thought for your life, what ye shall eat, or what ye shall drink; nor yet for your body, what ye shall put on. Is not the life more than meat, and the body than raiment? Behold the fowls of the air: for they sow not, neither do they reap, nor gather into barns; yet your heavenly Father feedeth them. Are ye not much better than they? Which of you by taking thought can add one cubit unto his stature?

In the light of much contemporary language about prosperity, this passage is not a guarantee that if we are righteous and have enough faith, then we will never be in need. The reality is that there are Christians in some of the poorest countries in the world who go to bed every night hungry and without the proper clothing. What about God's people in the world, or innocent children who die of starvation in countries all over the world because of war and famine? In the land of famine everything dies; even sparrows and lilies do not grow.

Some might think that this seems like a strange theological idea. But it is consistent with both Old and New Testament narratives. Many of the people of God were in need of some of the basic of human needs in the Old Testament (see 1 Kings 17, for example). Rather than a promise or the assurance of prosperity, Jesus was teaching on the importance of trusting in God. Douglas R. Hare said, in his *Commentary on Matthew*: "Birds and lilies are not models to be imitated but powerful symbols of God's providential care.... It is a calmer vision of God's bountiful care in the natural world." For our teaching, Jesus used an example from the most primal of human needs—food and drink (verse 25). He issued a prohibition against worrying about your life. Then Jesus became specific about what were some of the worries of life: "what you will eat or drink; or about…what you will wear" (NIV). In our world, there are those who worry about what they will eat and drink, and what they will wear. This is not the culture to which Jesus spoke. These are the concerns of an affluent culture.

However, the word *worry* carries the idea of being anxious and is used in this section of chapter 6 (verses 25, 27, 28, 31, and 34) two times. Jesus was calling us to a greater appreciation of divine providence, as reflected in the balance of nature. The image that comes to mind as we read this text is Elijah and a famine that afflicted Israel in the days of Ahab. It was God who caused the famine, and it was God who sent the prophet Elijah to a brook east of the Jordan River. It was God who sent a raven to feed Elijah morning and evening until the brook dried up (see 1 Kings 17:1-6). To worry about food and drink is to learn nothing from nature or biblical history. Likewise, Jesus was calling His followers to realize that life in its fullest was not based on things, but on one's relationship with God. Jesus made it plain in verse 27 that worry is useless and adds nothing to one's life. It will not change the outcome of any situation in life and undermines faith in God. The profound truth in Jesus' admonition is not prosperity, but the great biblical teaching about trust: "Trust in the Lord and lean not on your own understanding" (see Proverbs 3:5).

B. Trusting God beyond Status Symbols (Matthew 6:28-30)

And why take ye thought for raiment? Consider the lilies of the field, how they grow; they toil not, neither do they spin: And yet I say unto you, That even Solomon in all his glory was not arrayed like one of these. Wherefore, if God so clothe the grass of the field, which to day is, and to morrow is cast into the oven, shall he not much more clothe you, O ye of little faith?

In these verses, Jesus shifts from the biological needs of food and water, to the sociological need of clothing. Indeed, in America we are a vain people who go to great lengths to eat the best of foods and dress in the latest styles, regardless of the price. There are many people who are so preoccupied with dress and appearance that they have hocked their future, worrying about their social status. There are stories of persons who boast that they will not wear the same garment twice, or will not wear it again if they know of someone who has the same outfit. Not only does worry add nothing to our lives, but neither do the things that we tend to grasp for.

Jesus used the lilies of the field and how they grew (lilies do not labor but are arrayed in beauty and splendor like King Solomon) as an example of providential care. King Solomon was king of ancient Israel and was known for his wealth and splendor. But then in verse 30, Jesus shifted to contrasting something that was even more basic and temporary in nature— grass. How much more than grass are we who are created in the image of God? "If God so clothes the grass of the field, which today is, and tomorrow is thrown into the oven, will He not much more clothe you, O you of little faith?" (verse 30, NKJV).

Use of the expression "little faith" affirmed that the multitude had faith, but their faith was hesitant and doubtful and needed assurance. Of course, "little" modifies the noun *faith*, which meant that their faith was not strong or sufficient enough to prevent worry. Jesus is encouraging the believer to have faith enough in the One who called us to live radical lives. God will provide our most basic needs. For some commentators, this is a reference to Jesus' disciples, who left vocations and all earthly possessions to follow Jesus. Like Jesus' disciples, who left their individual vocations and earthly possessions to follow Jesus, we, too, are expected to put all our trust in God.

C. Trusting One Trinity for the Other (Matthew 6:31-34)

Therefore take no thought, saying, What shall we eat? or, What shall we drink? or, Wherewithal shall we be clothed? (For after all these things do the Gentiles seek:) for your heavenly Father knoweth that ye have need of all these things. But seek ye first the kingdom of God, and his righteousness; and all these things shall be added unto you. Take therefore no thought for the morrow: for the morrow shall take thought for the things of itself. Sufficient unto the day is the evil thereof.

There are three rhetorical questions according to verse 31 (NKJV): "Therefore do not worry, saying, 'What shall we eat?' or 'What shall we drink?' or 'What shall we wear?'" Do not worry about things like food, drink, and clothes. These are the things that the pagans worry about. The word *pagan* represents those who are worldly and who are not a part of the kingdom of heaven. Jesus compared and contrasted the ways of the world to the ways of the kingdom of heaven. This contrast and comparison was consistent with Jesus' teachings in the Sermon on the Mount, in which Jesus warned His followers not to strive to be like the world in love, forgiveness, or prayer, but to live by a different standard—a kingdom standard.

The world is absorbed with self-fulfillment and possessions. This absorption often steers humanity away from God. It was Abraham Maslow, in *A Theory of Human Motivation* (1943), who introduced to the world the theory of the hierarchy of needs. He said, "The most primal needs of human beings are food, clothing, and shelter (physiological requirements and safety). Humans cannot move up the ladder of higher needs like self-actualization, loving/belonging, and self-esteem until their most basic needs are met." We cannot be sure where Maslow would place faith and spirituality on his hierarchy-of-needs scale, but Jesus had a different theory: "Seek first his kingdom and his righteousness, and all these things will be given to you as well" (see verse 33).

The operative word in verse 33 is *first*. "Seek first" is not an admonition against having other pursuits. Rather, the first pursuit should be the kingdom of heaven. Steven Covey's principle of leadership, "First things first," says that an effective leader prioritizes his or her agenda with things that are most important. Now if this is a worldly principle of effectiveness and results, how much more important is the principle that Jesus taught—"Seek first his kingdom and his righteousness"? The promise is that if we seek first the kingdom and God's righteousness, then we need not worry about our most basic needs, because of God's providential care. Finally, the word *worry* is repeated six times in ten verses, which means that for Jesus, worry was a very real aspect of life. "Do not worry about tomorrow, for tomorrow will worry about itself. Each day has enough trouble of its own" (verse 34, NIV). We are to address each problem as it comes, with confidence that life is in the hands of a loving and benevolent God who cares for us. The psalmist assured us that "The earth is the LORD's and everything in it, the world, and all who live in it" (Psalm 24:1, NIV). Assurance and confidence are the hallmarks of Jesus' teachings. The world and all that is in it is in the Lord's hand, and worrying cannot change its outcomes.

However, we must be clear that this is not an assurance that money problems will be solved by an unquestionable confidence in God. What it means is that God's providential care will provide for those who accept the call to follow Him.

III. CONCLUDING REFLECTION

Worry is both irreverent and irrelevant for the people of God. It is irreverent in that it fails to recognize God's care for creation and His compassion toward us. It is irrelevant because it does not change the outcome of anything. It is an exercise in futility. Jesus used seemingly the most insignificant things in nature—birds, lilies, and grass—to illustrate providential care and concluded that if God cares for these things in nature that are easily taken for granted by humanity, how much more are we, the people of God who are created "just a little lower than angels" (Psalm 8:5). The late Howard Thurman, in his book *Jesus and the Disinherited* (p. 147), captured the essence of this lesson when he said, "The core of the analysis of Jesus is that man [humanity] is a child of God, the God of life that sustains all nature and guarantees all the intricacies of the life process itself. It is quite unreasonable to assume that God whose creative activity is expressed even in such details of nature [birds, lilies, and grass] would exclude from His concern the life of the man himself."

This is the summation of the lesson from the Sermon on the Mount. This text is not about prosperity—as it is often taught and understood by preachers and pastors—but it is about the providential care of God, who provides for (not makes rich) those who will leave all to follow Jesus. Jesus provides for our *needs*. To move from "what shall we eat and drink" to mansions, luxury cars, and designer clothes is a stretch of man's imagination and not God's true intent. We can face worry with the reality that God is aware of our needs and will provide for us.

PRAYER

Lord of all creation, we humbly bow in total submission to You. Thanks for Your provisions of not only salvation, but also for our daily bread. Now, increase our faith so that we may trust You in a more excellent way. In Jesus' name we pray. Amen.

WORD POWER

Worry *(mérimna)*—means "to be anxious" and is often translated as "care, worry, or anxiety."
Life *(psuchē)*—vitality; it refers to the total person—body, mind, and soul.
Pagan *(ethnē)*—Gentile, heathen nation, or those who are worldly who seek after worldly things.
Seek *(zēteite)*—to search out or to demand or crave for.
Little faith *(oligopistos)*—this concept means incredulous—i.e., lacking confidence (in Christ).

HOME DAILY BIBLE READINGS
(November 21-27, 2011)

Trusting as God's People

MONDAY, November 21: "Do Not Fret" (Psalm 37:1-8)

TUESDAY, November 22: "The Consequences of Worry" (Matthew 13:18-23)

WEDNESDAY, November 23: "Guard against Worry" (Luke 21:29-36)

THURSDAY, November 24: "Do Not Be Afraid" (Matthew 10:24-31)

FRIDAY, November 25: "The Spirit as Our Resource" (Matthew 10:16-20)

SATURDAY, November 26: "Give Your Worries to God" (1 Peter 5:6-11)

SUNDAY, November 27: "Don't Worry about Tomorrow" (Matthew 6:25-34)

God Establishes a Faithful People

GENERAL INTRODUCTION

The study this quarter focuses on God's covenant through Abraham. The theological emphasis is on faith. God promised Abraham that through him all the nations of the earth would be blessed. That promise was passed on from generation to generation until it was ultimately fulfilled in Christ. The lessons for this quarter are taken from the books of Genesis, Exodus, Luke, and Galatians.

The four lessons of **Unit I**, *God's Covenant*, tell the story of God's promise to Abraham. The first three lessons are studies in the book of Genesis. These narratives from the book of Genesis are appropriate for Advent because they point us to Christ's coming. The fourth lesson (the Christmas lesson) leaps forward from the book of Genesis to the books of Luke and Galatians, where it is heard from Mary's lips that she will give birth to Christ, the seed of Abraham's promise.

Unit II, *God's Protection*, has five lessons. The first four lessons consider Joseph's story in Genesis 39–50. We see how God's promise to Abraham is passed on from generation to generation and carried with Abraham's descendants into Egypt. The final lesson of the unit considers the songs of Moses and Miriam in Exodus 15. God delivered Israel and led them to safety in the desert. God's covenant faithfulness is proved again.

Unit III, *God's Redemption*, has four lessons. These lessons from Paul's letter to the Galatians emphasize the New Testament interpretation of the Law, of justification by faith, and of Christ's disciples as heirs of Abraham's promise.

LESSON 1   December 4, 2011

A BLESSING FOR ALL NATIONS

DEVOTIONAL READING: **Hebrews 6:13-20**
PRINT PASSAGE: **Genesis 12:1-9**

BACKGROUND SCRIPTURE: **Genesis 12:1-9**
KEY VERSE: **Genesis 12:2**

Genesis 12:1-9—KJV

NOW THE LORD had said unto Abram, Get thee out of thy country, and from thy kindred, and from thy father's house, unto a land that I will shew thee:

2 And I will make of thee a great nation, and I will bless thee, and make thy name great; and thou shalt be a blessing:

3 And I will bless them that bless thee, and curse him that curseth thee: and in thee shall all families of the earth be blessed.

4 So Abram departed, as the LORD had spoken unto him; and Lot went with him: and Abram was seventy and five years old when he departed out of Haran.

5 And Abram took Sarai his wife, and Lot his brother's son, and all their substance that they had gathered, and the souls that they had gotten in Haran; and they went forth to go into the land of Canaan; and into the land of Canaan they came.

6 And Abram passed through the land unto the place of Sichem, unto the plain of Moreh. And the Canaanite was then in the land.

7 And the LORD appeared unto Abram, and said, Unto thy seed will I give this land: and there builded he an altar unto the LORD, who appeared unto him.

8 And he removed from thence unto a mountain on the east of Bethel, and pitched his tent, having Bethel on the west, and Hai on the east: and there he builded an altar unto the LORD, and called upon the name of the LORD.

9 And Abram journeyed, going on still toward the south.

Genesis 12:1-9—NIV

THE LORD had said to Abram, "Leave your country, your people and your father's household and go to the land I will show you.

2 I will make you into a great nation and I will bless you; I will make your name great, and you will be a blessing.

3 I will bless those who bless you, and whoever curses you I will curse; and all peoples on earth will be blessed through you."

4 So Abram left, as the LORD had told him; and Lot went with him. Abram was seventy-five years old when he set out from Haran.

5 He took his wife Sarai, his nephew Lot, all the possessions they had accumulated and the people they had acquired in Haran, and they set out for the land of Canaan, and they arrived there.

6 Abram traveled through the land as far as the site of the great tree of Moreh at Shechem. At that time the Canaanites were in the land.

7 The LORD appeared to Abram and said, "To your offspring I will give this land." So he built an altar there to the LORD, who had appeared to him.

8 From there he went on toward the hills east of Bethel and pitched his tent, with Bethel on the west and Ai on the east. There he built an altar to the LORD and called on the name of the LORD.

9 Then Abram set out and continued toward the Negev.

UNIFYING LESSON PRINCIPLE

Sometimes people are asked to do incredibly difficult things with only promises of reward to motivate them. How much are some people willing to endure and risk in exchange for promises? In their old age, Abram and Sarai risked everything to move their family and all their possessions to a new land, because of their faith in God's promises.

TOPICAL OUTLINE OF THE LESSON

I. Introduction
   A. Transition Is Challenging
   B. Biblical Background

II. Exposition and Application of the Scripture
   A. The Call of Abram
       (Genesis 12:1-3)
   B. Age Is Nothing but a Number
       (Genesis 12:4-5a)
   C. Altars to God
       (Genesis 12:5b-9)

III. Concluding Reflection

LESSON OBJECTIVES

Upon the completion of this lesson, the students will know that:

1. The calling of God sometimes means that one must take drastic measures, which may mean that one must leave family and close friends;
2. Our social locations, such as age or gender, do not matter to God; and,
3. After responding to God's call, one must maintain one's focus on Him through prayer.

POINTS TO BE EMPHASIZED

ADULT/YOUTH
Adult Topic: Sharing Good Fortune
Youth Topic: A Blessing to All Nations
Adult/Youth Key Verse: Genesis 12:2
Print Passage: Genesis 12:1-9

—Abraham's name was initially Abram.
—Abram was a descendant of Noah through Shem and Terah (see Genesis 9:10-26; 11:26).
—Abram's move, at age seventy-five, from Haran to Canaan was motivated by God's call, promise, and direction.
—God's promise to Abram of land, posterity, and greatness was reaffirmed to Abram several times (see Genesis 13:15-17; 15:5-7, 18-21; 22:17-18).
—Abram built altars of worship and called on God's name.
—Abraham's wealth did not keep him from responding to God's call.
—God promised a reciprocal response to persons in accordance with how they treated Abram and Sarai.
—Abram arrived in the land of Canaan with his wife Sarai, his nephew Lot, and all their possessions and built an altar (they worshipped God).
—This is a story about faith in God and the beginning of the nation of Israel.

CHILDREN
Children Topic: A Promise to Abram
Key Verse: Genesis 12:2
Print Passage: Genesis 12:1-9

—The Lord made specific promises to Abram.
—God promised to make Abram great.
—Abram displayed obedience to God's Word.
—God promised to make Abram a blessing to all people.
—Abram responded to God's promises by worshipping God.

I. INTRODUCTION

A. Transition Is Challenging

One of the most difficult things for a person to do is leave a place of comfort to follow the paths of the unknown. In various stages of our lives, we experience transitioning from one place to another. As toddlers, there is separation anxiety when it is time to leave home and parents to go to day care. After getting comfortable with day-care and kindergarten teachers, young kids leave this place to go to the unknown again—elementary school. A few years later, it is time to enter high school; as young adults, we venture off to college to travel new paths that set the course for our adult lives. Finally, after our college days, we face the unknown of life as full adults. In each stage, we leave a place of comfort to venture into the unknown. However, God is with us in each new stage, leading and guiding us to the promised destination.

Abram was also in a new stage of his life when God called him to go to a new place. The divine command insisted that Abram leave his country and his father's house to settle in the land that God had designated. To respond to God, Abram had to take the drastic measure of uprooting himself, leaving all that he knew in order to show his faithfulness to God. In the midst of uncertainty, human flaws, and errors in decision making, God was with Abram, leading and guiding him to the promised destination.

B. Biblical Background

The call of Abram, as seen in Genesis 12:1-9, contrasts with the Hebrew writer's explication of the descendents of Terah. Genesis 11:27-32 contains brief details of Terah and his family. Terah was the father of Abram, Nahor, and Haran. Haran was the father of Lot, who eventually traveled with Abram as Abram followed the call of God. While in Ur, the land of the Chaldeans, Haran died and Abram and his remaining brother, Nahor, took wives. The Hebrew writer alerted us that Sarah was barren—she could not conceive. Eventually, Terah and his family left Ur of the Chaldeans to go to Canaan. However, when they came to the place called Haran, the family settled there. Terah, the patriarch of Abram's family, died in Haran.

Terah ventured out toward new lands, but did not make it to his destination. Later, God called Abram to continue the journey by leaving his father's house, his extended family, and his country. He told Abram that He would bless and make Abram's name great so that he would be a blessing. At the age of seventy-five, Abram followed the command of God. He and his family took all their possessions and left Haran. Like his father Terah, Abram set out for Canaan; this time, however, he was traveling with the promised of God.

II. EXPOSITION AND APPLICATION OF THE SCRIPTURE

A. The Call of Abram
(Genesis 12:1-3)

NOW THE LORD had said unto Abram, Get thee out of thy country, and from thy kindred, and from thy father's house, unto a land that I will shew thee: And I will make of thee a great nation, and I will bless thee, and make thy name great; and thou shalt be a blessing: And I will bless them that bless thee, and curse him that curseth thee: and in thee shall all families of the earth be blessed.

God's call was to a special family in an unusual time. Abram's family had experienced loss and uncertainty. Abram's father, Terah, failed to make it to Canaan. Terah died in Haran, leaving Abram as the family patriarch. Abram's wife, Sarai, was barren; she had no children. Thus, Abram did not yet have an heir. Moreover, Lot, the son of Nahor, was Abram's responsibility along with all the family's possessions. How was Abram to deal with the upheaval and uncertainty in his life? God's divine call demanded drastic measures. To be found faithful, it was imperative that Abram follow the call of God.

The divine directive was a call to abandonment and relinquishment (*Genesis*, Brueggemann, p. 118). It was a call to leave what could be considered a safe and secure world. The act of abandonment entails giving something up with the intent of never again claiming a right or interest in it. Abram was called to abandon family members and the place that he called home. Therefore, he was giving up his rights to the family land and relationships, never again to seek to claim an interest. The call of God also was a call to relinquishment. Abram relinquished to God his control, care, and protection of self. When Abram decided to follow the command of God, he relinquished self to

divine protection and guidance. Like Abram, the divine call upon our lives forces us to take drastic measures.

In our lives, the call of God is not just a divine call, but a directive that leads and guides us toward a better quality of life. However, when Abram departed his home to travel unknown paths, God had spoken specific promises. God declared that Abram would be blessed to be a great nation with a great name, so that Abram would be a blessing. Abram was not traveling blind. His journey was undergirded by the Word of God. Just as Abram had the Word and divine injunction of God, we, too, must have the Word of God in our lives before we take off on new paths. When God calls one to a specific task, He has specific ends to be met.

B. Age Is Nothing but a Number
(Genesis 12:4-5a)

So Abram departed, as the LORD had spoken unto him; and Lot went with him: and Abram was seventy and five years old when he departed out of Haran. And Abram took Sarai his wife, and Lot his brother's son, and all their substance that they had gathered, and the souls that they had gotten in Haran.

Many times, people are granted open doors and new opportunities in life, but are afraid to move forward. For some, the fear of leaving family and friends is too large a burden to overcome. Others simply fear the unknown. There are some who are afraid to take advantage of a new opportunity because they tell themselves that they are too old. The messages from contemporary society tell us that only young people follow dreams or take chances on new opportunities. Old age is symbolic of a settled life. Many persons look forward to the idea of "retirement" in order to rid themselves of the daily hustle and bustle—to be free of the capitalistic work life. The settled life suggests easygoing days without problems. Persons envision enjoying their daily lives by getting up in the morning and reading the newspaper while drinking morning coffee. There will be no more rushing out of the house to sit in traffic just to get to work late again. During the course of the day, the settled life in old age points to rest and naps, lunch at noon, time to run errands before the evening traffic, dinner at six, and more rest and relaxation before one goes to bed after the nightly news. The settled life is not one that cultivates uncommon ideas or starts far-fetched ventures.

Old age also symbolizes security. Security is the freedom from danger, fear, or anxiety. It is the state of feeling secure in one's existence. Many people have spent their lifetimes working to pay mortgages, car notes, and other bills. By the time of retirement, people look forward to the security of paid-off homes and cars. They want to feel secure in knowing that now that they are older, they have a roof over their heads, food in the refrigerator, reliable transportation to run daily errands, and funds to take care of their physical health. Thus, one may be apprehensive about taking drastic measures in order to follow the divine call of God. However, our security does not lie in what we have accomplished and accumulated. Our security is in being faithful witnesses to God's divine call by heeding and participating in the call of God.

Finally, old age is not only a time of settled lives and security, but the time to move over and allow younger persons to take the reins. We are taught to believe that it is only young persons who have something new to contribute to society. The wisdom and life experiences of older persons are regarded as passé. Antiquity is out and novelty is in. Yet, God inspires whom God pleases in order to bring about His kingdom and life-giving situations.

When God provides an opportunity, age is not God's concern—nor should it be our concern. Abram was seventy-five years old (what we in contemporary times consider old) when he left Haran. He took his wife, nephew Lot, and all his possessions on the journey. Despite his age, Abram began the journey to Canaan, which is synonymous with beginning the journey of faith.

C. Altars to God
(Genesis 12:5b-9)

And they went forth to go into the land of Canaan; and into the land of Canaan they came. And Abram passed through the land unto the place of Sichem, unto the plain of Moreh. And the Canaanite was then in the land. And the Lord appeared unto Abram, and said, Unto thy seed will I give this land: and there builded he an altar unto the Lord, who appeared unto him. And he removed from thence unto a mountain on the east of Bethel, and pitched his tent, having Bethel on the west, and Hai on the east: and there he builded an altar unto the Lord, and called upon the name of the Lord. And Abram journeyed, going on still toward the south.

Once we accept the call of God and begin our faith journeys, our success is rooted in our willingness to stay connected to God through prayer. All too often, we begin a task or assignment only to quit before it is completed. We see the same phenomenon when new persons come to Christ and become members of a local body of believers. There is faithful church attendance and participation in ministry events. There is also consistent Bible study at home.

There are new conversations and sometimes even new friends. Moreover, the new convert is always in prayer, seeking to commune with God and expecting a response from God. But as time passes and daily life appears to be the same, weariness sets in and some new converts drift away from God. They miss one or two Sundays here and there. They have to work extra hours and therefore cannot participate in ministry events. When God has not answered or when it seems that God is not going to answer their continuous prayers, disappointment and even anger set in. At this point, we are near the point of abandoning and relinquishing our faith. While on the journey, we have no idea of the challenges that may come before us. Our task is to overcome the challenges by keeping our eyes on God and our ears listening for God. The task of building altars helps us to do this. We build altars to God not only in our private prayer time, but also when we secure prayer partners, find godly mentors, and make the attempt to practice living out Christian principles. In the moments when we are not able to pray, our prayer partners and mentors can pray for and encourage us. Those whom we have encouraged and demonstrated the love of God to may also serve us by demonstrating that same love of God in our moments of despair. Building altars to God is the foundation for sustaining us in our faith and on our journeys with God.

The biblical text states that the Canaanites were in the land when Abraham traveled through the land as far as the site of the great tree of Moreh at Shechem. While we do not know the demeanor of the Canaanites or how they would have reacted to Abram and his family, it is easy to see that Abram was potentially facing a challenge. Although on a journey ordained by God, he entered someone else's territory. It is here that the Lord appeared to Abram and made the promise that He would give that land to Abram's offspring. Rather than exhibit foolish rejoicing, Abram built an altar to God. From there, Abram traveled toward the hills east of Bethel and pitched his tent. The biblical witness says that Abram built another altar and called on the name of the Lord. To build altars and call on the name of God signified that Abram had decided to trust in God—who made specific promises. In our faith journeys, what altars are we building to God? Are we calling on the name of God as we journey? The divine call of God and its attending journey are fraught with challenges; we overcome those challenges by clinging to God, who is leading and guiding us.

III. CONCLUDING REFLECTION

The calling of God upon our lives normally means that we will need to make uncomfortable choices if we are to be found faithful to God and God's call. God's call is not determined by our social situations such as age, gender, socio-economic status, or education. Rather, God's call is determined by His timing and desired ends. While individuals are blessed for following God, the bigger picture is that God desires to do a great thing. The "great thing" of God may not be toward our immediate families and friends. The "great thing" may be for someone else or a situation of which we are unaware. As followers of God, our calling does not include worrying about the "great thing" in God's big picture. Our job is to simply be faithful and continue with the task that God has given us.

For those chosen to begin the journey to the Promised Land, prayer and communion with God is what helps us to reach the desired destination. The Promised Land comes in a variety of ways. In all instances, God is the source of the Promised Land and the guide that leads us to the Promised Land. Our altars to God, by way of prayer, build and sustain us so that we can persevere and make it to our destinations. Persons such as Harriett Tubman, Frederick Douglass, Ella Baker, Martin Luther King Jr., Marva Collins, and Malcolm X exhibited the call of God on their lives so that human flourishing could come to a multitude of African Americans. They are examples of those who did their part so that the "great thing" could come to many. It takes one willing vessel to open the door of blessings for a multitude of God's people.

PRAYER

Dear God, open our eyes so that we may see You; open our ears so that we may hear You; open our hearts so that we may perceive You. Give us the faith to follow Your promptings, knowing that in doing so, we are open to receive Your greater good. Protect us and strengthen us as we accept Your call and begin our journeys to the designated land that You have promised. In Jesus' name we pray. Amen.

WORD POWER

Barren—Sarai was described as being barren; she had no children. Yet, *barren* may take on more meaning than "one without children." If barrenness is the state of lack or failure to be fruitful, then in what ways does barrenness manifest itself in our contemporary times?

HOME DAILY BIBLE READINGS
(November 28–December 4, 2011)

A Blessing for All Nations

> **MONDAY, November 28:** "Abraham's Story" (Acts 7:1-8)
>
> **TUESDAY, November 29:** "A God So Near" (Deuteronomy 4:5-9)
>
> **WEDNESDAY, November 30:** "The Lord Heard Our Voices" (Deuteronomy 26:1-11)
>
> **THURSDAY, December 1:** "Look to Abraham" (Isaiah 51:1-6)
>
> **FRIDAY, December 2:** "Abraham, Our Ancestor?" (Matthew 3:1-10)
>
> **SATURDAY, December 3:** "We Have This Hope" (Hebrews 6:13-20)
>
> **SUNDAY, December 4:** "God's Call to Bless" (Genesis 12:1-9)

LESSON 2   December 11, 2011

A PROMISE TO ABRAHAM

DEVOTIONAL READING: **Hebrews 13:17-22**   BACKGROUND SCRIPTURE: **Genesis 15:1-21**
PRINT PASSAGE: **Genesis 15:1-6, 12-18**   KEY VERSE: **Genesis 15:6**

Genesis 15:1-6, 12-18—KJV

AFTER THESE things the word of the LORD came unto Abram in a vision, saying, Fear not, Abram: I am thy shield, and thy exceeding great reward.

2 And Abram said, Lord GOD, what wilt thou give me, seeing I go childless, and the steward of my house is this Eliezer of Damascus?

3 And Abram said, Behold, to me thou hast given no seed: and, lo, one born in my house is mine heir.

4 And, behold, the word of the LORD came unto him, saying, This shall not be thine heir; but he that shall come forth out of thine own bowels shall be thine heir.

5 And he brought him forth abroad, and said, Look now toward heaven, and tell the stars, if thou be able to number them: and he said unto him, So shall thy seed be.

6 And he believed in the LORD; and he counted it to him for righteousness.

.....

12 And when the sun was going down, a deep sleep fell upon Abram; and, lo, an horror of great darkness fell upon him.

13 And he said unto Abram, Know of a surety that thy seed shall be a stranger in a land that is not theirs, and shall serve them; and they shall afflict them four hundred years;

14 And also that nation, whom they shall serve, will I judge: and afterward shall they come out with great substance.

15 And thou shalt go to thy fathers in peace; thou shalt be buried in a good old age.

16 But in the fourth generation they shall come hither again: for the iniquity of the Amorites is not yet full.

Genesis 15:1-6, 12-18—NIV

AFTER THIS, the word of the LORD came to Abram in a vision: "Do not be afraid, Abram. I am your shield, your very great reward."

2 But Abram said, "O Sovereign LORD, what can you give me since I remain childless and the one who will inherit my estate is Eliezer of Damascus?"

3 And Abram said, "You have given me no children; so a servant in my household will be my heir."

4 Then the word of the LORD came to him: "This man will not be your heir, but a son coming from your own body will be your heir."

5 He took him outside and said, "Look up at the heavens and count the stars—if indeed you can count them." Then he said to him, "So shall your offspring be."

6 Abram believed the LORD, and he credited it to him as righteousness.

.....

12 As the sun was setting, Abram fell into a deep sleep, and a thick and dreadful darkness came over him.

13 Then the LORD said to him, "Know for certain that your descendants will be strangers in a country not their own, and they will be enslaved and mistreated four hundred years.

14 But I will punish the nation they serve as slaves, and afterward they will come out with great possessions.

15 You, however, will go to your fathers in peace and be buried at a good old age.

16 In the fourth generation your descendants will come back here, for the sin of the Amorites has not yet reached its full measure."

UNIFYING LESSON PRINCIPLE

Sometimes people are asked to believe the unbelievable, even the impossible. How far can some peoples' ability to believe be stretched? Even though he and his wife were long beyond the age of childbearing, because of his faith in God, Abram believed God when told that he would have descendants more numerous than the stars.

17 And it came to pass, that, when the sun went down, and it was dark, behold a smoking furnace, and a burning lamp that passed between those pieces.

18 In the same day the LORD made a covenant with Abram, saying, Unto thy seed have I given this land, from the river of Egypt unto the great river, the river Euphrates.

17 When the sun had set and darkness had fallen, a smoking firepot with a blazing torch appeared and passed between the pieces.

18 On that day the LORD made a covenant with Abram and said, "To your descendants I give this land, from the river of Egypt to the great river, the Euphrates."

TOPICAL OUTLINE OF THE LESSON

I. Introduction
A. In the Midst of Following God
B. Biblical Background

II. Exposition and Application of the Scripture
A. Will the Promises Take Place? (Genesis 15:1-6)
B. God's Reassurance and Revelation Concerning the Community (Genesis 15:12-14)
C. God's Reassurance and Revelation Concerning Abram (Genesis 15:15-18)

III. Concluding Reflection

LESSON OBJECTIVES

Upon the completion of this lesson, the students will know:

1. How to stand in faith even if it appears that the promises of God may not manifest;
2. That it is in moments of peace rather than turmoil when we are ready to hear from God; and,
3. God is faithful and ready to reassure us in times of uncertainty.

POINTS TO BE EMPHASIZED
ADULT/YOUTH

Adult Topic: Believing the Impossible
Youth Topic: An Enormous Family
Adult Key Verse: Genesis 15:6
Youth Key Verse: Genesis 15:5
Print Passage: Genesis 15:1-6, 12-18

—God communicated with Abram and others through dreams.
—God rewards those who by faith accept divine promises of future developments.
—God allotted land to Abram's family that was occupied by other peoples at that time.
—God predicted the experiences of the Hebrew people several generations in advance.
—Abram's belief in God's promises is an example of what it means to be righteous.
—The text provides the oldest and most important Abrahamic tradition of faith and covenant.

—Abram saw his lack of a descendant as a real obstacle to God's blessing.

—God told Abram in a dream that his descendants would experience a time of slavery, but that they would come out of it with great possessions.

—God made the covenant with Abram; however, it was God's responsibility to fulfill all components of that covenant.

CHILDREN
Children Topic: Expect God to Keep His Promises
Key Verse: Genesis 15:1

Print Passage: Genesis 15:1-7

—God was Abram's protector.

—This passage speaks to the passing down and receiving of the family inheritance in biblical times.

—God's promises are unlimited.

—God responded to Abram's question and his concern.

—God honors and rewards a person's faithfulness.

—Abram believed in what God promised, even when he could not see God's promises or understand how they would happen.

I. INTRODUCTION

A. In the Midst of Following God

In the midst of following God, there are times when we have doubts about God's promises' being fulfilled. Many of us have made the drastic choice to do all that we can in the name of following God. We have "abandoned" our families and friends, and all that is familiar. We have "relinquished" our control, care, and protection of ourselves into the hands of God. We faithfully began the journey to our new destination in life and in God, unaware of the challenges that lay ahead. We do all of this, only to come to a point where we wonder if it was worth it all. This is a familiar scenario with new Christians. The excitement of a new life in God fills one with energy and desire to do the work of God. We listen to every word of the pastor; we avail ourselves to a variety of ministries in the church. God seems to be answering every prayer and uttered word. We begin to believe that God will do the impossible, things that we never thought about asking for. Then, a few months down the road, we hit a stumbling block. We realize that we have been on our faith journey for some time, but have not seen the desired rewards of this new faith life. At the first opportunity, we question ourselves and God. We ask God, "Where are You?" We ask ourselves whether our new lives are worth it all. It is in times like these that we see how God has grown us. Moreover, in times of doubt, if we stay the course, we grow to our next level in faith.

B. Biblical Background

Abram and his family left Ur, the land of the Chaldeans, in obedience to the call of God and in pursuit of the promises of God. While in Shechem, Abram built an altar symbolizing his trust in God. After communing with God, Abram continued his journey to his promised land, but encountered a variety of challenges. His family traveled to Egypt seeking relief from a famine. Upon entering Egypt, Abram made an unwise decision by asking his wife Sarai to tell the Egyptians that she was his sister. Abram believed that if the Egyptians knew Sarai was his wife, they would kill him because of her beauty and desirability. The Egyptians did indeed view Sarai as a beautiful woman and Pharaoh took her into his palace. In return, Pharaoh gave Abram cattle and servants. Abram's deceitfulness caused God to inflict disease upon Pharaoh, who then confronted Abram and asked him to leave Egypt. After leaving Egypt, Abram and Lot decided to separate because the land could not support both men's possessions. After Lot left Abram, God appeared to Abram and reminded him of a promise. God said that He would give all the land that Abram could see to Abram and his offspring. In the midst of a multitude of challenges, God showed Himself to be faithful to His promise. But, yet, Abram would deal with another adventure. He had to rescue his nephew Lot from four kings in the region of Sodom and Gomorrah. After the rescue, Abram ate bread and wine with Melchizedek—king of Solomon—and gave him a tenth of all that he had.

II. EXPOSITION AND APPLICATION OF THE SCRIPTURE

A. Will the Promises Take Place?
(Genesis 15:1-6)

AFTER THESE things the word of the LORD came unto Abram in a vision, saying, Fear not, Abram: I am thy shield, and thy exceeding great reward. And Abram said, Lord GOD, what wilt thou give me, seeing I go childless, and the steward of my house is this Eliezer of Damascus? And Abram said, Behold, to me thou hast given no seed: and, lo, one born in my house is mine heir. And, behold, the word of the LORD came unto him, saying, This shall not be thine heir; but he that shall come forth out of thine own bowels shall be thine heir. And he brought him forth abroad, and said, Look now toward heaven, and tell the stars, if thou be able to number them: and he said unto him, So shall thy seed be. And he believed in the LORD; and he counted it to him for righteousness.

New and seasoned Christians alike often have moments of doubt. To doubt a thing is to show a lack of confidence in uncertainty, or even distrust. When one doubts that God will keep a promise, there is indeed a lack of confidence in or distrust of God. New Christians may exhibit doubt toward God by becoming fearful and impatient. They fear that God will not keep His promises and they become impatient while waiting for the promises to be fulfilled. Conversely, those who have been committed to God for a number of years also have doubts. Seasoned Christians sometimes get caught up in the needs of the moment. They forget to look at their track record with God that shows how God has brought them through tough situations. New Christians do not necessarily have track records with God that they can recognize. In each case, doubting sometimes leads to poor decision making and can be a hindrance to receiving the promises of God. As one waits on God, it is important to be in community with other believers who are seeking and waiting on God, and those who have received some promises from God. It is our fellowship with other Christians that strengthens us in God. The stronger that one becomes in God, the more one has the ability to walk with God.

Similar to the behavior of a new Christian, Abram became impatient with the waiting on the promises of God. God said to Abram, "I am your shield, your reward shall be very great." This very statement was a promise from God, but one that Abram could not hear as a new person to faith. God neither said what He was shielding, nor did He give an idea of Abram's reward. God simply spoke in a manner that showed Abram that he should continue to be faithful. Abram, new to faith and heeding a divine call, was yet strong enough to hear the simple but deep promise of God. After being on his faith journey and experiencing a few challenges, Abram reminded God that he wanted a child. He said, "What can you give me since I remain childless?" Here, rather than exercising faith, Abram seemed to have resorted to negotiation. It was at that point that God explained His promise by telling Abram that the slave would not be Abram's heir. God further encouraged Abram by explaining to him that if he could count the stars, Abram's descendants would be as many. God supplies moments of reassurance through His Word, other people, or miraculous situations to alert us that He is still with us. It is up to faithful people to continue in faith so that they receive what is promised.

B. God's Reassurance and Revelation Concerning the Community (Genesis 15:12-14)

And when the sun was going down, a deep sleep fell upon Abram; and, lo, an horror of great darkness fell upon him. And he said unto Abram, Know of a surety that thy seed shall be a stranger in a land that is not theirs, and shall serve them; and they shall afflict them four hundred years; And also that nation, whom they shall serve, will I judge: and afterward shall they come out with great substance.

As God reassured Abram that his heir would be a son coming from his own body, Abram believed God and it was credited to Abram as righteousness. However, although Abram believed God, his words and actions told another story. After God reminded Abram that He would give him the land, Abram still asked God, "How can I know that I will gain possession of it?" Christians tend to "believe" the Word of God externally, but their actions show what they believe internally. God is faithful and patient with this human flaw and is not quick to dismiss us as inept or unbelieving. Rather, God told Abram to gather sacrificial animals; in the midst of his weary faith, Abram responded to God by bringing a heifer, a goat, a ram, a dove, and a pigeon. Before finishing the offering ritual, the sun set and Abram fell into a "deep sleep." The text describes the situation as deep sleep with "dreadful darkness." Here, the text suggests divine activity. While a thick darkness came over him, the Lord said to him in a dream for Abram to know that his descendants would be strangers in a country not their own. God informed Abram that they would be enslaved and mistreated for four hundred years. However, God said that the nation that Abram's descendants served would be punished and the descendants would come out with great possessions.

Although not every part of the Lord's speech may have been pleasant for Abram, it was and is during peaceful moments that the voice of the Lord rings with clarity. Peaceful moments are not only the times of quietness, but also lie in being free from oppressive thoughts or emotions. Thus, times of turmoil and chaos are the most difficult times to hear the voice of God. Therefore, it is always in our best interests to seek refuge and a quiet place so that we may have the best opportunity to hear the plans and instructions of the Lord. In the book of Isaiah, the prophet stated that "in quietness and trust is your strength" (Isaiah 30:15, NIV). Sometimes, we must stop what we are doing and get into a reflective mood. All too often, one misses the importance of the Word of the Lord that comes from times of reflection. It is our duty as persons of faith to find new ways to hear the voice of God. Therefore, we must find the quiet spot, engage the silence, and wait on God. This exemplifies the strength that we now have. It also grows us to our next levels of strength and confidence.

C. God's Reassurance and Revelation Concerning Abram (Genesis 15:15-18)

And thou shalt go to thy fathers in peace; thou shalt be buried in a good old age. But in the fourth generation they shall come hither again: for the iniquity of the Amorites is not yet full. And it came to pass, that, when the sun went down, and it was dark, behold a smoking furnace, and a burning lamp that passed between those pieces. In the same day the Lord made a covenant with Abram, saying, Unto thy seed have I given this land, from the river of Egypt unto the great river, the river Euphrates.

While Abram was in a deep sleep, God reaffirmed His promise to Abram concerning his offspring. In addition, God not only outlined what was to happen to Abram's offspring, but also promised Abram that he would live to a ripe old age. Abram would then be buried with his fathers. Afterwards, God consummated a covenant with Abram and said, "To your descendants I give this land, from the river of Egypt to the great river, the river Euphrates" (verse 18, NRSV). The beauty of these promises and the ending covenant was that it was a one-sided commitment on the part of God to Abram, and exacted no comparable allegiance from Abram to God. God is the Supreme Being who has created us to worship and look to Him for guidance and sustenance. There is nothing more that we (as the created) can offer

to God. Our task is to worship and live out our faith as a response to God's blessings upon us. God is not quick to throw us away because of our faults. At the same time, God is quick to be consistent and patient with us in the midst of those same faults. Unlike humanity, when God makes a promise, God does not renege on the promise. God is not human beings. He will not lie, nor is He like mortals—that He should change His mind. Has He promised, and will He not do it? Has He spoken, and will He not fulfill it? (See Numbers 23:19.)

Like He did with Abram, God is in our midst to reassure us in times of uncertainty. The current economic woes within the United States and around the world show the necessity for looking to God for certainty. God has promised that He knows the plans that He has for us. He has promised to prosper us and not harm us (see Jeremiah 29:11). God has also promised that when we are weary or burdened, He will give us rest (see Matthew 11:28). God is also faithful and gives us more than we need to sustain ourselves. He has promised that if we ask anything according to His will, He will hear us so that whatever we ask, we know that we will receive it (see 1 John 5:14-15). In the black church tradition, we famously say that you cannot beat God's giving. The promises of God are evident in the biblical text. In those words, we find how God continuously gives to us. We find how God is continuously in our midst. We find how God is continuously leading and guiding us to the fulfillment of His promises. There is nothing that we can give to God other than our faith. We cannot outdo God, negotiate with God, or scam God. God reigns supreme and is the giver and sustainer of life. As Abram maintained his faith in the promise of God, his descendants were able to benefit from his steadfastness. God promised that He would give them land even though Abram and Sarai had not been given a child. Let our descendants also benefit from our steadfastness, so that they, too, will receive the promises that God has made to us. In our moments of faith crisis, we need only to trust God—because God's faithfulness is free, unconditional, and trustworthy.

III. CONCLUDING REFLECTION

Genesis 15 teaches that the life of faith is not only a life of waiting, but also one of trusting while waiting. If we are disgruntled or disheartened for too long in what we call waiting, we are not waiting on God at all. We are then striving against God. Ironically, those who have trusted most passionately and for the longest time sometimes find that their faith has not yet yielded the promise. It is in these moments that one is tempted to abandon the faith for "no faith at all."

In our contemporary society, many people are caught in the web of instant gratification. We do not entertain the aspect of waiting that Abram endured. Conversely, in the African-American church tradition, our ancestors had a long history of waiting while on their faith journeys. Although there were crisis-of-faith moments, like Abram, our ancestors were inspired to be faithful in the midst of chaotic times. The life of faith is a life of waiting, but our successful waiting is dependent on how much we lean on God and allow Him into our presence.

PRAYER

Lord, we come to You, asking that You give us the fortitude to continue in our faith. Build us up where we may be torn down; speak strength and wisdom into our lives; forgive us for our moments of lapse as we continue to pursue the call upon our lives. In Jesus' name we pray. Amen.

WORD POWER

Doubt—To doubt a thing is to show a lack of confidence in, uncertainty, or even distrust.

HOME DAILY BIBLE READINGS
(December 5-11, 2011)

A Promise to Abraham

LESSON 3   December 18, 2011

THE LORD PROVIDES

DEVOTIONAL READING: **Philippians 4:15-20**   BACKGROUND SCRIPTURE: **Genesis 22:1-14**
PRINT PASSAGE: **Genesis 22:1-2, 6-14**   KEY VERSE: **Genesis 22:12**

Genesis 22:1-2, 6-14—KJV

AND IT came to pass after these things, that God did tempt Abraham, and said unto him, Abraham: and he said, Behold, here I am.

2 And he said, Take now thy son, thine only son Isaac, whom thou lovest, and get thee into the land of Moriah; and offer him there for a burnt offering upon one of the mountains which I will tell thee of.

.....

6 And Abraham took the wood of the burnt offering, and laid it upon Isaac his son; and he took the fire in his hand, and a knife; and they went both of them together.

7 And Isaac spake unto Abraham his father, and said, My father: and he said, Here am I, my son. And he said, Behold the fire and the wood: but where is the lamb for a burnt offering?

8 And Abraham said, My son, God will provide himself a lamb for a burnt offering: so they went both of them together.

9 And they came to the place which God had told him of; and Abraham built an altar there, and laid the wood in order, and bound Isaac his son, and laid him on the altar upon the wood.

10 And Abraham stretched forth his hand, and took the knife to slay his son.

11 And the angel of the LORD called unto him out of heaven, and said, Abraham, Abraham: and he said, Here am I.

12 And he said, Lay not thine hand upon the lad, neither do thou any thing unto him: for now I know that thou fearest God, seeing thou hast not withheld thy son, thine only son from me.

Genesis 22:1-2, 6-14—NIV

SOME TIME later God tested Abraham. He said to him, "Abraham!" "Here I am," he replied.

2 Then God said, "Take your son, your only son, Isaac, whom you love, and go to the region of Moriah. Sacrifice him there as a burnt offering on one of the mountains I will tell you about."

.....

6 Abraham took the wood for the burnt offering and placed it on his son Isaac, and he himself carried the fire and the knife. As the two of them went on together,

7 Isaac spoke up and said to his father Abraham, "Father?" "Yes, my son?" Abraham replied. "The fire and wood are here," Isaac said, "but where is the lamb for the burnt offering?"

8 Abraham answered, "God himself will provide the lamb for the burnt offering, my son." And the two of them went on together.

9 When they reached the place God had told him about, Abraham built an altar there and arranged the wood on it. He bound his son Isaac and laid him on the altar, on top of the wood.

10 Then he reached out his hand and took the knife to slay his son.

11 But the angel of the LORD called out to him from heaven, "Abraham! Abraham!" "Here I am," he replied.

12 "Do not lay a hand on the boy," he said. "Do not do anything to him. Now I know that you fear God, because you have not withheld from me your son, your only son."

13 And Abraham lifted up his eyes, and looked, and behold behind him a ram caught in a thicket by his horns: and Abraham went and took the ram, and offered him up for a burnt offering in the stead of his son.

14 And Abraham called the name of that place Jehovah-jireh: as it is said to this day, In the mount of the Lord it shall be seen.

13 Abraham looked up and there in a thicket he saw a ram caught by its horns. He went over and took the ram and sacrificed it as a burnt offering instead of his son.

14 So Abraham called that place The Lord Will Provide. And to this day it is said, "On the mountain of the Lord it will be provided."

TOPICAL OUTLINE OF THE LESSON

I. Introduction
    A. Our Faith Journeys
    B. Biblical Background

II. Exposition and Application of the Scripture
    A. Tests Are a Part of Life (Genesis 22:1-2)
    B. Tests Enable Us to See Ourselves as Stewards (Genesis 22:6-10)
    C. God Is Always Near (Genesis 22:11-14)

III. Concluding Reflection

LESSON OBJECTIVES

Upon the completion of this lesson, the students will know that:

1. Our faith journeys include times of testing;
2. We are stewards instead of owners; and,
3. God is near to us and our circumstances even if it feels as if He is afar.

POINTS TO BE EMPHASIZED

ADULT/YOUTH
Adult Topic: Passing the Test
Youth Topic: The Ultimate Test
Adult Key Verse: Genesis 22:12
Youth Key Verse: Genesis 22:8
Print Passage: Genesis 22:1-2, 6-14

—Abraham did not question God's command to sacrifice his only son, Isaac.

—Child sacrifice was a practice of other religions in the ancient Near East.

—Abraham's faithfulness was rewarded with God's provision of a ram to be sacrificed in place of Isaac.

—The practice of presenting *burnt offerings* (involving sacrificing an animal on the altar as atonement for sin) was common before it was commanded in the Mosaic covenant.

—Abraham's readiness to sacrifice his son was a foretaste of God's action to do the same.

—Abraham bound Isaac and was prepared to kill him, but God intervened.

—Abraham's test took place in the land of Moriah.

—God told Abraham to offer his son as a sacrifice.

—God provided the sacrifice for Abraham in place of Isaac.

I. INTRODUCTION

A. Our Faith Journeys

Faith is not static. It is dynamic—meaning it is alive, always moving, and always encountering something new. Our faith journeys have the potential to take us places that we have never imagined. Faithful preachers preach in a multitude of places. Faithful teachers get the opportunity to teach and impact a variety of students. Faithful parents have the opportunity to see the fruits of their labors manifest in their children. Faithful students have the opportunity to explore the world through learning. The life of faith is pervasive. It consumes the person that practices faith because being faithful to God should be the overarching purpose in our daily endeavors. However, just as we encounter the good things of life during our faith journeys, there are also challenging moments and encounters.

The life of faith always brings tests our way. The tests may seem to come at the most inopportune times, but they are for the purpose of strengthening us. Abraham began his faith journey by responding to the call of God to leave Ur and his family. He encountered challenges while on the journey and had a crisis of faith. Yet, God was always near to his situation. After reassuring Abraham that the promises were going to come true, Abraham's faith was tested. Tests are part of the life of faith. Just as tests in a classroom situation show what we have obtained and how we have grown with the added knowledge, faith tests show how much we have grown and what we have obtained with our added knowledge about God. Thus, how we respond to the tests determines how we continue in our journeys of faith.

B. Biblical Background

The passage of Scripture designated for this lesson begins with the words: "And it came to pass after these things" (Genesis 22:1). The logical question we should ask is this: After *what* things? It was after all the things that Abraham and his family had endured up to this point as detailed in chapter 21: the birth of Isaac, who was identified as the promised son, and the sending away of Hagar and Ishmael. Now, at the point when Abraham perhaps felt that his home life was at peace and in some semblance of tranquility, God interrupted it. The word came to Abraham in the form of a test. The writer of this book went to great lengths to let us know that God was testing Abraham. It is important to understand this, because nowhere else in biblical history does God ever ask a person to sacrifice his or her child as a burnt offering. God did not and does not act in a capricious manner as the worshippers of idol gods believe their gods demand. It can be concluded that God's command to Abraham at this juncture in his life was harsh. However, Abraham trusted God to do the right thing. God tested Abraham and asked him to take his only son Isaac and sacrifice him as a burnt offering. Abraham and Isaac traveled to the place of offering that God had designated. As Abraham prepared to sacrifice Isaac, the angel of the Lord said to Abraham not to lay a hand on Isaac. Because of his willingness to sacrifice Isaac, Abraham proved his fear of God. God provided a ram in the bush for the sacrifice. The ultimate question to be asked in this context is this: Would we be willing to entrust our futures unhesitatingly to the God whom Abraham trusted?

II. EXPOSITION AND APPLICATION OF THE SCRIPTURE

A. Tests Are a Part of Life
(Genesis 22:1-2)

AND IT came to pass after these things, that God did tempt Abraham, and said unto him, Abraham: and he said, Behold, here I am. And he said, Take now thy son, thine only son Isaac, whom thou lovest, and get thee into the land of Moriah; and offer him there for a burnt offering upon one of the mountains which I will tell thee of.

God's request and challenge to Abraham is among the best known and, theologically, most demanding communications from God in the Abraham tradition. It poses acute questions about the nature of faith and the way of God with His faithful people (*Genesis*, Brueggemann, p. 185). God's tests are part of the faith journey. Without testing, the people of God do not get the opportunity to see how much they have grown in the Lord. Ironically, the tests tell us how far we have come, but also push us to the next levels of faith in God. Faith is not static, but dynamic; the tests of God are like bloodlines to our living faith. One dimension of faith is the temptation to accommodate the world, and to yield to its pressures, which lead to a compromised state. The world tells us to look out for ourselves and our own desires. If we place ourselves in Abraham's shoes, it is almost a certainty that

we would have been tempted not to do what God asked. God asked Abram to take his son, his only son Isaac—whom he loved—and go to the region of Moriah. "Sacrifice him there as a burnt offering on one of the mountains I will tell you about" (Genesis 22:2, NIV).

To sacrifice one's own child does not make sense! Surely, God could not view this as the best course of action, especially since Abraham and Sarah had waited so long for this promised child. The testings of God make clear the conflict between the purposes of God and our own desires. Additionally, the testings of God show that what is normal in the world may not be normal with God. The prophet Isaiah reminded us that God's thoughts are not our thoughts. His ways are not our ways (see Isaiah 55:8). To accept a test from God shows that we seek to be faithful to God. To run away from the test shows that we may not be as ready to do everything for God as we have proclaimed.

The tests of God do not look the same for everyone. For many of us, the test comes in the form of continuing faith without seeing the immediate rewards. God has promised a thing and we have been faithful. Yet, we begin to ask, "How long, Lord?" The test then becomes a quest to see how long we can keep our eyes focused on God. For pastors and other ministry leaders, God's testing comes in the form of challenges within the church and the operations of ministries. Will the pastor continue to see the Spirit of God as the people of the church commit godless actions? Will ministry leaders continue to serve the church in the midst of waning church attendance, participation, and finances? Again, the test is to see how we can continue looking to and following God. Abraham's test was of mitigating circumstances. God asked him to give up his one and only son. Isaac was the son for whom Abraham endured the challenges of his faith journey. Imagine the angst of Abraham when he heard God tell him to go to the region of Moriah and sacrifice his only son. If the test exposed conflict between the purposes of God and the purposes of the world, Abraham had no choice if he was to be found faithful. There was no escaping the test. The test had to be taken.

B. Tests Enable Us to See Ourselves as Stewards (Genesis 22:6-10)

And Abraham took the wood of the burnt offering, and laid it upon Isaac his son; and he took the fire in his hand, and a knife; and they went both of them together. And Isaac spake unto Abraham his father, and said, My father: and he said, Here am I, my son. And he said, Behold the fire and the wood: but where is the lamb for a burnt offering? And Abraham said, My son, God will provide himself a lamb for a burnt offering: so they went both of them together. And they came to the place which God had told him of; and Abraham built an altar there, and laid the wood in order, and bound Isaac his son, and laid him on the altar upon the wood. And Abraham stretched forth his hand, and took the knife to slay his son.

God's testing may ask us to give up something that is dear to us. In Abraham's case, it was his son, Isaac. In our own tests, we may need to give up money, personal time, specific desires, or even certain people such as family members or friends. When one is asked to give up something, God may want to see where our loyalties lie. The testing of God shows us that we are stewards of God's gifts rather than owners of the gifts.

Today, we may not be asked to sacrifice our children as a response to the testing of God. But, the testing we may have to undergo may require us to release that which we have in hand. Therefore, to follow God and be found faithful, we must view ourselves as stewards of God's gifts instead of owners of God's gifts. At any time, God's testing may require that we give up something very close and dear to us. Understanding ourselves as stewards allows us to have freedom in following God and God's divine calls and instructions. In the midst of anguish, Abraham was ready to sacrifice his beloved Isaac in faithfulness to God. Abraham's actions suggest that he came to the realization that he was a steward over Isaac and not the owner of Isaac.

A *steward* is someone appointed to manage affairs and to supervise and distribute provisions. As God's stewards, we are called to manage our affairs in a worthy manner, while supervising and distributing the provisions that God makes available to us.

C. God Is Always Near (Genesis 22:11-14)

And the angel of the LORD called unto him out of heaven, and said, Abraham, Abraham: and he said, Here am I. And he said, Lay not thine hand upon the lad, neither do thou any thing unto him: for now I know that thou fearest God, seeing thou hast not withheld thy son, thine only son from me. And Abraham lifted up his eyes, and looked, and behold behind him a ram caught in a thicket by his horns: and Abraham went and took the ram, and offered him up for a burnt offering in the stead of his son. And

Abraham called the name of that place Jehovah-jireh: as it is said to this day, In the mount of the Lord it shall be seen.

As Abraham was about to go through with the sacrificing of Isaac, the angel of the Lord intervened in order to stop Abraham. Abraham responded with, "Here I am" (verse 11, NIV). The angel of the Lord said, "Do not lay a hand on the boy....Do not do anything to him. Now I know that you fear God, because you have not withheld from me your son, your only son" (verse 12, NIV). Abraham was commended for reverencing God by his willingness to give up his son, Isaac. The bigger picture, here, is that Abraham was willing to give up what was dearest to him. To regard the meaning here as only about Isaac is to miss the larger lesson that God desires us to understand. There cannot be persons, places, or things that separate us from God. The apostle Paul explained our connection to God through Christ: "For I am convinced that neither death nor life, neither angels nor demons, neither the present nor the future, nor any powers, neither height nor depth, nor anything else in all creation, will be able to separate us from the love of God that is in Christ Jesus our Lord" (Romans 8:38-39, NIV). To follow the call of God and to be faithful requires that we be "slaves" to Christ by not operating from our own autonomy. Abraham looked up to see a ram caught in the thicket. He used the ram as a burnt offering instead of Isaac. He named the place of the sacrifice "The Lord will provide." On our faith journeys and in times of testing, it may appear that we are walking alone. When we embark on new journeys or try out new ideas, there must be the resolve that God is near and will sustain us because there are times when we cannot feel the presence of God nor see the results of the hand of God in our lives. God may seem distant and unable to hear our calls. It is in these times that we must be intentional that nothing will separate us from God. As we continue in that strength, God will give us what we need to make it to the desired destination. Isaac did not become a barrier between Abraham and God. In turn, God provided the ram in the bush so that Abraham could make a sacrifice, as required.

Abraham's example of continuing faith during challenging times is a model for contemporary Christians. Life's challenges are numerous, particularly for African Americans. God will provide the ram in the bush by using those who heed the divine call and follow through in faith. It is up to us to continue in faith. It is God's provision that brings success and order. Similarly, Abraham was assigned a part to keep in the journey and he decided to follow through. As he continued to exemplify faithfulness, God provided a resolution to the situation. The chaos of sacrificing his son was brought to order when God supplied what was needed. God is transcendent, but also imminent. Our faith keeps us close to God, even during the moments when God seems far away.

III. CONCLUDING REFLECTION

Faith is not static. It is dynamic, always moving, and seeking that which is fresh and new. Faith is also pervasive and consuming. It is the driving force that keeps us connected to God and moving toward the fulfillment of God's promises. Yet, times of testing are part of our faith journeys. The tests provide ways in which we see our growth and move to the next stages of faith. Genesis 22 is unique in that it not only affirms the testing by God, but also affirms God's way of providing. God is the tester at the beginning of the chapter, but at the end, God is the provider. God as tester is the God who seems distant. God the provider is the God who is near to our circumstances. In either case, God is in the midst—leading us. The life of Abraham is set by this text in the midst of the contradiction between the testing of God and the providing of by God. The call to Abraham was a call to live in the presence of this God who moves both toward us and apart from us (*Genesis*, Brueggemann, p. 192). African Americans have a long history of living between the contradiction of testing and provision. We are tested daily with low wages, lack of job opportunities, and limited education. We are plagued by a sinful system that takes away human flourishing. Yet, the provision of God enables us to have food on our tables and roofs over our heads. God's provision also provides education for our children. Most importantly, God's provision allows African Americans to live peaceably in a culture ruled by the whims and thoughts of the dominant race. God tests us, but God also provides for us. That is the way of faith, and that is how God communes with His people.

PRAYER

Lord, we come to You thanking You for our times of testing. We know that Your testing is a part of the way of faith. Your tests are not designed to harm us, but to build us up. We ask that You give us the ability to pass the test so that we are able to continue on our faith journeys. In Jesus' name we pray. Amen.

WORD POWER

Stewardship—the careful and responsible management of something entrusted to one's care.

HOME DAILY BIBLE READINGS
(December 12-18, 2011)

The Lord Provides

MONDAY, December 12: "All Your Needs" (Philippians 4:15-20)

TUESDAY, December 13: "Born through the Promise" (Galatians 4:21-28)

WEDNESDAY, December 14: "Not Withholding His Only Son" (Genesis 22:15-19)

THURSDAY, December 15: "Faith Completed by Works" (James 2:14-24)

FRIDAY, December 16: "Concern for Our Descendants" (Joshua 22:21-29)

SATURDAY, December 17: "Righteousness and Justice" (Proverbs 21:1-5)

SUNDAY, December 18: "The Challenge to Commitment" (Genesis 22:1-2, 6-14)

ACCORDING TO THE PROMISE

DEVOTIONAL READING: **2 Corinthians 1:18-22**
PRINT PASSAGE: **Luke 1:46-55**
KEY VERSES: **Luke 1:46-47**

BACKGROUND SCRIPTURE: **Luke 1:26-56;**
Galatians 3:6-18

Luke 1:46-55—KJV

46 And Mary said, My soul doth magnify the Lord,
47 And my spirit hath rejoiced in God my Saviour.
48 For he hath regarded the low estate of his handmaiden: for, behold, from henceforth all generations shall call me blessed.
49 For he that is mighty hath done to me great things; and holy is his name.
50 And his mercy is on them that fear him from generation to generation.
51 He hath shewed strength with his arm; he hath scattered the proud in the imagination of their hearts.
52 He hath put down the mighty from their seats, and exalted them of low degree.
53 He hath filled the hungry with good things; and the rich he hath sent empty away.
54 He hath holpen his servant Israel, in remembrance of his mercy;
55 As he spake to our fathers, to Abraham, and to his seed for ever.

Luke 1:46-55—NIV

46 And Mary said: "My soul glorifies the Lord
47 and my spirit rejoices in God my Savior,
48 for he has been mindful of the humble state of his servant. From now on all generations will call me blessed,
49 for the Mighty One has done great things for me—holy is his name.
50 His mercy extends to those who fear him, from generation to generation.
51 He has performed mighty deeds with his arm; he has scattered those who are proud in their inmost thoughts.
52 He has brought down rulers from their thrones but has lifted up the humble.
53 He has filled the hungry with good things but has sent the rich away empty.
54 He has helped his servant Israel, remembering to be merciful
55 to Abraham and his descendants forever, even as he said to our fathers."

BIBLE FACT

GOD'S PROMISE

There are many more promises in Scripture. The promise of a Savior that was fulfilled in the book of Luke was made in the book of Genesis. In theological terms, that promise is called the *proto-evangelium* (the first Gospel). God promised that through the Seed (i.e., descendant) of a woman (Eve) would come one who would crush the head of Satan. This is the first promise of a Savior and the first great act of God's grace after our tragic act of rebellion.

UNIFYING LESSON PRINCIPLE

Faithfulness has timeless benefits. How can acts of faithfulness be rewarded in a time far from the actual acts? Because Abraham was faithful to God and God was faithful to the promise to give Abraham many descendants, God acknowledged Mary's faithfulness to Him by choosing her to be the mother of the Savior.

TOPICAL OUTLINE OF THE LESSON

I. Introduction
   A. A Cause for Celebration
   B. Biblical Background

II. Exposition and Application of the Scripture
   A. God's Plan for the Poor and Lowly
      (Luke 1:46-53)
   B. God's Magnificence and Mary's Response
      (Luke 1:54-55)

III. Concluding Reflection

LESSON OBJECTIVES

Upon the completion of this lesson, the students will understand:

1. The place of praise in the lives of Christians;
2. That God had a plan and that He works to save humanity; and,
3. That God is a liberator of the poor and oppressed.

POINTS TO BE EMPHASIZED

ADULT/YOUTH
Adult Topic: **Celebrating Promises Fulfilled**
Youth Topic: **A Timeless Promise**
Adult Key Verses: **Luke 1:46-47**
Youth Key Verses: **Luke 1:54-55**
Print Passage: **Luke 1:46-55**

—This passage is called "The Magnificat," or "Mary's Song of Praise," and glorifies God for what He has done.
—Mary's song of praise echoes Hannah's song in 1 Samuel 2:1-10.
—Support for the Virgin Birth (Luke 1:34) is also found in Isaiah 7:14 and Matthew 1:24-25.
—Both Mary and her cousin Elizabeth were recipients of God's miraculous action and blessing.
—God often chooses the poor and lowly to accomplish His purposes.
—Mary praised God, her Savior, for choosing her.
—Mary recognized the availability of God's mercy to all who fear God.
—Mary recognized the nature of God's kingdom—humbling the proud and rich and uplifting the humble and the hungry.
—Mary recognized that in the birth of Christ the promise to Abraham and his descendants would be fulfilled.

CHILDREN
Children Topic: **The Joy of Jesus' Birth**
Key Verse: **Luke 2:10**
Print Passage: **Luke 2:1-16**
—The stable was a cave area.
—The shepherds were the first persons to visit Jesus.

—The shepherds were able to overcome their fear of the bright light and the angels.

—God's promise of the Messiah was fulfilled in Jesus.

—The shepherds were willing to share the Good News with others.

—Mary and Joseph were faithful and obedient to God.

I. INTRODUCTION

A. A Cause for Celebration

Birth announcements are celebratory occasions. Women learn that they will soon become mothers; men learn that they will soon become fathers; and parents learn that they will soon become grandparents. Birth announcements remind us all of the miracle of birth, and that the world would soon be blessed with a gift from God: a baby. Women often testify to the marvel of feeling life growing within their own bodies, and the privilege of sharing in a divine activity: the miracle of life. Imagine being told by a celestial messenger that the child you carry will be Jesus, the Savior of the world! This holy announcement came to Mary when she was barely more than a child herself. Most biblical scholars estimate that Mary was probably between the ages of thirteen and fifteen when she conceived Jesus.

The birth of Jesus in the gospel of Luke is unique on many levels. It is only in Luke's account that we hear about Jesus' being born in a manger, and shepherds' being present at His birth (see Luke 2:7-8). Only Luke provided us with a narrative about Jesus' infancy (see Luke 2:21-38), and only in the book of Luke do we read anything about Jesus' childhood (see Luke 2:41-52). Juxtaposed between the foretelling of the births of John the Baptist and Jesus is the Magnificat of Mary (see Luke 1:46-55), or Mary's song of thanksgiving. This has become a song of praise used in liturgies in churches around the world. The Magnificat of Mary is a praise coming from the mother of the Christ. The word *Magnificat* is Latin in origin and means "magnify." Praise is a recurring theme in the gospel of Luke: a blind man gave praise to God in Luke 18:43, and even upon the death of Jesus a centurion gave praise to God in Luke 23:47. When Mary heard from God that He had a divine purpose for her womb, her response was praise.

B. Biblical Background

The author of the gospel of Luke did not begin his account with details about Jesus, as did the authors of the other Synoptic Gospels—Matthew and Mark—which both immediately start with information about Jesus. The gospel of Luke begins by letting us know that the purpose of this gospel was to provide an "orderly account" for someone named Theophilus (see Luke 1:1-4).

In the culture of the ancient world, there was a social structure known as *client* and *patron*. A patron often assisted a client financially. It is possible that Theophilus may have been Luke's patron, and perhaps even paid Luke's research expenses for the writing of this gospel. Luke's reference to him as "most excellent Theophilus" (Luke 1:3) may have been an official title. This means that Theophilus may have been a government official, or a member of the upper class—or he may have had some significant social status. The reference to "things about which you have been instructed" may indicate that Theophilus had previously received some Christian instruction. There is also another possibility: that Theophilus was a code name for believers. In Greek, *Theophilus* means "beloved of God." It can be deduced that the purpose of the gospel of Luke was either to instruct an individual about the ways of Christ, or to provide assurance to a group of believers who would recognize the name *Theophilus* as coded language meant for them. This was not an uncommon practice among oppressed peoples. During American slavery, slaves would often use the spirituals to communicate messages that the slaveholders would not understand; it was a tool of the Underground Railroad. For example, to announce the arrival of Harriet Tubman, slaves might sing a particular song that may seem innocent on its face, but for the slaves the message was clear: if you were planning to run away to the North, tonight would be your opportunity to do so.

But the gospel of Luke does not move from Theophilus to Jesus. The gospel of Luke moves from Theophilus to John the Baptist. Luke provides one of the most thorough accounts of preparation for the mission of Jesus by beginning with the narrative of Jesus' frontrunner, John the Baptist, and the visit of an angel to Mary, a self-described "lowly servant."

As important a character as she is to the history of Christianity, there is not a lot that can be confirmed about Mary, the mother of Jesus. One of the first challenges to any investigation of Mary is the frequency with which this name appears in the New Testament: in addition to Jesus' mother, there were Mary, the sister of Martha (see Luke 10:39-42); Mary Magdalene (see John 20:1)—one of the most prominent female disciples; Mary the mother of James and Joses (see Mark 15:40); Mary the mother of John Mark (see Acts 12:12); and a Mary apart from Mary Magdalene, who stood by the cross and watched Jesus die (see John 19:25). Even Paul's writings reference a Mary who worked diligently in the church of Rome (see Romans 16:6). Clearly, Mary was quite a popular name in first-century Palestine at the time of Jesus. The Greek form of her name is *Maria*, and the Hebrew form is *Miriam* or *Mariamme*.

In this reference to Mary in the beginning of the gospel of Luke, Mary is introduced between stories about Elizabeth and Zechariah, the parents of John the Baptist. The Scriptures reveal that an angel appeared to Mary, letting her know that she would bear a son who was to be named Jesus, and that this already-overwhelming event would happen *outside of the natural order of childbirth*. Imagine the impact of hearing that one would conceive supernaturally through the Holy Spirit! In fact, both Mary and Elizabeth were informed by celestial messengers that not only would they conceive, but that God would use their sons mightily in His plan of salvation. Only in the gospel of Luke is this divine familial relationship revealed—that Jesus and John the Baptist were related (see Luke 1:36), and that their ministries would work together in God's plan (see Luke 3:1–4:13).

II. EXPOSITION AND APPLICATION OF THE SCRIPTURE

A. God's Plan for the Poor and Lowly
(Luke 1:46-53)

And Mary said, My soul doth magnify the Lord, And my spirit hath rejoiced in God my Saviour. For he hath regarded the low estate of his handmaiden: for, behold, from henceforth all generations shall call me blessed. For he that is mighty hath done to me great things; and holy is his name. And his mercy is on them that fear him from generation to generation. He hath shewed strength with his arm; he hath scattered the proud in the imagination of their hearts. He hath put down the mighty from their seats, and exalted them of low degree. He hath filled the hungry with good things; and the rich he hath sent empty away.

When Mary received word from the angel Gabriel that she had found favor with God, her response was uniquely devoid of any sense of haughtiness or pride. Instead, Mary stood in solidarity with the oppressed, the poor, and the lowly. There is quite a bit of talk about the oppressed and the poor in the gospel of Luke. God is presented as one who is faithful to the downtrodden and to the outcast of society. It is only in the book of Luke where Jesus announced that His mission was to preach to the poor, heal the brokenhearted, and announce the release of captives (see Luke 4:16-18).

Mary's song of praise talks about another theme prevalent in the gospel of Luke—the theme of reversal: "[God] has brought down the powerful from their thrones, and lifted up the lowly; he has filled the hungry with good things, and sent the rich away empty" (Luke 1:52-53, NIV). This theme of reversal seems to indicate a reversal between the rich and the poor—that those at the top of the social echelon would trade places with those who had been outcast. Mary's song of praise seems to foreshadow the tone of Jesus' ministry as

it is presented in the book of Luke (see Luke 4:16-30); Jesus established His mission by announcing that He had come to set the captives free, to recover sight for the blind, to let the oppressed go free, and to bring good news to the poor. The poor, those on the bottom of the social-status totem pole, had high priority in Jesus' mission. The lowly were at the forefront of what Jesus understood His task to be, for Jesus understood Himself to be sent to those who were considered to be at the bottom of the social register at that time: the sick, the poor, and women.

Women had prominent roles in the gospel of Luke, and are often in socially surprising roles: God is imaged as a woman in the parable of the lost coin, and Mary Magdalene, Joanna, Susanna, and many other women provided for Jesus out of their own resources (see Luke 8:1-3). It is also worth noting that most women of the ancient Near East were described in terms of the men with whom they were associated. In verse 3, Joanna was described as the wife of Herod's own steward Chuza, yet Mary Magdalene was named for where she came from—Magdala—a fishing village on the Sea of Galilee. These images of women in socially significant roles suggest that God is compassionate toward those whom society deems as unworthy.

Mary's Magnificat speaks about how those whom society deems as "respectable" (those at the top) are replaced by those who are considered socially marginalized—those at the bottom. The gospel of Luke is filled with images, not of the righteous as central figures, but rather the sinners, the poor, the sick, and outcasts. This is a powerful message for those who are oppressed—for as Mary's story reveals, God uses the lowly for divine purposes. Marginalized peoples have roles in God's plan for salvation. This is a message of hope!

B. God's Magnificence and Mary's Response (Luke 1:54-55)

He hath holpen his servant Israel, in remembrance of his mercy; As he spake to our fathers, to Abraham, and to his seed for ever.

Although quite a bit has been said about the concept of a Virgin Birth, perhaps a deeper investigation would consider how the information about Mary's pregnancy is used within the narrative. As demonstrated via Hannah's prayer (see 1 Samuel 2:1-10), there have been several cases in Scripture where a barren woman was blessed with a child. This often was an indication that the child was special and would be used by God in some form or fashion. In the case of Jesus, however, the birth was more than special—it was miraculous. Mary had a bit of a struggle taking it all in, as was made evident in her asking, "How can this be?" (Luke 1:34, NRSV).

Mary's response to all of this is quite remarkable, considering the tight spot that it placed her in. It is important to understand that Mary was not yet married to Joseph; she was *betrothed* (or promised) to him. Mary knew that Joseph would be within his rights to spurn a pregnant fiancée; in fact, he could have made her a public spectacle and allowed her to be stoned to death for being found with child before they were married. Even today, there is a certain stigma and shame attached to unwed teenage pregnancy, and yet Mary was willing to put herself at risk. It is also worth noting that God sought Mary's consent to the pregnancy, but did not seek Joseph's input at all in the gospel of Luke. The Magnificat of Mary suggests that God did not simply impose His will upon a young girl without her permission. The Magnificat of Mary is her surrender and submission to God's will.

One can only marvel at the quiet confidence displayed by the young Mary when she was told that God would use her. We can learn a lot from her example: we learn from Mary that one is never too small in one's own eyes and never too inadequate in one's own estimation to be used by God for a divine purpose. Mary praised God for it! Mary praised God for choosing her to participate in that divine activity; she also praised God for allowing her to witness the fulfillment of the promise that He made to Abraham. Mary's encounter with God reveals Him to be all-powerful. Through Mary's simple act of obedience—in yielding to God's will—we witness that God is faithful, and God's faithfulness does unexpected things. In one simple act by a young girl, God is shown to be both the fulfiller of promises to Israel, and the merciful God who offers compassion and salvation to "the least of these." The Magnificat of Mary is a powerful reminder that God saves in unexpected ways.

III. CONCLUDING REFLECTION

Mary was an eyewitness to the ministry of Jesus—from the moment He drew His first breath to the moment He breathed His last upon the cross. Mary was there when a young Jesus told her that He had to be about God's business, and she pondered His sayings in her heart. Mary was present, and some might argue the catalyst, for the first miracle (or "sign") that Jesus performed in the gospel of John: when He turned water into wine at a wedding in Cana (see John 2:1-11). Mary knew what it was like to have a son falsely accused, and then bear the pain of watching Him be condemned, beaten with rods, whips, and fists, and then nailed to a cross, where He would hang until He died. Mary witnessed her oldest child endure a public execution meant to both torture and shame the victim. She watched the Roman guards thrust a spear into His side to be sure that His death was certain. She stood by as they pulled the nails out of His flesh and lowered His body to the ground. Mary was present in the upper room (see Acts 1:14) and played a significant role as the church was born. Mary was blessed beyond measure, as was foretold by the angel Gabriel—who announced that she had favor with God (see Luke 1:30).

This encounter with the angel Gabriel, when Mary was informed of God's plan for her, is one of the most poignant scenes in Scripture. A young girl barely into her teens demonstrated great faith and confidence in God. Mary was willing to yield to the Almighty, regardless of what it may have cost her in social status. God used one with the lowest social status of the times—an unmarried, teenage Jewish girl—to bring Jesus into the world. God made this covenant not with the high priest, not with a Pharisee, not with a prophet, but with a young girl who had no social power. Mary displayed no detectable fear of what could happen to her. Mary did not respond like Moses and request that someone else be given the task. Mary's response to God was yes.

PRAYER

Merciful God, help us to respond like Mary whenever You call on us. Help us to live lives that testify to others that nothing is impossible with You. In Jesus' name we pray. Amen.

WORD POWER

Magnificat—a song of praise sung by Mary after her conception of Jesus.

HOME DAILY BIBLE READINGS
(December 19-25, 2011)

According to the Promise

MONDAY, December 19: "God Is Faithful" (2 Corinthians 1:18-22)

TUESDAY, December 20: "A Faithful Heart" (Nehemiah 9:6-10)

WEDNESDAY, December 21: "Descendants of Abraham" (Galatians 3:6-12)

THURSDAY, December 22: "Inheritance through the Promise" (Galatians 3:13-18)

FRIDAY, December 23: "Jesus' Birth Foretold" (Luke 1:26-38)

SATURDAY, December 24: "Elizabeth's Blessing" (Luke 1:39-45)

SUNDAY, December 25: "Mary's Song of Praise" (Luke 1:46-55)

LESSON 5   January 1, 2012

GOD WATCHES OVER JOSEPH

DEVOTIONAL READING: **1 Corinthians 10:1-13**
PRINT PASSAGE: **Genesis 39:7-21a**

BACKGROUND SCRIPTURE: **Genesis 39:1-23**
KEY VERSE: **Genesis 39:9**

Genesis 39:7-21a—KJV

7 And it came to pass after these things, that his master's wife cast her eyes upon Joseph; and she said, Lie with me.

8 But he refused, and said unto his master's wife, Behold, my master wotteth not what is with me in the house, and he hath committed all that he hath to my hand;

9 There is none greater in this house than I; neither hath he kept back any thing from me but thee, because thou art his wife: how then can I do this great wickedness, and sin against God?

10 And it came to pass, as she spake to Joseph day by day, that he hearkened not unto her, to lie by her, or to be with her.

11 And it came to pass about this time, that Joseph went into the house to do his business; and there was none of the men of the house there within.

12 And she caught him by his garment, saying, Lie with me: and he left his garment in her hand, and fled, and got him out.

13 And it came to pass, when she saw that he had left his garment in her hand, and was fled forth,

14 That she called unto the men of her house, and spake unto them, saying, See, he hath brought in an Hebrew unto us to mock us; he came in unto me to lie with me, and I cried with a loud voice:

15 And it came to pass, when he heard that I lifted up my voice and cried, that he left his garment with me, and fled, and got him out.

16 And she laid up his garment by her, until his lord came home.

17 And she spake unto him according to these words, saying, The Hebrew servant, which thou hast brought unto us, came in unto me to mock me:

18 And it came to pass, as I lifted up my voice and cried, that he left his garment with me, and fled out.

Genesis 39:7-21a—NIV

7 and after a while his master's wife took notice of Joseph and said, "Come to bed with me!"

8 But he refused. "With me in charge," he told her, "my master does not concern himself with anything in the house; everything he owns he has entrusted to my care.

9 No one is greater in this house than I am. My master has withheld nothing from me except you, because you are his wife. How then could I do such a wicked thing and sin against God?"

10 And though she spoke to Joseph day after day, he refused to go to bed with her or even be with her.

11 One day he went into the house to attend to his duties, and none of the household servants was inside.

12 She caught him by his cloak and said, "Come to bed with me!" But he left his cloak in her hand and ran out of the house.

13 When she saw that he had left his cloak in her hand and had run out of the house,

14 she called her household servants. "Look," she said to them, "this Hebrew has been brought to us to make sport of us! He came in here to sleep with me, but I screamed.

15 When he heard me scream for help, he left his cloak beside me and ran out of the house."

16 She kept his cloak beside her until his master came home.

17 Then she told him this story: "That Hebrew slave you brought us came to me to make sport of me.

18 But as soon as I screamed for help, he left his cloak beside me and ran out of the house."

19 And it came to pass, when his master heard the words of his wife, which she spake unto him, saying, After this manner did thy servant to me; that his wrath was kindled.
20 And Joseph's master took him, and put him into the prison, a place where the king's prisoners were bound: and he was there in the prison.
21 But the LORD was with Joseph, and shewed him mercy.

19 When his master heard the story his wife told him, saying, "This is how your slave treated me," he burned with anger.
20 Joseph's master took him and put him in prison, the place where the king's prisoners were confined. But while Joseph was there in the prison,
21 the LORD was with him; he showed him kindness.

TOPICAL OUTLINE OF THE LESSON

I. **Introduction**
   A. Employer-employee Relations
   B. Biblical Background

II. **Exposition and Application of the Scripture**
   A. Sexual Temptation: "Ain't Nobody Watchin'" (Genesis 39:7-12)
   B. Public Humiliation and False Witness (Genesis 39:13-18)
   C. Suffering: What to Do when Life Seems Unfair (Genesis 39:19-21a)

III. **Concluding Reflection**

LESSON OBJECTIVES

Upon the completion of this lesson, the students will understand that:
1. Adversity and hardship build maturity and shape faith;
2. In the face of temptations, there are always options to escape evil;
3. A life of integrity lines up with God's purposes; and,
4. Great things happen in life when our dreams become one with God's dream.

POINTS TO BE EMPHASIZED
ADULT/YOUTH

Adult Topic: A Life of Integrity
Youth Topic: No Means No!
Adult Key Verse: Genesis 39:9
Youth Key Verse: Genesis 39:21
Print Passage: Genesis 39:7-21a

—The story of Joseph's fleeing Potiphar's wife illustrates the teaching of Proverbs 7.
—Joseph's and Potiphar's wife's value systems differed.
—Slaves in Bible times could be promoted to positions of high responsibility.
—A lack of witnesses can have serious consequences.
—The Lord does not necessarily correct injustice immediately.
—Joseph was a trusted administrator under Potiphar, one of Pharaoh's officials.
—Potiphar's wife falsely accused Joseph when he would not sleep with her.

—Potiphar believed his wife, became angry with Joseph, and threw him in prison.

—The Lord was with Joseph through everything he endured.

CHILDREN

Children Topic: A Faithful Young Man

Key Verse: Genesis 39:21

Print Passage: Genesis 39:7-21a

—Potiphar's wife was a wicked woman who desired to be romantic with Joseph.

—Joseph maintained his integrity in spite of the pleas of Potiphar's wife.

—Potiphar's wife tried to ensnare Joseph as he was completing household tasks.

—In her rage, Potiphar's wife falsely accused Joseph of attempted rape.

—Potiphar had Joseph thrown into prison.

—God was with Joseph and gave him favor with the keeper of the prison.

I. INTRODUCTION

A. Employer-employee Relations

If there were a meeting at a church on any given Wednesday night and the members of that church were given an "open mike" session to air their faith challenges, a topic that would be sure to come up would be ways to deal with the people they work with, particularly their bosses. The recent downturn of the economy has forced many employers to downsize their number of employees as a means of cutting back. This has resulted in the formerly employed people's duties' being redistributed among those still on the job, often with no additional compensation for taking on extra work and longer hours. To further complicate matters, there may appear to be one employee who is favored by the employer—one who is paid more, yet works significantly less than his colleagues. And to elevate the levels of stress even higher, in some cases there may be a supervisor who says and does things that make the employees feel both uncomfortable and powerless, because they know that they need their jobs in order to pay the bills. There have been far too many instances of people in positions of authority taking unfair advantage of those who work for them. In some cases, authority figures often take their own frustrations, shortcomings, and insecurities out on their employees.

This scenario can help us to understand a bit of the tension that Joseph must have felt when the wife of the man he worked for as a slave propositioned him. It could be argued that Joseph was sexually harassed on the job! After his own brothers sold him into slavery, Joseph was purchased by Potiphar and put to work in his household. Joseph became the overseer of Potiphar's home, and in time had a fateful encounter with his wife that would even further change the course of his life.

B. Biblical Background

Joseph is one of the most pivotal figures of the Hebrew Bible/Old Testament. The story of Joseph is part of a recurring theme in Israel's history—the theme of the Israelites' experiencing domination by a foreign power. The story of Joseph and his trials and tribulations in Egypt is part of the Jewish ancestor tradition. In other words, Joseph was linked to the sons and daughters of God's promise to Israel through Abraham. Joseph was the older son of Jacob and Rachel. Jacob, once known as the trickster who stole his brother Esau's birthright, received a promise from God in Genesis 28:13-15 that God would bless him and his offspring with land.

Joseph was born to Jacob and his favorite wife, Rachel. Rachel and her sister Leah bore several sons for Jacob, and are mentioned as matriarchs of Israel in Ruth 4:11. It could be argued that Joseph, as the older son of Jacob's favored wife, received so much special favor and preference from his father that it offended his brothers to the point of murder! His brothers were more than likely jealous of the attention that Joseph received, and Joseph probably did not help his case much when he shared his dreams with them. Joseph's dreams always seemed to involve his being elevated above others. Apparently, Joseph the teenager had not quite mastered the fine art of knowing when to keep certain things to himself!

According to the biblical narrative, Joseph had several siblings. We learn from Genesis 37:3 that Jacob preferred Joseph over all of his children. One can imagine the tension not only between Israel's wives and their maids, who also bore children for him, but also among the children themselves! Although it does not justify or excuse their actions, it becomes easy to see how Joseph's brothers would grow weary of hearing their younger brother brag all the time about his dreams. Sibling rivalry is complicated enough when a parent favors one child over another. Joseph's brothers looked on as Jacob affirmed Joseph and loved him and shared special moments with him. When Joseph was not getting special attention from their father, he was busy telling them how they would bow down to him someday!

Joseph was guilty of sharing his dreams to his brothers. Imagine if you had to listen to your father praise your brother all day long, and as soon as that was over, you got to hear the brother tell you every chance he got that you would serve him someday. Joseph's dreams spoke clearly of his elevated status within his own family as Joseph revealed to his brothers that in his dream, "the sun and moon and eleven stars were bowing down to me" (Genesis 37:9, NIV).

In a fit of rage and jealousy, the brothers began to plot the murder of their own brother, but ended up setting the stage for Joseph to be sold to Midianite merchants, who in turn sold him to Potiphar, an Egyptian official of Pharaoh and captain of the guard (see Genesis 39:1). It is believed that Potiphar had some type of connection to the royal palace, because he was named as the "captain of the guard" (Genesis 39:1). Potiphar must have held some power, since he was able to get Joseph tossed into jail. In any event, Potiphar's purchase of this handsome Hebrew boy set Joseph on a path that would land him squarely within the sights of Potiphar's wife, who tried to seduce him.

II. EXPOSITION AND APPLICATION OF THE SCRIPTURE

A. Sexual Temptation: "Ain't Nobody Watchin'" (Genesis 39:7-12)

And it came to pass after these things, that his master's wife cast her eyes upon Joseph; and she said, Lie with me. But he refused, and said unto his master's wife, Behold, my master wotteth not what is with me in the house, and he hath committed all that he hath to my hand; There is none greater in this house than I; neither hath he kept back any thing from me but thee, because thou art his wife: how then can I do this great wickedness, and sin against God? And it came to pass, as she spake to Joseph day by day, that he hearkened not unto her, to lie by her, or to be with her. And it came to pass about this time, that Joseph went into the house to do his business; and there was none of the men of the house there within. And she caught him by his garment, saying, Lie with me: and he left his garment in her hand, and fled, and got him out.

Sexual temptation is one of many recurring themes that appear throughout the Hebrew Bible/Old Testament. Young Hebrew boys are warned to keep a safe distance from the seductive powers of foreign women, and there are quite a few parallels between Potiphar's wife and the foreign woman of Proverbs 7:16-21. The "strange woman" of the book of Proverbs cast a net of sexual temptation as she described her bedroom to her would-be suitor (see Proverbs 7:16-17). It is a common theme in ancient literature to beware of women who are "different" because they could potentially tempt young, virile Hebrew men into sexual sin. What made a woman "different," "strange" or "foreign" was primarily cultural in tone; it was a way of speaking of women who were not Jewish.

Joseph was tempted to sin sexually by a non-Jewish foreign woman—the wife of Potiphar. We are not made privy of her motivations for wanting Joseph to "sleep with her." Were her motivations purely sexual gratification and lust, or did she simply want a child? Some Bible scholars believe Potiphar was a eunuch and therefore would have been incapable of producing offspring. If Potiphar were a eunuch, then he would have been castrated before he hit puberty. Another theory is the idea that Potiphar's wife was making a bid (which turned out to be a successful one) to remove Joseph from his place as the "overseer in his (Potiphar's) house" (Genesis 39:5), so that she could hold that title herself. Was the wife of Potiphar informed that Joseph was joining the staff? And better yet, did Joseph now have more authority in her own household than she did? One element of the story that is left purely to our own imaginations is Mrs. Potiphar's motives. Why did she set Joseph up? Was she being purely vindictive? Or did she fear reprisals from her husband? Was she trying to get pregnant? Or was she simply jealous that Joseph held a higher status in her own house than she did? Potiphar's wife is one of many women portrayed negatively in the Hebrew Bible/Old Testament. Her story ended with her accusation, and we never hear about her again.

Whether the wife of Potiphar was acting out of jealousy and resentment over Joseph's new status in her house, responding to her biological clock's ticking, or wanting to act out her lust with a handsome young Hebrew boy, we can conclude that she was operating out of basic human desires that are familiar to all of us. Although Joseph resisted her, Potiphar's wife gained the upper hand quickly by telling the lie that Joseph tried to seduce her and used Joseph's torn clothes as evidence against him.

Unfortunately for Joseph, Potiphar believed his wife and tossed Joseph in jail on trumped-up charges of attempted seduction.

Regardless of her motivations, this Egyptian woman put Joseph between a rock and a hard place because she was married to his master. Potiphar's wife was Joseph's mistress, but not in the modern sexual sense of the word. Potiphar's wife was not Joseph's mistress as though the two of them were carrying on an affair; rather, she was his owner who had the power to send him to jail based on her false testimony against him. Thanks to a plan put into motion by his own brothers, Joseph found himself pressed for sex by a woman he technically should not be able to refuse, because he was her slave. Yet Joseph rebuked her. This account in Genesis 39 is a highlighting of Joseph's refusal to give in to her temptation, when he pulled away from her and exclaimed, "How then can I do this great wickedness, and sin against God?" Joseph's statement reveals quite a bit about his relationship with God. It is worth noting that Joseph did not say, "How can I do this great wickedness, because it could land me in jail?" Joseph also did not say, "How can I do this great wickedness, and risk losing my standing with Potiphar?" Joseph refused to sexually engage the wife of Potiphar, not because he was concerned about anything coming back on him, but, rather, he was more concerned with offending God. Joseph's response to the wife of Potiphar is theological, not personal.

Temptation is often used in the Bible to reveal one's commitment to God. In this Scripture passage, Joseph was falsely accused of seduction, and he suffered because of it.

B. Public Humiliation and False Witness (Genesis 39:13-18)

And it came to pass, when she saw that he had left his garment in her hand, and was fled forth, That she called unto the men of her house, and spake unto them, saying, See, he hath brought in an Hebrew unto us to mock us; he came in unto me to lie with me, and I cried with a loud voice: And it came to pass, when he heard that I lifted up my voice and cried, that he left his garment with me, and fled, and got him out. And she laid up his garment by her, until his lord came home. And she spake unto him according to these words, saying, The Hebrew servant, which thou hast brought unto us, came in unto me to mock me: And it came to pass, as I lifted up my voice and cried, that he left his garment with me, and fled out.

Joseph seemed to have had some real challenges with holding on to his clothes. First, we see him stripped of his coat of many colors when his own brothers left him for dead. In Genesis 39, Joseph once again lost his clothes, actually leaving a piece of his garment in the hands of Potiphar's wife in his haste to flee from her attempts at seduction.

This pattern of Joseph's losing his clothing can be symbolic on many levels. It could represent exposure, vulnerability, and the need for some type of shield or protection from shame. Uncovering shame—the removal of Joseph's clothing—could also be a form of public humiliation. In our own time, we have witnessed countless episodes of public humiliation and uncovered shame in relatively recent political scandals: President Bill Clinton and Monica Lewinsky and an incriminating blue dress; New York Governor Eliot Spitzer and his visitation of prostitutes; and South Carolina Governor Mark Sanford and his lying to his own state about his whereabouts (he claimed to be on an Appalachian hiking trail when he was really with his Argentinean mistress). Although these cases are similar to Joseph's experience of public humiliation and false witness, there is one key difference: despite many public denials, many of the political scandals have been proven to be true. The charges and allegations were correct. In Joseph's case, however, the allegations against him were false—but that fact did not keep him from suffering.

C. Suffering: What to Do when Life Seems Unfair (Genesis 39:19-21a)

And it came to pass, when his master heard the words of his wife, which she spake unto him, saying, After this manner did thy servant to me; that his wrath was kindled. And Joseph's master took him, and put him into the prison, a place where the king's prisoners were bound: and he was there in the prison. But the LORD was with Joseph, and shewed him mercy.

There is a saying that goes, "Suffering is inevitable, but misery is a choice." The message is clear: even when we feel that we have no control over our circumstances, we still control how we *react* to those circumstances. Psychologists argue that suffering is one of the most persistent human problems. All of us will encounter some form of pain and/or distress. Some of us will experience suffering with more frequency than others. Suffering comes in many forms: shattered dreams, frustrated hopes, pain in the body, grief, despair, loneliness, anxiety, crises of spirit, and depression. It should come as no shock that these unpleasant expressions find their way into the lives of Bible-believing Christians.

Joseph's experiences in Egypt remind us that even those who are used by God for divine purposes are not exempt from suffering. Joseph coped by believing in the power of God to change his circumstances. This suggests that one must look beyond the pain and remain focused on God. Joseph did not focus on the temptation before him; he focused rather on the God whom he served. He did not focus on the shapely form of Potiphar's Egyptian wife; he kept his eyes toward heaven and concentrated instead on how his actions would look in God's eyes. Imagine what would happen if we used our suffering to focus our attention on God—how would that make God feel? And what would it say to those who are watching us suffer? Joseph suffered unjustly due to a false accusation, but he did not allow it to make him bitter.

It is worth noting that the general public watches very carefully those who profess themselves to be Christians. For those who have even the slightest curiosity about what a relationship with God is like, suffering provides an opportunity for them to see if God is real. If you have experienced the peace of Jehovah-Shalom, your demeanor will reflect it. People will begin to wonder how someone in the midst of great calamity can remain in a peaceful state. For some people, the only God that they will ever see in their lives is the God reflected in us.

III. CONCLUDING REFLECTION

Even though it was a foreign woman who seduced Joseph and made false charges against him, Joseph eventually married an Egyptian woman, Asenath, and had two sons with her—Manasseh and Ephraim. At least one other prominent figure from the history of Israel did indeed marry a woman who would have been considered different and foreign: Moses who married Zipporah, who was a Cushite/Ethiopian (see Numbers 12:1). Zipporah bore Moses two sons: Gershom and Eliezer (see Exodus 18:2-4).

Much like the genetic makeup of many African Americans, Joseph's children were multiethnic. Many of us who are the descendants of kidnapped Africans forced to labor until death as slaves are also multiethnic—as we carry the blood of European slaveholders. Many African Americans also have Native-American and Latino ancestry as well. This is significant, because Joseph was counted among the ancestors of Jesus, which means that Jesus has a unique, multicultural bloodline. This reminds us that the face of God is not flat and static, but rather three-dimensional, with strands of every race, ethnicity, and culture known to humanity.

PRAYER

Almighty God, help us to remember that what we do lingers far longer than what we say. Help us to remember that others are watching us in our time of suffering for any sign of You. Help us to be the brightest light for a world that has a flickering, dim faith. In Jesus' name we pray. Amen.

WORD POWER

Wickedness—In this context, it refers to a willful act of sin and rebellion.

HOME DAILY BIBLE READINGS
(December 26, 2011–January 1, 2012)

God Watches over Joseph

MONDAY, December 26: "A Man Sent Ahead" (Psalm 105:16-22)

TUESDAY, December 27: "Joseph's Story" (Acts 7:9-16)

WEDNESDAY, December 28: "Facing Temptation" (Luke 22:39-46)

THURSDAY, December 29: "Enduring Temptation" (1 Corinthians 10:1-13)

FRIDAY, December 30: "Choosing the Way of Faithfulness" (Psalm 119:25-32)

SATURDAY, December 31: "A Responsible Servant" (Genesis 39:1-6)

SUNDAY, January 1: "Guided by a Loving Lord" (Genesis 39:7-21a)

LESSON 6   January 8, 2012

JOSEPH FINDS FAVOR

DEVOTIONAL READING: **Genesis 49:22-26**
PRINT PASSAGE: **Genesis 41:37-45, 50-52**

BACKGROUND SCRIPTURE: **Genesis 41:1-52**
KEY VERSE: **Genesis 41:38**

Genesis 41:37-45, 50-52—KJV

37 And the thing was good in the eyes of Pharaoh, and in the eyes of all his servants.

38 And Pharaoh said unto his servants, Can we find such a one as this is, a man in whom the Spirit of God is?

39 And Pharaoh said unto Joseph, Forasmuch as God hath shewed thee all this, there is none so discreet and wise as thou art:

40 Thou shalt be over my house, and according unto thy word shall all my people be ruled: only in the throne will I be greater than thou.

41 And Pharaoh said unto Joseph, See, I have set thee over all the land of Egypt.

42 And Pharaoh took off his ring from his hand, and put it upon Joseph's hand, and arrayed him in vestures of fine linen, and put a gold chain about his neck;

43 And he made him to ride in the second chariot which he had; and they cried before him, Bow the knee: and he made him ruler over all the land of Egypt.

44 And Pharaoh said unto Joseph, I am Pharaoh, and without thee shall no man lift up his hand or foot in all the land of Egypt.

45 And Pharaoh called Joseph's name Zaphnath-paaneah; and he gave him to wife Asenath the daughter of Poti-pherah priest of On. And Joseph went out over all the land of Egypt.

     .....

50 And unto Joseph were born two sons before the years of famine came, which Asenath the daughter of Poti-pherah priest of On bare unto him.

51 And Joseph called the name of the firstborn Manasseh: For God, said he, hath made me forget all my toil, and all my father's house.

52 And the name of the second called he Ephraim:

Genesis 41:37-45, 50-52—NIV

37 The plan seemed good to Pharaoh and to all his officials.

38 So Pharaoh asked them, "Can we find anyone like this man, one in whom is the spirit of God?"

39 Then Pharaoh said to Joseph, "Since God has made all this known to you, there is no one so discerning and wise as you.

40 You shall be in charge of my palace, and all my people are to submit to your orders. Only with respect to the throne will I be greater than you."

41 So Pharaoh said to Joseph, "I hereby put you in charge of the whole land of Egypt."

42 Then Pharaoh took his signet ring from his finger and put it on Joseph's finger. He dressed him in robes of fine linen and put a gold chain around his neck.

43 He had him ride in a chariot as his second-in-command, and men shouted before him, "Make way!" Thus he put him in charge of the whole land of Egypt.

44 Then Pharaoh said to Joseph, "I am Pharaoh, but without your word no one will lift hand or foot in all Egypt."

45 Pharaoh gave Joseph the name Zaphenath-Paneah and gave him Asenath daughter of Potiphera, priest of On, to be his wife. And Joseph went throughout the land of Egypt.

     .....

50 Before the years of famine came, two sons were born to Joseph by Asenath daughter of Potiphera, priest of On.

51 Joseph named his firstborn Manasseh and said, "It is because God has made me forget all my trouble and all my father's household."

52 The second son he named Ephraim and said, "It

UNIFYING LESSON PRINCIPLE

Earning other people's faith in us can lead to great responsibility and honor. What results can we expect when others have faith in us? Because Joseph performed so well for the Egyptian king, Pharaoh had faith in Joseph's abilities, elevated him to the second position in all of Egypt, and gave him responsibility for ruling the day-to-day activities of the kingdom.

For God hath caused me to be fruitful in the land of my affliction.

is because God has made me fruitful in the land of my suffering."

TOPICAL OUTLINE OF THE LESSON

I. **Introduction**
   A. Available for God's Use
   B. Biblical Background

II. **Exposition and Application of the Scripture**
   A. How to Get Along with Your Boss
      (Genesis 41:37-45)
   B. God's Blessings in the Midst of Adverse Circumstances
      (Genesis 41:50-52)

III. **Concluding Reflection**

LESSON OBJECTIVES

Upon the completion of this lesson, the students will understand that:

1. Pharaoh acted positively in regards to his faith in Joseph's abilities;
2. Superior performance can lead to greater responsibility and eventual honors by leaders and the community; and,
3. Learners can articulate a connection between their faith and the effort they put into their relationships and responsibilities.

POINTS TO BE EMPHASIZED
ADULT/YOUTH

Adult Topic: Real Success
Youth Topic: From the Prison to the Palace
Adult Key Verse: Genesis 41:38
Youth Key Verse: Genesis 41:40
Print Passage: Genesis 41:37-45, 50-52

—Slaves in ancient cultures could rise to high positions.
—Parents in Bible times often gave their children meaningful names.
—The injustices done to Joseph formed an important backdrop to his being selected as second-in-command in Egypt.
—Even pagan rulers were/are able to recognize the workings of God.
—The names of Joseph's two sons served as permanent reminders of God's blessings.
—Pharaoh had two dreams that greatly troubled him.
—Joseph interpreted Pharaoh's dreams as meaning that Egypt would enjoy seven years of abundance, followed by seven years of famine.
—Joseph advised Pharaoh to appoint commissioners to store up food during the times of plenty so they would be prepared for the years of famine.
—Pharaoh recognized the Spirit of God in Joseph's life and abilities.
—This is a story about one leader's recognizing another's God-given gifts of leadership.

CHILDREN

Children Topic: **Faithfulness Is Rewarded**

Key Verse: **Genesis 41:41**

Print Passage: **Genesis 41:37-45, 50-52**

—Pharaoh wanted a man of wisdom to oversee Egypt during the imminent famine.

—Pharaoh chose Joseph for the task because he possessed the Spirit of God.

—Pharaoh gave Joseph great authority and influence over the kingdom of Egypt.

—Pharaoh gave Joseph a wife.

—Joseph's wife bore him two children; he gave them names that reflected the deliverance of the Lord.

I. INTRODUCTION

A. Available for God's Use

There is a recurring theme in ancient Jewish literature where the fate of the Israelites was often placed in the hands of a young Jewish boy or girl. In the Hebrew Bible/Old Testament, the Israelites, God's chosen people, found themselves being targeted for mass murder—they were at the mercy of foreign oppressors who had conquered them and scattered them from the land that God promised for them, and were in danger of mass starvation. These calamities were averted when young Jewish boys and girls made themselves available for God's purpose. We see this in the case of Daniel, Esther, and particularly Joseph. All three of these towering figures of Hebrew history served as "salvation agents" because of their efforts to save their people. Daniel saved the Jews from the Babylonian kings during the period of the Exile; Esther saved her people from a plan to exterminate them when Haman, the prime minister of the Persian king Ahasuerus, vowed to destroy the Jews when Mordecai (Esther's cousin) refused to bow down to him; and Joseph prevented a famine when he interpreted the Egyptian king's dream that warned of the coming famine, then suggested a plan that would store up food ahead of time. Both Joseph and Daniel had the gift of dream interpretation and used that gift to help others. In cases, we learn quickly that the Jews had some prophet inclination that the Egyptian and Babylonian authorities did not. This suggests that this type of prophetic gift comes only from God.

B. Biblical Background

In Genesis 41, we see that Joseph had been thrown into prison for the alleged crime of seduction against the wife of Potiphar, but years later he was brought into the royal court to help the king interpret a dream that the king had. When Joseph interpreted the king's dreams, he was not only set free, but was also rewarded by the king for his assistance.

Much of Joseph's story is immediately to the hundreds of African-American families with sons and daughters in jail. Recent statistics reveal that 60 percent of all incarcerated people are racial and ethnic minorities. In the case of African-American males in their twenties, one out of every eight is presently incarcerated. If this trend continues into the next generation, one out of every three black males born today can expect to be incarcerated. Like Joseph, many of these will be incarcerated under false pretenses, and accused and convicted of crimes they did not commit. Unfortunately for Joseph, there was no prospect of DNA evidence to exonerate him in the ancient world. It was God's favor that saved him from his predicament.

II. EXPOSITION AND APPLICATION OF THE SCRIPTURE

A. How to Get Along with Your Boss
(Genesis 41:37-45)

And the thing was good in the eyes of Pharaoh, and in the eyes of all his servants. And Pharaoh said unto his servants, Can we find such a one as this is, a man in whom the Spirit of God is? And Pharaoh said unto Joseph, Forasmuch as God hath shewed thee all this, there is none so discreet and wise as thou art: Thou shalt be over my house, and according unto thy word shall all my people be ruled: only in the throne will I be greater than thou. And Pharaoh said unto Joseph, See, I have set thee over all the land of Egypt. And Pharaoh took off his ring from his hand, and put it upon Joseph's hand, and arrayed him in vestures of fine linen, and put a gold chain about his neck; And he made him to ride in the second chariot which he had; and they cried before him, Bow the knee: and he made him ruler over all the land of Egypt. And Pharaoh said unto Joseph, I am Pharaoh, and without thee shall no man lift up his hand or foot in all the land of Egypt. And Pharaoh called Joseph's name Zaphnath-paaneah; and he gave him to wife Asenath the daughter of Poti-pherah priest of On. And Joseph went out over all the land of Egypt.

I once heard a pastor joke that he could get so much more work done if only he did not have a congregation. Humor allows us the freedom to tell truths that we probably would not say otherwise, and his joke speaks to a real issue regarding pastors and their congregations: one of the biggest challenges one faces when discovering that God has a call on your life is realizing that the call is not a protective force that keeps all hardships at bay. One who is called of God may encounter friction from the very persons who voted him in. One who is called by God to lead others may experience resistance from those members who never miss a Bible study. God's servants often discover that they have families in their churches that get along like the Hatfields and the McCoys! The church may be the body of Christ, but it is far from perfect. The miracle of the church is that God is able to use the church toward His divine end in spite of its many flaws! Despite this knowledge, however, depression, bewilderment, and frustration still find their way into the lives of many of God's servants. This is why those who commit themselves to serving others must make the time to "fill their own gas tanks" every now and then.

Anyone who is used by God to do anything must learn how to get along with others, even in unpleasant circumstances. Ministry is a *communal* activity, and those in ministry must find ways to "get along" with their church members, even when they may feel that they have been wronged by the very congregation that they serve. Even though Joseph had been wronged by various people—brothers, Potiphar and his wife, and the forgetful cupbearer—in varying degrees, he did not allow his present circumstances to dictate either his attitude or his behavior. Throughout our lives, we will encounter flawed persons whom we will either have to lead or be led by. Some people live under very demeaning circumstances such as poverty, verbal, sexual, or physical abuse, have alcoholic parent or alcoholic spouse, or are experiencing varying degrees of drug abuse. In some capacity or another, all of us have either worked with or for someone who has dressed up these dysfunctions and brought them into the church, on the job, or in the very homes in which we live. Our task is to remember that even in ministry, we will encounter imperfection and not allow it to distract us from our task. Joseph did not take his opportunity in front of the king to blame him for everything that had gone wrong in his life. He did not take his time in front of the king to plead his case and beg for mercy. Instead, Joseph did what God empowered him to do—help the king by interpreting his dreams.

Although he might have been resentful, Joseph did not have a chip on his shoulder as a result of his past experiences. Joseph did not cop an attitude with his oppressors. If he were angry, Joseph kept it under control (temperance) to such a degree that it was undetectable by the Egyptian king. At this point, it would be easy to imagine that Joseph was bitter. Joseph would have been justified in being angry: his own brothers sold him into slavery, he was falsely accused of seduction, and he was thrown in jail for a crime that he did not commit. Joseph would have been within his rights to seethe, and stew, and plot revenge against everybody who wronged him. But he did not allow ill feelings to fester.

Joseph knew his purpose in the midst of his trials and tribulations. When gold is put through a furnace, all of its impurities are extracted. What we can learn from Joseph's experiences in Egypt is that everything that happens to us is an opportunity for God to remove the impurities from our lives. When we allow God to burn our grudges, harsh feelings, self-righteousness, and pride in the furnace of our trials and tribulations, they are replaced with perseverance, patience, and forgiveness— all traits embodied by Joseph. Joseph trusted God and believed that God would answer him—and He did.

When Pharaoh asked his servants (in verse 38) whether there was anyone else in the land like Joseph, it was a very significant moment. All of Joseph's trials and tests came to a head in this one question posed by the king, because Pharaoh's question demonstrated that Joseph did not suffer in vain. The Egyptian king's question shows that Joseph put his faith in the One who is worthy. Pharaoh's question actually testifies to the hand of God in Joseph's life because a non-Jew, someone outside of the covenant of Abraham, recognized and acknowledged the power of God at work in Joseph. Not only did Pharaoh ask if there was anyone else like him, but he also recognized a power higher than himself: the Spirit of God. The word *spirit* has multiple meanings in the Bible. In Hebrew, it is *ruach* and in Greek it is *pnuema*, both words meaning "wind" or "breath" and can be understood as life-giving elements—the Breath of Life. Once coupled with *Holy*, the word *Spirit* becomes a reference to the mysterious power of the Almighty either as it is demonstrated in creation, or present within certain individuals or communities. The Holy Spirit (or the Spirit of God) is understood as that entity which has the ability to inspire or empower a person with qualities that the person would not have otherwise. In the Hebrew Bible/Old Testament, Spirit wind is described as being present during Creation and the revealer of the mighty works of God (see Genesis 1:2). There are also several examples of the prophets who "as the Spirit gave them utterance" (Acts 2:4). And the Spirit was so evident in Joseph that even a foreign leader recognized its presence.

B. God's Blessings in the Midst of Adverse Circumstances (Genesis 41:50-52)

And unto Joseph were born two sons before the years of famine came, which Asenath the daughter of Poti-pherah priest of On bare unto him. And Joseph called the name of the firstborn Manasseh: For God, said he, hath made me forget all my toil, and all my father's house. And the name of the second called he Ephraim: For God hath caused me to be fruitful in the land of my affliction.

God had a plan for Joseph to escape his circumstances. Although Joseph was left for dead by his brothers and then put into jail by an accusation of seduction by the wife of Potiphar, the Egyptian king had need of him, even when everyone else had all but forgotten about him. Joseph appeared before the king, and was able to do what even his closest aides could not: interpret his troubling dreams. Notice that Joseph did not take the credit for his gift but, rather, directed praise to God. Joseph was the classic biblical example of the "underdog," the Rocky Balboa type of character who manages to succeed against the odds.

We see that Joseph matured in Egypt. Joseph clearly did not exercise good judgment by sharing his own dreams with his brothers. Joseph informed them often that not only would they bow to him, but the sun and the moon would, too (see Genesis 37:9-11). Some thirteen years behind bars had matured Joseph to a degree that he began to think before he spoke. Joseph learned to demonstrate modesty and self-control along with some humility. We

see that Joseph had not previously been able to control himself. The one who taunted his brothers to such a degree that they sought to murder him had now proven himself worthy to handle power and administrative authority.

In these verses (verses 50-52), we see the culmination of Joseph's experiences as God blessed him to have offspring: two sons were born to him prior to the coming of the famine. The names given to them reveal how Joseph recognized the hand of God in his life. Joseph named his first son Manesseh, which meant "making to forget." Joseph saw the power of God evident in his life, enabling him to stop dwelling on the hurtful things that had transpired in his life. The second son he named Ephraim, which meant "to be fruitful." Joseph realized that God enables a person to forget his or her trials and to be fruitful as a result of those trials.

III. CONCLUDING REFLECTION

One of the most difficult things for a Christian to do is reshape his or her definition of success. Success by the world's definition can be markedly different from what makes one successful as a Christian. Being virtuous is not necessarily a trait the world admires—and in Joseph's case, the payoff for being virtuous did not pay off right away; in fact, it landed him in jail! But Christians are expected to display virtue. Faith is the cornerstone of God's celestial home. Christians ought to display great faith—yet, like Joseph, we can find ourselves in predicaments where our faith is tested to such a degree that we may even feel that it is not worth it. It is easy to imagine that being in jail on trumped-up charges would cause anyone to have serious doubts. But Joseph remained steadfast. Being thrown in jail did not cause Joseph to doubt the greatness that God promised him. Joseph learned that the road to the palace had some pits, twists, and turns. But he continued operating in his God-given gift to interpret dreams.

Joseph was aware that God had given him the gift of interpreting dreams, and he worked diligently at being the best that he could be at it. God's gifts are given to us not for ourselves, but for the benefit of others. Joseph used his gifts to help his boss—the Egyptian king—and was given his freedom and what we today would consider a good job with benefits. Would this have happened if Joseph had not honed his craft?

The successful Christian's life should show signs of virtue, temperance, and great faith. However, in order for a Christian to be successful, he or she must have a sense of what he or she was purposed by God to do. There is an old saying that goes, "He who aims at nothing will surely hit it." There are far too many among us with aimless souls, living aimless existences. Joseph, the dreamer, showed us that it is our dreams that keep us going in spite of our circumstances. We should hold on to our dreams even when it may appear that they will not be fulfilled. There are many things that we can learn from Joseph's example, and one of the most important is how to be diligent about our faith. Faith is not something one picks up from the store when he or she needs it; it is something we already have—all we have to do is use it. Joseph displayed great faith that God would look with favor upon him. It took time for all of this to happen—but it did happen.

PRAYER

Almighty God, help us to remember that simply being Your children is not a shield that protects us from hard times. Remind us often that trouble truly does not last always, and help us to remain steadfast and unmovable when we face the obstacles of life, so that we may accomplish Your will and purpose to the best of our abilities. In Jesus' name we pray. Amen.

WORD POWER

Spirit of God—In the context of this lesson, the primary meaning of this name would refer to wisdom and insight, which are characteristics of the Spirit of God.

HOME DAILY BIBLE READINGS
(January 2-8, 2012)

Joseph Finds Favor

MONDAY, January 2: "Interpretations Belong to God" (Genesis 40:1-8)

TUESDAY, January 3: "Restored to Office" (Genesis 40:9-15)

WEDNESDAY, January 4: "The Predictions Come True" (Genesis 40:16-23)

THURSDAY, January 5: "The Interpreter Remembered" (Genesis 41:1-13)

FRIDAY, January 6: "Pharaoh's Dreams" (Genesis 41:14-24)

SATURDAY, January 7: "The Dreams Interpreted" (Genesis 41:25-36)

SUNDAY, January 8: "A Discerning and Wise Leader" (Genesis 41:37-45, 50-52)

LESSON 7   **January 15, 2012**

GOD PRESERVES A REMNANT

DEVOTIONAL READING: **Psalm 81:1-10**   BACKGROUND SCRIPTURE: **Genesis 42:1-38; 45:1-28**
PRINT PASSAGE: **Genesis 45:3-15**   KEY VERSE: **Genesis 45:8**

Genesis 45:3-15—KJV

3 And Joseph said unto his brethren, I am Joseph; doth my father yet live? And his brethren could not answer him; for they were troubled at his presence.
4 And Joseph said unto his brethren, Come near to me, I pray you. And they came near. And he said, I am Joseph your brother, whom ye sold into Egypt.
5 Now therefore be not grieved, nor angry with yourselves, that ye sold me hither: for God did send me before you to preserve life.
6 For these two years hath the famine been in the land: and yet there are five years, in the which there shall neither be earing nor harvest.
7 And God sent me before you to preserve you a posterity in the earth, and to save your lives by a great deliverance.
8 So now it was not you that sent me hither, but God: and he hath made me a father to Pharaoh, and lord of all his house, and a ruler throughout all the land of Egypt.
9 Haste ye, and go up to my father, and say unto him, Thus saith thy son Joseph, God hath made me lord of all Egypt: come down unto me, tarry not:
10 And thou shalt dwell in the land of Goshen, and thou shalt be near unto me, thou, and thy children, and thy children's children, and thy flocks, and thy herds, and all that thou hast:
11 And there will I nourish thee; for yet there are five years of famine; lest thou, and thy household, and all that thou hast, come to poverty.
12 And, behold, your eyes see, and the eyes of my brother Benjamin, that it is my mouth that speaketh unto you.
13 And ye shall tell my father of all my glory in Egypt, and of all that ye have seen; and ye shall haste and bring down my father hither.

Genesis 45:3-15—NIV

3 Joseph said to his brothers, "I am Joseph! Is my father still living?" But his brothers were not able to answer him, because they were terrified at his presence.
4 Then Joseph said to his brothers, "Come close to me." When they had done so, he said, "I am your brother Joseph, the one you sold into Egypt!
5 And now, do not be distressed and do not be angry with yourselves for selling me here, because it was to save lives that God sent me ahead of you.
6 For two years now there has been famine in the land, and for the next five years there will not be plowing and reaping.
7 But God sent me ahead of you to preserve for you a remnant on earth and to save your lives by a great deliverance.
8 So then, it was not you who sent me here, but God. He made me father to Pharaoh, lord of his entire household and ruler of all Egypt.
9 Now hurry back to my father and say to him, 'This is what your son Joseph says: God has made me lord of all Egypt. Come down to me; don't delay.
10 You shall live in the region of Goshen and be near me—you, your children and grandchildren, your flocks and herds, and all you have.
11 I will provide for you there, because five years of famine are still to come. Otherwise you and your household and all who belong to you will become destitute.'
12 You can see for yourselves, and so can my brother Benjamin, that it is really I who am speaking to you.
13 Tell my father about all the honor accorded me in Egypt and about everything you have seen. And bring my father down here quickly."

When people are mutually faithful to each other, they support and protect each other. What can faithful people expect from other faithful people? Because Jacob and Joseph were both faithful to God, God remained faithful to His promise to Abraham by putting Joseph in a position to save the entire family from death by starvation.

14 And he fell upon his brother Benjamin's neck, and wept; and Benjamin wept upon his neck.	14 Then he threw his arms around his brother Benjamin and wept, and Benjamin embraced him, weeping.
15 Moreover he kissed all his brethren, and wept upon them: and after that his brethren talked with him.	15 And he kissed all his brothers and wept over them. Afterward his brothers talked with him.

TOPICAL OUTLINE OF THE LESSON

I. **Introduction**
   A. Divine Design
   B. Biblical Background

II. **Exposition and Application of the Scripture**
   A. Sibling Rivalry: Actions Have Unintended Consequences (Genesis 45:3-4)
   B. Resisting Revenge and Seeking Reconciliation (Genesis 45:5-15)

III. **Concluding Reflection**

LESSON OBJECTIVES

Upon the completion of this lesson, the students will understand that:

1. God can heal broken relationships;
2. It may take many years for God's plan to unfold; and,
3. A proper attitude is crucial for handling life situations that are beyond our control.

POINTS TO BE EMPHASIZED

ADULT/YOUTH

Adult Topic: **Sharing Blessings**

Youth Topic: **Preserving the Family Line**

Adult Key Verse: **Genesis 45:8**

Youth Key Verse: **Genesis 45:7**

Print Passage: **Genesis 45:3-15**

—God brought good out of an intended evil.

—Joseph correctly perceived the bigger picture and believed that God sent him to Egypt to save his family.

—Joseph was not vindictive.

—A foreign slave in an ancient culture could serve in an important position.

—God used negative circumstances (famine, slavery) to accomplish a larger purpose.

—Reconciliation resulted in weeping.

—This is a story about Joseph's faith in God that enabled him to forgive his brothers and provide for the needs of his family.

—After Joseph's brothers had been with him in Egypt for a while, Joseph finally revealed himself to them.

—Joseph's brothers were afraid that he would try to take revenge against them.

—Joseph wanted his brothers to know that it was God's plan that he be sent before them to preserve life.

—Joseph welcomed his brothers and told them to bring the entire family to Egypt so that he could care for them during the seven-year drought.

—Faithfulness to God was part of Joseph's family heritage, starting with Abraham.

CHILDREN

Children Topic: A Surprise Reunion

Key Verse: Genesis 45:7

Print Passage: Genesis 45:1-9

—Joseph was unable to continue hiding his identity from his brothers.

—When Joseph revealed his identity to his brothers, they became fearful.

—Joseph refrained from vengeful actions, choosing to forgive his brothers.

—Joseph recognized in his own life God's plan to preserve his family's life and heritage.

—Joseph asked that his father be brought to Egypt.

I. INTRODUCTION
A. Divine Design

It is hard not to notice the similarities between the experiences of Joseph in Egypt with those of Jesus the Christ. Jesus spent time in Egypt when He was a child. Joseph and Mary fled with the baby Jesus to Egypt to escape King Herod's wrath (see Matthew 2:13-15). Jesus was estimated to be around thirty years old at the beginning of His ministry (see Luke 3:23), and Joseph was thirty years old when he began his leadership role in Egypt (see Genesis 41:46). Joseph had been betrayed by a brother and Jesus by a friend. They were both sold out for pieces of silver (see Genesis 37:28; Matthew 26:15). Jesus and Joseph were both tempted to sin, but remained blameless; they both experienced rejection, and neither of them made any defense for themselves against the charges levied against them; they both were handed over to Gentiles (anyone who was not Jewish was considered a Gentile), and both Jesus and Joseph endured unjust punishment.

Joseph and Jesus were both associated with two criminals—one who received pardon for his crimes, and the other who did not. In Joseph's case, he was imprisoned with two officers of Pharaoh, his chief baker and his chief cupbearer. The cupbearer was spared and was restored to his rightful position, but the chief baker was hanged (see Genesis 40:16-23). In Jesus' case, He was condemned and sentenced to death with two thieves who were crucified with Him. One of them received grace and pardon while on the cross (see Luke 23:32-43). And finally, both Jesus and Joseph shared the experience of having persons who were not under the covenant of Abraham, recognizing the power of God's working in them. In Joseph's case, it was the recognition of the Egyptian Pharaoh who proclaimed, "Can we find anyone else like this—one in whom is the spirit of God?" (Genesis 41:38, NRSV). In Jesus' case, it was the Roman centurion who exclaimed at the moment of Jesus' death, "Truly this man was God's Son!" (see Matthew 27:54).

B. Biblical Background

Famine in the ancient world was a harsh, brutal reality. Typically, a famine referred not only to a period when there was a massive shortage of food that impacted large numbers of persons, but famine could also represent hunger in the Hebrew language (*ra-ab*). At the time of Joseph, the people lived in an agrarian economy, which meant that people thrived not by "buying low and selling high," but rather lived or died by what they could grow. An inadequate rainfall had the potential to cut off the production of grain. Grain crops were such a staple in an agrarian economy that just one bad crop could lead to mass starvation.

There are several references to famine in the Bible. Famine is mentioned in Genesis 12 and Genesis 26 during the time of Abraham and Isaac; in the books of 1 and 2 Kings during the time of Elisha; and in the book of Deuteronomy, there is an instance of a famine so severe that people resorted to cannibalism (see Deuteronomy 28:47-57). Famine was also believed to be a curse that God sent when the people were disobedient as a sign of God's wrath and displeasure (see Deuteronomy 28:48). Famines were greatly feared in the ancient world because any imbalance in the process of food production could easily bring about disaster. In the ancient world, famines would cause geographical shifts as people moved where the food supplies were plentiful.

II. EXPOSITION AND APPLICATION OF THE SCRIPTURE

A. Sibling Rivalry: Actions Have Unintended Consequences (Genesis 45:3-4)

And Joseph said unto his brethren, I am Joseph; doth my father yet live? And his brethren could not answer him; for they were troubled at his presence. And Joseph said unto his brethren, Come near to me, I pray you. And they came near. And he said, I am Joseph your brother, whom ye sold into Egypt.

Although the term *brothers* speaks primarily to blood relations, African-American culture uses the term to speak of close male associates. The word *brother* can also reflect religious affiliations, an expression that indicates a spiritual or fraternal relationship such as monks in a monastery or brothers in a fraternity or lodge.

Joseph and his brothers are the group of brothers whose names reflect the twelve-tribe alliance that made up ancient Israel. How ironic it is that the nation of God's chosen people is named for twelve brothers who were fractured by an act of jealousy so extreme that one of these brothers ended up sold into slavery in a foreign land. Like many of us, Joseph's family had its fair share of strife. Joseph's own brothers sold him into slavery, but an important element of the story that should not be overlooked is the fact that Joseph's brothers also allowed their father to believe his son was dead, having been torn to bits by some wild animal (see Genesis 37:31-36). In order to make their lie even more convincing, the brothers of Joseph slaughtered a goat, dipped Joseph's garment in the blood, and presented the stained garment to their father. Talk about strife!

This type of familial discord is a theme prevalent throughout the Bible. There are countless stories of brothers at odds with each other: Cain and Abel, David and his brothers who resented his being present on the battlefield against Goliath and the Philistine army, and the twin brothers (one of whom was Joseph's own father), Jacob and Esau. Although they were twins, it was Esau who was born first and therefore had certain privileges as the firstborn. An example of this privilege dealt with inheritance rights: the firstborn son would receive a double portion of his father's estate (see Deuteronomy 21:15-17), while the remaining children would split one-third. Knowing this, Jacob manipulated his older brother out of his birthright with a bowl of stew. Esau came in from the fields and was so hungry that he was willing to sell his birthright to Jacob for something to eat (see Genesis 25:29-34). It would appear that discord was handed down in Joseph's family from one generation to the next.

The famine that Joseph saw in his dream and told to Pharaoh was the trigger that brought his brothers back into his life. This famine was so severe that it lasted seven years; as a result, Jacob sent his sons to Egypt to look for food because the famine that Joseph foresaw in his dream had reached all the way to Canaan. While in Egypt, they crossed paths with the brother whom they had left for dead. They did not recognize Joseph immediately, but he recognized them. Have you ever had a chance encounter with someone who did you tremendous harm? Have you ever been in a position to retaliate against the person for what he or she did? This was the dilemma Joseph was in. Joseph did not reveal himself to his brothers immediately, but when he did, it must have been a moment of sheer horror for them. They realized quickly that the one whom they had left for dead in the pit held the power of life and death in his hands. The brothers must have feared reprisal by Joseph,

who was now in a position to take whatever revenge he wanted to on his brothers.

B. Resisting Revenge and Seeking Reconciliation (Genesis 45:5-15)

Now therefore be not grieved, nor angry with yourselves, that ye sold me hither: for God did send me before you to preserve life. For these two years hath the famine been in the land: and yet there are five years, in the which there shall neither be earing nor harvest. And God sent me before you to preserve you a posterity in the earth, and to save your lives by a great deliverance. So now it was not you that sent me hither, but God: and he hath made me a father to Pharaoh, and lord of all his house, and a ruler throughout all the land of Egypt. Haste ye, and go up to my father, and say unto him, Thus saith thy son Joseph, God hath made me lord of all Egypt: come down unto me, tarry not: And thou shalt dwell in the land of Goshen, and thou shalt be near unto me, thou, and thy children, and thy children's children, and thy flocks, and thy herds, and all that thou hast: And there will I nourish thee; for yet there are five years of famine; lest thou, and thy household, and all that thou hast, come to poverty. And, behold, your eyes see, and the eyes of my brother Benjamin, that it is my mouth that speaketh unto you. And ye shall tell my father of all my glory in Egypt, and of all that ye have seen; and ye shall haste and bring down my father hither. And he fell upon his brother Benjamin's neck, and wept; and Benjamin wept upon his neck. Moreover he kissed all his brethren, and wept upon them: and after that his brethren talked with him.

Revenge becomes more complicated when it is examined in the Bible because there are some mixed messages: it would seem that God endorsed revenge in Genesis 9:5-6, but Jesus taught that we are not to take revenge on those who do us harm (see Matthew 5:38-42). What is the believer to make of this contradiction?

The Genesis account speaks of "blood vengeance," which refers to the execution of a murderer: "For your own lifeblood I will surely require a reckoning for human life. Whoever sheds the blood of a human, by a human shall that person's blood be shed." However, the references to revenge in the New Testament (see Romans 12:17-19; 1 Thessalonians 4:6; Revelation 19:2) speak of God as the One who will send vengeance upon those who cause the faithful to suffer. Joseph opted for another choice in his dealings with his brothers after they were reconciled in Egypt: forgiveness.

One of the aspects of Joseph's personality that paralleled that of Jesus' was his ability to resist the very human desire to exact revenge on those who have caused hurt. Certain medical studies confirm that even having thoughts of revenge and carrying around resentment can have a detrimental effect on the body. It would follow, then, that not practicing forgiveness can lead to stress in the body, and can even trigger certain health problems.

Reconciling with another person is a difficult task, and it is seldom an easy one. The reason for this is the degree of difficulty required to reconcile with someone who has offended you: you must acknowledge that you were hurt and why, you must forgive the offender, and you must negotiate a new relationship with that person where you once were isolated and far removed from that person. Now you must replace your bad feelings toward that person with feelings of peace and restored fellowship. This is not an easy task, indeed; in fact, Joseph seemed to struggle when facing his brothers—at first. He spoke to them through an interpreter, and then set up several tests to see if they would recognize him. Joseph sent them to jail for three days and demanded that they bring back his brother Benjamin, the only other child Jacob had with Joseph's mother, Rachel. Joseph put his brothers through the paces, perhaps because he needed time to deal with his feelings after seeing them again, or maybe he needed to determine their remorse and repentance over what they had done to him.

Perhaps the enormity of this task is what caused Joseph to break down and cry. There is a lot to be said for the cleansing power of tears. Joseph had himself a good cry; in fact, he wailed so loudly that he could be heard from a distance! (See Genesis 45:2.) One can speculate that Joseph released any and all lingering bad feelings toward his brothers in that cry. Broken relationships are difficult to mend, and we see that in Genesis 42:6-9 when Joseph immediately recognized his brothers and spoke harshly to them, even treating them like strangers. Joseph accused them of lying to him and coming to Egypt to spy out the land. The last time Joseph laid his eyes on his brothers, they were looking down on him in the pit that they had cast him into. Many would argue that Joseph would have been justified if he had become bitter and determined that he would blame them for the rest of their lives; but Joseph decided that was a weight that was just too heavy for him to carry. Joseph chose to reconcile with his brothers and extend grace and forgiveness to them. Joseph resisted the temptation to let his brothers sweat, and told them that he held no resentment and would take no revenge on them for what they had done to him. Joseph realized that there was divine purpose in what he had gone through: being sold into slavery, falsely accused by Potiphar's wife, and imprisoned. Joseph recognized that although his brothers meant him harm, God used their bad acts to bring about good.

III. CONCLUDING REFLECTION

Those who are used by God for divine purposes must learn to relinquish control and learn to both live with and manage high levels of uncertainty. Allowing God to use your life means that you may be asked to quit your job and go back to school, or put your search for a spouse on hold while you work with the poor, or learn to live beneath your means so that you can give as God asks of you. One of the hardest things for many of us to do is accept the fact that some things are simply beyond our control. The only constant in life is change. One of the many meaningful lessons we can learn from Joseph is that what starts off as a negative does not always end up as one. Joseph received a small hint of his purpose when he dreamed that his brothers would bow down to him; however, his dream did not come with a guide book, a road map, or an instruction manual as to exactly how that would come to pass.

Joseph believed that God had sent him to Egypt to preserve a remnant. The biblical understanding of a *remnant* is "the portion that is left over after a piece of that portion has been removed." The remnant may have referred to plant life, animal life, or human life, particularly when used in speaking about persons who escaped exile. A theological understanding of the word *remnant* would refer to those who have been or will be redeemed by God. The remnant signifies relationship with God. This is pregnant with potential meanings.

Joseph did not focus on the stress of his situation; he remained fixated on the One who could do something about his situation. The way Joseph handled himself gives new meaning to the question, "What are *you* looking at?"

PRAYER

Dear God, please show us any areas of strife in our lives and release us from its bondage. Reveal to us every secret place in us where we are holding grudges and resentment toward another person and lead us on the path of reconciliation. Remind us to take good care of our physical selves, our emotional selves, and our spiritual selves so that we might serve You better. In Jesus' name we pray. Amen.

WORD POWER

Posterity—the offspring of one progenitor to the furthest generation.
Revenge—to avenge by retaliating in kind or degree.

HOME DAILY BIBLE READINGS
(January 9-15, 2012)

God Preserves a Remnant

MONDAY, January 9: "A Famine in Canaan" (Genesis 42:1-5)
TUESDAY, January 10: "Joseph Recognized His Brothers" (Genesis 42:6-17)
WEDNESDAY, January 11: "Paying the Penalty" (Genesis 42:18-25)
THURSDAY, January 12: "Hold Me Accountable" (Genesis 43:1-14)
FRIDAY, January 13: "Benjamin Detained in Egypt" (Genesis 44:1-13)
SATURDAY, January 14: "A Father's Suffering" (Genesis 44:24-34)
SUNDAY, January 15: "A Brother Revealed" (Genesis 45:3-15)

JOSEPH TRANSMITS ABRAHAM'S PROMISE

DEVOTIONAL READING: **Deuteronomy 7:6-11**
PRINT PASSAGE: **Genesis 50:15-26**

BACKGROUND SCRIPTURE: **Genesis 50:1-26**
KEY VERSE: **Genesis 50:20**

Genesis 50:15-26—KJV

15 And when Joseph's brethren saw that their father was dead, they said, Joseph will peradventure hate us, and will certainly requite us all the evil which we did unto him.

16 And they sent a messenger unto Joseph, saying, Thy father did command before he died, saying,

17 So shall ye say unto Joseph, Forgive, I pray thee now, the trespass of thy brethren, and their sin; for they did unto thee evil: and now, we pray thee, forgive the trespass of the servants of the God of thy father. And Joseph wept when they spake unto him.

18 And his brethren also went and fell down before his face; and they said, Behold, we be thy servants.

19 And Joseph said unto them, Fear not: for am I in the place of God?

20 But as for you, ye thought evil against me; but God meant it unto good, to bring to pass, as it is this day, to save much people alive.

21 Now therefore fear ye not: I will nourish you, and your little ones. And he comforted them, and spake kindly unto them.

22 And Joseph dwelt in Egypt, he, and his father's house: and Joseph lived an hundred and ten years.

23 And Joseph saw Ephraim's children of the third generation: the children also of Machir the son Manasseh were brought up upon Joseph's knees.

24 And Joseph said unto his brethren, I die: and God will surely visit you, and bring you out of this land unto the land which he sware to Abraham, to Isaac, and to Jacob.

Genesis 50:15-26—NIV

15 When Joseph's brothers saw that their father was dead, they said, "What if Joseph holds a grudge against us and pays us back for all the wrongs we did to him?"

16 So they sent word to Joseph, saying, "Your father left these instructions before he died:

17 'This is what you are to say to Joseph: I ask you to forgive your brothers the sins and the wrongs they committed in treating you so badly.' Now please forgive the sins of the servants of the God of your father." When their message came to him, Joseph wept.

18 His brothers then came and threw themselves down before him. "We are your slaves," they said.

19 But Joseph said to them, "Don't be afraid. Am I in the place of God?

20 You intended to harm me, but God intended it for good to accomplish what is now being done, the saving of many lives.

21 So then, don't be afraid. I will provide for you and your children." And he reassured them and spoke kindly to them.

22 Joseph stayed in Egypt, along with all his father's family. He lived a hundred and ten years

23 and saw the third generation of Ephraim's children. Also the children of Makir son of Manasseh were placed at birth on Joseph's knees.

24 Then Joseph said to his brothers, "I am about to die. But God will surely come to your aid and take you up out of this land to the land he promised on oath to Abraham, Isaac and Jacob."

UNIFYING LESSON PRINCIPLE

Even though some people commit acts of faithlessness, they may be overcome by acts of others' faithfulness. Who can forgive acts of faithlessness? Because Jacob and Joseph were both faithful to God, Joseph was able to forgive his brothers' treachery enacted many years before.

25 And Joseph took an oath of the children of Israel, saying, God will surely visit you, and ye shall carry up my bones from hence.

26 So Joseph died, being an hundred and ten years old: and they embalmed him, and he was put in a coffin in Egypt.

25 And Joseph made the sons of Israel swear an oath and said, "God will surely come to your aid, and then you must carry my bones up from this place."

26 So Joseph died at the age of a hundred and ten. And after they embalmed him, he was placed in a coffin in Egypt.

TOPICAL OUTLINE OF THE LESSON

I. Introduction
  A. Transition
  B. Biblical Background

II. Exposition and Application of the Scripture
  A. Death Causes a Reevaluation of Life
      (Genesis 50:15-18)
  B. The Scope of Forgiveness
      (Genesis 50:19-26)

III. Concluding Reflection

LESSON OBJECTIVES

Upon the completion of this lesson, the students will understand that:

1. Forgiveness is more for the offended than it is for the offender;

2. People often lie in order to avoid facing the consequences of their actions; and,

3. It is important to see the bigger picture when facing trials and tribulations.

POINTS TO BE EMPHASIZED

ADULT/YOUTH

Adult Topic: **The Power of Forgiveness**

Youth Topic: **I'm Not a Hater!**

Adult/Youth Key Verse: **Genesis 50:20**

Print Passage: **Genesis 50:15-26**

—A father's instructions were considered mandatory in a patriarchal society.

—Reminders of God's promises were important to fledgling Israel.

—God may take hundreds of years to bring a plan to fruition.

—The request for forgiveness indicates that the previous forgiveness was not considered final.

—Joseph could see a bigger picture when his brothers could not.

—Joseph remembered God's promises even on his deathbed at age 110.

—After Jacob died, Joseph's brothers were afraid that Joseph would take revenge against them.

—Joseph's brothers implored Joseph to forgive their past treatment of him.

—Joseph wept because his brothers still thought that he was angry with them.

—Joseph, through a kind voice and words, assured his brothers of his acceptance of them.

—By faith, Joseph spoke of the exodus of the Israelites on his deathbed and gave instructions about his burial (see Hebrews 11:22).

—Joseph forgave his brothers, not because of a paternal mandate, but rather because of his own faith relationship with God.

CHILDREN

Children Topic: Victory from Hardship
Key Verse: Genesis 50:20

Print Passage: Genesis 50:15-26

—When Jacob died, Joseph's brothers assumed that he would exact revenge against them.

—When the brothers visited Joseph, he extended mercy and comfort.

—Before Joseph died at the age of 110 years, he prophesied to his brothers and asked that his bones be carried to the Promised Land one day.

—Joseph promised to provide for his brothers and their families.

I. INTRODUCTION

A. Transition

The book of Genesis is practically a Bible in and of itself. It is revered because the book of Genesis not only provides the stories of the Creation, the Garden of Eden, the Fall of humanity, and the Flood, but it also provides the stories of the patriarchs: Abraham, Isaac, and Jacob. The most common definition of a patriarch is the male leader of a family or clan, but the Old Testament/Hebrew Bible understanding is a specific reference to Abraham (see Genesis 12–24), Isaac (see Genesis 17–26), and Jacob (see Genesis 36–50), who are considered by many to be the forerunners in biblical faith.

Abraham is held in high regard because he was esteemed as one through whom God provided revelation. The death of Jacob helps us to develop a fuller appreciation for the significance of God's promise to Abraham. God's promise to Abraham is affirmed in His promises to the Israelites. That promise looked forward to the continuation of God's plan of redemption in the person of Jesus the Christ, who, like Joseph, traced His lineage back to the patriarchs.

B. Biblical Background

Our reconciling with a loved one has the ability to heal us. There is healing power in human connectedness, and human beings were created to be social beings. Joseph's ability to reconnect with his father had healing power not only for the two of them, but also for the entire family.

In the last chapters of the book of Genesis, we see that Joseph was fortunate in that he had the opportunity to be reconciled with his father before he died, and Jacob was able to lay his eyes once again upon the son he believed had been dead for nearly twenty years. There is no other figure in the Hebrew Bible/Old Testament whose death received as much honor and detailed attention as did Jacob's; he was the last link to the patriarchs.

Embalming was not a part of the typical Hebrew burial ritual, but because Jacob died while he was in Egypt, he was buried according to their practices and mummified (see Genesis 50:2-3, 26). Jacob was mourned for more than two months upon his death. Joseph was also embalmed in Egypt, but wanted to be buried in the land of his ancestors so his coffin remained above ground for almost four hundred years, and he was buried in the Promised Land after Moses led the Israelites out of Egypt in the Exodus.

II. EXPOSITION AND APPLICATION OF THE SCRIPTURE

A. Death Causes a Reevaluation of Life (Genesis 50:15-18)

And when Joseph's brethren saw that their father was dead, they said, Joseph will peradventure hate us, and will certainly requite us all the evil which we did unto him. And they sent a messenger unto Joseph, saying, Thy father did command before he died, saying, So shall ye say unto Joseph, Forgive, I pray thee now, the trespass of thy brethren, and their sin; for they did unto thee evil: and now, we pray thee, forgive the trespass of the servants of the God of thy father. And Joseph wept when they spake unto him. And his brethren also went and fell down before his face; and they said, Behold, we be thy servants.

In the last chapter of the book of Genesis, Jacob's death caused his sons to reevaluate their treatment of Joseph. They believed that since their father had died, there would be nothing to stop Joseph from taking revenge on them if he so desired. "What if Joseph still bears a grudge against us and pays us back in full for all the wrong that we did to him?" (verse 15, NRSV). When reading accounts about the history of slavery in America, the one thing that slave owners feared the most was slave uprisings. One theory is that those who held slaves feared what the slaves would do to them if they ever gained the upper hand. Joseph's brothers were experiencing this type of fear that was driven out of guilt: they knew that they had done Joseph harm. They were so anxious about what Joseph might do that they sent word to him, saying, "Your father left these instructions before he died:...I ask you to forgive your brothers the sins and the wrongs they committed in treating you so badly" (verses 16, 17, NIV). This is an interesting twist in the story, for there was no evidence in the biblical text that Jacob ever made this request. It would appear to be yet another fabrication told by Joseph's brothers, this time as a means of shielding them from Joseph's wrath.

In one of the most moving scenes in Scripture, Joseph broke into tears. The reason for these tears is not as clear as the previous one. In Genesis 45, Joseph cried at the prospect of reconciling with his brothers. In Genesis 50, it is left up to us to determine whether Joseph wept because he knew his brothers were lying, or because he was hurt that they did not fully trust him. Perhaps the brothers did not feel that they had a right to approach Joseph directly to ask him to deal mercifully with them because their sin against him was so great.

B. The Scope of Forgiveness (Genesis 50:19-26)

And Joseph said unto them, Fear not: for am I in the place of God? But as for you, ye thought evil against me; but God meant it unto good, to bring to pass, as it is this day, to save much people alive. Now therefore fear ye not: I will nourish you, and your little ones. And he comforted

them, and spake kindly unto them. And Joseph dwelt in Egypt, he, and his father's house: and Joseph lived an hundred and ten years. And Joseph saw Ephraim's children of the third generation: the children also of Machir the son Manasseh were brought up upon Joseph's knees. And Joseph said unto his brethren, I die: and God will surely visit you, and bring you out of this land unto the land which he sware to Abraham, to Isaac, and to Jacob. And Joseph took an oath of the children of Israel, saying, God will surely visit you, and ye shall carry up my bones from hence. So Joseph died, being an hundred and ten years old: and they embalmed him, and he was put in a coffin in Egypt.

Forgiveness is a complicated process. Some people outright refuse to forgive, simply because they have developed a certain level of comfort with their anger. Some people refuse to forgive because they feel that forgiving the people who wronged them is somehow giving the offender a pass and it feels too much like justifying the wrong that was done to them. Medical experts suggest that being unwilling to forgive someone who harmed you is like having extra weight applied to your mid-section—tugging at your heart and lungs all day, weighing you down as you climb stairs, making your sleep uncomfortable, and draining you of your energy. In a recent article on the impact of forgiveness on cardiovascular activity, it was found that forgiveness was linked to lowered blood pressure as well as lower rates of anxiety, depression, and stress levels, and even lowered cholesterol levels.

Joseph assured his brothers that he would take no revenge. Instead, he spoke kind words to them and promised to provide not only for them but for their children as well. Joseph provided a powerful example of humility when he gently rebuked his brothers with the question, "Am I in the place of God?" (verse 19). Even though Joseph was in a position of great power and privilege, he knew it was not his job to take revenge on his brothers. Even though Joseph would have been well within his rights to exercise his own brand of vigilante justice—and there was no one who could have stopped him—he recognized that it was not he who should determine his brothers' fate; that was God's option alone.

Joseph did not sugarcoat the wrong that his brothers did to him; he told them quite clearly, "You meant evil against me," but the good news in Joseph's declaration was that God is able to turn any evil act into good. Here, Joseph demonstrated a rule for living that every believer should strive for: to remain focused on the hand of God in our lives—the hand that has the sovereign ability to use any of our negative experiences for good.

The heart of Joseph's story is that we, through this story, learn that God both forgives and heals human guilt and shame. More importantly, Joseph's story reveals the protective care of God—in that God always has the power and the ability to overrule any evil purpose and turn it into a good end. Forgiveness is a means of working with divinity to reach that end.

III. CONCLUDING REFLECTION

The deaths of Jacob and Joseph in the last chapter of the book of Genesis provide us with an opportunity to reflect upon remembering God's promises. In Genesis 28:14-15 (NKJV), God promised Jacob that his seed would be "as the dust of the earth; you shall spread abroad to the west and the east, to the north and the south; and in you and in your seed all the families of the earth shall be blessed." We certainly see that come full circle in these past few lessons about Joseph. God showed Joseph (in a dream)—when he was very young—that he would have a status so lofty that people, including his own brothers, would bow to him.

Joseph's experiences teach us how crucial faith is to the life of the Christian. Reading chapter 11 of the book of Hebrews should not only remind us of the biblical figures who died in faith, but also should garner special meaning of the African-American figures who died—most of them brutally executed—before experiencing the type of freedom that we have today.

One way to watch the movement of God in our lives is to begin to journal about our experiences with God. We should keep a personal log of our prayers and petitions and note when they come to pass. Not only will this exercise help us develop discipline in the area of patience, where so many of us struggle, but also it will strengthen our faith. It will remind us that the God of Joseph is a very present help in times of our own temptations, trials, and tests.

PRAYER

Creator God, thank You for Your majestic power and willingness to use it to intervene in our lives. Help us to remember Your promises whenever we are tempted to give up. In Jesus' name we pray. Amen.

WORD POWER

Adversity—a state, condition, or instance of serious or continued difficulty or adverse fortune.
Patriarch—the male leader of a family or clan.

HOME DAILY BIBLE READINGS
(January 16-22, 2012)

Joseph Transmits Abraham's Promise

MONDAY, January 16: "A Divine Confirmation" (Genesis 46:1-7)

TUESDAY, January 17: "Settled in a New Land" (Genesis 46:28–47:6)

WEDNESDAY, January 18: "A Father's Heritage" (Genesis 48:8-16)

THURSDAY, January 19: "A Father's Blessing" (Genesis 49:22-26)

FRIDAY, January 20: "A Father's Final Wish" (Genesis 49:29–50:6)

SATURDAY, January 21: "A Child's Final Duty" (Genesis 50:7-14)

SUNDAY, January 22: "Reconciliation in the Family" (Genesis 50:15-26)

OUT OF EGYPT

DEVOTIONAL READING: **Psalm 77:11-20**
PRINT PASSAGE: **Exodus 15:1-3, 19, 22-26**

BACKGROUND SCRIPTURE: **Exodus 1:8-14; 15:1-27**
KEY VERSE: **Exodus 15:19**

Exodus 15:1-3, 19, 22-26—KJV

THEN SANG Moses and the children of Israel this song unto the LORD, and spake, saying, I will sing unto the LORD, for he hath triumphed gloriously: the horse and his rider hath he thrown into the sea.

2 The LORD is my strength and song, and he is become my salvation: he is my God, and I will prepare him an habitation; my father's God, and I will exalt him.

3 The LORD is a man of war: the LORD is his name.

.....

19 For the horse of Pharaoh went in with his chariots and with his horsemen into the sea, and the LORD brought again the waters of the sea upon them; but the children of Israel went on dry land in the midst of the sea.

.....

22 So Moses brought Israel from the Red sea, and they went out into the wilderness of Shur; and they went three days in the wilderness, and found no water.

23 And when they came to Marah, they could not drink of the waters of Marah, for they were bitter: therefore the name of it was called Marah.

24 And the people murmured against Moses, saying, What shall we drink?

25 And he cried unto the LORD; and the LORD shewed him a tree, which when he had cast into the waters, the waters were made sweet: there he made for them a statute and an ordinance, and there he proved them,

26 And said, If thou wilt diligently hearken to the voice of the LORD thy God, and wilt do that which is right in his sight, and wilt give ear to his commandments, and keep all his statutes, I will put none of these diseases upon thee, which I have brought upon the Egyptians: for I am the LORD that healeth thee.

Exodus 15:1-3, 19, 22-26—NIV

THEN MOSES and the Israelites sang this song to the LORD: "I will sing to the LORD, for he is highly exalted. The horse and its rider he has hurled into the sea.

2 The LORD is my strength and my song; he has become my salvation. He is my God, and I will praise him, my father's God, and I will exalt him.

3 The LORD is a warrior; the LORD is his name."

.....

19 When Pharaoh's horses, chariots and horsemen went into the sea, the Lord brought the waters of the sea back over them, but the Israelites walked through the sea on dry ground.

.....

22 Then Moses led Israel from the Red Sea and they went into the Desert of Shur. For three days they traveled in the desert without finding water.

23 When they came to Marah, they could not drink its water because it was bitter. (That is why the place is called Marah.)

24 So the people grumbled against Moses, saying, "What are we to drink?"

25 Then Moses cried out to the LORD, and the LORD showed him a piece of wood. He threw it into the water, and the water became sweet. There the LORD made a decree and a law for them, and there he tested them.

26 He said, "If you listen carefully to the voice of the LORD your God and do what is right in his eyes, if you pay attention to his commands and keep all his decrees, I will not bring on you any of the diseases I brought on the Egyptians, for I am the LORD, who heals you."

UNIFYING LESSON PRINCIPLE

People will often follow a trusted leader even into dangerous places. What inspires such trust? Because Moses had faith in God, the Israelites followed him into the Red Sea, where God saved them from the Egyptians and from drowning.

TOPICAL OUTLINE OF THE LESSON

I. Introduction
   A. God's Presence
   B. Biblical Background

II. Exposition and Application of the Scripture
   A. A Song: Moses and the Israelites (Exodus 15:1-3)
   B. A Miracle: Israel versus Pharaoh and His Army (Exodus 15:19)
   C. The People Grumbled against Moses (Exodus 15:22-26)

III. Concluding Reflection

LESSON OBJECTIVES

Upon the completion of this lesson, the students will understand that:

1. Humanity can experience freedom from the tyranny of social, political, and religious oppression by following God;
2. Human salvation requires a remembrance of the narratives of captivity to fully celebrate deliverance; and,
3. Leaders who depend on God should be governed by a "holy intentionality."

POINTS TO BE EMPHASIZED

ADULT/YOUTH

Adult Topic: Following a Trusted Leader

Youth Topic: Free!

Adult Key Verse: Exodus 15:19

Youth Key Verse: Exodus 15:1

Print Passage: Exodus 15:1-3, 19, 22-26

—The writing of commemorative songs was part of Israel's history.

—The Israelites recognized a power greater than themselves.

—The Exodus involved the death of the pursuers.

—The Israelites could not have defeated the Egyptian army without God's help.

—God tested the Israelites on more than one occasion.

—God expects complete obedience and trust.

—Moses and the Israelites sang about all that God had done for them, after witnessing the miraculous parting of the sea and walking through on dry ground.

—The Israelites viewed their deliverance from bondage as an act of God.

—Moses and the Israelites acknowledged that God had guided them physically and miraculously in their flight from Egypt.

—The parting of the Red Sea and its subsequent drowning of Pharaoh's armies was a particular highlight of God's rescue of the Israelites.

CHILDREN

Children Topic: Rescued from the Enemy

Key Verse: Exodus 15:19

Print Passage: Exodus 15:1-3, 19, 22-26

—Verses 1-3 introduce the song of victory created and sung by Moses and the Israelites.

—The children of Israel gave glory to God for delivering them from the Egyptian army.

—Shortly thereafter, the Israelites grumbled for lack of fresh water.

—When Moses prayed for help, God prompted him to throw a tree branch into the water, which then became clean and sweet.

—Moses reminded the Israelites of their covenant with the Lord.

—Moses encouraged the people to be faithful to God so that they would not experience disaster.

I. INTRODUCTION

A. God's Presence

Early in Israel's history, it was threatened by a political regime. From the time of Moses's birth, danger threatened his life. But Moses's mother Jochebed (see Exodus 6), Pharaoh's daughter, and Moses's sister Miriam defied Pharaoh's evil plot and determined that Moses, a Hebrew boy, would not only live, but also flourish during his formative years in the royal palace. In this unique story, God honored the faith of a few and used that faith as an instrument of liberation for many. When Moses got a little older, God revealed His plans to Moses from a burning bush. God also summoned the universe to participate in the struggle for freedom. In the story of the Exodus, the natural world actively participated in Israel's cry for liberation. Phenomenal events unfolded over Egypt: blood in the Nile, frogs across the land, a gathering of gnats and flies, the death of livestock, boils, hail, locusts, darkness, and the death of the firstborn. Each plague sent a devastating message to Pharaoh that God heard and responded to the cry of freedom. Throughout Israel's experiences, God was present.

B. Biblical Background

In the Exodus story, we are eyewitnesses of a tale of two leaders. One emerged from the royal ancestral lineage—a pharaoh—and another emerged from a lineage of the oppressed—Moses. The writers of the biblical text saw Pharaoh and his henchmen as people who imposed bitter hardship upon the Hebrew people. In Exodus 1:14 (NIV), the Egyptians "made their lives bitter with hard labor in brick and mortar and with all kinds of work in the fields; in all their hard labor the Egyptians used them ruthlessly." But given this harsh setting, Moses emerged in the text as a pragmatic solution to Hebrew slavery, a savior figure who had not experienced slavery but shared common ancestry, a son of Israel. Moses was instrumental in Israel's liberation. And his faithful leadership was prefigured by two women.

The strategic leaders in the Exodus story were Shiphrah and Puah, the midwives originally sent by Pharaoh as ambassadors of death. While they may have been Egyptian women given Hebrew names, they refused complicity in Pharaoh's executive order. With tenacity and courage, they found a way to honor the will of God (see Exodus 1:17), thereby denying the evil mandate of Pharaoh.

II. EXPOSITION AND APPLICATION OF THE SCRIPTURE

A. A Song: Moses and the Israelites
(Exodus 15:1-3)

THEN SANG Moses and the children of Israel this song unto the Lord, and spake, saying, I will sing unto the Lord, for he hath triumphed gloriously: the horse and his rider hath he thrown into the sea. The Lord is my strength and song, and he is become my salvation: he is my God, and I will prepare him an habitation; my father's God, and I will exalt him. The Lord is a man of war: the Lord is his name.

This text begins in verse 1 with Moses and the people gathered together to worship the Lord—Yahweh—for great and mighty acts. The victory won over the Egyptians was significant to Israel. In fact, verses 1-3 seems to serve as the theme of the song. It praises God as a mighty "warrior." A phrase commonly used by the psalmist—"If it was not for the Lord on our side"—seems to find its nativity in these verses. It is used quite frequently by the psalmist to suggest how much of a significant role God played in Israel's early history. The crossing of the Red Sea is a benchmark episode. Even in modern times, Jews and Christians celebrate the significance of its meaning.

According to Frank S. Frick, the biblical scholar and author of the "Song of Moses" "is given special status in the traditional Jewish synagogue. When it is read in the synagogue, people stand, out of respect for its unique importance (a tradition also observed during the readings of the Ten Commandments)" (221, *A Journey Through the Hebrew Scriptures*). A brief look at Israel's history reveals a pattern. Israel regularly gathered to celebrate or to commemorate the salvation of the Lord on their behalf. Here are some examples: Moses led the children of Israel in the Feast of Unleavened Bread (see Exodus 12:17); commemorating God's devotion during their flight from Egypt, he led them in the Passover Feast (see Exodus 15:43); commemorating God commitment to bring Israel out of Egypt, Moses led them in the Feast of Tabernacles to recognize God's deliverance and protection during the wilderness wanderings; and Queen Esther led the Hebrew people in the Feast of Purim to commemorate God's deliverance from Haman's evil plot (see Esther 9:18). Celebration was an important aspect of Israel's historical narrative. It was a practical, pedagogical tool for teaching future generations about the significant details in its history and its unique relationship with the Lord. It also made real each event, so that God's covenantal promise was again and again remembered and reestablished with God's people.

The first half of the poem/song is focused on God. There is no mention of the Israelites until verse 13: "The people you have redeemed." The attention was drawn to God and God's mighty acts; the picture that was painted in the song was that where the people had no strength, the Lord became that strength. Where the people had no other salvation, God becomes the source of salvation. This was the song of liberation from a free people, a newly freed people, who associated this God with the God of their fathers and mothers. In other words, while this event was of course unique to the lives of those crossing the Red Sea, they also worshipped because they associated this God as the same God of Abraham, Isaac, and Jacob. There was a deep respect for God that stretched through the generations.

B. A Miracle: Israel versus Pharaoh and His Army (Exodus 15:19)

For the horse of Pharaoh went in with his chariots and with his horsemen into the sea, and the LORD brought again the waters of the sea upon them; but the children of Israel went on dry land in the midst of the sea.

One way to interpret verse 19 is to highlight God's intervention in human affairs. God is present in many episodes throughout the Exodus narrative. For example, "God was kind to the midwives" (1:20, NIV). God heard the groans of the slaves and remembered the covenant made with them (see 2:24). God called Moses from the burning bush and sent him to Pharaoh to demand their release (chapter 3). God orchestrated a number of supernatural occurrences that we understand as plagues to get the attention of Pharaoh. God sent Aaron to accompany Moses as they both attempted to convince Pharaoh of the power of their God. God intervened on many levels. The song, however, exalted the hand of God in the climactic event of Israel's escape through the Red Sea. The people of Israel witnessed the utter destruction of Pharaoh and his armies.

Verse 19 is written in prose rather than in the poetic form in verses 1-18. It brings closure to the song of Moses, recapturing two fundamental truths. Verse 19 is a reminder of two miracles. God created a footpath for Israel through the waters of the Red Sea. They walked on dry ground. The second reminder was the drowning of Pharaoh's armies, "chariots and horsemen." While the waters separated for the children of Israel, it came back together upon the Pharaoh's horses and henchmen. The children of Israel escaped via the hand and intervention of the Lord. What Israel sang that day is what Israel proves again and again throughout the sacred record and that is the fact that their God has no rival. It was through events like this that the reputation of God spread.

Even though the song has strong military imagery, which raises some problems, it highlights themes that were consistent with the way that Israel understood its relationship with God. God rescues and delivers. God throws down oppressors and lifts up the oppressed. It is God, not Pharaoh, who would reign forever. When other nations heard of this God, they would tremble. Many nations fight each other today in the name of God. They understand themselves to be involved in a holy war. This verse is not meant to authorize war, but to explain the ancient memory of a people intimately involved with a God invested in humanity's story. It is true that Israel celebrated God with a sense of abandonment made even clearer by the episode with Miriam and the women. Their worship was exuberant praise and public theater that alerted surrounding nations that there was no God like Yahweh.

C. The People Grumbled against Moses (Exodus 15:22-26)

So Moses brought Israel from the Red sea, and they went out into the wilderness of Shur; and they went three days in the wilderness, and found no water. And when they came to Marah, they could not drink of the waters of Marah, for they were bitter: therefore the name of it was called Marah. And the people murmured against Moses, saying, What shall we drink? And he cried unto the LORD; and the LORD shewed him a tree, which when he had cast into the waters, the waters were made sweet: there he made for them a statute and an ordinance, and there he proved them, And said, If thou wilt diligently hearken to the voice of the LORD thy God, and wilt do that which is right in his sight, and wilt give ear to his commandments,

and keep all his statutes, I will put none of these diseases upon thee, which I have brought upon the Egyptians: for I am the LORD that healeth thee.

Exodus 15:22 is a record of a shift in the text. Worship and praise fell to the side. Faith and assurance wavered as Moses and the children of Israel met their first wilderness test. How quickly they forgot the extraordinary divine intervention through years of slavery that culminated in the dramatic Exodus event. In the desert of Shur, they found themselves wanting. They were in need of water. Quite literally they were thirsty with no water in sight. The waters of Marah were bitter. They had no other options that were available. At the root of their complaint was the fear of death. Water was in fact a necessity. But even metaphorically they were experiencing the dry spell that often accompanies many relationships, the place where need goes unfilled and looming overhead is the fear of abandonment and neglect. Just like the children of Israel, we become desperate and are tempted to doubt.

Verse 24 reads, "So the people grumbled against Moses...then Moses cried out to the LORD." Three days into the wilderness of Shur, which was also the site of an oasis, located between Negeb and Egypt, the children of Israel were tempted to lose faith. They grumbled against Moses but they could have been indirectly questioning God's dependability as well. The story of the children in the wilderness is a story of faith. The wilderness narrative is a prototypical faith story. Each of the elements of covenantal relationship was involved—humanity's oppression and subsequent cry for help, God's response, deliverance, and liberation, the journey toward promise, wilderness wandering, temptation to complain and follow other gods, divine intervention, and the return to religious devotion. The story also reveals the leaders' capacity to lead with a sense of integrity and patience.

In verse 25, Moses cried out to God and the Lord showed him how to quickly remedy the situation. The answer was found in a piece of wood. After he threw it into the water, the water became sweet enough to drink. Often the remedies are just as close, but they are only most often found in prayer. Not until Moses prayed did the solution become clear.

In verse 26, God went on to stress the importance of listening carefully and paying attention. In other words, God told them that they would need to listen carefully to what He said, and do what was right. Following trusted leaders has to do with disciplining ourselves with the spiritual practice of prayer, and developing a deep trust that God can and will move on our behalf.

III. CONCLUDING REFLECTION

An image of the baby Moses floating in the Nile in a basket is similar to the image in Alex Haley's ancestral narrative, the movie *Roots,* when at the end of the movie a new baby was born and held high above his father's head. That one swift act of a father's raising his son as a presentation to God and to the community becomes a sign to those who behold the event that one child—a babe, an infant—can represent cultural and social transformation. The symbolic "raising" signals hope, excitement, and possibilities that generations before may never have tasted. However, present generations can predict with theological certainty that something new and good is on the horizon. It suggests that God still raises up leaders to the work of the kingdom.

Despite the obstacles found in the book of Exodus, Moses and the children celebrated with a sense of abandonment for all that God had done in and through the life of Israel. And despite the fact that sometimes we endure severe circumstances and conditions in which to flourish it is impossible, those are possibilities and opportunities that still exist. God has not left us.

We who identify with Christ have a steadfast anchor of the soul in a seemingly hopeless and war-devastated world. We still have hope in a world high on drugs like crystal methamphetamine, cocaine, and heroin. We still have hope, though storms rage in our lives and floodwaters overflow their banks. We still have hope. We still have hope, even when fathers are estranged from their children and mothers turn deaf ears. We still have hope in the possibility for renewed relationships between generations. We still have hope.

Moses and the children of Israel are historic witnesses that the God of our weary years and the God of our silent tears has not failed us.

PRAYER

O God, You delivered Moses and the children of Israel from the hands of Pharaoh. You deliver us from difficult trials. Guide Your leaders with integrity, and Your people with compassion. Help us live fully submitted and deeply committed to Your purposes. In Jesus' name we pray. Amen.

WORD POWER

Liberation—God's work in the world. As Moses was inspired to join God's work of liberation, we, too, are called to this work to set the oppressed free.

HOME DAILY BIBLE READINGS
(January 23-29, 2012)

Out of Egypt

MONDAY, January 23: "A Mighty Redemption" (Psalm 77:11-20)

TUESDAY, January 24: "A Strong People" (Exodus 1:1-7)

WEDNESDAY, January 25: "A New King" (Exodus 1:8-14)

THURSDAY, January 26: "A Treacherous Plan" (Exodus 1:15-22)

FRIDAY, January 27: "A Divine Intervention" (Exodus 15:4-10)

SATURDAY, January 28: "An Unsurpassable God" (Exodus 15:11-18)

SUNDAY, January 29: "A New Ordinance" (Exodus 15:1-3, 19, 22-26)

LESSON 10   February 5, 2012

JUSTIFIED BY FAITH IN CHRIST

DEVOTIONAL READING: **Luke 18:9-14**
PRINT PASSAGE: **Galatians 2:15-21**

BACKGROUND SCRIPTURE: **Galatians 1:1–2:21**
KEY VERSES: **Galatians 2:19-20**

Galatians 2:15-21—KJV

15 We who are Jews by nature, and not sinners of the Gentiles,

16 Knowing that a man is not justified by the works of the law, but by the faith of Jesus Christ, even we have believed in Jesus Christ, that we might be justified by the faith of Christ, and not by the works of the law: for by the works of the law shall no flesh be justified.

17 But if, while we seek to be justified by Christ, we ourselves also are found sinners, is therefore Christ the minister of sin? God forbid.

18 For if I build again the things which I destroyed, I make myself a transgressor.

19 For I through the law am dead to the law, that I might live unto God.

20 I am crucified with Christ: nevertheless I live; yet not I, but Christ liveth in me: and the life which I now live in the flesh I live by the faith of the Son of God, who loved me, and gave himself for me.

21 I do not frustrate the grace of God: for if righteousness come by the law, then Christ is dead in vain.

Galatians 2:15-21—NIV

15 "We who are Jews by birth and not 'Gentile sinners'

16 know that a man is not justified by observing the law, but by faith in Jesus Christ. So we, too, have put our faith in Christ Jesus that we may be justified by faith in Christ and not by observing the law, because by observing the law no one will be justified.

17 If, while we seek to be justified in Christ, it becomes evident that we ourselves are sinners, does that mean that Christ promotes sin? Absolutely not!

18 If I rebuild what I destroyed, I prove that I am a lawbreaker.

19 For through the law I died to the law so that I might live for God.

20 I have been crucified with Christ and I no longer live, but Christ lives in me. The life I live in the body, I live by faith in the Son of God, who loved me and gave himself for me.

21 I do not set aside the grace of God, for if righteousness could be gained through the law, Christ died for nothing!"

BIBLE FACT

GOD'S PROMISE OF JUSTIFICATION

Justification is a legal sentence or declaration issued by God in which He pronounces the person in question free from any fault or guilt, and acceptable in His sight. The person is declared to have met all the requirements of God's holy law and to possess a perfect righteousness. (From *Romans: An Interpretive Outline,* by David N. Steele and Curtis C. Thomas, Presbyterian and Reformed Publishing Co.)

UNIFYING LESSON PRINCIPLE

Having faith in someone else is the greatest gift that one can give to another. Why is faith greater than any other gift? Paul stated that Jesus died in vain if we place our faith in anything other than Him.

TOPICAL OUTLINE OF THE LESSON

I. **Introduction**
   A. Unity in Diversity
   B. Biblical Background

II. **Exposition and Application of the Scripture**
   A. Faith in Christ (Galatians 2:15)
   B. Justified in Christ (Galatians 2:16-18)
   C. Crucified with Christ (Galatians 2:19-21)

III. **Concluding Reflection**

LESSON OBJECTIVES

Upon the completion of this lesson, the students will understand:

1. The necessity of faith;
2. The necessity of blessing of justification; and,
3. The transformation in Christ.

POINTS TO BE EMPHASIZED

ADULT/YOUTH

Adult Topic: **Seeking Something to Believe In**
Youth Topic: **Got Faith?**
Adult Key Verses: **Galatians 2:19-20**
Youth Key Verse: **Galatians 2:16**
Print Passage: **Galatians 2:15-21**

—Paul's struggle in the book of Galatians was with people who thought that they could be saved by obeying the Law of Moses.

—When the writer spoke of being justified by faith instead of works, he meant the works of the Law of Moses.

—Gentiles were sinners simply by virtue of being Gentiles; they had been excluded from citizenship in Israel; they were "strangers to the covenants of promise, having no hope and without God in the world" (Ephesians 2:11-12, NIV).

—The Jews who could claim all the privileges of the chosen people did not realize that no one could be justified by observing the Law.

—All who have believed in Christ are justified by faith in Jesus Christ.

—Works, regardless of their merit, will not justify us before God—only faith in Jesus Christ will do this.

—The benefit of grace is ignored when one continues to seek justification by obeying the Law.

—Paul considered himself crucified with Christ and that Christ was now alive in him; his current life was lived by faith in Jesus Christ.

—Paul said that we must die to the Law in order to live for God.

—God's favor to us is manifested in the plan of salvation by the living Christ.

Children Topic: **I Believe**

Key Verse: **Galatians 2:20**

Print Passage: **Galatians 2:15-21**

—God showed His love for us by sending His Son, Jesus.

—God gives us grace.

—Christ wants us to live for Him.

—Christ wants us to love one another.

I. INTRODUCTION

A. Unity in Diversity

The controversy between rival missionary groups in Galatia—Peter and his "circumcision" faction, and Paul and his "uncircumcision" faction—introduce several issues for contemporary Christians inhabiting intercontinental worlds and engaging in interreligious dialogue. Many distinctions today between Christian groups are based not on theological but, rather, on social differences related to class and aesthetic tastes, race and ethnicity, geography, or even nationality. It is sometimes difficult to separate religious belief from the cultural beliefs that most groups pass on through the elders, but we are made better by recognizing our biases and prejudices upfront.

The way that Paul chose to handle controversy involved several elements. First, he established that he had been "entrusted with the gospel." He acknowledged that he received apostolic commissioning to go to the Gentiles. Paul also acknowledged that even though he and Peter disagreed with the necessity of circumcision as a requirement for belief, they both agreed that ministry to the poor was non-negotiable. Though their controversy is the subject of most of the letter to the Galatians, Peter and Paul agreed that the most significant aspect of their leadership was ministry to the poor. Paul's eagerness to make the poor a central part of his ministry can be seen again and again in his letter to the Romans (see Romans 15:25-27), and in both the books of 1 and 2 Corinthians (see 1 Corinthians 16:1-4 and 2 Corinthians 8:1–9:15).

B. Biblical Background

The letter to the Galatians is the only one attributed to Paul that does not begin with thanksgiving, which provides a clue to the reader. Paul was serious about the allegations that certain leaders were "misinterpreting" Christian responsibility. Rather than demand that new converts be bound to the legal customs and religious practices of Judaism, Paul encouraged the church in Galatia to lift the burden of tradition. His message: new converts would be saved by grace through faith in the person and work of Christ.

By what authority did Paul speak? Paul established in the salutation that he was commissioned to speak on this controversy—not from human authority, but from God, and supported by a group of believers who were in agreement with him. The issue Paul addressed to the two culturally distinct audiences (Jewish Christians and

Gentile Christians) was a culturally sensitive one: the Jewish religious custom of circumcision, and later the issue of Jewish eating customs.

Paul was sympathetic to the problem of Jewish religious customs, because his heritage and ambition as a Jewish zealot is clearly recorded in Scripture. None persecuted the early church more—before the Damascus experience—than Paul. One may sense that Paul had to come to a point of theological clarity for himself. He had to determine for himself what faith looked like before he could share an understanding with anyone else. Born out of his own sense of faithfulness and humility, Paul, more than anyone, moved the early church to understand the impact that belief has upon the Christian life.

The letter to the Galatians is meant to offer a definitive response to these "intra-Christian" disputes. Paul wrote the letter prior to the split between church and synagogue—and in this transitory period, Paul identified himself as one who could speak with "apostolic" authority. Paul interpreted faith in Christ as justification (placed in right relationship with God). In other words, Paul took literally that Christ lives within the convert, and thereby the believer takes on the righteousness of Christ in accepting this belief by faith. For Paul, accepting God's grace meant accepting the new life of Christ which is present in all believers, regardless of any particular physical signs depicted on the body.

II. EXPOSITION AND APPLICATION OF THE SCRIPTURE

A. Faith in Christ
(Galatians 2:15)

We who are Jews by nature, and not sinners of the Gentiles.

In verse 15, Paul raised a critical point significant to the early church, but with lasting implications for the contemporary church. It is a point related to the influences of culture, ethnicity, nationalism, and any number of ways that we identify each other as believers. For Peter and the Jerusalem church, establishing standards for salvation based upon culturally significant attributes should have been obligatory for all persons seeking a relationship with God. Paul disagreed. Paul did not say that there was anything wrong with the Law (in fact, the Law had its purposes and significance in the life of Israel). But what Paul did argue

was that to require allegiance to the old law by new converts was to deny the work of the Spirit through the life of Christ.

In other words, when we value our heritage over and above the work of the Spirit, we deny the Spirit His freedom and His power. This is not to suggest that heritage and ethnicity cannot be celebrated in church. The fact of the matter is that when we celebrate our culture and ethnicity by recalling special moments where the Spirit has triumphed over evil and oppression, we are establishing an important standard for worship. We are implicitly demonstrating that the Spirit is one; it is involved in one work—that of unifying and reconciling us to God and each other. Furthermore, we are showing forth the characteristics of the Spirit across the kingdom. We are calling attention to the work of the Spirit in the lives of people everywhere. However, when we confuse Christianity with capitalism (unable to critique our own greed and consumerism), we merely associate the "American Dream" with some vision of what it means to be saved, missing the more radical claims of Jesus that we should be dedicated to ministry to the poor, oppressed, imprisoned, and broken.

Jesus' interpretation of the purpose of Christian ministry is recorded in Luke 4:18; Jesus established at the beginning of His ministry that He was given spiritual authority "to preach good news to the poor" (NIV). While some over-spiritualize the interpretation of Jesus' words, focusing on spiritual uplift and inspiration, in the book of Galatians the emphasis is not just on the spiritual care for the poor, but on meeting their practical and tangible needs as well. Jesus demonstrated throughout His ministry a twofold focus. Spiritual need is never separated from physical need. While Jesus preached and taught, He also fed and healed. The early disciples understood that these two needs should not be separated or denied.

When James, Peter, John, and Paul acknowledged Jesus' teaching, they put their theological differences aside and established that ministry to the poor must be the focal point of any ministry. Their actions set a theological precedent for contemporary Christians.

B. Justified in Christ
(Galatians 2:16-18)

Knowing that a man is not justified by the works of the law, but by the faith of Jesus Christ, even we have believed in Jesus Christ, that we might be justified by the faith of Christ, and not by the works of the law: for by the works of the law shall no flesh be justified. But if, while we seek to be justified by Christ, we ourselves also are found sinners, is therefore Christ the minister of sin? God forbid. For if I build again the things which I destroyed, I make myself a transgressor.

In verse 16, Paul was still addressing Peter. Because both Peter and Paul had Jewish backgrounds and leadership responsibilities in their respective regions (Paul, in this case, in Galatia, and Peter in Jerusalem), they were seeking to come to theological agreement. Paul was concerned that recent missionaries who were probably Jewish converts (or maybe even sent by the Jerusalem church) were teaching that Gentile converts still needed to observe the Law. The Jewish missionaries refused to envision life without the Law because for as long as they could remember, dating back to the first stories of their people—the exodus out of Egypt—the Law had been central to their personal and communal identities. Passed down from generation to generation, they had heard the Law read in the synagogue and taught in their homes. It was a part of their daily existence. They were introduced to the ideas of morality and religion under the Law. The question naturally became this: If the Law or the "Torah" was the rule of life given by God and used to show God's people how to conduct their lives, then how could one abandon a century-long system of belief for an entirely new narrative? If Jesus came to fulfill the Law, then should not Gentile converts be encouraged to accept it as well?

In verses 16-17, Paul's message was for the Jewish converts as well as the Gentiles. For Paul, justification by faith in Christ suggests several things: (1) that "to live in Christ" is "to die to the law"; (2) that human effort is nullified by God's grace; and (3) that righteousness is not earned through works, but by faith in Christ. In other words, the life, death, and resurrection of Christ were the single most important facts to the early church. Paul was attempting to switch the focal point from the Law to the personhood of Christ. Clearly, Paul's message was that people were justified through Christ alone—made right with God not by their obedience to Jewish Law, but through faith in Christ.

Paul indicated that people have access to and membership in the family of God and the seed of Abraham through Christ. Paul suggested that it is through Christ, Abraham's seed, that all become heirs of the promise of the covenant that God made with Israel. Faith in Christ is a warranty for the promise. It is by faith that believers are justified and by faith that they can now participate in the freedom and responsibilities given to members of the family of God. In fact, Paul insisted that those who are determined to follow the Law place their emphasis on the wrong things: human effort, human ability, and human will. Paul attempted to shift the emphasis from self-reliance to total reliance on the Spirit of God.

In verse 18, Paul was clear that Christ was no lawbreaker. Ultimately, following Christ means following someone who submitted Himself to the Law, fulfilled it, and then ultimately stamped it null and void.

C. Crucified with Christ
(Galatians 2:19-21)

For I through the law am dead to the law, that I might live unto God. I am crucified with Christ: nevertheless I live; yet not I, but Christ liveth in me: and the life which I now live in the flesh I live by the faith of the Son of God, who loved me, and gave himself for me. I do not frustrate the grace of God: for if righteousness come by the law, then Christ is dead in vain.

Paul struck an interesting position in verse 19. He stated that he was "dead to the law." Scholars are not entirely sure what this death signifies. It may mean nothing more than that Paul put aside strict observance of the Law and faithful reliance on human effort to refocus. His new focus seemed to have been based on the idea of the free gift of grace, based upon faith in Christ Jesus. It was not the case that Paul was "taking the easy way out." It is neither the case that Paul was unfamiliar with what keeping the Law entailed. Paul had reasons to be confident in the flesh. In other words, the tone of the statement is that Paul felt that he conquered his flesh. He knew the Law, studied it, and became a master of it. He took it seriously and practiced it to the fullest.

The contrast Paul made in these verses is a demonstration of radical humility. Paul put ego aside to be "crucified with Christ." In other words, his faith and belief in the story of Jesus caused him to encounter the Christ within himself. As Christ was faithful to the point of death, so Paul pursued that same trajectory. Though the notion of spiritual experience is not explicitly stated in the text, clearly that is the move in verse 20.

Verse 20 is not merely an example of the Bible Bowl Scriptures that high school students may memorize for the Sunday school class competition; it depicts an acknowledgment or a personal statement of belief based upon a personal experience with Christ. "I have been crucified with Christ and I no longer live, but Christ lives in me" captures the shift in consciousness. By comparison, the life of Christ marked a level of faithfulness that superseded Paul's zealousness as a Pharisee. Until the Damascus Road experience, Paul had been responsible for taking lives but had not given up his own. What Paul experienced in his conversion and continued to reflect on throughout his life was the person of Jesus, His ministry, His death, and His resurrection. In that experience, Paul witnessed the grace of God acting through the life of Christ and spent the remainder of his life attempting to draw people into the story so as to spread the Good News.

III. CONCLUDING REFLECTION

Paul suggested that what distinguished Christians from other people were not external markings, but rather our common interest and commitment to charity and advocacy on behalf of the poor. The church too often is guilty of neglecting its singular mandate: to love and do justice. Sometimes our theological disputes serve to help us avoid the real work of the ministry. In the worst cases, the only casualties of our theological wars are those people who have a genuine desire to serve. The letter to the Galatians challenges the church to face its in-house disputes. Paul challenged us to extend welcome and hospitality to all who express faith in Christ Jesus. The Christian community is to be hospitable to all people, remembering Paul's fierce opposition to discrimination and prejudice in the early church. Finally, Paul emphasized that the Good News, for both the Gentile and the Jew, is that we can rely upon the Spirit of God to grant insight on how we should live and treat our neighbors.

PRAYER

O God, we thank You that Your grace reaches far and wide. Bless our faith. Help us to love each other extravagantly, and to remember that in loving each other, we show love to You. Grant us the tools that we need in order to reconcile with one another in patience and joy. In Jesus' name we pray. Amen.

WORD POWER

Imitation—doing what someone else does. Paul attempted to imitate the life of Christ, a life fully committed to God. In that imitation, he felt the full grace of God and sought to convert others.

HOME DAILY BIBLE READINGS
(January 30–February 5, 2012)

Justified by Faith in Christ

LESSON 11   February 12, 2012

FREED FROM LAW THROUGH CHRIST

DEVOTIONAL READING: **Matthew 19:16-23**
PRINT PASSAGE: **Galatians 3:1-14**

BACKGROUND SCRIPTURE: **Galatians 3:1-14**
KEY VERSE: **Galatians 3:14**

Galatians 3:1-14—KJV

O FOOLISH Galatians, who hath bewitched you, that ye should not obey the truth, before whose eyes Jesus Christ hath been evidently set forth, crucified among you?

2 This only would I learn of you, Received ye the Spirit by the works of the law, or by the hearing of faith?

3 Are ye so foolish? having begun in the Spirit, are ye now made perfect by the flesh?

4 Have ye suffered so many things in vain? if it be yet in vain.

5 He therefore that ministereth to you the Spirit, and worketh miracles among you, doeth he it by the works of the law, or by the hearing of faith?

6 Even as Abraham believed God, and it was accounted to him for righteousness.

7 Know ye therefore that they which are of faith, the same are the children of Abraham.

8 And the scripture, foreseeing that God would justify the heathen through faith, preached before the gospel unto Abraham, saying, In thee shall all nations be blessed.

9 So then they which be of faith are blessed with faithful Abraham.

10 For as many as are of the works of the law are under the curse: for it is written, Cursed is every one that continueth not in all things which are written in the book of the law to do them.

11 But that no man is justified by the law in the sight of God, it is evident: for, The just shall live by faith.

12 And the law is not of faith: but, The man that doeth them shall live in them.

13 Christ hath redeemed us from the curse of the law, being made a curse for us: for it is written, Cursed is every one that hangeth on a tree:

Galatians 3:1-14—NIV

YOU FOOLISH Galatians! Who has bewitched you? Before your very eyes Jesus Christ was clearly portrayed as crucified.

2 I would like to learn just one thing from you: Did you receive the Spirit by observing the law, or by believing what you heard?

3 Are you so foolish? After beginning with the Spirit, are you now trying to attain your goal by human effort?

4 Have you suffered so much for nothing—if it really was for nothing?

5 Does God give you his Spirit and work miracles among you because you observe the law, or because you believe what you heard?

6 Consider Abraham: "He believed God, and it was credited to him as righteousness."

7 Understand, then, that those who believe are children of Abraham.

8 The Scripture foresaw that God would justify the Gentiles by faith, and announced the gospel in advance to Abraham: "All nations will be blessed through you."

9 So those who have faith are blessed along with Abraham, the man of faith.

10 All who rely on observing the law are under a curse, for it is written: "Cursed is everyone who does not continue to do everything written in the Book of the Law."

11 Clearly no one is justified before God by the law, because, "The righteous will live by faith."

12 The law is not based on faith; on the contrary, "The man who does these things will live by them."

13 Christ redeemed us from the curse of the law by becoming a curse for us, for it is written: "Cursed is everyone who is hung on a tree."

14 That the blessing of Abraham might come on the Gentiles through Jesus Christ; that we might receive the promise of the Spirit through faith.

14 He redeemed us in order that the blessing given to Abraham might come to the Gentiles through Christ Jesus, so that by faith we might receive the promise of the Spirit.

TOPICAL OUTLINE OF THE LESSON

I. **Introduction**
   A. This, Not That
   B. Biblical Background

II. **Exposition and Application of the Scripture**
   A. The Demands of Faith (Galatians 3:1-6)
   B. The Role of Faith (Galatians 3:7-11)
   C. The Blessing of Faith (Galatians 3:12-14)

III. **Concluding Reflection**

LESSON OBJECTIVES

Upon the completion of this lesson, the students will understand that:

1. Faith is a necessity in the life of the believer;
2. There is a crucial role that faith plays in the body of Christ; and,
3. Believers are to be admonished and encouraged to receive the blessings of faith in Christ.

POINTS TO BE EMPHASIZED
ADULT/YOUTH

Adult Topic: The Place of Ultimate Trust
Youth Topic: Free at Last!
Adult Key Verse: Galatians 3:14
Youth Key Verse: Galatians 3:13
Print Passage: Galatians 3:1-14

—The Galatians' conduct was foolish or irrational. This passage suggests the actions of one who can think but fails to use his or her powers of perception (see Romans 1:14; 1 Timothy 6:9; Titus 3:3).

—The true Gospel had been clearly preached to them, so their defection from the crucified Christ is incomprehensible.

—All Jews, including Paul's opponents, would look back to Abraham as their father in the faith and as their example. "Abraham believed God, and it was reckoned to him as righteousness" (verse 6, NASU).

—Since the blessing of Abraham is declared to have been intended for the Gentiles also, how could the Gentiles be blessed except by faith? (See verses 8-9.)

—All who depend on observing the Law for justification will experience "the curse of the law" (verse 13), for a curse is attached to any failure to keep it, no matter how small. Since all fail, all are under the curse.

—Christ redeemed all people (who place their faith in Him) from the curse of the Law.

—Paul saw that the Galatians had gone back to trying to observe the Law instead of following Christ.

—Without God's Spirit, rules can be neither meaningful nor adhered to consistently.

CHILDREN
Children Topic: I Am Free
Key Verse: Galatians 3:12
Print Passage: Galatians 3:1-14
—The righteous will live by faith.

—Those who follow the Law and do the works will live by them.
—Those who believe in the Spirit will be faithful to the Word of God.
—Miracles take place through the power of God's intervening in people's lives.
—Those who are righteous will live by faith.
—Through Christ, redemption is accomplished.

I. INTRODUCTION
A. This, Not That

Paul painted a clear picture throughout the book of Galatians, indicating that followers of Christ are not obligated to keep the Law. In other words, Paul made clear distinctions between what the Gospel is and what it is not. Paul suggested that the Galatian church and hence all Gentile Christians have been converted under a different gospel—a gospel that he referred to as "the grace of Christ," and "the Gospel of Christ." They were not obligated, Paul wrote, to bear the same cultural marks as their Jewish Christian counterparts did. Paul said that they would receive the same blessing as the children of Abraham, but without the looming possibility of being cursed for failing to follow everything written in the Law.

Paul may have seemingly overemphasized the point, but he defended his passion by stating that false teachers were confusing what should have been a clear theological concept. While Paul negated observing the Law, he also painted a clear picture of what living in the Spirit should look like, which he summarized, "Do not use your freedom to indulge the sinful nature; rather, serve one another in love" (Galatians 5:13, NIV). The Christian is not under the command to observe the Law, but, rather, to live by the Gospel of Christ, which is to love.

B. Biblical Background

Galatians 3 lays the biblical and theological foundation for how the churches in Galatia should deal with the controversy about the Law in their lives. Paul attempted to remove this burden. Paul's argument was that if they received Christ by faith, then they should continue to live by faith in the grace that God extends to those who believe. Like Abraham, whom Paul said was counted as righteous for "believing," the Galatians also should believe. In other words, Paul's emphasis was not on external manifestations of the Law, but rather on internal change based upon one's faith in Christ and a believer's reliance upon the workings of the Spirit.

The questions that introduce the chapter were meant to call the attention of the Galatians to their conversion to the church (see Galatians 3:2-5). Paul asked (rhetorically), "Did you receive the Spirit by observing the law or through hearing and believing what you heard? Are you foolish? After having been initiated into the faith by the Spirit, are you now relying on human effort to continue? Are you doing this to yourself for nothing? Does God reward you by the signs and wonders that follow you because you observe the law or because of your belief?"

Paul emphasized that "observing the law" is not a part of their requirements; he advised that they receive the Spirit (see Galatians 3:2) and believe the Gospel of Jesus Christ. No other prerequisites for salvation exist.

II. EXPOSITION AND APPLICATION OF THE SCRIPTURE

A. The Demands of Faith
(Galatians 3:1-6)

O FOOLISH Galatians, who hath bewitched you, that ye should not obey the truth, before whose eyes Jesus Christ hath been evidently set forth, crucified among you? This only would I learn of you, Received ye the Spirit by the works of the law, or by the hearing of faith? Are ye so foolish? having begun in the Spirit, are ye now made perfect by the flesh? Have ye suffered so many things in vain? if it be yet in vain. He therefore that ministereth to you the Spirit, and worketh miracles among you, doeth he it by the works of the law, or by the hearing of faith? Even as Abraham believed God, and it was accounted to him for righteousness.

Verse 1 begins with a strong appeal by Paul not to forget basic truths of the faith, which for him crystallized into a single point: "Christ crucified." The way that this phrase is written, using the present participle of the word *crucified*, suggests that Paul was encouraging the church in Galatia to remember that though the Crucifixion was a past event, it has present results. Christ is *always* the crucified one. By casting their faith upon that truth, they entered into a new relationship with the Spirit of God. Paul's argument was founded upon belief in the crucified Christ.

It is suggested in verses 2-3 that *belief* was the method by which they entered this "new life," and it would be the centerpiece upon which this new life was based. Paul laid out the logic. If they entered this new life by faith, it would be faith that would sustain this new life. If observing the Law was a prerequisite for entering the faith, then they would need to spend their lives observing the Law. For Paul, the means of justification verified the ends of salvation. This point is further made in verse 3. If this new life was based upon human effort, then one would be required to observe the Law; but since it was not, God gave His Spirit. Faith in this free gift is the only requirement for discipleship. In other words, the terms of membership were fixed. They need not worry about the opposing teachings from rogue missionaries who demanded that they observe the Law.

Faith demands that we believe God. Paul used Abraham in verse 6 as an example to teach us about faith. Paul used Abraham, not as an exemplar of someone who followed the Law, but as one who walked by faith and obeyed the Spirit of God through faith. Abraham was an example of faithfulness: "By faith Abraham obeyed when he was called to go out to the place which he would receive as an inheritance. And he went out, not knowing where he was going. By faith he dwelt in the land of promise as in a foreign country, dwelling in tents with Isaac and Jacob, the heirs with him of the same promise; for he waited for the city which has foundations, whose builder and maker is God" (Hebrews 11:8-10, NKJV). Like the example of the baby, Abraham responded to God; Abraham provided an example to all believers and he was rewarded because of his faithfulness.

In this section of the book of Galatians, the choice was simple: live by faith or abide by the Law. Paul did not lower the bar for Gentiles, but, rather, introduced them to the freedom that awaited them as they followed Christ through faith.

B. The Role of Faith
(Galatians 3:7-11)

Know ye therefore that they which are of faith, the same are the children of Abraham. And the scripture, foreseeing that God would justify the heathen through faith, preached before the gospel unto Abraham, saying, In thee shall all nations be blessed. So then they which be of faith are blessed with faithful Abraham. For as many as are of the works of the law are under the curse: for it is written, Cursed is every one that continueth not in all things which are written in the book of the law to do them. But that no man is justified by the law in the sight of God, it is evident: for, The just shall live by faith.

In verse 8, Paul wrote that the Gospel had been given in advance to Abraham. Again, Paul stressed how unnecessary it was to follow the Law, because those who had faith were blessed right along with the man of faith—Abraham. The righteous do live by faith. But what is faith? *Faith* is trust in that which we cannot see, and assurance in what we hope for. Faith is a guttural response to God and ultimately that

which alone pleases God. Even after making a personal notation that the scales of inequality and discrimination may tip against us, Howard Thurman and later Dr. Martin Luther King Jr. both suggested that the arc of the universe is long, but it bends toward justice. Faith is an unwavering and indomitable trust that God *is*. Paul taught that we are made right by our faith in Christ.

Paul emphasized that the church models its belief after Christ. Christ, being fully aware of Jewish Law, understood the standards of morality that were taught to Him by the regulations and ritual policies of the Law—but Christ understood that the spirit of those laws was born out of love: love of God, love of self, and love of neighbor. Jesus taught very simply that the fruit of the religion is love. Paul suggested a new center of focus to early Jewish Christians and Gentiles. Paul suggested that they move from focusing on the Law to focusing on love; moving from observing a list of commands to observing one command summarized as, "loving God, neighbor and self." In other words, Paul was suggesting that the new grading scale was based upon love. The ethical expectation was that believers base their actions and even order their lives by the rule of love. No where is the ethical command to love made more evident than in the life of Jesus.

We get a clear picture of the role of love as we glimpse the totality of faith by which Jesus lived His life. Jesus was radically given over to love because of His deep faith in the presence and power of God. Jesus clarified in His mind that nothing would separate Him from the love of God—not even death. Through the life of Christ we learn something about the possibilities that exist for all believers when we have faith.

When Paul established faith as a necessity for redemption, he was not merely talking about a spiritual redemption, but saying that God claimed our beings wholly to live by faith in Him. The call for every believer is to share this Good News with those who have not heard that we are made right in and through our faith. We are justified by faith.

C. The Blessing of Faith
(Galatians 3:12-14)

And the law is not of faith: but, The man that doeth them shall live in them. Christ hath redeemed us from the curse of the law, being made a curse for us: for it is written, Cursed is every one that hangeth on a tree: That the blessing of Abraham might come on the Gentiles through Jesus Christ; that we might receive the promise of the Spirit through faith.

Verses 12 and 13 again stress the point that the Law was not based upon experience. Paul again made the claim that the Gentile convert is exempt from observances of the law through Christ. Christ met that qualification in two ways: He redeemed the Gentile from the curse by becoming a curse (because He hung on a tree, fitting the standard that everyone who "hangs on a tree" is cursed), and Christ is an heir of Abraham. Once in Christ, one receives the inheritance only promised to the heirs of Abraham.

Abraham's blessing may seem insignificant, but Abraham and Sarah were unlikely candidates to be progenitors of generations of people; they were past the child-bearing age. But they did not allow their circumstances to determine God's outcomes. They put their trust in the promises of God rather than relying on a kind of self-sufficiency. For their faithfulness, they were blessed, and so were their descendants. And though we are Gentiles,

"through Christ Jesus" by faith we receive the promise of the Spirits.

The book of Galatians names a number of blessings that believers receive as a result of their faith. These blessings are individual and communal, spiritual and material. They have residuals now and through eternity. The following is not meant to be an exhaustive list, but these blessings include the following:

- Watching God work in the ministry and mission of the church;
- Being assured of God's pleasure in our faithfulness;
- Witnessing the Spirit's manifestation and felt presence in a person's life: comforting, teaching, and removing unnecessary burdens to "perform" or be "successful" by human effort alone;
- Receiving the gift of freedom from the burden of following religious norms that demand an external mark of righteousness;
- Experiencing the liberation to follow and serve the purpose of God;
- Receiving the ancient blessing of Abraham, through faith in the Spirit, by being reclaimed as whole and fully liberated in and reconciled to God;
- Being added to the number of those who walk with God out of their faith in God's promises.

Ultimately, the blessing of faith serves to draw the believers to understand at the depth of their beings that they have been set free from any yoke that prevents them from feeling a sense of personal wholeness and reconciliation to God—for what can separate us from the love of God? Paul communicated to the church in Galatia the possibility for a profound relationship with God. This would not only please God in seeing their faith, but, because of God's initial promise to Abraham, the Gentiles also became recipients of the inheritance that God promised Abraham: access to God now and a vision of the city's being prepared.

III. CONCLUDING REFLECTION

It may be easier to have a "checklist" kind of faith—where rather than contemplating what Jesus Christ means to one's life socially, politically, and ethically, one may simply follow a list of rules and regulations. However, Paul was warning, throughout the book of Galatians, that rather than emphasizing legalism, the church should emphasize faith in Christ. Paul asserted that critical attention ought to be given to the power of the Spirit of God. We are encouraged to place our faith in Christ.

Faith in Christ Jesus introduces a new paradigm for living. Faith in Christ Jesus propels one to consider what it means to love God and humanity. Faith in Christ Jesus situates one to think critically about Paul's statements about the passing away of the Law. Yes, we ought to give special attention to what the Gospel means for us spiritually, but also to how it manifests in the body of Christ. Living with full awareness of the Spirit of God suggests a level of quickening that should be associated with every believer.

PRAYER

Our Father, help us in our quest to live as Your sons and daughters, guided by the Spirit. In our striving, let us not throw love aside. In our loving, help us not to throw justice aside. Holy One, guard us with Your mighty arm. In Jesus' name we pray. Amen.

WORD POWER
Faith—defined as "the substance of things hoped for, the evidence of things not seen" (Hebrews 11:1).

HOME DAILY BIBLE READINGS
(February 6-12, 2012)

Freed from Law through Christ

MONDAY, February 6: "Blessing All Nations" (Genesis 18:16-21)

TUESDAY, February 7: "Keep the Law and Live" (Leviticus 18:1-5)

WEDNESDAY, February 8: "The Curse of Sin" (Deuteronomy 27:15-26)

THURSDAY, February 9: "The Righteous Live by Their Faith" (Habakkuk 2:1-5)

FRIDAY, February 10: "Faith and Salvation" (Hebrews 10:32-39)

SATURDAY, February 11: "What Do I Still Lack?" (Matthew 19:16-26)

SUNDAY, February 12: "The Blessing for All" (Galatians 3:1-14)

HEIRS TO THE PROMISE

DEVOTIONAL READING: **Romans 4:1-8**
PRINT PASSAGE: **Galatians 3:15-18; 4:1-7**
KEY VERSE: **Galatians 4:7**

BACKGROUND SCRIPTURE: **Galatians 3:15-29; 4:1–5:1**

Galatians 3:15-18; 4:1-7—KJV

15 Brethren, I speak after the manner of men; Though it be but a man's covenant, yet if it be confirmed, no man disannulleth, or addeth thereto.
16 Now to Abraham and his seed were the promises made. He saith not, And to seeds, as of many; but as of one, And to thy seed, which is Christ.
17 And this I say, that the covenant, that was confirmed before of God in Christ, the law, which was four hundred and thirty years after, cannot disannul, that it should make the promise of none effect.
18 For if the inheritance be of the law, it is no more of promise: but God gave it to Abraham by promise.

.....

NOW I say, That the heir, as long as he is a child, differeth nothing from a servant, though he be lord of all;
2 But is under tutors and governors until the time appointed of the father.
3 Even so we, when we were children, were in bondage under the elements of the world:
4 But when the fulness of the time was come, God sent forth his Son, made of a woman, made under the law,
5 To redeem them that were under the law, that we might receive the adoption of sons.
6 And because ye are sons, God hath sent forth the Spirit of his Son into your hearts, crying, Abba, Father.
7 Wherefore thou art no more a servant, but a son; and if a son, then an heir of God through Christ.

Galatians 3:15-18; 4:1-7—NIV

15 Brothers, let me take an example from everyday life. Just as no one can set aside or add to a human covenant that has been duly established, so it is in this case.
16 The promises were spoken to Abraham and to his seed. The Scripture does not say "and to seeds," meaning many people, but "and to your seed," meaning one person, who is Christ.
17 What I mean is this: The law, introduced 430 years later, does not set aside the covenant previously established by God and thus do away with the promise.
18 For if the inheritance depends on the law, then it no longer depends on a promise; but God in his grace gave it to Abraham through a promise.

.....

WHAT I am saying is that as long as the heir is a child, he is no different from a slave, although he owns the whole estate.
2 He is subject to guardians and trustees until the time set by his father.
3 So also, when we were children, we were in slavery under the basic principles of the world.
4 But when the time had fully come, God sent his Son, born of a woman, born under law,
5 to redeem those under law, that we might receive the full rights of sons.
6 Because you are sons, God sent the Spirit of his Son into our hearts, the Spirit who calls out, "Abba, Father."
7 So you are no longer a slave, but a son; and since you are a son, God has made you also an heir.

UNIFYING LESSON PRINCIPLE

Sometimes a person inherits a system of values without personally investigating the appropriateness of such values. Why is it important to understand, rather than merely inherit, the values by which we live? Paul stated that Gentiles received God's blessing as heirs of Abraham, but had to accept the promise for themselves by maturing in their faith in Jesus Christ.

TOPICAL OUTLINE OF THE LESSON

I. Introduction
   A.   Covenant with God
   B.   Biblical Background

II. Exposition and Application of the Scripture
   A.   The Heart of the Promise (Galatians 3:15-18)
   B.   The Spirit of Sonship (Galatians 4:1-5)
   C.   No Longer Slaves (Galatians 4:6-7)

III. Concluding Reflection

LESSON OBJECTIVES

Upon the completion of this lesson, the students will understand:

1. The meaning of the inheritance given to the children of God;
2. The significance of the extension of the promise given to Abraham; and,
3. What it means to inspire a life of freedom in Christ.

POINTS TO BE EMPHASIZED
ADULT/YOUTH

Adult Topic: Understanding Values
Youth Topic: The Benefits of Adoption
Adult/Youth Key Verse: Galatians 4:7
Print Passage: Galatians 3:15-18; 4:1-7

—Paul observed that the promises of God were made to Abraham and his seed. The singular reference is Christ.
—Paul used an example from everyday life to illustrate God's promise to Abraham and his heirs.
—Nothing can annul the covenant already ratified.
—The situation of church life in Galatia sets an example for everyone.
—Paul believed that all people who believe can become children of God.
—God made the promise of Christ's coming to Abraham and his descendants.
—When the time was right, God sent His Son so that we might become heirs of the promise.
—Paul said that children have limited rights just as slaves do.
—As heirs of the promise through Christ, we now can call God "Abba, Father," an expression Paul used to explain the kind of relationship that everyone can have with Christ.

CHILDREN

Children Topic: I Am Growing
Key Verse: Galatians 3:26
Print Passage: Galatians 3:15-18, 21-29

—God made a promise to Abraham.
—If we belong to Christ, we will receive the promise given to Abraham.
—All people who are baptized in Christ will become one with Him and with one another.
—Christ overcomes barriers among people.

I. INTRODUCTION

A. Covenant with God

African-American Christians have an affinity for the Exodus story and many biblical references regarding the quest for freedom. Lewis V. Baldwin, professor of Religious History at Vanderbilt University, writes of the spiritual "Go Down, Moses" that "[It] is a spiritual with revolutionary content and meanings. The biblical references and the call for freedom were applied by the slaves to their own situation of living in bondage. Used as a musical code for slaves escaping on the Underground Railroad, 'Go Down, Moses' was very important to the slave community because of its double meaning. Masters and other whites hearing the song were only impressed by the strong biblical themes. However, to escaping slaves and persons helping them along the way, this spiritual also represented hidden meaning, hints, messages, and signals" (*Plenty Good Room*, 15).

In the oft-repeated refrain of the song, "Let My People Go," God is depicted as summoning Moses for the purpose of leading the people of Israel out of bondage. Black Americans immediately identify with the story and the implications of a radical God intimately involved in the quest for liberation. Baldwin and other scholars of the black experience indicate that when enslaved Africans sang this tune, they believed that God was still acting on the behalf of those enslaved by modern, cruel pharaohs. The song was a theological reminder that God still acts, and a social code that God was presently acting in monumental and strategic ways to ensure freedom and salvation in the face of evil.

African Americans have historically put their faith in a covenantal relationship with God. Black people may have suffered and still suffer because of the ambiguities of the law to serve black communities justly—but where the legal system fails, black history proves that persons have successfully challenged and successfully demanded that the country live up to its highest ideals. The resolve to struggle in the face of inconsistencies and injustice is nurtured by the belief that God is just. If God is just, then God's children are justified in securing justice for all those who are threatened by systems of injustice.

B. Biblical Background

Galatians 4:7 has a companion Scripture: Romans 8:16-17. The Galatians text reads, "So you are no longer a slave, but a son; and since you are a son, God has made you also an heir" (NIV). The Scripture connotes a move from servanthood to sonship, and then from sonship to inheritor. Notice the Romans text. It reads similarly, "The Spirit himself testifies with our spirit that we are God's children. Now if we are children, then we are heirs—heirs of God and co-heirs with Christ" (NIV). Paul was establishing the concept of the fullness of God's love extended to the mature Spirit-led believer. For Paul, the determining factor in progressing from the slave metaphor to the son-ship metaphor is obedience to the Spirit. Paul noted a move from basic principles (law) to faith in the Spirit of God. For Paul, the church was challenged to be a community of people who eventually moved from the basic principles of the Law to life in the Spirit. Moving from an emphasis on Law to an emphasis on Spirit is like moving from the metaphor of slave to son, servant to heir—in other words, the relationship changes. Life in the Spirit reorients our relationship to God.

Paul's parental imagery is key to a fuller understanding of the text. Paul taught a profound truth—the image of God as a divine parent. Paul attributed the Spirit of God as that which draws us to God, and the Spirit as that which develops and nurtures our faith over time. The full picture that Paul painted is a picture of a God who creates, hovers over creation, calls creation into relationship, and sustains that relationship by a living Spirit. The emphasis is on the Spirit because, for Paul, the Spirit is the supply of living water for the church. It is the source of life from which all Christians draw.

Paul made clear distinctions between Judaism and Christianity, which was being interpreted by Jewish Christian leaders. The primary difference seemed to have been interpretations of how the Law should be used. For Paul, the Law acted as a tutor, not a disciplinarian. The Gospel of Christ is a gospel of freedom *from* the Law, a new life under the guidance of the Spirit—as chapter 5 begins with "It is for freedom that Christ has set us free." Paul was clear: this freedom is not a license to "indulge the sinful nature," but rather for us to "serve one another in love" (see Galatians 5:13); neither sin nor love was proscribed by legalistic interpretations, but rather determined by the Spirit's witness. In other words, Paul was arguing that the Spirit should be, for the children of God, an internal governing witness. Christians then are invited to live by the Spirit.

II. EXPOSITION AND APPLICATION OF THE SCRIPTURE

A. The Heart of the Promise
(Galatians 3:15-18)

Brethren, I speak after the manner of men; Though it be but a man's covenant, yet if it be confirmed, no man disannulleth, or addeth thereto. Now to Abraham and his seed were the promises made. He saith not, And to seeds, as of many; but as of one, And to thy seed, which is Christ. And this I say, that the covenant, that was confirmed before of God in Christ, the law, which was four hundred and thirty years after, cannot disannul, that it should make the promise of none effect. For if the inheritance be of the law, it is no more of promise: but God gave it to Abraham by promise.

Verse 15 contains a reintroduction to the language of covenant. *Nelson's Expository Dictionary of the Old Testament* says this about covenant: "Occasionally, Israel made a covenant before the Lord, to walk after the Lord, and keep his commandments...to perform the words of this covenant that were written in this book" (2 Kings 23:3). Israel did not propose terms or a basis of union with God. They responded to God's covenant. In other words, what Paul was suggesting was that just like Israel, Christian believers do not come to the proverbial negotiating table with God, to bargain for additional perks or clauses in a covenant with God—we are merely responding to what has been initiated by God already.

It is stated in verse 16 that somehow

Abraham's progeny trickled down to a single heir—Christ. However, Abraham's seed was plenteous. The point is that Paul was attempting to strengthen his argument that inheritance did not depend upon the Law, but depended upon a promise, ultimately given to Christ, the sole heir of Abraham. This argument contributed to a number of problems because it glossed over much of Israel's recorded history. The argument covered over numerous stories about Abraham's heirs (through Isaac, Rebekah, and Rachel) and their relationship with God. It neglected Abraham's progeny through Ishmael, Hagar's son. It is quite clear that Paul was making a case for the Gentiles. Paul's concern was to establish a direct lineage from Abraham to Christ, thus legitimizing the promise to the Gentiles.

Verse 18 establishes that God gave the promise directly to Abraham. The grace of God was active in that decision, and ultimately situated Abraham and his descendants to have access to the promise of God through eternity. Paul's argument mimics a legal argument. He was clear about what was at stake. He was establishing a legal precedent for Gentile believers.

Throughout the book of Galatians, Paul was establishing and reconfirming his objective: to show that observance of the Law was not necessary for those who confessed Christ. It was a circular argument. Paul showed God's giving Abraham the promise. Paul then proved Christ to be the seed of Abraham. From there, Paul proved how through Christ, believers become heirs of the promise. The promise symbolizes access. Through the promise, believers have access to God and all the promises that accompany that access.

B. The Spirit of Sonship
(Galatians 4:1-5)

NOW I say, That the heir, as long as he is a child, differeth nothing from a servant, though he be lord of all; But is under tutors and governors until the time appointed of the father. Even so we, when we were children, were in bondage under the elements of the world: But when the fulness of the time was come, God sent forth his Son, made of a woman, made under the law, To redeem them that were under the law, that we might receive the adoption of sons.

This passage summarily indicates that all believers in Christ eventually progress to sonship in God. Through sonship we are entitled to legal inheritance. Carolyn Osiek, professor of New Testament, argues that because of the culture that Paul's letter addresses—one in which daughters did not have the same legal rights as sons—he used the image of sonship as a way to most accurately capture the equity by which the inheritance is distributed. Both male and female in Christ, "have the equivalent legal status of son before God—that is, all stand with Christ as heirs of eternal life" (*Women's Bible Commentary, 424).*

According to Osiek, a son was more a legal nomenclature, as daughters would have still legally needed an arbiter for any inherited personal wealth. This interpretation is consistent with Paul's ongoing views of the men and women who served the early church. They established churches and used their homes to serve as hosts, consistent with the phrase that Paul used to refer to both men and women who labored in the kingdom as "fellow workers." The spirit of sonship was meant to capture the concept that it is the Spirit of God who empowers the church, *without respect to gender.* It is reminiscent of the work of the Spirit in the book of Acts, where the apostles remembered a comment from the prophet Joel, "In the last days, God says, I will pour out my Spirit on all people" (see Acts 2:17).

It further offers clarity on those cultural markers by which we are identified. Paul's argument was that whether Jew or Gentile, everybody in Christ is an heir to the promise. One does not have to take on "Jewishness" (by rule or ritual) to gain access to the inheritance won for us by Christ. We are all "in" Christ as new creatures. The concept of inheritance foreshadows an issue that Paul later tackled. Our place as the "sons" of God grants us access, agency, and authority as heirs of God. Our redemption is not based upon our genders, statuses, or heritage. Our redemption is solely based upon our faith in Christ.

C. No Longer Slaves
(Galatians 4:6-7)

And because ye are sons, God hath sent forth the Spirit of his Son into your hearts, crying, Abba, Father. Wherefore thou art no more a servant, but a son; and if a son, then an heir of God through Christ.

It is argued in verse 6 that every believer is given access to the Spirit. And it is through the Spirit that each person is now identified. Because of the Spirit, believers share a family resemblance. We each have equal access to God.

It is stated in verse 7 that every believer is an heir. But what shall we inherit? Certainly the glory of Christ, but also the sufferings (see Romans 8:17 and Philippians 3:10). Believers are not exempt from suffering. Believers suffer in a world that does not aim toward the building of close communities. We suffer physically, emotionally, spiritually, and

materially. The suffering that these Scriptures refer to have some relationship with the suffering that comes as a result of attempting to follow in the ministry of Christ—or suffering that is worsened by one's commitment to the ministry of Christ. Suffering, in this sense, refers to that which is suffered on the behalf of the poor, the oppressed, the imprisoned, and the disinherited. Suffering often comes from the dangerous oppositions that challenge one's beliefs. But Soren Kierkegaard, in *The Sickness Unto Death,* remarks that courage is gained when suffering itself is not feared but is, rather, put into perspective.

Suffering is inevitable because Christ warned that the world did not know Him and, therefore, would not know us. Suffering is also the result of having so few laborers when the harvest is plenty. Suffering will come as a result of teaching, preaching, and ministering in socially liberating ways so that the fullness of humanity will experience the kingdom of God come near. But good news is found in the Romans companion text, which reminds us and exhorts us that as we participate in the sufferings, so shall we share in the glory of Christ.

The content of our inheritance is both suffering and glory. Such has been the case with believers who through time have suffered persecution and martyrdom. Such has also been the case with those who have participated in small and great acts of love. But more glory awaits! John the Revelator's vision of glory in Revelation 21 was a "new heaven and a new earth come down...coming down out of heaven from God." In that sense, the glory that awaits is "the dwelling of God...with men." This will be the inheritance of the children of God.

We glimpse the glory whenever a child prays. In that one instant we witness the perpetuation of the Gospel from one generation to the next. As believers and "heirs according to the promise," we inherit both sufferings and glory. In every age, we are graced to witness the triumph of the glory, just as in every age we sing, "Glory, Glory, Hallelujah! Our God Is Marching On!"

III. CONCLUDING REFLECTION

Faithfulness in Christ will teach every believer what he or she needs to know to fulfill God's command *to be*. The Spirit, according to the book of Galatians, can be trusted as the new tutor. The Spirit can be trusted to guide and to instruct. Paul offered a sustained argument about the Spirit's work. As churches reconnect with the life of the Spirit, new energy will grow around the ways in which God is still moving in the world. More study of the function of the Spirit might reintroduce to churches the necessity for being led by the Spirit's unction toward the purposes of God in the world today. More study of the function and personality of the Spirit might help churches reflect more broadly around the possibilities for unity in our world today. The Spirit's effectual work gives believers new tongues and heartier worship—but the Spirit also teaches, comforts, struggles alongside the sufferer, thirsts for unity, and hungers for righteousness. The church's prayer ought to be this: "Let not our hearts quench the Spirit, O God."

PRAYER

O God, we drink deep from Your living Spirit, the wellspring of life. Help us to travel with full awareness of Your presence. Guide us through clear paths as we seek to make life-giving choices and struggle beyond the pain of our lives. In Jesus' name we pray. Amen.

WORD POWER

Inheritance—refers to the fact that we have received a legacy as heirs of the promise. That promise was initially given to Abraham, but we inherit it through Christ.

HOME DAILY BIBLE READINGS
(February 13-19, 2012)

Heirs to the Promise

MONDAY, February 13: "Ancestor to a Multitude of Nations" (Genesis 17:1-8)
TUESDAY, February 14: "The Promise Is for You" (Acts 2:32-39)
WEDNESDAY, February 15: "The Gift of Righteousness" (Romans 4:1-8)
THURSDAY, February 16: "Now that Faith Has Come" (Galatians 3:19-29)
FRIDAY, February 17: "Until Christ Is Formed in You" (Galatians 4:12-20)
SATURDAY, February 18: "Stand Firm in Christ's Freedom" (Galatians 4:28–5:1)
SUNDAY, February 19: "Heirs to the Promise" (Galatians 3:15-18; 4:1-7)

LESSON 13   February 26, 2012

FRUITS OF REDEMPTION

DEVOTIONAL READING: **2 Peter 1:3-8**
PRINT PASSAGE: **Galatians 5:22-26; 6:1-10**

BACKGROUND SCRIPTURE: **Galatians 5:2–6:18**
KEY VERSES: **Galatians 5:22-23**

Galatians 5:22-26; 6:1-10—KJV

22 But the fruit of the Spirit is love, joy, peace, long-suffering, gentleness, goodness, faith,

23 Meekness, temperance: against such there is no law.

24 And they that are Christ's have crucified the flesh with the affections and lusts.

25 If we live in the Spirit, let us also walk in the Spirit.

26 Let us not be desirous of vain glory, provoking one another, envying one another.

.…..

BRETHREN, IF a man be overtaken in a fault, ye which are spiritual, restore such an one in the spirit of meekness; considering thyself, lest thou also be tempted.

2 Bear ye one another's burdens, and so fulfil the law of Christ.

3 For if a man think himself to be something, when he is nothing, he deceiveth himself.

4 But let every man prove his own work, and then shall he have rejoicing in himself alone, and not in another.

5 For every man shall bear his own burden.

6 Let him that is taught in the word communicate unto him that teacheth in all good things.

7 Be not deceived; God is not mocked: for whatsoever a man soweth, that shall he also reap.

8 For he that soweth to his flesh shall of the flesh reap corruption; but he that soweth to the Spirit shall of the Spirit reap life everlasting.

9 And let us not be weary in well doing: for in due season we shall reap, if we faint not.

10 As we have therefore opportunity, let us do good unto all men, especially unto them who are of the household of faith.

Galatians 5:22-26; 6:1-10—NIV

22 But the fruit of the Spirit is love, joy, peace, patience, kindness, goodness, faithfulness,

23 gentleness and self-control. Against such things there is no law.

24 Those who belong to Christ Jesus have crucified the sinful nature with its passions and desires.

25 Since we live by the Spirit, let us keep in step with the Spirit.

26 Let us not become conceited, provoking and envying each other.

.…..

BROTHERS, IF someone is caught in a sin, you who are spiritual should restore him gently. But watch yourself, or you also may be tempted.

2 Carry each other's burdens, and in this way you will fulfill the law of Christ.

3 If anyone thinks he is something when he is nothing, he deceives himself.

4 Each one should test his own actions. Then he can take pride in himself, without comparing himself to somebody else,

5 for each one should carry his own load.

6 Anyone who receives instruction in the word must share all good things with his instructor.

7 Do not be deceived: God cannot be mocked. A man reaps what he sows.

8 The one who sows to please his sinful nature, from that nature will reap destruction; the one who sows to please the Spirit, from the Spirit will reap eternal life.

9 Let us not become weary in doing good, for at the proper time we will reap a harvest if we do not give up.

10 Therefore, as we have opportunity, let us do good to all people, especially to those who belong to the family of believers.

UNIFYING LESSON PRINCIPLE

While faith in something or someone must come first, acts beneficial to others will follow. Why is it important to act on faith? Paul said that faithfulness is one of the gifts of the Holy Spirit and that, whenever possible, believers should work for the good of all—especially for those in the family of faith.

TOPICAL OUTLINE OF THE LESSON

I. Introduction
   A. Communal Emphasis
   B. Biblical Background

II. Exposition and Application of the Scripture
   A. A Spiritual Harvest (Galatians 5:22-24)
   B. Life in the Spirit (Galatians 5:25-26)
   C. Heavy Lifting (Galatians 6:1-5)
   D. Sowing and Reaping (Galatians 6:6-10)

III. Concluding Reflection

LESSON OBJECTIVES

Upon the completion of this lesson, the students will understand that:
1. Life in the Spirit produces fruit;
2. There is an experience referred to as the discipline of the Spirit; and,
3. We are called to recognize the burdens of the Spirit.

POINTS TO BE EMPHASIZED

ADULT/YOUTH
Adult Topic: **Bearing One Another's Burdens**
Youth Topic: **Fruit Does a Body Good**
Adult Key Verses: **Galatians 5:22-23**
Youth Key Verse: **Galatians 6:10**
Print Passage: **Galatians 5:22-26; 6:1-10**

—The nine virtues that are the Spirit's fruit seem to fall into three categories of three each—general aspects, relationships to others, and personal concerns of others.
—The Law was given to restrain evil. The fruits of the Spirit do not need to be restrained. Hence, no law opposes these fruits.
—Paul was discussing repentance in this passage.
—Paul was discussing the leadership of the Spirit in this passage.
—Living by God's Spirit produces the fruit of the Spirit in our lives.
—The practice of being sensitive and obedient to God's Spirit helps us to have right relationships with others.
—Paul encouraged us to gently restore those who sin and to guard ourselves against temptation.
—Paul encouraged us to support one another, to stay humble, and to share with others.
—Paul encouraged us to do good, since we will reap what we sow.
—In this passage, Paul revealed what it means to be led by God's Spirit.

CHILDREN
Children Topic: **I Am Helpful**
Key Verse: **Galatians 6:10**
Print Passage: **Galatians 5:22-26; 6:1-10**
—The fruit of the Spirit is love, joy, peace, patience, kindness, generosity, faithfulness, gentleness, and self-control.

—Christ wants us to work for the good of others.

—The grace of God is with us.

—We must use the grace that God has given us to help restore others.

—Christians are never to have an attitude of self-importance.

—We are called to help support others.

I. INTRODUCTION

A. Communal Emphasis

Many churches emphasize the work of the Spirit as that which enlivens worship: ecstatic utterances (speaking in tongues), powerful singing, and thoughtful and fiery preaching. These are usually markers that signify to believers whether or not the "Spirit was in the house" on Sunday morning. But contrast that with what Paul considered the fruits of the Spirit: love, joy, peace, patience, kindness, goodness, faithfulness, gentleness, and self-control. Are these two examples of the Spirit's work in contrast with each other? Are there other examples of the Spirit's work in sacred Scripture? Jesus declared in the gospel of Luke that "the Spirit of the Lord" came upon Him and anointed Him for radical proclamation. In the Galatians text, there are at least two other examples of the Spirit's work: submission to the Spirit leads to exemption from the Law, and sowing to the Spirit leads to reaping from the Spirit (see Galatians 5:18; 6:8). The Spirit moves us to worship; He shapes character; He anoints for ministry; and He leads to certain spiritual rewards.

Scripture also teaches that the Spirit works within us to discipline, instruct, and clarify any confusion that we may have about our identities in Christ. If we continue in the life of the Spirit, then it is inevitable that we will experience spiritual growth. Paul encouraged the churches around Galatia to continue growing in grace, but not only as a self-reflective act—whereby they were concerned about personal growth as believers—but also as that which contributed to the Spirit's guidance to nurture the work of the church. That work may include restoring a fellow believer; it also might include sharing the Spirit's witness and thereby offering encouragement to another. The work of the Spirit should help keep us from falling short of real community. In fact, Paul urged that if one transgressed, violated, or threatened the ethics of the community, then those who had received the Spirit ought to restore the violator with spirits of gentleness. The close reader of the book of Galatians will find varied examples of the church's life in the Spirit.

B. Biblical Background

Paul named nine fruits of the Spirit: love, joy, peace, patience, kindness, generosity, faithfulness, gentleness, and self-control. The fruit of the Spirit has implications for individual believers, for the local and universal church, as well as for the global community in which we live. These nine characteristics—what we might call norms—if they regularly govern the ways in which we interact with each other, have great potential to change our politics, our business practices, our leadership styles, and our theories about education and public policy. In essence, they become ethical norms that order thought and behavior, and that come into direct contrast with discriminatory and prejudicial practices daily witnessed in the public sphere.

If the effects of a spiritual life are that a spiritual life bears fruit and bears particular kinds of fruit, then it might be argued that where there is no fruit, perhaps there is no Spirit. The Spirit is a barely definable, hardly recognizable, scarcely measureable entity. In classical Christian terms, we identify the Spirit as the third Person of the Trinity, so the best evidence for the presence of the Spirit in the life of the believer may just be the fruit. The biblical text indicates that there are at least four residual effects of life in the Spirit: (1) Life in the Spirit motivates one for transformative proclamation to the poor, the brokenhearted, the prisoner, and the captive. (2) Life in the Spirit exempts one from the penalties of the Mosaic Law. (3) Life in the Spirit disciplines character. (4) Life in the Spirit governs our relationships with each other. There is at least one additional work of the Spirit: the call to love.

II. EXPOSITION AND APPLICATION OF THE SCRIPTURE

A. A Spiritual Harvest
(Galatians 5:22-24)

But the fruit of the Spirit is love, joy, peace, longsuffering, gentleness, goodness, faith, Meekness, temperance: against such there is no law. And they that are Christ's have crucified the flesh with the affections and lusts.

Paul argued in the book of Galatians that faith in Christ and submission to the Spirit were daily disciplines that, if practiced, would have a particular kind of effect upon the human condition. The characteristics of the fruit of the Spirit are a penetrating regard for oneself and others. Paul argued that living with that kind of self-discipline produces fruit that is beneficial for individuals and the body of Christ. Furthermore, Paul's argument supports the harvest metaphor of reaping and sowing.

In an agricultural society the image is clear. If I purchase and plant a certain kind of seed, I can expect that my seed will produce its own kind. If I plant an apple seed, I can expect to get apple trees. If I plant a grapevine, I can expect to get grapes. The same is true in human relationships. If I plant or sow discord, I can expect to reap conflict. In other words, whatever kinds of characteristics and ethical norms a person lives by will be the same kind that he or she reaps. In light of Paul's argument, it is plausible to suggest that whatever the believer sows in the context of the larger society will also be reaped. If we sow violence, we will reap violence; if we sow peace, we will reap peace. This is all the more reason for believers to be aware of the larger effects that life in the Spirit can have.

Every believer is called upon and challenged by the demand to be a peacemaker. "Blessed are the peacemakers: for they shall be called the children of God" (Matthew 5:9). While lessons and commentaries providing exegetical remarks on the fruits of the Spirit rarely expose the more radical nature of these demands, a more integrative approach to Scripture cannot do otherwise. Believers are called to live out the command to love in the church as well as in the world. Given the increasingly violent nature of our society, America's participation in two wars, and the almost daily commentary we hear in the news on terrorism and violence among teens, the church has a window to witness publicly the Gospel of peace. Not only is the church's voice welcomed to offer an alternative vision for the world in which we live—but also, the church's response is a necessity. The Gospel of Christ is a gospel which requires the church to provoke others to live in peace, not war. The Prince of Peace came proclaiming a new hope: that all God's children would live out of its understanding of the call to love.

Sometimes passages of Scripture like the one emphasizing the fruit of the Spirit are interpreted to mean that the Christian should maintain a quiet resignation or passive indignation toward issues in the public sphere. That is to the contrary. There is nothing quiet and passive about love when we are called to share love with the death-row inmate or when we are called upon to stand in solidarity with the poor. The fruit of the Spirit has a political ideology: nonviolent protest. Martin Luther King Jr. spoke poignantly when he wrote, "The great tragedy is that Christianity failed to see that it had the revolutionary edge. You don't have to go to Karl Marx to learn how to be a revolutionary. I did not get my inspiration from Karl Marx; I got it from a man named Jesus, a Galilean saint who said He was anointed to heal the brokenhearted. He was anointed to deal with the problems of the poor. And that is where we get our inspiration" (*The Autobiography of Martin Luther King Jr.,* 351).

King found in the Scriptures a deep and profound sense of love and an operational model for pursuing love in the world. When the Christian exercises his or her right and responsibility to love, we might be able to say, "The kingdom of God is near" and "the Spirit of God is at work." It is through the fruit of the Spirit that believers witness maturity in the Christian's life.

B. Life in the Spirit (Galatians 5:25-26)

If we live in the Spirit, let us also walk in the Spirit. Let us not be desirous of vain glory, provoking one another, envying one another.

As children, we often linked arms with our best buddies or suddenly realized that while we were walking with them, we had begun to step in sequence with each other—like a marching band in a city parade or a military brigade whose steps are in sync to a distinct rhythm. As kids, we kept time and mirrored each other one leg at a time. The image Paul gave in verse 25 is just that, keeping in step with the Spirit. But just as easily as two friends become distracted by playful invitations from the latest neighborhood games, so are we distracted, too. We may get turned away from the Spirit by many of the same things that Satan used to tempt Jesus with in the wilderness: the temptation to rule and to feed our hunger for power and easy success. But Paul encouraged us to keep living by the Spirit. He encouraged us to keep in step with whatever feeds the Spirit.

Maintaining the kind of discipline required by the believer to keep step with the Spirit may be exhausting. What does tending to the Spirit look like? The kinds of disciplines associated with the spiritual life are prayer and meditation, devotional Scriptures, listening to music, reading, and tending to the care of the soul through journaling. There are perhaps other practices that each individual could add to the list. Thomas 'a Kempis, in *The Imitation of Christ,* found great solace in meditating on the life of Christ to get a better understanding of human nature.

Howard Thurman, Thomas More, George Fox, Emilie Townes, and Dorothee Soelle are modern figures committed to writing and teaching on the life of the Spirit. They are committed to thinking about the Spirit as that part of humanity that communicates directly with God. They are also committed to the idea that spirituality and the physical existence of humanity are two sides of the same coin. "The pneuma" or the "breath" is that which enlivens humanity. The most poignant example is the early Garden of Eden narrative where God breathed life into *Adam,* the Hebrew word for "humanity." The body comes alive by way of the Spirit.

Paul's exhortation has particular importance for believers who journey through difficult times. For believers who find themselves in an economy distraught by recession and uncertainty in world markets, Paul said not to grow weary of doing the right thing. It is easy to be overcome by economic, social, and political issues that tend to undermine human community by promoting unhealthy competition and distrust; but do not get tired of doing the right thing. In times like these, ancient biblical witness rings true yet again: do not get tired of doing the right thing.

In other words, these may seem like dark times, but Walter Brueggemann admonishes that energy comes from embracing the "inscrutable darkness"—because God is moving in the dark in ways that the "prince of darkness" cannot even discern. Just as a seed is planted in the shadows of the soil and begins to grow there and flourish in the rich underbrush, so the Spirit of God is moving in indescribable ways. We are only to trust the consistency of the Spirit.

C. Heavy Lifting (Galatians 6:1-5)

BRETHREN, IF a man be overtaken in a fault, ye which are spiritual, restore such an one in the spirit of meekness; considering thyself, lest thou also be tempted. Bear ye one another's burdens, and so fulfil the law of Christ. For if a man think himself to be something, when he is nothing, he deceiveth himself. But let every man prove his own work, and then shall he have rejoicing in himself alone, and not in another. For every man shall bear his own burden.

On the one hand, Paul said to carry each other's burdens. On the other, Paul said to carry your own load! In both cases, Paul was suggesting some heavy lifting. Carrying the load of another is "fulfilling the law of Christ." While each of us should carry our own loads, let's face it—sometimes a helping hand is good medicine for the soul. Another message is also clear: in helping someone else, we show a kind of loyalty and ultimate devotion to Christ; in helping someone else, we "fulfil the law of Christ" (Galatians 6:2).

Paul said that "fulfilling the law of Christ" may be the single most important example of the fruit of the Spirit at work. In fact, Paul evoked the "law of Christ" because Jesus submitted Himself to the law of God. The Cross represented the worst of human cruelty: betrayal in friendship, duplicity in religious leadership, and inconsistency in government. And yet, when Jesus hung on the cross amid the contradictions of human goodness and justice, He still managed to show the manifestation of His spiritual life, a life ultimately devoted to the will of God. He still managed to operate out of the larger purpose of His life. Jesus still managed to show the effects of a Spirit-led life. His last words marked the degree to which He was grounded in the life of the Spirit. Jesus' last words foreshadowed the fruit of the Spirit which Paul would later write about. We live in the shadow of that Cross.

The Cross was a juxtaposition of the best of human devotion and the worst of human deceit. The Cross represents humanity's utter loyalty to the regulation and punishment of those ideas not supported by religious hierarchies or sanctioned by state officials. Yet, the Cross also represents the failure of evil to completely overshadow good. It represents the indomitable power of love. It represents the incomprehensible power of faith. Lifted high, Scripture teaches, the Cross in all of its multiple meanings will draw humanity to Christ.

Boasting in the Cross of Christ reveals a radical commitment to life in the Spirit, whatever may come as a result. Radical commitment to life in the Spirit is captured brilliantly in the beloved hymn of the church, "When I Survey the Wondrous Cross." The first line of the hymn reads, "When I survey the wondrous cross/On which the Prince of Glory died/My richest gain I count but loss/And pour contempt on all my pride." The song, written by Sir Isaac Watts, shows a reflective encounter with the Cross. Until one thinks about the Cross over time and relates it to his or her own personal reflection about what it means to be committed to death, a revelation of the meaning of the Cross will be stagnant—devoid of human emotion and religious substance.

D. Sowing and Reaping
(Galatians 6:6-10)

Let him that is taught in the word communicate unto him that teacheth in all good things. Be not deceived; God is not mocked: for whatsoever a man soweth, that shall he also reap. For he that soweth to his flesh shall of the flesh reap corruption; but he that soweth to the Spirit shall of the Spirit reap life everlasting. And let us not be weary in well doing: for in due season we shall reap, if we faint not. As we have therefore opportunity, let us do good unto all men, especially unto them who are of the household of faith.

It is noteworthy to observe that there is a sudden change in the tone and topic of Paul's presentation in this sixth chapter. He abruptly brought up the topic of sharing in the context of what that means in living life in the Spirit. Paul was attempting to get across to his readers that those who live under the influence of the Spirit of God will want to adequately take care of those who live off their ministry of teaching the people of God. This is interpreted in the context of "sowing and reaping." When teachers/ministers sow into the lives of others, it is expected that they will reap from the harvest that eventually comes about.

Verses 7-10 expand upon this idea of sowing and reaping. God oversees the entire process. God cannot be fooled or mocked. It is a law of nature, both physically and spiritually, that whatever is sown will be reaped. This suggests, as Paul so ably put it, that if we live primarily to please our physical lives, then we will find ourselves spiritually depleted because we did not sow to the Spirit. However, if we live by the Spirit, then we will see the fruit of those efforts because we have a rich reward awaiting us in heaven.

III. CONCLUDING REFLECTION

The church has a responsibility to witness the work of the Spirit in the world. In a world filled with hate, the most radical response a believer may offer is love. The believer has a radical call to show forth joy where there is despair; to offer peace where there is war; to move with intentional patience where there is a frantic pace; to offer kindness in the face of greed; and to offer goodness where there is evil, faithfulness where there is lack of commitment, and gentleness and self-control where there is unchecked power. While the fruits of the Spirit should be our creative response to each other in the church, they should also function as the battle cry to do justice in the land. The fruits of the Spirit offer alternative ethical norms by which to govern ourselves and the work of the Spirit in the world.

PRAYER

Dear God, You have given us a great sense of Your abiding love. Help us stay the course and model that love to the dark corners of the earth. May we learn to understand the urgent work that we have through the Spirit. Guide our hearts and stir our imaginations to do Your work. In Jesus' name we pray. Amen.

WORD POWER

Spirit (pneuma)—the third Person of the Trinity. Paul made the distinction that the believer should trust in the work of the Holy Spirit, who perfects us in Christ.

HOME DAILY BIBLE READINGS
(February 20-26, 2012)

Fruits of Redemption

MONDAY, February 20: "Renewed by the Holy Spirit" (Titus 3:1-7)

TUESDAY, February 21: "Chosen to Be Obedient" (1 Peter 1:1-5)

WEDNESDAY, February 22: "Supporting Your Faith" (2 Peter 1:3-8)

THURSDAY, February 23: "Faith Working through Love" (Galatians 5:2-6)

FRIDAY, February 24: "Called to Freedom" (Galatians 5:7-15)

SATURDAY, February 25: "The Works of the Flesh" (Galatians 5:16-21)

SUNDAY, February 26: "Living by the Spirit" (Galatians 5:22–6:10)

God's Creative Word

GENERAL INTRODUCTION

The spring quarter is an in-depth study of John's gospel through the theological lens of creation. Creation was more than God's one-time action of bringing the world into existence; it involved God's ongoing action of reconciling and recreating, now and in eternity. God's creating Word was, is, and shall be making all things good.

Unit I, *The Word Was in the Beginning,* has six lessons. The first two lessons stress the creative power of God's Word and the many nuances of understanding the meaning behind the Word. Lesson 3 looks at the power of Jesus' words to change water into wine, to clear the Temple, to address the longing of the human heart, and to heal. Lesson 4 looks at the power of the Word for salvation. On Palm Sunday and Easter Sunday, we look at the death and resurrection of Jesus as recorded in John.

The three lessons of **Unit II,** *The Word Is Here and Now,* offer a study in the power of Jesus' words as He lived among us as a human being. Jesus' words had the power to purify the Temple, to restore human life, and to heal.

Unit III, *The Word Will Be,* has four lessons. These lessons look at some of the "I am" sayings of Jesus. They give us a sense of the divinity of Jesus and of his eternal power to promise us life, security, resurrection, and the way to God.

WISDOM'S PART IN CREATION

DEVOTIONAL READING: **Psalm 8**
PRINT PASSAGE: **Proverbs 8:22-35**

BACKGROUND SCRIPTURE: **Proverbs 8**
KEY VERSE: **Proverbs 8:33**

Proverbs 8:22-35—KJV

22 The LORD possessed me in the beginning of his way, before his works of old.

23 I was set up from everlasting, from the beginning, or ever the earth was.

24 When there were no depths, I was brought forth; when there were no fountains abounding with water.

25 Before the mountains were settled, before the hills was I brought forth:

26 While as yet he had not made the earth, nor the fields, nor the highest part of the dust of the world.

27 When he prepared the heavens, I was there: when he set a compass upon the face of the depth:

28 When he established the clouds above: when he strengthened the fountains of the deep:

29 When he gave to the sea his decree, that the waters should not pass his commandment: when he appointed the foundations of the earth:

30 Then I was by him, as one brought up with him: and I was daily his delight, rejoicing always before him;

31 Rejoicing in the habitable part of his earth; and my delights were with the sons of men.

32 Now therefore hearken unto me, O ye children: for blessed are they that keep my ways.

33 Hear instruction, and be wise, and refuse it not.

34 Blessed is the man that heareth me, watching daily at my gates, waiting at the posts of my doors.

35 For whoso findeth me findeth life, and shall obtain favour of the LORD.

Proverbs 8:22-35—NIV

22 "The LORD brought me forth as the first of his works, before his deeds of old;

23 I was appointed from eternity, from the beginning, before the world began.

24 When there were no oceans, I was given birth, when there were no springs abounding with water;

25 before the mountains were settled in place, before the hills, I was given birth,

26 before he made the earth or its fields or any of the dust of the world.

27 I was there when he set the heavens in place, when he marked out the horizon on the face of the deep,

28 when he established the clouds above and fixed securely the fountains of the deep,

29 when he gave the sea its boundary so the waters would not overstep his command, and when he marked out the foundations of the earth.

30 Then I was the craftsman at his side. I was filled with delight day after day, rejoicing always in his presence,

31 rejoicing in his whole world and delighting in mankind.

32 Now then, my sons, listen to me; blessed are those who keep my ways.

33 Listen to my instruction and be wise; do not ignore it.

34 Blessed is the man who listens to me, watching daily at my doors, waiting at my doorway.

35 For whoever finds me finds life and receives favor from the LORD."

UNIFYING LESSON PRINCIPLE

People appreciate wisdom and yearn for a depth of wisdom for themselves and others. What is the root of this longing for wisdom? The writer of the book of Proverbs speaks about Wisdom's having a divine origin, being present as God created all things, and having a role with God in Creation.

TOPICAL OUTLINE OF THE LESSON

I. **Introduction**
   A. The Value of Wisdom
   B. Biblical Background

II. **Exposition and Application of the Scripture**
   A. Wise Up to God
      (Proverbs 8:22-26)
   B. Wise Up to Jesus
      (Proverbs 8:27-29)
   C. Wise Up to Life
      (Proverbs 8:30-35)

III. **Concluding Reflection**

LESSON OBJECTIVES

Upon the completion of this lesson, the students will know:

1. That God's wisdom was crucial to the creation of the world;
2. How to connect the biblical narrative to stories of wisdom manifesting in their own lives;
3. That wisdom is available to the discerning person; and,
4. That wisdom is needed for fulfilled living.

POINTS TO BE EMPHASIZED
ADULT/YOUTH

Adult Topic: Wise Up!
Youth Topic: Got Wisdom?
Adult/Youth Key Verse: Proverbs 8:33
Print Passage: Proverbs 8:22-35

—Some people wrestle with the idea of Wisdom's being an eternal quality of God and, yet, it is spoken of here as being created.

—Some commentators take this description of wisdom to be a description of the pre-incarnate Word of God, Jesus.

—Like God's grace, wisdom is offered to humans and must be accepted by them to be effective.

—As wisdom delights in God, so God delights in wisdom—and in any who would attain wisdom as well.

—Since the creation of wisdom is not included in either Genesis story, its position in creation is sometimes confusing to Christians.

—The word *created* in verse 22 can also be translated as "got, possessed, or acquired."

CHILDREN

Children Topic: Learn from Wisdom
Key Verse: Proverbs 8:22
Print Passage: Proverbs 8:22-35

—Wisdom was God's first creation.

—Wisdom was a witness to and a participant in the creation of the heavens and earth.

—Wisdom rejoiced in the created order, including humankind.

—Humans are urged to learn from Wisdom's instruction.

—Those who apply wisdom are pleasing to God.

I. INTRODUCTION

A. The Value of Wisdom

People around the world, and in every culture, place a high value on wisdom. Sages, griots, and wise women and men are esteemed in their particular communities for acquiring a deep understanding of the arts, sciences, professional arenas, religions, and other areas. There is a general expectation among people that the elders of the community possess a certain degree of wisdom by virtue of their years. It is also generally understood that all persons can access wisdom through study, sensitivity, and spiritual discipline. God instituted creation through the implementation of wisdom. Wisdom is indeed a witness to creation and was present as God unfolded the universe. Acquiring wisdom, then, becomes an important goal of Christians. Upon acquiring it, we affirm the presence of God within us through our wise thinking and wise actions.

Youth and *folly* are seen as enemies of wisdom. Being young and foolish makes us more susceptible to distraction. Failure to pay attention to what is going on around us can lead to disaster—so those of us who seek to gain wisdom must constantly pray for our children and young people who are not yet clear as to the benefit of wise action.

Ego and greed may also impede many adults' use of wisdom. The inability to control our appetites and our needs for self-satisfaction can cause even the elderly to reject wisdom. The need to acquire and consume beyond what our means will allow can lead to unwise courses of action in us all. It becomes important for God's people, then, to seek to be guided by God's wisdom daily as we negotiate the trials of life.

B. Biblical Background

It is generally accepted that King Solomon wrote most of the book of Proverbs, including the passage that is studied in this lesson. Chapters 30 and 31 are attributed to "Agur" and "King Lemuel," respectively. Chapter 25 mentions that the "men of Hezekiah" copied that section of the book of Proverbs, also authored by King Solomon. These facts and other internal evidence suggests that the book was compiled over several hundred years. Proverbs 8 is part of a larger section devoted to the subject of wisdom. There are similar sections that discuss adultery, the "adultress," and folly. In Proverbs 8–9, wisdom is described in feminine form.

Though feminine in form, conventional definitions of *chokmah* (pronounced "kok MAH") have to do with a group of learned men who specialized in rhetoric and clever arguments. Wisdom itself was reflective of the cleverness of females who were notorious for winning more arguments than men. More than that, because wisdom was feminine, she was intimately associated with creation. But we must be careful to understand that the writer employed the literary tool of personification here (as he did with *folly* in Proverbs 9:13-18), and not revealing some deeper understanding about the Creation. Ideally, we can understand wisdom to be an attribute of God that is available in good quantity to those who ask God for it.

That metaphorical connection notwithstanding, wisdom may be understood as the intentional and refined skill of engaging life with a clear understanding of and sense of respect for the dangers and pitfalls that present themselves as obstacles during the journey. Proverbs 8:22-35 presents wisdom as being present in creation: before it began; during its unfolding; and after its completion. We may view wisdom as a way to overcome life's obstacles without repeating the same mistakes, since we tend to repeat our mistakes if we do not learn from them the first time.

II. EXPOSITION AND APPLICATION OF THE SCRIPTURE

A. Wise Up to God
(Proverbs 8:22-26)

The Lord possessed me in the beginning of his way, before his works of old. I was set up from everlasting, from the beginning, or ever the earth was. When there were no depths, I was brought forth; when there were no fountains abounding with water. Before the mountains were settled, before the hills was I brought forth: While as yet he had not made the earth, nor the fields, nor the highest part of the dust of the world.

In the Old Testament, *wisdom* (*binah*) in the Hebrew is defined in terms of teaching, understanding, or intelligence. It may also refer to *skill* (*chokmah, chokmoth*) and/or "craftiness, subtlety" (*ormah*), among other similarly related terms. In the New Testament, the Greek rendering of the word *wisdom* is from the term *sophia*. The primacy of wisdom is established beginning in verse 22 of Proverbs 8. The author employs rich metaphors to describe the role of wisdom in the Creation. Wisdom is introduced here as an attribute of God that is revealed to those who have the sensitivity to perceive "her" presence. Wisdom, in this text, is presented as a necessary component of creation. The very earth upon which we stand is founded upon the wisdom of God. Born before the oceans, the mountains, or the hills, wisdom sits apart. Even before the heavens were flung into place God's intelligence was manifested through God's creative power.

Verses 22-31 actually comprise a hymn that beautifully portrays the movement of wisdom as coming forth from God before any of God's ancient actions. Wisdom is described as being "appointed" (verse 23) by God even before God made the universe. In other wisdom texts found in the Bible, specifically the books of Psalms and Job, there is language that describes the sea and the mountains as being brought forth by God. In the book of Genesis, the "fountains of the deep" are highlighted as being foundational to creation. In the book of Proverbs, great effort is expended to help the reader visualize the order of creation as requiring the presence of wisdom before anything else could come forth through the power of God. As the verses of this hymn unfold, the voice of wisdom is established as a primordial presence. Wisdom is in place as God sets the boundaries and limitations of the earth. Wisdom is the witness to God's handiwork and shows herself to those who are able to discern her.

B. Wise Up to Jesus
(Proverbs 8:27-29)

When he prepared the heavens, I was there: when he set a compass upon the face of the depth: When he established the clouds above: when he strengthened the fountains of the deep: When he gave to the sea his decree, that the waters should not pass his commandment: when he appointed the foundations of the earth.

Some commentators have used this description of wisdom found in Proverbs 8 to point to the pre-incarnate Word of God—Jesus the Christ. Though the character of Christ may be located in the descriptive verses of Proverbs 8, they should not be viewed as a direct description of Jesus Christ. Without a doubt, however, the life of Christ is one that is characterized by the embodiment of wisdom and right thinking. And the pre-incarnate Christ was present with God from before creation, being equal and eternal with God. Indeed, Paul did refer to Christ as the "wisdom of God" (see 1 Corinthians 1:24). However, this passage cannot be lifted in its entirety and applied as a prophetic reference to Christ.

The key aspect of the lesson is presented to us in the Key Verse of Scripture. Verse 33 reads, "Hear instruction, and be wise, and refuse it not." The text admonishes us to listen for the voice of instruction, which suggests that wisdom may be imparted from one person to another. It is seemingly suggested in this verse that we should not only pay attention to the voice within, but also listen to the voices that emerge from those around us. The word *instruction* here is translated from the Hebrew word *musar*, which could mean "chastisement"

or "teaching." There is a price to pay for wisdom. One must be willing to listen to others and to endure hard teachings that at times may make us feel uncomfortable. God's wisdom may be contained in vessels that we did not expect to carry it. Those of us who wish to be wise will have to be sensitive to the voices that may not speak loudly or authoritatively but, yet, hold the keys to the wisdom that we need in order to become our best selves.

C. Wise Up to Life
(Proverbs 8:30-35)

Then I was by him, as one brought up with him: and I was daily his delight, rejoicing always before him; Rejoicing in the habitable part of his earth; and my delights were with the sons of men. Now therefore hearken unto me, O ye children: for blessed are they that keep my ways. Hear instruction, and be wise, and refuse it not. Blessed is the man that heareth me, watching daily at my gates, waiting at the posts of my doors. For whoso findeth me findeth life, and shall obtain favour of the LORD.

Wisdom is described as a "craftsman" (verse 30, NIV) that was at God's side during the unfolding of creation. A major part in the development of Christian maturity is found in the acquisition of wisdom. Wisdom, however, is not always easily acquired. Some wisdom takes time, patience, and experience to grasp. We are admonished by James to ask God for wisdom. And God will give it—some immediately, some through the process of time. No one is born wise. "We live and we learn" is an old adage that holds its worth and value. While this does not always refer to godly wisdom, it definitely is about acquiring beneficial experience. As one sage professor said to a group of eager students, "We do not learn from experience, we learn through reflection upon our experiences."

Acquiring a more natural form of wisdom is conveyed through a story that is told of a young woman who was unemployed. She had just graduated from college with a freshly minted degree in hand. Because of her hard work and long hours of study, her grades were excellent. She graduated at the top of her class and embarked upon the task of finding a job with determination and a true sense of expectation. She had diligently prepared herself to make the best impression at the interviews that she had secured. Her interview suit was always freshly dry-cleaned, and her hair was always professionally coiffed. She stayed on prayer, loved the Lord, and was dedicated to her family, her church, and her community. She seemed to have everything she needed to be employable, but despite all of her preparation and sincere effort, she was unable to get a job because she had no experience. Finally, after a long day of fruitless encounters, she was interviewed by a "sistah" who had risen to the position of bank president. This woman was savvy and sagacious. She knew the "ins and outs" of the banking industry because she paid attention to every detail of the business as she climbed the corporate ladder—shattering glass ceiling after glass ceiling as she rose to the top of her field.

Although frustrated and disappointed, the young woman collected her confidence and walked into the office of the bank president. She placed her portfolio on the desk of the president and began the interview process. After a few minutes of professional exchange, the knowing glance of this wise and compassionate "seasoned" sister disarmed the young lady and she began to weep under the weight of her being disappointed by having not found

work. Through her tears, the young woman asked the older, "How in the world will I ever become as successful as you?" The seasoned "sistah" said, "by making good decisions." The younger lady said, "How do I make good decisions?" The older woman replied, "Experience." The younger woman then asked, "How do I get experience?" to which the older woman replied, "By making bad decisions." Experience is a tough teacher, but the lessons learned through experience will result in the acquisition of wisdom, if we pay attention to the process.

III. CONCLUDING REFLECTION

Wisdom has been defined as "the ability to use the best means at the best time to accomplish the best end." It means taking what you have and making the best use of whatever that may be. It means considering the needs of the community to bring about the greatest good for the poor and suffering persons around us. We are called by God to creatively resist forces that continue our suffering. By studying God's Word, acquiring knowledge and understanding through formal education, and paying attention to people and our surroundings, we can "increase in wisdom and stature" as Jesus did. Jesus created ways to encounter and engage in relationship with the people in the community around Him. He creatively "healed" them out of His compassion for them—according to the wisdom that was within Him. Jesus understood the pain and the plight of the people, and His understanding propelled Him into action so that issues would be addressed.

It has been stated that wisdom, like the pre-incarnate Christ, was present before the world was created—because God needed wisdom to create the awesome and intricate interconnecting systems of operation in creation. God's wisdom is manifest throughout the wonder of creation, and the biblical text found in Proverbs 8 relies heavily on the literary technique known as *personification* to illustrate the function of wisdom among those who would apply it in their lives. Wisdom is seen as a feminine being who calls out to everyone. Those who would reject her find themselves lacking, but the one who accepts her becomes wise. "I love those who love me" is a phrase attributed to wisdom that reflects the reality of an intimate connection between those who embrace her and, likewise, the disconnection from those who refuse her love.

To love wisdom is to make oneself available to be a lifelong learner. This is what it means to resist "ignoring" wisdom's instruction. One who pursues wisdom can never assume that he or she has learned it all. Being open to learning makes wisdom more accessible—because a closed mind, like a closed mouth, is unable to receive. As we listen to hear the voice of wisdom speak, we do so with expectation of receiving for the purpose of sharing. Wisdom, like love, becomes much more valuable when it is shared with others who are in need.

PRAYER

Dear God, we thank You for the wisdom that gives us the power to be creative vessels of knowledge and understanding, who work together to strengthen Your church and community. In Jesus' name we pray. Amen.

WORD POWER

Wisdom (Hebrew: *chokmaw* [kok MAW]): "skillful; wit"—This term is used to refer to special abilities—mental or physical—that are exceptional and that show one's uniqueness or distinction.

Wisdom (Greek: *sophia* [soh FEE ah])—This term is akin to a term that means "clear." As it refers to Jesus Christ in 1 Corinthians 1:24, Christ is the "clear" expression of God. He is clearer than seeing God's power in creation, the birth of a child, or any other natural experiences that raise our awareness of the spiritual realm.

HOME DAILY BIBLE READINGS
(February 27–March 4, 2012)

Wisdom's Part in Creation

MONDAY, February 27: "The Call of Wisdom" (Proverbs 8:1-11)

TUESDAY, February 28: "The Gifts of Wisdom" (Proverbs 8:12-21)

WEDNESDAY, February 29: "Before the Foundation of the World" (Ephesians 1:3-10)

THURSDAY, March 1: "The Handiwork of God" (Psalm 8)

FRIDAY, March 2: "The Firstborn of All Creation" (Colossians 1:15-19)

SATURDAY, March 3: "Creation Awaits Glory" (Romans 8:18-25)

SUNDAY, March 4: "Find Wisdom, Find Life" (Proverbs 8:22-35)

LESSON 2   March 11, 2012

THE WORD BECAME FLESH

DEVOTIONAL READING: **Isaiah 40:21-26**
PRINT PASSAGE: **John 1:1-14**

BACKGROUND SCRIPTURE: **John 1:1-14**
KEY VERSE: **John 1:14**

John 1:1-14—KJV

IN THE beginning was the Word, and the Word was with God, and the Word was God.

2 The same was in the beginning with God.

3 All things were made by him; and without him was not any thing made that was made.

4 In him was life; and the life was the light of men.

5 And the light shineth in darkness; and the darkness comprehended it not.

6 There was a man sent from God, whose name was John.

7 The same came for a witness, to bear witness of the Light, that all men through him might believe.

8 He was not that Light, but was sent to bear witness of that Light.

9 That was the true Light, which lighteth every man that cometh into the world.

10 He was in the world, and the world was made by him, and the world knew him not.

11 He came unto his own, and his own received him not.

12 But as many as received him, to them gave he power to become the sons of God, even to them that believe on his name:

13 Which were born, not of blood, nor of the will of the flesh, nor of the will of man, but of God.

14 And the Word was made flesh, and dwelt among us, (and we beheld his glory, the glory as of the only begotten of the Father,) full of grace and truth.

John 1:1-14—NIV

IN THE beginning was the Word, and the Word was with God, and the Word was God.

2 He was with God in the beginning.

3 Through him all things were made; without him nothing was made that has been made.

4 In him was life, and that life was the light of men.

5 The light shines in the darkness, but the darkness has not understood it.

6 There came a man who was sent from God; his name was John.

7 He came as a witness to testify concerning that light, so that through him all men might believe.

8 He himself was not the light; he came only as a witness to the light.

9 The true light that gives light to every man was coming into the world.

10 He was in the world, and though the world was made through him, the world did not recognize him.

11 He came to that which was his own, but his own did not receive him.

12 Yet to all who received him, to those who believed in his name, he gave the right to become children of God—

13 children born not of natural descent, nor of human decision or a husband's will, but born of God.

14 The Word became flesh and made his dwelling among us. We have seen his glory, the glory of the One and Only, who came from the Father, full of grace and truth.

UNIFYING LESSON PRINCIPLE

People are often curious about how things began. How are we to answer our own and others' questions about the origins of faith? Jesus, who was fully human and fully involved in human society, was also personally divine from the beginning, and was God's agent in the world, creating and redeeming.

TOPICAL OUTLINE OF THE LESSON

I. Introduction
A. A Picture of Jesus
B. Biblical Background

II. Exposition and Application of the Scripture
A. The Word in the Beginning (John 1:1-5)
B. The Life and Light of the Word (John 1:6-9)
C. A Witness of the Word (John 1:10-14)

III. Concluding Reflection

LESSON OBJECTIVES

Upon the completion of this lesson, the students will:

1. Be acquainted with the uniqueness of the theological claims in the gospel of John;
2. Know how to consider the impact of the "Word made flesh" upon the world; and,
3. Know the uniqueness of the personality of the Christ.

POINTS TO BE EMPHASIZED
ADULT/YOUTH

Adult Topic: **From the Beginning**
Youth Topic: **Always Been There**
Adult/Youth Key Verse: **John 1:14**
Print Passage: **John 1:1-14**

—John 1:3 refutes the Greek idea that reality was separated into spiritual and material realms.
—Light and darkness are significant themes in the book of John.
—The word *overcome* in verse 5 is translated "understood" or "comprehend" in some versions. The Greek word *katalambano* has a double meaning similar to the English word *grasp*: one can grasp an idea (i.e., "understand") or grasp a person (i.e., "apprehend, overcome"). The double meaning may well be deliberate: Jesus' enemies could not understand Him, so they tried, in vain, to overcome Him.
—Colossians 1:16 supports the idea that the Word (Jesus) was active in creation (see John 1:3, 10).
—"Coming into the world" (birth) describes everyone, but it is a familiar description of Christ in the writings of this evangelist (see John 12:46; 16:28; 18:37; 1 Timothy 1:15; 1 John 4:9).
—In John's gospel, light and darkness are two physical qualities that are used to symbolize articles of faith.

CHILDREN

Children Topic: **In the Beginning**
Key Verse: **John 1:14**
Print Passage: **John 1:1-14**

—The Word is usually associated with the Son but is also understood to be God.

—The Word brought life and light into the world.

—John gave testimony to the Incarnate Word.

—The Word gives believers direct access to God.

—Most of the world did not accept the Word.

I. INTRODUCTION

A. A Picture of Jesus

To better appreciate John's theological picture of Jesus, we need to examine the literary frame that John used to portray this magnanimous, one-of-a-kind God-human person called Jesus of Nazareth. Jesus is the Word of God made flesh, communicating and revealing divine truth through the humanity of Jesus, who is the living God in human form. Human speech is limited in its communication. Yet, God uses human language as a channel for the expression of divine truth. The Greek term *logos* (translated "Word") found in John 1:1 shows God's desire and ability to speak, communicate, or reveal divine truth to the human family. God's *Logos*, which Jesus represents, acts as a bridge between God and human life, and fulfills the need for human beings to listen to God by receiving divine truth as embodied and lived out through the life and deeds of Jesus Christ. The principle of the *Logos* opens up to the human understanding the idea of the living God of creation—who in the beginning brought the world into existence. Without the principle of Jesus as the divine *Logos,* then an understanding of God's personality as love and God's will and power as a living and active force in the world would be incomprehensible. The humanity of Jesus gives God's love flesh with which we can identify as the Word dwells among the human family, revealing and validating God's love for His creation.

B. Biblical Background

The Bible embraces various aspects of literature, including use of allegory, historical narratives, parables, sermons, apocalyptic literature, poetry, letters, and epic poetry. Each literary genre has its own rules through which to interpret what the author intends to say. This is coupled with the fact that it is God who has inspired the Scriptures, so this must be the guidepost for our final interpretation and application. John's introduction or prologue features a special literary genre known as Semitic poetry. Semitic poetry contains a powerful communicative feature called parallel sense-making. It is perfect for meditation and worship. In this literary genre, one line in the poem states a truth, and then the next line restates that same truth using slightly different words. A clear example of parallel sense-making in Semitic poetry is in Psalm 24:1, which reads, "The earth is the LORD's and the fulness thereof; the world, and they that dwell therein."

The intent is to line up and match up similar ideas. Each truth is carefully aligned. The logic of the poetry is precisely and carefully constructed, even layered, placing matching ideas on top of each other. This is also a rhythmic device providing a clue to its reading for us. The *Broadman Commentary* observes the type of parallelism in John's prologue as "climactic or stair-step parallelism." In climactic or step parallelism, a new line carries forward a key element contained in the preceding line. In most versions of Scripture, John's prologue is framed in the sentence format—this way, the reader immediately notices a rhythmic lyrical pattern in this stair-step parallelism:

- In the beginning was the Word/and the Word was with God/and the Word was God (or the Word is what God was).

We see this feature again in verses 4-5:

- In him was life/and the life was the light of men/and the light shineth in darkness/ And the darkness comprehended it not.

Each line contains an element of the previous line, yet it carries the reader forward to another related idea in a stair-step pattern. It is a masterful way of handling a profound idea—if it is true that "less is more." In this language format, it is what might be characterized as "economy of statement." It has no excess verbiage—none at all—just a few tiny words conveying tons of meaning, and it does it instantly! Instant impact of a profound truth has power and can move us to feel what is not just profound, but what is majestic about that truth. Perhaps this is the reason why so many scholars and commentaries like *The Broadman Bible Commentary* refer to John 1:1-18 as a "majestic prologue" or a poetic meditation on the Word of God.

II. EXPOSITION AND APPLICATION OF THE SCRIPTURE

A. The Word in the Beginning
(John 1:1-5)

IN THE beginning was the Word, and the Word was with God, and the Word was God. The same was in the beginning with God. All things were made by him; and without him was not any thing made that was made. In him was life; and the life was the light of men. And the light shineth in darkness; and the darkness comprehended it not.

The ancient use and understanding of the *Logos*/Word implies something majestic, profound, and grandiose in creation. It points the human mind to the invisible, timeless origin of visible reality. It attempts to usher human awareness to an area behind the scenes of observable phenomena to the underlying ordering principle behind creation and the invisible spiritual glue holding it all together. The material world is second-generation reality brought about by spiritual forces. This is more than mere thought. It is a majestic insight that illuminates our lack of intelligence concerning an almost unfathomable mystery. This mystery is fully disclosed in the Word, or *Logos*, in the beginning. The presence of Jesus marks this mystery as revealed, but humankind did not recognize or know it. The value of John's version is that John knew this mystery in a unique sense. He asserted that Jesus is eternal and identical to and intimately connected with God before creation. Jesus is what is holding creation together. Jesus is both behind it all yet present in it all. To go further, the genius of these short five stanzas according to *The Broadman Bible Commentary* is that John grappled with three of the most profound issues of human existence: the relationship of eternity to time, of spirit to matter, and of good to evil. Learned men from every culture and clime have ceaselessly pondered over the relationship between eternity and time. According to John's prologue, Jesus is eternity in time, not eternity existing *outside* of time. He is God in human flesh, or (as in Matthew's gospel) He is called *Immanuel*, which means "God with us."

Adolphus Huxley said, "Man is always examining this wonderful frame that he finds himself living in." The author of the book of John declared that it was Jesus, the Word (or *Logos)* of God, who created this wonderful frame called our universe. In other words, the Word dwells among us. Whether detectable by an electron microscope or revealed, John declared that it is Jesus who is holding this wonderful frame together. Modern science has yet to name this entity that is holding the atoms together in all material phenomena. They see the atoms moving at tremendous speeds, yet not spinning out of control. This mysterious organizing principle keeps the atoms in our bodies, our cars, the tables we eat on, the floors we stand on, and the trees we sit under moving around in the same basic space all day. If not, every material thing in the observable universe would fall apart.

Verse 4 of John 1 reads, "In Him was life; and the life was the light of men." This is a further development of John's idea of Jesus as *Logos*/Word. The Greeks were satisfied with the *Logos'* being some ordering principle that held matter together. John's association of Jesus as the *Logos*/Word transcended the Greek notion of *Logos*/Word's being a mere scientific principle or axiom. It is a mysterious, luminous, divine living entity dwelling among and with humanity. It is life. One can refer to the phenomenon of light literally or metaphorically—meaning "right conduct, intelligence, and/or a manifestation of the presence of God." The problem of the cosmic conflict between the forces of good and the forces of evil is resolved in verse 5. It was thought to exist prior to man's arrival on the planet. Evil is characterized as darkness, and light as good. Men in this realm are in darkness, but Jesus—as the light of God—has come to this dark realm for us and the forces of darkness will lose, or as John put it: "The darkness comprehended it not" (John 1:5).

B. The Life and Light of the Word (John 1:6-9)

There was a man sent from God, whose name was John. The same came for a witness, to bear witness of the Light, that all men through him might believe. He was not that Light, but was sent to bear witness of that Light. That was the true Light, which lighteth every man that cometh into the world.

John the Baptist was an extraordinary religious figure when Jesus came on the scene. His was a voice crying in the wilderness of Judea to make straight the way of the Lord. John's voice was heard in Palestine. Each day (except on the Sabbath), the Jews went to the marketplaces to buy and sell. Their voices mingled with Greek and Roman merchants selling their wares. There were beggars crying out for alms. Once in a while, the blast from a royal trumpet could be heard for miles as a prelude to some royal edict's being announced from Caesar or a governor. Yet, in the very airwaves that came through the marketplace and among the cacophony of voices crying, John's voice was heard crying in the wilderness. People by the droves went out to the Jordan and were further captivated by a lone figure dressed in camel hair. He was compelling in his witness and made many disciples. Large crowds followed John. It was easy for unthinking people to confuse John's as the voice of the Promised Messiah. The author of this text found a way to affirm John the Baptist as a compelling religious figure connected with the mission and ministry of the Word; yet, it distinguished him from the Word. It is stated in verse 7 that John was a witness who was sent to bear witness of the Light. It is stated in verse 8 that John was not that Light, but was sent to bear witness of that Light.

C. A Witness of the Word
(John 1:10-14)

He was in the world, and the world was made by him, and the world knew him not. He came unto his own, and his own received him not. But as many as received him, to them gave he power to become the sons of God, even to them that believe on his name: Which were born, not of blood, nor of the will of the flesh, nor of the will of man, but of God. And the Word was made flesh, and dwelt among us, (and we beheld his glory, the glory as of the only begotten of the Father,) full of grace and truth.

It is stated in verse 10 that the Word (Jesus) was in the world, and the world was made by Him, and the world knew Him not. What a painful irony presented here of Jesus as Creator, rejected by creatures that He Himself had made. Notice that, initially, John presented Jesus as a person so magnanimous and elevated. He employed the same stair-step parallelism

of Semitic poetry toward the closing of this prologue to contrast this world's response.

He was in the world/and the world was made by Him/and the world knew Him not/ He came unto His own/and His own received Him not. Jesus is one-of-a-kind—a divine personality in human flesh, full of grace and truth. The divine character, personality, and nature of Jesus alone were not recognized by the covenant community of which He was a member by birth, nationality, and race. The reason for this is rooted in a phenomenon that was deeper than birth, nationality, and race. Spiritual darkness could not comprehend the light of the revealed reality. This darkness is deeper than blood ties, tribal connections, and patriotism combined. Humanity's reasoning can be darkened. One can be conceptually blind, not recognizing the ideas and concepts that a teacher is sharing. Once shared, however, it is up to the individual to choose to live in conceptual blindness or allow his or her mind to become host to new thoughts and ideas. In other words, let the voice of God speak and be heard. New ideas have a way of stretching the mind. One writer said that a mind stretched by a new idea never returns to its original dimensions. Perhaps this is why so many people are comfortable with the familiar and have placed a "Do Not Disturb" sign on their minds. This could never be the case with God. Jesus is the manifested idea of God's redemptive plan for God's children, an illumination that darkness cannot shut out. Some people work hard to stay in darkness because the light of God hurts their human eyes. But when humanity awakens to God, it is different from the world's reality. The light of the Word does not come from human origins, nor can it be comprehended by human intellect alone. Thus, to live in darkness becomes problematic when the light of life dwells in human flesh. Another way to speak of this truth is to recognize that the humanity of God has moved into the human neighborhood.

III. CONCLUDING REFLECTION

What occurred in the beginning with God continues today. God is yet illuminating divine truth through the humanity, life, and deeds of Jesus. As one scholar puts it, Jesus is the parable of God. We can know how human life was intended to be lived by the parable of Jesus' life. Why does humanity choose to live in darkness when the light of God shines upon us? This is the question of the Gospel as well as the response of God to our need for God's loving grace and gift of salvation. We are encouraged to walk in the light of the *Logos,* or Word of God.

PRAYER

Dear God, help us to learn and grow and to be changed by what we experience of the Word of God as a reality in our lives. In Jesus' name we pray. Amen.

WORD POWER

Beginning (Greek: *arkhay* [ar KAY])—a commencement. Academic graduation ceremonies, or commencements, mark the beginning of a new life for graduates. Much study, time, parental sacrifice, money, meals, and many other things brought them to the place of that new beginning. In the same way, Christ is the source of our commencement—our beginning.

HOME DAILY BIBLE READINGS
(March 5-11, 2012)

The Word Became Flesh

MONDAY, March 5: "The Beginning of the Year" (Exodus 12:1-8)

TUESDAY, March 6: "The Beginning of Wisdom" (Psalm 111)

WEDNESDAY, March 7: "In the Beginning, God..." (Genesis 1:1-5)

THURSDAY, March 8: "From the Foundations of the Earth" (Isaiah 40:21-26)

FRIDAY, March 9: "The Beginning of the Gospel" (Mark 1:1-8)

SATURDAY, March 10: "Beginning from Jerusalem" (Luke 24:44-49)

SUNDAY, March 11: "In the Beginning, the Word..." (John 1:1-14)

LESSON 3   March 18, 2012

THE WEDDING AT CANA

DEVOTIONAL READING: **John 17:1-5**
PRINT PASSAGE: **John 2:1-12**

BACKGROUND SCRIPTURE: **John 2:1-12**
KEY VERSE: **John 2:11**

John 2:1-12—KJV

AND THE third day there was a marriage in Cana of Galilee; and the mother of Jesus was there:

2 And both Jesus was called, and his disciples, to the marriage.

3 And when they wanted wine, the mother of Jesus saith unto him, They have no wine.

4 Jesus saith unto her, Woman, what have I to do with thee? mine hour is not yet come.

5 His mother saith unto the servants, Whatsoever he saith unto you, do it.

6 And there were set there six waterpots of stone, after the manner of the purifying of the Jews, containing two or three firkins apiece.

7 Jesus saith unto them, Fill the waterpots with water. And they filled them up to the brim.

8 And he saith unto them, Draw out now, and bear unto the governor of the feast. And they bare it.

9 When the ruler of the feast had tasted the water that was made wine, and knew not whence it was: (but the servants which drew the water knew;) the governor of the feast called the bridegroom,

10 And saith unto him, Every man at the beginning doth set forth good wine; and when men have well drunk, then that which is worse: but thou hast kept the good wine until now.

11 This beginning of miracles did Jesus in Cana of Galilee, and manifested forth his glory; and his disciples believed on him.

12 After this he went down to Capernaum, he, and his mother, and his brethren, and his disciples: and they continued there not many days.

John 2:1-12—NIV

ON THE third day a wedding took place at Cana in Galilee. Jesus' mother was there,

2 and Jesus and his disciples had also been invited to the wedding.

3 When the wine was gone, Jesus' mother said to him, "They have no more wine."

4 "Dear woman, why do you involve me?" Jesus replied. "My time has not yet come."

5 His mother said to the servants, "Do whatever he tells you."

6 Nearby stood six stone water jars, the kind used by the Jews for ceremonial washing, each holding from twenty to thirty gallons.

7 Jesus said to the servants, "Fill the jars with water"; so they filled them to the brim.

8 Then he told them, "Now draw some out and take it to the master of the banquet." They did so,

9 and the master of the banquet tasted the water that had been turned into wine. He did not realize where it had come from, though the servants who had drawn the water knew. Then he called the bridegroom aside

10 and said, "Everyone brings out the choice wine first and then the cheaper wine after the guests have had too much to drink; but you have saved the best till now."

11 This, the first of his miraculous signs, Jesus performed at Cana in Galilee. He thus revealed his glory, and his disciples put their faith in him.

12 After this he went down to Capernaum with his mother and brothers and his disciples. There they stayed for a few days.

UNIFYING LESSON PRINCIPLE

When faced with possibly embarrassing or difficult situations, many people hope for a miracle to bring order out of chaos. Where and how can we find these miracles? Jesus' first miracle during the wedding in Cana revealed His power by creating something good, and the disciples believed in Him.

TOPICAL OUTLINE OF THE LESSON

I. Introduction
   A. Jesus: Human and Divine
   B. Biblical Background

II. Exposition and Application of the Scripture
   A. Crisis of Hospitality (John 2:1-5)
   B. Simple Obedience (John 2:6-8)
   C. The Sign of God's Purity (John 2:9-12)

III. Concluding Reflection

LESSON OBJECTIVES

Upon the completion of this lesson, the students will:

1. Present Jesus as a relational being, engaged in the life of family, friends, and community;
2. Be exposed to the power of obedience to Jesus' commands; and,
3. Begin to see the possibility of the miraculous in everyday living.

POINTS TO BE EMPHASIZED

ADULT/YOUTH

Adult Topic: **The Good Stuff**
Youth Topic: **He's Got the Power!**
Adult/Youth Key Verse: **John 2:11**
Print Passage: **John 2:1-12**

—Jesus' reply that His hour had not yet come represents the first of many references in the book of John to an hour's (especially Jesus' hour) having come or not come. See also John 4:21, 23; 5:25, 28; 7:30; 8:20; 12:23, 27; 13:1; 16:2, 4, 21, 25, 32; 17:1.

—Jesus made it clear that He was no longer under Mary's control (see 2:4). In the Synoptic Gospels, it is a later event that establishes Jesus' independence from parental authority (Matthew 12:46-50; Mark 3:31-35 [Mark's only mention of Mary]; Luke 8:19-21).

—John's note that this was "the first of his signs" points to signs as a major theme in John's gospel.

—The word *sign,* while often rendered "miracle," is important in explaining the purpose of Jesus' miracles: they were *significant* in declaring Jesus' identity and leading people to faith (see John 20:30-31).

—Mary's order to the servants after Jesus' rebuke of her indicated both her complete belief in His powers and her certainty that He would use them.

—Chapters 2–4 form a discrete section framed by references to Cana and signs (see 2:11; 4:46, 54).

CHILDREN

Children Topic: **Good Things Come when Needed**
Key Verse: **John 2:11**
Print Passage: **John 2:1-12**

—Jesus and His disciples joined His mother as guests at a wedding.

—Jesus was reluctant to intervene when a crisis arose at the wedding dinner, but He complied with His mother's request.

—Jesus asked the servants to fill the empty jars with water—which He turned into wine.

—Jesus' turning water into wine was the first of many miracles that attested to His identity and His power over nature.

I. INTRODUCTION

A. Jesus: Human and Divine

Jesus and His disciples had social lives. They retreated often to desert places and the mountains to rest and to pray. However, Jesus lived a balanced life. He prayed often and went to synagogue, but He also ministered to people where they were in their daily lives. Jesus valued relationships. In Cana, Jesus was reunited with His mother, and possibly His brothers (see verse 12). His mother and brothers went down to Capernaum with Him and the disciples after the wedding in Cana. Cana was a little more than four miles northeast of Nazareth. What an excellent gesture to invite Jesus to grace one's marriage with His presence, and then to be blessed with a miracle! Of all the memorable things done and said at this wedding, it is the miracle that stood out because it took the sacredness of the occasion to another level. Jesus was revealed to the few who were aware of the miracle as one with divine and sacred identity as a result of His actions at the wedding in Cana. Divinity is tied to Jesus' humanity in an eternal way that brings transformation even to a social setting like the wedding where relationships were defined and life was affirmed. It is important to note that Jesus functioned in normal daily life and was always alert to opportunities to share God's vision of love for everyone in every situation.

B. Biblical Background

Jesus' visit to Cana of Galilee marked the beginning of His many miracles. Cana was a village that was much like Nazareth—where He grew up. As Jesus and His entourage entered the village of Cana, He was probably welcomed by the people of the town. Some scholars believe that His mother, Mary, who also attended the wedding, was possibly a dear friend of one or both of the families of the bride and groom. This would have made the wedding a communal event and possibly indicates that Jesus and His mother were honored guests.

Some biblical expositors describe the festive event in the following manner: women dressed in their best clothes, possibly outer cloaks over linen tunics; some may have worn linen sashes or thick flax cords around their waists. Young women pulled the hoods attached to their cloaks down over their hair, shielding their faces so that they were modestly veiled. Men also wore their best clothes.

The bride would have been sequestered within her own household until the wedding. Some experts on ancient weddings believe that a bride's hair would have been combed with olive oil—scented with cassia flowers and aloes. She would have worn it in braids wound around her head, covered by a net. For her wedding, she might have worn purple eye shadow, colored with expensive Phoenician dye. She would have been wrapped in two thick linen sashes: one accentuated the curve of her hips, and the other would have been wound around her waist.

The people of Cana and the surrounding villages would eventually come to know Jesus as a powerful teacher who reminded people of God's love and told them how they should live. But they did not realize that He was divine.

II. EXPOSITION AND APPLICATION OF THE SCRIPTURE

A. Crisis of Hospitality
(John 2:1-5)

AND THE third day there was a marriage in Cana of Galilee; and the mother of Jesus was there: And both Jesus was called, and his disciples, to the marriage. And when they wanted wine, the mother of Jesus saith unto him, They have no wine. Jesus saith unto her, Woman, what have I to do with thee? mine hour is not yet come. His mother saith unto the servants, Whatsoever he saith unto you, do it.

Chapter 2 of the gospel of John opens with a time identity of "the third day." This may be in reference to the time that had passed since John acknowledged Jesus as the Lamb of God, and subsequently began to turn over His disciples to Jesus. Thus, we begin to mark the transition from John's ministry to that of Jesus'.

Another distinguishing mark is Jesus' presence at this wedding feast. It does not seem like John the Baptist would have attended such a gathering. He was a hermit, having "lived in the desert" until he began his public ministry (see Luke 1:80). It seems that Mary, Jesus, and the handful of men who had recently begun to follow Him were invited to the wedding. This suggests that it may have been an affair held by relatives of Mary's, or at least some close friends. Like many women at high-profile social events, Mary was attentive to the details that distinguished the celebration. All things needed to have been carefully planned. Imagine all of the time and energy put into this affair. Imagine the attention given to the color scheme.

Imagine all of the fun and the tension in the air of the family courtyard. The moment of marriage was scarcely what we would call a religious service. During that time in eastern culture, there would have been music from flutes, harps, and drums, and dancing as the wedding party entered the courtyard. Imagine the bride coming down the aisle and the nervousness of the bride and groom as the marriage covenant was read or recited by an elder. Then there would have been singing of psalms and portions of the Song of Songs. The new couple had their first dance as the feasting and drinking began. The wedding would have taken place in the late morning, and by the early afternoon everyone would have been well fed and tipsy. It was then that a social disaster loomed. The wedding feast ran out of wine, a crisis of hospitality that threatened to ruin the occasion.

Mary was quick and to the point. She said to Jesus: "They have no wine." Jesus responded with a Hebrew idiomatic expression: "Woman, what have I to do with thee?" It means, "That is of no concern to me," or, rather, that the matter was the concern of the wedding planner. He added, "My hour has not yet come." Jesus was quite clear on when and where He should use His godly powers and reveal Himself as the God-man. It almost appears that He did not see this as an opportunity to perform a sign in order to show people who He really was. In verse 12, it was clear that He did it to engender His own disciples' belief in Him.

B. Simple Obedience
(John 2:6-8)

And there were set there six waterpots of stone, after the manner of the purifying of the Jews, containing two or three firkins apiece. Jesus saith unto them, Fill the waterpots with water. And they filled them up to the brim. And he saith unto them, Draw out now, and bear unto the governor of the feast. And they bare it.

Jesus' treatment of the crisis of hospitality at the wedding feast was casual and abrupt, but also surreal. It was a feast, and yet the wine, which would normally be abundant on such an occasion, was suddenly in short supply. At weddings, people want everything to be perfect. Running short on food and drink would have caused untold embarrassment. Mary's friends would have been the talk of the town for months to come. It was a good thing that Mary was not put off by Jesus' initial response. She said to the servants of the host:

"Whatsoever He saith unto you, do it." The lesson here is one of simple *obedience*. It may have been a rather tense moment and perhaps one of great expectancy. What in the world was Jesus going to do?

Jesus looked around the room and saw the water pots. There was a lack of wine, but there was also an abundance of water—the essential ingredient in wine. These water pots were the type used in a Jewish household or gathering for ceremonial cleansing and perhaps for hand washing before meals. But they were empty, or at least not full. Jesus ordered the servants to fill the huge pots—six in all—with water normally used for ceremonial purification. This water would be served up as wine.

C. The Sign of God's Purity
(John 2:9-12)

When the ruler of the feast had tasted the water that was made wine, and knew not whence it was: (but the servants which drew the water knew;) the governor of the feast called the bridegroom, And saith unto him, Every man at the beginning doth set forth good wine; and when men have well drunk, then that which is worse: but thou hast kept the good wine until now. This beginning of miracles did Jesus in Cana of Galilee, and manifested forth his glory; and his disciples believed on him. After this he went down to Capernaum, he, and his mother, and his brethren, and his disciples: and they continued there not many days.

The manager of the feast tasted "water that had been turned into wine" (see verse 9). The gospel of John refers to what happened in Cana as a miracle. The miracle in Cana happened, but not without simple obedience. The same Jesus who would later demonstrate His power over the wind-tossed sea revealed His power over still water by changing its form. This miracle, like many other miracles which God is willing to perform for us, occurred through simple obedience and faith in Jesus' ability to do so. The servants saw no wine, but they did as they were told. They filled the water pots to the brim. One source has said that each water pot held ten gallons and two pints of water, while the biblical information estimates the pots to have held up to thirty gallons. Jesus gave a second command, which was, "Draw out now, and bear unto the governor of the feast. And they bare it" (John 2:8). That was the turning point where the power of God manifested in the midst of the particular circumstances that confronted them. In verses 9-10, John recorded the reaction of the wedding coordinator. He called the bridegroom over. He said (in essence), "This is wonderful stuff. You're different from most. Usually a host uses the best wine first, and afterwards, when everyone is full and does not care, then he brings out the less expensive brands. But you have kept the best for the last." This response suggests that the wedding managers were clueless about what Jesus had done and oblivious to this miraculous display of power. This miracle enjoys particular significance because it is the first recorded miracle attributed to Jesus.

Archeologists have discovered the kind of stone jars described in Cana in John 2:6. How Jesus used those peculiar emblems of Jewish identity was, in the symbolic language of early Judaism, even more radical than changing water into wine. By using the ceremonial cleansing water during the miracle, and having others join Him, He insisted that the purity of Israel was indeed to begin from the inside, and from God's covenant people. This was the sign or epiphany that happened in Cana; Jesus, God's Son, brought purity (integrity) to life. The final victory of purity over uncleanness (incompleteness), of the divine over any human hegemony (dominant force of influence or authority over others), of God's chosen people over all the nations of the world was the essential hope that was awakened through the actions of Jesus at the wedding in Cana. Jesus simply put purity into practice with the trust that God would act in His own time. Christians are an extension of God's purity in Jesus. By Christians' holding to purity (inner and outer integrity toward God) in their relations with the world around them, they are living signs of God's kingdom. Jesus taught that the kingdom of God is an inward reality as it is also a "not yet" which will be our outer reality when Jesus comes. Even at a social event such as a wedding feast, the sign of God's kingdom can become an example. The way we remain alert to this Christian faith possibility is dependent on our obedience to and trust in Jesus Christ.

III. CONCLUDING REFLECTION

It is said that a college student and his friends were on summer break and were having a discussion about faith. They had declared philosophy as their major. It was a robust dialogue, each one enthusiastically tossing around philosophical data and theories. All of them were reluctant to back down from the assertions they were making about what faith is. The student who lived there recalled that his grandmother said that she lived by faith. He suggested that he and his colleagues refer this matter to someone who was more knowledgeable about this matter. So they did. They asked her, "Grandma, what is faith?" She said, "If God asks me to get up and walk through that door, I'd get up and walk through that door." This disturbed each of them. Her grandson looked for her glasses and suggested that she put them on. They repeated the question. "Grandma, what is faith?" Again, she said, "If God told me to get up and walk through that door, I'd get up and walk through that door." This was too much for them. They said, "Grandma, your eyes must really be bad or perhaps senility has set in, for there is no door there." She said, "I know that." Her grandson's eyebrows by this time were knitted together in a frown of confusion. "How, Grandma, can you walk through a door that is not there? All we see is a wall." She said, "That's all I see, too. But that is what faith is. If God tells me to get up and walk through that door, it's my business to get up and start walking, and it is God's business to put a door there when I get there." She continued, "Faith, my children, is simple obedience to what God asks you to do in spite of what you don't see." It is the substance of things hoped for and the evidence of things not seen.

In verse 12, it is interesting to note that Jesus returned to Capernaum after the wedding in the company of His mother and brothers, as well as with His disciples. Family and community had been present when He did the miraculous. It was His disciples, though, who grasped that life-changing moment with the Savior. The next few years would be filled with other great miracles, but also with great conflict and challenges.

PRAYER

God, help us to celebrate each day, knowing that obedience to You makes space for miracles each day we live. In Jesus' name we pray. Amen.

WORD POWER

Miracle (Greek: *semeion* [say mih on])—an indication. Jesus' act was not the focus; His act was an indication of His true identity; He is God's only begotten Son who came to take away sin for those who trust in Him.

HOME DAILY BIBLE READINGS
(March 12-18, 2012)

The Wedding at Cana

MONDAY, March 12: "Glorify Your Son" (John 17:1-5)

TUESDAY, March 13: "Glory that Comes from God" (John 5:39-47)

WEDNESDAY, March 14: "Glory that Belongs to God" (John 7:10-18)

THURSDAY, March 15: "God Glorifies the Son" (John 8:48-59)

FRIDAY, March 16: "Loving Human Glory" (John 12:36b-43)

SATURDAY, March 17: "Glory for the Sake of Unity" (John 17:20-24)

SUNDAY, March 18: "Glory Revealed" (John 2:1-12)

LESSON 4   **March 25, 2012**

GOD'S WORD SAVES

DEVOTIONAL READING: **Matthew 5:13-16**
PRINT PASSAGE: **John 3:11-21**
KEY VERSE: **John 3:16**

BACKGROUND SCRIPTURE: **Numbers 21:4-8;**
John 3:11-21

John 3:11-21—KJV

11 Verily, verily, I say unto thee, We speak that we do know, and testify that we have seen; and ye receive not our witness.

12 If I have told you earthly things, and ye believe not, how shall ye believe, if I tell you of heavenly things?

13 And no man hath ascended up to heaven, but he that came down from heaven, even the Son of man which is in heaven.

14 And as Moses lifted up the serpent in the wilderness, even so must the Son of man be lifted up:

15 That whosoever believeth in him should not perish, but have eternal life.

16 For God so loved the world, that he gave his only begotten Son, that whosoever believeth in him should not perish, but have everlasting life.

17 For God sent not his Son into the world to condemn the world; but that the world through him might be saved.

18 He that believeth on him is not condemned: but he that believeth not is condemned already, because he hath not believed in the name of the only begotten Son of God.

19 And this is the condemnation, that light is come into the world, and men loved darkness rather than light, because their deeds were evil.

20 For every one that doeth evil hateth the light, neither cometh to the light, lest his deeds should be reproved.

21 But he that doeth truth cometh to the light, that his deeds may be made manifest, that they are wrought in God.

John 3:11-21—NIV

11 "I tell you the truth, we speak of what we know, and we testify to what we have seen, but still you people do not accept our testimony.

12 I have spoken to you of earthly things and you do not believe; how then will you believe if I speak of heavenly things?

13 No one has ever gone into heaven except the one who came from heaven—the Son of Man.

14 Just as Moses lifted up the snake in the desert, so the Son of Man must be lifted up,

15 that everyone who believes in him may have eternal life.

16 For God so loved the world that he gave his one and only Son, that whoever believes in him shall not perish but have eternal life.

17 For God did not send his Son into the world to condemn the world, but to save the world through him.

18 Whoever believes in him is not condemned, but whoever does not believe stands condemned already because he has not believed in the name of God's one and only Son.

19 This is the verdict: Light has come into the world, but men loved darkness instead of light because their deeds were evil.

20 Everyone who does evil hates the light, and will not come into the light for fear that his deeds will be exposed.

21 But whoever lives by the truth comes into the light, so that it may be seen plainly that what he has done has been done through God."

UNIFYING LESSON PRINCIPLE

People understand that their behavior has consequences. How can we be saved from the consequences of our poor choices? The writer of the book of John gave assurance that, regardless of our choices, God loves us and sent Jesus so the world might be restored to a right relationship with God.

TOPICAL OUTLINE OF THE LESSON

I. **Introduction**
  A. Birth: Natural and Spiritual
  B. Biblical Background

II. **Exposition and Application of the Scripture**
  A. We Know What We Say (John 3:11-13)
  B. The Knowledge of God Lifted Up (John 3:14-15)
  C. Knowledge of God (John 3:16-21)

III. **Concluding Reflection**

LESSON OBJECTIVES

Upon the completion of this lesson, the students will:

1. Know how to present Jesus as proof of God's unconditional love for all people;
2. Be exposed to the effects of God's salvific act through Jesus; and,
3. Be made aware of God's eternal and unconditional love for humankind.

POINTS TO BE EMPHASIZED

ADULT/YOUTH

Adult Topic: **A New Life**
Youth Topic: **Saved!**
Adult/Youth Key Verse: **John 3:16**
Print Passage: **John 3:11-21**

—Both the "you" in verses 11 and 12 and the second-person verbs in this passage are plural, different from the earlier part of the conversation, when they were singular (directed exclusively at Nicodemus).
—The Print Passage represents Jesus' answer to Nicodemus's request for an explanation about the earlier part of the conversation.
—Verses 14-15 allude to the incident in Numbers 21:4-8.
—Our understanding of Jesus' discussion about light and darkness in verses 19-21 is informed by John's prologue, specifically John 1:4, 5, 9-11.
—The Greek term used for "life" in verse 16, *zoe*, implies far more than mere physical existence.
—The setting for this passage is found in John 3:1-10.

CHILDREN

Children Topic: **Love Leads to Action**
Key Verse: **John 3:16**
Print Passage: **John 3:11-21**

—Jesus spoke to Nicodemus about the difference between temporal and eternal truths and values.
—Jesus explained the underlying reason that God sent His Son into the world.
—Those who believe in Jesus receive the gift of life, but those who do not believe are condemned.
—Followers of Jesus live in the light of Christ and should not be afraid when the world criticizes their deeds.

I. INTRODUCTION

A. Birth: Natural and Spiritual

None of us chose the time and place where we would be born. We did not choose our race, our parents, or our nationality. It was all arranged without our say-so or our approval. No one consulted us. Often people who travel long distances research the deals that travel agencies offer in order to get good travel packages. Our appearance on planet earth was providentially arranged, and the travel package itself—including the mode of transportation—was attended to by angels who were given charge after our conception to minister to us in our brief, yet agonizing sojourn from our mothers' wombs to the outside world.

The same cannot be said about our second births. The new birth experience is one that we choose. It is one where the stakes of believing or not believing are ultimate. Jesus spelled out in thirteen words the consequences of believing or not believing on Jesus and His love. This choice is a choice that determines our destinies. In choosing this, we are able to see what is happening and which way we are headed. This is why John 3:16 is so valuable.

B. Biblical Background

John 3:16 is one of the most well-known verses in the history of Christianity. It really focuses our attention on what God had in mind by sending Christ into the world. Because Jesus responded to a variety of concerns and human needs, it is easy to become confused about His central mission or the basic idea behind His life here on earth. One way to resolve this issue about Jesus' identity and mission is to avoid boxing Him into one or two categories. You might say that Jesus is beyond being categorized. Jesus was clearly identified as "Wonderful Counselor," "Prince of Peace," "Lord of Lords," "Alpha and Omega," and "Lamb of God." He was both master and servant. Based on the scathing rebukes in the latter part of Matthew's gospel, He can be seen as an uncompromising nonconformist or a prophet hurling scathing rebukes at corrupt leaders. At Caesarea Philippi, Jesus asked His disciples, "Whom do men say that I the Son of man am?" Jesus seems to have labored on this matter with Nicodemus, perhaps because He sensed how desperately Nicodemus wanted an answer. He knew that Nicodemus's thoughts on God's love were limited to his own political nationalistic interests. Popular messianic expectations in Palestine looked for a political Messiah from David's lineage who would overthrow the Roman government by force and restore the Israelites to a former place of international prominence. This would elevate Jesus to the status of a political Savior for Israel, but not for the world. For centuries, Judaism boxed God into the narrow confines of their nationalistic interest. They understood God only in relationship to Old Testament covenant theology and its promises to them. The Scribes and Pharisees dogmatized this truth (or non-truth), and it was too narrow to state Jesus' mission. Jesus saw Nicodemus as one who needed new life, a spiritual revolution of his core values, his definition of life, and his relationship to God and the world around him.

II. EXPOSITION AND APPLICATION OF THE SCRIPTURE

A. We Know What We Say
(John 3:11-13)

Verily, verily, I say unto thee, We speak that we do know, and testify that we have seen; and ye receive not our witness. If I have told you earthly things, and ye believe not, how shall ye believe, if I tell you of heavenly things? And no man hath ascended up to heaven, but he that came down from heaven, even the Son of man which is in heaven.

Jesus began the discourse by speaking in the first-person plural. The exposition of Jesus' words in the Greek (translated into English) means "what we know we say." This word order is important because it means that the beginning of Jesus' discourse and Nicodemus's opening words to Jesus (verse 3) were the same: "we know." Knowledge and belief support our sense of what we can confirm as true. We believe in what we know, and we know what we believe. The question is not what we believe we know, but, rather, whether what we believe we know makes sense or authenticates our relationship to God and the world around us.

The key issue of Jesus' knowledge of God was His belief that the Spirit of God gave identity to His very being. Thus, the state of our relationships with Jesus leads us to believe that His spiritual identity in God is an identity that defines and shapes our relationship with God. We choose to believe on Him. In doing so, we "shall not perish but shall have everlasting life." Jesus speaks what He knows or testifies of what He knows for the sake of the world's salvation and transformation. Nicodemus and his community serve to represent all people who do not receive Jesus' witness of God. The concept of earthly things (human knowledge) in contrast to heavenly knowledge was at the heart of Nicodemus's confusion about Jesus' statement, "You must be born again." Things about God are revealed through the Spirit of God, not through the human intellect. God is the origin of this knowledge. Jesus' privileged access to God is open to all who believe and receive the gift of God's Spirit. Jesus moves between heaven and earth and brings the two together, which yields divine knowledge of heavenly things. As Moses went up the mountain and then descended with God's Word, so did Jesus, who descended with knowledge of God. The things of God are not just to be known but to be believed or embodied in the human heart.

B. The Knowledge of God Lifted Up
(John 3:14-15)

And as Moses lifted up the serpent in the wilderness, even so must the Son of man be lifted up: That whosoever believeth in him should not perish, but have eternal life.

John 3:14 is one of three statements about the "lifting up" of Jesus (see also John 8:28; 12:32-34). These statements point to the passion or crucifixion of Jesus. As is made clear in verse 14, there is no exaltation apart from the crucifixion or cross of Jesus. The overlap of crucifixion and exaltation provides the context for interpreting how knowledge of God brings new birth or new life. Jesus' relationship to God and to the Word is salvific, because Jesus is endowed with the very Spirit and being of God—the Word made flesh. Jesus committed Himself to the principle of self-sacrifice or self-annihilation as a lifelong process of purification and renewal: "Whosoever loses one's life will save it" (Mark 8:35). When this knowledge of God is lifted up and believed, transformation of people and social circumstances miraculously occur (see Luke 47–48).

The whole experience of being born from above and choosing to change our citizenship from this world to heaven is the most pivotal, life-changing, awesome, and indescribable experience ever. It is not an overstatement to say that the moment that you choose to believe on Jesus a great drama begins; again and again we embrace the shattering of self for holistic communion with God's love for us and the entire creation. When young people encounter this transformation, it is more dramatic and exciting than a two-thumbs-up, fast-paced action thriller—because the experience of being born-again is God-given. When one is born from above, one literally exchanges realms of existence as well as creature-hood. One writer said that man on planet earth looks up and sees the cloud, but God looks down from heaven and sees the sun. Imagine the panoramic view accorded to a person whose mind, heart, and soul are focused on God, and who is like, but not equal to, God in grace, wisdom, and power. From this transformation, one receives a whole new outlook on the human drama that we call

life. However, explaining this to people with a worldly focus is difficult. It was not easy for Jesus, even though He was a master teacher. "Verily, verily, I say unto thee, We speak that we do know, and testify that we have seen; and ye receive not our witness. If I have told you of earthly things, and ye believe not, how shall ye believe, if I tell you of heavenly things?" (verses 11-12).

C. Knowledge of God (John 3:16-21)

For God so loved the world, that he gave his only begotten Son, that whosoever believeth in him should not perish, but have everlasting life. For God sent not his Son into the world to condemn the world; but that the world through him might be saved. He that believeth on him is not condemned: but he that believeth not is condemned already, because he hath not believed in the name of the only begotten Son of God. And this is the condemnation, that light is come into the world, and men loved darkness rather than light, because their deeds were evil. For every one that doeth evil hateth the light, neither cometh to the light, lest his deeds should be reproved. But he that doeth truth cometh to the light, that his deeds may be made manifest, that they are wrought in God.

Verse 16 is the most familiar verse in all of Christendom. It is a statement of God's love as an unconditional gift to those who believe. God is the source of what Jesus offers the world; "God so loved the world, that he gave his only begotten Son." The key words are *love* and *gave*. God gave or *sent* Jesus so that human beings might know the will of God—that is, God's love for all and in all. This is God's will. God's gift of Jesus, which culminated in Jesus' death, is the fullest expression of divine love. If one believes, then his or her life is transformed by the gift of eternal life, and trust in God that brings eternal life. If one does not believe, then he or she will perish without the knowledge of God's love.

These words of Jesus were strong, yet gentle—firm, yet delicate. Jesus understood what was difficult for Nicodemus to understand. Trying to explain the colors of a sunset to a blind person can be challenging. So how does one do it? You make use of what the person already knows and go from there. Nicodemus knew about earthly things, so Jesus used the idea of natural birth and wind as metaphors. However, it seemed that these were not sufficient. Nicodemus was still in a quandary. He could not receive Jesus' witness. The witness was crucial at this point, because it indicated that Jesus was not talking about a place where He had not been. Jesus was a resident of heaven who came down to earth. He was an eyewitness to glory, but it was difficult for humanity to understand this glory. Nicodemus discovered God at the feet of Jesus (see John 3:10-17).

Nicodemus had been taught that obedience and strict adherence to rabbinical law and the tradition of the elders would yield knowledge of God on earth. As with many other religious approaches, it was believed that through some human practice man could ascend to heaven. Jesus as the Son of Man had to descend to earth from heaven and bring God to humanity. The heavenly state of being is a marvelous, majestic, mysterious, magical realm of love, peace, joy, and harmony. God's gift of Jesus to the world began the judgment of the world. "No man has ascended up to heaven, but he that came down from heaven, even the Son of Man which is in heaven" (verse 13). Verses 17-21 explain this judgment as the judgment of God's love against all in the world who reject divine love. It is what biblical scholars call "realized escha-tology," meaning that God's judgment of the world is not a cosmic future event but is under way in the present, initiated by Jesus' coming into the world. In other words, God's love is the "urgency of now" for everyone to receive and believe. There is an eastern spiritual axiom that goes, "Every bit of it is all of it." Though Jesus is God incarnate in human form, He brought all of heaven with Him.

The way a person acts in the presence of love (the light of God) is the defining mark of a person's eternal identity. People's responses to Jesus determine who they are inside. These verses (14-15, 17-21) provide a telling conclusion to the Nicodemus narrative. Nicodemus may have thought to himself, "I now have a grasp of who Jesus is." Jesus used the ancient symbol of Moses's lifting up the emblem of a brazen serpent in the wilderness. The snakes coiled on the staff—embossed on medical uniforms and letterheads—represent healing and curing. It was a revered Egyptian-created medical symbol associated with powerful magic that relieved human suffering. All this was known by Nicodemus. However, Jesus took the meaning of this to another dimension. The cure for mankind's illness was Jesus' being lifted up on the cross at Calvary. "For God so loved the world that he gave his only begotten Son, that whosoever believeth in Him should not perish but have everlasting life" (verse 16). Nicodemus came to Jesus in the dark, but left in God's cosmic light of love (see John 19:38-40).

III. CONCLUDING REFLECTION

The same God who made heaven and earth and all the people on the planet contained enough love for all the people on the planet. God has an unquenchable love for mankind. His Old Testament plan was to covenant with one nation and reveal to the world what God's true nature is—which is love. In the history of mankind, there were and continues to be tribal religions and national deities whose understanding of God positioned that particular tribe or nation as God's chosen people. What we see in John 3:16 is a theological insight or truth that comes from God to man, as opposed to man's truth about God. The truth of the matter is clear in this often-quoted and well-known verse. It is simply this:

God loves all tribes and all nations. This love became incarnate in Christ and was revealed in its most dramatic form at Calvary. Jesus can be claimed by all people, but owned exclusively by none. He is the Light of the World and the Savior of all mankind. A radical understanding of Jesus is a constant challenge to a world that resists God's love. God's judgment of the world arises precisely out of God's love for the world, which was prominently disclosed in Jesus.

PRAYER

God, make us truly thankful for the gift of eternal love and life through Jesus Christ. In Jesus' name we pray. Amen.

WORD POWER

"Whoever believes"—some words that are eternal in scope. They ring out into the destiny of humanity and define the parameters of our future existence.

HOME DAILY BIBLE READINGS
(March 19-25, 2012)

God's Word Saves

MONDAY, March 19: "The Light of the World" (Matthew 5:13-16)

TUESDAY, March 20: "Lovers of Darkness" (Job 24:13-17)

WEDNESDAY, March 21: "Loving Evil More than Good" (Psalm 52)

THURSDAY, March 22: "Look and Live" (Numbers 21:4-9)

FRIDAY, March 23: "Wrongly Worshipping the Symbol" (2 Kings 18:1-7a)

SATURDAY, March 24: "Light for the Way" (Nehemiah 9:9-15)

SUNDAY, March 25: "Whoever Believes in Him" (John 3:11-21)

LESSON 5   April 1, 2012 (Palm Sunday)

JESUS TESTIFIES TO THE TRUTH

DEVOTIONAL READING: **John 8:28-38**
PRINT PASSAGE: **John 18:28-37**

BACKGROUND SCRIPTURE: **John 18–19**
KEY VERSE: **John 18:37**

John 18:28-37—KJV

28 Then led they Jesus from Caiaphas unto the hall of judgment: and it was early; and they themselves went not into the judgment hall, lest they should be defiled; but that they might eat the passover.
29 Pilate then went out unto them, and said, What accusation bring ye against this man?
30 They answered and said unto him, If he were not a malefactor, we would not have delivered him up unto thee.
31 Then said Pilate unto them, Take ye him, and judge him according to your law. The Jews therefore said unto him, It is not lawful for us to put any man to death:
32 That the saying of Jesus might be fulfilled, which he spake, signifying what death he should die.
33 Then Pilate entered into the judgment hall again, and called Jesus, and said unto him, Art thou the King of the Jews?
34 Jesus answered him, Sayest thou this thing of thyself, or did others tell it thee of me?
35 Pilate answered, Am I a Jew? Thine own nation and the chief priests have delivered thee unto me: what hast thou done?
36 Jesus answered, My kingdom is not of this world: if my kingdom were of this world, then would my servants fight, that I should not be delivered to the Jews: but now is my kingdom not from hence.
37 Pilate therefore said unto him, Art thou a king then? Jesus answered, Thou sayest that I am a king. To this end was I born, and for this cause came I into the world, that I should bear witness unto the truth. Every one that is of the truth heareth my voice.

John 18:28-37—NIV

28 Then the Jews led Jesus from Caiaphas to the palace of the Roman governor. By now it was early morning, and to avoid ceremonial uncleanness the Jews did not enter the palace; they wanted to be able to eat the Passover.
29 So Pilate came out to them and asked, "What charges are you bringing against this man?"
30 "If he were not a criminal," they replied, "we would not have handed him over to you."
31 Pilate said, "Take him yourselves and judge him by your own law." "But we have no right to execute anyone," the Jews objected.
32 This happened so that the words Jesus had spoken indicating the kind of death he was going to die would be fulfilled.
33 Pilate then went back inside the palace, summoned Jesus and asked him, "Are you the king of the Jews?"
34 "Is that your own idea," Jesus asked, "or did others talk to you about me?"
35 "Am I a Jew?" Pilate replied. "It was your people and your chief priests who handed you over to me. What is it you have done?"
36 Jesus said, "My kingdom is not of this world. If it were, my servants would fight to prevent my arrest by the Jews. But now my kingdom is from another place."
37 "You are a king, then!" said Pilate. Jesus answered, "You are right in saying I am a king. In fact, for this reason I was born, and for this I came into the world, to testify to the truth. Everyone on the side of truth listens to me."

TOPICAL OUTLINE OF THE LESSON

I. Introduction
A. Jesus' Ministry: Divinely Designed
B. Biblical Background

II. Exposition and Application of the Scripture
A. The Hypocrisy of the Jews (John 18:28-32)
B. Pilate's Inquisition (John 18:33-36)
C. Jesus' Purpose (John 18:37)

III. Concluding Reflection

LESSON OBJECTIVES

Upon the completion of this lesson, the students will know that:

1. Knowing and accepting God's purpose for your life will govern your life;
2. One's profession is validated by his or her action; and,
3. Speaking and living the truth will cause controversy.

POINTS TO BE EMPHASIZED

ADULT/YOUTH
Adult Topic: **No Foolin'!**
Youth Topic: **Keeping It Real**
Adult/Youth Key Verse: **John 18:37**
Print Passage: **John 18:28-37**

—John's gospel reports that Jesus was sent from Annas to Caiaphas (18:24) and then from Caiaphas to Pilate (18:28). The reader must rely on the synoptic gospels for information about what happened in Caiaphas's court (Matthew 26:57-68; Mark 14:53-65; Luke 22:66-71).

—This Scripture uses irony in two ways. First, the Jewish leaders refuse to enter Pilate's headquarters so they will not be "defiled" and unable to eat the Passover, but they see nothing defiling about sending an innocent man to His death! Second, Pilate's last question to Jesus, "What is truth?" is ironic because the truth intended for the Jews was rejected by them but asked for by the Gentile Pilate.

—John agreed with the Synoptic Gospels that Pilate's first question to Jesus was, "Are you the king of the Jews?"

—While Pilate wanted to talk politics ("Are you a king?"), Jesus wanted to "testify to the truth."

—The word *my* in verse 36 is in the emphatic position in the Greek text all four times it appears—twice in reference to "my kingdom," once as "my servants," and once in "my arrest."

—John 18:36 does not mean that Christians should not be involved in politics. For many Christians, participation in the political process is a means of working for the kingdom of God.

CHILDREN
Children Topic: **Action Requires Courage**
Key Verse: **John 18:37**
Print Passage: **John 18:28-37**

—Jesus was betrayed, arrested, and brought to trial before the Jewish authorities before being sent to Pilate.

—Jesus appeared for trial before Pilate, the representative of Rome, after being condemned by the high priest and other Jewish authorities.

—Pilate tried to avoid making a decision about Jesus' fate.

—When Pilate asked Jesus if He were King of the Jews, Jesus spoke of a realm beyond the earth.

—Jesus explained that His purpose in life was to testify to the truth about God.

I. INTRODUCTION

A. Jesus' Ministry: Divinely Designed

The ministry of Jesus as a whole challenged and motivated people to take responsibility for their own lives through faith in God's Word, rather than to depend upon the egotistical, ritualistic, and lifeless practices of those in religious authority. Jesus' teaching galvanized the people to the point of giving them hope. His ministry moved them so much that they began to proclaim Him as their Christ, the Anointed One of God.

Quite naturally, this movement threatened the status of those in religious authority, relegating them to a place of insignificance. They were forced to find a way to thwart this movement, and that was to convince the people that the ministry of Jesus was not of God. What better way to do that than to misrepresent the truth of what Jesus was saying and doing as injurious to the core of the traditions and customs that had been practiced by the people down through generations? This required the assistance of those who were loyal to the religious leaders and those who were opposed to change. Israel had longed for God to send them a Messiah to deliver them from the oppression that they were experiencing at the hands of other nations. Ironically, when God fulfilled His promise of deliverance to them, they rejected it because it was not in accordance with what they had been taught. God sent them spiritual deliverance, but they desired physical deliverance.

B. Biblical Background

Much has been presented about the arrest and trial of Jesus, and each of the Gospel writers presented the events in his own way. John wrote that after Jesus had been betrayed by Judas and arrested according to the orders of the religious leaders, Jesus was brought before the high priest to answer the charges which had been leveled against Him. John did not mention the trial of Jesus before the Sanhedrin Council, where He was accused and found guilty of blasphemy. Desperate people will resort to any means to eliminate persons who threaten their position(s). The charges against Jesus were made up; the trial was illegal; and the Jews, under Roman rule, did not possess the authority to exercise capital punishment in any case except in situations that violated the sanctity of the Jerusalem Temple.

Since the Jews were intent on killing Jesus, and since the Jewish religious authority did not have the legal right to put Jesus to death, they had to cunningly get the Roman government to carry out their dastardly deed. Pontius Pilate was the Roman governor in Judea at that time—so the case was brought before him.

Normally, the Roman governor resided in Caesarea, but during the Jewish celebration of the Passover, he thought it more prudent for him to be in Jerusalem in the event of an insurrection—because the emotions of the Jews ran high as they remembered their deliverance from bondage in Egypt.

II. EXPOSITION AND APPLICATION OF THE SCRIPTURE

A. The Hypocrisy of the Jews
(John 18:28-32)

Then led they Jesus from Caiaphas unto the hall of judgment: and it was early; and they themselves went not into the judgment hall, lest they should be defiled; but that they might eat the passover. Pilate then went out unto them, and said, What accusation bring ye against this man? They answered and said unto him, If he were not a malefactor, we would not have delivered him up unto thee. Then said Pilate unto them, Take ye him, and judge him according to your law. The Jews therefore said unto him, It is not lawful for us to put any man to death: That the saying of Jesus might be fulfilled, which he spake, signifying what death he should die.

Now that the first stage of the Jewish leaders' plan had been successfully completed (that of falsely convicting Jesus of a punishment worthy of death), they then had to manipulate the Roman governor into being part of this farce in order to bring their plan to completion. They did not have the legal right to put Jesus to death, so they resorted to whatever means that were available. The hypocrisy of their actions is highlighted when John stated, "Then the Jews led Jesus from Caiaphas to the palace of the Roman governor. By now it was early morning, and to avoid ceremonial uncleanness the Jews did not enter the palace; they wanted to be able to eat the Passover" (verse 28, NIV). In their eagerness to carry out their scheme, the religious leaders disregarded a law within

their tradition that did not allow a sentence and execution to be carried out on the same day. They had determined that the death of Jesus would take place no matter what the cost. They knew that they could not rightfully carry it out; so, they turned to the civil authorities to do their dirty work. This was a sad indictment of "religion" and its practices, and it may also reflect what is happening today in some of our churches. When those who are in religious authority purpose in their hearts to keep themselves in power, they will stoop to any level to accomplish this aim. The church should not involve the civil authority in matters that relate to spiritual governance.

The pinnacle of their hypocrisy is revealed in the statement, "To avoid ceremonial uncleanness the Jews did not enter the palace; they wanted to be able to eat the Passover" (verse 28). According to Jewish tradition, during Passover a Jew would be considered unclean if he entered a house that contained leaven—thus rendering him ceremonially defiled. Therefore, the religious leaders would not enter the residence of a Gentile during the Passover. The gall of one's being more concerned about being defiled during the Passover than with the total disregard for shedding innocent blood demonstrated the disposition of one who is totally void of God-consciousness. It confirmed Jesus' description of them as being those who would "strain at a gnat and swallow a camel." As believers, we have to make sure that all of our motives for doing things are pure motives. The motives for whatever we do should be based on God's Word. The truth of God's Word will always expose hypocrisy.

B. Pilate's Inquisition
(John 18:33-36)

Then Pilate entered into the judgment hall again, and called Jesus, and said unto him, Art thou the King of the Jews? Jesus answered him, Sayest thou this thing of thyself, or did others tell it thee of me? Pilate answered, Am I a Jew? Thine own nation and the chief priests have delivered thee unto me: what hast thou done? Jesus answered, My kingdom is not of this world: if my kingdom were of this world, then would my servants fight, that I should not be delivered to the Jews: but now is my kingdom not from hence.

The Jewish leaders wanted Pilate to confirm their sentence based solely upon their actions. They had no interest in a fair and just trial; they simply wanted Pilate to carry out their sentence of death. The dialogue between Jesus and Pilate was focused on one of the major themes in the story of Jesus' death which is somewhat of a comparison-contrast that is presented by John—that being that, earlier in the Gospel account, Jesus had put forth the idea that He was the Lamb of God dying for the sins of the world, and now Pilate was referring to Him as the *King of the Jews*. This is important because in order for the religious leaders to get the Roman government to facilitate their plan, there had to be a direct threat to the Roman government's authority. The religious claim of Jesus' being the "Lamb of God"

would not provoke the Roman governor's involvement into this matter, but the claim "King of the Jews" would definitely get Pilate's attention, because it would be viewed as a treasonous offense, and a guilty verdict would be punishable by death. One must take into account that Messianic claims were nothing new to the Roman government, because several others had been made during the Maccabean and post-Maccabean periods—which spurred Jewish uprisings.

Jesus' response to Pilate's question of whether or not He was the King of the Jews was (in essence), "Is that your own idea, or did others talk to you about me?" Posing this question served to determine the reason and the source of Pilate's question. The play on words between Jesus and Pilate helps us to understand that as believers, we cannot allow what people say about us to determine our identities. Who God says we are outweighs the opinions of others, especially in times of great crisis. Our profession of who we are should be confirmed by our behavior, and the challenges we are confronted by should not cause us to deny who we have become. As adult believers, this perspective must be an example before our children, so that when they are faced with criticism for choosing to live the Christian life, God will strengthen them to overcome their fears.

The disdain that the Romans had for the Jews was reflected in Pilate's rhetorical question, "Am I a Jew?" Once again, Jesus' reply provides our example as to how we should respond when we are questioned about our loyalty to our beliefs. One's response based on Christian principles will always be in contrast with the world's responses, and will draw the ire of those who feel that their principles are superior to the principles of Christians. However, we must be explicitly clear as to the source of our response to certain situations. All too often, some people give the impression that being a Christian is something that they *do* rather than who they *are*.

C. Jesus' Purpose
(John 18:37)

Pilate therefore said unto him, Art thou a king then? Jesus answered, Thou sayest that I am a king. To this end was I born, and for this cause came I into the world, that I should bear witness unto the truth. Every one that is of the truth heareth my voice.

Jesus' purpose for coming into the world would radically change the lives of people if they would accept it. Jesus knew what His purpose in life was, and it governed and guided everything He did. In moments of great challenge, He relied on His purpose as the means to overcome difficulty. Many people strive to know their purposes in life. What makes it so difficult for us to determine our purposes in life is that we try to determine a spiritual perspective by using human means. Our purpose in life is determined by God, and if we would ask God to show us His purpose for our lives, then it would not be so difficult to grasp. There are times when God has shown us our purpose in life, but we have not accepted it for whatever reason. Many young people allow the things of the world to influence them in determining their purpose in life; however, many of us have learned that we have spent vast amounts of energy and resources pursuing worldly dreams. His is not an indictment against dreams, but it is counsel directed toward knowing and accepting God's purpose for one's life.

Jesus expressed His purpose for being in the world as "to testify to the truth" (John 18:37, NIV). From this it could be deduced that coming to know one's purpose in life is related to knowing the truth about one's life. The question that many have asked is this: "How does one come to know the truth about his or her life?" Jesus, in dialogue with His disciple Philip, said, "I am the way and the truth and the life" (John 14:6). This statement suggests that for one to come to know the truth about his or her life he or she would have to come to know Jesus. Jesus presented Himself as the fulfillment of God's promise as presented in God's Word. Because He did not conform to their interpretations and beliefs, the Jews rejected Him. In spite of what they believed, He lived and operated in accordance with the purpose of His life. This lets us know that once we ask God to tell us what our purpose in life is, He expects us to live our lives governed by the truth that He has given us. Faithfulness to the truth will give us strength to meet the challenges we will face in life. Just as growing from a child into an adult happens over a period of time, the same is true for growing in faith—it happens over a period of time. Just as Jesus' knowing the purpose of His life governed what He did and was the source of His strength, in the same vein, our knowing our purposes in life will give us guidance and strength for our lives.

III. CONCLUDING REFLECTION

The trial of Jesus by Pilate was the Jews' way of bringing their plans of killing Jesus to completion. Much has been written about how illegitimate it was and how wrong it was. However, if one views it from Jesus' perspective, he or she would come to see the plan of salvation being unfolded. Jesus made use of this spectacle to reveal God's purpose for His coming into the world. Jesus, in obedience to God's will, suffered shame in the eyesight of men to reveal God's love for humankind. The Jews were determined to kill Jesus, and Jesus was determined to die. The Jews thought that taking Christ's life would end His threat to them, but Jesus knew that giving His life would bring about transformation in the lives of many. In this, we see that it can be a powerful thing for one to know his or her purpose in life. Jesus knew His purpose in life, and it enabled Him to meet all that this world could throw at Him. Once again, the enemy meant for bad what God meant for good. Just as Joseph was sold into slavery by his brothers, Jesus was betrayed by one of His disciples, arrested by the ungodly, abandoned by His followers, tried, convicted, sentenced to death by an unjust court, and questioned by those who lacked authority; yet, it was all part of His fulfilling His purpose in life. It may be difficult to comprehend all that this trial by Pilate reveals, but the most important concept that one should grasp from this scenario is that just our knowing our purposes in life is not all that God expects of us. God expects us to live out our purposes so that others can benefit from them. Jesus said, "For this cause came I into the world, that I should bear witness unto the truth" (John 18:37).

PRAYER

Father, in the name of Jesus, we thank You for revealing to us how to come to know our purposes in life. We pray that after coming to know our purposes, You would give us the resolve to live them. In Jesus' name we pray. Amen.

WORD POWER

Testify ("Witness," KJV) (Greek: *martureo* [mahr too reh oh])—to bear record; to report. In eastern thought, a person's oral testimony was more valuable than a written record (cf. Acts 15:27), which is why bearing false witness is a breach of God's holy law.

HOME DAILY BIBLE READINGS
(March 26–April 1, 2012)

Jesus Testifies to the Truth

LESSON 6   April 8, 2012 (Easter)

THE LIVING WORD

DEVOTIONAL READING: **Psalm 31:1-5**
PRINT PASSAGE: **John 20:1-10, 19-20**

BACKGROUND SCRIPTURE: **John 20:1-23**
KEY VERSE: **John 20:20**

John 20:1-10, 19-20—KJV

THE FIRST day of the week cometh Mary Magdalene early, when it was yet dark, unto the sepulchre, and seeth the stone taken away from the sepulchre.

2 Then she runneth, and cometh to Simon Peter, and to the other disciple, whom Jesus loved, and saith unto them, They have taken away the Lord out of the sepulchre, and we know not where they have laid him.

3 Peter therefore went forth, and that other disciple, and came to the sepulchre.

4 So they ran both together: and the other disciple did outrun Peter, and came first to the sepulchre.

5 And he stooping down, and looking in, saw the linen clothes lying; yet went he not in.

6 Then cometh Simon Peter following him, and went into the sepulchre, and seeth the linen clothes lie,

7 And the napkin, that was about his head, not lying with the linen clothes, but wrapped together in a place by itself.

8 Then went in also that other disciple, which came first to the sepulchre, and he saw, and believed.

9 For as yet they knew not the scripture, that he must rise again from the dead.

10 Then the disciples went away again unto their own home.

.....

19 Then the same day at evening, being the first day of the week, when the doors were shut where the disciples were assembled for fear of the Jews, came Jesus and stood in the midst, and saith unto them, Peace be unto you.

20 And when he had so said, he shewed unto them his hands and his side. Then were the disciples glad, when they saw the Lord.

John 20:1-10, 19-20—NIV

EARLY ON the first day of the week, while it was still dark, Mary Magdalene went to the tomb and saw that the stone had been removed from the entrance.

2 So she came running to Simon Peter and the other disciple, the one Jesus loved, and said, "They have taken the Lord out of the tomb, and we don't know where they have put him!"

3 So Peter and the other disciple started for the tomb.

4 Both were running, but the other disciple outran Peter and reached the tomb first.

5 He bent over and looked in at the strips of linen lying there but did not go in.

6 Then Simon Peter, who was behind him, arrived and went into the tomb. He saw the strips of linen lying there,

7 as well as the burial cloth that had been around Jesus' head. The cloth was folded up by itself, separate from the linen.

8 Finally the other disciple, who had reached the tomb first, also went inside. He saw and believed.

9 (They still did not understand from Scripture that Jesus had to rise from the dead.)

10 Then the disciples went back to their homes.

.....

19 On the evening of that first day of the week, when the disciples were together, with the doors locked for fear of the Jews, Jesus came and stood among them and said, "Peace be with you!"

20 After he said this, he showed them his hands and side. The disciples were overjoyed when they saw the Lord.

UNIFYING LESSON PRINCIPLE

People have always wondered about what happens to our human spirits after physical death. Is there a life after death? Jesus' followers were confused when His body was missing, but when the resurrected Jesus appeared to them, they rejoiced.

TOPICAL OUTLINE OF THE LESSON

I. Introduction
   A. Hope in Despair
   B. Biblical Background

II. Exposition and Application of the Scripture
   A. The Response to an Empty Tomb (John 20:1-10)
   B. Resurrection and the Gift of Peace (John 20:19-20)

III. Concluding Reflection

LESSON OBJECTIVES

Upon the completion of this lesson, the students will know:

1. That the resurrection story of Christ is essential to the de-velopment of Christian faith;
2. How to examine their feelings about the Resurrection; and,
3. That they will find the con-temporary message within the resurrection story of Jesus Christ.

POINTS TO BE EMPHASIZED

ADULT/YOUTH

Adult Topic: **Dawn of a New Day**
Youth Topic: **The Word Lives On!**
Adult/Youth Key Verse: **John 20:20**
Print Passage: **John 20:1-10, 19-20**

—In the book of John, "light" and "dark" take on spiritual significance. Thus, not only was Mary coming in the pre-dawn darkness, but since the Resurrection was yet unknown, a spiritual darkness reigned as well.
—The details given here and in the Synoptic Gospels make it clear that the disciples did not expect a resurrection, in spite of Jesus' many predictions before His death. The disciples' later testimony is that of men and women who had to be convinced with tangible, observable facts.
—In verse 8, the other disciple believed in Jesus' resurrection solely on the evidence of the empty tomb.

CHILDREN

Children Topic: **Rejoicing in New Life**
Key Verse: **John 20:20**
Print Passage: **John 20:1-10, 19-20**

—Mary Magdalene was the first visitor to Jesus' empty tomb.
—Peter and another disciple rushed to the tomb and entered it, but did not find Jesus.
—Later the same day the disciples met in fear behind locked doors.
—Jesus appeared among the disciples, showed them His crucifixion wounds, and said, "Peace be with you," and the disciples were filled with joy.

I. INTRODUCTION

A. Hope in Despair

Fatalism is an attitude that makes one live as a passive victim of exterior circumstances beyond his or her control. It is a belief that events are fixed in advance so that human beings are powerless to change them. Examples of fatalism are statements like the following: "I guess since they said I would never amount to anything, it should not be a surprise that I ended up in jail"; "He comes from a single-parent home, so it is no surprise that he ended up in divorce"; "She was a terrible child, so why do you expect her to be anything different as an adult?" "I came out of the projects; we lived below the poverty level and I cannot read or write, so it is no surprise that I ended up being on welfare"; "It makes no sense to vote"; "I go to church"; "I don't do drugs"; "I am not into the party scene; I guess that's why I am always alone." These scenarios are very similar to the ones that people were experiencing during the time of Jesus.

People were in bondage physically and spiritually. The Roman government was taking advantage of them, and the religious systems did not help them in their areas of need. The climate was right for the infusion of hope; all it took was someone to show up who appeared to be sensitive to the plight of the people with a message that challenged the status quo. John's gospel presents Jesus as that someone who not only offered a temporary resolution to their problems, but also extended eternal reconciliation to a people desperate for a relationship. Jesus' short but impactful ministry attracted the attention of many, and it provided the hope that people needed in the midst of despondency and despair. However, much of what Jesus said and did was misunderstood, because His actions were interpreted from a human perspective. Just as they misunderstood His life, His death was even more confusing, because the people could not fathom the idea of the Messiah, the Anointed One, succumbing to death. Jesus' resurrection represented more than what it appeared; it offered hope in the midst of despair.

B. Biblical Background

The death, burial, and resurrection of Christ are of the only events that all four gospel writers had in common in their stories. John presented the story from a universal perspective, making it possible for all who accept Christ by faith to benefit from the message. Jesus had informed His disciples of His impending death, but also of His resurrection—but they did not receive the message. Because they could not accept the prediction of His death, the prediction of His resurrection fell on deaf ears.

II. EXPOSITION AND APPLICATION OF THE SCRIPTURE

A. The Response to an Empty Tomb
(John 20:1-10)

THE FIRST day of the week cometh Mary Magdalene early, when it was yet dark, unto the sepulchre, and seeth the stone taken away from the sepulchre. Then she runneth, and cometh to Simon Peter, and to the other disciple, whom Jesus loved, and saith unto them, They have taken away the Lord out of the sepulchre, and we know not where they have laid him. Peter therefore went forth, and that other disciple, and came to the sepulchre. So they ran both together: and the other disciple did outrun Peter, and came first to the sepulchre. And he stooping down, and looking in, saw the linen clothes lying; yet went he not in. Then cometh Simon Peter following him, and went into the sepulchre, and seeth the linen clothes lie, And the napkin, that was about his head, not lying with the linen clothes, but wrapped together in a place by itself. Then went in also that other disciple, which came first to the sepulchre, and he saw, and believed. For as yet they knew not the scripture, that he must rise again from the dead. Then the disciples went away again unto their own home.

Culture and tradition many times determine how people respond to certain events. Jesus' death occurred close to the Sabbath, and because of tradition, He could not receive proper burial. His followers hurriedly placed His body in the tomb with the intentions of going back after the Sabbath to complete the ceremony. They were devastated by His death. The death of a loved one or close friend impacts us in much the same way, especially if it is unexpected. We often ponder the event until all of our emotions and thoughts are consumed by it. Just as Jesus' death overwhelmed His disciples, the death of our loved ones has the same effect: it becomes difficult to talk about.

Even though the subject of death is an unpleasant topic, it is one that adults who are growing older should discuss. The fact of death and its impact on us and those we love should be given some thought. As believers in Christ, we should draw from the experiences of those in the Bible as to how we should approach the subject of death. Jesus had informed His disciples of His impending death and the implications associated with it. They should not have been surprised by this death, but because of their unwillingness to accept the fact of His message, it caught them unprepared. The events of life often reveal to us the reality of death, but because we ignore the signs and refuse to talk about it, we, too, are unprepared for death when it happens. If we as adults find it difficult to talk about death, it must be twice as difficult for children to talk about it. The painful reality of death must be extremely difficult for them. It is important that they learn that the death of a loved one or a friend does make one sad, but if they come to learn that God loves them, then they will know that God will provide comfort and peace to take away their fear and pain.

Mary Magdalene went to the sepulchre expecting to find the body of Jesus, but it was not there. Naturally, the human response would be to think that someone had taken Jesus' body. Based upon her assumptions, Mary then ran to tell the disciples what she had discovered. The actions of Peter and John in response to the news presented by Mary are also indicative of logical deduction. They, too, ran to the grave with the frame of mind that someone had taken the body of Jesus. The theological implication in their response to Jesus' body's being gone from the grave reveals disbelief in what Jesus had said. Because of their disbelief, their sadness because of Jesus' death continued. It is important for us to recognize that faith in God's Word is the only means that we can use to confront issues of uncertainty. There was no visible evidence of what happened to Jesus' body; so the disciples came to the conclusion that someone had stolen His body. If those who walked with Jesus and heard His teaching firsthand had difficulty accepting the foretelling of His resurrection, then it should not be difficult to understand why people today waver in their belief in His resurrection.

In times of uncertainty and difficulty, faith in the resurrection of Christ may be all that we can rely on to get us through. Human wisdom will often fail us, but faith in what Jesus said will never let us down. Jesus knew that His death would greatly challenge His disciples. He knew His absence would take away the security that they had relied upon for three and a half years. To encourage them through that difficult moment, Jesus told them that in three days, He would rise from the dead; but because of their disbelief, they suffered unnecessarily. The resurrection of Jesus was to be a sign of the faithfulness of God's Word. Jesus wanted His followers to know that all of His teachings were true, and that if they would trust His teachings, then they would receive the blessings promised. The resurrection of Christ is God's way of revealing to us that God is faithful to His Word. During the most difficult moments of our lives, if we can trust and obey God's Word, then He will bring His Word to pass.

B. Resurrection and the Gift of Peace (John 20:19-20)

Then the same day at evening, being the first day of the week, when the doors were shut where the disciples were assembled for fear of the Jews, came Jesus and stood in the midst, and saith unto them, Peace be unto you. And when he had so said, he shewed unto them his hands and his side. Then were the disciples glad, when they saw the Lord.

Mary and the disciples, after seeing the empty grave and hearing the report, allowed human reasoning to influence their responses to what they had seen and heard rather than believing what Jesus had said. John's gospel reads, "Then the disciples went away again unto their own home. But Mary stood without at the sepulchre weeping: and as she wept, she stooped down, and looked into the sepulchre" (John 20:10-11). Mary Magdalene, totally distraught by what she had seen, began to weep. The sight of the empty grave fostered feelings of hopelessness and defeat for her and the disciples. Their reactions to Jesus' body's being absent from the grave suggest that they may have asked the questions: "What do we do now?" "How do we make it now?"

The word *resurrection* is eschatological in tone with the indication of future potential. However, the contemporary message that is presented in the text is that through faith in Christ's resurrection one can have victory over present and future situations. The resurrection of Christ reveals God's power and authority over present-day circumstances and situations. The disciples possibly could have forgotten Jesus' act of raising Lazarus from the grave. They may not have paid any attention to what He said in His prayer immediately before He called Lazarus from the grave: "Father, I thank thee that thou hast heard me. And I knew that thou hearest me always: but because of the people which stand by I said it, that they may believe that thou hast sent me" (John 11:41b-42).

The power that raised Jesus from the grave is available to all who receive Christ as Savior and Lord; and if that power was able to raise Jesus from the dead, then it can also give us victory over the challenges that we face in this life.

When Jesus spoke to Mary, and she recognized His voice, she was able to be delivered from her state of despair, hopelessness, and defeat. The Resurrection assures the believer of life after death, but it also gives peace and the strength to face the challenges of the here and now. This is the message that the church must present to today's young people who are resorting to worldly means to combat the pressures of life. The power of Christ's resurrection is available to all regardless of age, ethnicity, or gender.

The experience of Jesus' death cast the disciples into a state of anxiety and fear. They had not only lost their leader, but they could possibly be blamed for the disappearance of His body as a means to further their cause. They sought refuge in seclusion and hoped for the best. They were threatened by resurrection. John 20:19 reads, "The same day at evening… when the doors were shut where the disciples were assembled for fear of the Jews." Fear has the tendency to amplify a situation to seem worse. It was evening, but because of fear, it may have seemed like midnight to the disciples. The scene was probably one of doom and gloom, with little hope of the situation getting better. As believers, some of us are facing, and unfortunately will face, situations that bring about this same feeling of hopelessness. In our state of feeling hopeless, the one thing that we can take courage in is our knowing that Jesus is alive, and that He will show up in the midst of our situations.

Jesus had appeared to Mary Magdalene, but had not as yet appeared to the other eleven. She told them that she had seen Him and He spoke to her, but they had not seen Him for themselves. There are times when the testimony of others will give us courage to endure our problems, but personal experience is far more beneficial and reliable during difficult times. In spite of Mary's testimony, the disciples continued to fear for their safety. There is a wise old saying: "It gets darkest before the dawn"—which suggests that if one can make it through the night, then a new day brings about hope for change. Psalm 30:5b reads, "Weeping may endure for a night, but joy cometh in the morning." The dawn of a new day brings about joy.

As the disciples sat in fear, Jesus, while the doors were shut, appeared to them. One would think that just His appearance would calm the fears of the disciples; however, Jesus, knowing them as He did, showed them His hands and His side to confirm that it was truly Him. They saw for themselves how He was crucified, and they believed that He was dead but arose. Evidence of His wounds confirmed to them that it was the same Christ who rose from the dead and was now alive. Once they believed that Jesus was alive, it brought them great joy. At the darkest hour of their lives, the reality of the Resurrection gave them hope once again. It was the dawn of a new day.

III. CONCLUDING REFLECTION

Life today is much like it was during biblical times, as presented in the gospel of John. The struggles of today are nothing new; however, we should not even compare our situations to theirs. The people of that day faced far greater trials and struggles than do people in America today. People in biblical times experienced horrific suffering and persecution. They did not have the conveniences, freedoms, and privileges that we have today. The vast majority was poor and underprivileged, but they continued to believe that God cared. Many of them held on to the idea that God is faithful to His Word. God had promised that He would send a Messiah, a Deliverer who would free them from the oppression of that day. The mistake that the people made was that they expected physical deliverance rather than spiritual deliverance. Even though God had given them the means by which to recognize the Messiah, through misinterpretation of God's Word, they did not accept God's way of meeting their needs. Jesus was the Messiah whom they were longing for, but because of their lack of faith in His teachings, even His closest followers did not understand the significance of His death and burial, and failed to even grasp the fact of His resurrection. The defining moment in history became the darkest day of their lives. However, God knew their faults, their failures, and their weaknesses—and God did not abandon them. God demonstrated to them His faithfulness through the resurrection of Jesus Christ. Faith in the resurrection of Jesus brought them great joy. It gave them not only hope for the future, but also strength to face present challenges. It was the dawn of a new day. The story of the resurrection of Christ presented in John's gospel is God's way of revealing to us today that if we (through faith) can believe that Jesus is alive today, then we can also experience the dawn of a new day.

PRAYER

Dear God, we know that You love us and care for us even when we fail to trust Your Word. We ask that You continue to be faithful to Your Word by giving us what we need rather than what we want. In Jesus' name we pray. Amen.

WORD POWER

Believe (Greek: *pisteuo* [pist yoo oh])—to have faith. Another application is "to extend credit." Credit is given based on collateral. The disciples believed that Jesus rose based on the evidence at the grave.

HOME DAILY BIBLE READINGS
(April 2-8, 2012)

The Living Word
MONDAY, April 2: "To Save Sinners like Me" (1 Timothy 1:12-17)
TUESDAY, April 3: "Judgment of Jesus" (John 19:4-16)
WEDNESDAY, April 4: "We Have a Law" (Leviticus 24:10-16)
THURSDAY, April 5: "Crucifixion of Jesus" (John 19:17-25)
FRIDAY, April 6: "Father, into Your Hands" (Psalm 31:1-5)
SATURDAY, April 7: "Burial of Jesus" (John 19:38-42)
SUNDAY, April 8: "Resurrection of Jesus" (John 20:1-10, 19-20)

LESSON 7   April 15, 2012

CLEANSING THE TEMPLE

DEVOTIONAL READING: **Psalm 122**
PRINT PASSAGE: **John 2:13-22**

BACKGROUND SCRIPTURE: **John 2:13-22**
KEY VERSE: **John 2:16**

John 2:13-22—KJV

13 And the Jews' passover was at hand, and Jesus went up to Jerusalem,

14 And found in the temple those that sold oxen and sheep and doves, and the changers of money sitting:

15 And when he had made a scourge of small cords, he drove them all out of the temple, and the sheep, and the oxen; and poured out the changers' money, and overthrew the tables;

16 And said unto them that sold doves, Take these things hence; make not my Father's house an house of merchandise.

17 And his disciples remembered that it was written, The zeal of thine house hath eaten me up.

18 Then answered the Jews and said unto him, What sign shewest thou unto us, seeing that thou doest these things?

19 Jesus answered and said unto them, Destroy this temple, and in three days I will raise it up.

20 Then said the Jews, Forty and six years was this temple in building, and wilt thou rear it up in three days?

21 But he spake of the temple of his body.

22 When therefore he was risen from the dead, his disciples remembered that he had said this unto them; and they believed the scripture, and the word which Jesus had said.

John 2:13-22—NIV

13 When it was almost time for the Jewish Passover, Jesus went up to Jerusalem.

14 In the temple courts he found men selling cattle, sheep and doves, and others sitting at tables exchanging money.

15 So he made a whip out of cords, and drove all from the temple area, both sheep and cattle; he scattered the coins of the money changers and overturned their tables.

16 To those who sold doves he said, ""Get these out of here! How dare you turn my Father's house into a market!"

17 His disciples remembered that it is written: "Zeal for your house will consume me."

18 Then the Jews demanded of him, "What miraculous sign can you show us to prove your authority to do all this?"

19 Jesus answered them, "Destroy this temple, and I will raise it again in three days."

20 The Jews replied, "It has taken forty-six years to build this temple, and you are going to raise it in three days?"

21 But the temple he had spoken of was his body.

22 After he was raised from the dead, his disciples recalled what he had said. Then they believed the Scripture and the words that Jesus had spoken.

BIBLE FACT

Hebrew history is rife with *symbols* and *types* that inform the Christian life. Jesus' cleansing of the Temple is symbolic of His cleansing work in the hearts of believers, for we are the temples of the Holy Ghost, who lives in us (see 1 Corinthians 3:16).

UNIFYING LESSON PRINCIPLE

Many people stray from their central purpose in life and need restoration. What can help people recognize their need for restoration and re-creation? Jesus' action in cleansing the Temple was intended to restore God's central place in worship and in the lives of the people.

TOPICAL OUTLINE OF THE LESSON

I. **Introduction**
   A. The Place of True Worship
   B. Biblical Background

II. **Exposition and Application of the Scripture**
   A. Jesus in the Temple (John 2:13-14)
   B. Jesus' Zeal for the Temple (John 2:15-17)
   C. Restoration of the Temple (John 2:18-22)

III. **Concluding Reflection**

LESSON OBJECTIVES

Upon the completion of this lesson, the students will know:

1. The theology associated with the Temple;

2. That Jesus was talking not only about the defilement of the Tem-ple building in Jerusalem, but also about the defilement of lives; and,

3. How to reorder (recreate/restore) what is important in their lives so that worship of God is central.

POINTS TO BE EMPHASIZED

ADULT/YOUTH

Adult Topic: **Restoration and Re-creation**
Youth Topic: **Cleaning Up and Setting It Right!**
Adult/Youth Key Verse: **John 2:16**
Print Passage: **John 2:13-22**

—Cattle, sheep, and doves were required for burnt offerings in the Temple (verse 14).

—Many coming to worship in the Temple would have journeyed a great distance and would not have brought animals with them.

—The Temple tax could not be paid in Greek or Roman coinage because of the human image (the emperor's head) on these coins.

—The disciples did not play an active role in this story but served as interpretive witnesses for the future.

—This story happens near the beginning of Jesus' ministry in the gospel of John, while it appears late in Jesus' ministry in the Synoptic Gospels.

—Jesus' response to the inquiry for a sign of His authority was to use the Temple as a symbol for His body as the dwelling place for God.

CHILDREN

Children Topic: **Jesus Brings Order**
Key Verse: **John 2:16**
Print Passage: **John 2:13-22**

—Jesus attended the weeklong Feast of Unleavened Bread during which the Jews celebrated Passover.

—Religious leaders allowed the money changers and mer-chants to set up selling booths in the outer courts of the Temple.

—The money changers and merchants cheated persons who came to purchase animals for sacrifices and to exchange foreign money.

—The use of the Temple as a temporary market interfered with the spiritual lives of the people and with worship of God.

—Jesus showed His anger for the misuse of God's house of worship by the sellers.

—After Jesus chased the sellers and animals out of the Temple, He told His that disciples He was the Son of God.

I. INTRODUCTION

A. The Place of True Worship

God valued worship from Israel so much that He provided the means and the place by which Israel could express their love and gratitude. The place was designed in such a manner as to allow God to register His presence as a sign that He was pleased with what was offered. First, it was the tabernacle constructed by Moses in the wilderness, and later it was the Temple. When true worship was offered up to God, it was considered by God to be a "sweet-smelling savor" in His nostrils. When God was pleased with Israel's worship, He expressed His pleasure by exalting them above every nation on earth, and by providing for them beyond measure and protection from their enemies.

Unfortunately, Israel took God's blessing for granted. As history will show, insincere worship and the worship of idols were the things that placed Israel in direct disobedience to God. It was the insincere offering of sacrifices that became the tell-tale sign that Israel was seeking after other gods. God is a jealous God, which was clearly stated in the commandments given to Moses by God. After having been in captivity as punishment for their lack of true worship, one would think that Israel would have learned her lesson.

B. Biblical Background

For years, the Israelites wished to be restored back to the state of prominence which they once enjoyed. Their ingratitude and disobedience had relegated them to serf status; they were dominated by other nations. Therefore, they were governed by the systems of other nations, which created difficulty for them in following the laws that governed Temple regulations for the offering of sacrifices. The Law of Moses required that any animal offered in sacrifice be unblemished, and that every Jewish male over nineteen years of age should pay a Temple tax. As a result, tax collectors and inspectors of sacrificial animals were present at the Temple. Israel was under the Roman Empire's authority and Roman money was used. To put Roman money, which bore the image of the Roman emperor whom the pagans worshiped as a god, into the Temple treasury would be considered as an offense against God. So, in order to accommodate those visitors in need of animals and the right kinds of coins, animal merchants and money changers operated within the outer court of the Temple.

Unfortunately, these inspectors, tax collectors, and money exchangers defrauded the people by imposing higher taxes and charging higher prices. Jesus, who was from Nazareth, saw the unjust practices that went on in the Temple worship. When He established His earthly ministry, which was to offer the Jewish people restoration of their relationship with God and re-creation of the form of worship that pleased God, Jesus made it a priority to start at the place that was instrumental in causing the disconnect and insincerity—the Temple.

II. EXPOSITION AND APPLICATION OF THE SCRIPTURE

A. Jesus in the Temple
(John 2:13-14)

And the Jews' passover was at hand, and Jesus went up to Jerusalem, And found in the temple those that sold oxen and sheep and doves, and the changers of money sitting.

Jesus was a Jew, and He honored all of the traditions that were associated with the Jewish lifestyle. One of the most important traditions to observe was the celebration of the Passover, which was the observance of God's deliverance of Israel from bondage in Egypt. Since He was in Capernaum, which was not far from Jerusalem, it would seem logical for Jesus to go to Jerusalem to celebrate the Passover. Celebration of the Passover attracted many people to Jerusalem. Jerusalem was the city of David, the city where the Temple was built and also the place where Jews and Jewish converts worshipped God. For the Jew, Jerusalem was considered the center of the world. The Temple was observed as the focal point of worship to God. Any time Jesus went to Jerusalem, He was going to the Temple. If Jesus was going to start His earthly ministry, what would be a more fitting place than Jerusalem and the Temple?

The theological essence of the Temple was that it was the house of God. Generation after generation recognized the Temple as the place of God's presence. It was the visible sign of Israel's being the chosen people of God. It was to reflect the holiness of God. It stood as a reminder of God's redemptive love. Last but not least, the Temple was a physical sign of the covenant that God had established with Israel. The life of Israel was centered on the Temple, and it also represented the totality of their existence as a nation of people.

Jesus identified with the Temple from two perspectives—human and divine. From a human perspective, Jesus was born a Jew. Jesus was associated with all that the Temple represented to Israel as whole. From early childhood up through the establishment of the new dispensation, Jesus participated in all traditions and rituals associated with Temple activity. Jesus revealed to believers that it is important to value and identify with the place we designate as our place of worship, and also to know and participate in traditions and rituals associated with it. As Christians, we should take great pride in being identified in such manner, and the place where we gather to worship should also be held in high esteem. Our traditions and rituals should be more than what we *do*—they should also exemplify who we *are* as Christians. Jesus was proud to be a Jew, and He cherished and honored His place of worship and the traditions and rituals associated with it.

From the perspective of divinity, Jesus had come to accept who He really was; He was the Son of God—and as the Son of God, He would be justified in His claim that the Temple was His Father's house. Our children often lay claim to our possessions as theirs; so, we can understand His claim. Therefore, the Temple was more than just a place of worship in the eyesight of Jesus. God's interest in, concern about, and passion and zeal for the Temple became Jesus' concern.

B. Jesus' Zeal for the Temple
(John 2:15-17)

And when he had made a scourge of small cords, he drove them all out of the temple, and the sheep, and the oxen; and poured out the changers' money, and overthrew the tables; And said unto them that sold doves, Take these things hence; make not my Father's house an house of merchandise. And his disciples remembered that it was written, The zeal of thine house hath eaten me up.

Jesus had visited the Temple on several occasions, but this visit had special meaning. He purposely designed the launching of His ministry in the Temple because the imagery of the activity of sacrifice taking place in the Temple would provide direct correlation to the reason for His coming into the world—the Lamb of God's dying for the sin of the world. The Temple was supposed to reflect the holy character of God, and the activity taking place within the Temple was to encourage the people to imitate and emulate God's character. However, some of the activity that was taking place in the Temple at the time when Jesus entered contradicted the sanctity of the Temple. It also did not reflect the Old Testament prophetic view of the role that the Temple had in worship. The zeal that Jesus had

for the Temple and what it was supposed to represent moved Him to respond to that which was occurring with righteous indignation.

Jesus became indignant because the Jews had desecrated the Temple by using it for their own self-serving interests. The Temple was designed for the worship of God, and it was not meant to be turned into a marketplace or a house of business. The activity taking place may have had some significance because animals were used for sacrifice and money was given for offerings. However, Jesus' objection may not have been based upon *what* was being done but *how* it was being done. He was aware that those traveling from afar may have needed to purchase animals to be offered as sacrifices, and money may have had to be exchanged; so it was probably the misuse and the abuse that took place that prompted Jesus to act in anger. Jesus' action challenges us to be mindful of the things that we do in the name of the Lord. Even if something seems right to us, we still have to ask ourselves if it lines up with the Word of God. Many of the religious programs in the church today are not biblically based and, therefore, should be discontinued. In an attempt to make worship attractive and appealing, some have resorted to secularism and humanism. As believers, we, too, should become upset to the point whereby we will not stand idly by and allow an activity that does not bring glory to God to occur in our places of worship.

C. Restoration of the Temple
(John 2:18-22)

Then answered the Jews and said unto him, What sign shewest thou unto us, seeing that thou doest these things? Jesus answered and said unto them, Destroy this temple, and in three days I will raise it up. Then said the

Jews, Forty and six years was this temple in building, and wilt thou rear it up in three days? But he spake of the temple of his body. When therefore he was risen from the dead, his disciples remembered that he had said this unto them; and they believed the scripture, and the word which Jesus had said.

The indignation that Jesus displayed toward the actions of the tax collectors and money changers was based upon His zeal for restoring God's holiness, restoring a righteous relationship between God and the people, and re-creating an atmosphere whereby true worship could take place. Casual perusal of this passage would lead one to believe that Jesus was basically concerned about the condition of the Temple. However, Jesus was addressing not only human activity, but also spiritual activity. Much of the activity that took place in the Temple was a direct reflection of the spiritual lives of the people. The way we live as believers reflects what we believe about God. We confirm what we believe about God by what we do. The way we treat our physical bodies is often an indication of where we are spiritually in our lives. Those in authority questioned Jesus about His right to make the statements that He made and take the actions that He took. Jesus responded in a manner that totally confused them; He said, "Destroy this temple, and in three days I will raise it up" (verse 19). They thought that He was talking about the physical building, but He was referring to His body. Once again, Jesus used this situation as a means to set forth His ministry. The destruction and the rebuilding of the Temple was His way of presenting His death and resurrection.

The destroying and raising of the Temple discussed by Jesus were also indications that restoration of relationship with God and re-creating the true worship of God were necessary. Many of the problems that the people were facing were directly related to lack of relationship with God and insincere worship offered to God. God was offering them the means to restore fellowship with Him and once again experience the joy of true worship. Due to their misunderstanding this, they only perceived what Jesus said on the physical or surface level—so they were unaware that He was offering them restoration and re-creation. Unless we give attention to our physical lives, we may not know that spiritually we are deficient. We may be going through all of the traditions and rituals, but, spiritually, we are not rendering true worship and praise unto God. The symbolic cleansing of the Temple was God's way of physically revealing to the Jews their spiritual condition. Jesus' whole ministry was to offer them restoration and re-creation, and the means by which this would be done was to accept Him as the Lamb of God who would take away their sins. They also needed to believe in His death and resurrection. Upon our having faith in Christ, God is offering us the same things.

III. CONCLUDING REFLECTION

Jesus' cleansing of the Temple is about more than that which meets the eye; it is a revelation of God's great love for His people. The Jewish leaders misunderstood His actions and what He was saying; therefore, they could not see what God was trying to say to them. The struggles of Israel were directly connected to how they viewed the Temple and the activity that took place in the Temple. God gave them the Temple as a sign of His holiness, as a sign of His redemptive love, and as a physical sign of the covenant that He had established with them. It was there for them to come and express their love and gratitude to God through worship. The Temple was there to provide the means to worship God until the true means to worship God came in the presence of His Son, Jesus the Christ. Jesus would replace the Temple and bring about restoration and re-creation in their lives. The continual sacrifice of animals would no longer be necessary for the forgiveness of sins, and the keeping of rituals would no longer be required—because faith in the death and resurrection of the Lamb of God would take away their sins and pay the price for eternal life. As believers in Christ, we need to keep in mind that God is still holy, and still offering redemptive love, and that the new covenant is still available—all of which are made available to us through Jesus Christ. It is important that we take pride in our places of worship, and most of all, we should be careful of the type of worship that we offer to God. It cannot be polluted with secularism and humanism, and we must be willing to stand against those who attempt to do so. It is important for us to remember our purposes in life and make every effort to create the atmosphere whereby true worship can take place and people can come and find restoration and re-creation for their lives.

PRAYER

Dear God, we know that Your love for us is great, and You demonstrated it by sending Your Son Jesus to die for our sins, providing the means by which we can have continual fellowship with You. Help us to never forget what You have done for us. In Jesus' name we pray. Amen.

WORD POWER

Temple (Greek: *hieron* and *naos* [hee er on; nah os]—*Hieron* is used in reference to the "sacred building"; *naos* refers to the "shrine as a dwelling," or the Christian believer in whom the Spirit of God dwells.

HOME DAILY BIBLE READINGS
(April 9-15, 2012)

Cleansing the Temple

MONDAY, April 9: "Building the Temple" (1 Chronicles 28:1-10)

TUESDAY, April 10: "The Lord Has Chosen Zion" (Psalm 132:1-14)

WEDNESDAY, April 11: "Keeping the Passover" (2 Chronicles 30:1-9)

THURSDAY, April 12: "The House of the Lord" (Psalm 122)

FRIDAY, April 13: "My Father's House" (Luke 2:41-51)

SATURDAY, April 14: "Zeal for God's House" (Psalm 69:6-15)

SUNDAY, April 15: "Cleansing the Temple" (John 2:13-22)

LESSON 8   April 22, 2012

WOMAN OF SAMARIA

DEVOTIONAL READING: **Revelation 22:10-17**
PRINT PASSAGE: **John 4:7-15, 23-26, 28-30**

BACKGROUND SCRIPTURE: **John 4:1-42**
KEY VERSE: **John 4:14**

John 4:7-15, 23-26, 28-30—KJV

7 There cometh a woman of Samaria to draw water: Jesus saith unto her, Give me to drink.

8 (For his disciples were gone away unto the city to buy meat.)

9 Then saith the woman of Samaria unto him, How is it that thou, being a Jew, askest drink of me, which am a woman of Samaria? for the Jews have no dealings with the Samaritans.

10 Jesus answered and said unto her, If thou knewest the gift of God, and who it is that saith to thee, Give me to drink; thou wouldest have asked of him, and he would have given thee living water.

11 The woman saith unto him, Sir, thou hast nothing to draw with, and the well is deep: from whence then hast thou that living water?

12 Art thou greater than our father Jacob, which gave us the well, and drank thereof himself, and his children, and his cattle?

13 Jesus answered and said unto her, Whosoever drinketh of this water shall thirst again:

14 But whosoever drinketh of the water that I shall give him shall never thirst; but the water that I shall give him shall be in him a well of water springing up into everlasting life.

15 The woman saith unto him, Sir, give me this water, that I thirst not, neither come hither to draw.

.....

23 But the hour cometh, and now is, when the true worshippers shall worship the Father in spirit and in truth: for the Father seeketh such to worship him.

24 God is a Spirit: and they that worship him must worship him in spirit and in truth.

John 4:7-15, 23-26, 28-30—NIV

7 When a Samaritan woman came to draw water, Jesus said to her, "Will you give me a drink?"

8 (His disciples had gone into the town to buy food.)

9 The Samaritan woman said to him, "You are a Jew and I am a Samaritan woman. How can you ask me for a drink?" (For Jews do not associate with Samaritans.)

10 Jesus answered her, "If you knew the gift of God and who it is that asks you for a drink, you would have asked him and he would have given you living water."

11 "Sir," the woman said, "you have nothing to draw with and the well is deep. Where can you get this living water?

12 Are you greater than our father Jacob, who gave us the well and drank from it himself, as did also his sons and his flocks and herds?"

13 Jesus answered, "Everyone who drinks this water will be thirsty again,

14 but whoever drinks the water I give him will never thirst. Indeed, the water I give him will become in him a spring of water welling up to eternal life."

15 The woman said to him, "Sir, give me this water so that I won't get thirsty and have to keep coming here to draw water."

.....

23 "Yet a time is coming and has now come when the true worshipers will worship the Father in spirit and truth, for they are the kind of worshipers the Father seeks.

24 God is spirit, and his worshipers must worship in spirit and in truth."

25 The woman saith unto him, I know that Messias cometh, which is called Christ: when he is come, he will tell us all things.
26 Jesus saith unto her, I that speak unto thee am he.

.....

28 The woman then left her waterpot, and went her way into the city, and saith to the men,
29 Come, see a man, which told me all things that ever I did: is not this the Christ?
30 Then they went out of the city, and came unto him.

25 The woman said, "I know that Messiah" (called Christ) "is coming. When he comes, he will explain everything to us."
26 Then Jesus declared, "I who speak to you am he."

.....

28 Then, leaving her water jar, the woman went back to the town and said to the people,
29 "Come, see a man who told me everything I ever did. Could this be the Christ?"
30 They came out of the town and made their way toward him.

TOPICAL OUTLINE OF THE LESSON

I. Introduction
   A. Jesus: Unbiased
   B. Biblical Background

II. Exposition and Application of the Scripture
   A. Jesus Travels to Samaria (John 4:7-15)
   B. Jesus Encounters an Oppressed Woman (John 4:23-26)
   C. The Water of Life (John 4:28-30)

III. Concluding Reflection

LESSON OBJECTIVES

Upon the completion of this lesson, the students will know that:

1. The humanity and spirituality of Jesus are gifts from God;

2. God's gift of radical freedom transforms life from all forms of spiritual and social oppression; and,

3. A Christian spirituality of love, justice, freedom, and spirituality are indivisible qualities of the Gospel.

POINTS TO BE EMPHASIZED
ADULT/YOUTH

Adult Topic: Turning Life Around
Youth Topic: The Thirst Quencher
Adult/Youth Key Verse: John 4:14
Print Passage: John 4:7-15, 23-26, 28-30

—The Samaritan woman is portrayed as a model of growing faith.

—"Living water" has two possible meanings. It can mean fresh, running water (spring water as opposed to water from a cistern), or it can mean life-giving water. The author used a word with a double meaning.

—Jesus' conversation with a woman was surprising for three reasons. A Jewish man would not initiate a conversation with an unknown woman. A Jewish teacher would not engage in public discussion with a woman. Jews and Samaritans did not invite contact with one another.

—This story challenges boundaries regarding gender. Jesus did not act on society's fears and prejudices and treated the woman as fully human.

—It is striking that a Samaritan woman recognized and proclaimed Jesus' identity before the disciples made this declaration.

—Jesus crossed two cultural boundaries in this story: the boundary between two peoples—Jews ("chosen people") and Samaritans ("rejected people")—and between men and women.

CHILDREN

Children Topic: Jesus Restores Life

Key Verse: John 4:14

Print Passage: **John 4:7-15, 23-26, 28-30**

—Jesus violated Jewish customs when He shared the Gospel with a Samaritan woman at Jacob's well.

—Jesus stated His claim that He was the Messiah by offering the woman Living Water that would bring her eternal life.

—Jesus Christ is the Living Water that can satisfy all spiritual needs.

—Attitude in worship is much more important than the location of worship.

—Since God is Spirit, we can worship God anywhere.

I. INTRODUCTION

A. Jesus: Unbiased

Jesus lived with a radical sense of freedom and openness to God. For Jesus, God's Spirit was radically free to everyone in every place as an eternal gift. No social barriers of race, gender, ethnicity, or social location could hinder the transforming power of God's Spirit to touch and transform life. The story of Jesus' encounter with the woman of Samaria at Jacob's Well illustrates the transformation that is possible for a life oppressed by social conditions and barriers that distort and abuse individuals and communities. Jesus' encounter with the Samaritan woman illustrates that life is not isolated but must be lived in community with others. The Samaritan woman was trapped in a cultural wasteland with a history of ethnic hostilities between Jews and Samaritans. It was a culture of male dominance and patriarchy wherein exploitative relationships between men and women were the social norm in the Jewish community and the larger Roman Empire. Based on His own experience of the "living water" baptism of John in the wilderness pools of Judah, Jesus lived with a radical spirituality and openness to God that broadened His vision to see that every good person deserved unhindered access to God's gift of radical freedom. The openness of Jesus to God's Spirit allowed Him to live without division based on race and gender. In an ancient culture where ethnicity and tribal identity fueled prejudice and bias, Jesus was able to overcome social division because He believed that the Spirit of God touched all life. This lesson will illustrate how God's Spirit overcomes all barriers, illusions, and social definitions of race and gender and sets people free.

B. Biblical Background

Jesus traveled into Samaria with two of John's former disciples—Nathaniel and Philip (see John 1:43-51). By the time Jesus traveled to Samaria, He had become a radical public theologian and popular prophetic figure. Because of the hostile political climate that developed in the empire, it was necessary for Jesus to avoid the search parties of Herod, who was anxious to arrest him. Jesus traveled through the village of Samaria, knowing the ancient history of ethnic hatred and cultural demise that existed between Jews and Samaritans. Typically, Galilean and Judean Jews viewed Samaritans as a people apart from Israel, even though many Samaritans were members of the twelve tribes who had accepted God's covenant with Abraham and Moses. The Samaritans sacrificed to Yahweh in a different location than other Jews. They worshipped God and offered sacrifice on Mount Gerizim, not at the Temple in Jerusalem. That made Samaritans, in the view of other Jews, impure idolaters.

The Samaritan people had deliberately broken with mainstream Judaism because they had been oppressed. Although King David and his son Solomon, who succeeded him, are portrayed as heroes in Jewish history, it is described in the book of 1 Kings how they used the centralized power of the Judean monarchy to impose their will on all of Israel. To build the Temple, they enslaved their fellow Israelites, especially those from the territory that became known as Samaria. Many Jews outside Judea hoped slavery would cease when Solomon died in 922 BCE. But his son Rehoboam only intensified the practice (see 1 Kings 12:10). The result was an overt and successful revolution (see 1 Kings 12) in the same year that Solomon died. The rebellion led to a Jewish clan who settled in the land north of Judea where on Mount Gerizim they built their own temple, and eventually built their resplendent capital city, Samaria.

Over the years, Samaritans became more prosperous and powerful than the Judeans and became a dominant force in shaping the religion of Israel. But the Assyrians besieged Samaria in 722 BCE, exiled the political and religious leaders and settled non-Israelites in the Samaritans' land. The Israelites of Samaria fell victim to the cultural genocide of the Assyrians. To the Judeans in the south who worshipped and made their sacrifice to God at the Temple in Jerusalem, the Samaritans were a perfect example of what the people of God should not become—mixed with the Gentiles. Hostility developed between Jews and Samaritans to the extent that Jews and Samaritans sought to have no dealings with each other. The study of this lesson will challenge students to reflect critically about how the Gospel seeks the transformation of life for all persons who suffer from injustices based on race and gender.

II. EXPOSITION AND APPLICATION OF THE SCRIPTURE

A. Jesus Travels to Samaria
(John 4:7-15)

There cometh a woman of Samaria to draw water: Jesus saith unto her, Give me to drink. (For his disciples were gone away unto the city to buy meat.) Then saith the woman of Samaria unto him, How is it that thou, being a Jew, askest drink of me, which am a woman of Samaria? for the Jews have no dealings with the Samaritans. Jesus answered and said unto her, If thou knewest the gift of God, and who it is that saith to thee, Give me to drink;

thou wouldest have asked of him, and he would have given thee living water. The woman saith unto him, Sir, thou hast nothing to draw with, and the well is deep: from whence then hast thou that living water? Art thou greater than our father Jacob, which gave us the well, and drank thereof himself, and his children, and his cattle? Jesus answered and said unto her, Whosoever drinketh of this water shall thirst again: But whosoever drinketh of the water that I shall give him shall never thirst; but the water that I shall give him shall be in him a well of water springing up into everlasting life. The woman saith unto him, Sir, give me this water, that I thirst not, neither come hither to draw.

By the time Jesus traveled to Samaria, He had become a radical religious teacher and a popular prophetic figure. Arrest parties under the command of Herod were roaming the land to find Jesus and arrest Him. Jesus traveled through northern Judea to avoid the soldiers and find a safe haven to avoid arrest. Having grown up in Nazareth, Jesus was very much aware of the Galilean prejudice and racial hostility against Samaritans. Outside the small village of Sychar, Jesus came to a well. Nathaniel and Philip had gone on to the village to seek bread. The well was a hole in the ground, a couple of feet wide. Jesus stood in the hot sun with no way to draw water. A woman appeared at the well, clearly past her youth, with water pots, a wooden dipper, and a flaxen cord with which to draw water. Both the Samaritan woman and Jesus had a need for water to quench their physical thirst and to fulfill a spiritual need.

The Samaritan woman needed more than physical water; she needed Jesus' liberating vision of God. The life of the Samaritan woman had been shaped by the Judaic attitudes of cultural and political oppression towards the Samaritans. Jesus lived without human barriers and did not allow hostility, racism, or gender oppression to stop Him from having a conversation with the Samaritan woman. Race, class, and gender differences can get in the way of social exchange and authentic relationships. Social histories of racism and prejudice, the possibility of danger, and violence did not prevent Jesus from traveling through Samaria. During racial segregation in the American South, there were certain places and cities that were dangerous for black people to travel through. In places like Money, Mississippi, where Emmett Till, a fourteen-year-old boy from Chicago, was murdered in August of 1955, it was dangerous to travel alone day or night. Jesus traveled in dangerous hostile territory, where He encountered a woman who was bound by racial hatred and did not know and had not experienced God's Spirit and love that transcend all human barriers.

B. Jesus Encounters an Oppressed Woman (John 4:23-26)

But the hour cometh, and now is, when the true worshippers shall worship the Father in spirit and in truth: for the Father seeketh such to worship him. God is a Spirit: and they that worship him must worship him in spirit and in truth. The woman saith unto him, I know that Messias cometh, which is called Christ: when he is come, he will tell us all things. Jesus saith unto her, I that speak unto thee am he.

The Samaritan woman whom Jesus encountered at Jacob's Well existed in a cultural wasteland where truth and tradition, love and hate, and alienation and community clashed. It was as the poet T. S. Eliot described, "A culture of broken images, where the sun beats, and dead trees give shelter," where one's life was vulnerable and exposed to the chaos and aridity of the world. It was a wasteland of non-caring people that lacked relationships that nurtured genuine community. When Jesus saw this woman coming to Jacob's Well, after making a simple request for a drink of water and the woman's responding, "Jews had no dealing with Samaritans," He perhaps saw her as a composite of fear squeezed into a handful of dust, desperate and dying, trapped in a cultural wasteland of sexism, racism, and ethnic hostility, living in an empire of oppression. The interior life of the woman was like dry stone—waterless. Her life was a series of humiliations due to her having had several failed relationships with Jewish men. Patriarchalism and sexism around her had become part of her. She was alienated from family, and the community had cut her off from emotional nurture and a sense of belonging. Just as much as Jesus was thirsty for physical water, the Samaritan woman needed "living water" to heal her broken identity and spiritual emptiness. Jesus did not make a judgment about the Samaritan woman's life; Jesus offered her the salvation that could heal her life.

In the pews of the churches sit persons like the Samaritan woman—deeply wounded by racism, bound by the limits of social poverty, and abused by social habits and sexism. Through the worship of the church, the message of love and liberation, and the communal affirmation of God's Spirit and presence is the "living water" that they seek. The Samaritan woman asked Jesus for "living water." Like Jesus, the church is God's agent in the world who should offer the world of hurting people this water.

C. The Water of Life
(John 4:28-30)

The woman then left her waterpot, and went her way into the city, and saith to the men, Come, see a man, which told me all things that ever I did: is not this the Christ? Then they went out of the city, and came unto him.

The life of the Samaritan woman calls to mind the unusual patterns of human society and conflict that develop when people are broken by racial and gender bias and social divisions. We see this brokenness in the life of famed poet and novelist James Baldwin. In his own struggle for his identity, he said, "All the fears with which I had grown up, like a wall between the world and me and controlled my vision of the world, rose up like a wall between the world and me, drove me into the church." In the church, Baldwin felt himself needing "to belong," somewhere, to someone—to surrender to something. Baldwin discovered that even in the black church, care was then and is now a scandal. Baldwin ultimately left the church because "religion" in general and Christianity in particular failed to meet the basic needs of people trapped in a wasteland—the need for "living water."

Tradition often blinds us to truth. It takes courage to break the tradition of cultural oppression. The Samaritan woman knew the tradition of race, the social exploitation and function of women, and the way of law and custom by which women were governed. When Jesus engaged in public conversation with her and asked her for a drink of water, He broke with tradition. This exchange was not acceptable in a society where racism and sexism had propriety. Jesus broke with the tradition by asking the woman for a drink of water. Jews and Samaritans had no dealings with each other in public spaces. The woman's social and gender conditioning immediately alerted her to the fact that the request was loaded with wasteland realities and social violations. But Jesus spoke to the woman, because her hearing the truth was more important for her than the cultural traditions that bound her.

III. CONCLUDING REFLECTION

Jesus was able to overcome the identity crisis and social wounding the Samaritan woman had experienced. Jesus introduced the Samaritan woman to the living water of God. To know that God cares is "living water." To discover that worship is an open encounter with God not bound by race, class, or social position is "living water." To worship God in "spirit and truth" and be liberated to a new vision of self in the world is "living water." The Samaritan woman was confused at all levels of relationship with God. When she discovered that God's love and Spirit were free gifts to all, without conditions, the Samaritan woman was set free.

We meet people daily like the woman of Samaria. They have endured the language of sexism and racism and may no longer believe that there is true love and care in the world. Life is a broken narrative—and these people are lonely, isolated, and desperate to encounter a healing discourse, a prophetic compassion that humanizes life in the midst of their existential pain. They need "living water" in order to turn their lives around.

PRAYER

Loving and liberating God, lead us to the well of living water. Heal our souls of racial and gender hostilities that keep us from worshipping God in Spirit and in truth. In Jesus' name we pray. Amen.

WORD POWER

Living Water—the life-restoring flow of God's love in our world. It is the incarnation, habitation, crucifixion, and resurrection of Jesus Christ, the power of God.

HOME DAILY BIBLE READINGS
(April 16-22, 2012)

Woman of Samaria

MONDAY, April 16: "Planted by Streams of Water" (Psalm 1)

TUESDAY, April 17: "Longing for God" (Psalm 42)

WEDNESDAY, April 18: "The Water of Life" (Revelation 22:10-17)

THURSDAY, April 19: "The Samaritans' Heresy" (2 Kings 17:26-34)

FRIDAY, April 20: "Worshipping What You Do Not Know" (John 4:16-22)

SATURDAY, April 21: "Fields Ripe for Harvest" (John 4:35-42)

SUNDAY, April 22: "'Come and See'" (John 4:7-15, 23-26, 28-30)

HEALING THE BLIND MAN

DEVOTIONAL READING: **Isaiah 29:17-21**
PRINT PASSAGE: **John 9:1-17**

BACKGROUND SCRIPTURE: **John 9**
KEY VERSE: **John 9:16**

John 9:1-17—KJV

AND AS Jesus passed by, he saw a man which was blind from his birth.

2 And his disciples asked him, saying, Master, who did sin, this man, or his parents, that he was born blind?

3 Jesus answered, Neither hath this man sinned, nor his parents: but that the works of God should be made manifest in him.

4 I must work the works of him that sent me, while it is day: the night cometh, when no man can work.

5 As long as I am in the world, I am the light of the world.

6 When he had thus spoken, he spat on the ground, and made clay of the spittle, and he anointed the eyes of the blind man with the clay,

7 And said unto him, Go, wash in the pool of Siloam, (which is by interpretation, Sent.) He went his way therefore, and washed, and came seeing.

8 The neighbours therefore, and they which before had seen him that he was blind, said, Is not this he that sat and begged?

9 Some said, This is he: others said, He is like him: but he said, I am he.

10 Therefore said they unto him, How were thine eyes opened?

11 He answered and said, A man that is called Jesus made clay, and anointed mine eyes, and said unto me, Go to the pool of Siloam, and wash: and I went and washed, and I received sight.

12 Then said they unto him, Where is he? He said, I know not.

13 They brought to the Pharisees him that aforetime was blind.

14 And it was the sabbath day when Jesus made the clay, and opened his eyes.

John 9:1-17—NIV

AS HE went along, he saw a man blind from birth.

2 His disciples asked him, "Rabbi, who sinned, this man or his parents, that he was born blind?"

3 "Neither this man nor his parents sinned," said Jesus, "but this happened so that the work of God might be displayed in his life.

4 As long as it is day, we must do the work of him who sent me. Night is coming, when no one can work.

5 While I am in the world, I am the light of the world."

6 Having said this, he spit on the ground, made some mud with the saliva, and put it on the man's eyes.

7 "Go," he told him, "wash in the Pool of Siloam" (this word means Sent). So the man went and washed, and came home seeing.

8 His neighbors and those who had formerly seen him begging asked, "Isn't this the same man who used to sit and beg?"

9 Some claimed that he was. Others said, "No, he only looks like him." But he himself insisted, "I am the man."

10 "How then were your eyes opened?" they demanded.

11 He replied, "The man they call Jesus made some mud and put it on my eyes. He told me to go to Siloam and wash. So I went and washed, and then I could see."

12 "Where is this man?" they asked him. "I don't know," he said.

13 They brought to the Pharisees the man who had been blind.

14 Now the day on which Jesus had made the mud and opened the man's eyes was a Sabbath.

15 Then again the Pharisees also asked him how he had received his sight. He said unto them, He put clay upon mine eyes, and I washed, and do see. 16 Therefore said some of the Pharisees, This man is not of God, because he keepeth not the sabbath day. Others said, How can a man that is a sinner do such miracles? And there was a division among them.

17 They say unto the blind man again, What sayest thou of him, that he hath opened thine eyes? He said, He is a prophet.

15 Therefore the Pharisees also asked him how he had received his sight. "He put mud on my eyes," the man replied, "and I washed, and now I see." 16 Some of the Pharisees said, "This man is not from God, for he does not keep the Sabbath." But others asked, "How can a sinner do such miraculous signs?" So they were divided.

17 Finally they turned again to the blind man, "What have you to say about him? It was your eyes he opened." The man replied, "He is a prophet."

TOPICAL OUTLINE OF THE LESSON

I. **Introduction**
   A. Enabled!
   B. Biblical Background

II. **Exposition and Application of the Scripture**
   A. Who Sinned? (John 9:1-5)
   B. Jesus Makes Mud (John 9:6)
   C. Go Wash Yourself (John 9:7-11)
   D. The Pharisees' Investigation (John 9:12-17)

III. **Concluding Reflection**

LESSON OBJECTIVES

Upon the completion of this lesson, the students will know that:

1. People born with physical disabilities are not being punished for human sin;

2. God is compassionate toward those born with physical disabilities;

3. God's love allows no limitations or barriers to get in the way of healing those born with physical abnormalities; and,

4. Healing is the work of love and compassion.

POINTS TO BE EMPHASIZED

ADULT/YOUTH

Adult Topic: **What Comes First?**

Youth Topic: **Rules You Don't Keep**

Adult Key Verse: **John 9:16**

Youth Key Verse: **John 9:14**

Print Passage: **John 9:1-17**

—Stories of Jesus' giving sight to a blind man are found in all of the Gospels.

—This story has the three formal elements of a miracle story: the situation of need, the miracle, and the attestation to the miracle.

—The healing power of clay made with spittle was a popular element in healing stories in the Greco-Roman world.

—John's gospel presents sight in a metaphorical sense. Sometimes a person can look, but not see. Here, the blind man received not only the ability to use his eyes, but also the gift to see the truth.

—People in the first century believed that any disability was a result of divine judgment.

CHILDREN
Children Topic: Jesus Heals
Key Verse: John 9:7
Print Passage: John 9:1-17

—The Pharisees, the neighbors, the parents of the blind man, and the healed man all had different reactions to Jesus' healing of the man born blind.

—The Jewish culture commonly believed that suffering was the result of some great sin.

—Jesus used the blind man's suffering to teach about faith and to glorify God.

—The Pharisees were envious of Jesus' popularity and great influence on the people.

I. INTRODUCTION
A. Enabled!
There seems to be a lingering curiosity associated with how it is that persons come to be differently enabled. It is as if we need someone to blame for the natural occurrence of genetic anomaly. The tendency is either to pity or to blame the physically or mentally challenged person or those who were responsible for his or her care from childhood—the mother and/or the father. This was true for people in biblical times, and it is also true for us now.

Many laws and restrictions are instituted to ensure the maintenance of the status quo in society. The ruling classes keep their rule by controlling the behavior, actions, and movements of the poor and powerless. If their behavior can be criminalized, they can be punished. The fear of punishment serves as a deterrent to the exercise of freedom among the marginalized persons of society.

B. Biblical Background
Such is the case in the text found in John 9. The religious powers accused Jesus of being a sinner because He violated the law of the synagogue that prohibited work of any kind on the Sabbath. This accusation appears to have been totally politically motivated and was debunked by Jesus. Jesus was concerned with bringing healing to the hurting persons in the community to which He belonged. He would not willingly submit to unjust laws that curtailed His ability to do the work that He had been assigned to do by God.

II. EXPOSITION AND APPLICATION OF THE SCRIPTURE

A. Who Sinned?
(John 9:1-5)

AND AS Jesus passed by, he saw a man which was blind from his birth. And his disciples asked him, saying, Master, who did sin, this man, or his parents, that he was born blind? Jesus answered, Neither hath this man sinned, nor his parents: but that the works of God should be made manifest in him. I must work the works of him that sent

me, while it is day: the night cometh, when no man can work. As long as I am in the world, I am the light of the world.

In 2004, the motion picture *Ray* was released and was predicted to be "the best movie of the year" as well as "the movie to beat at the Oscars." Multitalented performer Jamie Foxx, who won the Oscar for "best actor" in the film, starred in the lead role as Ray Charles, the talented musician whose playing, composition, and vocal skills propelled him to international fame and recognition despite his vision impairment. Ray Charles became ill as a child and the illness resulted in his losing his vision. His blindness did not serve to limit his abilities, however, because his mother insisted that he learn to be self-sufficient in spite of being unable to see.

Neither Ray nor his mother was at fault for his blindness. And in spite of his lack of physical sight, God's creative power was indeed manifested through Ray Charles's musical talent. Though his natural eyesight was limited, he was able to see what others could not see.

Such was the case with this man in the biblical text who was described as having been blind since the day he was born. Chapter 9 begins with an interesting question being raised by Jesus' disciples about this man's condition. In verse 2 of the text, the disciples referred to Jesus as *Rabbi*, which means "teacher," and then posed the query, "Who did sin, this man or his parents, that he was born blind?" This question is colored by an understanding of the teaching of other rabbis, who taught that, "There is no death without sin, and there is no suffering without iniquity." Their teachings were informed by the idea that a child could sin while yet in his or her mother's womb. They were given to believe, for example, that a child could be pronounced guilty of idolatry if his or her mother worshipped in a heathen temple while pregnant.

Jesus roundly rejected this line of thinking and, in verse 3, comprehensively answered the indictment of this innocent blind man; Jesus said, "Neither this man nor his parents sinned…but this happened so that the work of God might be displayed in his life" (NIV). Jesus then expressed concern that the work of attending to the needs of hurting persons be done while the opportunity availed itself. He said in verse 4 (NIV), "As long as it is day, we must do the work of him who sent me. Night is coming, when no one can work." In verse 5 (NIV), Jesus declared, "While I am in the world, I am the light of the world." Jesus represents light, illumination, discernment, and intellect. This light comes from God, the Creator of light, and those who receive this light shine as they reflect the light of the Son.

Blindness is a kind of darkness that not only physically affects persons, but also has spiritual implications. Jesus, who was known to "hit a straight lick with a crooked stick," may have been referring to religious, academic, political, economic, and social blindness from which persons who are obsessed with control can often suffer. It is also highly probable that Jesus was referring to the spiritual blindness that predisposes persons to lack discernment in the areas of spiritual significance. The light of care, kindness, and healing shone brightly from the face of Jesus, helping those who are willing to see the injustices and possibilities for transformation that exist before us.

B. Jesus Makes Mud
(John 9:6)

When he had thus spoken, he spat on the ground, and

made clay of the spittle, and he anointed the eyes of the blind man with the clay.

As the opportunity to embody the ministry of healing presented itself, Jesus responded by making mud—that is to say that Jesus used what was available to Him to bless, to heal, and to restore wholeness where suffering, shame, and pain once existed.

There is evidence that substantiates that saliva has medicinal qualities. The dirt on the ground contains the elements that God's breath animated during God's creative process. Jesus, through the making of mud, engaged in the process of giving sight to a blind man. Through the making of mud from spit and dirt, He also revealed the power that rested within Him to the witnesses of His work. The mud that Jesus made was spread on the eyes of the blind man, but the healing power of Christ was not made manifest only in the mud. The man's transformation was not complete without the man's personal faith investment.

C. Go Wash Yourself
(John 9:7-11)

And said unto him, Go, wash in the pool of Siloam, (which is by interpretation, Sent.) He went his way therefore, and washed, and came seeing. The neighbours therefore, and they which before had seen him that he was blind, said, Is not this he that sat and begged? Some said, This is he: others said, He is like him: but he said, I am he. Therefore said they unto him, How were thine eyes opened? He answered and said, A man that is called Jesus made clay, and anointed mine eyes, and said unto me, Go to the pool of Siloam, and wash: and I went and washed, and I received sight.

Jesus instructed the man to "Go wash in the pool of Siloam" in verse 7. This was a key aspect of the miracle. Jesus empowered the man to self-identify as a person with agency,

ability, and ashé. Ashé is an African term that means "the power to make things happen." All persons have ashé. Jesus invited the man to participate in his own healing. There was no magic to the miracle; it is rather an exercise in enablement. Jesus, in a sense, invited the man to participate in the re-creation of himself as a whole person, lacking nothing.

No one else was enlisted to aid the man. He was instructed to go and do something for himself, and the result was restoration of his sight. The pool of Siloam was located on the south end of Jerusalem, and was the source of water for the Festival of Shelters. The text also reveals the double meaning of the term *Siloam* which means "sent." Interestingly, Jesus, the one who was "sent" by God, "sent" the man who would be healed to go and wash in a pool called "sent." The man did as he was directed by Jesus—washing his eyes in the pool that he was sent to, and returning to the community whole, healed, clean, and cured.

As members of the community noticed the transformation in the man's life, they wondered among themselves how the change had occurred. It is as if the man's identity had changed and they no longer knew him as he had been. When he was questioned about the source of his healing, the man simply replied in verse 11 (NIV), "The man they call Jesus made some mud and put it on my eyes…So I went [to the pool of Siloam] and washed, and then I could see."

D. The Pharisees' Investigation
(John 9:12-17)

Then said they unto him, Where is he? He said, I know not. They brought to the Pharisees him that aforetime was blind. And it was the sabbath day when Jesus made

the clay, and opened his eyes. Then again the Pharisees also asked him how he had received his sight. He said unto them, He put clay upon mine eyes, and I washed, and do see. Therefore said some of the Pharisees, This man is not of God, because he keepeth not the sabbath day. Others said, How can a man that is a sinner do such miracles? And there was a division among them. They say unto the blind man again, What sayest thou of him, that he hath opened thine eyes? He said, He is a prophet.

One might imagine that every member of the community would be overjoyed upon learning of the miraculous acts of Christ that had happened in their midst. But this was not so. Certain members of the community thought it proper to consult the Pharisees concerning this miracle—because Jesus made the mud on the Sabbath. And so the Pharisees immediately launched an investigation into Jesus' behaviors, actions, and movements within the community. After interrogating the newly enabled man over and over again, and having discussed the matter among themselves, some of the Pharisees made the determination (in verse 16) that "this man is not from God, for he does not keep the Sabbath" (NIV). It appears that the Pharisees were invested in the politics of the Sabbath to the extent that they were unable to show compassion to their brother.

The suffering of the society is magnified and intensified when there is division among the members of the community. Verse 16b reveals the paradox that caused their division. It reads, "'How can a sinner do such miraculous signs?' So they were divided." Often, what we see does not reflect the true reality of a situation. The Pharisees' obsession with seeing things through the rigid legal restriction limited their ability to see the things of the Spirit. From the perspective of the Pharisees, Jesus was a sinner. The letter of the law did not allow for Him to be seen otherwise by those who saw it as their responsibility to maintain control over the people. The man who had been blind from birth had a sense of spiritual vision that allowed him to see Jesus as a "prophet," a holy man—one sent from God. The deception inherent in the systems of this world does not allow many today to see the truth in Jesus' words of healing, justice, and liberation.

III. CONCLUDING REFLECTION

In our lesson for today, we find the Pharisees placing more importance upon their traditions and laws than they did the people for whom the traditions and laws were established. This behavior is still more common than one might imagine, because people tend to pay more attention to what others cannot do rather than who they were created to be. There is a story told about a traveling man whose wandering led him to a small village one day. His travels had taken him many places, and he had learned much along the journey. As he approached this small village he noticed people gathered together in a nearby field. They appeared to be worshipping, dancing, singing, and shouting, so he went closer to see what was going on. When he got close enough to join them he discovered that at the center of all the commotion was a watermelon. This traveler then asked the person who seemed to be leading the people what it was that they were doing. The leader replied, "We are worshipping our god." The man was perplexed and amused. In all the man's moving about he had never witnessed anything so ridiculous, and so he decided to share with them some of the wisdom of his travels. He said, "Ladies and gentlemen,

I hate to burst your bubble, but this god that you worship is merely a watermelon." They looked at him in astonishment and replied, "O no, this is our god and it must be worshipped." The man said, "No, this is a watermelon and it is really quite a tasty treat." And he kneeled down, picked the melon up, broke it open over a rock and began to eat the reddish-pink flesh. The juice ran down his arms as he said, "See, this is a fruit that is meant to be eaten; please eat it with me."

With looks of shock, horror, and disapproval on the people's faces, the leader said, "You have killed our god; now you must die," and the members of their community began to stone the man to death. The moral of the story is that introducing new ideas to people who are invested in a particular system can be very dangerous. People will go to great lengths to preserve the legitimacy of their traditions. Jesus understood that and thus chose to operate out of a spirit of courage, placing a higher value on persons than He did on traditions, laws, or cultic restrictions.

PRAYER

Lord, help us to learn how to value people over systems, traditions, and things. In Jesus' name we pray. Amen.

WORD POWER

Blind (Greek: *tuphlos* [toof los])—This is derived from the Greek word for "pride." Self-conceit and pride obscure the truth, like smoke or fog obscures the road while driving. The prideful person is blind to things that are obvious to everyone else.

HOME DAILY BIBLE READINGS
(April 23-29, 2012)

Healing the Blind Man

MONDAY, April 23: "Hope for the Future" (Isaiah 29:17-21)

TUESDAY, April 24: "Separating Light from Darkness" (Genesis 1:14-19)

WEDNESDAY, April 25: "Light for the Journey" (Exodus 13:17-22)

THURSDAY, April 26: "The Blind Questioning Blindness" (John 9:18-23)

FRIDAY, April 27: "Teaching the Un-teachable" (John 9:24-34)

SATURDAY, April 28: "Seeing, but Not 'Seeing'" (John 9:35-41)

SUNDAY, April 29: "The Light of the World" (John 9:1-17)

LESSON 10   May 6, 2012

THE BREAD OF LIFE

DEVOTIONAL READING: **Psalm 107:1-9**   BACKGROUND SCRIPTURE: **John 6**
PRINT PASSAGE: **John 6:22-35**   KEY VERSE: **John 6:35**

John 6:22-35—KJV

22 The day following, when the people which stood on the other side of the sea saw that there was none other boat there, save that one whereinto his disciples were entered, and that Jesus went not with his disciples into the boat, but that his disciples were gone away alone;

23 (Howbeit there came other boats from Tiberias nigh unto the place where they did eat bread, after that the Lord had given thanks:)

24 When the people therefore saw that Jesus was not there, neither his disciples, they also took shipping, and came to Capernaum, seeking for Jesus.

25 And when they had found him on the other side of the sea, they said unto him, Rabbi, when camest thou hither?

26 Jesus answered them and said, Verily, verily, I say unto you, Ye seek me, not because ye saw the miracles, but because ye did eat of the loaves, and were filled.

27 Labour not for the meat which perisheth, but for that meat which endureth unto everlasting life, which the Son of man shall give unto you: for him hath God the Father sealed.

28 Then said they unto him, What shall we do, that we might work the works of God?

29 Jesus answered and said unto them, This is the work of God, that ye believe on him whom he hath sent.

30 They said therefore unto him, What sign shewest thou then, that we may see, and believe thee? what dost thou work?

31 Our fathers did eat manna in the desert; as it is written, He gave them bread from heaven to eat.

32 Then Jesus said unto them, Verily, verily, I say unto you, Moses gave you not that bread from

John 6:22-35—NIV

22 The next day the crowd that had stayed on the opposite shore of the lake realized that only one boat had been there, and that Jesus had not entered it with his disciples, but that they had gone away alone.

23 Then some boats from Tiberias landed near the place where the people had eaten the bread after the Lord had given thanks.

24 Once the crowd realized that neither Jesus nor his disciples were there, they got into the boats and went to Capernaum in search of Jesus.

25 When they found him on the other side of the lake, they asked him, "Rabbi, when did you get here?"

26 Jesus answered, "I tell you the truth, you are looking for me, not because you saw miraculous signs but because you ate the loaves and had your fill.

27 Do not work for food that spoils, but for food that endures to eternal life, which the Son of Man will give you. On him God the Father has placed his seal of approval."

28 Then they asked him, "What must we do to do the works God requires?"

29 Jesus answered, "The work of God is this: to believe in the one he has sent."

30 So they asked him, "What miraculous sign then will you give that we may see it and believe you? What will you do?

31 Our forefathers ate the manna in the desert; as it is written: 'He gave them bread from heaven to eat.'"

32 Jesus said to them, "I tell you the truth, it is not Moses who has given you the bread from heaven,

but it is my Father who gives you the true bread from heaven.

33 For the bread of God is he who comes down from heaven and gives life to the world."

34 "Sir," they said, "from now on give us this bread."

35 Then Jesus declared, "I am the bread of life. He who comes to me will never go hungry, and he who believes in me will never be thirsty."

UNIFYING LESSON PRINCIPLE

Many people are hungering for what will make their lives complete. Where do we find what is missing in our lives? Jesus promised His followers that they would never be hungry or thirsty if they would come to Him.

TOPICAL OUTLINE OF THE LESSON

I. **Introduction**
   A. The "I Am"
   B. Biblical Background

II. **Exposition and Application of the Scripture**
   A. Anxious for Bread (John 6:22-26)
   B. Bread from Heaven (John 6:27-31)
   C. Bread for Life (John 6:32-35)

III. **Concluding Reflection**

LESSON OBJECTIVES

Upon the completion of this lesson, the students should know that:

1. Life is incomplete and something is missing without the spiritual nourishment that God provides;

2. The acquiring of friends and possessions will not make life more complete without God; and,

3. Spiritual hunger and thirst are more intense than physical hunger.

POINTS TO BE EMPHASIZED

ADULT/YOUTH

Adult Topic: **Nourishment for Life**

Youth Topic: **Better than Bread!**

Adult/Youth Key Verse: **John 6:35**

Print Passage: **John 6:22-35**

—The story of the feeding of the five thousand is recorded in all four gospels.

—The stories in this passage make many allusions to stories in the Hebrew Scriptures.

—The ceremony of meals and table fellowship informs the symbols of bread and life in this passage.

—The "I am" sayings form the distinctive core of Jesus' self-revelation in the gospel of John.

—In this story as in others in John's writings, Jesus uses ordinary things like bread and water to speak metaphorically about great spiritual truths.

CHILDREN

Children Topic: Jesus Is the Living Bread

Key Verse: John 6:35

Print Passage: John 6:22-35

—Jesus criticized those who followed Him only for physical and transient benefits rather than for the fulfillment of their spiritual hunger.

—Many who followed Jesus had self-centered or negative motives.

—To believe that Jesus is who He claims to be and to obey His commands pleases God.

—The only way we can satisfy our spiritual hunger and be Christlike is through a right relationship with Jesus Christ.

I. INTRODUCTION

A. The "I Am"

The "I am" sayings of Jesus form the distinctive core of Jesus' identity and self-revelation in the gospel of John. With the "I am the bread of life" statement, Jesus used the ordinary commodity—the image of bread as food—to speak metaphorically about the seal of God's truth on His life. Jesus' self-understanding as "the bread of life" did not emerge without struggle. Previously, Jesus retreated with His closest disciples to the coast of Caesarea Philippi. There, Jesus raised questions about His identity that were a matter of intense debate among the people. Jesus had resisted any public acclamation as the Messiah, but He was unwavering in His conviction that God's Spirit had anointed Him (see Luke 4:18). "Who do you say that I am?" (see Luke 9:20) was the question Jesus put to the disciples. Jesus knew the meaning of His prophetic vocation and His identity as the Son of God. God's kingdom was the only thing that really mattered, and He was fully committed to its fulfillment. Jesus was an example of the presence of God in the world and among the people. However, awakening the disciples and the common people to this fact was not easy; they demanded a sign of the work of God.

Jesus knew that the abundance of God was the spiritual sustenance that the people needed for their struggle against the oppressive realities of the Roman Empire. That profound spirituality was Jesus' reality. It was the basis on which John's gospel identified Jesus as "the bread of life" (John 6:35).

B. Biblical Background

Jesus' hunger for the fulfillment of the will of God made Him acutely conscious of God's promise to ancient Israel (see Isaiah 2:2-4; 11:6-9; and Luke 14:21). The promise of God's kingdom burned so strongly within Jesus that it seemed imminently present as a reality in His own life. There was no separation in Jesus' consciousness between the kingdom's reality and His own identity (see John 17:21). Jesus was acutely aware of how deeply God cared for human beings. Jesus' intense longing for God gave Him the assurance that God loves and cares for every life. The pure desire for God, like the pure desire for an absent loved one, was itself an assurance of the power of God's love in the world, to which Jesus' own life was completely devoted. The nearness of the kingdom of God awakened more than love and compassion in Jesus. He also came to have a clear vision of His prophetic vocation. Jesus taught that truth, justice, and compassion were within the people's grasp, if only the people would seize them. The manifestation of these spiritual qualities in Jesus' life inspired the miraculous feeding of the five thousand (see John 6:1-13). Believing in Jesus and hearing and accepting His teachings satisfy the deepest hungers of life. When the Israelites wandered in the wilderness, God provided for their hunger and thirst through the gift of manna (see Exodus 16) and water from the rock (see Numbers 20:9-13). God's provisions for Israel continued through Jesus' teachings and works. What people need for life is available in Jesus. This is the message of John's gospel: Jesus is the Bread of Life.

II. EXPOSITION AND APPLICATION OF THE SCRIPTURE

A. Anxious for Bread
(John 6:22-26)

The day following, when the people which stood on the other side of the sea saw that there was none other boat there, save that one whereinto his disciples were entered, and that Jesus went not with his disciples into the boat, but that his disciples were gone away alone; (Howbeit there came other boats from Tiberias nigh unto the place where they did eat bread, after that the Lord had given thanks:) When the people therefore saw that Jesus was not there, neither his disciples, they also took shipping, and came to Capernaum, seeking for Jesus. And when they had found him on the other side of the sea, they said unto him, Rabbi, when camest thou hither? Jesus answered them and said, Verily, verily, I say unto you, Ye seek me, not because ye saw the miracles, but because ye did eat of the loaves, and were filled.

In first-century Palestine, the shortage of food was a constant concern and anxiety due to the ever-present threat of famine and drought. Local villagers struggled to find ways to meet the needs of their families. The daily anxiety of needing more and the fear of not finding resources necessary for survival were constantly on their minds. When their ancestors entered the Canaanite territory, they were often tempted to worship the idol gods of fertility believing that these fertility gods would provide for their need for food and water.

Jesus was aware that insecurities and fears of scarcity were the chief motivation of the villagers and the cause of their lack of faith. Jesus wanted to connect people who followed Him with the infinite supply of the "goods of the Spirit." The people had a tendency to overvalue their physical needs, while love, compassion, trust, and caring were in short supply. Jesus saw deeply into the people's real need. "Man shall not live by bread alone, but by every word that proceedeth out of the mouth of God" (Matthew 4:4). There was no separation in Jesus' consciousness among mind, body, and soul; life was a complete unit. How often do we base our associations and relationships with God and others on the acquisition of material possessions, when the real problem of our spirituality is the inner life? This is perhaps the basis of all human envying and strife—the drive or instinct to get more, the feeling that there is not enough to go around. God's abundance is grounded in love and grace which is sufficient for all human need.

B. Bread from Heaven
(John 6:27-31)

Labour not for the meat which perisheth, but for that meat which endureth unto everlasting life, which the Son of man shall give unto you: for him hath God the Father sealed. Then said they unto him, What shall we do, that we might work the works of God? Jesus answered and said unto them, This is the work of God, that ye believe on him whom he hath sent. They said therefore unto him, What sign shewest thou then, that we may see, and believe thee? what dost thou work? Our fathers did eat manna in the desert; as it is written, He gave them bread from heaven to eat.

The people who followed Jesus were anxious for a sign that validated Jesus as one who did the work of God. Jesus cast His lot with the poor and oppressed and taught them not to be anxious for physical security, but the crowd saw the relevance of Jesus and His teaching only in terms of a full stomach, not as a sign of God's true abundance. Jesus contrasted the crowd's anxiety and toil for food that perished with working for food that "endures to eternal life." The reference to food that perishes links with Jesus' earlier admonition about the perishable manna of Exodus 16:18-21. In His instructions, Jesus sought to free them from the shackles of their gross materialism.

The food that endures to eternal life, much like the living water of John 4:14, comes only from God, whose love is fully disclosed in Jesus. Jesus is God's gift of the abundant life. This is the sign that the people could not grasp or accept. It is ironic that the crowd asked Jesus for a sign of God's abundance immediately after the feeding miracle of five thousand in which they shared (see John 6:14, 26). They missed the sign of God's work and abundance in the identity of Jesus. The response of the people to Jesus' claim that He was sent by God with the seal of God's truth was to ask for a sign or revelation. "What sign therefore are you doing that we may come to see and believe you?" The crowd cited the fact that their fathers had eaten manna in the desert, and reminded Jesus that it was predicted that the Messiah would do even greater things than Moses, who had given their ancestors bread in the wilderness. Jesus corrected their false understanding of God's provision in the wilderness by pointing out that the miracle of that manna (provided so many years before) was not comparable to the true bread from heaven. The manna ceased after Moses's death, but the true bread from heaven endures to eternal life. It was not Moses who gave them bread from heaven, but God. God is the eternal donor, giver, and creator of both spiritual and physical food. To trust God's abundance is to accept God's offer of Jesus Christ. God is the true source of bread from heaven that does not perish. All other bread perishes. The Exodus gift of manna during Moses's time does not compare with the bread that Jesus offers. The Law came through Moses; grace and truth came through Jesus Christ (see John 1:17). Jesus is the medium of revelation between God and the world. One who believes in Jesus already has and will have eternal life. This truth is the truth that the crowd did not grasp. Jesus was the Bread of Life in two senses: there was life (Spirit-life of God) in Him—and Jesus imparted life to others. Jesus is the Bread of Life.

C. Bread for Life
(John 6:32-35)

Then Jesus said unto them, Verily, verily, I say unto you, Moses gave you not that bread from heaven; but my

Father giveth you the true bread from heaven. For the bread of God is he which cometh down from heaven, and giveth life unto the world. Then said they unto him, Lord, evermore give us this bread. And Jesus said unto them, I am the bread of life: he that cometh to me shall never hunger; and he that believeth on me shall never thirst.

Today, the social systems and structures that govern our economy are driven by consumerism, excessive greed, and capitalism. People live with a mentality of scarcity amid a land of abundance. The crowd that followed Jesus became anxious consumers of what they believed Jesus would do for them and were less concerned about what God's Spirit could do in them. They were less concerned about Jesus' vision of God's presence among them for the re-creation of the world in love and justice. In Jesus' understanding, the bounty of the land—crops, wine, beasts, and fruit—belonged and still belongs to God and it was/is through God's grace and love that all persons can know and share in His sufficiency. The church today might ask itself in our consumerist society how the people of God can demonstrate faith in the sufficiency of God. Christians affirm that everything people need for life is available through a relationship with Jesus. People of faith understand that the bread Jesus offers is nourishment for the mind, body, and soul. The Bread of Life is divine love, divine justice, divine compassion, and divine truth as the center of all human relations. This is what Jesus understood as His mission.

God's abundance is everywhere—in nature, the soil, the oceans, and fertile lands. Properly treated, nature seems capable of infinite self-replenishment. Seeds sown in fertile soil supply an abundance of fruit and food. God's abundance is everywhere; what is in short supply are fruits of the Spirit—the bread God offers to set one free from the anxieties of debt-acquired wealth, greed, and excessive consumerism. In the midst of God's abundance in the world, how can we explain the mentality of scarcity that many people have today? Surrounded by divine grace capable of meeting all human needs, how did we end up with love, justice, and compassion in short supply? Paul wrote, "God is able to provide you with every blessing in abundance so that you may have enough and may provide in abundance for every work" (see 2 Corinthians 9:8). Jesus' life—teachings, love, giving, and ultimate sacrifice—is God's abundance capable of meeting all needs of mind, body, and soul. Jesus is the Bread of Life.

III. CONCLUDING REFLECTION

Many people's identities and sense of self are tied to their places of work that provide them access to the wider world. By gaining identity from the possession of things, we establish those material goods as gods in our lives. We give these perishable gods the power to make us happy or miserable. By attaching our identities to that which is transient, we ignore the intrinsic spirituality of all human life. When the material world has more value to us than the spiritual qualities of relationships, we help maintain social structures that perpetuate materialism, a value system based on what people own rather than who people are in their deepest meaning and relationship to God and others around them. Those who seek well-being—who grasp for more than their share—will find life in the pinch of fear and anxiety. Those who live this way will reap only the anxiety of needing more and more, and the fear that someday it will all be taken away.

Jesus taught that "life is more than meat and drink" (see Luke 12:23). In other words, we are more than what we possess, more than what we eat or drink. The body has physical needs, but the fulfillment of bodily needs is not the end goal or ultimate concern of the Spirit within us. Jesus teaches us that true abundance comes to persons whose life meanings and purposes are sustained by faith in God. Those who live in ways that allow possession and profit to become more important than service and love to others fail to understand that Jesus offers the enduring qualities of the Spirit to sustain life. Jesus lived with confidence in God's grace and abundance. When people live with confidence in the spiritual realm of God's abundance, they find lives of plenty, which transcend the economies of scarcity and the anxieties and fears associated with it. Jesus offers us lives that move us away from obsessive consumerism and capitalism. The spiritual lesson Jesus teaches us is that we cannot buy the love and security we seek through material possession. "Be on your guard against all kinds of greed; a man's life does not consist in the abundance of his possessions" (Luke 12:15, NIV). They are not the bread that nurtures the spiritual qualities of the soul—but a confident love and a sustainable sense of life that come to us only as we let go of existential anxieties and live in the grace of God. We must accept the true Bread of Life that God offers us. Jesus is the Bread that God offers to nurture the soul, the true bread that will endure to eternal life.

PRAYER

Holy God, grant that we may live with trust in Your love every day. Grant that we share with the world the true Bread of Life that You offer in Christ. In Jesus' name we pray. Amen.

WORD POWER

"I Am"—Jesus' use of this designation evokes memories of God's pronouncement to Moses that God is "I AM." Thus, Christ again affirms His eternality and all-sufficiency.

HOME DAILY BIBLE READINGS
(April 30–May 6, 2012)

The Bread of Life

MONDAY, April 30: "Feeding the Hungry" (John 6:1-15)

TUESDAY, May 1: "Walking on Water" (John 6:16-21)

WEDNESDAY, May 2: "Giving Eternal Life" (John 6:36-40)

THURSDAY, May 3: "Offering Living Bread" (John 6:41-51)

FRIDAY, May 4: "The Life-giving Spirit" (John 6:60-65)

SATURDAY, May 5: "To Whom Can We Go?" (John 6:66-71)

SUNDAY, May 6: "The True Bread of Heaven" (John 6:22-35)

LESSON 11   May 13, 2012

THE GOOD SHEPHERD

DEVOTIONAL READING: **Psalm 28**
PRINT PASSAGE: **John 10:7-18**

BACKGROUND SCRIPTURE: **John 10:1-18**
KEY VERSE: **John 10:4**

John 10:7-18—KJV

7 Then said Jesus unto them again, Verily, verily, I say unto you, I am the door of the sheep.

8 All that ever came before me are thieves and robbers: but the sheep did not hear them.

9 I am the door: by me if any man enter in, he shall be saved, and shall go in and out, and find pasture.

10 The thief cometh not, but for to steal, and to kill, and to destroy: I am come that they might have life, and that they might have it more abundantly.

11 I am the good shepherd: the good shepherd giveth his life for the sheep.

12 But he that is an hireling, and not the shepherd, whose own the sheep are not, seeth the wolf coming, and leaveth the sheep, and fleeth: and the wolf catcheth them, and scattereth the sheep.

13 The hireling fleeth, because he is an hireling, and careth not for the sheep.

14 I am the good shepherd, and know my sheep, and am known of mine.

15 As the Father knoweth me, even so know I the Father: and I lay down my life for the sheep.

16 And other sheep I have, which are not of this fold: them also I must bring, and they shall hear my voice; and there shall be one fold, and one shepherd.

17 Therefore doth my Father love me, because I lay down my life, that I might take it again.

18 No man taketh it from me, but I lay it down of myself. I have power to lay it down, and I have power to take it again. This commandment have I received of my Father.

John 10:7-18—NIV

7 Therefore Jesus said again, "I tell you the truth, I am the gate for the sheep.

8 All who ever came before me were thieves and robbers, but the sheep did not listen to them.

9 I am the gate; whoever enters through me will be saved. He will come in and go out, and find pasture.

10 The thief comes only to steal and kill and destroy; I have come that they may have life, and have it to the full.

11 I am the good shepherd. The good shepherd lays down his life for the sheep.

12 The hired hand is not the shepherd who owns the sheep. So when he sees the wolf coming, he abandons the sheep and runs away. Then the wolf attacks the flock and scatters it.

13 The man runs away because he is a hired hand and cares nothing for the sheep.

14 I am the good shepherd; I know my sheep and my sheep know me—

15 just as the Father knows me and I know the Father—and I lay down my life for the sheep.

16 I have other sheep that are not of this sheep pen. I must bring them also. They too will listen to my voice, and there shall be one flock and one shepherd.

17 The reason my Father loves me is that I lay down my life—only to take it up again.

18 No one takes it from me, but I lay it down of my own accord. I have authority to lay it down and authority to take it up again. This command I received from my Father."

UNIFYING LESSON PRINCIPLE

People often follow strong leaders who may or may not have their best interests at heart. How do we know which leaders have our best interests at heart? Jesus was a strong leader whom people followed and who was willing to give up His life to save them from harm.

TOPICAL OUTLINE OF THE LESSON

I. Introduction
   A. The True Shepherd
   B. Biblical Background

II. Exposition and Application of the Scripture
   A. The Actions of a Good Shepherd-leader (John 10:7-10)
   B. The Model of a Good Shepherd-leader (John 10:11-16)
   C. The Sacrifice of the Good Shepherd-leader (John 10:17-18)

III. Concluding Reflection

LESSON OBJECTIVES

Upon the completion of this lesson, the students should know that:

1. Jesus was the Good Shepherd, in contrast to the Pharisees and false teachers who were before Him;
2. Jesus is the door, the only authentic access point to His sheep; and,
3. This analogy cannot be fully applied to individual congregations and local pastors.

POINTS TO BE EMPHASIZED

ADULT/YOUTH

Adult Topic: Following Good Leaders
Youth Topic: Leaders You Don't Follow
Adult Key Verse: John 10:4
Youth Key Verse: John 10:10
Print Passage: John 10:7-18

—There are two Greek words for *good*. The first, not used in this passage, is *agathos*, which describes the moral quality of a thing. The second, used here, is *kalos*, which means "model" or "true," implying that a thing or a person is not only good but also that in the goodness, there is a quality of winsomeness, loveliness, and attractiveness.

—This passage reflects the image of the shepherd in Ezekiel 34:11-16.

—In ancient Palestine, shepherds may have had to risk their lives to prevent wild animals from destroying the flock.

—There are two terms that accompany the "I am" passages in John 10:1-18: *gate* and *good shepherd*.

—The shepherd was a common image used for rulers, from ancient Egypt to Israel. It reflected both versatile strength and nurture. It was an image of engaged leadership. The word *pastor* comes from the Latin word for "shepherd." In many traditions, the ordained minister is referred to as the "pastor," and ministerial care of the congregation is referred to as "pastoral care."

CHILDREN

Children Topic: The Good Shepherd
Key Verse: John 10:14
Print Passage: John 10:7-18

—Jesus watches over believers and protects them from harm.
—Followers of Jesus should turn away from leaders who may harm, abandon, or even destroy them.

—Believers know that Jesus loves them and knows each of them by name.

—Believers know that Jesus protects them and serves as the gate to salvation for them.

—Jesus was completely in control of everything when He died for all, and He knew He would live again.

I. INTRODUCTION
A. The True Shepherd

Using the pastoral image of shepherd life, Jesus contrasted false leaders and good teachers with a self-explanatory allegory of the good shepherd. Jesus made the contrast between Himself and the Pharisees. Jesus started out with a general statement about the distinguishing attributes of the true versus the false shepherds (teachers and leaders). The true shepherd came through the door of the sheepfold, which was a roofless enclosure where sheep were herded. Any other person climbing up by some other way over the wall was a thief who came to steal, or a bandit-robber who stole by violence. A true shepherd would open the door and the sheep would listen to his voice. He would call his own sheep and lead them out. The loneliness of pastoral life bound the shepherd and his sheep together in companionship, dangers, and the support both mutually enjoyed. There were the dangers of ditches, floods, wolves, thirst, winter storms, steep mountains, and straying, when the sheep looked to their shepherd for protection. There were occasions of care and tenderness shown from the true shepherd for the sheep, leading his flock out in the morning and returning with them to the safety of the fold at nightfall. The sheep knew the shepherd's manner and his voice. The shepherd led the sheep out on many occasions, and so they trusted him. The sheep would not follow a stranger, but would flee from him as from a wolf.

From the tenderness of this intimate relationship, Jesus drew the lesson of the true or good shepherd-teacher. The Pharisees were so absorbed in their own religious piety that they did not understand Jesus' allegory of using them as examples of false leaders and teachers. The lesson should be revealing and helpful to churches who want to cultivate good spiritual leadership. The impact of good leaders in contrast to poor ones—and the wide difference between caring teachers and false teachers—ought to be of grave concern for the church today. Jesus' exemplary model of leadership is a spiritual paradigm or pattern of God's love for humanity.

B. Biblical Background

Among the "I am" sayings of Jesus is the solemn declaration: "I am the door of the sheep." This reminds us of other declarations that Jesus made about His identity, nature, and mission: "I Am the Bread of Life," "the Living Water," "the True Vine," and "Light of the World." When Jesus called Himself "the Light of the World" or "the Bread of Life," He infuriated those who saw Jesus as a poor peasant lad from Nazareth. For Jesus, the Spirit of God gave authentication to His being and provided purity and healing by means of His own love and compassion (see John 9:1-7). The people saw Jesus differently from the Scribes and Pharisees, whose teaching was empty of care. Jesus taught as one with the authority of the Spirit. Jesus claimed a spiritual authority implicitly greater than that of priests in the Temple. Jesus' mind and character consisted of a combination of love, faith, and compassion, qualities that made Him a good leader. It was this visionary fervor coupled with a sense of oneness with the Spirit of God that propelled Jesus' self-revelation as the good and true Shepherd of God's people.

II. EXPOSITION AND APPLICATION OF THE SCRIPTURE

A. The Actions of a Good Shepherd-leader (John 10:7-10)

Then said Jesus unto them again, Verily, verily, I say unto you, I am the door of the sheep. All that ever came before me are thieves and robbers: but the sheep did not hear them. I am the door: by me if any man enter in, he shall be saved, and shall go in and out, and find pasture. The thief cometh not, but for to steal, and to kill, and to destroy: I am come that they might have life, and that they might have it more abundantly.

Jesus compared His relationship to the sheep to the actions of a good shepherd-leader who entered the shepherd gate or door the right way. The sheepfold (entrance way) was usually constructed adjoining the house, and had a separate entrance gate. The only access to the sheepfold was through the gate. The shepherd came through the door of the sheepfold in a pastoral way that the sheep were familiar with and knew, calling them by name, and leading them. The sheep would respond to the good shepherd who entered the gate properly, but would refuse to respond to the stranger, the thief, and the bandit.

The *Interpreter's Bible* provides an insightful exposition of John 10 that puts the good shepherd-leader imagery in theological perspective. "The image of sheep and shepherd were frequently used with metaphorical significance within the Old Testament. Traditionally, God is understood as the shepherd and God's people as sheep (see Psalm 23:1; 74:1; 79:13; 80:1; 95:7; 100:3). Of particular importance for the background of Jesus' use of the pastoral imagery of a good shepherd is Ezekiel 34, in which the kings of Israel are the bad shepherds who endanger and exploit the flock (see Ezekiel 34:1-10). God is the good shepherd who will rescue the sheep and who will place them in the care of 'my servant David' (verse 23, that is, a restored monarchy)." In Psalm 23, God is depicted as the good Shepherd who provides for the flock's every need.

Jesus claimed to be the only door of the spiritual fold by which the true shepherd entered. There had been many false messiahs and self-appointed leaders who had wreaked havoc with the flock. The scribes and Pharisees had just given an illustration of this by excommunicating the poor beggar whom Jesus healed. But Pharisees and Scribes did not understand

Jesus' statement that "I am the door" by which they themselves must enter the spiritual fold if they wished to be saved. Jesus repeated, "If anyone enters through me, he shall be saved, and shall come in and go out in the daily routine of the flock and shall go on finding pasture" (see verse 9). Jesus drew the contrast between Himself and false teachers. The thief did not come except to steal, kill, and destroy. In contrast, Jesus came that His followers may go on having life and a surplus or overflowing of blessings.

Jesus identified Himself as the gate of the sheep (in verse 7, one's identity as a member of the flock was determined exclusively by one's relationship to Jesus as the gate). Those who enter the fold by ways other than the gate are thieves and bandits. By identifying Himself as the door, Jesus declared Himself as the point of access to God for the flock. The central affirmation of the Gospel is that Jesus came to bring life (see John 3:16; 5:24; 6:40).

B. The Model of a Good Shepherd-leader (John 10:11-16)

I am the good shepherd: the good shepherd giveth his life for the sheep. But he that is an hireling, and not the shepherd, whose own the sheep are not, seeth the wolf coming, and leaveth the sheep, and fleeth: and the wolf catcheth them, and scattereth the sheep. The hireling fleeth, because he is an hireling, and careth not for the sheep. I am the good shepherd, and know my sheep, and am known of mine. As the Father knoweth me, even so know I the Father: and I lay down my life for the sheep. And other sheep I have, which are not of this fold: them also I must bring, and they shall hear my voice; and there shall be one fold, and one shepherd.

The adjective that John used for *good* means "model" or "true." Biblically, it has reference to a model shepherd-leader as described in Ezekiel

34. According to Ezekiel 34:11-16, God the Good Shepherd cares for the sheep, liberating them from the places to which they have been scattered, feeding them, and tending to the weak, the injured, and the lost. By identifying Himself as the Good Shepherd, Jesus upheld Himself as the model fulfilling God's promises and doing God's work (see John 4:34; 17:4). The Pharisees and scribes were poor models of the "good shepherd" tradition of Ezekiel. Unlike Jesus, they exploited the people with yokes of the Law and neglected to practice the weightiest matters of the Law, which were love and compassion. The Pharisees' and scribes' leadership contrasted that of Jesus'—in that they were unwilling to lay down their lives for the sheep (see Zechariah 13:7-9); the death of the shepherd is required so that the flock can be purified.

In ancient Israel, kings were expected to "tend" their subjects (sheep) justly, especially those who were most vulnerable to abuse—widows, orphans, the poor, the infirm, and the displaced. The Pharisees and scribes whom Jesus encountered in the villages knew the history of Israel's past shepherds who neglected such responsibilities of care and protection of the sheep. How a society and its leaders treat those who struggle against disadvantages speaks volumes about that society's true values—not the ones it professes to hold, but those revealed in policy and action. American society provides all-too-stark examples of our failure to imitate the divine/good shepherd-leader.

God stands against the bad shepherds and false teachers and prophets who cause vulnerable sheep to stray. Jesus is God's response to the evil perpetuated by false teachers and leaders. Jesus' model of leadership calls for an end to the irresponsible tending of sheep, leaders who indulge themselves at the sheep's expense. As the good shepherd, Jesus will rescue God's flock from bad leaders. When the sheepfold is denied the care and protection of a good shepherd, the sheep are left as prey for ravaging beasts. The shepherd/flock metaphor is an enduring model of effective spiritual leadership of God's people. Its significance for Christian ministry is reflected in our use of the word *pastor* to refer to ordained ministers. Ministers serve as shepherds who are obedient to God. They are not self-appointed, nor are they engaged primarily by the flock. Instead, they are called by God to divine service. The pastoral function is not, however, the sole responsibility of ordained ministers. Authentic leadership requires "pastoral care" from all spiritual disciples of Christ. Everyone in a congregation of care and love should consider how the shepherd-leader metaphor might impact his or her actions. As leaders of care and compassion, shepherds are servant-leaders who do not use persons, things, and situations for personal advantage or exploitation. The servant-leader who is a good shepherd acts as God's steward of care and love, protecting the spirituality of the people and providing for those who are entrusted to his or her care. Servant leaders recognize that the people, the flock, belong to God.

C. The Sacrifice of the Good Shepherd-leader (John 10:17-18)

Therefore doth my Father love me, because I lay down my life, that I might take it again. No man taketh it from me, but I lay it down of myself. I have power to lay it down, and I have power to take it again. This commandment have I received of my Father.

The exposition in the *Interpreter's Bible*

indicates that the discourse of John 10:17-18 deals with Jesus' death and relationship to God. These verses focus on three theological themes that are essential to understanding the statement that Jesus made that the good shepherd lays down his life for the sheep. The whole of Jesus' life was a sacrifice for revealing the love and Spirit of God to the world (see John 3:16). God endorsed and anointed Jesus because Jesus lived out and embodied God's commandment fully. The core commitment and value by which the model of the good shepherd-leader was fulfilled was love. Love was at the core of Jesus' willingness to lay down his life for the disciples. Jesus passed on the commandment to love to the disciples, to live fully in the love of God and love of God's flock. Jesus' sacrifice of His life for the sheep was the ultimate expression of the love relationship that defines who He is and what He does and how He enacts God's will for the world.

Jesus made it clear that laying down His life was an act not forced upon Him but freely chosen as obedience to God. Jesus was not a victim in death nor a martyr against His will; "Father, if you are willing, take this cup from me; yet not my will, but yours be done" (Luke 22:42, NIV). Jesus revealed God's will for the world not only in His death, but also in His victory over death. Because Jesus' life completely embodied the love of God, because the Spirit of God was deeply alive and active in Jesus' being and manifested in His every action, and because the teaching and revelation of Jesus was the Word of God, God transformed Jesus' death into resurrection. As Jesus is the Good Shepherd of God's flock, His leadership is the eternal model and exemplar of God's loving and liberating leadership in the world.

III. CONCLUDING REFLECTION

Although many people today will have had little or no direct contact with the imagery of shepherds or sheep, the metaphor remains powerful. Witness the popularity of Psalm 23, which affirms that even as God's sheep "walk through the valley of the shadow of death," they do not fear, for God is with them as protector and guide. For many Christians, Jesus assumes the role of the Good Shepherd-leader. As one biblical scholar observes, "The image of Jesus as the good shepherd has a perennial hold on Christian imagination and piety. As the exposition of John 10:11 indicates, Jesus appropriates the 'good shepherd leader' metaphor because he, like a good shepherd, 'lays down his life for the sheep.'" The image of Jesus as the Good Shepherd has a perennial hold on Christian imaginations as the supreme model of a good leader. The imagery of Jesus as the Good Shepherd has influenced the church's view of its leaders, so that in many leadership traditions, the ordained clergy is referred to as the "pastor" or shepherd of the flock. Ministerial practices that involve congregational nurture are referred to as "pastoral care." Behind Jesus' model of a good shepherd, the ministerial vocation is a calling to lead in the steps of Jesus' leadership. The model of the good shepherd-leader has much to say about leaders at all levels of society, be they politicians, health care providers, supervisors, teachers, pastors, or parents.

PRAYER

Dear Lord, as the Good Shepherd of life, thank You for the sacrifice of Your love for our salvation. May the example of Your love guide us in our actions and decisions to love as You have loved and to give as You have given. In Jesus' name we pray. Amen.

WORD POWER

Servant-leader—This term is most accurately and fully depicted in Jesus Christ, the Good Shepherd. He is fully servant in that He cares for all of the heads or the sheep, up to giving His life for them. He is fully leader in that He calls His own unto Himself.

HOME DAILY BIBLE READINGS
(May 7-13, 2012)

The Good Shepherd

MONDAY, May 7: "Sheep without a Shepherd" (2 Chronicles 18:12-22)
TUESDAY, May 8: "A New Shepherd for Israel" (Numbers 27:12-20)
WEDNESDAY, May 9: "The Shepherd David" (Psalm 78:67-72)
THURSDAY, May 10: "Lord, Be Our Shepherd" (Psalm 28)
FRIDAY, May 11: "Shepherd of Israel, Restore Us" (Psalm 80:1-7)
SATURDAY, May 12: "The Sheep Follow" (John 10:1-6)
SUNDAY, May 13: "'I Am the Good Shepherd'" (John 10:7-18)

LESSON 12   May 20, 2012

THE RESURRECTION AND THE LIFE

DEVOTIONAL READING: **1 Corinthians 15:50-58**   BACKGROUND SCRIPTURE: **John 11:1-27**
PRINT PASSAGE: **John 11:17-27**   KEY VERSE: **John 11:25**

John 11:17-27—KJV

17 Then when Jesus came, he found that he had lain in the grave four days already.
18 Now Bethany was nigh unto Jerusalem, about fifteen furlongs off:
19 And many of the Jews came to Martha and Mary, to comfort them concerning their brother.
20 Then Martha, as soon as she heard that Jesus was coming, went and met him: but Mary sat still in the house.
21 Then said Martha unto Jesus, Lord, if thou hadst been here, my brother had not died.
22 But I know, that even now, whatsoever thou wilt ask of God, God will give it thee.
23 Jesus saith unto her, Thy brother shall rise again.
24 Martha saith unto him, I know that he shall rise again in the resurrection at the last day.
25 Jesus said unto her, I am the resurrection, and the life: he that believeth in me, though he were dead, yet shall he live:
26 And whosoever liveth and believeth in me shall never die. Believest thou this?
27 She saith unto him, Yea, Lord: I believe that thou art the Christ, the Son of God, which should come into the world.

John 11:17-27—NIV

17 On his arrival, Jesus found that Lazarus had already been in the tomb for four days.
18 Bethany was less than two miles from Jerusalem,
19 and many Jews had come to Martha and Mary to comfort them in the loss of their brother.
20 When Martha heard that Jesus was coming, she went out to meet him, but Mary stayed at home.
21 "Lord," Martha said to Jesus, "if you had been here, my brother would not have died.
22 But I know that even now God will give you whatever you ask."
23 Jesus said to her, "Your brother will rise again."
24 Martha answered, "I know he will rise again in the resurrection at the last day."
25 Jesus said to her, "I am the resurrection and the life. He who believes in me will live, even though he dies;
26 and whoever lives and believes in me will never die. Do you believe this?"
27 "Yes, Lord," she told him, "I believe that you are the Christ, the Son of God, who was to come into the world."

BIBLE FACT

Resurrection and *resuscitation* are different in that resurrection is eternal. Lazarus was raised only to die again; Jesus was raised once forever. Thus, He *is* the resurrection. As such, Jesus treats death as we treat sleep. So great is the Lord's power to raise us from death that it can be compared to an adult's awakening a sleeping child.

UNIFYING LESSON PRINCIPLE

People often think that death separates us from everything we know. How can we have confidence that death is not the end, but a transformation? Jesus promised that those who believe in Him will—even though they die—have a new relationship with God.

TOPICAL OUTLINE OF THE LESSON

I. Introduction
A. Jesus Confronts Death
B. Biblical Background

II. Exposition and Application of the Scripture
A. The Choice of Life over Death (John 11:17-19)
B. The Gateway to Life (John 11:20-27)

III. Concluding Reflection

LESSON OBJECTIVES

Upon the completion of this lesson, the students will know that:

1. Death does not separate us from the love of God;
2. Losing a loved one to death does not mean losing the meaning and value of the loved one; and,
3. The immortality of God's love in the life and spirit of a believer is eternal.

POINTS TO BE EMPHASIZED

ADULT/YOUTH
Adult Topic: **Life that Does Not End**
Youth Topic: **Life that Doesn't End**
Adult/Youth Key Verse: **John 11:25**
Print Passage: **John 11:17-27**

—As a cultural norm, Mary and Martha, as single women, would have been dependent on Lazarus for their livelihood. Losing Lazarus would have meant losing a brother and losing their means of living.
—Jesus told the disciples that Lazarus was asleep (*kekoimetai*) and that Jesus was going to awaken (*exupniso*) him. Both *kekoimetai* and *exupniso* can be understood in two ways. The former means "asleep," but it is also a euphemism for "death." The latter means "awaken," but it can also mean "save."
—Jesus' conversation with Martha helped her affirm her belief in Jesus as the Messiah.
—The word *believe* means more than assenting to a truth. The roots of the word suggest giving one's love and commitment to that truth.
—Both sisters affirmed that if Jesus had arrived sooner, Lazarus would not have died.

CHILDREN
Children Topic: **He Lives Again**
Key Verse: **John 11:25**
Print Passage: **John 11:17-19, 32-44**

—Jesus cares for us and has experienced what we feel.
—Jesus empathized with the grief and helplessness of those who mourned at Lazarus's tomb.
—Jesus prayed prior to raising Lazarus from the grave so that those in His presence would know that God the Father sent Him.
—Jesus has power over life and death.

I. INTRODUCTION

A. Jesus Confronts Death

The miraculous events in Bethany brought about a new level of political exposure for Jesus. Bethany was a small village that Jesus often visited—specifically the home of Martha and Mary, as a place for refuge. Unfortunately, Jesus was away at the time of Lazarus' death, because He feared stoning at the hands of His opponents (see John 11:7-9). Jesus wanted to avoid any action that Pilate or Caiaphas might take against Him. He also wanted to avoid the deteriorating situation that simmered among those loyal to the high priest, due to His teaching and actions in the Temple.

When word came to Jesus about the severe illness of Lazarus, His response to this family crisis deeply disturbed Mary and Martha and created what grief counselors call "an emotional or spiritual impasse" for the grieving family. The death of Lazarus caused Mary and Martha to confront the limitations imposed upon life through death. The death of Lazarus was their "dark night of the soul." In such an experience of human limitation, the Spirit of God calls us beyond ourselves, beyond where we are, into transcendence. We are challenged to make the journey from loving, serving, and "being with"—because of the pleasure and joy it gives us—to loving and serving regardless of the cost or circumstance. This, to say the least, is not easy but difficult on all levels of emotions and spirituality that we only can know by going through the experience.

B. Biblical Background

The home of Lazarus and his sisters was situated some two miles southeast of Jerusalem, on the slope of the Mount of Olives. Mary was identified by John as the one who anointed Jesus with expensive ointment in the home of Simon, who had been cured of leprosy. This anointing took place some weeks after the raising of Lazarus and not long before the Crucifixion. The act of devotion of Mary to Jesus stood out in the memory of John as his narrative mentioned her in the gospel account. Mary's eagerness to learn at Jesus' feet was commended by Jesus on His frequent visits to this hospitable home (see Luke 10:38). In the narrative, Martha, the pragmatist, was more concerned with housework and meal preparation than listening to the teaching of Jesus. The individual personalities of Martha and Mary became even more pronounced during the illness and eventual death of their brother.

Illness and death challenge the depths of our relationships with loved ones. The message of Mary and Martha to Jesus about the illness of their brother was sent with anxious hearts, and revealed a complete confidence in Jesus' friendship. When the messenger delivered the message, Jesus sent back the reply: "This illness is not to end in death, but is for the glory or honor of God, that the Son of God may be glorified through it." In His reply, Jesus gave them His view of the experience of illness—that illness is a part of life and thus is useful in the providence of God. The illness of Lazarus would be "for the glory of God." John's narrative helps us toward an understanding of Jesus' theological perspective of death. We think of life as moving us to the point of death; we rarely think of death moving us to life. What did Jesus mean when He said to Mary and Martha (in John 11:25), "I am the resurrection, and the life: he that believeth in me, though he were dead, yet shall he live"? The study of this lesson will help us grasp the meaning of Jesus' words for our life and death experiences.

II. EXPOSITION AND APPLICATION OF THE SCRIPTURE

A. The Choice of Life over Death
(John 11:17-19)

Then when Jesus came, he found that he had lain in the grave four days already. Now Bethany was nigh unto Jerusalem, about fifteen furlongs off: And many of the Jews came to Martha and Mary, to comfort them concerning their brother.

The life system on which one depends breaks down at death. One's usual way of functioning or relating provides no satisfaction and does not work. What formerly was essential for growth and fidelity now hinders growth. One cannot relate to the loved one as he or she did before. Certainty and pleasure may give way to ambiguity, misunderstanding, and a sense of abandonment. There seems to be no possibility of moving forward. This occurred in the lives of Martha and Mary when their beloved brother died. Lazarus was dead and everything stalled; beyond his death, there was no hope.

The message that Mary and Martha sent to Jesus was, "He whom You love is sick" (John 11:3, NASB)—which garnered a response from Jesus that they did not expect. Jesus' response to the family crisis turned the focus away from the illness of Lazarus and to an understanding of the illness as an occasion for the revelation of the glory of God (see John 1:14; 2:11). That is, from the theological perspective of John's gospel, the character and identity of God would be revealed in crisis. This is difficult to grasp when a loved one is deeply grieved over after his or her prolonged illness and subsequent death. Through this illness and death of Lazarus, the gift of life would reveal the glory of God. The gift of life would reveal Jesus' relationship with God. John's gospel narrative links Lazarus's death with Jesus' own death and refers to His resurrection and ascension (see John 12:16, 23, 28; 13:31).

Lazarus's illness was not ultimately about death—it was about life. It was about life that comes through the power of God that was evident in Jesus' life on earth. John's gospel highlighted this event to dramatize the symbolic picture of Jesus as one whose life, power, and love is stronger than death. At their brother's death, Martha and Mary were inconsolable. Martha rebuked Jesus for not getting there in time, and Mary flatly refused to leave the house to see Him as He approached Bethany (see John 11: 17-21). The description of Jesus' own pain over Lazarus's death includes the shortest verse in the English Bible: "Jesus wept" (John 11:35). Never was Jesus more grieved: "He censured himself in the spirit" and "shook himself" (see John 11:33, 38). Those people who were present were deeply moved by Jesus' depth of weeping.

Human pain and joy are not alien emotions separate from the brooding Spirit of God. People touch God just as God touches people.

The message, here, is that death and dying yield meaningful revelations about life.

In making the decision to return to Bethany, Jesus chose life over death. This is the constant struggle and choice we face daily. Death keeps life imprisoned in fear and hinders decisions. Jesus referred to Lazarus's death as being "sleep." The disciples did not understand why Jesus would risk His life by returning to Judea if Lazarus was only "asleep." Jesus saw the cessation of physical life of Lazarus as a moment to deepen the disciples' faith in God's power over life and death. The great challenge to Jesus' disciples and us is to trust God's love in every situation or circumstance of life and death. When we lose a family member or friend to death or when we become jobless—when we live through a separation or a divorce, or an earthquake or flood destroys our homes or touches us—the question of "why" spontaneously emerges. "Why me?" "Why now?" "Why here?" Martha and Mary also wondered "why," but without an answer. The unanswered "why" question moved them to place blame on Jesus: "If you had been here, then Lazarus would not have died" (see verse 21). In the brokenness of death, we are tempted to try to rationalize the death over which we have no control with our conscious or unconscious evaluation of what happened or who could have prevented it from happening. Our effort to explain death is futile; our capacity for life beyond death is open to our trust in God. This is what Martha and Mary discovered by trusting Jesus; they placed their brokenness under His love and power.

B. The Gateway to Life
(John 11:20-27)

Then Martha, as soon as she heard that Jesus was coming, went and met him: but Mary sat still in the house. Then said Martha unto Jesus, Lord, if thou hadst been here, my brother had not died. But I know, that even now, whatsoever thou wilt ask of God, God will give it thee. Jesus saith unto her, Thy brother shall rise again. Martha saith unto him, I know that he shall rise again in the resurrection at the last day. Jesus said unto her, I am the resurrection, and the life: he that believeth in me, though he were dead, yet shall he live: And whosoever liveth and believeth in me shall never die. Believest thou this? She saith unto him, Yea, Lord: I believe that thou art the Christ, the Son of God, which should come into the world.

John's gospel has notions of life and death very different from the view of those which we have today. Whereas we think of life as the continuing functioning of the individual organism and death as the cessation of such functioning, the Gospel understands life and death as realities related to God. Life and death are profound expressions of relatedness—that is, they have a symbiotic relationship, meaning that one cannot exist without the other. Life's purpose and meaning cannot be understood apart from understanding life's relationship to death. The miracle of the raising of Lazarus from the dead illustrates the relatedness of Jesus, not only to life and death, but to God—as He declared, "I am the resurrection and the life. The one who believes in me, even if he dies, will live" (see verses 25 and 26). When Jesus identifies Himself with the images of the resurrection and the life, He gives concrete expression to His unity with God and God's creation. In the "I am the resurrection, and the life" statement, Jesus declares that God's power over life and death is shared with Him (see John 5:21-29). When an individual believes in Jesus, he or she accepts God's love and will for the salvation of the world. Thus, theologically, "the resurrection and the life" manifests the power of God not as a continuation of physical life, but as power to continue the meaning and purpose of life beyond death. Jesus defeated the power of death because in Him, the world met the power of the love of God incarnate (see Romans 8:35-39). God's full sharing of the power of life and death with Jesus is an expression of God's love for Jesus and the world. Thus, life is grounded in God's love, from which neither death, affliction, anguish, or persecution can separate us.

Life and death are not simply the state of the individual person, but are expressions of the relationship between the person and the community, as related to and governed by God's love. Life in the Gospel means relatedness to divine love over which death has no power. The deep truth is that human suffering and death need not be obstacles to the joy and peace that God desires for us, but can, instead, become the means to the gateway of life.

III. CONCLUDING REFLECTION

Death and dying make the demand that we hand over our powerlessness to the inspiration and power of God. John's gospel reminds us that Jesus' powerful announcement to Mary and Martha suggests that the church needs to embrace Jesus as the Resurrection and the Life. This is true not only at times of death, but also in the daily moments of our human lives. It is time, because these moments—whether or not one is conscious of them—are also lived in the face of death. The story of Mary and Martha prompts the church to reflect on death and dying as related to God's love, a love that in the life of Jesus gives Him power over death—not only in the crisis moment of death, but also for all moments in life. Jesus invites the church to claim that death is indeed an inescapable part of the believer's life, but that it also belongs to the ongoing, life-giving power of God.

PRAYER

Dear God, help us to know Your love as the deepest reality of life. Fill us with divine love so that we live—without fear of death, but in the joy of life. In Jesus' name we pray. Amen.

WORD POWER

Resurrection—it is "a standing up" or "a recovery." Martha saw resurrection as an event; Jesus revealed that resurrection is a person. He is the "standing up." He is our "recovery."

HOME DAILY BIBLE READINGS
(May 14-20, 2012)

The Resurrection and the Life

LESSON 13   May 27, 2012

THE WAY, THE TRUTH, AND THE LIFE

DEVOTIONAL READING: **Matthew 7:13-20**
PRINT PASSAGE: **John 14:1-14**

BACKGROUND SCRIPTURE: **John 14:1-14**
KEY VERSE: **John 14:6**

John 14:1-14—KJV

LET NOT your heart be troubled: ye believe in God, believe also in me.

2 In my Father's house are many mansions: if it were not so, I would have told you. I go to prepare a place for you.

3 And if I go and prepare a place for you, I will come again, and receive you unto myself; that where I am, there ye may be also.

4 And whither I go ye know, and the way ye know.

5 Thomas saith unto him, Lord, we know not whither thou goest; and how can we know the way?

6 Jesus saith unto him, I am the way, the truth, and the life: no man cometh unto the Father, but by me.

7 If ye had known me, ye should have known my Father also: and from henceforth ye know him, and have seen him.

8 Philip saith unto him, Lord, shew us the Father, and it sufficeth us.

9 Jesus saith unto him, Have I been so long time with you, and yet hast thou not known me, Philip? he that hath seen me hath seen the Father; and how sayest thou then, Shew us the Father?

10 Believest thou not that I am in the Father, and the Father in me? the words that I speak unto you I speak not of myself: but the Father that dwelleth in me, he doeth the works.

11 Believe me that I am in the Father, and the Father in me: or else believe me for the very works' sake.

12 Verily, verily, I say unto you, He that believeth on me, the works that I do shall he do also; and greater works than these shall he do; because I go unto my Father.

13 And whatsoever ye shall ask in my name, that will I do, that the Father may be glorified in the Son.

14 If ye shall ask any thing in my name, I will do it.

John 14:1-14—NIV

"DO NOT let your hearts be troubled. Trust in God; trust also in me.

2 In my Father's house are many rooms; if it were not so, I would have told you. I am going there to prepare a place for you.

3 And if I go and prepare a place for you, I will come back and take you to be with me that you also may be where I am.

4 You know the way to the place where I am going."

5 Thomas said to him, "Lord, we don't know where you are going, so how can we know the way?"

6 Jesus answered, "I am the way and the truth and the life. No one comes to the Father except through me.

7 If you really knew me, you would know my Father as well. From now on, you do know him and have seen him."

8 Philip said, "Lord, show us the Father and that will be enough for us."

9 Jesus answered: "Don't you know me, Philip, even after I have been among you such a long time? Anyone who has seen me has seen the Father. How can you say, 'Show us the Father'?

10 Don't you believe that I am in the Father, and that the Father is in me? The words I say to you are not just my own. Rather, it is the Father, living in me, who is doing his work.

11 Believe me when I say that I am in the Father and the Father is in me; or at least believe on the evidence of the miracles themselves.

12 I tell you the truth, anyone who has faith in me will do what I have been doing. He will do even greater things than these, because I am going to the Father.

13 And I will do whatever you ask in my name, so that the Son may bring glory to the Father.

14 You may ask me for anything in my name, and I will do it."

People always try to find direction in their lives. How can we know which way to go? Jesus proclaimed that He was the way people would come to God—because He was in God and God was in Him.

TOPICAL OUTLINE OF THE LESSON

I. **Introduction**
   A. Jesus Is the Way!
   B. Biblical Background

II. **Exposition and Application of the Scripture**
   A. How to Be Untroubled (John 14:1-4)
   B. There Is Always God (John 14:5-10)
   C. Following Jesus' Model of Service (John 14:11-14)

III. **Concluding Reflection**

LESSON OBJECTIVES

Upon the completion of this lesson, the students should know that:

1. Jesus' life provided spiritual elements essential for Christian discipleship;

2. Faith in Jesus is the only pathway to faith in God;

3. Believers find in Jesus' ministry a model for their own service; and,

4. Trusting the promises of Jesus for direction in the midst of uncertainty is the way to fulfill God's purpose in life.

POINTS TO BE EMPHASIZED

ADULT/YOUTH

Adult Topic: Finding Direction for Life
Youth Topic: No Other Way!
Adult/Youth Key Verse: John 14:6
Print Passage: John 14:1-14

—The word *oikia*, often translated as "house," a physical structure, may also be translated as "household," a community of people.

—This passage is the beginning of a "farewell" address that Jesus gave to the disciples.

—The Greek term for *believe* may also be translated "have confidence and obey" or "be assured and follow."

—The word *dwell* is used to talk about believers' relationship with God and Jesus.

—Thomas misunderstood Jesus' use of "way" as a geographical term.

—The word *hodos* can be translated as "road" or "way."

CHILDREN

Children Topic: Jesus Gives True Life
Key Verse: John 14:6
Print Passage: John 14:1-14

—Jesus assures us that our way to eternal life is to trust in Him.

—Jesus will bring all believers to a prepared place.

—The only way to God the Father is through God the Son.

—Even though the disciples had been with Jesus for some time, it was necessary for Jesus to identify Himself.

—Jesus is the totally human and totally divine visible image of the invisible God, who completely reveals to us what God is like.

—When believers' prayers are aligned with the character and will of God, God grants their requests.

I. INTRODUCTION

A. Jesus Is the Way!

Before one can know what Jesus meant by the words "I am the way, the truth, and the life," the context in which He spoke those words must be understood. The context was not one absent of fears, tension, and conflict. In fact, mounting fears surrounded Jesus and His disciples as Herod Antipas reacted to Jesus' prophetic ministry. The reaction of Herod Antipas to Jesus is understandable, given the fact that the Roman Empire was a mere generation old, and its policy of violently protecting its power was as necessary as it was ruthless to maintain its world status. Because of Jesus' prophetic character, Galileans compared Jesus to Elijah, the prophet of Mt. Carmel. Jesus spoke and acted with prophetic authority in His teachings (see Luke 11:49). Jesus knew that prophets in the mold of Elijah or Elisha had entered into direct conflict with the kings of their time, demanding they conform to the rule of divine justice. Although Jesus never formed a military group, Herod Antipas would have seen Jesus and His disciples as a potential army, a band of rabble rousers who could ignite the fire of revolution in Galilee. Herod Antipas would not tolerate Jesus' revolutionary speech about the reign of God, an irreversible change in the system values of the Empire. It was in this context that the disciples of Jesus became deeply concerned about the kind of revolution that Jesus was leading, and this moved Jesus to say to His disciples in John 13:33 (NIV), "My children, I will be with you only a little longer. You will look for me, and just as I told the Jews, so I tell you now: Where I am going, you cannot come." This profession only intensified the fears and tension of the disciples, to which Jesus responded by saying these comforting words to them: "Do not let your hearts be troubled. Believe in God, believe also in me" (John 14:1, NRSV). The key phrase to remember in the study of this lesson is "believe also in me," or "trust Jesus" for life's direction.

B. Biblical Background

Jesus' prophetic pronouncements about the imminent coming of the kingdom of God signaled a revolution in the name of God to the disciples. This was also in the mind of Herod Antipas and created conflict for Herod between the kingdom of God and Herod's empire. Elijah's authority had been confirmed by the prophetic feats that brought drought and floods (see 1 Kings 17:1-7; 18:25-38); and the killing of the prophets of Baal (see 1 Kings 18:39-40). Many Jews believed that God would again send Elijah, whose signs would herald the fire and healing of the divine kingdom (see Malachi 4:1-2). The prophetic fame of Jesus branded Him as a potentially greater threat than John the Baptist, whom Herod Antipas had beheaded. Jesus' healing miracles became a sign for the restoration of the community of Israel.

In studying this lesson, it is important to note that perhaps Jesus was concerned about the fear in the communities of His disciples who lived on the dangerous edge and tension of political and cultural estrangement within the Roman Empire. In His teachings, Jesus stressed His growing conviction that the power of God's Spirit and the coming kingdom of God would see the disciples through any threat. Jesus' sense of the violence around Him, and the conflict between fear and confidence, compassion and judgment were all resolved in His complete trust in the Spirit of God and the divine kingdom. Although events at the time were moving quickly both in the politics of Galilee and in His own spiritual quest, Jesus' deep trust in God's kingdom gave Him confidence to teach the disciples to trust His truth and way to God.

II. EXPOSITION AND APPLICATION OF THE SCRIPTURE

A. How to Be Untroubled
(John 14:1-4)

LET NOT your heart be troubled: ye believe in God, believe also in me. In my Father's house are many mansions: if it were not so, I would have told you. I go to prepare a place for you. And if I go and prepare a place for you, I will come again, and receive you unto myself; that where I am, there ye may be also. And whither I go ye know, and the way ye know.

While these comforting words of Jesus' have sustained many through periods of grief, Jesus spoke these words in a context of hostility and conflict that had developed around His prophetic life. Confronting a hostile world and having to trust Jesus' revolutionary teachings created uncertainty and fears within the disciples. Jesus knew that His disciples were bewildered as they shared in the hope of His salvation. They all became hunted men. The difficulty of their grasping Jesus' teachings coupled with questions of uncertainty about where and how God was present in the midst of them perpetuated the disciples' fears. Jesus understood Himself to be the embodiment of a new world in which God's kingdom was the only source of life. Jesus' teachings were aimed at helping the disciples not only to trust in God, but also, more specifically, to believe and have confidence in Him as the authentic path to the divine kingdom. Jesus Himself—or, rather, what He stood for—had become the core of the meaning of His teaching.

Jesus understood that He was to be the presence of the kingdom in the disciples' midst. "Believe in God, believe also in me" (verse 1) was how Jesus responded to the fears of the disciples. Faith in Jesus is the only true faith in God. The Greek term for the word *believe* may also be translated "have confidence and obey" or "be assured and follow." Even in the light of Jesus' impending betrayal, separation, and death (see John 11:33; 12:27; 13:21), Jesus commanded the disciples to "Love one another; as I have loved you" (John 13:34). Love for God's kingdom, love for one another, and self-denial on behalf of the kingdom were the ways to overcome fear. The love that the disciples expressed toward God was the same love that Jesus commanded His disciples to have toward one another. In other words, faith in Jesus is the only true faith in God; and love is the way that such faith is expressed. This faith does not remove external threats, but it puts human fears in the right perspective. In addition to the command to love one another, Jesus sought to comfort the troubling fears of the disciples by teaching them that their present anxieties, fears, and threats to their futures were not larger or more powerful than the futures that God had prepared for them. "Let not your heart be troubled"—because God had secured their futures. The present fears and trials were real, but temporary. The presence of God's kingdom was in their midst, as Jesus was its embodiment of love and healing power. Jesus followed up the phrase "Let not your heart be troubled" with, "Believe in God, believe also in me." Jesus' healings, His confrontation with demons, His miraculous feeding of the thousands, and His teachings had all become prophetic signs, incursions from the divine kingdom into the world of the disciples. Thus, Jesus' identification of Himself as one with God was an act of faith, a trust in the power of God to bring Him and His disciples to God's spiritual home—the true place of restoration. In this place of restoration, God's salvation would have plenty of "mansions" for all who believed to find peace and transformation.

B. There Is Always God
   (John 14:5-10)

Thomas saith unto him, Lord, we know not whither thou goest; and how can we know the way? Jesus saith unto him, I am the way, the truth, and the life: no man cometh unto the Father, but by me. If ye had known me, ye should have known my Father also: and from henceforth ye know him, and have seen him. Philip saith unto him, Lord, shew us the Father, and it sufficeth us. Jesus saith unto him, Have I been so long time with you, and yet hast thou not known me, Philip? he that hath seen me hath seen the Father; and how sayest thou then, Shew us the Father? Believest thou not that I am in the Father,
and the Father in me? the words that I speak unto you I speak not of myself: but the Father that dwelleth in me, he doeth the works.

Living with untroubled faith is grounded in the confidence that "there is always God." God's reality, His truth, His love, His justice, and His purpose will have the last and final word about the future of the world and our humanity. The world of the Roman Empire loomed so large in the lives of the ancients that it was difficult for them to grasp that there was another reality more powerful than the governance of the Empire. Jesus simply taught the disciples that to believe in God is to realize that you are never alone to manage life for yourself and by yourself—that you can always trust that God is working in the world, bringing to fruition divine justice and divine purposes. When life threatens us, our belief in God's love guides and sustains our faith. The Reverend Dr. Martin Luther King Jr. told the story of his confrontation with the threats that occurred during the Montgomery Bus Boycott in 1955. The black community faced daily threats of physical violence as they sought to end segregation and discrimination. One night, just as Dr. King was retiring for rest, he received a threatening telephone call from an anonymous caller whose display of hatred unsettled the spirit of Dr. King: "Nigger, you will regret having ever come to Montgomery." At that moment, Dr. King decided not to awaken his wife but went into the kitchen and prayed to God as he had never prayed before: "I am here taking a stand for what I believe is right. But now I am afraid. The people are looking to me for leadership, and if I stand before them without strength and courage, they, too, will falter. I am at the end of my powers. I have nothing left. I've come to the point where I can't face it alone." At that moment, Dr. King reported that he "experienced the presence of the Divine as he had never experienced God before. It seemed as though I could hear the quiet assurance of an inner voice saying, 'Stand up for justice, stand up for truth; and God will be at your side forever.'" Christians must have the spiritual resolve and commitment to do God's will as Jesus did—"Not my will but Thy will be done."

Jesus' belief in God and His sense of one-ness with God's presence and purpose in the world is the key to understanding why Jesus insisted that the disciples believe in Him also. As with the disciples, in some real measure over the course of history, Jesus has taught us also to believe in Him. We might have questions like the one Philip of Bethsaida had in John 14:8, but Jesus points us to the demonstration of "works" of God in our historical transfor-mations. The end of slavery, social justice, and radical change in the social lives of black people in America are but a few examples. The works of God uncompromisingly validate that God's power is for us, with us, and in us as we stand for divine justice and love in the world. Godly lives become possible—even amid threats—when they are undergirded by belief in God. This is Jesus' way, and is our only way to God.

Thomas, one of the disciples of Jesus, asked Him about the "Way"; he asked, "Lord, we don't know where you are going, so how can we know the way?" (John 14:5, NIV). Many may think that the raising of this question by Thomas to Jesus indicated Thomas's doubt and lack of faith. However, we might consider that good theological questions are the foundation for growing authentic faith. "I am the way and

the truth and the life," Jesus declared. This declaration indicated Jesus' own faith in God, whom He believed had endorsed Him, His agency, His teachings, and His truth as one with those of God; through Him persons can attain salvation and life in God's kingdom.

C. Following Jesus' Model of Service (John 14:11-14)

Believe me that I am in the Father, and the Father in me: or else believe me for the very works' sake. Verily, verily, I say unto you, He that believeth on me, the works that I do shall he do also; and greater works than these shall he do; because I go unto my Father. And whatsoever ye shall ask in my name, that will I do, that the Father may be glorified in the Son. If ye shall ask any thing in my name, I will do it.

Christians believe that in all that Jesus said and did, He was the express image of God's very person, the Word that conveys to us God's very thoughts and mind and heart. Jesus calls us to live in solidarity with Him as the only way to God. Jesus has set an example of love that opens up a pathway to God. This was what Jesus meant by the words, "Believe me that I am in the Father, and the Father in me: or else believe me for the very works' sake" (verse 11). Jesus made the promise to His disciples that by believing in Him they would do greater works than the works that He performed. It is incredible to affirm in our faith "the greater works" of God. God's love, His compassion, His justice, and His liberation and salvation are the ongoing work of the kingdom of God. When believers trust God's power, the promise of Jesus is that human brokenness turns to heal-ing, poverty of body and soul turn to abundant life, and guilty souls can turn to souls of joy and restoration. These are the greater works to which every believer is called. If we follow in the model of Jesus' love and service—while it may seem that our service is little—then God will take it and expand His kingdom.

In the black church, I remember the song "Serving the Lord Will Pay Off after While." Little did I know as a boy that the seed was being planted in my spirit for God's work, nor was I aware of the dividends of faith that would yield a harvest for God's kingdom. Now as a proclaimer of the Gospel, a Christian theological educator, and leader of a Christian college, I have been graciously called to the greater works of God's kingdom. Jesus promises to grant us the power to do the works of the kingdom. Only inasmuch as we advance kingdom causes can we expect God's Spirit to be with us.

III. CONCLUDING REFLECTION

Jesus is the way to God, the way to life and truth. This is what this lesson teaches us. The way of God is love. The way of God is divine justice. The way of God is divine truth unhindered in the world. The way of God brings authentic life. Only when God's love and pain for the world become our love and pain for the world are we following in the servant model of Jesus. In the world of fears and threats, we, like the disciples of Jesus, can easily allow the world to blur our thinking and drain us of faith and energy to do the work of God. We must learn that our spiritual service or kingdom work must exist in faith and belief in Jesus as "the way, the truth, and the life."

PRAYER

Thank You, Lord, for Your sacrifice of love that helps us overcome fear. Cultivate in our hearts trust in Your love, so that we can bring glory to Your kingdom on earth. In Jesus' name we pray. Amen.

WORD POWER

The eastern understanding of the word *kingdom* focuses more on the royalty than the realm. There is more attention placed on the king than on the dominated territory. As such, Jesus calls us unto Himself before He calls us to labor in His vineyard.

HOME DAILY BIBLE READINGS
(May 21-27, 2012)

The Way, the Truth, and the Life

MONDAY, May 21: "Making Known the Way of God" (Exodus 18:13-23)

TUESDAY, May 22: "Turning Aside from the Way" (Exodus 32:7-14)

WEDNESDAY, May 23: "Seeking Truth Within" (Psalm 51:1-7)

THURSDAY, May 24: "Speaking Truth from the Heart" (Psalm 15)

FRIDAY, May 25: "Telling the Whole Message" (Acts 5:17-21)

SATURDAY, May 26: "Choosing the Hard Road" (Matthew 7:13-20)

SUNDAY, May 27: "'How Can We Know the Way?'" (John 14:1-14)

God Calls for Justice—Old Testament Survey

GENERAL INTRODUCTION

The study this quarter is a survey of the Old Testament. Its three units follow the theme of "justice" as it pertains to God's ongoing relationship with Israel and all the peoples of the earth.

Unit I, *Justice Defined,* has four lessons. These lessons are explorations of the fundamental teachings of the Law, as laid out in the books of Exodus, Leviticus, and Deuteronomy.

Unit II has five lessons of *Justice Enacted,* which are examinations of the justice of God as it was enacted through some of Israel's righteous leaders. The first lesson is a consideration of Samuel. The next three lessons are studies of David and Solomon. The final lesson of the unit is an examination of the judicial reforms that were carried out under Jehoshaphat.

Unit III, *Justice Promised,* has four lessons. The lessons are examinations of some of the Old Testament texts that prophesy concerning God's coming judgments. The first lesson is from Psalm 146. The remaining lessons are from the Major Prophets: Isaiah, Jeremiah, and Ezekiel.

LESSON 1　　　　　　　　　　　　　　　　　　　　June 3, 2012

RULES FOR JUST LIVING

DEVOTIONAL READING: **Deuteronomy 32:1-7**　　　BACKGROUND SCRIPTURE: **Exodus 22:1–23:9**
PRINT PASSAGE: **Exodus 23:1-9**　　　　　　　　　KEY VERSE: **Exodus 23:2**

Exodus 23:1-9—KJV

THOU SHALT not raise a false report: put not thine hand with the wicked to be an unrighteous witness.
2 Thou shalt not follow a multitude to do evil; neither shalt thou speak in a cause to decline after many to wrest judgment:
3 Neither shalt thou countenance a poor man in his cause.
4 If thou meet thine enemy's ox or his ass going astray, thou shalt surely bring it back to him again.
5 If thou see the ass of him that hateth thee lying under his burden, and wouldest forbear to help him, thou shalt surely help with him.
6 Thou shalt not wrest the judgment of thy poor in his cause.
7 Keep thee far from a false matter; and the innocent and righteous slay thou not: for I will not justify the wicked.
8 And thou shalt take no gift: for the gift blindeth the wise, and perverteth the words of the righteous.
9 Also thou shalt not oppress a stranger: for ye know the heart of a stranger, seeing ye were strangers in the land of Egypt.

Exodus 23:1-9—NIV

"DO NOT spread false reports. Do not help a wicked man by being a malicious witness.
2 Do not follow the crowd in doing wrong. When you give testimony in a lawsuit, do not pervert justice by siding with the crowd,
3 and do not show favoritism to a poor man in his lawsuit.
4 If you come across your enemy's ox or donkey wandering off, be sure to take it back to him.
5 If you see the donkey of someone who hates you fallen down under its load, do not leave it there; be sure you help him with it.
6 Do not deny justice to your poor people in their lawsuits.
7 Have nothing to do with a false charge and do not put an innocent or honest person to death, for I will not acquit the guilty.
8 Do not accept a bribe, for a bribe blinds those who see and twists the words of the righteous.
9 Do not oppress an alien; you yourselves know how it feels to be aliens, because you were aliens in Egypt."

BIBLE FACT

Exodus 20:22–23:33 contain what is known as God's lawcode for Israel. It is known by biblical scholars as "the book of the covenant." We are told that it is the oldest record we have of Jewish law. It consists of judgments and statutes. It is important to note that the whole code rests on the authority of God, not of a king. We also note that there is no division between civil and religious law. (*Eerdman's Handbook to the Bible,* Lion Publishing, England, p. 164)

Everyone desires and deserves justice. How do we act justly toward friend and foe? By treating everyone the same, we reflect the justice of God.

TOPICAL OUTLINE OF THE LESSON

I. Introduction
A. Practicing Justice
B. Biblical Background

II. Exposition and Application of the Scripture
A. Justice in the Courts (Exodus 23:1-3)
B. Justice and One's Enemies (Exodus 23:4-5)
C. Justice and the Poor (Exodus 23:6-7)
D. Justice, Bribes, and Aliens (Exodus 23:8-9)

III. Concluding Reflection

LESSON OBJECTIVES

Upon the completion of the lesson, the students will be able to:

1. Explain the ways that justice was to be exacted on the Hebrew people; and,

2. Recognize and be willing to adhere to the imperatives of practicing justice as outlined in the Bible.

POINTS TO BE EMPHASIZED

ADULT/YOUTH

Adult Topic: Justice for All
Youth Topic: Don't Twist Justice
Adult Key Verse: Exodus 23:2
Youth Key Verse: Exodus 23:1
Print Passage: Exodus 23:1-9

—This passage is part of what is known as "the book of the covenant" (Exodus 20:22–23:33), the oldest extant record of Jewish law. Unlike other ancient law codes of the ancient Near East, it rests on the authority of God rather than on that of a king.

—The text suggests that legal, moral, and religious laws are inseparable, showing God's concern for the whole of life.

—Leviticus 19:15 is similar to Exodus 23:3, but it calls attention to both the great and the poor.

—Regulations in this passage specify protecting the weak and helpless such as aliens and the poor.

—It appears that the writer was concerned with right attitudes, which form the basis for ethics in these matters—not merely the letter of the judicial code.

CHILDREN

Children Topic: Doing What's Fair!
Key Verse: Psalm 106:3
Print Passage: Exodus 23:1-9

—God forbids treating others in an unfair manner.

—We must apply justice impartially in all situations to both our friends and our enemies.

—The rights of the poor and those who are strangers in our midst must be protected at all times.

—God will not hold guiltless those who falsely charge or kill others.

—God forbids us to join with others to harm another person.

—God expects us to do the right thing, even when no one is watching.

I. INTRODUCTION

A. Practicing Justice

One of the major themes of the Old Testament—and particularly the ancient Hebrew legal codes (*Torah*)—was the emphasis on the practice of justice within ancient Israelite society. God commanded that Israel live in and create a just social community. They were to treat each other with dignity and respect. They were not to commit fraud or deception in their dealings with each other. They were not to take brides nor pervert justice in favor of the rich and powerful, nor were they to tilt the scales of justice in favor of the poor. Israel was not to charge interest nor exact high rates of surety in their business dealings (see Deuteronomy 15:1-11; 16:18-20; 24:10-22).

A great deal of the preaching of the Hebrew prophets focused on social, economic, and political justice issues (see Isaiah 1:16-17; 55:7; 56:1-2; Jeremiah 5:25-29; Amos 5:10-15; Micah 6:6-8). This particular lesson points out that God was concerned about the treatment of the poor within the context of the Hebrew community. As you study the lesson today, make a list of the forms of social, economic, political, and legal injustices you see being practiced in your city or county. Look for stories that you may find in the local newspapers that highlight the practice of injustice in the community. During your discussion of the lesson, make a list of the ways that you can become involved in helping to fight injustice in your city, county, or state.

B. Biblical Background

The lesson today comes from a portion of the Old Testament known as "the Book of the Covenant" (see Exodus 20:22–23:33), the oldest existing record of Jewish law—the name of which is derived from Exodus 24:7. The Book of the Covenant is one of four distinct groups of laws in the Pentateuch. The other three are the Deuteronomic Code (see Deuteronomy 12–26), the Holiness Code (see Leviticus 17–26), and the Priestly Code (see Exodus 25-31; 34:29–Leviticus 16; portions of the book of Numbers). There are two types of laws in the Old Testament. The first type of Old Testament law is *casuistic law*. The word *casuistic* means "case-by-case law." These were legal codes that applied only in specific circumstances. They can be identified in the Old Testament by the words "If... then...." The second type of Old Testament law is called *apodictic law*. It includes direct commands that Israel could not violate. There were no exceptions to these laws. They applied to all Israelites and provided direction and instruction on things that they could and could not do. The performance of these laws was the condition for fulfilling the terms of the covenant between God and Israel. The characteristic form of this type of law is "You shall or shall not"; "Thou shalt or thou shalt not." The text contains both types of laws.

It is made clear in the lesson that God is concerned about the practice of justice and equity in society. Israel was to ensure that there would not be two standards of justice but, rather, that there was one law regardless of one's social or economic status. Furthermore, the Law was also concerned about the treatment of aliens who may have lived among the Israelites. Justice was to be meted out equally and without partiality.

II. EXPOSITION AND APPLICATION OF THE SCRIPTURE

A. Justice in the Courts
(Exodus 23:1-3)

THOU SHALT not raise a false report: put not thine hand with the wicked to be an unrighteous witness. Thou shalt not follow a multitude to do evil; neither shalt thou speak in a cause to decline after many to wrest judgment: Neither shalt thou countenance a poor man in his cause.

Verses 1-3 are *apodictic laws* (direct commands), which set the tone for what was to follow. Justice would never be served by the spreading of "false reports" about another member of the community. The list of prohibitions begins with, "Do not spread false reports." The Hebrew word translated into "spread" also has in it the idea of "supporting and sustaining" false reports. Why are false reports damaging? First, because they can forever damage an individual's reputation. Second, individuals may be falsely accused of crimes or infractions that they did not commit. Third—and this is particularly true in faith communities—divisions can begin when one group believes a report to be true and spreads it without regard for its impact upon the whole community. Likewise, a second or third group may not believe the report and may seek to counter the claims of others. Communities are negatively impacted when information about others is spread with no regard for the truth.

The second prohibition states, "Do not help a wicked man by being a malicious witness." The Hebrew people were cautioned against joining forces with persons whose intentions were devilish, particularly when it came to acting as false witnesses. Deuteronomy 17:6 and 19:15 established the criteria that there must be two or three witnesses to corroborate a matter in the courts. Imagine that two or three people might come together and conspire to frame someone for a crime or an infraction that he or she did not commit. Under Hebrew law, the person would have virtually no chance because the testimony of credible witnesses was deemed sufficient for any matter. This is what happened during the trial of Jesus: false witnesses were lined up against Him.

It is suggested in verse 2 that when a person gives testimony in a lawsuit, the person is not to pervert justice by going along with the crowd. This next prohibition was intended to prevent mob violence in matters that might occur within the community. There was always the possibility that the crowd was wrong and that to join in with the crowd would be to participate in a worse crime. Further, one was not to pervert justice by joining in a popular position held by the masses. Poverty is not grounds for receiving favorable treatment or verdicts. The law was to be administered equally to the rich as well as the poor (see verse 3).

B. Justice and One's Enemies
(Exodus 23:4-5)

If thou meet thine enemy's ox or his ass going astray, thou shalt surely bring it back to him again. If thou see

the ass of him that hateth thee lying under his burden, and wouldest forbear to help him, thou shalt surely help with him.

This section contains hypothetical situations that could arise within any ancient Hebrew community. The laws in this group are termed as *casuistic* law or case laws. One might raise the question of who the enemy was. Clearly, the reference was not to someone outside the Hebrew community, since the laws were given to govern their internal relationships. How should one respond to his or her enemies? Deuteronomy 22:1-3 contains a fuller discussion regarding the way that the members of the community were to assist others in times of need. Verse 4 (NIV) reads, "If you come across your enemy's ox or donkey wandering off, be sure to take it back to him." Oxen and donkeys were very valuable in the ancient world (and even today); in developing countries, they are extremely valuable property. Donkeys were used for transportation and the carrying of goods to market in ancient times. Oxen were used primarily for tilling the soil and pulling heavy loads. Therefore, to lose an animal would lead to serious economic hardship.

Within ancient Hebrew society, the Law drew no distinction between how one was to treat an enemy or one's friend. The community was built around a covenant relationship which meant that all would be treated equally in whatever situation they found themselves in. The Scriptures never recommended hatred of one's enemies; rather, love was always the guiding principle (see Job 31:29; Proverbs 25:21-22; compare them with Romans 12:17-21). In this case, if one came across the ox or donkey of an enemy, then the easiest thing to do would be to ignore it.

Additionally, in verse 5, we see a similar scenario to the one expressed in verse 4—only in this one, the enemy is someone who hates you, as opposed to someone whom one may dislike or hate. The law stresses that people in trouble or who had trouble were not to be ignored because of personal differences. Moreover, God's people were/are held to a higher standard of altruistic love and compassion. "These requirements are neither about the legal system per se nor about oxen or donkeys only, they are expressions of Yahweh's expectations for His people that concentrate on general social attitudes using situations involving lost or stumbling animals as paradigmatic examples" (*New American Commentary—New American Commentary* Volume 2: *Exodus*, p. 525).

C. Justice and the Poor (Exodus 23:6-7)

Thou shalt not wrest the judgment of thy poor in his cause. Keep thee far from a false matter; and the innocent and righteous slay thou not: for I will not justify the wicked.

This section of the lesson gets to the basic fabric of any society: the administration of justice among all of the people regardless of social or economic background. When the legal system denies the rights of people based on things other than equity and righteousness, that society will not prosper. Such is the case in many countries in Africa, Asia, and Latin and South America, where the legal system is tilted to the rich and powerful. This was not to be the case among the people of God. The society's well-being was based upon the capacity of the people to practice equality in the society.

The meaning of the law in the statement, "Do not deny justice to your poor people in their lawsuits" (verse 6, NIV) could not be any clearer. The poor were not to be denied due process when it came to lawsuits. Those with vast sums of money are able to buy the best lawyers and even buy the judges. In some developing countries, the rampant corruption ensures that a few people keep and the government control the wealth of the people. The legal system and even the parliament make it easy for people to be abused and exploited by the wealthy and leaders. It becomes easy to manipulate the laws for one's personal benefit when the poor have no voice.

The prohibition of verse 7 was intended to prevent the senseless and wrongful conviction of someone who was innocent. God strictly forbade the Hebrew people from falsely accusing a person. The epitome of false accusation is when a man or woman is executed for a crime he or she did not commit. Those who are guilty of setting up the innocent with false charges and who participate in the execution of the innocent will not go unpunished by God.

D. Justice, Bribes, and Aliens (Exodus 23:8-9)

And thou shalt take no gift: for the gift blindeth the wise, and perverteth the words of the righteous. Also thou shalt not oppress a stranger: for ye know the heart of a stranger, seeing ye were strangers in the land of Egypt.

In his first letter of instruction to Timothy, the apostle Paul strongly cautioned him about the love of money's being the root of all kinds of evil (see 1 Timothy 6:10). Nowhere is the love of money more dangerous than in the legal and government systems of a nation. The perversion of justice is easy when the people responsible for the administration of justice can be bought and sold with ease. The Lord God forbade the giving and receiving of bribes.

In verse 8, the Hebrew word *bribe* comes from a word that means "gift." A *bribe* is an unlawful gift given for the purpose of perverting the law. The Hebrew people were told not to take bribes because they blind one to the truth of the circumstances and lead one to turn away from the truth. Bribes also lead to fabrications of the truth. The one who is bribed may forget what he or she saw and/or make up information to support the lie. The ancient Hebrew prophets preached against the practice of bribery (see Isaiah 1:23; 5:23; Micah 3:11).

In developing nations where the legal system is easily bought and sold, bribery is the common means by which business is conducted. The breakdown of the legal system by bribery causes the people to become filled with cynicism and disrespect for their leaders and the government. Many large multinational corporations use bribery as a means of manipulating the economic and legal systems to their advantage in many of the poorer nations of the world.

In verse 9, we are exposed to the admonition against the mistreatment of people who were not part of the covenant community. Aliens were people who were not Hebrew by birth, but who lived among them. There was to be no discrimination by the people of God because they, too, had experienced social isolation and discrimination. Who would better understand oppression than the man or woman who has been oppressed and has lived with it?

III. CONCLUDING REFLECTION

In today's lesson, we have taken a brief look at the concept of social justice as it related to a portion of the ancient Hebrew law. As

Christians, we must not only learn to apply the law appropriately, but we must also take our cues from Jesus Christ. Jesus came preaching a message that mirrored the preaching of the ancient Hebrew prophets. His ministry focused a great deal of attention on the need for social reform within the Jewish society. Jesus lived and preached during a period when there were masses of hungry and disinherited people.

Jesus clearly aligned Himself with the prophetic work of those who had preceded Him. Jesus came announcing that the kingdom of God would be characterized by preaching the Good News to the poor, preaching deliverance to the captives, healing the brokenhearted, restoring the sight of the blind, and setting at liberty those who were bruised. A great deal of the ministry time of Jesus was spent among the disinherited and disenfranchised (those deprived of a right or privilege; see also Matthew 25:31-46 and Mark 6:30-44).

The apostles not only learned social responsibility from the Book of the Law, but they also received many practical lessons from Jesus that carried over into their preaching and teaching ministries. They were with Jesus as He traveled among the villages and small towns in Galilee, healing and ministering to the people of the land (see Matthew 4:23-25).

The early Christian church practiced social responsibility among themselves, especially in regard to the poor and widows in their midst. They cared for each other and made sure that there were no members in the local congregation whose needs were not met.

PRAYER

Lord, teach us to love who You love and to hate what You hate. Grant that we will be moved to action as we consider the teachings of the Scriptures that call us to action. In Jesus' name we pray. Amen.

WORD POWER

Community—people with common interests living in a particular area.

Justice—the maintenance or administration of what is just, especially by the impartial adjustment of conflicting claims; the administration of law.

HOME DAILY BIBLE READINGS
(May 28–June 3, 2012)

Rules for Just Living

MONDAY, May 28: "Punishment for False Witnesses" (Deuteronomy 19:15-20)

TUESDAY, May 29: "God Holds Court" (Psalm 82)

WEDNESDAY, May 30: "The Day of Punishment" (Isaiah 10:1-4)

THURSDAY, May 31: "Rescued from the Wicked and Unjust" (Psalm 71:1-6)

FRIDAY, June 1: "A God of Justice" (Isaiah 30:18-22)

SATURDAY, June 2: "God's Ways Are Just" (Deuteronomy 31:30–32:7)

SUNDAY, June 3: "Justice for All" (Exodus 23:1-9)

LESSON 2   June 10, 2012

LIVING AS GOD'S JUST PEOPLE

DEVOTIONAL READING: **Luke 10:25-37**
PRINT PASSAGE: **Leviticus 19:9-18, 33-37**

BACKGROUND SCRIPTURE: **Leviticus 19:9-18, 33-37**
KEY VERSE: **Leviticus 19:34**

Leviticus 19:9-18, 33-37—KJV

9 And when ye reap the harvest of your land, thou shalt not wholly reap the corners of thy field, neither shalt thou gather the gleanings of thy harvest.

10 And thou shalt not glean thy vineyard, neither shalt thou gather every grape of thy vineyard; thou shalt leave them for the poor and stranger: I am the LORD your God.

11 Ye shall not steal, neither deal falsely, neither lie one to another.

12 And ye shall not swear by my name falsely, neither shalt thou profane the name of thy God: I am the LORD.

13 Thou shalt not defraud thy neighbour, neither rob him: the wages of him that is hired shall not abide with thee all night until the morning.

14 Thou shalt not curse the deaf, nor put a stumblingblock before the blind, but shalt fear thy God: I am the LORD.

15 Ye shall do no unrighteousness in judgment: thou shalt not respect the person of the poor, nor honour the person of the mighty: but in righteousness shalt thou judge thy neighbour.

16 Thou shalt not go up and down as a talebearer among thy people: neither shalt thou stand against the blood of thy neighbour: I am the LORD.

17 Thou shalt not hate thy brother in thine heart: thou shalt in any wise rebuke thy neighbour, and not suffer sin upon him.

18 Thou shalt not avenge, nor bear any grudge against the children of thy people, but thou shalt love thy neighbour as thyself: I am the LORD.

.....

33 And if a stranger sojourn with thee in your land, ye shall not vex him.

34 But the stranger that dwelleth with you shall be unto you as one born among you, and thou shalt love him as thyself; for ye were strangers in the land

Leviticus 19:9-18, 33-37—NIV

9 "'When you reap the harvest of your land, do not reap to the very edges of your field or gather the gleanings of your harvest.

10 Do not go over your vineyard a second time or pick up the grapes that have fallen. Leave them for the poor and the alien. I am the LORD your God.

11 Do not steal. Do not lie. Do not deceive one another.

12 Do not swear falsely by my name and so profane the name of your God. I am the LORD.

13 Do not defraud your neighbor or rob him. Do not hold back the wages of a hired man overnight.

14 Do not curse the deaf or put a stumbling block in front of the blind, but fear your God. I am the LORD.

15 Do not pervert justice; do not show partiality to the poor or favoritism to the great, but judge your neighbor fairly.

16 Do not go about spreading slander among your people. Do not do anything that endangers your neighbor's life. I am the LORD.

17 Do not hate your brother in your heart. Rebuke your neighbor frankly so you will not share in his guilt.

18 Do not seek revenge or bear a grudge against one of your people, but love your neighbor as yourself. I am the LORD.'"

.....

33 "'When an alien lives with you in your land, do not mistreat him.

34 The alien living with you must be treated as one of your native-born. Love him as yourself, for you were

People want to feel significant. How do we assure others that they are valued? We treat them with love, justice, and generosity.

of Egypt: I am the LORD your God.

35 Ye shall do no unrighteousness in judgment, in meteyard, in weight, or in measure.

36 Just balances, just weights, a just ephah, and a just hin, shall ye have: I am the LORD your God, which brought you out of the land of Egypt.

37 Therefore shall ye observe all my statutes, and all my judgments, and do them: I am the LORD.

aliens in Egypt. I am the LORD your God.

35 Do not use dishonest standards when measuring length, weight or quantity.

36 Use honest scales and honest weights, an honest ephah and an honest hin. I am the LORD your God, who brought you out of Egypt.

37 Keep all my decrees and all my laws and follow them. I am the LORD.'"

TOPICAL OUTLINE OF THE LESSON

I. Introduction
   A. The Need for Compassionate Living
   B. Biblical Background

II. Exposition and Application of the Scripture
   A. Laws Regarding the Harvest (Leviticus 19:9-10)
   B. Laws Regarding Honesty (Leviticus 19:11-12)
   C. Laws Regarding the Exploitation of the Weak (Leviticus 19:13-14)
   D. Laws Regarding One's Neighbor (Leviticus 19:15-18)
   E. Laws Regarding the Alien and Commerce (Leviticus 19:33-37)

III. Concluding Reflection

LESSON OBJECTIVES

Upon the completion of this lesson, the students will be able to:

1. Cite biblical sources that guide the development of compassionate living;
2. Name the ways that believers can practice holiness; and,
3. Discuss ways that faith communities can respond to situations of injustice.

POINTS TO BE EMPHASIZED

ADULT/YOUTH

Adult Topic: Acting with Compassion
Youth Topic: Justice by Caring
Adult Key Verse: Leviticus 19:34
Youth Key Verse: Leviticus 19:18
Print Passage: Leviticus 19:9-18, 33-37

—This chapter begins with a call to reflect the nature of God: "You shall be holy, for I the LORD your God am holy" (verse 2).

—The holiness of the people is to reflect God's holiness in concern for the needy (verses 9-10, 14, 20), truthfulness coupled with fair and impartial justice (verses 11, 13, 15), and in respect for human life and reputation (verses 16-18).

—Gentiles were unable to own land in Israel. When landowners purposely left some grain and fruit during harvest, it enabled the poor and aliens to gather food (verses 9-10).

—It was customary to pay workers each day, because laborers lived on the margins of society with little, if any, cash reserves. Thoughtlessly or callously holding funds, even "until morning" (verse 13), would have caused hardship for some families.

—In dealing with the state of the heart that prompts actions, verses 17 and 18 go to the root of what is to motivate the people of God as they act in accordance with the stipulations of the preceding and following verses.

—The admonition to love one's *neighbor* (verse 18) was generally interpreted, in the Jewish community, to refer to fellow Israelites. That understanding, however, was broadened in verse 34 to include non-Israelites—that is, to "love [the alien] as thyself" (verse 34).

CHILDREN

Children Topic: Just Do It!

Key Verse: Leviticus 19:18b

Print Passage: Leviticus 19:9-18, 33-37

—God requires believers to share their earnings with the poor and with strangers.

—The faithful show compassion and fairness to others and walk humbly before God.

—Equity in relationships with others allows everyone to be treated fairly.

—God's kindness should remind us to be kind to others.

—We should not seek to profit from the misfortunes of others.

—God repeatedly echoes the refrain: "I am the LORD."

I. INTRODUCTION

A. The Need for Compassionate Living

The lesson today gives us practical help in developing meaningful strategies for how to respond to the presence of aliens (undocumented persons) in our midst. The Israelites in ancient times lived in an environment where they were surrounded by different ethnic groups, many of whom lived in Israel's tribal areas. According to the law of God, the Israelites were not to oppress the aliens in their midst; rather, their responses were to be always guided by love, compassion, and fairness. As the people of God, the church is called to live at a higher standard of righteousness and holiness. As you study the lesson, look for ways that you can make others aware of the practices of injustice in the world today. Consider doing an Internet search of the word *injustice* to see what you find and where injustice is allowed to flourish in the world today. Make a list of your discoveries and share them with people in your class.

B. Biblical Background

Leviticus 19 begins with the Lord's telling Moses to speak to the people of Israel and command them to live holy because He is holy (see verse 1). Holiness is not an abstract religious concept, but, rather, has its basis in the very nature and character of God—who is just, righteous, and pure. Leviticus 19 reads like a recitation of the Ten Commandments or a list of "do's and don'ts." Holiness, then, is a reflection of one's personal integrity and character when it comes to dealing with other people. The holiness of the people was to reflect the holiness of God through their concern for the poor, the needy, and those who were aliens living in their midst. In ancient Israelite society, Gentiles were not allowed to own land. However, landowners were instructed to purposely leave some of the grain and fruit in the fields during the time of harvest. This would enable the poor and the aliens to have something to eat (see Ruth 2:1-3).

The laws in the lesson were *apodictic*, which were laws that could not be violated. Throughout the chapter, Israel was given very practical ways to demonstrate that their lives reflected the life and character of God.

II. EXPOSITION AND APPLICATION OF THE SCRIPTURE

A. Laws Regarding the Harvest (Leviticus 19:9-10)

And when ye reap the harvest of your land, thou shalt not wholly reap the corners of thy field, neither shalt thou gather the gleanings of thy harvest. And thou shalt not glean thy vineyard, neither shalt thou gather every grape of thy vineyard; thou shalt leave them for the poor and stranger: I am the LORD your God.

Poverty and the treatment of the poor were and are major concerns of the Lord God. In these laws, the Lord wanted to make sure that Israel treated the poor with dignity and respect. We cannot be sure as to how many people in ancient Israel lived in poverty, but it is certain that there were large numbers of them. At the time when these laws were given, Israel was still trying to overcome the legacy of slavery in Egypt. The Lord commanded that Israel not ignore the plight of the poor, many of whom did not own land. Israelite farmers were to allow the poor to glean the leftover grain and fruit from their fields. Farmers were forbidden to harvest to edges of the field, thereby stripping the field of its crops. They were not to go through their fields or their vineyards a second time to gather grapes that had fallen to the ground or the grain that had been left.

B. Laws Regarding Honesty (Leviticus 19:11-12)

Ye shall not steal, neither deal falsely, neither lie one to another. And ye shall not swear by my name falsely, neither shalt thou profane the name of thy God: I am the LORD.

Verses 11-18 form a large block of laws related to the social behavior and interaction of the Israelites. There are four commands in verses 11-12 that deal with honesty and the need for the society to be free of corruption. The impetus for doing the right thing was the call to be like God and the fact that God was the One who issued the command: "I am the LORD." The first of these laws is a recitation of the eighth commandment found in Exodus 20:15. It is interesting to note that this command is placed immediately after the command for farmers not to harvest everything that their fields produce. Personal greed on the part of the wealthy and a covetous attitude on the part of the people would create an environment for theft and dishonesty to grow and flourish.

Throughout the Old Testament and in the teachings of the early Christian church, stealing, lying, deception, and swearing falsely were all signs of a sinful heart (see Jeremiah 9:3-5; Acts 5:3-4; Romans 3:4; 1 Corinthians 6:8-10; Ephesians 4:25, 28; Colossians 3:9; and 1 Timothy 1:10). In the preaching of Jeremiah, stealing was seen as an abomination as heinous as idolatry (see Jeremiah 7:9-11). Using the Lord's names as the basis for supporting a lie or deception leads to the act of profaning the name of God. The word *profane* is a strong word and has in it the idea of desecrating the name of God. All four of these acts are detrimental to the social fabric of the community and do not reflect the image of God's holiness and character.

C. Laws Regarding the Exploitation of the Weak (Leviticus 19:13-14)

Thou shalt not defraud thy neighbour, neither rob him: the wages of him that is hired shall not abide with thee all night until the morning. Thou shalt not curse the deaf, nor put a stumblingblock before the blind, but shalt fear thy God: I am the Lord.

Exploitation of the weak, helpless, and defenseless was a serious matter in ancient Hebrew society. The series of commands detailed in this passage dealt with the treatment of one's neighbor. Being holy means that one does not cheat people or rob them of what is rightfully theirs. *Robbing* is the taking of another's possessions either by force or deception. The Old Testament took a very harsh view toward robbers and people who committed crimes against other people (see Proverbs 20:10; 22:22; Jeremiah 22:3). The worst robbers are those who believe that they can rob God and get away with it (see Malachi 3:8-10). Congregations can be guilty of robbing other churches by failing to adequately compensate their pastors who must preach and teach in other churches to earn a living (see 2 Corinthians 11:8).

The ancient Hebrews were not to exploit their workers. In the ancient world, as it is today, many people worked during the day and looked to be compensated at the end of the day (see Matthew 20:1-2). Wages were not to be held back until a more convenient time for the one who did the hiring (see Deuteronomy 24:14-15; Jeremiah 22:13; Malachi 3:5; and James 5:4). Christians must never believe that it is acceptable not to adequately compensate people for their labor. When we have it within our means to pay, we should pay them and not put off payment for a more convenient time for us.

Equity and righteousness mean that in a just society all stand upon the same foundation of impartiality. When laws are tilted toward the poor, the rights of the wealthy are negated and vice versa. The Scriptures point out that God does not show favoritism or partiality and neither must we (see Romans 2:11; 1 Peter 1:17; compare with Deuteronomy 1:17; 16:19; 25:13-16; 27:19; 2 Chronicles 19:6-7; Psalm 82:2; Proverbs 18:5; 24:23; and James 2:6-9). The Lord made it clear that it was not Moses who was issuing these commands, but that He was "for I am the Lord."

D. Laws Regarding One's Neighbor (Leviticus 19:15-18)

Ye shall do no unrighteousness in judgment: thou shalt not respect the person of the poor, nor honour the person of the mighty: but in righteousness shalt thou judge thy neighbour. Thou shalt not go up and down as a talebearer among thy people: neither shalt thou stand against the blood of thy neighbour: I am the Lord. Thou shalt not hate thy brother in thine heart: thou shalt in any wise rebuke

thy neighbour, and not suffer sin upon him. Thou shalt not avenge, nor bear any grudge against the children of thy people, but thou shalt love thy neighbour as thyself: I am the Lord.

Slandering the name of another person is one sure way to ruin that person's reputation. The Scriptures had a very negative view of slander and persons who bore false witness against others (see Exodus 23:1-9; 1 Samuel 15:3; Proverbs 11:13; 20:19; Jeremiah 6:28; Ezekiel 22:9; 1 Timothy 3:3; Titus 2:3; 1 Peter 2:1). Slander is a destructive form of false witnessing that can cost a person his or her livelihood, or even worse, his or her life. Such was the case with Naboth, who was victimized by Ahab's and Jezebel's wickedness (see 1 Kings 21:1-10).

The ancient Israelite society was to be built upon the love of neighbor. Hatred had no place in Israel (see Genesis 27:41; Proverbs 26:24-26; 1 John 2:9, 11; 3:12-15). The Scriptures teach that love is the supreme virtue (see 1 Corinthians 13). Love is best expressed not in what one says but rather in what one does (see Luke 10:25-37). The opposite of hatred is love; so the Israelites were to love their neighbors by not doing anything that would hurt them or endanger their lives. Genuine love is also expressed through the act of our correcting our neighbors when we know that their behavior or conduct is wrong.

Revenge is one of the most destructive practices in our society. The ancients were instructed not to seek revenge, which has in it the idea of retaliating. One of the points that we cannot forget about these laws is that they did not describe ways that the Israelites were to deal with their neighbors, but they spoke to the internal social fabric of the people. The reference to "your people" indicates that there were to be no distinctions in the treatment of either the poor or the wealthy. They were to love all and they were to hold no grudges against others for past wrongs committed against them. Rather, they were to love their neighbors as themselves, which Jesus considered to be the second part of the greatest commandment (see Matthew 22:34-40).

E. Laws Regarding the Alien and Commerce (Leviticus 19:33-37)

And if a stranger sojourn with thee in your land, ye shall not vex him. But the stranger that dwelleth with you shall be unto you as one born among you, and thou shalt love him as thyself; for ye were strangers in the land of Egypt: I am the Lord your God. Ye shall do no unrighteousness in judgment, in meteyard, in weight, or in measure. Just balances, just weights, a just ephah, and a just hin, shall ye have: I am the Lord your God, which brought you out of the land of Egypt. Therefore shall ye observe all my statutes, and all my judgments, and do them: I am the Lord.

Aliens were residents in Israel who were not ethnically Hebrew by birth. As early as in the book of Exodus, there were people who were among the Hebrews who were not native-born. The law recognized them as deserving the same treatment as those who were true Israelites by birth (see Exodus 12:48-49). Mistreatment was highly frowned upon by the Lord God, who reminded them repeatedly that they, too, had been aliens in a foreign land (see Exodus 22:21; 23:9; Deuteronomy 10:19; 24:17-18).

The theme of honesty not only applied to relationships, but it was also to permeate every part of Hebrew society, including its commerce (see Deuteronomy 25:13-16; Proverbs 11:1; 16:11; 20:10, 23; Hosea 12:7; Micah 6:11). Gold, silver, crops, and fruits were all exchanged according to weights. It would be easy to manipulate the value of precious metals and crops by using illegal weights and measures.

Americans know what can happen in a society when business leaders manipulate the economy for personal gain.

The chapter closes with a call for Israel not only to record or keep the laws of God, but also to follow them. How does one live a life of holiness? Holiness according to the Law is a matter concerning how we live among and before the world. Holiness is the practical expression of our lives of faith in the living God, according to Leviticus 19.

III. CONCLUDING REFLECTION

At the heart of this lesson is the summons to love our neighbor as we love ourselves. The imitation of the character of God is best seen and portrayed in the life of Jesus Christ. Christians are exhorted to take on the character and righteousness of Jesus Christ. Our lives conform to His likeness when we seek to live out what it means to be His disciples. In John 13:34-35, Jesus said that the real test of discipleship and the recognition of that by the world would be the love that His followers had one for one another.

PRAYER

Lord God, we bless You for the lessons that we have learned in our study of Your Word today. May the practical truths become a living reality in our lives and in the life of our church. In Jesus' name we pray. Amen.

WORD POWER

Holy (Hebrew: *Qodesh*)—apartness, holiness, sacredness, hallowed, holy (ASV, RSV, similar). The noun *qodesh* connotes the concept of "holiness" (i.e., the essential nature of that which belongs to the sphere of the sacred and which is thus distinct from the common or profane). This distinction is evident in Leviticus 10:10 and Ezekiel 22:26, where *qodesh* occurs as the antithesis of hôl ("profane," "common").[1]

HOME DAILY BIBLE READINGS
(June 4-10, 2012)

Living as God's Just People

End Notes

[1]R. Laird Harris, Gleason L. Archer, Jr. And Bruce K. Waltke, *Theological Wordbook of the Old Testament,* Vol. II, (Chicago: Moody Press, 1980), p. 787.

LESSON 3   June 17, 2012

CELEBRATE JUBILEE

Devotional Reading: **Nehemiah 1:5-11**
Print Passage: **Leviticus 25:8-12, 25, 35-36, 39-40, 47-48, 55**

Background Scripture: **Leviticus 25:8-55**
Key Verse: **Leviticus 25:10**

Leviticus 25:8-12, 25, 35-36, 39-40, 47-48, 55—KJV

8 And thou shalt number seven sabbaths of years unto thee, seven times seven years; and the space of the seven sabbaths of years shall be unto thee forty and nine years.

9 Then shalt thou cause the trumpet of the jubile to sound on the tenth day of the seventh month, in the day of atonement shall ye make the trumpet sound throughout all your land.

10 And ye shall hallow the fiftieth year, and proclaim liberty throughout all the land unto all the inhabitants thereof: it shall be a jubile unto you; and ye shall return every man unto his possession, and ye shall return every man unto his family.

11 A jubile shall that fiftieth year be unto you: ye shall not sow, neither reap that which groweth of itself in it, nor gather the grapes in it of thy vine undressed.

12 For it is the jubile; it shall be holy unto you: ye shall eat the increase thereof out of the field.

…..

25 If thy brother be waxen poor, and hath sold away some of his possession, and if any of his kin come to redeem it, then shall he redeem that which his brother sold.

…..

35 And if thy brother be waxen poor, and fallen in decay with thee; then thou shalt relieve him: yea, though he be a stranger, or a sojourner; that he may live with thee.

36 Take thou no usury of him, or increase: but fear thy God; that thy brother may live with thee.

…..

39 And if thy brother that dwelleth by thee be waxen

Leviticus 25:8-12, 25, 35-36, 39-40, 47-48, 55—NIV

8 "'Count off seven sabbaths of years—seven times seven years—so that the seven sabbaths of years amount to a period of forty-nine years.

9 Then have the trumpet sounded everywhere on the tenth day of the seventh month; on the Day of Atonement sound the trumpet throughout your land.

10 Consecrate the fiftieth year and proclaim liberty throughout the land to all its inhabitants. It shall be a jubilee for you; each one of you is to return to his family property and each to his own clan.

11 The fiftieth year shall be a jubilee for you; do not sow and do not reap what grows of itself or harvest the untended vines.

12 For it is a jubilee and is to be holy for you; eat only what is taken directly from the fields.'"

…..

25 "'If one of your countrymen becomes poor and sells some of his property, his nearest relative is to come and redeem what his countryman has sold.'"

…..

35 "'If one of your countrymen becomes poor and is unable to support himself among you, help him as you would an alien or a temporary resident, so he can continue to live among you.

36 Do not take interest of any kind from him, but fear your God, so that your countryman may continue to live among you.'"

…..

39 "'If one of your countrymen becomes poor among you and sells himself to you, do not make him work as a slave.

UNIFYING LESSON PRINCIPLE

Some people are oppressed because of the unjust circumstances into which they are born and live. How can all people be treated fairly regardless of their life circumstances? By observing a Year of Jubilee, those who were oppressed were given the means for making a fresh start.

poor, and be sold unto thee; thou shalt not compel him to serve as a bondservant:

40 But as an hired servant, and as a sojourner, he shall be with thee, and shall serve thee unto the year of jubilee.

.....

47 And if a sojourner or stranger wax rich by thee, and thy brother that dwelleth by him wax poor, and sell himself unto the stranger or sojourner by thee, or to the stock of the stranger's family:

48 After that he is sold he may be redeemed again; one of his brethren may redeem him.

.....

55 For unto me the children of Israel are servants; they are my servants whom I brought forth out of the land of Egypt: I am the LORD your God.

40 He is to be treated as a hired worker or a temporary resident among you; he is to work for you until the Year of Jubilee.'"

.....

47 "'If an alien or a temporary resident among you becomes rich and one of your countrymen becomes poor and sells himself to the alien living among you or to a member of the alien's clan,

48 he retains the right of redemption after he has sold himself. One of his relatives may redeem him.'"

.....

55 "'for the Israelites belong to me as servants. They are my servants, whom I brought out of Egypt. I am the LORD your God.'"

TOPICAL OUTLINE OF THE LESSON

I. **Introduction**
  A. The Need for Economic Justice
  B. Biblical Background

II. **Exposition and Application of the Scripture**
  A. God Announces the Year of Jubilee (Leviticus 25:8-12)
  B. God Ordains the Law of Redemption (Leviticus 25:25)
  C. God Annuls Economic Slavery (Leviticus 25:35-36, 39-40, 47-48)
  D. God Is the Architect of the Hebrew Nation (Leviticus 25:55)

III. **Concluding Reflection**

LESSON OBJECTIVES

Upon the completion of this lesson, the students will be able to:

1. Summarize the principles of Jubilee;

2. Recognize the scope and implications of economic justice and equity; and,

3. Apply the principles of economic justice and equity.

POINTS TO BE EMPHASIZED

ADULT/YOUTH

Adult Topic: Making a Fresh Start

Youth Topic: Justice that Frees

Adult/Youth Key Verse: Leviticus 25:10

Print Passage: Leviticus 25:8-12, 25, 35-36, 39-40, 47-48, 55

—The word *jubilee* comes from the Hebrew *yobel*, probably referring to a ram's horn. The Jubilee Year began when the ram's horn sounded on the Day of Atonement (verse 9).

—The Jubilee Year was a year of "release" when people returned to their homes and property reverted to its ancestral owner. An Israelite who had sold himself into bondage because of poverty was released.

—In Israel, God was considered the true owner of the land. It was the *crop value* of the land that was sold between jubilee years.

—Among other things, the Jubilee Year was designed to prevent wealth from accumulating in the hands of a powerful few and to give those who had fallen on hard times a fresh start.

—The law against taking interest from a fellow Israelite was part of an effort to eliminate profiteering at the expense of the less fortunate members of society (verses 36-37).

CHILDREN

Children Topic: Let Freedom Ring!

Key Verse: Leviticus 25:10

Print Passage: Leviticus 25:8-22

—Spiritual rejuvenation and renewal can occur by resting from work and reflecting on God.

—Faithful believers understand that justice can be achieved by giving generously to others.

—God calls us to recognize and celebrate His provision.

—Compromise, rather than domination, is useful in resolving problematic situations.

—God calls us to restore relationships with the land, our neighbors, and others.

I. INTRODUCTION

A. The Need for Economic Justice

The Bible makes it clear that God is concerned about the practice of justice in all of its forms: social, economic, political, and religious (see Genesis 18:19; Deuteronomy 16:18-19; Isaiah 56:1; Micah 6:6-8). One of the central aims of today's lesson is to focus our attention on economic justice as the framework for developing a healthy and prosperous society. God included the celebration of Jubilee in the Law of Moses as a means for ensuring that no one in ancient Hebrew society would be able to accumulate large sums of wealth to the exclusion of others.

What is economic justice and why is it important in any society? The Center for Social and Economic Justice defines *economic justice* as that which "encompasses the moral principles which guide us in designing our economic institutions. These institutions determine how each person earns a living, enters into contracts, exchanges goods and services with others and otherwise produces an independent material foundation for his or her economic sustenance."[1] Why is economic justice important in a society? It is important because an economically just society affords each individual an equal right to participate in the commercial part of society and to pursue his or her ambitions without being denied or hindered by others. Unfortunately, economic justice is more an ideal than it is a reality, especially when 2 percent of the world's population own more than 50 percent of the world's wealth. As you study the lesson today, make a list of the times when you needed a second chance because of the mistakes you had made. Find the addresses and telephone numbers of the local homeless shelters in your community. Find out what kind of services they offer and ask how you can become involved in their work. Ask the Holy Spirit to reveal to you ways to make the teachings of the lesson applicable in your life.

B. Biblical Background

The Jubilee is the culmination of a forty-nine-year cycle (Leviticus 25:8). The word *jubilee* comes from the Hebrew word *yobel*, which refers to the ram's horn. The Year of Jubilee began with the blowing of the ram's horn on the Day of Atonement (verse 9). The Jubilee was a year of "release" when people returned to their homes and property reverted back to its ancestral owners. Allen Ross noted that "it provided a general overhaul of economic and social life to restore people and properties to their rightful conditions."[2] Israelites who had sold themselves into slavery were to be released and people were released from all indebtedness. These things were done for several reasons. First, it would give people who had fallen into poverty and deep debt the opportunity to have a fresh start. Second, it would prevent the concentration of wealth into the hands of a few powerfully rich farmers and land owners. Third, it would deter Israelites from profiteering from the misfortunes of fellow Israelites and aliens who lived within their borders. Fourth, it would ensure that the people would never lose sight of the fact that the land belonged to God; they were His servants serving His purpose.

II. EXPOSITION AND APPLICATION OF THE SCRIPTURE

A. God Announces the Year of Jubilee (Leviticus 25:8-12)

And thou shalt number seven sabbaths of years unto thee, seven times seven years; and the space of the seven sabbaths of years shall be unto thee forty and nine years. Then shalt thou cause the trumpet of the jubile to sound on the tenth day of the seventh month, in the day of atonement shall ye make the trumpet sound throughout all your land. And ye shall hallow the fiftieth year, and proclaim liberty throughout all the land unto all the inhabitants thereof: it shall be a jubile unto you; and ye shall return every man unto his possession, and ye shall return every man unto his family. A jubile shall that fiftieth year be unto you: ye shall not sow, neither reap that which groweth of itself in it, nor gather the grapes in it of thy vine undressed. For it is the jubile; it shall be holy unto you: ye shall eat the increase thereof out of the field.

In the Hebrew language, *Sabbath* means "rest." It refers to the cessation of work. The Sabbath is first mentioned in Genesis 2:2-3 of the Old Testament; God instituted the Sabbath as a day of rest when He had finished all of the work of creating the heavens and the earth: "And by the seventh day God completed

His work which He had done, and He rested on the seventh day from all His work which He had done. Then God blessed the seventh day and sanctified it, because in it He rested from all His work which God had created and made" (NASB). The Sabbath is the first and oldest of all of the holy days.[3] It represented Israel's affirmation of the Sinai Covenant (see Exodus 20:8-10). The Sabbath as Israel's day of rest was applicable only to Israel as God's covenant people. Christians are not bound to this law but worship on Sunday, which is the Lord's Day (or first day of the week). In Exodus 31:12-17, God commanded Moses to speak to the people, telling them to honor the Sabbath. It was to be a "perpetual sign" of the covenant between Israel and God. Sabbath observance was not kept by any of the other nations surrounding Israel. Observance of the Sabbath set Israel apart from the surrounding nations. Sabbath begins at sunset on Fridays and ends at sunset on Saturdays, which is the length of the Jewish day. Alfred Edersheim writes that "The day was computed from sunset to sunset, or rather to the appearance of the first three stars with which a new day commenced."[4] In the Jewish reckoning of time, the first hour of the day corresponds roughly to 6:00 a.m. or first light.[5]

Every seventh year, there was to be a Sabbath of rest for the land so that it could regenerate itself (verses 1-7). "Seven" was the number of completion or perfection. Jubilee was an extension of the Sabbath rest of the land, a time when no crops were to be planted. Every forty-ninth year was to be the start of the Year of Jubilee (verse 8). The priests were to blow the trumpets throughout the land, which would mark the start of the celebration. Jubilee

would begin on the Day of Atonement after the people had made the appropriate sacrifices and been forgiven of all their sins (see Leviticus 16).

The fiftieth year was to be consecrated to the Lord, just as the other holy days were consecrated to the Lord. One of the prominent themes of the Jubilee was liberty, not just for a few but for the entire nation. Everyone was to return to their ancestral homes and tribal lands (verse 10). The word *liberty* comes from the Hebrew word *derowr,* and it has in it the idea of "freedom of movement," or "free flowing." Jubilee would create a climate of safety when men who had been slaves or had sold themselves into servitude because of indebtedness would be free to return to their homes and families. In many African countries, there are seasons of the year when people return to their ancestral villages for national holidays and celebrations. During the Jubilee Year, the people were not to plant any seeds nor were they to reap the crops that grew in the fields, nor harvest any untended vines. The Lord would provide enough in the year prior to Jubilee to last for three years (see Leviticus 25:21). The Jubilee was a special time in ancient Israel; it was holy and they were to eat only what was taken directly from the fields.

What were the key themes of Jubilee? First, reconciliation and repentance were signified by Jubilee, commencing on the Day of Atonement—the most holy day in ancient Israel. Second, there was the theme of rest, both for the land and for the people. All sacred days were days of rest when no work was to be done throughout the land. Third, it was a time of release from slavery, indebtedness, and the other forms of servitude that limited human progress. At the very heart of this message for

Christians is the need to value physical rest and regeneration of the human spirit. The constant grind of ministry can wear down the strongest of believers. God allows for periods of regeneration and restoration.

B. God Ordains the Law of Redemption (Leviticus 25:25)

If thy brother be waxen poor, and hath sold away some of his possession, and if any of his kin come to redeem it, then shall he redeem that which his brother sold.

In ancient Israel, God was the owner of all of the land; therefore, it could not be bought and sold for profit (see verses 23-24). These laws were given prior to the settlement of the Hebrew people in the land of Canaan. They would ensure that no family would ever lose their inheritance because of poverty or some other unfortunate event. This is the first in a series of hypothetical situations that could arise within a typical Hebrew family regarding personal financial misfortunes. The question answered in this law had to do with family responsibility in helping to relieve the suffering and poverty of another family member. If a man became poor and was forced to sell portions or all of his property and possessions to cover the debt, then the nearest relative must serve as his redeemer, or "goel." The nearest relative must buy back the land of the impoverished family member and return it to him without obligation (see Ruth 4 and Jeremiah 32:7-8 for examples of redemption). In the New Testament, Jesus Christ became the redeemer of a broken and sin-ridden humanity. He paid the price for the sins of the whole world (see John 1:14; 2 Corinthians 8:9; Hebrews 2:13-14; Revelation 5:9).

C. God Annuls Economic Slavery (Leviticus 25:35-36, 39-40, 47-48)

And if thy brother be waxen poor, and fallen in decay with thee; then thou shalt relieve him: yea, though he be a stranger, or a sojourner; that he may live with thee. Take thou no usury of him, or increase: but fear thy God; that thy brother may live with thee.... And if thy brother that dwelleth by thee be waxen poor, and be sold unto thee; thou shalt not compel him to serve as a bondservant: But as an hired servant, and as a sojourner, he shall be with thee, and shall serve thee unto the year of jubilee... And if a sojourner or stranger wax rich by thee, and thy brother that dwelleth by him wax poor, and sell himself unto the stranger or sojourner by thee, or to the stock of the stranger's family: After that he is sold he may be redeemed again; one of his brethren may redeem him.

In this part of the lesson, we have three additional hypothetical situations that could arise within the ancient Hebrew community, each beginning with the word *if*. The first in verses 35-36 involves a countryman who became poor and was unable to support himself. In this situation, the man was forced to sell everything and still fell into poverty. The question answered had to do with community responsibility toward the poor in their midst. Israel was a covenant community, with all members being descendants of Abraham; hence, they were more than a nation—God considered them to be a family (see Amos 3:2). Another important observation in this group of laws was God's concern for the alien or strangers who might live among the Hebrew people. It would be easy to oppress them and see them as social outcasts and economic burdens. However, because Israel knew how it felt to be aliens in a strange land, they were to show kindness and compassion to the aliens in their midst (see Leviticus 19:34; 23:9; Deuteronomy 10:18-19; Matthew 25:35; Hebrews 13:2).

What were Israel's obligations to the poor

(see Deuteronomy 15:7-8; compare with Proverbs 14:20; 17:5; 19:17)? First, they were not to ignore the plight of their poor countrymen (see James 2:14-18 for a New Testament understanding of this principle). Second, they were not to see someone else's misfortune as an opportunity for acquiring greater wealth (see 1 Kings 9:22; 2 Kings 4:1). Third, they were to see the situation of the destitute countryman as an obligation to make sure that he was able to continue to live in the community. Fourth, they were not to charge high interest rates on borrowed money (see verse 36; compare with Exodus 22:25 and Deuteronomy 23:19-20, which are laws against high interest rates' being charged to the poor).

The ancient Hebrews were to offer whatever support would be needed to make sure that the poor person would be able to live among them. The destitute Hebrew was to be given the same compassion and care that would be shown to a resident alien. In fact, he was to be treated with even greater respect because he was a fellow countryman.

Leviticus 25:39-40 is an introduction to the second hypothetical situation that could arise. Suppose one's countryman became poor and sold himself to another Hebrew. What obligation did he have toward the one who voluntarily sold himself into servitude? First, under no circumstance was the person to be treated as a slave. He could not be required to work as if he were a slave with no rights and consideration. Second, he was to be treated with the same respect and dignity as a hired worker. Although he was working to pay off a debt, he was not to be abused nor mistreated. Third, this was not an open-ended obligation. The person would work until the Year of Jubilee, at which time he would be released.

Leviticus 25:47-48 comprise the third hypothetical situation that could arise within the covenant community. The scenario is set up in the reverse order in which an alien came to Israel and became wealthy. Did he have an obligation to the poor and was he obligated to follow the laws of Israel regarding the undue accumulation of wealth at the expense of the poor? Suppose a man became poor and sold himself into the hands of a wealthy resident alien or a member of the alien's family for the purpose of paying off a debt—how is he to be treated? The law required that he be treated the same way. The land belonged to God; and it could not be permanently sold to anyone. The person was accorded the same rights when sold to an alien as he would be when sold to a fellow Hebrew.

D. God Is the Architect of the Hebrew Nation (Leviticus 25:55)

For unto me the children of Israel are servants; they are my servants whom I brought forth out of the land of Egypt: I am the LORD your God.

This final verse in the biblical text describes Israel's relationship to God. They belonged to Him by virtue of their covenant relationship (see Exodus 19:1-7). Israel was to be the servant of the Lord, because it was He who had redeemed them out of the hand of Pharaoh. As their redeemer and as owner of the land, God had every right to decide and dictate how they would relate to each other and to Him. He was the Lord their God!

III. CONCLUDING REFLECTION

On the surface, one would assume that this ancient practice of Jubilee would have no application to Christians living in the twenty-first century. However, it is clear that the principles outlined are applicable in every age and in every country. One of the biggest challenges that all societies have is the concentration of wealth into the hands of the privileged few. The poor, the disenfranchised, and the politically disconnected continue to struggle just as much in developed nations as they do in the developing countries. God's will is that all men and women would be treated equally and fairly.

Spend a few minutes reflecting over the truths of this lesson and jot down your thoughts about how to apply these principles in your life.

PRAYER

Lord God, we pray that we might learn how to be just and kind to those who are our employees, and how to honor You by standing up for the rights of the poor. In Jesus' name we pray. Amen.

WORD POWER
Jubilee—refers to the institution of a fiftieth-year celebration ordained by God.

HOME DAILY BIBLE READINGS
(June 11-17, 2012)

Celebrate Jubilee

MONDAY, June 11: "Turning Back from Repentance" (Jeremiah 34:8-17)

TUESDAY, June 12: "If You Return to Me" (Nehemiah 1:5-11)

WEDNESDAY, June 13: "Walking at Liberty" (Psalm 119:41-48)

THURSDAY, June 14: "The Spirit and Freedom" (2 Corinthians 3:12-18)

FRIDAY, June 15: "When Liberty Becomes a Stumbling Block" (1 Corinthians 8)

SATURDAY, June 16: "The Perfect Law of Liberty" (James 1:19-27)

SUNDAY, June 17: "Proclaiming Liberty throughout the Land" (Leviticus 25:8-12, 25, 35-36, 39-40, 47-48, 55)

End Notes

[1]From *Defining Social and Economic Justice*, http://www.cesj.org/thirdway/*economicjustice-defined.htm;* Internet.
[2]Allen P. Ross, *Holiness to the Lord: A Guide to the Exposition of the Book of Leviticus* (Grand Rapids: Baker Academic, 2002), p. 456.
[3]Ibid. p. 396.
[4]Alfred Edersheim, *The Temple: Its Ministry and Services,* Peabody, MA: Hendrickson Publishers, 1994), p. 159.
[5]Ibid.

LESSON 4   June 24, 2012

THE HEART OF THE LAW

DEVOTIONAL READING: **Micah 6:1-8**

BACKGROUND SCRIPTURE: **Deuteronomy 10:1-22;**

PRINT PASSAGE: **Deuteronomy 10:12-22; 16:18-20**   **16:18-20**

KEY VERSES: **Deuteronomy 10:12-13**

Deuteronomy 10:12-22; 16:18-20—KJV

12 And now, Israel, what doth the LORD thy God require of thee, but to fear the LORD thy God, to walk in all his ways, and to love him, and to serve the LORD thy God with all thy heart and with all thy soul,

13 To keep the commandments of the Lord, and his statutes, which I command thee this day for thy good?

14 Behold, the heaven and the heaven of heavens is the LORD's thy God, the earth also, with all that therein is.

15 Only the LORD had a delight in thy fathers to love them, and he chose their seed after them, even you above all people, as it is this day.

16 Circumcise therefore the foreskin of your heart, and be no more stiffnecked.

17 For the LORD your God is God of gods, and Lord of lords, a great God, a mighty, and a terrible, which regardeth not persons, nor taketh reward:

18 He doth execute the judgment of the fatherless and widow, and loveth the stranger, in giving him food and raiment.

19 Love ye therefore the stranger: for ye were strangers in the land of Egypt.

20 Thou shalt fear the LORD thy God; him shalt thou serve, and to him shalt thou cleave, and swear by his name.

21 He is thy praise, and he is thy God, that hath done for thee these great and terrible things, which thine eyes have seen.

22 Thy fathers went down into Egypt with threescore and ten persons; and now the LORD thy God hath made thee as the stars of heaven for multitude.

          .....

18 Judges and officers shalt thou make thee in all thy gates, which the LORD thy God giveth thee,

Deuteronomy 10:12-22; 16:18-20—NIV

12 And now, O Israel, what does the LORD your God ask of you but to fear the LORD your God, to walk in all his ways, to love him, to serve the LORD your God with all your heart and with all your soul,

13 and to observe the LORD's commands and decrees that I am giving you today for your own good?

14 To the LORD your God belong the heavens, even the highest heavens, the earth and everything in it.

15 Yet the LORD set his affection on your forefathers and loved them, and he chose you, their descendants, above all the nations, as it is today.

16 Circumcise your hearts, therefore, and do not be stiff-necked any longer.

17 For the LORD your God is God of gods and Lord of lords, the great God, mighty and awesome, who shows no partiality and accepts no bribes.

18 He defends the cause of the fatherless and the widow, and loves the alien, giving him food and clothing.

19 And you are to love those who are aliens, for you yourselves were aliens in Egypt.

20 Fear the LORD your God and serve him. Hold fast to him and take your oaths in his name.

21 He is your praise; he is your God, who performed for you those great and awesome wonders you saw with your own eyes.

22 Your forefathers who went down into Egypt were seventy in all, and now the LORD your God has made you as numerous as the stars in the sky.

          .....

People respond in various ways to being loved. How should someone respond when he or she is the recipient of love? As recipients of God's love, we are expected to be fair, act justly, and love others.

throughout thy tribes: and they shall judge the people with just judgment.

19 Thou shalt not wrest judgment; thou shalt not respect persons, neither take a gift: for a gift doth blind the eyes of the wise, and pervert the words of the righteous.

20 That which is altogether just shalt thou follow, that thou mayest live, and inherit the land which the LORD thy God giveth thee.

18 Appoint judges and officials for each of your tribes in every town the LORD your God is giving you, and they shall judge the people fairly.

19 Do not pervert justice or show partiality. Do not accept a bribe, for a bribe blinds the eyes of the wise and twists the words of the righteous.

20 Follow justice and justice alone, so that you may live and possess the land the LORD your God is giving you.

TOPICAL OUTLINE OF THE LESSON

I. **Introduction**
   A. Divine Love
   B. Biblical Background

II. **Exposition and Application of the Scripture**
   A. The Lord's Requirements (Deuteronomy 10:12-13)
   B. The Lord Owns Everything (Deuteronomy 10:14-16)
   C. The Great God: Mighty and Awesome (Deuteronomy 10:17-19)
   D. Fear the Lord (Deuteronomy 10:20-22)
   E. Organized for Justice (Deuteronomy 16:18-20)

III. **Concluding Reflection**

LESSON OBJECTIVES

Upon the completion of the lesson, the students will be able to:

1. List ways that the people of Israel were to respond to God's love;

2. Examine the various ways that people respond to being loved; and,

3. Discuss the importance of love as the framework for doing ministry today.

POINTS TO BE EMPHASIZED

ADULT/YOUTH

Adult Topic: Loving as We Are Loved

Youth Topic: The Heart of the Matter

Adult/Youth Key Verses: Deuteronomy 10:12-13

Print Passage: Deuteronomy 10:12-22; 16:18-20

—The principle underlying justice, in this passage, does not originate in humankind but in the nature of God.

—Loving God involves more than a sentimental response; it means serving God with one's heart and soul (Deuteronomy 10:12).

—Why is it that one should love God? Our love for God is the response to God's love for us (Deuteronomy 10:14-15).

—Loving God means loving what and whom God loves: justice for the orphan and widow, mercy and compassion for the stranger, and concern for the weak and oppressed.

—"Circumcise . . . your heart" (Deuteronomy 10:16) is a metaphorical expression meaning "to open the heart (including the mind and will) in order to be receptive and responsive to God's direction."

—Deuteronomy 16:19 speaks against positional influence and bribery, which were common means of securing favorable decisions in courts of the ancient Near East.

CHILDREN

Children Topic: What God Requires

Key Verse: Deuteronomy 10:12

Print Passage: Deuteronomy 10:12-22

—Believers are required to fear, walk like, love, serve, and obey God.

—Just as the God who owns everything cared for our ancestors, God the Creator still cares for us today.

—We must exercise obedience to God's requirements through tangible, effective acts of service to one another.

—Our love for an awesome God motivates us to love God and others enough to act justly at all times.

I. INTRODUCTION

A. Divine Love

Divine love was at the center of the covenant relationship between God and Israel (see Deuteronomy 7:7-9; Jeremiah 31:1-3). God's love for Israel could not be measured, nor were there words strong enough to adequately describe it. God expected the Israelites to demonstrate their love by being faithful to the covenant. The one requirement that God placed upon Israel was that they love Him with all their hearts, minds, and souls, and that they would serve only Him (see Exodus 19:1-7; Deuteronomy 6:5). Yet, Israel often had trouble remaining faithful to God, as is evidenced in the preaching of the prophets (see 1 Kings 18:20-35; Isaiah 1:1-4; Jeremiah 3:6-10).

This lesson raises very serious questions for believers living in the twenty-first century about the nature of their love for God and other human beings. What does it mean to be a believer who loves others without showing partiality? We live in a time when people with privilege are accorded the latitude to go back to the former ways without being held accountable for their crimes and sins. In our world, often those who are at the bottom of the socio-economic ladder are ostracized and taken advantage of by institutions and systems that favor the rich and powerful. Yet, there stands at the heart of the Christian faith the cross of Jesus Christ, which is the symbol of God's unparalleled love for the whole world (see John 3:16; 2 Corinthians 8:9). The Cross is the clearest demonstration that God's love extends to all people in every place. As you study the lesson today, make a mental note of the people in your congregation whom you find it difficult to relate to. Make a list of the reasons that keep you from expressing authentic love and fellowship. Ask the Holy Spirit to reveal to you ways to make the teachings of the lesson applicable in your life.

B. Biblical Background

Today, we conclude our brief study of the Books of the Law and their teachings regarding social and economic justice. Deuteronomy is the last book in the Pentateuch (or first five books of the Old Testament); the name means "second law." There has been much debate about the authorship and date of the book, but tradition and the internal evidence of the book hold that Moses was the author (see Deuteronomy 1:1; 5:1; 6:1; 27:1). The book of Deuteronomy is set within the context of Israel's final days of wilderness wandering when they were nearing the land promised to Abraham, Isaac, and Jacob (see Deuteronomy 1:1-5).

The book of Deuteronomy is among the most highly valued of the Old Testament Books of Law because of its teaching about God's love and faithfulness to Israel; one of its most important themes is the call to "remember" (see Deuteronomy 5:15; 7:18; 8:2, 18; 9:7; 15:15; 16:3, 12; 24:9, 18; 32:7). Israel was reminded by Moses to remember the past and let it serve as the guide for the future. A second theme of equal importance is the call to "hear and obey." As a nation, they would only be blessed by following the commandments of God without reservation. A third theme of critical significance is the motif of "covenant" which appears twenty-seven times in the book (see Deuteronomy 4:13, 23, 31; 5:2-3; 8:18; 9:9). Covenant (Hebrew, *berith)* has in it the idea of "alliance or agreement." Israel was a nation shaped by her covenant with God. That covenant was first made with the patriarch Abraham (see Genesis 12:1-3).

From the passage we are studying today we learn that justice did not originate in humankind, but in the very nature of God. Why are we called to love God? According to the lesson, our love for God is the response of God's love for us (verses 14-15). When we love God, we will not only do what He says, but also we will love the people and things that matter most to Him. God is to be loved because of the greatness of His might. Once Israel entered the Promised Land, they were to appoint judges who would ensure that the laws were executed in fairness and equity.

II. EXPOSITION AND APPLICATION OF THE SCRIPTURE

A. The Lord's Requirements
(Deuteronomy 10:12-13)

And now, Israel, what doth the Lord thy God require of thee, but to fear the Lord thy God, to walk in all his ways, and to love him, and to serve the Lord thy God with all thy heart and with all thy soul, To keep the commandments of the Lord, and his statutes, which I command thee this day for thy good?

"And now" is a transitional phrase and signals the beginning of a new discussion regarding how Israel was to live within the borders of the Promised Land (see Deuteronomy 9:1). Moses addressed Israel by asking a rhetorical question: "What does the Lord your God ask of you?" (verse 12, NIV). He specifically asked that they obey five imperative commands: fear, walk, love, serve, and observe. Here there is a sharp contrast between the gods of the surrounding nations—with whom Israel would certainly have to live—and the God who brought them out of Egypt with mighty signs and wonders. The answer to the question comes in the form of five requirements.

First, Israel was to fear the Lord. *Fear* (Hebrew, *yare*) has in it the idea of dread, but at a deeper level it means honor, respect, astonishment, and awe.

Second, Israel's reverent respect for the Lord would lead to the second requirement— walking in all of His ways. *Walk* (Hebrew, *Balak*) not only means "to proceed," but more often refers to one's manner of life.

Third, Israel was to love God. *Love* (Hebrew, *châshaq*) refers to love in all of its various dimensions. In this context, it is specifically directed towards Israel's love for God being expressed through her faithfulness to the covenant relationship.

Fourth, the Israelites were to serve the Lord with all of their hearts and souls. Everything that they did was to be done wholeheartedly. *Serve* (Hebrew, *abad*) has in it the idea of labor and work. It also has reference to worship and following other gods. Israel served the Lord by following Him, honoring the covenant, and worshipping Him only.

Fifth, the Israelites were to observe the Lord's commands and decrees. *Observe* (Hebrew, *shamar*) means "to keep, guard, watch or perform." Israel was told to observe both the commands and the decrees by doing it (see Deuteronomy 6:3, 25; 8:1; 11:32; 24:8; 2 Kings 21:8). God gave the Israelites the commandments for their own good. They were not barriers to social and economic growth but, rather, were guides for ensuring that the society was just and fair for all people.

B. The Lord Owns Everything (Deuteronomy 10:14-16)

Behold, the heaven and the heaven of heavens is the LORD's thy God, the earth also, with all that therein is. Only the LORD had a delight in thy fathers to love them, and he chose their seed after them, even you above all people, as it is this day. Circumcise therefore the foreskin of your heart, and be no more stiffnecked.

Moses made the declaration that God was the sole owner of the universe. While the other nations surrounding them all had a concept of God, their concept was of the works of human hands and thus not real (see Deuteronomy 4:28; 2 Kings 19:18; Psalms 115:4; 135:15; Isaiah 37:19; Acts 17:25). God is the Lord of the heavens, and therefore He can choose whomever He wishes to choose. Yet, it was upon Abraham and his descendants that God set His love above all of the nations of the earth. *Chose* (Hebrew, *bachar*) means "to take a keen look at with the idea of picking out the choicest one." This definition is used in several places in the Old Testament (see Genesis 13:11; 1 Samuel 17:40). The word is used to express that choosing which has ultimate and eternal significance. On the one hand, God chooses a people (Psalm 135:4), certain tribes (Psalm 78:68), specific individuals (1 Kings 8:16; 1 Chronicles 28:5; 1 Samuel 10:24; 2 Samuel 6:21), and a place for his name (Deuteronomy 12:5; etc.).[1]

Circumcision was the sign of the covenant between God and Abraham (see Genesis 17:10-14). One of the things that often happens with religious practices is their elevation to a status never intended by God. This is precisely what happened with the act of circumcision—it became the mark of divine selection without regard for keeping the Law. "The prophets became aware of this perversion and preached against mere circumcision of the flesh, that is, circumcision not accompanied by living faith. Jeremiah spoke of the circumcision of the heart. He said, "Circumcise yourselves to the Lord, and take away the foreskins of your heart, ye men of Judah" (Jeremiah 4:4). But long before Jeremiah, the people had been warned of this danger. Indeed, Jeremiah was quoting Deuteronomy 10:16. The use of the verb in Deuteronomy 30:6 proves the statement above—that circumcision symbolized the deepest spiritual reality of the Hebrew religion.[2]

The term *stiff-necked* refers to "being hard, difficult to manage, obstinate, unresponsive, un-submissive, and uncooperative." In the Old Testament, it is used as a metaphor for people who are unwilling to be obedient to God or to their masters (see Exodus 32:9; 33:3, 5; 34:9; Deuteronomy 9:6, 13; 2 Chronicles 30:8). The generation that was comprised of adults when Israel had come out of Egypt had all died, and a new generation had come along who were just as stubborn and hard to lead as the first. If they were to prosper in the Promised Land, then Israel must learn to walk in humility and uprightness before the Lord God.

C. The Great God: Mighty and Awesome (Deuteronomy 10:17-19)

For the Lord your God is God of gods, and Lord of lords, a great God, a mighty, and a terrible, which regardeth not persons, nor taketh reward: He doth execute the judgment of the fatherless and widow, and loveth the stranger, in giving him food and raiment. Love ye therefore the stranger: for ye were strangers in the land of Egypt.

Israel was exhorted to take note of the person of their God. He was not like the local deities, who lacked power and might and were nothing more than mere idols. Rather, He is "God of gods and Lord of lords"—a phrase that denotes His incomparable and incomprehensible nature (see Isaiah 40:18-26; compare with Ephesians 3:14-21). Three adjectives were used to describe God: *great, mighty,* and *awesome.* Yet, He is the God who shows no partiality. He cannot be tricked, coerced, or duped into showing favoritism to any one group, people, or individual (see 1 Chronicles 16:25-26; Psalm 136:3; Daniel 2:47; Acts 10:34; Colossians 3:25; Revelation 17:14). God cannot be bribed by false loyalty, empty praise, or perfunctory worship (see Amos 5:21-24).

What is this God like? Moses answered the question, although it was not asked. He defended those who were the least of the earth, the fatherless, widows, and the aliens. He provided for their basic needs. The fatherless and widows, who were often mentioned with aliens, were the objects of God's special concern. The quality of one's devotion and obedience to God was measured by how one treated the fatherless, widow, and alien.

Israel was to be especially sensitive to the aliens in their midst, because they were at one time aliens themselves. They were mistreated and made to make bricks without straw (see Exodus 1:6-14; 5:1-14). God's people are called to imitate His character and actions (see 1 Peter 1:13-15). We are most like the Lord Jesus Christ when we take seriously the needs of those who are victimized by the unjust social and economic structures.

D. Fear the Lord (Deuteronomy 10:20-22)

Thou shalt fear the Lord thy God; him shalt thou serve, and to him shalt thou cleave, and swear by his name. He is thy praise, and he is thy God, that hath done for thee

these great and terrible things, which thine eyes have seen. Thy fathers went down into Egypt with threescore and ten persons; and now the LORD thy God hath made thee as the stars of heaven for multitude.

These verses conclude this section of the lesson and passage. Verse 20 is a repeat of the previous commands to fear the Lord and serve Him, but to this is added the additional requirement to "hold fast" (NIV), which means to cling or stick close to (see Deuteronomy 4:4; 11:22; 13:4; Joshua 23:8; Acts 11:23; Romans 12:9) and "take your oaths in His name" (NIV), which literally meant to pledge one's complete allegiance to the Lord (see Deuteronomy 6:13; Psalm 63:11; Isaiah 45:3).

Praise (Hebrew, *tehillah*) means "laudation, a hymn, praising God in singing" (see Psalms 22:25; 48:10; 145). The main section in a psalm of praise is the section that extols and celebrates the mighty acts of God. Throughout the Bible, God is celebrated as the Creator of the ends of the earth (see Job 38:8-11; Psalm 102:25-26; Isaiah 40:12-26). He is the one who keeps His people safe and delivers them from their enemies (see Psalms 27:1ff; 37:1f; 121). He is the only One worthy of praise and adoration. God has absolute power; therefore, He is free to do for His people as He pleases. As we bless Him, we are in turn blessed by the Lord.

Two main reasons are given for Israel's praise in verses 21 and 22. First, Israel sang the praises of God because of the great and wonderful things that He had done. God is to be praised for who He is and what He does. Second, because the descendants of Abraham went to Egypt there were only about seventy people, but over time God grew them into a mighty nation (see Genesis 46:27, and compare it with Genesis 15:5; Deuteronomy 1:10; 28:62; and Nehemiah 9:23).

E. Organized for Justice
(Deuteronomy 16:18-20)

Judges and officers shalt thou make thee in all thy gates, which the LORD thy God giveth thee, throughout thy tribes: and they shall judge the people with just judgment. Thou shalt not wrest judgment; thou shalt not respect persons, neither take a gift: for a gift doth blind the eyes of the wise, and pervert the words of the righteous. That which is altogether just shalt thou follow, that thou mayest live, and inherit the land which the LORD thy God giveth thee.

The concluding section of the lesson deals with how Israel was to organize her government upon reaching the Promised Land. They were to appoint *judges* (Hebrew, *shaphat*) and *officers* (Hebrew, *shoter*). Within these two groups of leaders, the *judges* would have overall responsibility for the conduct of the civil affairs of government to ensure that the laws of God were carried out equitably and fairly. The *officers* were a lower level of leaders whose primary role was probably that of assisting the judge or carrying out some other duties. What is important in this passage is that every town was to have credible leaders who would treat the people fairly, not perverting justice or accepting bribes and tainting the overall social structure of the community. The reason for not permitting bribes was twofold: to prevent "[the] blind[ing] [of] the eyes of the wise, and [the] pervert[ing] [of] the words of the righteous" (verse 19).

The leaders were to follow *justice* (Hebrew, *misphat)*, which is a very important Old Testament word and concept. It is found nearly 218 times in the Old Testament and was used to prescribe a range of legal and social standards by which Israel was to live. When justice is practiced and all have equal access to the security of the law, the society will prosper and all will live the abundant life.

III. CONCLUDING REFLECTION

One of the major church leadership challenges today lies in helping believers of this generation to see and sense the need to become champions for justice and righteousness. The farther we move from the heyday of the Civil Rights Movement, the more people become relaxed and at ease with things the way that they are. This lesson reminds us that love for God translates into dynamic and responsible social activism. We are required to love the least, last, and left out in our society, not just by what we *say*, but more importantly by what we *do*. How is your church engaged in the ministry of social and economic justice? What do you see as your role in the fight for equality today? It may be that the lives of the saints will be greatly enhanced when we move back to the center of what it means to be Christian in a broken world.

PRAYER

Our Father, we thank You that You have entrusted us with the obligation to show love to the oppressed, the despised, and the neglected. Help us to truly show forth this love to all with whom we come into contact. In Jesus' name we pray. Amen.

WORD POWER

Fear (Hebrew: *yare*)—**This word has in it the idea of dread, but at a deeper level it means honor, respect, astonishment, and awe.**

Praise (Hebrew: *tehillah*)—**means laudation; a hymn; praising God in singing.**

HOME DAILY BIBLE READINGS
(June 18-24, 2012)

The Heart of the Law

MONDAY, **June 18: "God of Gods, Lord of Lords" (Psalm 136:1-9)**

TUESDAY, **June 19: "Spiritual Matters of the Heart" (Romans 2:25-29)**

WEDNESDAY, **June 20: "God's Faithfulness and Justice" (Romans 3:1-9)**

THURSDAY, **June 21: "Hold Fast to the Traditions" (2 Thessalonians 2:13-17)**

FRIDAY, **June 22: "What the Lord Requires" (Micah 6:1-8)**

SATURDAY, **June 23: "Just and True Are Your Ways" (Revelation 15:1-4)**

SUNDAY, **June 24: "Loving God and Justice" (Deuteronomy 10:12-22; 16:18-20)**

End Notes

[1]Harris, R. Laird; Harris, Robert Laird; Archer, Gleason Leonard; Waltke, Bruce K.: *Theological Wordbook of the Old Testament*. Electronic ed. Chicago: Moody Press, 1999, c1980, 100.

[2]Harris, R. Laird; Harris, Robert Laird; Archer, Gleason Leonard; Waltke, Bruce K.: *Theological Wordbook of the Old Testament*. Electronic ed. Chicago: Moody Press, 1999, c1980, S. 495.

LESSON 5   July 1, 2012

SAMUEL ADMINISTERS JUSTICE

Devotional Reading: **Ezekiel 18:25-32**
Print Passage: **1 Samuel 7:3-11, 15-17**

Background Scripture: **1 Samuel 7:3-17**
Key Verse: **1 Samuel 7:3**

1 Samuel 7:3-11, 15-17—KJV

3 And Samuel spake unto all the house of Israel, saying, If ye do return unto the Lord with all your hearts, then put away the strange gods and Ashtaroth from among you, and prepare your hearts unto the Lord, and serve him only: and he will deliver you out of the hand of the Philistines.

4 Then the children of Israel did put away Baalim and Ashtaroth, and served the Lord only.

5 And Samuel said, Gather all Israel to Mizpeh, and I will pray for you unto the Lord.

6 And they gathered together to Mizpeh, and drew water, and poured it out before the Lord, and fasted on that day, and said there, We have sinned against the Lord. And Samuel judged the children of Israel in Mizpeh.

7 And when the Philistines heard that the children of Israel were gathered together to Mizpeh, the lords of the Philistines went up against Israel. And when the children of Israel heard it, they were afraid of the Philistines.

8 And the children of Israel said to Samuel, Cease not to cry unto the Lord our God for us, that he will save us out of the hand of the Philistines.

9 And Samuel took a sucking lamb, and offered it for a burnt offering wholly unto the Lord: and Samuel cried unto the Lord for Israel; and the Lord heard him.

10 And as Samuel was offering up the burnt offering, the Philistines drew near to battle against Israel: but the Lord thundered with a great thunder on that day upon the Philistines, and discomfited them; and they were smitten before Israel.

11 And the men of Israel went out of Mizpeh, and pursued the Philistines, and smote them, until they came under Beth-car.

1 Samuel 7:3-11, 15-17—NIV

3 And Samuel said to the whole house of Israel, "If you are returning to the Lord with all your hearts, then rid yourselves of the foreign gods and the Ashtoreths and commit yourselves to the Lord and serve him only, and he will deliver you out of the hand of the Philistines."

4 So the Israelites put away their Baals and Ashtoreths, and served the Lord only.

5 Then Samuel said, "Assemble all Israel at Mizpah and I will intercede with the Lord for you."

6 When they had assembled at Mizpah, they drew water and poured it out before the Lord. On that day they fasted and there they confessed, "We have sinned against the Lord." And Samuel was leader of Israel at Mizpah.

7 When the Philistines heard that Israel had assembled at Mizpah, the rulers of the Philistines came up to attack them. And when the Israelites heard of it, they were afraid because of the Philistines.

8 They said to Samuel, "Do not stop crying out to the Lord our God for us, that he may rescue us from the hand of the Philistines."

9 Then Samuel took a suckling lamb and offered it up as a whole burnt offering to the Lord. He cried out to the Lord on Israel's behalf, and the Lord answered him.

10 While Samuel was sacrificing the burnt offering, the Philistines drew near to engage Israel in battle. But that day the Lord thundered with loud thunder against the Philistines and threw them into such a panic that they were routed before the Israelites.

11 The men of Israel rushed out of Mizpah and pursued the Philistines, slaughtering them along the way to a point below Beth Car.

UNIFYING LESSON PRINCIPLE

People want to feel safe. What gives people a sense of security? Samuel taught the people that their security was a direct result of their loyalty and obedience to God.

.....

15 And Samuel judged Israel all the days of his life. 16 And he went from year to year in circuit to Bethel, and Gilgal, and Mizpeh, and judged Israel in all those places. 17 And his return was to Ramah; for there was his house; and there he judged Israel; and there he built an altar unto the LORD.

.....

15 Samuel continued as judge over Israel all the days of his life. 16 From year to year he went on a circuit from Bethel to Gilgal to Mizpah, judging Israel in all those places. 17 But he always went back to Ramah, where his home was, and there he also judged Israel. And he built an altar there to the LORD.

TOPICAL OUTLINE OF THE LESSON

I. Introduction
A. The Need for Protection
B. Biblical Background

II. Exposition and Application of the Scripture
A. The Call to Return to the Lord (1 Samuel 7:3-4)
B. The Assembly at Mizpeh (1 Samuel 7:5-6)
C. The Threat of Philistine Invasion (1 Samuel 7:7-8)
D. Samuel Prayed and the Lord Answered (1 Samuel 7:9-11)
E. Samuel: The Faithful Judge (1 Samuel 7:15-17)

III. Concluding Reflection

LESSON OBJECTIVES

Upon the completion of the lesson, the students will be able to:

1. Retell the Bible story of Samuel's administration as judge;
2. Recall times when they were rescued from threatening situations; and,
3. Identify situations in their communities where people need help, and then be determined to make a difference.

POINTS TO BE EMPHASIZED
ADULT/YOUTH

Adult Topic: Rescued!
Youth Topic: Security through Justice
Adult/Youth Key Verse: 1 Samuel 7:3
Print Passage: 1 Samuel 7:3-11, 15-17

—Israel's repentance at Samuel's urging is a repetition of its behavior on many occasions before. The period of the judges was marked by cycles of prosperity, sin and idolatry, divine punishment at the hands of an invader, and the raising of a judge who led in repentance and deliverance.

—Samuel and Samson were both nazirites who contended against the Philistines and judged Israel.

—While some archaeologists have concluded that the worship of Astartes was part of the ancient worship of Yahweh, this passage makes it clear that while such practice did sometimes occur, it was a perversion of the true worship of Yahweh.

—Samuel could visit the three cities mentioned on his circuit and return home to Ramah in a trip of some thirty-five to forty miles.

—While Samuel "judged Israel all the days of his life" (verse

15), his role was less official in his latter years, as Saul was then reigning as king.

CHILDREN
Children Topic: Samuel: A Just Judge
Key Verse: 1 Samuel 7:3
Print Passage: 1 Samuel 7:3-11, 15-17
—Israel's difficulty was a direct result of disobedience to God's laws, and practicing of idolatry.
—Samuel instructed Israel that it was possible to return to God, but the removal of idols was necessary.

—Samuel as the prophet, priest, and judge took leadership by calling the people together, praying, fasting, and making a burnt offering to God.
—Studying Samuel is an excellent opportunity to see the significance of the role of leaders in enabling people to repent and practice justice.
—God responds with mercy and favor in seemingly impossible situations by using unexpected actions.
—The relationship of the Israelites to God was a key factor in their success.

I. INTRODUCTION
A. The Need for Protection
In our lesson today. Israel faced a serious threat from the Philistines, who were their historic enemies. Samuel, who was the national leader and judge, rose to the occasion and reassured the people that God would fight their battle. He still offers that same assurance to us today.

As you study the lesson today, look for ways that you can begin to pray for people who worship idols. Conduct an Internet search, look up the worship of idol gods, and make a list of the things that you discover. Make a mental note of the things that you have allowed to get in the way of your total surrender to the lordship of Jesus Christ. Ask the Holy Spirit to reveal to you ways to make the teachings of the lesson applicable in your life.

B. Biblical Background
First Samuel 7 serves as the transition from the period of the judges to the beginning of the Hebrew monarchy, which begins with chapter 8. During the period of the judges, Israel fell into a cycle that repeated itself again and again. The cycle usually followed this pattern: there was a period of prosperity, then a period of sin—including idolatry—resulting in divine punishment at the hands of an invader. There would then be a cry for forgiveness by the people and repentance, and God would then appoint a judge/leader (see Judges 2:11-23; 3:7-30). These were very dark days in Israel. The presence of the Lord no longer abode with them at Shiloh.

Samuel appeared at the right time. In chapter 3, verse 20, we are told that the Lord was with Samuel and that He continued to reveal Himself to Samuel at Shiloh. Samuel's word came to all Israel (seen in 4:1). Israel had fallen into a state of apostasy (turning away from God) and idolatry (worship of false gods). God had Samuel positioned for the right moment to lead Israel back to Him. Samuel called upon the people to repent and return to the Lord their God. However, at the same time that Samuel was leading Israel in a time of spiritual renewal and repentance, the Philistines were planning an invasion of Israel. Panic and fear gripped the hearts of the people and they appealed to Samuel to intercede to the Lord for them. God answered Samuel's prayer and delivered them out of the hands of the Philistines. The final verses are a summary of Samuel's time as judge and describe the manner in which he went about his work.

II. EXPOSITION AND APPLICATION OF THE SCRIPTURE

A. The Call to Return to the Lord
(1 Samuel 7:3-4)

And Samuel spake unto all the house of Israel, saying, If ye do return unto the LORD with all your hearts, then put away the strange gods and Ashtaroth from among you, and prepare your hearts unto the LORD, and serve him only: and he will deliver you out of the hand of the Philistines. Then the children of Israel did put away Baalim and Ashtaroth, and served the LORD only.

For more than twenty years, Israel had been in a state of spiritual and religious rebellion (verse 2). The ark of the covenant—which was the most sacred symbol of the presence of the Lord—had been sitting in the house of a man named Abinadab in the hill country of Kiriath Jearim (see Exodus 25:22 and Numbers 10:3; compare with 1 Samuel 4:1-11 for details of how the ark was lost). We are not told where Samuel was or what he had been doing all of these years. Clearly, he must have been engaged in some sort of preaching and prophetic ministry.

Verse 3: The people had come to Samuel to seek his help in two areas. First, they needed to return to the Lord God. Second, they wanted help in dealing with the Philistines. Samuel's response hints that he may have had doubts about their sincerity. He called upon them to be genuinely sincere in returning to the Lord *with all of their hearts* (a phrase meaning "with total commitment"; see also Deuteronomy 11:13; Joshua 22:5; 1 Samuel 12:24; Jeremiah 29:13). The language of return was common in ancient Hebrew prophetic preaching (see Isaiah 55:7; Hosea 6:1; 14:1; Joel 2:12). The word *rid* is an imperative command, meaning that it was absolutely necessary for them to depart from and remove the Ashtoreths and foreign gods without picking them up again. The Ashtoreths were the local goddesses of love and fertility to the Canaanites. Samuel called upon the Israelites to commit to the Lord by serving Him only. The word *commit* in Hebrew means "to be firmly directed toward a goal." It was only in turning completely away from the foreign gods that they could expect the Lord to deliver them from the hand of the Philistines.

Verse 4: The Israelites responded by putting away their Baals and Ashtoreths and they began to serve the Lord only. This suggests that there may have been periods when they tried to serve both the Lord God and others gods. Who was Baal? He was the male fertility god of the Canaanites and Phoenicians. Baal worship entered into the Israelites' religious lives shortly after Joshua's generation died (see Judges 2:6-14). As the tribes went to their tribal areas during the settlement of Canaan, there was no central leader to keep them focused on the

Law and the Lord. Hence, the people adopted many of the practices of the people around them—including their religious practices.

B. The Assembly at Mizpeh
(1 Samuel 7:5-6)

And Samuel said, Gather all Israel to Mizpeh, and I will pray for you unto the Lord. And they gathered together to Mizpeh, and drew water, and poured it out before the Lord, and fasted on that day, and said there, We have sinned against the Lord. And Samuel judged the children of Israel in Mizpeh.

Verse 5: Use of the adverb *then* (NIV) points to the actions that Samuel took after the people repented and committed themselves to returning to the Lord. He called for a national convocation of the people at Mizpah (as it is spelled in NIV), which was located eight miles north of Jerusalem in the tribal area of Benjamin. It is not likely that the entire nation gathered at Mizpah because it would take many weeks to gather the entire nation and the area would not be able to contain all of the people. More than likely this was a gathering of the primary tribal and clan leaders. Samuel promised to intercede for them at Mizpah, which was also his home.

Verse 6: The people came together at Mizpah at the appointed time. The act of the pouring out of water has raised more questions than answers because there are no paralleled acts in Israel's history. There are other instances when we see the pouring out of water, but they all seemed to have different purposes (see 1 Kings 18; 2 Samuel 23:13-17).[1] It is possible that they poured out the water as a sign of their willingness to make the ultimate sacrifice of their lives, given the scarceness of water in that part of the world. The people fasted and confessed their sins against the Lord. The concluding statement is a summary of the leadership role of Samuel. He had led the nation back to the Lord God by leading them into a renewed commitment to serve and worship Him.

C. The Threat of Philistine Invasion
(1 Samuel 7:7-8)

And when the Philistines heard that the children of Israel were gathered together to Mizpeh, the lords of the Philistines went up against Israel. And when the children of Israel heard it, they were afraid of the Philistines. And the children of Israel said to Samuel, Cease not to cry unto the Lord our God for us, that he will save us out of the hand of the Philistines.

Verse 7: The Philistines had been Israel's enemies for years—and they would look for any opportunity to attack them. While the Israelites were in the midst of a religious convocation, the Philistines saw it as an opportunity to launch an attack. When the news of the pending attack reached the leaders at Mizpah, they were gripped by fear (see Exodus 14:10; 1 Samuel 13:6; 17:11; and 2 Chronicles 20:3).

Verse 8: The leaders cried out to Samuel, asking him not to stop crying out to the Lord. The appeal of the people revealed three things about their hearts: First, their repentance and turning from the Ashtoreth and Baal gods were genuine. They were not looking for help from Baal (see Psalm 121:1). Second, it revealed that they were willing to acknowledge the Lord God to be their Lord. Third, they believed that prayer would make the difference in this situation, not their appeal to a symbol.

D. Samuel Prayed and the Lord Answered
(1 Samuel 7:9-11)

And Samuel took a sucking lamb, and offered it for a burnt offering wholly unto the Lord: and Samuel cried unto the Lord for Israel; and the Lord heard him. And as Samuel was offering up the burnt offering, the Philistines drew

near to battle against Israel: but the Lord thundered with a great thunder on that day upon the Philistines, and discomfited them; and they were smitten before Israel. And the men of Israel went out of Mizpeh, and pursued the Philistines, and smote them, until they came under Beth-car.

Verse 9: Samuel built an altar and presented a burnt offering of a suckling lamb to the Lord. The burnt offering was one of several offerings prescribed in the book of Leviticus. Each of the offerings served a specific purpose. "The distinguishing mark of this offering was that it was wholly consumed on the altar, while in other animal sacrifices only the fat portions were burned. The purpose of the offering was propitiation; but with this idea was united another, the entire consecration of the worshiper to the Lord. Because of the regularity and frequency with which it was offered, it was called the "continual" burnt offering (Exodus 29:42); and because no part was left for human consumption, it was also called the "whole burnt offering" (Psalm 51:19)".[2]

Samuel called upon the name of the Lord and the Lord heard his cry and answered. In this act, we have a clear example of how to approach God in worship and prayer. Samuel did not just bring an offering with the intention of trying to appease God. He brought the best—a young lamb without spot or blemish. Sincere worship always involves sacrifice and giving. We must never appear before the Lord empty-handed and expect to receive abundance and blessings.

Verse 10: While Samuel was offering the sacrifice, the Philistines continued to approach Mizpah. One would think that Samuel would have mustered the army, but he kept on sacrificing and worshipping. "The Lord thundered" was probably a phrase used to refer to a mighty rainstorm that the Lord sent which created panic within the Philistine ranks. Whatever happened, they knew that the sounds, wind, and rain were no ordinary event (see Exodus 9:23; 1 Samuel 2:10; Psalm 18:11; Revelation 16:18). They knew that the God of the Israelites was mighty and that He could defeat an army without a sword or spear (see Deuteronomy 20:3; Joshua 10:10; Zechariah 4:6). The Philistines were thrown into a state of panic and began to run in fear. Samuel's worship was not interrupted because of the Philistine threat.

Verse 11: The Israelites were encouraged and pursued the Philistines and annihilated the army. The exact location of Beth-car is not known. A nation that had at one time been filled with fear at the mere mention of their enemies had won a great victory with the help of the Lord God. There have been occasions when God answered our prayers. These become the springboard for increasing our faith and enlarging our vision of God's service.

E. Samuel: The Faithful Judge
(1 Samuel 7:15-17)

And Samuel judged Israel all the days of his life. And he went from year to year in circuit to Bethel, and Gilgal, and Mizpeh, and judged Israel in all those places. And his return was to Ramah; for there was his house; and there he judged Israel; and there he built an altar unto the Lord.

The chapter closes with a brief summary of Samuel's tenure as both judge and prophet. After the decisive victory over the Philistines at Mizpah, the Israelites recognized and respected Samuel as their leader all of the days of his life. Every year he would travel a circular route through the central highlands to Bethel, Gilgal, Mizpah, and back to his home in Ramah. During this time there was no central worship center, because Shiloh had been destroyed by the Philistines and the priestly family of Eli and his sons were dead (see 1 Samuel 4:1-18). Samuel demonstrated the primary traits of a godly leader. He honored God and he served the people, practicing justice and righteousness.

III. CONCLUDING REFLECTION

Millions of Christians will gather for worship today and perform many of the rituals and traditions associated with a typical worship service—but the question is this: Will real repentance and turning from sin take place? God demands that our service be backed up with genuine and sincere hearts and lifestyles that reflect our relationship with Him. It is always easier to talk about living the Christian life than it is to consistently walk upright before the Lord.

PRAYER

Lord God, we pray that the Holy Spirit will reveal to us ways that we may serve You in a more worthy manner. Teach us how to be fair and just in all our ways. May we model the life and teachings of Jesus Christ. In Jesus' name we pray. Amen.

WORD POWER

Heart (Hebrew: *shuwb*)—**refers to the seat of the human emotion and passion. There are more than 725 references to the heart in the Bible. The heart is the source of the intellect (see Isaiah 65:17), the seat of the imagination (see Genesis 6:5), and the seat of the human will (see Joshua 22:5). Man's heart can fail in times of crisis (see 1 Samuel 17:32), be rebellious (see Jeremiah 5:24), and be filled with evil (see Jeremiah 7:24). God is intimately concerned about our hearts and what lies within—for what comes out of the mouth is the expression of the desires, intentions, and feelings.**

HOME DAILY BIBLE READINGS
(June 25–July 1, 2012)

Samuel Administers Justice

MONDAY, June 25: "Repent and Turn" (Ezekiel 18:25-32)

TUESDAY, June 26: "An Earnest Petition" (1 Samuel 1:12-20)

WEDNESDAY, June 27: "A Gift to the Lord" (1 Samuel 2:11-21)

THURSDAY, June 28: "A Voice in the Night" (1 Samuel 3:1-14)

FRIDAY, June 29: "A Trustworthy Prophet" (1 Samuel 3:15–4:1a)

SATURDAY, June 30: "A Revered Prophet" (Psalm 99)

SUNDAY, July 1: "A Faithful Judge" (1 Samuel 7:3-11, 15-17)

End Notes

[1]Tony W. Cartledge, *1 & 2 Samuel: Smyth & Helwys Bible Commentary* (Macon: Smyth & Helwys Publishing Co., 2001), p. 99.

[2]Douglas, J.D.; Tenney, Merrill Chapin: *New International Bible Dictionary*. Grand Rapids, MI: Zondervan, 1987, S. 882.

LESSON 6   July 8, 2012

DAVID EMBODIES GOD'S JUSTICE

DEVOTIONAL READING: **Isaiah 32:1-8**
PRINT PASSAGE: **2 Samuel 23:1-7;**
1 Chronicles 18:14

BACKGROUND SCRIPTURE: **2 Samuel 22:1–23:7;**
1 Chronicles 18:14
KEY VERSE: **1 Chronicles 18:14**

2 Samuel 23:1-7; 1 Chronicles 18:14—KJV

NOW THESE be the last words of David. David the son of Jesse said, and the man who was raised up on high, the anointed of the God of Jacob, and the sweet psalmist of Israel, said,

2 The Spirit of the LORD spake by me, and his word was in my tongue.

3 The God of Israel said, the Rock of Israel spake to me, He that ruleth over men must be just, ruling in the fear of God.

4 And he shall be as the light of the morning, when the sun riseth, even a morning without clouds; as the tender grass springing out of the earth by clear shining after rain.

5 Although my house be not so with God; yet he hath made with me an everlasting covenant, ordered in all things, and sure: for this is all my salvation, and all my desire, although he make it not to grow.

6 But the sons of Belial shall be all of them as thorns thrust away, because they cannot be taken with hands:

7 But the man that shall touch them must be fenced with iron and the staff of a spear; and they shall be utterly burned with fire in the same place.

.....

14 So David reigned over all Israel, and executed judgment and justice among all his people.

2 Samuel 23:1-7; 1 Chronicles 18:14—NIV

THESE ARE the last words of David: "The oracle of David son of Jesse, the oracle of the man exalted by the Most High, the man anointed by the God of Jacob, Israel's singer of songs:

2 The Spirit of the LORD spoke through me; his word was on my tongue.

3 The God of Israel spoke, the Rock of Israel said to me: 'When one rules over men in righteousness, when he rules in the fear of God,

4 he is like the light of morning at sunrise on a cloudless morning, like the brightness after rain that brings the grass from the earth.'

5 Is not my house right with God? Has he not made with me an everlasting covenant, arranged and secured in every part? Will he not bring to fruition my salvation and grant me my every desire?

6 But evil men are all to be cast aside like thorns, which are not gathered with the hand.

7 Whoever touches thorns uses a tool of iron or the shaft of a spear; they are burned up where they lie."

.....

14 David reigned over all Israel, doing what was just and right for all his people.

UNIFYING LESSON PRINCIPLE

People want their lives to have meaning. How do we discover our purposes in life? Acknowledging God's authority in our lives enables us to become the persons whom God created us to be.

TOPICAL OUTLINE OF THE LESSON

I. Introduction
   A. Life's Memoirs
   B. Biblical Background

II. Exposition and Application of the Scripture
   A. The Life of a Just King (2 Samuel 23:1-2)
   B. The Leadership of a Just King (2 Samuel 23:3-5)
   C. The Fates of Evil Rulers (2 Samuel 23:6-7)
   D. The Summary of David's Life (1 Chronicles 18:14)

III. Concluding Reflection

LESSON OBJECTIVES

Upon the completion of the lesson, the students will be able to:

1. Describe the results of being an instrument of God's justice;
2. Reflect on what it means to live a life that is well-pleasing to God; and,
3. Write a short summary of their beliefs regarding the biblical meaning of *justice*.

POINTS TO BE EMPHASIZED

ADULT/YOUTH

Adult Topic: **True to the End**
Youth Topic: **Significance through Justice**
Adult/Youth Key Verse: **1 Chronicles 18:14**
Print Passage: **2 Samuel 23:1-7; 1 Chronicles 18:14**

—The so-called last words of David are not the last words he spoke before he died (see 1 Kings 2:1-9). This passage from the book of 2 Samuel is rather the last prophetic or inspired utterance ("oracle") of the king.

—In David's exaltation from humble beginnings to king of Israel, he became a type of Christ.

—The NRSV translation of the last phrase of 2 Samuel 23:1 is curious. Virtually every other translation (including the earlier RSV) has "sweet psalmist of Israel" or something very close to that.

—Regarding David's "house" and God's covenant with him, see 2 Samuel 7 and 1 Chronicles 17:10.

—This passage is more than a description of David's reign; it is a prediction of the Messiah's perfect reign of justice and the blessings that will come to all those in the Messiah's kingdom.

—The 2 Samuel 23 passage is part of a set of passages (collectively called by some an appendix or aside) arranged not chronologically in the book, but topically and poetically—in particular, as a chiasmus.

CHILDREN

Children Topic: **David: A Just King**
Key Verse: **1 Chronicles 18:14**
Print Passage: **2 Samuel 23:1-7; 1 Chronicles 18:14**

—When God blesses, the one who is blessed should give praise and thanksgiving.

—David's life provides a portrait of a leader who practiced justice and allowed God to work through him.

—Because David allowed God to be his guide, David could practice justice and fairness for all people.

—Recalling the faithfulness of God to David helps affirm God's infinite ability to be faithful.

I. INTRODUCTION

A. Life's Memoirs

One of the rites of passage of the office of the American presidency is the writing and publication of a presidential memoir. These often self-congratulatory and defensive publications are written with the intention of giving the reader a glamour shot of the particular president's tenure in office.

Today's lesson can be compared to a presidential memoir. King David was approaching the final days of his life. While the first verse declares that these were the last words of David, they actually were not. David's last words are recorded in 1 Kings 2:1-9. What is remarkable about these words are the glowing terms with which David spoke of his personal relationship and experience with the God of Israel. Is this not a model for all believers who love the name of the Lord? As you study the lesson today, make a list of the final words or words of friends or family members who have died that have meant the most in your life. Make a mental note of the things that you would say to your own children or friends if you were to give a final speech to them.

B. Biblical Background

Today's lesson comes from one of the two songs of praise by David (see 2 Samuel 22:1-51 for the first of these songs). These poems of praise were written some time during the latter days of David's life (verse 1). In 1 Samuel 22:1-51, David reflected upon how God had delivered him from the hands of his enemy and exalted him to be the king. In 1 Samuel 23:1-8, he looked forward to the future and the promise of God to honor the covenant which He made with him. The two poems are considered to be "royal theology" which looks forward to the coming of God's anointed ruler who would reverse the injustices of the world and incorporate God's rule among His people.[1] Some Old Testament scholars view this passage as a counterpart to Hannah's song, which also looked forward to the time when God would reverse the fortunes of the downtrodden and poor (see 1 Samuel 2:1-10).

David was the most revered and greatest king in the history of Israel. He stood alone and was the standard by which all other kings were judged and evaluated (see 1 Kings 15:1-3; 2 Kings 14:3; 16:2; 18:3; 22:1-2). Indeed, David's life, like those of all people, was filled with its moments of failure and high drama (see 2 Samuel 11:1–12:23; 18:1-33). Yet, it must be remembered that he was still God's anointed leader, who was favored and blessed as one who loved God with both heart and soul.

Second Samuel 23 begins with the declaration that "these are the last words of David." However, they were not the *final* words of David, as previously stated. In the poem, David rejoiced that God had exalted him to be the ruler of the heritage of Jacob. His life and reign were under the anointing of the Spirit of the Lord who spoke through him (verse 2). God desired that rulers lead in righteousness and in the fear of God (verse 3). Ultimately, those who seek to lead unjustly fail, and they are cast aside like thorns destroyed (verses 6-7).

II. EXPOSITION AND APPLICATION OF THE SCRIPTURE

A. The Life of a Just King
(2 Samuel 23:1-2)

NOW THESE be the last words of David. David the son of Jesse said, and the man who was raised up on high, the anointed of the God of Jacob, and the sweet psalmist of Israel, said, The Spirit of the LORD spake by me, and his word was in my tongue.

David began this passage by announcing that these were his last words Throughout the Scriptures there are records of the final words of the saints (see Genesis 49:1; Deuteronomy 33:1; Joshua 23:1-24; Psalm 72:20; 2 Timothy 4:6-8; 2 Peter 1:13-15). More than likely, we are reading the final words that David put in writing. He announced that he was speaking as an "oracle" (see Word Power for a fuller discussion). David looked back over his life and the forty years when he was king over Israel. He reflected over the blessing of having been chosen by God to be the leader of His people. In these verses, he made four statements about himself. First, he was the son of Jesse (see Ruth 4:17-20; Samuel 16:1). Jesse was also a descendant of Nahshon, who was chief of the tribe of Judah during the time of Moses (see Numbers 1:1-7; compare with Matthew 1:1-6).

Second, David pointed out that it was God who exalted him to be king over Israel (see 1 Samuel 13:14; 2 Samuel 6:21; 7:8-9). David never sought to be king. Even during the time when Saul sought his life, David never lost respect for him and continued to see Saul as God's chosen king all of the days of his life (see 1 Samuel 24:1-7; 2 Samuel 1:17-27).

Third, David declared that he was the man anointed by God. The word *anointed* is translated from a Hebrew word that means "messiah," but we must not confuse the Old Testament understanding of this concept with the New Testament understanding. In the Old Testament, the act of anointing was used to dedicate people, places, or objects to the service of the Lord. It was a common practice for priests, prophets, and kings to be anointed through a special ceremony of consecration. The kings were anointed with oil by the prophet as a sign that God had chosen them to be the ruler over His people (see 1 Samuel 9:16; 10:1; 15:1; 16:3; 1 Kings 1:34; 2 Kings 9:3, 6). In ancient Hebrew culture, it was strictly forbidden to do harm to the Lord's anointed servant (see 1 Samuel 24:1-6, 10; 26:6-12; 2 Samuel 1:1-16).

Fourth, David said that he was the singer of Israel's songs, which was a reference to his role as the organizer of the Temple worship and the composer of numerous psalms of praise. All of the psalms that are recorded in the Scriptures that David wrote bear his name in the superscription as the author (see Psalms 3–6; 8; 9; 15; 18–19; 27–41). Everything that David said and wrote was given to him. It was not the product of his own intellect; rather, it was the Spirit of the Lord who gave the inspiration. David declared that it was the Word of the Lord that was on his tongue (see Matthew 22:43; Mark 12:36; Acts 2:25-31; and 1 Peter 1:21; compare with Psalm 119).

B. The Leadership of a Just King (2 Samuel 23:3-5)

The God of Israel said, the Rock of Israel spake to me, He that ruleth over men must be just, ruling in the fear of God. And he shall be as the light of the morning, when the sun riseth, even a morning without clouds; as the tender grass springing out of the earth by clear shining after rain. Although my house be not so with God; yet he hath made with me an everlasting covenant, ordered in all things, and sure: for this is all my salvation, and all my desire, although he make it not to grow.

Verses 3-4 are words spoken to David by God. In these verses, David revealed three statements about God and two about the requirements that He sought in leaders. First, God is the God of Israel (see Genesis 33:20; Exodus 3:15; 19:5-6; 20:2). Second, God is the one who speaks to His leaders (see Exodus 3:1-5; compare the first verse in every chapter of the book of Exodus and it becomes apparent that it is a record of all that God said to Moses in the early days preceding the Exodus and shortly afterward). Third, God is the Rock of Israel, a metaphor that denotes strength and stability (see Deuteronomy 32:4, 30-31; 2 Samuel 22:2, 32; Psalm 42:9).

The second part of verse 3 is an outlining of the two requirements for being a leader of God's people. These two character traits were not those that David created, nor were they recommended to him as a means of becoming a leader. Rather, they are central to what God looks for and are the very ones that He personally gave to David. The first is the willingness to rule in righteousness (Hebrew: *tsaddiyq*, meaning "righteous in government"). The king must be just and fair with all people. Second, the leader must rule or lead in the fear of God, meaning that he or she must have reverence and respect for the Lord God. The two traits mentioned by God were definitely a consistent fact of David's reign as king. He considered everyone to be on the same level when it came to sharing the blessings of God (see 1 Samuel 30:21-31; 2 Samuel 6:17-19).

In verse 4, there is a double simile that forms a comparison between the righteous leader and nature. The king who rules righteously is "like" the light of a bright, sunny morning that is free of clouds. He is "like" the brightness after the gentle rain causes the grass to grow. Birch noted, "The likeness of the just king to the bright sun of morning calls to mind eschatological images of Christ as one who shines like (or brighter than) the sun (Matthew 17:2; Acts 25:13; Revelation 1:16; 10:1; 21:23)."[2]

Verse 5 has been regarded by some commentators as standing alone and not connected to either thought in verses 3-4 or 6-7. At first glance, the words of verse 5 look to be filled with statements of arrogance and boasting. How could David make any claims to having a house that was right with God? The answer to the rhetorical question is found not in David's leadership, but in God's graciousness in keeping His covenant with David (see 2 Samuel 7:12-16). Birch rightly observes, "If justice and faithfulness were left to human capacities alone, all would be doomed to fail."[3] Although David made many mistakes and committed what we would consider to be horrendous sins, the fact that he remained as king and was blessed by God had nothing to do with just him. Rather, it was the faithfulness of God to His covenant that blessed the leader—not because of what he did, but at times because of what was in his heart (see 2 Chronicles 6:6-8). Though David did not live to see the fulfillment of the covenant promise, still he looked with expectancy to its completion in the future.

C. The Fates of Evil Rulers
(2 Samuel 23:6-7)

But the sons of Belial shall be all of them as thorns thrust away, because they cannot be taken with hands: But the man that shall touch them must be fenced with iron and the staff of a spear; and they shall be utterly burned with fire in the same place.

Verses 6-7 form an antithesis to the life and character of the just and righteous king. They are described as "evil men." The Hebrew word that is translated "evil" in the NIV is *beliya* (Belial), and it literally means "worthless" or "good for nothing." It is often used to express the depravity of character that is diametrically opposed to God's character. These evil leaders are like thorns that would be gathered and burned right where they lay. Thorns are sometimes used in the Scriptures as symbols of evil workers who stand against the kingdom of God or unhealthy spiritual growth (see Matthew 13:7, 22).

D. The Summary of David's Life
(1 Chronicles 18:14)

So David reigned over all Israel, and executed judgment and justice among all his people.

The lesson concludes with a summary statement of David's reign, as depicted by the chronicler of the kings of Israel. The books of 1 and 2 Chronicles are historical reflections of the lives and reigns of the kings of Israel and Judah, and how they related to the Temple religion. First Chronicles 18 is a summary of David's victories after he was made king over all Israel. David achieved what Saul never did nor could achieve. He united the entire nation of twelve tribes under one monarchy and created what came to be known as Israel's golden age of justice and righteousness. David was revered as the king who did what was right in the sight of God, and what was best for all of the people (see Jeremiah 22:13-16). In doing what was right and applying the rules of law justly, David ensured that God would always honor His promise and word to make of him a great nation.

III. CONCLUDING REFLECTION

One of the central questions raised in the lesson today pertains to congregational expectations of its leaders. Does a congregation have a right to expect that her leaders will be men and women who are filled with the Holy Spirit? Does the congregation have a right to expect that her leaders will always act in the best interests of the congregation? Does the congregation have a right to expect that her leaders will be men and women who seek God's mind in all things pertaining to the life of that congregation?

In this lesson, we are brought face-to-face with the need for God's people to understand the importance of choosing men and women who reflect His character and are driven by His purpose. God is not just the God of a song, shout, and dance; He demands and requires that we execute justice and righteousness. Many times churches are saddled with leaders who lack vision, courage, and the will to be open to God's will for the future.

PRAYER

Lord God, teach us to live in such a way that our lives will have meaning and value to those with whom we live and work. May the love and grace imparted to us be evident in the eyes of those whom we meet daily. In Jesus' name we pray. Amen.

WORD POWER

Oracle—The term *oracle* refers to an "utterance" or "declaration" of God. Many English Bible translations such as the NIV use the English word *oracle* to translate the Hebrew word *maśś*, a word frequently used by the Old Testament prophets. Several prophets begin their books with this word (Nahum 1:1; Habakkuk 1:1; Malachi 1:1). This word is also used often at the beginning of new prophetic units (Isaiah 13:1; 15:1; 17:1, etc.).

However, numerous times in the Old Testament *maśś* is used to mean "burden" or "load." Usually, the context is clear whether the word means "burden" or "oracle." However, the word occurs eight times in Jeremiah 23:33-38, and in this passage both meanings ("oracle" and "burden") can fit the context. Jeremiah loves to use wordplays, and in this passage he is probably playing off of both meanings.[4]

HOME DAILY BIBLE READINGS
(July 2-8, 2012)

David Embodies God's Justice

MONDAY, July 2: "Inquiring of the Lord" (2 Samuel 2:1-7)

TUESDAY, July 3: "Rejoicing in God's Deliverance" (2 Samuel 22:8-20)

WEDNESDAY, July 4: "Depending on God's Guidance" (2 Samuel 22:26-31)

THURSDAY, July 5: "Living in God's Strength" (2 Samuel 22:32-37)

FRIDAY, July 6: "Praising God's Steadfast Love" (2 Samuel 22:47-51)

SATURDAY, July 7: "Reigning in Righteousness" (Isaiah 32:1-8)

SUNDAY, July 8: "Ruling in the Fear of God" (2 Samuel 23:1-7; 1 Chronicles 18:14)

End Notes

[1]Bruce C. Birch, *The New Interpreter's Bible, Vol. II: The First and Second Books of Samuel* (Nashville: Abingdon Press, 1998), p. 1370.

[2]Tony W. Cartledge, *1 & 2 Samuel Smyth & Helwys Bible Commentary*, (Macon: Symth and Helwys Publishing, Incorporated, 2001), p. 676.

[3]Birch, *Interpreters*, p. 1371.

[4]Hays, J. Daniel; Duvall, J. Scott; Pate, C. Marvin: *Dictionary of Biblical Prophecy and End Times.* Grand Rapids, MI: Zondervan Publishing House, 2007, S. 322.

LESSON 7   **July 15, 2012**

SOLOMON JUDGES WITH WISDOM AND JUSTICE

DEVOTIONAL READING: **Psalm 37:27-34**   BACKGROUND SCRIPTURE: **1 Kings 3; 2 Chronicles 9:8**
PRINT PASSAGE: **1 Kings 3:16-28; 2 Chronicles 9:8**   KEY VERSE: **1 Kings 3:28**

1 Kings 3:16-28; 2 Chronicles 9:8—KJV

16 Then came there two women, that were harlots, unto the king, and stood before him.

17 And the one woman said, O my lord, I and this woman dwell in one house; and I was delivered of a child with her in the house.

18 And it came to pass the third day after that I was delivered, that this woman was delivered also: and we were together; there was no stranger with us in the house, save we two in the house.

19 And this woman's child died in the night; because she overlaid it.

20 And she arose at midnight, and took my son from beside me, while thine handmaid slept, and laid it in her bosom, and laid her dead child in my bosom.

21 And when I rose in the morning to give my child suck, behold, it was dead: but when I had considered it in the morning, behold, it was not my son, which I did bear.

22 And the other woman said, Nay; but the living is my son, and the dead is thy son. And this said, No; but the dead is thy son, and the living is my son. Thus they spake before the king.

23 Then said the king, The one saith, This is my son that liveth, and thy son is the dead: and the other saith, Nay; but thy son is the dead, and my son is the living.

24 And the king said, Bring me a sword. And they brought a sword before the king.

25 And the king said, Divide the living child in two, and give half to the one, and half to the other.

1 Kings 3:16-28; 2 Chronicles 9:8—NIV

16 Now two prostitutes came to the king and stood before him.

17 One of them said, "My lord, this woman and I live in the same house. I had a baby while she was there with me.

18 The third day after my child was born, this woman also had a baby. We were alone; there was no one in the house but the two of us.

19 During the night this woman's son died because she lay on him.

20 So she got up in the middle of the night and took my son from my side while I your servant was asleep. She put him by her breast and put her dead son by my breast.

21 The next morning, I got up to nurse my son—and he was dead! But when I looked at him closely in the morning light, I saw that it wasn't the son I had borne."

22 The other woman said, "No! The living one is my son; the dead one is yours." But the first one insisted, "No! The dead one is yours; the living one is mine." And so they argued before the king.

23 The king said, "This one says, 'My son is alive and your son is dead,' while that one says, 'No! Your son is dead and mine is alive.'"

24 Then the king said, "Bring me a sword." So they brought a sword for the king.

25 He then gave an order: "Cut the living child in two and give half to one and half to the other."

26 The woman whose son was alive was filled with

26 Then spake the woman whose the living child was unto the king, for her bowels yearned upon her son, and she said, O my lord, give her the living child, and in no wise slay it. But the other said, Let it be neither mine nor thine, but divide it.

27 Then the king answered and said, Give her the living child, and in no wise slay it: she is the mother thereof.

28 And all Israel heard of the judgment which the king had judged; and they feared the king: for they saw that the wisdom of God was in him, to do judgment.

.....

8 Blessed be the LORD thy God, which delighted in thee to set thee on his throne, to be king for the LORD thy God: because thy God loved Israel, to establish them for ever, therefore made he thee king over them, to do judgment and justice.

compassion for her son and said to the king, "Please, my lord, give her the living baby! Don't kill him!" But the other said, "Neither I nor you shall have him. Cut him in two!"

27 Then the king gave his ruling: "Give the living baby to the first woman. Do not kill him; she is his mother."

28 When all Israel heard the verdict the king had given, they held the king in awe, because they saw that he had wisdom from God to administer justice.

.....

8 "Praise be to the LORD your God, who has delighted in you and placed you on his throne as king to rule for the LORD your God. Because of the love of your God for Israel and his desire to uphold them forever, he has made you king over them, to maintain justice and righteousness."

TOPICAL OUTLINE OF THE LESSON

LESSON OBJECTIVES

Upon the completion of the lesson, the students will be able to:

1. Tell the story of Solomon and the two women who came to him seeking justice;

2. Describe a time when they needed someone to intervene on their behalf; and,

3. Identify a chronic community dilemma that could be resolved with acts of compassion.

POINTS TO BE EMPHASIZED

ADULT/YOUTH

Adult Topic: Wisdom and Justice

Youth Topic: Wisdom through Justice

Adult/Youth Key Verse: 1 Kings 3:28

Print Passage: 1 Kings 3:16-28; 2 Chronicles 9:8

—Probably the case of the two women had already been heard in court, but the court was unable to render a verdict, or the verdict rendered had been appealed to the king. The king's judgment was not typically the first recourse—at least for common people.

—The two women were undoubtedly poor, as they lived alone (no husbands, no servants) and supported themselves through socially unacceptable means (which they had not been able to practice for some months since they were pregnant), so it is somewhat surprising that they were able to get an audience with the king.

—Note that the proper procedures broke down and, instead of pleading their cases with the king, the women began arguing with one another.

—The NRSV picks up the sense of the Hebrew in verse 26 better than many versions when it says that the real mother's compassion "burned" within her; other translations speak of "yearning" and/or "compassion," but not the burning passion that is shown in the NRSV.

—The verse from the book of 2 Chronicles relates the judgment of the queen of Sheba when she visited Solomon and was amazed at his wisdom.

—The divine source of Solomon's wisdom (see 1 Kings 3:1-15) was apparent to the people of Israel (verse 28) and foreign people as well (2 Chronicles 9:8).

CHILDREN

Children Topic: Solomon: A Wise Judge

Key Verse: 1 Kings 3:28

Print Passage: 1 Kings 3:16-28

—God gives people wisdom to make wise decisions.

—Solomon's actions as a judge reveal the need for compassion and wisdom in making wise decisions.

—Solomon asked God to grant him wisdom so that he could make wise choices as a leader.

I. INTRODUCTION

A. The Importance of Making Just Decisions

In today's lesson, King Solomon was faced with an extremely difficult decision that literally was a matter of life and death. Solomon showed both courage and decisiveness. It took a lot of courage to choose the course of action that he did, especially since he had no idea how it would turn out. As you study the lesson today, look for signs and examples of wisdom that you can use in the exercise of justice and equity within the context of your ministry. Ask the Holy Spirit to reveal to you how you can become a person with greater spiritual wisdom and understanding.

B. Biblical Background

The lesson today comes from one of the best-known and perhaps most-beloved stories in the Bible. As a result of the judgment that he showed, Solomon developed the reputation for being one of the wisest men in history. Solomon had been king for only a short period when he was faced with his first big test of leadership. Earlier he had asked the Lord to give him a discerning heart so that he could govern the people and distinguish between right and wrong (see 1 Kings 3:9). In this passage, we see the fulfillment of the Lord's promise to give Solomon the things that he wanted most: wisdom and discernment. The case of these two prostitutes had probably been heard in a lower court or by one of the administrative judges in the land. Those who were not satisfied with the judgment of a lower-court official could appeal their cases to the king. We are not sure if kings in the ancient world heard every case that was appealed to them. However, this was an unusual case, one that required astute wisdom and discernment to solve.

The two women in the lesson were undoubtedly poor, as they lived alone and supported themselves through one of the most despised, yet accepted professions in ancient Israel (see Leviticus 19:29; Deuteronomy 23:17; Joshua 2:1). While standing before the king pleading their cases, the two women began to argue with one another. What the king proposed as a solution to the dispute was totally unacceptable to the real mother. The lesson closes with a statement of praise and adulation from the queen of Sheba, who was amazed at the depth of Solomon's wisdom and wealth.

II. EXPOSITION AND APPLICATION OF THE SCRIPTURE

A. The Case of the Two Prostitutes
(1 Kings 3:16-22)

Then came there two women, that were harlots, unto the king, and stood before him. And the one woman said, O my lord, I and this woman dwell in one house; and I was delivered of a child with her in the house. And it came to pass the third day after that I was delivered, that this woman was delivered also: and we were together; there was no stranger with us in the house, save we two in the house. And this woman's child died in the night; because she overlaid it. And she arose at midnight, and took my son from beside me, while thine handmaid slept, and laid it in her bosom, and laid her dead child in my bosom. And when I rose in the morning to give my child suck, behold, it was dead: but when I had considered it in the morning, behold, it was not my son, which I did bear. And the other woman said, Nay; but the living is my son, and the dead is thy son. And this said, No; but the dead is thy son, and the living is my son. Thus they spake before the king.

The biblical text is very straightforward in its description of the situation that faced King Solomon. Two women were granted permission to have an audience with the king in order to resolve a very sensitive and serious issue. The women were known prostitutes. One of the first things we notice about this situation is that the king did not condemn nor judge them for their profession. This is not to say that he condoned what they did for a living, either. Rather, they were citizens of the land and subjects of his kingdom, and they were entitled to their day in court.

One of the women stated why they were present. The woman doing the initial speaking was the one who brought the complaint before the king. She was the person who alleged that she had been wronged by the woman who lived with her in the same house. This speaks to their economic situation—that they were obviously very poor and because they were prostitutes they were unmarried. The one speaking reported that she had given birth to a baby boy during the time that they lived together (verse 17). Within three days the other woman also delivered a baby boy (verse 18). The babies were more than likely no more than a few days old when this incident took place. The perplexity of the situation was compounded by the fact that there were no other persons living in the house with them—thus, there were no witnesses to verify or confirm either of the women's testimony or to validate the identities of the babies. It was the word of one prostitute against the other.

The woman who brought the complaint continued to speak and explain to the king what had happened. She explained that during the course of the night the other woman's baby died because she unintentionally rolled over on him, smothering the child to death (verse 19). She continued, insisting that when the woman discovered what had happened during the night, she exchanged her dead baby for the other woman's living baby. On the surface, this would seem to be quite improbable. But remember that many people in that day and time lived in one-room homes, not unlike what we find in many poor countries today. It is quite conceivable that this could have happened without the other woman's having a clue as to what was happening.

As she began to prepare to nurse her baby, the woman whose baby had been exchanged for the dead baby discovered that her son was dead. It was only after the light of the morning sun had begun to break did she discover that the dead baby was not her son at all (verse 21). Every mother knows her own child, and is able to pick out her child's cry in a crowded room of crying babies. While she was speaking and laying out her complaint, the other woman exclaimed in a loud voice that the living baby was in fact *her* son. As the two women stood before the king, they began to argue with one another, compounding the gravity of the situation that Solomon faced (verse 22).

B. The Conclusion to the Problem (1 Kings 3:23-28)

Then said the king, The one saith, This is my son that liveth, and thy son is the dead: and the other saith, Nay; but thy son is the dead, and my son is the living. And the king said, Bring me a sword. And they brought a sword before the king. And the king said, Divide the living child in two, and give half to the one, and half to the other. Then spake the woman whose the living child was unto the king, for her bowels yearned upon her son, and she said, O my lord, give her the living child, and in no wise slay it. But the other said, Let it be neither mine nor thine, but divide it. Then the king answered and said, Give her the living child, and in no wise slay it: she is the mother thereof. And all Israel heard of the judgment which the king had judged; and they feared the king: for they saw that the wisdom of God was in him, to do judgment.

How would one resolve such a thorny issue, seeing as though there was no precedent upon which to base the decision? If there had been at least two witnesses who could verify the maternity and identity of the babies, then the matter could easily have been resolved. Ancient Hebrew law required that at least two witnesses confirm the truth of any legal matter (see Deuteronomy 19:15; Matthew 18:16). In this case, there were no DNA tests that could resolve this matter, nor were there any birth certificates or any other identifying birthmarks noted. Solomon more than likely thought carefully about the situation that he faced, pondering on what would be the best solution. Both women were claiming to be the rightful birth mother of the baby (verse 23).

The king ordered that a sword be brought to him (verse 24). He did not hesitate to order that the child be split down the middle and one half of the baby be given to each of the women (verse 25). This was a huge gamble on the part of the king. What would he have done if both women had seen this as the right thing and only thing to do? Solomon took a calculated risk, made a tough decision, and was prepared to live with the consequences.

Verse 26 brings the case to a climactic head. The birth mother of the living baby was filled with mercy, compassion, and tender love. She could not watch nor face the stark possibility that her child would be cut into two pieces to resolve this thorny legal wrangling. The birth mother's heart was burning with tenderness and love. How could she live with herself if the king's command had been carried out? She cried out, "Don't kill him!" She would rather the baby live with the other woman than die. Clearly, this reflected a mother's love that was both genuine and sacrificial. The other woman would rather have seen the baby die than live. Could it be that she was willing to see this child die because of her own brokenness over the loss of her baby? Maybe she was filled with anger or even jealousy. The gift that Solomon had asked the Lord to give him was utilized here. Finding that the real mother would rather see her child live with another woman than die, the king gave the baby back to the birth mother. He recognized who the real mother was (verse 27).

Solomon's fame and respect grew to make him a larger-than-life figure. The news of the decision and the wisdom displayed reverberated throughout the land. "All Israel heard the verdict of the king." This was such an astounding decision that there was not a single corner of Israel that did not hear about it.

C. The Queen of Sheba's Witness about God (2 Chronicles 9:8)

Blessed be the Lord thy God, which delighted in thee to set thee on his throne, to be king for the Lord thy God: because thy God loved Israel, to establish them for ever, therefore made he thee king over them, to do judgment and justice.

The lesson shifts from the book of 1 Kings to the book of 2 Chronicles. Briefly, the two books of Chronicles form a single record in the Hebrew Bible. They are collected records of the genealogical history of Israel. One of the primary purposes of the books was to record the history of God's interaction and dealings with His people. They also provide a portrait of the relationships of the kings of Israel and Judah to the Temple and the worship of Yahweh.

In chapter 9, we meet the queen of Sheba, who went to Jerusalem to confirm the words and stories that she had heard regarding the wisdom, wealth, and character of Solomon (verses 1-7). During her visit, she praised the name of the Lord God, who had chosen Solomon to be king over His people Israel. The queen praised God and declared that it was not because of anything that Solomon had done, but it was because God "delighted" in Solomon (see 1 Kings 10:9; Psalm 18:19; Isaiah 42:1; 62:4). It is also worthy of note to underscore that it was not David who conceded the throne to Solomon; the queen stated that it was God who placed him upon the throne. In this statement, she recognized that Israel was a theocracy, established by God and ruled by God.

God elevated Solomon to be king for three reasons: first, because He loved Israel with an everlasting love (see Deuteronomy 7:8; 1 Chronicles 17:22; 2 Chronicles 2:11; Jeremiah 31:3; Hosea 11:1; Malachi 1:2); second, God wanted to uphold or establish them forever; third, God had made Solomon king to uphold justice and righteousness (see 2 Samuel 8:15; 23:2; 1 Kings 3:28; Psalms 72:2; 99:4; Proverbs

21:3; Isaiah 11:1-5; 32:1-2; Jeremiah 33:15; Hebrews 1:8).

III. CONCLUDING REFLECTION

On the surface, it would appear that this passage would yield very little in terms of practical lessons on leadership and the practice of justice. Yet, there are at least three significant truths that can be gleaned from this passage. First, leaders are sometimes faced with situations that require them to make tough decisions and choose courses of action that astound their followers. Such was the case with Solomon in this lesson. What he ultimately did was not easy; a high drama played out before his face.

Second, justice has to be administered fairly to all people, regardless of how shady their social backgrounds may be. African Americans know something about this, given the fact that many times we have been denied true justice because of the color of our skin or our socio-economic levels. The women having the dispute were prostitutes, a profession that was outlawed and considered to be among the most sinful of practices in ancient Israel.

Third, leaders must be equipped to discern and to read between the lines, get beyond the rhetoric and emotions of a situation, and see the real facts of matters that require mature decision making and leadership that is guided by the Holy Spirit. Discernment is one of the gifts of the Holy Spirit. Solomon was keen to hear and perceive the larger issue at stake. His decision was one that flesh and blood did not reveal to him, but God the Father did. And He will do the same for believers.

PRAYER

Blessed heavenly Father, give us all wisdom to know the difference between right and wrong. Grant that we may hear clearly Your voice and without reservation do the things that matter most to You. In Jesus' name we pray. Amen.

WORD POWER

Wisdom—the ability to discern inner qualities and relationships, and to display understanding and knowledge.

HOME DAILY BIBLE READINGS
(July 9-15, 2012)

Solomon Judges with Wisdom and Justice
MONDAY, July 9: "A Prayer for Wisdom" (Ephesians 1:15-23)
TUESDAY, July 10: "The Lord Loves Justice" (Psalm 37:27-34)
WEDNESDAY, July 11: "Jedidiah—Beloved of the Lord" (2 Samuel 12:20-25)
THURSDAY, July 12: "Solomon Anointed as Israel's King" (1 Kings 1:28-37)
FRIDAY, July 13: "Grace for a Competitor" (1 Kings 1:41-53)
SATURDAY, July 14: "Solomon's Unsurpassed Wisdom" (1 Kings 4:29-34)
SUNDAY, July 15: "Solomon Puts Wisdom into Practice" (1 Kings 3:16-28; 2 Chronicles 9:8)

LESSON 8   July 22, 2012

A KING ACTS ON A WIDOW'S BEHALF

DEVOTIONAL READING: **Luke 15:11-24**
PRINT PASSAGE: **2 Kings 8:1-6**

BACKGROUND SCRIPTURE: **2 Kings 4:1-37; 8:1-6**
KEY VERSE: **2 Kings 8:6**

2 Kings 8:1-6—KJV

THEN SPAKE Elisha unto the woman, whose son he had restored to life, saying, Arise, and go thou and thine household, and sojourn wheresoever thou canst sojourn: for the LORD hath called for a famine; and it shall also come upon the land seven years.

2 And the woman arose, and did after the saying of the man of God: and she went with her household, and sojourned in the land of the Philistines seven years.

3 And it came to pass at the seven years' end, that the woman returned out of the land of the Philistines: and she went forth to cry unto the king for her house and for her land.

4 And the king talked with Gehazi the servant of the man of God, saying, Tell me, I pray thee, all the great things that Elisha hath done.

5 And it came to pass, as he was telling the king how he had restored a dead body to life, that, behold, the woman, whose son he had restored to life, cried to the king for her house and for her land. And Gehazi said, My lord, O king, this is the woman, and this is her son, whom Elisha restored to life.

6 And when the king asked the woman, she told him. So the king appointed unto her a certain officer, saying, Restore all that was hers, and all the fruits of the field since the day that she left the land, even until now.

2 Kings 8:1-6—NIV

NOW ELISHA had said to the woman whose son he had restored to life, "Go away with your family and stay for a while wherever you can, because the LORD has decreed a famine in the land that will last seven years."

2 The woman proceeded to do as the man of God said. She and her family went away and stayed in the land of the Philistines seven years.

3 At the end of the seven years she came back from the land of the Philistines and went to the king to beg for her house and land.

4 The king was talking to Gehazi, the servant of the man of God, and had said, "Tell me about all the great things Elisha has done."

5 Just as Gehazi was telling the king how Elisha had restored the dead to life, the woman whose son Elisha had brought back to life came to beg the king for her house and land. Gehazi said, "This is the woman, my lord the king, and this is her son whom Elisha restored to life."

6 The king asked the woman about it, and she told him. Then he assigned an official to her case and said to him, "Give back everything that belonged to her, including all the income from her land from the day she left the country until now."

BIBLE FACT

The significance of this narrative should not be overlooked. Within the context of the culture of this period, the king's action on behalf of this woman was significant. Culturally speaking, women had no voice within their society. Widows in particular were left to fend for themselves. This would be particularly traumatic if a woman had no male offspring. It is clear that there had to be "divine intervention" for the plight of the Shunammite woman.

TOPICAL OUTLINE OF THE LESSON

I. Introduction
   A. The Reality of Injustice
   B. Biblical Background

II. Exposition and Application of the Scripture
   A. God Is in Control (2 Kings 8:1-2)
   B. Facing the Uncertainty of Returning (2 Kings 8:3-5)
   C. Justice Prevailed (2 Kings 8:6)

III. Concluding Reflection

LESSON OBJECTIVES

Upon the completion of the lesson, the students will be able to:

1. Trace the sequence of events in the life of the Shunammite widow;
2. Describe how they feel when something lost has been restored to them; and,
3. Create modern-day scenarios in which restorative justice is required.

POINTS TO BE EMPHASIZED

ADULT/YOUTH

Adult Topic: Restorative Justice
Youth Topic: Restoration through Justice
Adult/Youth Key Verse: 2 Kings 8:6
Print Passage: 2 Kings 8:1-6

—In 2 Kings 4:12-13, Elisha had volunteered to intercede with the king on the Shunammite's behalf, but she declined. Ironically, he did intercede (indirectly and unintentionally) for her years later when she returned from the land of the Philistines.

—Gehazi had leprosy (see 2 Kings 5:27) and contact with him would have caused the king to be "unclean." Cultural norms suggest that the conversation between the two may have occurred by "long distance" or with a wall separating the two. (Some commentators thus place this incident chronologically before 2 Kings 5, to eliminate the problem of the king's conversing with a leper.)

—It is unclear whether the famine in Samaria (2 Kings 7) was the same famine as the seven-year famine mentioned here or was another one.

—The woman had a husband in the earlier narrative (2 Kings 4), but none is mentioned here. Perhaps the husband had died and his family had seized their kinsman's land while the woman was in the land of the Philistines, and they refused to grant her a kinsman-redeemer when she returned.

—God's providence is evident in Elisha's warning the woman to flee the famine and in the timing of her arrival before the king just as Gehazi was telling about her.

CHILDREN

Children Topic: Justice Restored
Key Verse: 2 Kings 8:6
Print Passage: 2 Kings 8:1-6

—Despite Elisha's restoration of life to the Shunammite woman's son, the family still faced natural disaster, which forced them to leave their home.

—When the Shunammite woman's land and earnings were restored, justice was served.

—God often provides witnesses to help accomplish justice.

—The woman's obedience to God influenced the king's just decision on her behalf.

I. INTRODUCTION

A. The Reality of Injustice

In 1997, an African-American farmer named Timothy Pigford became the lead plaintiff in a class action lawsuit against the United States Department of Agriculture (USDA) alleging racial discrimination. According to the suit, the USDA engaged in discrimination against black, Hispanic, Native American, and female farmers by failing to provide the same types of services to them as it did for white male farmers. Many people have never heard of Timothy Pigford or the lawsuit he filed. Shortly after filing the lawsuit, he was joined by four hundred other African-American farmers. The suit charged that the USDA treated black and other minority farmers unjustly, especially when it came to special subsidies, loan programs, disaster loans, and price support loans. The suit also alleged that the USDA failed to even process the discrimination request of the farmers. The case was settled in 1999 with each of the plaintiffs receiving $50,000 and the forgiveness of some farm loans. The case dragged on for several more years because many of the farmers never received the payments as a result of an administrative technicality. Finally, in 2010, President Barack Obama signed into law a settlement of $1.25 billion dollars that would settle the case and level the playing field once and for all. What happened to the African-American farmers is not an unusual story. American history is littered with the wrecked lives of men and women who were faced with injustice and discrimination because of their ethnicity or socio-economic backgrounds. In this case, justice prevailed for the farmers, many of whom were uneducated or undereducated.

In the lesson today, we see a similar type of situation, where a poor widow faced the prospect of losing her livelihood and property because of an unjust economic system. As you study the lesson, make a list of the problems that the woman in the story faced. Also, make a list of the kinds of problems that widows may face in our society today. Look for ways that you can become more involved with assisting the widows of your congregation to live fuller and more abundant lives. Ask the Holy Spirit to reveal to you ways to make the teachings of the lesson applicable in your life.

B. Biblical Background

Elisha was one of the great prophets in ancient Israel. His exploits and miracles put him ahead of many of the great writing prophets. In today's lesson, we are reintroduced to the woman from Shunem (see 2 Kings 4:8-37). More than seven years had elapsed since Elisha told her to leave her home because of a pending famine. When we first meet the woman she is identified as a woman of some wealth. She had a home, fields, servants, and animals. However, severe economic extremes can wipe out a person's wealth within a matter of months or even days. According to the background passage, the woman had shown considerable kindness to the prophet. He wanted to intercede on her behalf with the king, but she declined. Ironically, he would indirectly and unintentionally intercede for her at a time when she really needed a friend.

The events of this chapter probably took place prior to those recorded in 5:27, when Elisha's servant Gehazi was struck with leprosy. The primary explanation for this chronology of events has to do with the disease of leprosy itself. It is highly unlikely that Gehazi would have had an audience with the king if he were afflicted with such a severe and dreaded disease. This is not a real problem for the story nor the events described. Also, the famine mentioned in chapter 7 is more than likely the same famine referred to by Elisha.

In the earlier narrative of 2 Kings 4, the woman had a husband, though he was not mentioned in this section of Scripture. It may be that he died during the time that the family was living in the land of the Philistines. During her absence, the land that she owned was seized by someone. Maybe it was the family of the deceased husband, the king, or even people who lived in the area who could have done this. At any rate, we are not told who did it; what is essential to the story is the woman's appeal to the king, who just happened to be listening to Gehazi share accounts of the mighty works done by Elisha. In this woman's life we see the providential hand of God meeting her at every point at which she needed a helping hand and a hero to champion her cause. As you study this lesson, look for ways in your life that you can become an advocate for those who are not always able to speak for themselves.

II. EXPOSITION AND APPLICATION OF THE SCRIPTURE

A. God Is in Control
(2 Kings 8:1-2)

THEN SPAKE Elisha unto the woman, whose son he had restored to life, saying, Arise, and go thou and thine household, and sojourn wheresoever thou canst sojourn: for the LORD hath called for a famine; and it shall also come upon the land seven years. And the woman arose, and did after the saying of the man of God: and she went with her household, and sojourned in the land of the Philistines seven years.

One of the underlying truths of this narrative is that God is in control of the events of human life. There is nothing that happens by chance or without some divine purpose. God is always aware of our situations and the hindrances that we face in life (see Psalm 139:1-12). We are not sure when Elisha spoke to the woman of Shunem about a pending famine. It could have been shortly after he raised up her son from death, or a few months later. The text makes it clear that the woman whom Elisha spoke to was the same one whose son he had raised from the dead in 2 Kings 4:32-36. This woman had shown great respect for the man of God. She and her husband provided a room for the prophet whenever he was in or passing through their town/the area (see 2 Kings 4:8-10). Elisha never forgot the kindness that she had shown to him and his servant.

Elisha told the woman of Shunem to take her family and leave the area for a while because God had decreed that a famine would grip the land for seven years. Famines were and are horrific economic and social calamities. Depending upon how long the famine lasts, livestock, crops, and even people can be completely wiped out by these occurrences. God revealed to Elisha that a famine was coming. It was not unusual for God to reveal to the man of God what He was about to do (see Genesis 41:25, 28). There was no particular reason given for the famine. This was not a famine caused by dry-weather patterns. It may have been the continued rebellion and apostasy of the Omri Dynasty that had plunged Israel into idolatry and rebellion against God (see 1 Kings 16:25; compare with Leviticus 26:19-20, 26; Deuteronomy 28:22-24, 38-40; Psalms 105:16; 107:34). The fact that Elisha spoke directly to the woman suggests that she was the head of her household and that her husband, mentioned in chapter 4, was probably deceased. The woman did not delay; she quickly gathered her family's belongings and took them into the land of the Philistines; and there they lived for seven years (see verse 2).

B. Facing the Uncertainty of Returning
(2 Kings 8:3-5)

And it came to pass at the seven years' end, that the woman returned out of the land of the Philistines: and she went forth to cry unto the king for her house and for her land. And the king talked with Gehazi the servant of the man of God, saying, Tell me, I pray thee, all the great things that Elisha hath done. And it came to pass, as he was telling the king how he had restored a dead body to life, that, behold, the woman, whose son he had restored to life, cried to the king for her house and for her land. And Gehazi said, My lord, O king, this is the woman, and this is her son, whom Elisha restored to life.

Picture in your mind's eye the anxiety that the Shunammite woman faced as she made her way from the land of the Philistines back to her own land. She had been away for seven years and, therefore, had no idea what her land looked like nor what had transpired during her absence. Upon her arrival, she was met with the worst news. Her land was no longer hers—it was in the hands of someone else. It is possible that the people who seized the land may have thought that the woman and her son were either both dead or that they had no intention of returning to claim the land. Being a woman alone in a male-dominated culture placed this woman at a real disadvantage when it came to dealing with other men in regards to property rights and ownership. There were laws in Israel regarding the right of redemption of property (see Numbers 27:11; Ruth 2:1; Jeremiah 32:7-8).

When she discovered that the land had been seized, the woman sought an immediate audience with the king. In the story, we are not told the king's name. More than likely it was Joram, who had succeeded his father Ahab (see 2 Kings 3:1). It happened that as she made her way to meet with the king and beg for his help, Gehazi (the servant of Elisha) was having an audience with the king. The king must have sought out the servant of the man of God so that he could hear of the work and exploits of Elisha. The name of Elisha was a household word throughout Israel. His influence was greater than that of even the king's. Every pastor has probably experienced this—where he or she is greeted by the words, "I have heard of you or your church." The person who made the statement does so based purely upon what he or she has previously heard about the ministry. This was the case with Elisha; his name echoed across the land.

The king may have requested a personal audience with Elisha—and rather than go himself, he sent Gehazi. The king wanted to know about the great things that Elisha had done (verse 4). There is no doubt that the fame of Elisha had been widely known and circulated among the people of Israel. Gehazi was telling the king about how Elisha had raised the dead son of a woman of Shunem. The king may have already heard of the miracle, but he received a firsthand account from the mouth of Gehazi. As he spoke, the woman walked, crying out how she had been unjustly treated and that someone had seized her land. Gehazi pointed out that this was the very woman whose son was raised, and that she was accompanied by her son (verse 5).

C. Justice Prevailed
(2 Kings 8:6)

And when the king asked the woman, she told him. So the king appointed unto her a certain officer, saying, Restore all that was hers, and all the fruits of the field since the day that she left the land, even until now.

The king stopped everything and began to question the woman about the miracle. He probably asked her a battery of questions, as would any inquisitive person. The woman told the king everything that had happened. She may have related how she and her husband added a room for Elisha and his servant to stay in during their visits to the region. The highlight of her witness was the miracle that restored her son to life and how much it meant that he was alive. Her husband was deceased,

and the boy would become the rightful heir of all that was theirs.

The king was no doubt deeply moved and may have been angered that someone took her land. He did not just order that it be given back; moreover, he assigned a special officer of the king's court to see that his orders were carried out. The woman ended up receiving more than she sought. In addition to getting all of her land back, she received all of the proceeds from the crops that may have been grown, harvested, and subsequently sold during her seven-year absence. Does this mean that the famine did not last seven years? It did last seven years; there may have been brief periods when rains came—enabling something to grow—or the land may have been irrigated. In this act of restorative justice to the woman, the king demonstrated that he was looking after the welfare of the widows, as the law required.

III. CONCLUDING REFLECTION

In spending more time meditating upon the story and the things that occurred, it becomes obvious that there are several significant truths that we would all do well to apply. First, there was the woman's trust in Elisha's word. It is apparent that the prophet was a man with great credibility with this woman. He had prophesied that she would have a child, and this came true. He had raised her son from the dead. And when he asked her to leave everything for the uncertainty of life among the Philistines, that, too, was a giant leap of faith. Similarly, there are times when we are called upon to trust the word of the man or woman of God. This becomes easier to do when the man or woman of God has already demonstrated godly characteristics and lives a credible life before us.

Second, we learn from the lesson that life can turn quickly, leaving the wealthiest person in financial hardship. Remember, this woman's family had been considered to be rather wealthy. The coming of a famine would mean that her family faced the prospects of losing everything. The economic downturn of 2008–2011 left many families economically shattered. Even many families that were well-off prior to the collapse lost everything, and found themselves facing poverty and homelessness. In our day, the one lesson that should implant itself in our hearts is the need to become better stewards of our possessions. This is not to say that this woman was a poor steward—she had obviously been a good steward.

Third, people who face injustice must be willing to persevere, even if it means taking their cases to the very top of the legal system.

There are times when injustice and inequities cannot be remedied at lower levels of the legal system. This was the case with the Civil Rights Movement. Many of the lower courts were not willing to hear the complaints of African Americans—and even those who did were not always sympathetic to our plight. Only through the perseverance of our foreparents and elders have we achieved the legal status and rights that we now enjoy. There are two words that can be used to sum up today's lesson: *perseverance* and *trust*.

PRAYER

Lord God, teach us to never take for granted the law of justice and righteousness. May we live each day with the knowledge of what You require of us. In Jesus' name we pray. Amen.

WORD POWER

Famine—an extreme scarcity of food caused by natural phenomenon or through divine intervention.

HOME DAILY BIBLE READINGS
(July 16-22, 2012)

A King Acts on a Widow's Behalf

MONDAY, July 16: "A Son Restored" (Luke 15:11-24)

TUESDAY, July 17: "The Protector of Widows" (Psalm 68:1-6)

WEDNESDAY, July 18: "Greed and Generosity" (Luke 20:45–21:4)

THURSDAY, July 19: "A Promised Son" (2 Kings 4:8-17)

FRIDAY, July 20: "Seeking Help from the Prophet" (2 Kings 4:18-27)

SATURDAY, July 21: "A Child Restored" (2 Kings 4:28-37)

SUNDAY, July 22: "Justice for a Widow" (2 Kings 8:1-6)

JEHOSHAPHAT MAKES JUDICIAL REFORMS

DEVOTIONAL READING: **James 2:1-5**

PRINT PASSAGE: **2 Chronicles 19:4-11**

BACKGROUND SCRIPTURE: **2 Chronicles 18:28–19:11**

KEY VERSE: **2 Chronicles 19:6**

2 Chronicles 19:4-11—KJV

4 And Jehoshaphat dwelt at Jerusalem: and he went out again through the people from Beer-sheba to mount Ephraim, and brought them back unto the LORD God of their fathers.

5 And he set judges in the land throughout all the fenced cities of Judah, city by city,

6 And said to the judges, Take heed what ye do: for ye judge not for man, but for the LORD, who is with you in the judgment.

7 Wherefore now let the fear of the LORD be upon you; take heed and do it: for there is no iniquity with the LORD our God, nor respect of persons, nor taking of gifts.

8 Moreover in Jerusalem did Jehoshaphat set of the Levites, and of the priests, and of the chief of the fathers of Israel, for the judgment of the LORD, and for controversies, when they returned to Jerusalem.

9 And he charged them, saying, Thus shall ye do in the fear of the LORD, faithfully, and with a perfect heart.

10 And what cause soever shall come to you of your brethren that dwell in their cities, between blood and blood, between law and commandment, statutes and judgments, ye shall even warn them that they trespass not against the LORD, and so wrath come upon you, and upon your brethren: this do, and ye shall not trespass.

11 And, behold, Amariah the chief priest is over you in all matters of the LORD; and Zebadiah the son of Ishmael, the ruler of the house of Judah, for all the king's matters: also the Levites shall be officers before you. Deal courageously, and the LORD shall be with the good.

2 Chronicles 19:4-11—NIV

4 Jehoshaphat lived in Jerusalem, and he went out again among the people from Beersheba to the hill country of Ephraim and turned them back to the LORD, the God of their fathers.

5 He appointed judges in the land, in each of the fortified cities of Judah.

6 He told them, "Consider carefully what you do, because you are not judging for man but for the LORD, who is with you whenever you give a verdict.

7 Now let the fear of the LORD be upon you. Judge carefully, for with the LORD our God there is no injustice or partiality or bribery."

8 In Jerusalem also, Jehoshaphat appointed some of the Levites, priests and heads of Israelite families to administer the law of the LORD and to settle disputes. And they lived in Jerusalem.

9 He gave them these orders: "You must serve faithfully and wholeheartedly in the fear of the LORD.

10 In every case that comes before you from your fellow countrymen who live in the cities—whether bloodshed or other concerns of the law, commands, decrees or ordinances—you are to warn them not to sin against the LORD; otherwise his wrath will come on you and your brothers. Do this, and you will not sin.

11 Amariah the chief priest will be over you in any matter concerning the LORD, and Zebadiah son of Ishmael, the leader of the tribe of Judah, will be over you in any matter concerning the king, and the Levites will serve as officials before you. Act with courage, and may the LORD be with those who do well."

UNIFYING LESSON PRINCIPLE

People want to be judged fairly. How can we expect to receive justice? When human judges adhere to God's standards and fearlessly apply God's laws, there is no perversion of justice.

TOPICAL OUTLINE OF THE LESSON

I. Introduction
A. Corruption versus Compassion
B. Biblical Background

II. Exposition and Application of the Scripture
A. Jehoshaphat Leads the People Back to the Lord (2 Chronicles 19:4)
B. Jehoshaphat Appoints and Charges Judges (2 Chronicles 19:5-7)
C. Jehoshaphat Assigns New Duties to the Priests and Levites (2 Chronicles 19:8-10)
D. Jehoshaphat Establishes Administrative and Religious Order (2 Chronicles 19:11)

III. Concluding Reflection

LESSON OBJECTIVES

Upon the completion of the lesson, the students will be able to:

1. Compare the appointment of judges in biblical times with modern-day judicial appointments;
2. Share stories of times during which they (or someone they know) were treated fairly/unfairly; and,
3. Compare and contrast human justice and divine justice.

POINTS TO BE EMPHASIZED

ADULT/YOUTH

Adult Topic: **Return to Justice**
Youth Topic: **Fairness through Justice**
Adult Key Verse: **2 Chronicles 19:6**
Youth Key Verse: **2 Chronicles 19:7**
Print Passage: **2 Chronicles 19:4-11**

—This was the second time that Jehoshaphat sent officials out into the kingdom to instruct the people in matters of the law (2 Chronicles 17:7-9).

—By going into the hill country of Ephraim, Jehoshaphat was reaching into the northern kingdom to call some of the Israelites back to the Lord God. This occurred just after the death of Israel's wicked king, Ahab (2 Chronicles 18:28–19:3).

—The prophet Jehu had scolded Jehoshaphat for working with Ahab. His reforms may have been an attempt to atone for "help[ing] the wicked" (2 Chronicles 19:2).

—Jehoshaphat's establishment of district courts followed and expanded on the practice modeled by Moses (see Exodus 18:13-26; Deuteronomy 16:18).

—For all the good Jehoshaphat did, he also brought great harm to Judah with his alliance with Ahab and arranging for Ahab's daughter Athaliah to marry his son Jehoram (2 Kings 8:18). Athaliah would later wreak havoc on the royal family.

—Jehoshaphat's reforms had minimal effect on the people; by the end of his reign, "the people had not yet set their hearts upon the God of their ancestors" (2 Chronicles 20:33).

CHILDREN

Children Topic: **Be Fair with Everyone**

Key Verse: 2 Chronicles 19:9

Print Passage: 2 Chronicles 19:4-11

—Persons who stand for justice should not allow anything to interfere with the making of a just decision.

—Even when responsibilities are delegated by another, one is still ultimately held accountable to God.

—Leaders are challenged to be knowledgeable of God's standards.

—Leaders must not be swayed from God's standard by human law and understanding.

—King Jehoshaphat led Israel to restore justice in the law.

—God's justice is not always interpreted the way justice is interpreted in the human community.

I. INTRODUCTION

A. Corruption versus Compassion

Corruption is one of the most pervasive problems in the world. It exists on all continents and can be found to some degree in every government in the world. *The New World Dictionary* defines *corruption* as "evil or wicked behavior." I had no idea how destructive corruption could be to a nation until I traveled to Africa and saw and experienced the widespread corruption at every level of government. This is not to say that everyone was corrupt, but the corruption was systemic throughout the country. Corruption can occur in any institution or organization. Even churches can be caught in the clutches of corruption and wickedness. Americans tend to frown upon people in foreign countries where corruption is open and common. Yet, the United States has had its share of political corruption and influence in buying and selling. We have seen abuses of power and the misallocation of resources for the benefit of a few.

What happens to a people and a nation when the leaders are no longer interested in the welfare of the people, but are motivated by their own selfish interests? God has ordained leaders for the purpose of ensuring that justice and equity are practiced throughout society. In today's lesson, King Jehoshaphat was instrumental in bringing about reformation in ancient Judah and some portions of Israel. He appointed men who would execute justice for all. As you study the lesson, look for ways that you can become more attuned to instances of injustice in your community. Also, look for ways that you can become more involved in the political processes of your local government. Christians must not only be concerned about the spiritual life, but must also be concerned about the institutions that govern the lives of people. Ask the Holy Spirit to reveal to you ways to make the teachings of the lesson applicable in your life.

B. Biblical Background

Jehoshaphat became the fourth king of Judah sometime around 873 BC, and he reigned for twenty-five years in Jerusalem. He began his reign by initiating several religious reforms and sending the priests and Levites throughout the land to teach the people the law of God (see 2 Chronicles 17:7-9). He is described as a good king who walked in the ways of David (see 2 Chronicles 17:3-4). Among the most notable accomplishments were the abolition of idolatry and the destruction of the Asherah poles (see verses 3-6). One of his biggest mistakes was the formation of an alliance with King Ahab (whose wife was Jezebel) by giving his son in marriage to their daughter. Ahab convinced Jehoshaphat to join him in a war against Ramoth Gilead (see 2 Chronicles 18:3-34). During the raging battle, Jehoshaphat was mistaken for the king of Israel and survived only because the hand of the Lord protected him. He escaped and went back to Jerusalem to concentrate on leading Judah in the ways of the Lord.

The lesson today is the second time that Jehoshaphat sent officials out into the kingdom to instruct the people in matters relating to the law of God. Jehoshaphat reached out into the Northern Kingdom, going to Ephraim and appealing to the people to return to the Lord their God. Jehoshaphat appointed judges for civil matters and gave the Levites and priests additional duties in ceremonial or religious matters. Both groups were instructed to deal justly and honestly with the people because they were God's representatives. Jehoshaphat created an administrative organization to oversee all of the matters that related to civil and religious matters of the land.

As you read and study this lesson, look for ways that you can begin to incorporate the lessons and insights you gain from it. Also, make a list of the things that you can do to be more attuned to the matters of justice and equity in your community. Ask yourself what the Lord requires of you today as a result of this study.

II. EXPOSITION AND APPLICATION OF THE SCRIPTURE

A. Jehoshaphat Leads the People Back to the Lord (2 Chronicles 19:4)

And Jehoshaphat dwelt at Jerusalem: and he went out again through the people from Beer-sheba to mount Ephraim, and brought them back unto the Lord God of their fathers.

After his near fatal brush with death, Jehoshaphat returned to live in Jerusalem. He went out a second time among the people from Beersheba in the south to the hill country of Ephraim (see 2 Chronicles 17:7-9). Beersheba was the southernmost border of Judah in the region of the Negev. *Beersheba* means "well of the oath" and the place gets its name from Abraham, who made an oath with Abimelech in Genesis 21:31-34. The hill country of Ephraim, sometimes referred to as Mount Ephraim, refers to the central mountain range in Israel and later came to be known as Samaria.[1]

Jehoshaphat personally went throughout the land, seeking to lead the people back to the Lord God of their fathers. It is particularly significant that he went into the Northern Kingdom which separated from the south shortly after Solomon's death, and followed Jeroboam (see 1 Kings 12:1ff.). The north was deeply entrenched in idol worship—and to lead them back to God would be a major victory for Jehoshaphat.

B. Jehoshaphat Appoints and Charges Judges
(2 Chronicles 19:5-7)

And he set judges in the land throughout all the fenced cities of Judah, city by city, And said to the judges, Take heed what ye do: for ye judge not for man, but for the Lord, who is with you in the judgment. Wherefore now let the fear of the Lord be upon you; take heed and do it: for there is no iniquity with the Lord our God, nor respect of persons, nor taking of gifts.

One of the first acts of Jehoshaphat when he began his second round of reformation was the appointment of judges throughout the kingdom. The law that God had given Moses mandated that judges be appointed throughout all of Israel in every tribal area (see lesson 4, June 24, 2012). The judges were set up in the fortified cities. Andrew Hill stated that, "These cities are royal command centers and part of a network of defensive posts ringing Jerusalem."[2] Hill noted that the cities had a garrison of soldiers stationed within the borders and they also served as storehouses.[3] Because these cities were centrally located within Judah and near the capital city they were accessible to the majority of the population.[4]

The judges were to be very conscious of their roles and the responsibility that they had been given. The word *consider* is written as an imperative command in Hebrew and points to the need to give serious thought to a matter. The judges were commanded to weigh their decisions carefully. The reason was clear: while they had been appointed by the king, they were serving the Lord God (see verse 6). They were therefore accountable to the Lord for the execution of their assignments. The judges did not need to fear reprisal nor give thought to political retribution if they decided a case against a wealthy or powerful person. The Lord was with them whenever they gave a verdict.

The judges were to make decisions with the fear of the Lord upon them. This "fear" was not the fear of reverence or awe; it literally referred to the idea of *dread*. Judges were to be guided by the fact that they were accountable to God and hence the failure to make a decision based purely upon non-favoritism or impartiality would result in divine punishment. As judges, they represented the law of God, and therefore must execute it without partiality or favoritism (see verse 7). They were also cautioned against taking bribes. The judges were to ensure that the highest standards of justice and equity were maintained in the courts.

C. Jehoshaphat Assigns New Duties to the Priests and Levites
(2 Chronicles 19:8-10)

Moreover in Jerusalem did Jehoshaphat set of the Levites, and of the priests, and of the chief of the fathers of Israel, for the judgment of the Lord, and for controversies, when they returned to Jerusalem. And he charged them, saying, Thus shall ye do in the fear of the Lord, faithfully, and with a perfect heart. And what cause soever shall come to you of your brethren that dwell in their cities, between blood and blood, between law and commandment, statutes and judgments, ye shall even warn them that they trespass not against the Lord, and so wrath come upon you, and upon your brethren: this do, and ye shall not trespass.

Jehoshaphat was not finished establishing the judicial system upon his return to Jerusalem. The second thing he did was to set up a "supreme court," or a final court of appeals in Jerusalem. The judges for this court were the Levites, the priests, and the heads of Israelite families. This group was charged with the responsibility of administering the law and settling major disputes not settled at the lower-court level. All of these judges were to live in Jerusalem so that they could be accessible and available at any moment to hear and decide cases.

Jehoshaphat gave strict orders regarding how the work of judging the people was to be carried out. They were to serve *faithfully*, a word that has in it the idea of being loyal to the law, the king, and, most of all, to God (see verse 9). Use of the term *wholeheartedly* denotes "serving in such a way that the one who judges is always at peace with his verdict." The assignment was to be carried out in the fear of the Lord, which in this instance refers to moral reverence for the Word of God—that is, the judge does the right thing because it is the right thing in the eyes of God (see Deuteronomy 1:16; Isaiah 11:3-5).

The judges were to execute justice and righteousness without exception. They were to follow the rule of law in every case, whether it was a murder case or a civil matter. Furthermore, the people who would be giving a ruling for or against were their countrymen, people that they no doubt knew and lived among (see verse 10). Four categories of judicial responsibility were outlined by Jehoshaphat: (1) *Law* referred to the Torah or the Mosaic Law, which is described in the book of Deuteronomy. (2) *Commandments* refer to the whole range of commands that God gave to Moses to teach the children of Israel, specifically including the Ten Commandments and others (see Exodus 20:6; 24:12; 34:28). (3) *Statutes* included a whole range of civil laws that were given to regulate the social and community lives of the Hebrew people. These included laws against idolatry, prostitution, homosexuality, and a host of other social behaviors deemed to be immoral (see Leviticus 19:19, 26, 31, 37; 20:22; Deuteronomy 7:5, 25; 12:2-3). (4) *Judgment* is a translation of the Hebrew word *mishpat,* which is the most important concept for understanding the Hebrew concept of justice. It is used some four hundred times in the Bible, and

refers to the execution of justice in a manner that honors and glorifies God (see Psalms 36:6; 37:28; Proverbs 29:4; Isaiah 30:18; Micah 3:1; 6:8).

The gravity of the assignment is summed up in the last phrase. God's wrath would fall upon the judges themselves if they did not warn the people not to violate the laws of God, which would lead to sin. If, however, they warned the people, kept the commands, and followed the path of righteousness in their judging, then they would keep themselves from sinning.

D. Jehoshaphat Establishes Administrative and Religious Order (2 Chronicles 19:11)

And, behold, Amariah the chief priest is over you in all matters of the Lord; and Zebadiah the son of Ishmael, the ruler of the house of Judah, for all the king's matters: also the Levites shall be officers before you. Deal courageously, and the Lord shall be with the good.

Jehoshaphat set up what amounted to an executive leadership team to give guidance and organization to the work of the judges. Amariah, the high priest, would deal with all of the matters concerning the religious lives of the people. Ishmael would handle the civil matters. In doing this, Jehoshaphat established a clear separation of duties and created clear lines of authority. The Levites would serve as scribes and secretaries for the judges. They would record all of the legal documents and ensure that they were kept in a secure and safe place.

Finally, they were told to "act with courage," which would keep them from being bought or their opinions being sold to the highest bidder. They were working for the Lord, and He would surely do them well.

III. CONCLUDING REFLECTION

There are a number of lessons that emerge from today's session. First, we learn that the number-one task of spiritual leaders is to lead the people of God in the ways of the Lord. If people have gone astray, then the leader should seek to lead them back to the Lord. Second, there is no substitute for a fair and just legal system in any society. African Americans and poor people know the burden of being tried in courts where the system has stacked itself against them because of their ethnicity or their economic status. When judges are motivated more by righteousness and godliness, the whole society benefits because people will be treated fairly and impartially. Finally, there is the lesson of organization and a clear division of responsibility and authority. Within many churches, there is no clear line of demarcation between responsibility and authority. Churches operate best and with greater integrity when they operate within clearly defined lines of responsibility and authority.

PRAYER

Lord God, give us the minds and wills to serve You in righteousness and equity. May we be committed to the kind of justice that pleases You and honors the name of our Lord Jesus Christ. In Jesus' name we pray. Amen.

WORD POWER
Corruption—defined as "evil or wicked behavior."

HOME DAILY BIBLE READINGS
(July 23-29, 2012)

Jehoshaphat Makes Judicial Reforms

MONDAY, July 23: "The Lord Is Our Judge" (Isaiah 33:13-22)

TUESDAY, July 24: "May Righteousness Flourish" (Psalm 72:1-7)

WEDNESDAY, July 25: "Steadfast in Keeping God's Statutes" (Psalm 119:1-8)

THURSDAY, July 26: "Fear the Lord, Depart from Evil" (Job 28:20-28)

FRIDAY, July 27: "The Battle Is God's" (2 Chronicles 20:5-15)

SATURDAY, July 28: "Walking in God's Commandments" (2 Chronicles 17:1-6)

SUNDAY, July 29: "Judging on the Lord's Behalf" (2 Chronicles 19:4-11)

End Notes

[1] Charles R. Pfeiffer, *Baker's Bible Atlas*.

[2] Andrew Hill, *1 & 2 Chronicles: The New NIV Application Commentary*, (Grand Rapids: Zondervan Publishing Co., 2003), p. 486.

[3] Ibid.

[4] Ibid.

LESSON 10   August 5, 2012

PRAISE FOR GOD'S JUSTICE

DEVOTIONAL READING: **Luke 4:16-21**
PRINT PASSAGE: **Psalm 146:1-10**
KEY VERSES: **Psalm 146:5, 7**

BACKGROUND SCRIPTURE: **Exodus 21–23;**
Psalm 146:1-10; Isaiah 58

Psalm 146:1-10—KJV

PRAISE YE the LORD. Praise the LORD, O my soul.

2 While I live will I praise the LORD: I will sing praises unto my God while I have any being.

3 Put not your trust in princes, nor in the son of man, in whom there is no help.

4 His breath goeth forth, he returneth to his earth; in that very day his thoughts perish.

5 Happy is he that hath the God of Jacob for his help, whose hope is in the LORD his God:

6 Which made heaven, and earth, the sea, and all that therein is: which keepeth truth for ever:

7 Which executeth judgment for the oppressed: which giveth food to the hungry. The LORD looseth the prisoners:

8 The LORD openeth the eyes of the blind: the LORD raiseth them that are bowed down: the LORD loveth the righteous:

9 The LORD preserveth the strangers; he relieveth the fatherless and widow: but the way of the wicked he turneth upside down.

10 The LORD shall reign for ever, even thy God, O Zion, unto all generations. Praise ye the LORD.

Psalm 146:1-10—NIV

PRAISE THE LORD. Praise the LORD, O my soul.

2 I will praise the LORD all my life; I will sing praise to my God as long as I live.

3 Do not put your trust in princes, in mortal men, who cannot save.

4 When their spirit departs, they return to the ground; on that very day their plans come to nothing.

5 Blessed is he whose help is the God of Jacob, whose hope is in the LORD his God,

6 the Maker of heaven and earth, the sea, and everything in them—the LORD, who remains faithful forever.

7 He upholds the cause of the oppressed and gives food to the hungry. The LORD sets prisoners free,

8 the LORD gives sight to the blind, the LORD lifts up those who are bowed down, the LORD loves the righteous.

9 The LORD watches over the alien and sustains the fatherless and the widow, but he frustrates the ways of the wicked.

10 The LORD reigns forever, your God, O Zion, for all generations. Praise the LORD.

BIBLE FACT

Psalms 145–150 are referred to as a group of psalms in praise of God and are probably intended for public worship. We are told that they are used by Jews today in daily prayers. It is noteworthy that each of these psalms begins with the words "Praise ye the Lord" and ends with the same refrain of praise.

UNIFYING LESSON PRINCIPLE

People appreciate receiving lasting justice. Where can we look to find unshakable justice? God is the source of steadfast justice.

TOPICAL OUTLINE OF THE LESSON

I. **Introduction**
   A. Uncommon Courage
   B. Biblical Background

II. **Exposition and Application of the Scripture**
   A. Hallelujah!
      (Psalm 146:1-2)
   B. Trust Only in the Lord
      (Psalm 146:3-4)
   C. God's Compassion for the Weak
      (Psalm 146:5-10)

III. **Concluding Reflection**

LESSON OBJECTIVES

Upon the completion of the lesson, the students will be able to:

1. Explain the many ways that God cares for His human creation;
2. Acknowledge that God is faithful and just to those who place their hope in Him; and,
3. Discuss with others ways to get involved with helping the needy.

POINTS TO BE EMPHASIZED

ADULT/YOUTH

Adult Topic: Executing Justice
Youth Topic: Justice through Human Experience
Adult Key Verses: **Psalm 146:5, 7**
Youth Key Verse: **Psalm 146:5**
Print Passage: **Psalm 146:1-10**

—Psalm 146 is the first of five hallelujah psalms that conclude the Psalter.

—Its opening summons to the soul to praise the Lord and promise to praise God throughout life are a response to the commitment to lifelong praise at the end of Psalm 145.

—There is a warning exhortation not to put trust in human leaders because of their mortality.

—The psalmist praised the Lord, who supports widows and orphans.

—The Lord is described as giving help for a particular category of need: the oppressed, the hungry, and prisoners.

—The psalm concludes with a number of divine attributes that indicate the perfection of God and God's worthiness of praise.

CHILDREN

Children Topic: A God of Justice
Key Verses: **Psalm 146:5, 7**
Print Passage: **Psalm 146:1-10**

—God's help is contrasted with human help.

—God is faithful forever.

—God cares for people in need—those oppressed, hungry, imprisoned, blind, bowed down, and bereft.

—We are urged to praise the Lord as long as we live.

—Those who place their hope and trust in God for help will be satisfied.

I. INTRODUCTION

A. Uncommon Courage

The lesson today introduces us to the biblical concept of praise. God is praised not only with the fruit of our lips, but also through the works of our hands. God is glorified as we do good works (see Matthew 5:13-16; Ephesians 2:8-10). As you study this lesson, think of instances when you have been involved in an effort to overcome injustice. It may have been a situation on your job or something that occurred in your community. Throughout the lesson, make your own list of persons present or past whom you believe have been champions of social, political, or economic justice. Look for ways that you can model some of their actions.

B. Biblical Background

Today we begin Unit III, which is entitled *Justice Promised*. The four lessons in this unit examine some of the Old Testament texts that prophesy concerning God's coming judgment. These remaining lessons are from the Major Prophets: Isaiah, Jeremiah, and Ezekiel. The first lesson is from Psalm 146, which is the first of the five "Hallelujah Psalms" (146–150) that conclude the Psalter. Each of the five psalms has the same introductory and concluding formula: "Praise the Lord!" The main purpose of these psalms is to highlight the importance of giving God the praise that He is due.

The psalmist began with an opening summons to his soul to praise the Lord throughout all of his life. In the psalm, he warned that humans are not to put their trust in human leaders, because of their mortality. He declared that God is not just the God who creates, but He is the God who upholds and supports the widows and orphans. The Lord gives help to the oppressed, the hungry, and to those who are prisoners. In verses 6-10, the psalmist listed twelve attributes of the character of God which point to the worthiness of God to be praised.

One of the underlying truths of the lesson is that God is concerned about the plight of the least of the earth, which also makes their plight the concern of believers (see Matthew 25:31-46). As you read and study the passage today, consider ways that God has promised to help people who are oppressed and how God has kept His promise. Ask the Holy Spirit to reveal to you ways that you can become more involved in working with homeless families, men, or women in your community. Discuss with others in your class or church ways that you can live out the teachings of Psalm 146. Additionally, look for ways that you can join in the struggles of others who are fighting against injustice in their communities.

II. EXPOSITION AND APPLICATION OF THE SCRIPTURE

A. Hallelujah!
(Psalm 146:1-2)

PRAISE YE the LORD. Praise the LORD, O my soul. While I live will I praise the LORD: I will sing praises unto my God while I have any being.

These opening verses of Psalm 146 take the form of what is called "parallelism." Parallelism is where the same or similar ideas are presented in different sentences. Synonymous parallelism is the most frequently encountered form of parallelism in the entire Bible. In this form of parallelism, the first line of a verse is repeated in the second line, only in a different way.

The passage begins with the imperative declaration that his soul will "Praise the LORD." The phrase, "Praise the Lord!" is translated from the Hebrew word *halal*, which gives us the English word *Hallelujah*. It is the imperative summons to praise God. To *Halal* God is "to laud, boast, rave, and celebrate His unsearchable mercy and goodness" (see Psalms 22:22; 35:18; 56:4; 119:164, 175; 148). The psalmist did not just say that he would praise the Lord during the worship time; rather, to him, praise would be a lifelong pursuit. Only the living can praise the Lord and give His name glory and honor (see Psalms 63:4; 71:14-15; 104:33; 145:1-2; Revelation 7:9-17). For the people of God, praise is not an option—it is an imperative command. Praise is the highest form of personal adoration and reverence toward God. It is the supreme statement of personal piety and expression of our faith in God. All believers are to praise God because of who He is and what He has done.

B. Trust Only in the Lord
(Psalm 146:3-4)

Put not your trust in princes, nor in the son of man, in whom there is no help. His breath goeth forth, he returneth to his earth; in that very day his thoughts perish.

Verse 3 begins with an imperative command not to put one's trust in humans. The implication points to the futility of trusting human beings, even those who are princes. Why? They are mere mortals who lack the power to save anyone. They cannot even save themselves. The Scriptures teach repeatedly that we are not to trust in human beings (see Psalms 62:9; 118:8-9; Isaiah 2:22; 31:3; 37:6; Jeremiah 15:5-6).

Verse 4 gives additional reasons why we are not to trust in humans. When their spirits depart, their bodies return to the ground, as do those of all living creatures. Here, again, is the affirmation of the futility of trusting in someone who does not even have control over his or her own spirit or breath. The spirit of a person comes from God; thus, He can at any moment withdraw it from us (see Genesis 2:7; 6:17; Job 14:10; 17:1; 27:3; Psalm 104:29). It was from the dust that Adam and Eve—and hence all living creatures—were created, and it will be to the dust that we all return (see Genesis 3:9; Psalm 90:3; Ecclesiastes 12:7). At the moment of death, every plan, ambition, or goal planned by a man or woman goes into the grave along with him or her.

C. God's Compassion for the Weak
(Psalm 146:5-10)

Happy is he that hath the God of Jacob for his help, whose hope is in the LORD his God: Which made heaven, and earth, the sea, and all that therein is: which keepeth truth for ever: Which executeth judgment for the oppressed: which giveth food to the hungry. The LORD looseth the prisoners: The LORD openeth the eyes of the blind: the LORD

raiseth them that are bowed down: the LORD loveth the righteous: The LORD preserveth the strangers; he relieveth the fatherless and widow: but the way of the wicked he turneth upside down. The LORD shall reign for ever, even thy God, O Zion, unto all generations. Praise ye the LORD.

Verse 5 begins with a beatitude: "Blessed is he whose help is the God of Jacob" (NIV). Who are those who are blessed or happy? They are the ones who have anchored their lives in the God of creation (see Deuteronomy 33:29; Psalms 33:12; 84:12; 144:15). The word *help* indicates the state of being safeguarded by God. God's help not only defeats one's enemies, but it also lifts the downtrodden in their distress (see 2 Chronicles 20:9; Psalms 27:9; 37:40; 46:1).

In this verse, there is a backward look to the life of Jacob, who was one of the chief patriarchs of Israel. The psalmist did not view life in a vacuum; rather, His God is the same one who was the God of Jacob (see Genesis 32:24-29; compare with Genesis 50:17; Exodus 3:6; Psalms 46:7, 11; 84:8). The God of Jacob is the only one in whom men and women should hope (see 39:7; 71:5; Jeremiah 17:7; 1 Peter 1:3-5, 21). It is because He is Lord and sovereign over the entire universe that believers should hope in Him.

The psalmist made what is the central affirmation of the Scriptures—that God is the maker of the heavens and the earth (see Genesis 1-2; compare with Psalms 33:6; 136:5-6; 148:5-6; Jeremiah 10:11-12; John 1:1-4). There is nothing that exists in all of creation that was not made by God. The Lord, who is the Creator, is also the One who remains faithful. He can be counted on to do as He said He would (see Lamentations 3:22-23; Joshua 1:5-10).

Verses 7-9 begin a series of phrases that further define the God of Jacob. Many of the psalms recite the historical pilgrim of ancient Israel and how God delivered them at the Red Sea. Here, God is viewed as faithful because He is intimately concerned about the poor and helpless. In the course of a few lines, the psalmist captured what ought to be the ministry and mission focus of every church and believer. God is concerned about the oppressed.

Beginning at verse 8, the verses all begin with the same formula: "The LORD"—The Lord gives sight to the blind (see Isaiah 35:5; 42:16;, 18; Matthew 9:30 11:15; Luke 18:42; John 9:7-33; Acts 26:18; Ephesians 1:18; 1 Peter 2:9); He lifts up those who are bowed down (see Psalms 145:14; 147:6; Luke 13:11-13; 2 Corinthians 7:6); He loves the righteous (see Deuteronomy 33:3; Psalm 11:7; John 14:21-23; 16:7).

God is not just concerned about Israel, but He is Lord of all and creator of every race and nation of people. Thus, He watches the alien and sustains the fatherless (see Deuteronomy 10:18-19; 16:11; Psalm 68:5; Proverbs 15:25; Jeremiah 49:11; Hosea 14:3; Malachi 3:5); and finally, He frustrates the ways of the wicked (see 2 Samuel 15:31; 17:23; Esther 5:14; 7:10; 9:25; Psalms 18:26; 83:13-17; 145:20; 147:6; 1 Corinthians 3:19).

The psalm ends as it began—with a strong declaration of praise to the Lord. Hallelujah! The Lord is King forever. He was not the God of the Moabites, Ammonites, or Egyptians. He is the God who founded and called Israel into existence. The name *Zion* is another name for Jerusalem. God is to be praised because His protection of Zion is as sure as the mountains are that surround Jerusalem. Those who trust in the Lord are like Mount Zion—which cannot be shaken, but endures forever. As the mountains surround Jerusalem, so the Lord surrounds His people both now and forevermore (see Psalm 125:1-2).

III. CONCLUDING REFLECTION

The book of Psalms is one of the most important books in the Bible for increasing individual and corporate spirituality and faith. The psalms are among the diamonds and precious jewels of God's Word. Psalms are the remedy for our midnights of pain and heartache. From the psalter, we learn of the everlasting love of God, who keeps us from terror during the darkest moments of life. The book of Psalms offers us several spiritual benefits.

First and foremost, the psalms teach us how to worship and praise God. God was exalted in the psalter as the only one worthy of worship and praise. Israel was a worshipping community. God is the one to whom the community of faith came to present itself (see Psalm 95). It is before Him that we gather and bow down prostrate on the ground. He is the One who receives our singing and joyous celebration. God is to be worshipped with thanksgiving and gladness and loud shouts of celebration (see Psalm 95:1-2). When His people come before Him, they come with an offering (see Psalm 96:8). We do not just come before Him; rather, we come with hearts that are prepared to worship and adore Him.

Second, the psalms are a source of comfort in distress. How often we have found ourselves overwhelmed by vexing troubles, only to be strengthened by the words of a psalm: "God is our refuge and strength, a very present help in trouble" (Psalm 46:1). God is the one who keeps us by day and by night (see Psalm 121:5). God is the one who brings us out of terrible troubles when we cry out to Him (see Psalm 34). God is the one who prepares a table before us in the presence of our enemies (see Psalm 23).

PRAYER

Lord God, teach us how to trust in You with all our hearts and souls. We rejoice that You have been a constant source of help and hope. May we learn to bless and praise You without fear. In Jesus' name we pray. Amen.

WORD POWER

Hallelujah—translated from the Hebrew word *halal*.
Praise—the highest form of personal adoration and reverence toward God.

HOME DAILY BIBLE READINGS
(July 30–August 5, 2012)

Praise for God's Justice

LESSON 11   August 12, 2012

GOD PROMISED A RIGHTEOUS LORD

DEVOTIONAL READING: **John 8:12-19**
PRINT PASSAGE: **Isaiah 9:2-7**

BACKGROUND SCRIPTURE: **Isaiah 9:1-7**
KEY VERSE: **Isaiah 9:6**

Isaiah 9:2-7—KJV

2 The people that walked in darkness have seen a great light: they that dwell in the land of the shadow of death, upon them hath the light shined.

3 Thou hast multiplied the nation, and not increased the joy: they joy before thee according to the joy in harvest, and as men rejoice when they divide the spoil.

4 For thou hast broken the yoke of his burden, and the staff of his shoulder, the rod of his oppressor, as in the day of Midian.

5 For every battle of the warrior is with confused noise, and garments rolled in blood; but this shall be with burning and fuel of fire.

6 For unto us a child is born, unto us a son is given: and the government shall be upon his shoulder: and his name shall be called Wonderful, Counsellor, The mighty God, The everlasting Father, The Prince of Peace.

7 Of the increase of his government and peace there shall be no end, upon the throne of David, and upon his kingdom, to order it, and to establish it with judgment and with justice from henceforth even for ever. The zeal of the LORD of hosts will perform this.

Isaiah 9:2-7—NIV

2 The people walking in darkness have seen a great light; on those living in the land of the shadow of death a light has dawned.

3 You have enlarged the nation and increased their joy; they rejoice before you as people rejoice at the harvest, as men rejoice when dividing the plunder.

4 For as in the day of Midian's defeat, you have shattered the yoke that burdens them, the bar across their shoulders, the rod of their oppressor.

5 Every warrior's boot used in battle and every garment rolled in blood will be destined for burning, will be fuel for the fire.

6 For to us a child is born, to us a son is given, and the government will be on his shoulders. And he will be called Wonderful Counselor, Mighty God, Everlasting Father, Prince of Peace.

7 Of the increase of his government and peace there will be no end. He will reign on David's throne and over his kingdom, establishing and upholding it with justice and righteousness from that time on and forever. The zeal of the LORD Almighty will accomplish this.

BIBLE FACT

The prophet Isaiah has been identified as the prophet who stands at the head of "The Prophets"—that third great section of the Old Testament. *Eerdman's Handbook of the Bible* states that "there is nothing to equal Isaiah's tremendous vision of God and the glory in store for God's people." (*Eerdman's Handbook to the Bible*, Lion Publishing, England, p. 380)

UNIFYING LESSON PRINCIPLE

Discouraged people look for hope. Where can we find hope? Our hope is found in the coming Messiah, who established a just and right kingdom.

TOPICAL OUTLINE OF THE LESSON

I. Introduction
A. The Antidote to Despair
B. Biblical Background

II. Exposition and Application of the Scripture
A. God's Promise of Light to the People of Zebulun and Naphtali
(Isaiah 9:2)
B. God Promises to Give His People Joy
(Isaiah 9:3-5)
C. God's Promise of a Davidic King
(Isaiah 9:6-7)

III. Concluding Reflection

LESSON OBJECTIVES

Upon the completion of the lesson, the students will be able to:

1. Explain the historical context during which the ministry of Isaiah took place;
2. Identify the elements in the lesson that give them hope today; and,
3. Work with others in organizing a class project that offers hope to the hopeless.

POINTS TO BE EMPHASIZED

ADULT/YOUTH
Adult Topic: **Hope in spite of Darkness**
Youth Topic: **Justice Fulfilled**
Adult/Youth Key Verse: **Isaiah 9:6**
Print Passage: **Isaiah 9:2-7**

—The northern part of Israel, identified by the names of two tribes, Zebulun and Naphtali, is later known as upper and lower Galilee. Being in the far north of Israel, it was the first to tremble before the might of Assyria.
—This despised district was glorified when God honored it, and the fulfillment of the prophecy was realized when Jesus Christ the Son of God dwelt in Capernaum.
—Historically, the oppressor was the Assyrians, but in a far deeper sense, Assyria meted out the judgment of God on a disobedient Israel.
—There would be great rejoicing among God's people when God broke the yoke of foreign oppression. Ironically, the might of foreign armies was overcome by the humble birth of a child.
—The prediction of the birth of a child finds fulfillment in the birth of Christ (Matthew 4:12-16).
—Being established on the foundation stones of justice and righteousness, the Messiah's reign will be perpetual and progressive.

CHILDREN
Children Topic: **A Mighty Ruler**
Key Verse: **Isaiah 9:6**
Print Passage: **Isaiah 9:2-7**

—Isaiah's poem uses light and darkness as symbols of hope and hopelessness.
—The image of the yoke's being broken is used to symbolize the coming of justice and freedom.

—Prophecies of the coming of the Messiah are fulfilled in Jesus Christ.

—This passage speaks of the endless reign of the coming One.

I. INTRODUCTION

A. The Antidote to Despair

There has never been a time since the 1930s when the world has been covered with so much pessimism and despair. The massive economic downturn of 2007–2011 ripped the heart out of the global economy and left many people feeling financially doomed. Recently, the United States unemployment rate hit a record of nearly 9.8 percent according to the U.S. Bureau of Labor Statistics. Homelessness, unemployment, war, violence, famine, and drought are just a few of the reasons why hundreds of millions of people around the world have lost hope. Dr. Henry J. Venter—PhD, psychologist, speaker, and author—states, "Hopelessness is that state where I simply want to give up. I believe my circumstances can't change, that my life is over, that I will never find happiness, and everything looks dark and bleak. Hopeless individuals believe that their problems will never be solved and they will never succeed at what they attempt to do; they can't see the opportunities, only the failure and disappointments of yesterday."[1] How many people have you come across who express the attitude that their lives are hopeless? Are there individuals within your local congregation who see no way out of their plight? As you study today's lesson, make a list of the signs of despair that you see in the lesson. Compare these signs to the signs that you see in the community where you live. Ask the Holy Spirit to reveal to you ways that you can become involved in a local project or church ministry to help relieve the pain and suffering of people who are living without hope. Finally, ask the Lord to reveal to you ways that you can speak words of encouragement to people who have lost their way and who believe that life has but one outcome: despair and disappointment.

B. Biblical Background

Isaiah lived about 750 years before the birth of Christ. His work was centered in the southern kingdom which consisted of the tribes of Judah and Benjamin. He was one of the longest-living prophets and had one of the longest prophetic ministries of any of them as well. He lived and prophesied/preached during the tenure of four of Judah's kings (see Isaiah 1:1). The northern kingdom, which was referred to as Israel or Ephraim, was made up of the remaining ten tribes. These twelve tribes comprised the entire nation of Israel at one point in history; however, during the time of Isaiah's ministry, the nation was divided (see 1 Kings 11:26-39). During the days of Isaiah, there was constant conflict in the land of Israel, sometimes between the north and the south or with invaders. All of the major military powers of the ancient Near East wanted control of the land of Israel because of its strategic location. Israel formed the mainland route from Africa to Asia and Europe.

The northern part of Israel was identified by the names of the tribes Zebulun and Naphtali, and was later known as upper and lower Galilee. Being in the far north of Israel, it was the first part of the nation to feel the might of the Assyrian army. Galilee was an area that was despised and ridiculed, but God glorified the district when He honored it, through the fulfilling of prophecy when Jesus Christ dwelt in the land of Galilee (see Matthew 3:13).[2]

The prophet foretold of a time when the land would be filled with great rejoicing, highlighted by God's breaking the yoke of foreign oppression. Ironically, the might of foreign armies would be overcome by the humble birth of a child in Bethlehem. This birth found its fulfillment in the birth of Jesus Christ, as affirmed by the writer Matthew in quoting the prophet Isaiah (see Matthew 4:12-16). Isaiah was one in a long line of prophets who heralded the coming of the King—that King being Jesus Christ, the Son of God. There existed during the time of Isaiah a great anticipation over the arrival of the King.

II. EXPOSITION AND APPLICATION OF THE SCRIPTURE

A. God's Promise of Light to the People of Zebulun and Naphtali
(Isaiah 9:2)

The people that walked in darkness have seen a great light: they that dwell in the land of the shadow of death, upon them hath the light shined.

Verse 1 contains an explanation of the reason why the gloom of Isaiah 8:19-22 would be no more. The northern region of Israel lived with the constant threat of invasion and depopulation (see 2 Kings 17:5; 2 Chronicles 5:26; 16:4). The word *nevertheless* drew out the contrast between a time of gloom and a time of joy that would surely come in spite of the experiences of the past. Those in distress were the people of the tribal areas of Zebulun and Naphtali, which had been devastated by the invasion of King Tiglath-Pileser III of Assyria in 734 and 732 BC (see 2 Kings 15:29). The sins and rebellion of the past had been the primary reason why the Lord God had humbled the northern tribes. They worshipped idols, creating gods that were the works of men's hands. Their sins turned away the bounty and blessings of God, bringing the judgment of God upon them (see Leviticus 26:24, 28; Deuteronomy 28:15-26; Jeremiah 5:25).

Isaiah saw a time when the glory of the Lord would shine upon the people of Zebulun and Naphtali. This was the land of Galilee that had been despised by the Judeans. Why was the north despised by the Judeans? The proximity of the land of Galilee to areas inhabited by non-Israelites opened the way for different pagan and idolatrous influences to develop in the land. Therefore, Galileans were more likely to have contact with Gentiles in ways that the Judeans living in the south did not.

In the future, the honor that would be accorded to Galilee of the Gentiles would come to fruition in the life and ministry of Jesus Christ. "The way of the sea" referred to the main road that ran from Damascus through Capernaum and down along the coast. It was referred to as the Coastal Highway. The area around the Sea of Galilee is where Jesus spent the majority of His three-year ministry.

In verse 2, Isaiah declared that the people who had walked in darkness would one day experience the light of God's presence (see Isaiah 50:10; 60:1; Micah 7:8; Matthew 4:16; Luke 1:78; 2:32; John 8:12, 35, 46; Ephesians 5:13). In this verse, the reference was to the spiritual darkness that engulfed the north after the division of the tribes. The leaders, specifically Jeroboam, introduced idolatry on a massive scale in the land, and people never returned to their historical faith (see 1 Kings 12:10ff.). The practice of idolatry on such a large scale brought spiritual death to the north and eventually led to the total collapse of the northern kingdom in 722 BC (see 2 Kings 17).

B. God Promises to Give His People Joy (Isaiah 9:3-5)

Thou hast multiplied the nation, and not increased the joy: they joy before thee according to the joy in harvest, and as men rejoice when they divide the spoil. For thou hast broken the yoke of his burden, and the staff of his shoulder, the rod of his oppressor, as in the day of Midian. For every battle of the warrior is with confused noise, and garments rolled in blood; but this shall be with burning and fuel of fire.

Isaiah looked both backward and forward in these words. He looked back to the time when Israel was a united nation, living in peace and experiencing bounty, glory, and prosperity (see 1 Kings 4:20). He also looked forward to a time when the splintered and divided nation would once again be united. Isaiah described a time when the glory of the land would be filled with untold joy. God would increase the joy of the land (see Nehemiah 9:23; Psalm 107:38; Isaiah 26:15; 49:20-22 ; Zechariah 2:11; 8:23). The people would rejoice and celebrate the God of David. David, you would recall, was considered the foremost example of a godly leader. They would rejoice on two fronts. The first would be the kind of joy that comes when they have had a great harvest. The rains would have come and the land would have yielded more than enough for the people. The second example was the kind of joy that was experienced when the army divided the plunder and spoils of war (see 1 Samuel 30:16-31).

In verse 4, the Lord would give further evidence of His delight in His people by defeating their enemies, the Assyrians, just as Gideon defeated the Midianites (see Judges 7:7-25). The yoke of oppression and servitude to the Assyrians would be broken and the land would again be free to prosper (see Isaiah 10:27; 14:3, 25; 30:31; 47:6). We must remember that Israel and Judea lived with the constant threat of military invasion and conquest. Tyranny and oppression were not metaphorical images, but real possibilities all the time. The land would experience new peace. One of the expectations of the messianic age would be the cessation of war and violence. The prophets looked for a time when men would beat their weapons of war into instruments of peace and productivity (see Isaiah 2:4; Joel 3:10; Micah 4:3). The wars and conflicts of the past would be vanquished from the land. Every warrior's boot and garments worn in battle would be burned as a sign that there would be no more war in the land. Instead of being used as instruments of death, they would be used as fuel to produce heat and for cooking food.

C. God's Promise of a Davidic King (Isaiah 9:6-7)

For unto us a child is born, unto us a son is given: and the government shall be upon his shoulder: and his name shall be called Wonderful, Counsellor, The mighty God, The everlasting Father, The Prince of Peace. Of the increase of his government and peace there shall be no end, upon the throne of David, and upon his kingdom, to order it, and to establish it with judgment and with justice from henceforth even for ever. The zeal of the LORD of hosts will perform this.

Verses 6 and 7 are the most well-known and beloved words in the book of Isaiah. They are recited year after year in the retelling of the story of the birth of the Messiah. In these verses, we have the answer to how the land would experience the joy, peace, and prosperity that was promised in the previous verses. There would finally come One who would stand in the lineage of David and would be a ruler whose heart would be totally turned to the Lord. Upon this King's shoulders would rest the government, and He would uphold the laws of God. His rule would be characterized by justice and righteousness.

This new era began with the words, "Unto us a child is born, unto us a son is given" (verse 6). Was this the announcement of the birth of Hezekiah, who would reign in the place of his father, King Ahaz? Some interpreters see this prophecy as referring primarily to the birth of Hezekiah. There is no doubt that the prophecy referred to the near-term birth of Hezekiah, but it also looked off into the distant future to another King, who would fulfill the promise made to David in 2 Samuel 7:12-14. It has reference to the birth of Hezekiah and, yet, is a word that looks for so much more. God was raising up a leader for that time and one for the future. God gave the people a leader who would execute His will and lead the nation back to

Him. We see this in the reign of Hezekiah. Yet, there was One to come whom John said that he was not even "worthy to stoop down and untie" His shoelaces.

The new Davidic ruler would bear several titles: "Wonderful Counselor, Mighty God, Everlasting Father, Prince of Peace." He would be a Counselor whose wisdom exceeded even that of Solomon's. He leads us in the paths of righteousness. None need go astray when they follow Him. He is the Mighty God. In Him, there is no searching of His might (see Isaiah 40:18-26). His power is greater than the minds of all of the people who have ever lived can imagine together. He is the Everlasting Father who is the same yesterday, today, and forever. He lives in eternity, but His greatest works are in time. He is the Prince of Peace who will bring peace to the nation and establish peace. He promises to keep us in perfect peace when our minds are stayed upon Him. This is a prophecy that is not dependent upon human will to accomplish; rather, the very power of God will ensure that what has been promised will be accomplished. "The zeal of the Lord Almighty"; the word *zeal* comes from a Hebrew word that means "deep and very strong emotions." The central meaning of the word is "jealousy." God loved Israel with such deep passion that He guarded His relationship with her with passionate jealousy (see Exodus 20:5; 34:14; Numbers 5:14, 30; Deuteronomy 4:24; 5:9; and Zechariah 1:14; 8:2; compare with Amos 3:2).

III. CONCLUDING REFLECTION

One of the overarching truths of this lesson is the theme of hope. The prophets often preached to people who had fallen into sin and turned away from their God. Yet, their message, though laced at times with wrath and judgment, was also filled with words of hope and optimism about the future. They reminded the people of God that He had not forgotten them in spite of their willful disobedience. This must become the message of the church in the twenty-first century. Christians believe that the one and only hope for our communities, schools, families, and churches will not be more government control; not more conferences focusing on problems without real solutions—but a demonstration of the life and message of Jesus Christ.

We must make the message of hope live.

Romans 12:12 reads, "Rejoicing in hope; patient in tribulation; continuing instant in prayer." We worship and serve the God of all hope. Hope is the eternal expectation that God will bring a better and brighter day in the future. The message of hope is not just another message among many voices and messages; rather, it is God's Word to a dying world. We have the message of 2 Corinthians 5:17: "If any man be in Christ...."

PRAYER

Lord God almighty, grant that we may live with renewed hope. May the darkness of this world be filled by the light of Your presence manifested through us. In Jesus' name we pray. Amen.

WORD POWER

Idolatry—the worship of or allegiance to any god, thing, or person instead of the one true God.
Messianic Age—the period of the coming of the Messiah and all the hope that comes with that coming.

HOME DAILY BIBLE READINGS
(August 6-12, 2012)

God Promised a Righteous Lord
MONDAY, August 6: "A Heart Hardened to God's Righteousness" (Exodus 9:27-35)
TUESDAY, August 7: "Before God in Our Guilt" (Ezra 9:10-15)
WEDNESDAY, August 8: "Take Your Stand" (1 Samuel 12:6-16)
THURSDAY, August 9: "If We Confess Our Sins" (1 John 1:5-9)
FRIDAY, August 10: "The Righteous Judge" (2 Timothy 4:1-8)
SATURDAY, August 11: "The Light of the World" (John 8:12-19)
SUNDAY, August 12: "The Promise of a Righteous King" (Isaiah 9:2-7)

End Notes

[1] http://SearchWarp.com/swa536336-How-To-Conquer-Hopelessness-5-Steps-To-Break-The-Pattern-Of-Despair-And.htm.
[2] Edward J. Young, *The Book of Isaiah, Volume I, Chapters 1-18*, (Grand Rapids: William B. Eerdmans Publishing Co., 1965), p. 323.

LESSON 12   August 19, 2012

GOD PROMISED A RIGHTEOUS BRANCH

DEVOTIONAL READING: **Psalm 33:1-5**
PRINT PASSAGE: **Jeremiah 23:1-6; 33:14-18**
KEY VERSE: **Jeremiah 23:5**

BACKGROUND SCRIPTURE: **Jeremiah 23:1-6; 33:14-18**

Jeremiah 23:1-6; 33:14-18—KJV

WOE BE unto the pastors that destroy and scatter the sheep of my pasture! saith the LORD.

2 Therefore thus saith the LORD God of Israel against the pastors that feed my people; Ye have scattered my flock, and driven them away, and have not visited them: behold, I will visit upon you the evil of your doings, saith the LORD.

3 And I will gather the remnant of my flock out of all countries whither I have driven them, and will bring them again to their folds; and they shall be fruitful and increase.

4 And I will set up shepherds over them which shall feed them: and they shall fear no more, nor be dismayed, neither shall they be lacking, saith the LORD.

5 Behold, the days come, saith the LORD, that I will raise unto David a righteous Branch, and a King shall reign and prosper, and shall execute judgment and justice in the earth.

6 In his days Judah shall be saved, and Israel shall dwell safely: and this is his name whereby he shall be called, THE LORD OUR RIGHTEOUSNESS.

     .....

14 Behold, the days come, saith the LORD, that I will perform that good thing which I have promised unto the house of Israel and to the house of Judah.

15 In those days, and at that time, will I cause the Branch of righteousness to grow up unto David; and he shall execute judgment and righteousness in the land.

16 In those days shall Judah be saved, and Jerusalem shall dwell safely: and this is the name wherewith she shall be called, The LORD our righteousness.

Jeremiah 23:1-6; 33:14-18—NIV

"WOE TO the shepherds who are destroying and scattering the sheep of my pasture!" declares the LORD.

2 Therefore this is what the LORD, the God of Israel, says to the shepherds who tend my people: "Because you have scattered my flock and driven them away and have not bestowed care on them, I will bestow punishment on you for the evil you have done," declares the LORD.

3 "I myself will gather the remnant of my flock out of all the countries where I have driven them and will bring them back to their pasture, where they will be fruitful and increase in number.

4 I will place shepherds over them who will tend them, and they will no longer be afraid or terrified, nor will any be missing," declares the LORD.

5 "The days are coming," declares the LORD, "when I will raise up to David a righteous Branch, a King who will reign wisely and do what is just and right in the land.

6 In his days Judah will be saved and Israel will live in safety. This is the name by which he will be called: The LORD Our Righteousness."

     .....

14 "'The days are coming,' declares the LORD, 'when I will fulfill the gracious promise I made to the house of Israel and to the house of Judah.

15 In those days and at that time I will make a righteous Branch sprout from David's line; he will do what is just and right in the land.

16 In those days Judah will be saved and Jerusalem will live in safety. This is the name by which it will be called: The LORD Our Righteousness.'

17 For this is what the LORD says: 'David will never

17 For thus saith the Lord; David shall never want a man to sit upon the throne of the house of Israel; 18 Neither shall the priests the Levites want a man before me to offer burnt offerings, and to kindle meat offerings, and to do sacrifice continually.

fail to have a man to sit on the throne of the house of Israel, 18 nor will the priests, who are Levites, ever fail to have a man to stand before me continually to offer burnt offerings, to burn grain offerings and to present sacrifices.'"

TOPICAL OUTLINE OF THE LESSON

I. **Introduction**
   A. The Critical Dynamics of Leadership
   B. Biblical Background

II. **Exposition and Application of the Scripture**
   A. Woe to the Shepherds Who Scatter and Destroy the Sheep (Jeremiah 23:1-4)
   B. The Righteous King (Jeremiah 23:5-6)
   C. Restoration of the Davidic King and the Levitical Priesthood (Jeremiah 33:14-18)

III. **Concluding Reflection**

LESSON OBJECTIVES

Upon the completion of the lesson, the students will be able to:

1. Explain the benefits of being under the leadership of a righteous shepherd;
2. Define and identify the traits of a righteous spiritual leader; and,

3. Discuss strategies that churches can employ in order to train leaders for ministry.

POINTS TO BE EMPHASIZED

ADULT/YOUTH

Adult Topic: **The Just Leader**

Youth Topic: **Embrace the Righteous Shepherd**

Adult Key Verse: **Jeremiah 23:5**

Youth Key Verse: **Jeremiah 33:14**

Print Passage: **Jeremiah 23:1-6; 33:14-18**

—God condemned and repudiated the irresponsible shepherds of the past who misled the people and brought them to destruction.

—God promised to provide trustworthy and obedient shepherds who would care for the people and lead them with safety and care.

—The prophet expressed the hope that a king would be raised up, one who would bear the name "The Lord is our righteousness" (23:5).

—The promise of the restoration of the heirs of David was believed to be a sign of Israel's restored honor and prestige among nations.

—*Zedekiah*, the name of the last pre-exilic king, means "THE LORD OUR RIGHTEOUSNESS." This is a wordplay relating to verse 6.

—The "righteous branch" imagery (23:5 and 33:15) indicates the end of the dynasty of Jehoiakim's family and the beginning of a new Davidic reign.

CHILDREN

Children Topic: **A Just Leader**

Key Verse: **Jeremiah 33:15**

Print Passage: **Jeremiah 23:1-6; 33:14-18**

—The passage likens the Israelites and their leaders to sheep and unfaithful shepherds.

—God promised a just leader who would lead in right ways.

—God's promise through Jeremiah was of the righteous Branch, an ideal leader whose lineage would be from David's family tree.

—The name of this Branch would remind the people of their covenant relationship with God.

I. INTRODUCTION

A. The Critical Dynamics of Leadership

In our lesson today, we will study a period in the life of the ancient Hebrew prophet Jeremiah. God used him to preach against the religious and civil leaders who contributed to the demise of the nation of Judah. During the time of Jeremiah, the leaders could not be trusted. They betrayed the trust of the people, and thereby incurred the wrath of God. As you study the lesson today, look for leadership principles that will empower you to be a more effective leader. As you read and study the lesson, consider the history of your local church and legacy of her past leaders. Were there leaders whose legacy blessed the life of the congregation? If so, make a list of things that they did. Were there leaders whose legacies were harmful, and are there lingering effects today? Ask the Holy Spirit to reveal to you ways that you can be a more effective leader or follower in your church.

B. Biblical Background

Jeremiah lived and preached during a critical period in the history of Judah (see Jeremiah 1:1-2). There has never been real agreement among biblical scholars on the fact that every sense of civility and morality had all but collapsed. The army of Nebuchadnezzar was threatening to overthrow the once proud and powerful nation of Judah and make them another one of their puppet states. The social situation of Jerusalem was deplorable; the political machinery was corrupt, and the spiritual climate was no more than a religious sham. Given Judah's condition, it was no wonder that Jeremiah stood out in the midst of a desert wasteland. Judah's leaders were the central cause of the problems that had enveloped Jerusalem.

God called Jeremiah and sent him to preach a message of repudiation and condemnation to irresponsible shepherds who had misled the people and brought them to the brink of destruction. While the situation looked hopeless, God promised to provide trustworthy and obedient shepherds who would care for the people and lead them with safety and care. Throughout his preaching, Jeremiah expressed the hope that one day a king would be raised up by God, one who would bear the name "The Lord is our righteousness."

II. EXPOSITION AND APPLICATION OF THE SCRIPTURE

A. Woe to the Shepherds Who Scatter and Destroy the Sheep
(Jeremiah 23:1-4)

WOE BE unto the pastors that destroy and scatter the sheep of my pasture! saith the LORD. Therefore thus saith the LORD God of Israel against the pastors that feed my people; Ye have scattered my flock, and driven them away, and have not visited them: behold, I will visit upon you the evil of your doings, saith the LORD. And I will gather the remnant of my flock out of all countries whither I have driven them, and will bring them again to their folds; and they shall be fruitful and increase. And I will set up shepherds over them which shall feed them: and they shall fear no more, nor be dismayed, neither shall they be lacking, saith the LORD.

In these verses, Jeremiah brought to a conclusion a severe and scathing indictment that he initially brought against the king and the leaders of the nation (see Jeremiah 22:1-30). We are not sure of the exact historical date or the particular context during which these oracles were spoken. However, they do speak to the heart of what was the underlying problem with the nation: corrupt leaders at all levels of the government. In the passage, the shepherds are the leaders and the sheep are the people of God. Judah and Israel had to contend with leaders who were often more concerned about their personal welfares than the welfare of the people (see Jeremiah 12:10; 22:22; 50:6; 56:9; Ezekiel 22:25; Zephaniah 3:3). The prophets were guilty of creating their own visions and, in many cases, had not seen anything nor heard anything from the Lord. Hence, use of the word *woe* was a warning to them to watch out because the anger of God had reached its limit (see Jeremiah 2:8, 26; Ezekiel 13:3; Zechariah 11:7).

What was the sin of the shepherds? They were destroying the sheep. The term *destroying* has in it the idea of annihilation and extermination. Additionally, they were scattering the sheep. These were not just any people; rather, they were the people of Israel—descendants of Abraham, Isaac, and Jacob. They were the covenant people of God, who had been called to be a nation of priests (see Exodus 19:1-7). Although the leaders were responsible for caring for, guiding, and feeding the sheep, God was still the owner of the flock. How often are the people of God led astray by leaders who are more concerned about themselves than they are about the people they lead? Leaders are primarily responsible for caring for and safeguarding the flock of God.

The term *therefore* in verse 2 introduces the consequences of the irresponsible actions of the leaders. God would not allow their actions to go unchallenged or unpunished. He would punish them. We are not told what the punishment would be, but who would want to fall into the hands of an angry God? The leaders were not charged with making bad decisions or with being indecisive; rather, their crime was a matter of the heart. They simply did not care about the sheep. At the center of God's complaint against the leaders of Judah was the constant reminder that leaders were called to care about the people of God. Paul reminded the elders of Ephesus in his farewell address at Miletus that they must take heed to themselves and to all of the flock of God (see Acts 20:28).

Verse 3 is a statement of contrast between the current leaders of Judah and the Lord God, who declared that He was prepared to replace the earthly leaders for a time. These words are reminiscent of Exodus 3:7-8, where God told Moses that He had seen the affliction of His people and come down to personally deliver them out of the hand of the pharaoh of Egypt. Here, God spoke in a language that was emphatic. "I myself" is a statement that reflected God's personal intention to find new leaders and His inability to find a man who cared enough about the people to lead them in the right way (see Jeremiah 5:1). God is always looking for men and women who will divest themselves of their personal ambitions to serve His purposes.

God was going to gather them from the nations where He had driven them into exile. Israel, the northern kingdom, had been taken into exile in 722 BC by the Assyrians. Jerusalem was now about to be destroyed and its inhabitants carried into exile in Babylon. Yet, there was a word of hope that God would not allow them to remain in captivity forever. He was going to bring them out of captivity and bring them back to their homeland. The people would be prosperous once again, and the evidence of this new prosperity would be an increase in the number of people and the fruitfulness of the land and economy.

Finally, God said that He was going to place shepherds over the people who would not only lead them, but would also care for them. As a result, the people would not be afraid, nor would any of them be found missing (see verse 4).

B. The Righteous King
(Jeremiah 23:5-6)

Behold, the days come, saith the LORD, that I will raise unto David a righteous Branch, and a King shall reign and prosper, and shall execute judgment and justice in the earth. In his days Judah shall be saved, and Israel shall dwell safely: and this is his name whereby he shall be called, THE LORD OUR RIGHTEOUSNESS.

Jeremiah not only preached that judgment was coming upon the people of Judah, but also embedded in his message was a word of hope about the future. "The days are coming" is a phrase used sixteen times by Jeremiah to pronounce either judgment or redemption (see Jeremiah 7:35; 9:25; 16:14; 19:6; 31:38; 33:14; 49:2). In this instance, it was used to declare that the Lord would one day raise up a king from the line of David. That king was described as being a "righteous Branch" (verse 5). "Branch" is a word that is used to refer to the root or seed of David and is clearly messianic (see 2 Samuel 23:5; Psalm 132:17; Ezekiel 29:21; Zechariah 6:12). The king that the Lord would raise up would reign wisely, in stark contrast to the rulers described in Jeremiah 21–22. Jehoiakim was the king at the time and he was described as the king who built his palace on unrighteousness (see Jeremiah 22:13). The king whom the Lord would raise up would do what was just and right in the land. The righteousness that would characterize the reign of the new king was one that honored and obeyed the law of God. It would be a righteous king who held the right relationships between God and humanity. During his reign, Judah would be saved and Israel would live in safety.

C. Restoration of the Davidic King and the Levitical Priesthood
(Jeremiah 33:14-18)

Behold, the days come, saith the LORD, that I will perform that good thing which I have promised unto the house of Israel and to the house of Judah. In those days, and at that time, will I cause the Branch of righteousness to grow up unto David; and he shall execute judgment and righteousness in the land. **In those days shall Judah be saved, and Jerusalem shall dwell safely: and this is the name wherewith she shall be called, The Lord our righteousness. For thus saith the Lord; David shall never want a man to sit upon the throne of the house of Israel; Neither shall the priests the Levites want a man before me to offer burnt offerings, and to kindle meat offerings, and to do sacrifice continually.**

Walter Brueggemann stated that chapter 33 contains "seven promissory oracles, each of which announces God's resolve to invert the fortunes of Judah and to create a new season of well-being for Jerusalem."[1] The oracles all had the same introductory statements: "This is what the Lord says" or "The days are coming" (see verses 2-9, 10-11, 12-13, 14-15, 17-18, 19-20, 23-26). The oracle that forms the final section of our lesson looks back to Jeremiah 23:5-6 and repeats the promise that the "Branch" would come from the root of David.

The very first thing that we notice about this oracle of promise is the recipients. It was made to the house of Israel and the house of Judah, and it is a strand that runs throughout the Old Testament. The fact that Israel is mentioned first more than likely signals that God would bring the fractured nation back together and it would most likely begin with the return of the Judeans from Babylon (see Jeremiah 29:10).

"In those days and at that time" is a clear reference to the days of the Messiah. Here, again, we are face-to-face with Jeremiah's message of hope and restoration of the Davidic line or kingship. Unlike some of the previous kings who failed to measure up to the standards and practices of David, the messianic king would "do" what was just and right in the land. Often leaders would talk about doing what was right,

but would fail in many instances to live up to the principles of justice and righteousness.

Not only would the Lord send a righteous leader in those days, but also Judah would be saved and Jerusalem would live in safety. Here, the reference is not to spiritual salvation, although that can be assumed. Rather, it has reference to physical salvation. Judah had been devastated by the army of the Chaldeans and Babylonians. Jerusalem was ransacked, the walls torn down, the Temple desecrated, and all of the holy artifacts stolen (see 2 Kings 24:10-17; 25:8-21; compare with Jeremiah 39:8; 52:14). The destruction of the northern kingdom in 722 BC and the destruction of Jerusalem in 597 and 586 BC were two of the most humiliating events in the history of ancient Israel. Many of the people felt abandoned by God and felt that the gods of the Assyrians and Babylonians were greater. So, this backdrop is what makes the oracle of promise such an important word of encouragement. Jerusalem, the centerpiece of Judah's relationship with God and the capital of her faith, would thrive again in the future (see Jeremiah 32:6-15).

The passage concludes with the promise that there would not be a time when a descendant of David would not sit upon the throne of Israel. God's promises are sure and complete and can be counted on to come to fruition (see Joshua 1:3-5).

The question that is central to the lesson is this: At what point were these promises ultimately fulfilled? The final consummation of the promises reached their zenith in the life, death, burial, resurrection, ascension, and second return of Jesus Christ. He is both Prophet and

King who fulfills every promise of the Messiah in the Old Testament.

III. CONCLUDING REFLECTION

Central to the lesson is the realization that the people of God will always be first and foremost in the heart of God. Is God concerned about the quality of leadership that His people receive? The lesson emphatically points out that God is concerned so much that He holds leaders to a high level of accountability. Every church must take seriously the need to have leaders in place who have hearts for the things of God and who will care about the people of God. When leaders are selected because it is their turn to be in leadership positions, ultimately the ministry and mission efforts of the local church suffer immeasurable harm. Leaders in the local church should model themselves after Jesus Christ, who is the supreme and final example.

Make a list of the traits that you believe should characterize the leaders in your local church. Share that list with others and pray that God will raise up men and women who will seek to model those traits.

PRAYER

Lord God, Creator of the ends of the earth, the heavens continue to attest to the veracity of Your promises. Teach us to love and honor You, not simply by what we say, but even more so in our actions. In Jesus' name we pray. Amen.

WORD POWER

Oracle—a term used to denote a divine revelation communicated in a variety of ways and then recorded for future generations.

HOME DAILY BIBLE READINGS
(August 13-19, 2012)

God Promised a Righteous Branch

MONDAY, August 13: "Pursue Righteousness" (1 Timothy 6:11-16)

TUESDAY, August 14: "God's Children Now" (1 John 2:28–3:3)

WEDNESDAY, August 15: "The Righteous Will Flourish" (Proverbs 11:27-31)

THURSDAY, August 16: "All Shall Be Righteous" (Isaiah 60:17-22)

FRIDAY, August 17: "The Lord Loves Righteousness and Justice" (Psalm 33:1-5)

SATURDAY, August 18: "The Gracious and Righteous Lord" (Psalm 116:5-19)

SUNDAY, August 19: "The Lord Is Our Righteousness" (Jeremiah 23:1-6; 33:14-18)

End Notes

[1]Walter Brueggemann, *A Commentary on Jeremiah: Exile and Homecoming* (Grand Rapids: William B. Eerdmans Publishing Co., 1998), p. 312.

LESSON 13 ·   August 26, 2012

GOD PROMISED TO BE WITH US

DEVOTIONAL READING: **Psalm 23**
PRINT PASSAGE: **Ezekiel 34:23-31**

BACKGROUND SCRIPTURE: **Ezekiel 34**
KEY VERSE: **Ezekiel 34:23**

Ezekiel 34:23-31—KJV

23 And I will set up one shepherd over them, and he shall feed them, even my servant David; he shall feed them, and he shall be their shepherd.

24 And I the LORD will be their God, and my servant David a prince among them; I the LORD have spoken it.

25 And I will make with them a covenant of peace, and will cause the evil beasts to cease out of the land: and they shall dwell safely in the wilderness, and sleep in the woods.

26 And I will make them and the places round about my hill a blessing; and I will cause the shower to come down in his season; there shall be showers of blessing.

27 And the tree of the field shall yield her fruit, and the earth shall yield her increase, and they shall be safe in their land, and shall know that I am the LORD, when I have broken the bands of their yoke, and delivered them out of the hand of those that served themselves of them.

28 And they shall no more be a prey to the heathen, neither shall the beast of the land devour them; but they shall dwell safely, and none shall make them afraid.

29 And I will raise up for them a plant of renown, and they shall be no more consumed with hunger in the land, neither bear the shame of the heathen any more.

30 Thus shall they know that I the LORD their God am with them, and that they, even the house of Israel, are my people, saith the Lord GOD.

31 And ye my flock, the flock of my pasture, are men, and I am your God, saith the Lord GOD.

Ezekiel 34:23-31—NIV

23 "'I will place over them one shepherd, my servant David, and he will tend them; he will tend them and be their shepherd.

24 I the LORD will be their God, and my servant David will be prince among them. I the LORD have spoken.

25 I will make a covenant of peace with them and rid the land of wild beasts so that they may live in the desert and sleep in the forests in safety.

26 I will bless them and the places surrounding my hill. I will send down showers in season; there will be showers of blessing.

27 The trees of the field will yield their fruit and the ground will yield its crops; the people will be secure in their land. They will know that I am the LORD, when I break the bars of their yoke and rescue them from the hands of those who enslaved them.

28 They will no longer be plundered by the nations, nor will wild animals devour them. They will live in safety, and no one will make them afraid.

29 I will provide for them a land renowned for its crops, and they will no longer be victims of famine in the land or bear the scorn of the nations.

30 Then they will know that I, the LORD their God, am with them and that they, the house of Israel, are my people, declares the Sovereign LORD.

31 You my sheep, the sheep of my pasture, are people, and I am your God, declares the Sovereign LORD.'"

People are searching for tranquility and wholeness. Where can these things be found? A lasting relationship with God and an assurance that God is with us meets our deepest need.

TOPICAL OUTLINE OF THE LESSON

I. **Introduction**
   A. Showing the Right Example
   B. Biblical Background

II. **Exposition and Application of the Scripture**
   A. God Promises a Shepherd-King (Ezekiel 34:23-24)
   B. God's Covenant of Peace (Ezekiel 34:25-28)
   C. God's Promise of Provision (Ezekiel 34:29-31)

III. **Concluding Reflection**

LESSON OBJECTIVES

Upon the completion of the lesson, the students will be able to:

1. Recite the provisions of God's new covenant of peace with His people;
2. Identify situations in which they can find peace and wholeness; and,
3. Become involved in ministries that reflect their responses to God's presence in their lives.

POINTS TO BE EMPHASIZED
ADULT/YOUTH

Adult Topic: Meeting Our Deepest Need
Youth Topic: God's Covenant
Adult/Youth Key Verse: Ezekiel 34:23
Print Passage: Ezekiel 34:23-31

—Shepherding was a familiar metaphor for governing in the ancient Near East.
—The kings of Israel and Judah were bad shepherds; they were self-serving and neglected the needs of the people.
—The result of the shepherds' neglect is that the sheep are scattered and unprotected.
—God would restore order and justice under the Davidic ruler. There would be no more oppression, enslavement, and hunger.
—The Good Shepherd imagery is also reflected in the New Testament (Matthew 9:36; 18:12-14; Mark 14:27; Luke 15:1-7; John 10:1-30; 21:15-17).

CHILDREN

Children Topic: A Caring Presence
Key Verse: Ezekiel 34:30
Print Passage: Ezekiel 34:23-31

—God would send a shepherd, another David, to nurture the sheep—Israel.
—God speaks lovingly of a relationship with the people.
—God's covenant relationship brings peace: "You [are] my sheep" and "I am your God" (34:31, NIV).
—There are blessings in God's covenant of peace.

I. INTRODUCTION

A. Showing the Right Example

On January 4, 2011, Captain Owen Honors, then commander of the nuclear-powered aircraft carrier U.S.S. Enterprise, was relieved of his command. Being relieved of command in the military is the worst thing that can happen to any military officer. It virtually ends the person's career, regardless of how sterling and superior his or her military service record may be. Captain Honors was relieved of his command because he "showed 'exceptionally poor judgment' when he produced a series of raunchy videos and broadcast them for his crew in 2006 and 2007."[1] The irony of the demise of such a highly decorated naval officer is the claim that the videos were produced for the purpose of raising crew morale aboard the ship. U.S. naval warships are often subjected to very long, extremely lonely, and quite demanding deployments. The sexually oriented videos were allegedly produced to help relieve the tension of the wartime deployments. In his written remarks, Admiral John C. Harvey Jr. wrote that "The responsibility of the Commanding Officer for his or her command is absolute."[2] Captain Honors lost his command and ruined his naval career because he lost sight of what it meant to be an example for the six thousand men and women aboard the ship.

In today's lesson, God addressed the need of His people to live in peace and security. Their leaders had led the nation down the paths of social, political, and religious destruction. Israel's leaders were expected to be examples and to care for the people of God. They were charged with ensuring that justice and righteousness prevailed in the land. Instead of bringing justice, the people were often exploited. Instead of righteousness, the land was filled with hypocrisy.

As you study the lesson today, look for the various provisions that God spoke through the prophet Ezekiel to His people. See if you can identify the wonderful promises that God made to meet their needs. Finally, look at your life and identify the times and situations when God has met needs in your life.

B. Biblical Background

Today, our lesson comes from the prophetic writings of Ezekiel, who lived and preached during the period of the Babylonian Exile. He was probably taken into Babylon with the first deportation of 597 BC (see Ezekiel 1:1-3). He reported that he was among the captives near the Kebar River in Babylon. Kebar is sometimes spelled Chebar, and it was more a canal than a river that was used for irrigation. Psalm 137 is a description of the feeling of despair that filled the hearts of the Judeans as they pondered their future outside of Jerusalem.

Ezekiel's message was the right word at a time when the people of God needed hope that the future would be filled with peace and prosperity. There is no record that he ever returned to Jerusalem. Ezekiel was called by God to preach to a people who had all but lost hope in the God of Abraham and in their leaders. God used him to preach a message that He had not forgotten them nor had He abandoned them. Ezekiel reminded the people that one day God would bring them back together again and that He would appoint a shepherd over them who would be like David.

Judah and Israel had been plagued by the same form of diabolical leadership. The leaders of both nations exploited the people and neglected them, and their practices ultimately ended up causing the nation to be scattered into many places. God was going to restore order and justice under a Davidic ruler. There would be no more oppression, enslavement, and hunger. As you read the study lesson today, make comparisons between what you see in today's national and local leaders and what appeared to have been going on in Judah and Israel. Ask the Holy Spirit to reveal to you how to pray for the leaders of your church, city, and nation.

II. EXPOSITION AND APPLICATION OF THE SCRIPTURE

A. God Promises a Shepherd-King (Ezekiel 34:23-24)

And I will set up one shepherd over them, and he shall feed them, even my servant David; he shall feed them, and he shall be their shepherd. And I the Lord will be their God, and my servant David a prince among them; I the Lord have spoken it.

Verses 23-24 form the introduction to the covenant of peace which begins with verse 25 and concludes with verse 28. There are several questions that are raised in the passage. First, what is David's significance in these verses? Second, is the reference to David literal, figurative, or messianic? Initially, we can say that these verses are messianic in content and theology. They look back to the promise that God made to David that He would establish his throne forever and that there would always be one of his descendants sitting on the throne (see 2 Samuel 7:12-14). The verses look forward to a time when the disunity of the nation, caused by Israel's leaders—especially Jeroboam and Rehoboam—would be healed (see 1 Kings 12; compare with 1 Kings 11:26-39 for the explanation of why God allowed the nation to split between north and south). Under the new shepherd-king, the nation would be one nation, just as it was during the time of David and Solomon (see Ezekiel 37:21-24; compare with Jeremiah 23:4-6; 30:9; Hosea 3:5; Micah 5:2; Zechariah 13:7).

God said that He was going to place over them "one shepherd, my servant David." In all of Israel there was no king whose stature reached that of David's. He was the ideal king who was described as a man after God's own heart (see 1 Samuel 13:14). As a shepherd, he understood the needs of sheep for food, water, and protection. The "servant" theme highlights the fact that God was going to appoint someone of His own choosing who would carry out His will for the people and the land. This would be a servant who would not be driven by selfish ambitions, but one who would seek the will of the Father in all things (see Psalm 40:7-8; Isaiah 42:1; 53:11). We can conclude that these verses are messianic in that they look forward to the messianic age when the true King of Israel would come in the person of Jesus Christ. The shepherd motif is a ready reference to the Lord Jesus Christ, who declared that He was the Good Shepherd (see John 10:11-16).

In verse 24, God reminded the people that He had not abandoned them. The expression "I the LORD" is emphatic and was spoken to stress the continuing relationship between Israel and God. He was still their God who loved them with an everlasting love (see Ezekiel 36:28; 37:27; 39:22; compare Exodus 29:45; Isaiah 43:2; Jeremiah 31:3, 33; 32:28). These were no doubt welcomed words of comfort given that Judah had been literally ripped from her homeland and held captive to a strange land filled with idol gods and pagan practices.

B. God's Covenant of Peace
(Ezekiel 34:25-28)

And I will make with them a covenant of peace, and will cause the evil beasts to cease out of the land: and they shall dwell safely in the wilderness, and sleep in the woods. And I will make them and the places round about my hill a blessing; and I will cause the shower to come down in his season; there shall be showers of blessing. And the tree of the field shall yield her fruit, and the earth shall yield her increase, and they shall be safe in their land, and shall know that I am the LORD, when I have broken the bands of their yoke, and delivered them out of the hand of those that served themselves of them. And they shall no more be a prey to the heathen, neither shall the beast of the land devour them; but they shall dwell safely, and none shall make them afraid.

In verses 25-28, Ezekiel turned from speaking about the messianic king to sharing what the people could expect to see when they returned to Israel after their period of captivity in Babylon. It would be a land of both provision and protection. God promised to make a "covenant of peace" (see Ezekiel 37:26-28; 38:11-13; and 39:25-29). This was not the new covenant mentioned in Jeremiah 31:31-33 (compare with Luke 22:20). A *covenant* is an agreement between two or more individuals or nations. The word *peace* comes from the Hebrew word *shalom* and speaks of completeness and wholeness. It has in it the idea of a restored relationship. The covenant of peace referred to in this prophecy looks back to the covenant of peace between God and the Aaronic priesthood in which God promised to make the descendants of Aaron a perpetual priesthood (see Numbers 25:12; compare with Isaiah 54:10).

In the covenant of peace, God reaffirmed His commitment to His people. The land would have *shalom*, which would be characterized by prosperity and protection. The land was going to be rid of wild beasts and every place would be safe and secure (see Leviticus 26:6; Isaiah 11:6-9; 35:9; Hosea 2:18-23). The people would be able to even live in the desert, which is one of the harshest environments in Israel even today. Israel spent forty years in the desert (wilderness) and they were only able to survive because of the food and water that God provided daily.

The "hill" of verse 26 is an obvious reference to Mount Zion in Jerusalem (see Psalms 2:6; 68:16; 132:14; 133:3; Isaiah 2:2; 56:7; Ezekiel 20:40). David had conquered Zion and made it his capital and home (see 2 Samuel 5:1-10). During the time leading up to the ministry of Ezekiel, Jerusalem had been destroyed during the invasion of the Babylonians.

The Temple was ransacked and burned to the ground, and the walls were torn down as well. Rather than feeling that they were the blessed people of God, they must have felt cursed. The covenant of peace spoke of reversing the dismal past and opening up a new and bright future. God was going to bless them, and one of the primary ways was with rain to water the plants and crops. Rains would come in their seasons. In that part of the world the weather patterns can be unpredictable, which can lead to long periods of drought and famine. God was going to send showers of blessings rather than a deluge (see Deuteronomy 28:12; Psalm 68:9; Isaiah 32:15; 32:20; 44:3; Malachi 3:10).

According to verse 27, the trees would yield their fruit and the ground would yield its crops. Fruit and crops in abundance would be a sign of security. There would be enough food so that the people would not have to travel to foreign lands to buy grain. Israel had not known security in their land since the time of David and Solomon. For several hundred years, the land was plagued by either strife or conflict between the north and south or invaders from neighboring countries. The people would know with certainty that the God of their fathers was the Lord when He would come and break the yoke of their captors (see Exodus 3:6-8). *Yoke* is used figuratively in this passage to refer to Judah's political servitude and bondage to the Babylonians (see Deuteronomy 28:48; Jeremiah 27:8-12).

Verse 28 speaks of a time when Israel would be free from invasion by other nations. In the covenant of peace, they would no longer be subjected to foreign invasion. We are almost sure that this is a reference to a later time in Israel's history, because the land was invaded several times by the Greeks, Syrians, and eventually the Romans. The verse looks out in time to the period of the Messiah when Jesus Christ would come and reign on the earth and Jerusalem would no longer be conquered nor invaded by foreign nations.

C. God's Promise of Provision (Ezekiel 34:29-31)

And I will raise up for them a plant of renown, and they shall be no more consumed with hunger in the land, neither bear the shame of the heathen any more. Thus shall they know that I the LORD their God am with them, and that they, even the house of Israel, are my people, saith the Lord GOD. And ye my flock, the flock of my pasture, are men, and I am your God, saith the Lord GOD.

The final three verses are restatements of the provisions of the covenant of peace. First, God promised to make the land productive. They would never have to want for food because the land would be fertile, accompanied by the gentle rains in the growing season. Second, the land would be free of the scorn and ridicule that had made Israel and Judah the subject of the scorn of the nations. They were considered to be weak and helpless. Third, the promises would all rest upon the renewed relationship with the Lord. They would not have to worry about whether or not God would hold anything against them. As Sovereign Lord, God was and is free to do as He pleases—and it pleased Him to forgive and reconcile Judah and Israel to Himself. Israel would be the sheep of God's pasture and He would be their Lord (see Psalms 78:52; 95:7; 100:3; Ezekiel 36:38; Micah 7:14; John 10:26).

III. CONCLUDING REFLECTION

In the lesson today, God promised to meet the basic needs of His people Israel for food, water, and security. At the time when the words of the passage were spoken, the people of God were living through their worst nightmare. Yet, in the midst of their darkest moments God offered a word of hope through the prophets. Christians are an extension of the Lord Jesus Christ. We live in a world that has been broken by economic hardship, war, disease, crime, and family disintegration. All of these and many other problems have contributed to the feeling of hopelessness by millions of people in America and billions around the world. One of our responsibilities as believers is to minister to the hurting (see Matthew 25:31-46; Hebrews 6:10). As we reach out to the hurting we show the world that God is alive and that His love extends to all people. How do we preach and teach the Gospel today? Our witness is credible to the extent that we live out what we preach and teach.

PRAYER

Lord God, we beseech You by the presence of the Holy Spirit to make us more like Your Son Jesus Christ. May the indwelling presence of the Holy Spirit fill our lives with compassion for the weak, the lost, and the hurting. In Jesus' name we pray. Amen.

WORD POWER

Covenant—comes from the Hebrew word that refers to a "binding pact." It is used in reference to alliances between people. The highest covenant is of course that which God formed between Himself and His people Israel.

HOME DAILY BIBLE READINGS
(August 20-26, 2012)

God Promised to Be with Us

MONDAY, August 20: "The Lord Is My Shepherd" (Psalm 23)

TUESDAY, August 21: "I Will Be with You" (Genesis 28:10-17)

WEDNESDAY, August 22: "God Will Be with You" (Genesis 48:17-21)

THURSDAY, August 23: "I AM Has Sent Me" (Exodus 3:9-15)

FRIDAY, August 24: "I Am with You" (Haggai 1:7-14)

SATURDAY, August 25: "I Am with You Always" (Matthew 28:16-20)

SUNDAY, August 26: "'I Am Your God'" (Ezekiel 34:23-31)

End Notes

[1] Corinne Reilly, "I have lost Confidence in Capt. Honor's ability to lead effectively," *The Virginian-Pilot,* January 5, 2011., sec 1A, p. 1.

[2] Reilly, "lost confidence," sec 1A, p. 10.

GLOSSARY OF TERMS

FALL 2011

Lesson 1
Truth (Proverbs 3:3)—Hebrew: `*emeth* (eh'-meth): faithfulness, reliability; verity; assuredness; of divine instruction.

Lesson 2
Wisdom (verse 11)—Hebrew: *chokmah* (khok-maw'): shrewdness or skill; wits or prudence.

Lesson 3
Counsel (Proverbs 15:22)—Hebrew: *cowd* (sode): familiar converse; to have intimacy with God; secret; to be inward.

Lesson 4
Infamy (Proverbs 25:10)—Hebrew: *dibbah* (dib-baw'): to slander; an evil report; defamation.

Lesson 5
Transgression (Proverbs 29:16)—Hebrew: *pesha'* (peh'-shah): rebellion or sin (against God); to trespass.

Lesson 6
Besieged (Ecclesiastes 9:14)—Hebrew: *cabab* (saw-bab'): to compass; to turn, turn about, turn around or aside or back or towards, go about or around, surround, encircle, change direction.

Lesson 7
Heart (Ecclesiastes 11:9)—Hebrew: *leb* (labe): the inner man; mind, heart, and soul (of man); related to moral character; conscience.

Lesson 8
Heart (Song of Solomon 4:9)—Hebrew: *labab* (law-bab'): to ravish (my heart); to become enheartened.

Lesson 9
Blessed (Matthew 5:3)—Hebrew: *makarios* (mak-ar'-ee-os): to be happy; merrier.

Lesson 10
Destroy (Matthew 5:17)—Greek: *kataluo* (kat-al-oo'-o): dissolve; to disunite; to throw down or overthrow.

Lesson 11
Perfect (Matthew 5:48)—Greek: *teleios* (tel'-i-os): brought to its end, finished; wanting nothing necessary to completeness.

Lesson 12
Hypocrites (verse 5)—Greek: *hupokrites* (hoop-ok-ree-tace'): a dissembler; a pretender.

Lesson 13
Raiment (Matthew 6:25)—Greek: *enduma* (en'-doo-mah): garment; clothing; outer clothing.

WINTER 2011-2012

Lesson 1
Bless (Genesis 12:2)—Hebrew: *barak* (baw-rak`): to kneel; to be adored; to be praised; to congratulate.

Lesson 2
Vision (Genesis 15:1)—Hebrew: *machazeh* (makh-az-eh`): vision (in the ecstatic state).

Lesson 3
Tempt (Genesis 22:1)—Hebrew: *nacah* (naw-saw'): to test, try; prove; to put to the proof or test.

Lesson 4
Magnify (verse 46)—Greek: *megaluno* (meg-al-oo'-no): to make great; to enlarge; to esteem highly; to extol; laud or celebrate.

Lesson 5
Committed (verse 8)—Hebrew: *nathan* (naw-than'): to give; put or set; to recompense; to consecrate.

Lesson 6
Discreet (Genesis 41:39)—Hebrew: *biyn* (bene): to understand; to know (with the mind); to teach; to be prudent.

Lesson 7
Posterity (Genesis 45:7)—Hebrew: *sh@'eriyth* (sheh-ay-reeth'): rest; remnant; residue; what is left.

Lesson 8
Peradventure (Genesis 50:15)—Hebrew: *luw'* (loo): would God; would it might be; if only; oh that!

Lesson 9
Triumphed (Exodus 15:1)—Hebrew: *ga'ah* (gaw-aw'): to rise up; grow up; to be exalted in triumph.

Lesson 10
Justified (Galatians 2:16)—Greek: *dikaioo* (dik-ah-yo'-o): to declare or pronounce to be just or righteous; to be freed.

Lesson 11
Foolish (Galatians 3:1)—Greek: *anoetos* (an-o'-ay-tos): not understood; unintelligible; unwise; not understanding.

Lesson 12
Covenant (Galatians 3:15)—Greek: *diatheke* (dee-ath-ay'-kay): a testament or will; a disposition or arrangement.

Lesson 13
Fruit (Galatians 5:22)—Greek: *karpos* (kar-pos'): work; act or deed; an effect or result.

Lesson 1
Favor (Proverbs 8:35)—Hebrew *(rā ôn):* acceptance, goodwill, approval; from the root word meaning "to be pleased with."

Lesson 2
Word (John 1:1)—Greek *(logos):* "speaking." A message of God's full self-revelation through Jesus Christ; Word of God, Word of Life.

Lesson 3
Purification (John 2:6)—Greek *(katharismós):* to make clean, ritually cleansing from contamination or impurity; ceremonial washing practiced by the Jews who became defiled during the normal circumstances of daily life; the condition of cleanness (not the feeling) accomplished with the help of a mediator.

Lesson 4
Know (John 3:11)—Greek *(oída):* to have seen, to know intuitively or instinctively. It means "having come to a perception or realization of something"; to understand; comprehend.

Lesson 5
Defilement (John 18:28)—Greek *(miaínō):* stain, pollute; to cause something to be ceremonially impure.

Lesson 6
Believed (John 20:9)—Greek *(pisteuo):* think to be true; trust; put faith in; rely on.

Lesson 7
Zeal (John 2:17)—Greek *(zelos):* earnest concern; jealousy; to be hot, fervent; Jesus' zeal includes both reverence and holy wrath.

Lesson 8
Worship (John 4:23)—Greek *(proskuneo):* to prostrate oneself before; pay reverence and homage to a deity; render divine honors; adore, usually by kneeling.

Lesson 9
Work (John 9:4)—Greek *(ergazomai):* do business; perform by labor; to do, produce.

Lesson 10
Seal (John 6:27)—Greek *(sphragizo):* put a seal on; mark; means "to set a seal or mark upon a thing as a token of its authenticity or approvedness"; to attest, confirm, establish.

Lesson 11
Sheepfold (John 10:1)—Greek *(aule):* courtyard, dwelling; means "an enclosed space exposed to the open air; a place where sheep are housed."

Lesson 12
Console (John 11:19)—Greek *(paramutheomai):* to come close to someone's side and speak in a friendly manner, rousing up hope for a good outcome of what has happened.

Lesson 13
Believe (John 14:1)—Greek *(pisteuo):* to think to be true; trust; put faith in, rely on.

SUMMER 2012

Lesson 1
Pentateuch: the first five books of the Old Testament.

Lesson 2
Alien: a person who lives in a society other than his/her own.

Lesson 3
Day of Atonement: the tenth day of the seventh month of the Jewish calendar on which the high priest entered the inner sanctuary of the Temple to make reconciling sacrifices for the sins of the entire nation.

Lesson 4
Stewardship: responsibility to manage all the resources of life for the glory of God.

Lesson 5
Nazirites: a member of a class of individuals especially devoted to God. The Hebrew term means "consecration," "devotion," and "separation."

Lesson 6
Oracle: a divine revelation received from God through one who is made an instrument.

Lesson 7
Rendered: to return in kind; to give in reward or retribution.

Lesson 8
Kinsman: a man of the same race or family; one related by blood or sometimes marriage.

Lesson 9
Jehoshaphat: reigned as king of Judah for twenty-five years. He was one of the best, most pious and prosperous kings of Judah—the greatest since King Solomon.

Lesson 10
Hallelujah: highest praise given to God.

Lesson 11
Zebulun—Hebrew: means "dwelling or habitation"; his descendants made up the tribe of Zebulun.
Naphtali—Hebrew: "to obtain by wrestling"; one of the twelve tribes of Israel.

Lesson 12
Zedekiah: the last king of Judah and Jerusalem.

Lesson 13
Wholeness: to have nothing empty, broken, or missing.